NATIONAL BUREAU
OF
ECONOMIC RESEARCH
PUBLICATIONS
IN REPRINT

# BUSINESS CYCLES AND UNEMPLOYMENT

REPORT AND RECOMMENDATIONS

*OF A COMMITTEE*

OF THE PRESIDENT'S CONFERENCE ON UNEMPLOYMENT

WITH A FOREWORD

BY

HERBERT HOOVER

ARNO PRESS

A New York Times Company

New York – 1975

Editorial Supervision: Eve Nelson
Reprint Edition 1975 by Arno Press Inc.

NATIONAL BUREAU OF ECONOMIC RESEARCH
PUBLICATIONS IN REPRINT
ISBN for complete set: 0-405-07572-3
See last pages of this volume for titles.

Manufactured in the United States of America

———◆———

**Library of Congress Cataloging in Publication Data**

Conference on Unemployment, Washington, D. C. 1921.
    Committee on Unemployment and Business Cycles.
    Business cycles and unemployment.

    (National Bureau of Economic Research publications
in reprint)
    Reprint of the ed. published by McGraw-Hill, New York,
which was issued as no. 4 of National Bureau of Economic
Research's General series.
    1.  Unemployed--United States--Congresses.
2.  Business cycles--Congresses.  I.  Title.  II. Series.
III.  Series:  National Bureau of Economic Research.
General series ; no. 4.
HD5724.C69  1975      331.1'372'0973        75-19697
ISBN 0-405-07577-4

mmn
10/15

# BUSINESS CYCLES AND UNEMPLOYMENT

# BUSINESS CYCLES AND UNEMPLOYMENT

REPORT AND RECOMMENDATIONS

*OF A COMMITTEE*

OF THE PRESIDENT'S CONFERENCE ON UNEMPLOYMENT

WITH A FOREWORD

BY

HERBERT HOOVER

FIRST EDITION
FOURTH IMPRESSION

McGRAW-HILL BOOK COMPANY, INC.
NEW YORK: 370 SEVENTH AVENUE
LONDON: 6 & 8 BOUVERIE ST., E. C. 4
1923

THE MAPLE PRESS · YORK PA

# FOREWORD

The President's Conference on Unemployment which met in Washington in September, 1921, was called primarily to consider relief for four to five million unemployed resulting from the business slump of 1921. During the formulation of emergency measures, which subsequently proved successful in greatly alleviating the situation, the responsible business men, labor leaders, and economists of the Conference advanced the proposal that an exhaustive investigation should be made of the whole problem of unemployment and of methods of stabilizing business and industry so as to prevent the vast waves of suffering which result from the valleys in the so-called business cycle.

It was the view of the Conference that certain suggestions for controlling extremes of the business cycle so as to lessen the losses due to recurrent periods of unemployment were worthy of serious consideration and that in any event a thorough study of the business phenomena of booms and slumps would serve to advance public knowledge and stimulate thought toward constructive solution. Accordingly I appointed the following committee to undertake an investigation and report:

Owen D. Young, Chairman of the Board, General ElectricCo., Chairman; Joseph H. Defrees, Former President, U. S. Chamber of Commerce; Mary Van Kleeck, Russell Sage Foundation; Matthew Woll, Vice-president, American Federation of Labor; Clarence M. Woolley, President, American Radiator Co.; Edward Eyre Hunt, Secretary of the President's Conference on Unemployment, Secretary.

An exhaustive investigation was undertaken with the assistance of appropriations toward its cost from the Carnegie Foundation and with services contributed to the Committee by the National Bureau of Economic Research, the Russell Sage Foundation, the Federated American Engineering Societies, the U. S. Chamber of Commerce, the American Federation of Labor, the American Statistical Association, the American Economic Association, the Bureau of Railway Economics, the Department of Commerce, and a number of others.

The Committee has prepared the following short report after consideration of the facts and views developed. I am confident that it represents a definite advance in economic thought and offers practical constructive suggestions that should make for progress. A special volume will be issued at an early date, giving an exhaustive presentation of the facts and causes in relation to the business cycle and the views developed as to prevention and remedy.

Broadly, the business cycle is a constant recurrence of irregularly separated booms and slumps. The general conclusion of the Committee is that as the slumps are in the main due to the wastes, extravagance, speculation, inflation, over-expansion, and inefficiency in production developed during the booms, the strategic point of attack, therefore, is the reduction of these evils, mainly through the provision for such current economic information as will show the signs of danger, and its more general understanding and use by producers, distributors, and banks, inducing more constructive and safer policies. Furthermore, the Committee has developed some constructive suggestions as to the deferment of public work and construction work of large public-service corporations to periods of depression and unemployment, which, while in the nature of relief from evils already created, would tend both by their subtraction from production at the peak of the boom and addition of production in the valley of depression toward more even progress of business itself.

The report does not suggest panaceas or economic revolution but seeks to drive home the facts that the enlargement of judgment in individual business men as to the trend of business and consequent widened vision as to approaching dangers will greatly contribute to stability, and that the necessary information upon which such judgments can be based must be systematically recruited and distributed.

The investigation shows that many firms have pursued such policies and have come through the recent period of business disaster with success and stability, and that ignorance of determinable facts accounts for the disasters to many others.

The whole problem belongs to a vast category of issues which we must as a nation confront in the elimination of waste if we are to maintain and increase our high standards of living. No waste is greater than unemployment; no suffering is keener or more fraught with despair than that due to inability by those who wish to work to get jobs.

The public is indeed indebted to the Committee and to the very large group of its co-workers for the conduct of so able an investigation and the production of so much constructive thought. A constant feeling of the great human problem involved pervades the report and is in itself a tribute to the highest thought of American business.

HERBERT HOOVER.

WASHINGTON, D. C.
*March 1, 1923.*

# CONTENTS

|                                                                                             | PAGE   |
|---------------------------------------------------------------------------------------------|--------|
| FOREWORD, BY HERBERT HOOVER                                                                  | v      |
| REPORT AND RECOMMENDATIONS OF THE COMMITTEE ON UNEMPLOYMENT AND BUSINESS CYCLES              | xi     |
| QUESTIONS TO BE CONSIDERED                                                                   | xi     |
| WHAT IS THE BUSINESS CYCLE?                                                                  | xii    |
| A BUSINESS PROBLEM                                                                           | xiii   |
| THE NEED FOR FACTS                                                                           | xviii  |
| METHODS OF CONTROLLING THE BUSINESS CYCLE                                                    | xix    |
| RECOMMENDATIONS                                                                              | xix    |
| I. Collection of Fundamental Data                                                           | xix    |
| II. Larger Statistical Service                                                              | xxii   |
| III. Research                                                                               | xxiii  |
| IV. Control of Credit Expansion by Banks                                                     | xxiv   |
| V. Possible Control of Inflation by the Federal Reserve System                              | xxv    |
| VI. Control by Business Men of the Expansion of Their Own Industries                         | xxvii  |
| VII. Control of Private and Public Construction at the Peak                                  | xxvii  |
| VIII. Public Utilities                                                                       | xxix   |
| IX. Unemployment Reserve Funds                                                               | xxx    |
| X. Employment Bureaus                                                                        | xxxi   |
| QUESTIONS FOR DISCUSSION                                                                     | xxxii  |
| NOTE ON THE REPORT OF THE NATIONAL BUREAU OF ECONOMIC RESEARCH                               | xxxiii |
| ACKNOWLEDGMENTS                                                                              | xxxiii |
| PREFATORY NOTE                                                                               | xxxix  |

## PART I

## THE RELATION OF BUSINESS CYCLES TO UNEMPLOYMENT

INTRODUCTION . . . . . . . . . . . . . . . . . . . . . . . . . . . 1
By Wesley C. Mitchell, National Bureau of Economic Research.

### CHAPTER I

BUSINESS CYCLES . . . . . . . . . . . . . . . . . . . . . . . . . . 5
By Wesley C. Mitchell, National Bureau of Economic Research.

### CHAPTER II

INDIVIDUAL INDUSTRIES AND ENTERPRISES IN THE BUSINESS CYCLE . . . . . . 19
By Frederick R. Macaulay, National Bureau of Economic Research.

### CHAPTER III

THE ECONOMIC LOSSES CAUSED BY BUSINESS CYCLES . . . . . . . . . . . . 32
By Wesley C. Mitchell and Willford I. King, National Bureau of Economic Research.

# PART II

## CYCLICAL FLUCTUATIONS IN EMPLOYMENT

### CHAPTER IV

PAGE

WHAT THE PRESENT STATISTICS OF EMPLOYMENT SHOW. . . . . . . . . . 43
By William A. Berridge, Brown University.

### CHAPTER V

UNDER-EMPLOYMENT. . . . . . . . . . . . . . . . . . . . . . . . . 67
By Paul F. Brissenden, Columbia University.

### CHAPTER VI

CHANGES IN EMPLOYMENT IN THE PRINCIPAL INDUSTRIAL FIELDS, JANUARY 1,
1920 TO MARCH 31, 1922. . . . . . . . . . . . . . . . . . . . . 78
By Willford I. King, National Bureau of Economic Research.

### CHAPTER VII

THE EFFECT OF UNEMPLOYMENT UPON THE WORKER AND HIS FAMILY . . . . . . 99
By Stuart A. Rice, Columbia University.

# PART III

## PROPOSED REMEDIES FOR CYCLICAL UNEMPLOYMENT

### CHAPTER VIII

THE VARIOUS KINDS OF REMEDIES PROPOSED. . . . . . . . . . . . . . . 113
By Wesley C. Mitchell, National Bureau of Economic Research.

### CHAPTER IX

METHODS OF STABILIZING PRODUCTION OF TEXTILES, CLOTHING, AND NOVELTIES 116
By N. I. Stone, General Manager, Hickey-Freeman Company.

### CHAPTER X

METHODS OF STABILIZING PRODUCTION AND DISTRIBUTION . . . . . . . . . . 134
By Sanford E. Thompson, The Thompson and Lichtner Company, Engineers,
Boston.

### CHAPTER XI

THE PROBLEM OF "CANCELLATION" . . . . . . . . . . . . . . . . . . 170
By Gilbert H. Montague of the New York Bar.

### CHAPTER XII

METHODS OF STABILIZING WORK IN THE BUILDING INDUSTRIES. . . . . . . . 174
By Ernest S. Bradford, Vice-president of the American Statistical Association.

## CHAPTER XIII

PAGE

THE STABILITY OF RAILWAY OPERATIONS. . . . . . . . . . . . . . . . . 201
    By Julius H. Parmelee, Director of the Bureau of Railway Economics.

## CHAPTER XIV

THE LONG-RANGE PLANNING OF PUBLIC WORKS. . . . . . . . . . . . . . 231
    By Otto T. Mallery, Member of the Pennsylvania State Industrial Board.

## CHAPTER XV

FINANCIAL DEVICES FOR CONTROLLING OR MITIGATING THE SEVERITY OF
    BUSINESS CYCLES. . . . . . . . . . . . . . . . . . . . . . . . . 262
    By Thomas Sewall Adams, Yale University.

## CHAPTER XVI

PUBLIC EMPLOYMENT OFFICES AND UNEMPLOYMENT . . . . . . . . . . . . 272
    By Shelby M. Harrison, Director of Department of Surveys and Exhibits,
    Russell Sage Foundation.

## CHAPTER XVII

TRADE UNION OUT-OF-WORK BENEFITS . . . . . . . . . . . . . . . . . 293
    By John B. Andrews, Secretary of the American Association for Labor Legislation.

## CHAPTER XVIII

UNEMPLOYMENT INSURANCE . . . . . . . . . . . . . . . . . . . . . . 302
    By Leo Wolman, New School for Social Research.

## CHAPTER XIX

CHARTING THE COURSE OF EMPLOYMENT. . . . . . . . . . . . . . . . . 342
    By Mary Van Kleeck, Director of the Department of Industrial Studies,
    Russell Sage Foundation.

## CHAPTER XX

STATISTICAL INDEXES OF BUSINESS CONDITIONS AND THEIR USES . . . . . . . 361
    By Oswald W. Knauth, National Bureau of Economic Research.

## CHAPTER XXI

VARIOUS DEVICES USED FOR STABILIZING BUSINESS . . . . . . . . . . . . 378
    By a Committee of the Federated American Engineering Societies.

INDEX. . . . . . . . . . . . . . . . . . . . . . . . . . . . . . . 391

# REPORT AND RECOMMENDATIONS OF THE COMMITTEE ON UNEMPLOYMENT AND BUSINESS CYCLES

## QUESTIONS TO BE CONSIDERED

Can unemployment which results from recurrent business depression be reduced or prevented? Which of the proposals to relieve unemployment seem to offer prospects of practical service? What groups in the community can most effectively act?

These questions were forced upon the attention of the President's Conference on Unemployment when it met under Secretary Hoover's Chairmanship in Washington in September, 1921. Millions of wage-earners were out of work. The first responsibility of the Conference was to urge upon local communities plans to diminish suffering, but throughout the discussions it was clear that back of widespread unemployment were fundamental conditions which must be studied if more effective action were to be taken in the future than in the past. The depression of 1921 was obviously to some extent an aftermath of the great World War, but the War was not solely responsible. We were then in the midst of one of those periods of depression which inevitably follows abnormal activity. This upward and downward swing of business, recurring at intervals in the past century, has become known as the business cycle.

Before adjourning, the President's Conference on Unemployment provided for the appointment of a Committee to consider the underlying causes of recurrent depressions and specifically to analyze and present the more promising proposals for alleviating the extremes of the business cycle and reducing unemployment. To make this inquiry, Secretary Herbert Hoover, as Chairman of the Conference, appointed the Committee on Unemployment and Business Cycles. (See page xxxi.)

General business is now on the upward swing of the cycle, and unemployment has been greatly reduced. When business again declines men will be laid off and the problem of unemployment may again become serious. It will then be too late for any measures except relief for the unemployed unless we now address ourselves to the task of preventing, or at least reducing, these extreme fluctuations of business activity. Prevention as contrasted with relief is possible only through foresight.

The Committee on Unemployment and Business Cycles here presents to the public a preliminary discussion of the subject.

The Committee has been impressed with the scarcity of sound statistical and economic data regarding this fundamental problem. Extensive investigations and widespread public interest will undoubtedly be necessary before the business community will be able to deal adequately with the extremes of alternating booms and depressions. The Committee is confident that the destructive extremes of business cycles can in large measure be controlled.

If this report stimulates research and experiment by the various economic groups of this country in an effort to reduce periodic fluctuations in business and arouses them to cooperate with the Department of Commerce, the Department of Labor, and other agencies in the collection and distribution of any information they may require the Committee will feel that its work has been successful. Little in the way of definite and constructive programs can be advanced until the fundamental facts upon which action must be based are available in current and comparable form.

We hope that business organizations, banking associations, labor organizations, trade associations, and chambers of commerce, as well as individual business men and bankers, will consider and report back to us in detail upon these various proposals. (See page xxxii.)

Unless business men, bankers, and other economic groups at once begin investigation and study of these problems, leading to practical programs of action, solution will probably be attempted in ways unsound and unscientific.

## WHAT IS THE BUSINESS CYCLE?

The Committee uses the term "business cycle" to describe the series of changes in business conditions which are characterized by an upward movement toward a boom, followed by a downward movement into depression.

Business men know that the term "business cycle" is too simple to describe accurately the complexity of the problems involved. In reality the name covers a long series of influences in which a more or less unknown part is played by the individual establishment, by the industry of which it is a part, by conditions in other industries, and by credit conditions and policies.

In thus defining the cycle we are eliminating from consideration seasonal changes in particular trades or the total fluctuations which they produce. It is necessary to limit the scope of this report, and for that reason we hope that the seasonal problems will be the subject of study by other groups.

For a similar reason we have not been able to report on the problems of distribution, marketing, and finance in their relation to land ownership and agriculture.

Although a variety of reasons have been assigned for the upward and downward movement of business which appears to have occurred at intervals in all industrial countries, the general opinion is that the influences which cause the business cycle are conditions within business itself, and that the most productive results in controlling it are likely to be obtained from a consideration of business rather than from efforts to explore remote considerations.

Analyses of past cycles of business show certain common tendencies. If we begin the analysis when business is reviving, in general the characteristic features are increased volume of manufacturing, rising stock exchange prices followed by rising commodity prices, then by business expansion and increased demand for credit from both business men and speculators. As the result of the advance of commodity prices, money rates stiffen and credit gradually becomes strained, and these conditions may be accompanied by a curtailment of credit for speculative purposes. Then stock exchange prices fall; for a while longer general business continues to increase unevenly, transportation facilities are overburdened and deliveries are delayed, the apparent shortage of goods is intensified by speculative buying and duplication of orders by merchants and other buyers until credit expansion nears its limit. Public confidence is then shaken, resulting in widespread cancellation of orders if the cycle is extreme. This is always followed by liquidation of inventories and sharp and irregular fall of prices. During the period of depression there is always more or less widespread unemployment.

The cycle which ended in the depression of 1921 was unusual both in the extent of the preceding expansion, in the severity of the depression, and in the amount of unemployment. For this reason it is significant for us to review some examples of business difficulties caused by the last great fluctuation of business.

## A BUSINESS PROBLEM

In December, 1919, two manufacturers of silk went to their bank. One as a result of his study of business conditions—the degrees of over-expansion, inflation, and speculation—had decided that prosperity was beginning to assume the aspect of an unsafe boom. Although business was brisk and sales heavy, he told his bank that he did not propose to stock up during this period but that he would attempt to sell his goods with as rapid a turnover as possible.

The other manufacturer asked the bank for a large loan. Orders had been coming from his customers larger than those of any previous season, trade papers were emphasizing the scarcity of raw silk, traffic congestion made it seem imperative to increase his inventories, and he believed that it was necessary to expand in order to maintain his relative position in his trade. The bank gave him the loan because all the customary tests, such as the "two-to-one ratio" of quick assets to liabilities, usually relied upon to justify such an extension of credit, were met. Almost immediately the tide of prosperity turned in the silk industry, as the first manufacturer had predicted, and there came a severe drop in prices of both raw material and finished product. The second manufacturer found his factories stocked with high-priced raw material and with goods produced in the belief that good times and high prices would continue. The reduced value of his inventories made him unable to liquidate his loan, and his business was virtually bankrupt.

Was it wholly a defect in judgment upon the part of the second business man for which he alone was responsible? Did the bank use proper judgment? Did it have a responsibility which it did not exercise?

In the silk industry wholesale prices continued to rise until about February, 1920. Wholesalers and retailers talked of the great demand for silk and the great shortage of raw goods in the country. The men in the silk industry honestly believed that there was a lack of raw silk and that prices would continue to rise. The extent of the accumulation of speculative stocks was not realized in the trade. It was not until insurance companies discovered that the amount of silk which they had collectively insured was beyond their insurance limits that anyone understood that there was really an excess supply of silk in storage. Reacting to this news, all prices of silk dropped at once, and manufacturers, wholesalers, and retailers found themselves with huge inventories to liquidate. Manufacturers and wholesalers suffered from a general cancellation of orders, which still further added to their difficulties.

While the silk industry is peculiar in that most of the raw materials are imported, it shows the general developments leading to a depression market. It furnishes a striking example of the lack of information on the part of men within an industry as to the amount of stock in storage and the amount of stock in transit (which always increases during periods of business expansion), and, finally, of failure to take into consideration the great amount of speculative buying. The Committee finds that this lack of information is characteristic. Conditions in the silk industry could in this respect be duplicated in a large number of other industries.

It was not only manufacturers of silk who were faced with these problems in the early stages of the last business boom. In the autumn of 1919 the merchandise manager of a department store in New England began to make plans for the spring trade in one of his important lines. He knew the prices of raw and finished goods had been advancing steadily, and retailers had encountered difficulties in securing prompt deliveries. He was convinced that he must place his orders well in advance of his needs. His store, like that of other retailers, had sold an unprecedented amount of goods. Trade rumors appeared to indicate that the supply of raw materials was less than normal, and it was so difficult to secure deliveries that retailers duplicated orders with different manufacturers in order to be assured of the delivery of part of their requirements.

The merchandise manager thus decided to place in the autumn an order for the full requirements of the anticipated spring trade in 1920, for the purpose of avoiding the loss of prestige which the store would face if it were unable to supply its customers. To finance its purchases the company negotiated a bank loan at a time when money rates were rising, when wholesale and retail prices of all commodities were tending upward, and when the rapid advance—although the manager did not know this fact—had led to a good deal of speculation in the goods he wished to buy. The loan was obtained, the order given, and the result, of course, was a heavy loss.

It should here be pointed out that the retailer must carry stocks on hand. He must expect to take some losses in a period of depression. Some retailers believe that it is wise to build up a reserve in a rising market, fixing prices on a replacement value; they believe that it is good business to take losses early in a falling market by the same process of determining prices by replacement values. If information were provided to enable the retailer to change his present habits and buy "from hand to mouth" at the top of the boom and in larger quantities in a period of depression, bank credits would be relieved and cancellations decreased. It is the natural tendency at present to overstock in boom times and to stop buying in a depression. This tendency is strengthened by the difficulty of obtaining deliveries in a period of boom.

Early in 1920 a manufacturer of pulp and writing paper contracted to buy a large supply of pulp wood in order that the company's own extensive timber lands might be reserved for later use. The large sums expended for this purpose were listed as assets on the balance sheet of the company. For the first half of 1920 the company did the largest business in its history. Early in the following autumn cancellations began to pour in, and orders for spring delivery declined 50 per cent. Despite the fact that the company seemed to be efficiently organized and had standardized its products it was thrown into bankruptcy because of this error in judgment which caused it to accumulate raw materials at the peak of the cycle.

The object of giving so much space in this brief preliminary report to the difficulties of the business men is, first, to show by these cases the complexity of the problem of business cycles and, second, to emphasize the intricate decisions which confront business managers in their daily activities.

It might be said that our examples prove, in the case of the manufacturers of silk goods at least, that it was the conservative manager who succeeded and that the second manager, in seeking larger profits, took unwarranted speculative risks which resulted in failure. This is by no means universally true. The following instance of two manufacturers in the shoe industry illustrates the difference between what may be readily recognized as a conservative policy in one period of the business cycle and what just as clearly becomes a speculative policy in the other extreme of the cycle.

The first manufacturer of shoes, well along in the period of expansion, received more than normal orders from his customers. He knew the industry was overexpanded but he lacked any basis for judging how to handle his business at this time. Supplies of leather were apparently very small; congested railroad conditions made it imperative to have his raw material shipped to him several weeks before it was usually necessary; prices of leather were rapidly rising. The men in the industry did not question the price at which leather could be purchased but seemed willing to pay any price for raw material laid down at the factory. Under these conditions the manufacturer followed what must have seemed to him a conservative policy by purchasing raw material enough to cover his orders. Then came the break in leather prices; cancellations poured in, and he was unable to liquidate and experienced an enormous loss on his inventory of raw material.

Another manufacturer, under the same market conditions and at the same stage of the business cycle, convinced himself through a study of conditions that his orders were inflated and that it would be unwise to cover with raw material. He cut his orders to 25 per cent of his requirements. Other executives in his plant and particularly his sales organization opposed this policy. They prophesied not only that he would have to cover at high prices but that he would probably not be able to secure raw material at all and consequently his relative position in the industry would be destroyed. After the break this shoe manufacturer was able to purchase raw material to fill his requirements at much reduced prices, and he was able to send his sales organization into the field with a line of shoes produced at low cost, in competition with his competitors who were attempting to liquidate high-priced inventories.

It was not because one of these managers was conservative that he was more successful in coping with the problem of cyclical losses. The distinction which the Committee would emphasize is that the manager who knew and acted with reference to the fundamental facts of the relationship of his particular business to his industry and who had a sound knowledge of general business conditions from study of statistical data of trade generally was able, to a large extent, through policies planned in 1919 and 1920, to avoid the difficulties of 1921, while the manager who ran his business without reference to such factors was gambling in his most important decisions.

Another reason for reviewing these examples is to bring out the differences among industries in their relation to the general business cycle. The instances cited are interesting because the collapse of silk prices came before the depression in the shoe industry, and both came before the slump in paper. It is also of interest to point out that the drop in silk prices was one of the first signs of the general business depression and that paper was one of the last commodities to feel its full effects. The study of trends of our industries should thus become a safeguard.

In dealing with these problems the banks are in a position of great importance. The banks should realize sooner than the typical manufacturer when credit strain is approaching and should be in a position to warn their customers of impending danger. One of the difficulties which makes the banks in this respect less effective than they should be is the competitive situation. The individual borrower never likes to be told by his bank that his request for a loan is not granted, and if his credit standing is high the bank is apt to allow doubtful loans because it fears the loss of the customer's good will and his business through refusing them. This difficulty can be avoided only by placing proper research information in the hands of the bank in such form that the bank may use it with its customers without danger of losing business. The banks must realize that the responsibility for the overexpansion of loans rests upon them rather than upon their borrowers. Expansion of bank credit is a necessary condition of expansion of business operations. When the resources of the banks reach an end, a sudden contraction of loans is always a factor—generally the most compelling factor—in bringing about a business collapse. To meet the varying needs of modern business, credit must be elastic. There should be provisions for expansion as well as contraction. But an overexpansion of credit may so increase the purchasing power of business men that it will merely result in enabling them to bid against one another for limited supplies of goods and material so as to force prices above what consumers are willing and able to pay. Bank credit often expands so rapidly that it lifts the buying or investment power of business men out of line with the general buying power of the community. Because of their strategic position the banks have an unusual duty and an exceptional opportunity to give sound information and counsel to business men.

A problem which business men faced in 1920 and 1921 was the widespread uncertainty caused by cancellation of orders. From one standpoint these cancellations were entirely unjustifiable. Legally the orders constituted contracts and should have been carried out. It is important, however, to consider why widespread cancellations occurred. Their extent was undoubtedly due to at least two causes, both intensified by the wide fluctuations in that particular cycle.

First, in the period of inflation of 1919 to 1920 an unusual and perhaps unprecedented delay in securing deliveries was caused by the breakdown of transportation facilities near the peak of the boom. Many business men not only placed orders earlier than usual but also duplicated them, or ordered in larger quantities, with the expectation of having deliveries scaled down. When the slump came they had strong temptations to cancel.

Second, price levels had been on such a high plane when orders were placed and the fall in prices was so violent that many business men faced the alternative of cancellation or bankruptcy. Under these conditions it was wiser for the seller to accept cancellation than to deliver material to a customer who could not pay.

These two circumstances account for the fact that cancellations played such an extraordinary part in this cycle. There is reason to believe that in mild swings of the cycle, when inflation does not bring about such excessive commitments and when drops in prices are less drastic, cancellations are less important. The problem, however, should receive the earnest consideration of business men and their associations.

Contracts for purchase of materials should contain definite and substantial financial penalties for cancellation. It is clearly undesirable that contracts should be considered subject to cancellation except under conditions specified in advance, with such penalties as may be fair to both parties. Insistence on this principle and the inclusion in contracts of substantial penalties for cancellation will tend to prevent duplication of orders, to lessen the tendency to place orders far ahead of immediate requirements, and to prevent speculative buying by men who when they order have no intention of completing the purchase if prices drop.

## THE NEED FOR FACTS

From the illustrations of business experience which we have reviewed it is evident that knowledge of one's own business should be strengthened by knowledge of the conditions in the industry of which it is a part, and by information about current and future trends in general business conditions. The business man is placed thereby in a strong position to exercise judgment based on facts rather than on guesses, speculations, or approximations.

First, he must have available for his use current facts about general business conditions throughout the country and knowledge of the probable future trend of general business conditions.

Second, he must have the basic facts about his industry. Because his particular business is influenced by conditions affecting his entire industry, he must be in a position, with others in his industry, to study its peculiar industrial problems.

Third, he must secure enough facts about his own business to give him not merely statistics but a proper basis for judgment as to his general policies.

Fourth, he must inform himself in regard to the general credit situation and especially the attitude of his own bank toward extensions of loans.

## METHODS OF CONTROLLING THE BUSINESS CYCLE

Any consideration of methods to control the business cycle naturally divides itself into two parts—first, methods of preventing excessive expansion, such as occurred in the year 1919 and 1920, and second, methods of reducing the extent of the decline and of alleviating the distress caused by the depression. To a considerable extent these two are connected and interrelated. Anything which controls expansion tends also to lessen depression. Extreme expansion leads business men to dangerous over-extension, which is followed by collapse, whereas more moderate swings of the cycle stop short of this dangerous condition, with the result that more business men are able to maintain their business in a condition fundamentally sound. In cycles where this is typical the recovery of business is much more rapid.

The problem which the Committee has been asked to analyze is the possible prevention of widespread unemployment through the control of extreme fluctuations of the business cycle. The suggested remedies that have been included in the analysis made by the Committee relate both to the direct prevention of expansion or inflation and to the prevention of unemployment. In the order of their discussion these proposed remedies are:

Control of credit expansion by banks generally.

Possible control of inflation by the Federal Reserve System.

Control by individual business men of the expansion of their own industries.

Control of public and private construction, including construction by public utilities, at or near the peak of the business cycle.

Construction of public works in the depression.

Unemployment reserve funds.

Federal and State employment bureaus.

We are not here including a discussion of programs for relief of the unemployed and their families through social and charitable organizations and other agencies of the community charged with the prevention of distress, not because we underrate the importance of such programs, but because programs of relief of the poverty due to unemployment are not within the scope of this investigation.

## RECOMMENDATIONS

### RECOMMENDATION I

**Collection of Fundamental Data.**—Obviously the primary point for assembling data bearing upon trends of business is in each separate establishment. Many business organizations to day maintain intimate and complete statistics as to their production, stocks, orders, consumption, employment, and other pertinent questions not only as of the present but in comparison with former periods.  If, however, business men are to have the data necessary to form a judgment as to the trend of production and consumption in their own industries, and in other industries purchasing from them or selling to them, and to evaluate special influences that may affect productivity or consumption in business as a whole, they must be willing to contribute summaries of the data of their individual units to some common fund of information.

The first requisite in seeking such data is to assure the individual that the detailed facts about his business will not be divulged, except as these facts are included in a general total drawn from several sources.  The second important point is that only the essential facts in simplest possible form are required.

In many industries the cooperation necessary to form a common pool of fundamental facts is made possible through trade associations to which current figures are reported by their members.  In other industries such figures in whole or in part are supplied directly to Government bureaus.  Some of these statistical services have existed over many years and have become incorporated into the daily business life of the country.  They are not, however, sufficiently extensive to answer all needs.

In an endeavor to put in more available form the sum of information now current, and to add to it, Secretary Hoover has established in the Department of Commerce a monthly *SURVEY OF CURRENT BUSINESS* which summarizes the data available from all sources that bear upon this major problem of business trends.  This survey comprises not only the information collected directly by the Department of Commerce, but also the crucial facts collected by other Government bureaus and the material brought together through cooperation within trade associations. To a considerable degree the survey of current business has now covered the range of industry.  It is essential that the service should be maintained and expanded.

The greater part of the material presented by the Department of Commerce is based upon data furnished voluntarily either by industries or by trade associations.  One of the difficulties in making such returns effective for their purpose is the refusal of a few firms to contribute to the common pool through either of these channels.  Such refusal destroys the possibility of common knowledge in certain industries and seriously undermines the ability of business men in such industries to form proper judgments.  It also decreases the area of knowledge of the currents of business as a whole necessary to each separate business.

The vast majority of business men have given enlightened cooperation in these efforts.  But the minority who refuse to cooperate are doing injury to the business fabric as a whole.  Reluctance to reveal facts to competitors is not a valid reason for refusal, since individual returns supplied to the Department of Commerce are protected by special statute and are not available in their individual form for any other purpose either of the Government or of business.

It happens that information which is regarded by many students of the business cycle as most important is conspicuously lacking, namely, the actual stocks of different commodities on hand, whether in the place of manufacture or in transit, or in wholesale or retail warehouses. The practical use of such information may be illustrated if the experience of 1920 and 1921 be recalled. Early in 1920 the prevailing impression was that available goods were inadequate, and that orders must be placed far ahead to insure deliveries. In the summer of 1921, on the other hand, it was commonly believed that the goods on hand exceeded the consumer's demand. All of the facts, however, indicate that early in 1920 there was an excessive supply of goods, a condition which led shortly to collapse, while in the summer of 1921 stocks were very low and the resulting spread between stocks produced and consumers' demand inevitably brought about the current upward turn in the business cycle.

What is evidently needed is an increase in the resources of the Department of Commerce and a larger degree of cooperation with the Department in coordinating and extending business information, so that business men and bankers may know promptly the facts about the rate of production measured in physical units, the stocks on hand and in transit, the trend of prices, the volume of sales, and the trend in money rates. There is great need also for recording data as to the speed of freight movements so as to show whether the output of farms and factories is being promptly distributed to the consumer or is being delayed in transit because of freight congestion. Such congestion results in stimulating and duplicating orders and increasing inventories. Reliable information as to the extent of these delays would be very significant. It is important to emphasize the need of promptness in publishing statistical data and the fact that the failure of individual business units to make prompt returns delays the whole.

Of the various data needed, statistics of employment are highly important and are being collected with increasing efficiency by the federal Bureau of Labor Statistics. Conditions in business are invariably reflected in the volume of employment. Employment statistics reflect the economic welfare of wage-earners and are information of the greatest social importance.

When the Conference on Unemployment met in Washington in 1921 the federal Bureau of Labor Statistics was collecting monthly from a limited number of industries data as to the total number on pay-rolls each month and the total wages paid, which indicate whether industries are carrying their normal forces of employees or whether men are being laid off. From the State of New York the federal bureau secured its reports through the State Department of Labor, which was collecting identical facts extensive enough to chart the course of employment in the state. Duplication was thus avoided and only one report was required of any industrial plant, while both state and nation got the benefit of the information. The same plan has been in effect in Wisconsin since 1920. Recently Illinois and Massachusetts have arranged for the same sort of cooperation with the federal bureau. Once the plan has been launched in New York, Wisconsin, Illinois, and Massachusetts business men welcome the information and make reports promptly. Other states should now cooperate and the resources of the federal Bureau of Labor Statistics should be made sufficient for adequate work.

## RECOMMENDATION II

**Larger Statistical Service.**—The Committee recommends the expansion and standardization of the statistics now collected by state and federal bureaus, the publication of employment statistics by the federal Bureau of Labor Statistics, and the final summation and publication of all of these statistics by the Department of Commerce, in order that there may be promptly available a connected, uniform series of facts about the trend of business. It is important that agreements should be reached as to uniform definitions of terms and simplification of the material. Representatives of the various industries should aid Government bureaus in working out the questions to be asked and in securing the cooperation of their respective industries in establishing the habit of regular, prompt, and accurate reporting. It is the consensus of opinion of those who have most experience in the use of these periodical statistics that they should be as simple as possible and published promptly after they are collected.

With the exhaustive Census of Manufactures made by the Department of Commerce in five-year instead of two-year periods, it is possible annually to collect intermediate statistics of sufficient reliability by sampling methods, basing the ratio upon the five-year determinations, and to issue these figures promptly. Beyond this, monthly statistics of the same items are vital, although they need not be so exhaustive.

Expedition in publication is highly important, and while with the present limited resources of the Government departments and trade associations it is impossible to collect otherwise than by mail, it would be of the greatest possible value to business and commerce if the results of certain key industries could be collected by telegraph and published within the first ten days of each month; these to be followed by the more ample statistics collected by mail and relating to a larger spread and number of industries.

In collecting figures on stocks and production the following list of commodities has been suggested to the Committee by experts as most significant in showing the trend of the business cycle. Statistics of these commodities should be collected through a telegraphic service and should be issued immediately, as stated above. Later they should be published with more ample data in monthly publications, together with the statistics of many other industries which bear indirectly upon the question, all being finally related to the one-year and five-year periods. The list follows:

Raw wool and woolen textiles.
Raw cotton and cotton textiles.
Hides and leather and shoes.
Iron and steel and leading fabricated products, such as structural steel and standard tools.
Zinc, lead, and copper and leading products of each.
Bituminous coal.

The collection and dissemination of statistics must be current, periodic, and in comparable form for many industries. They should be uniform and continuous, and they should be collected officially, since complete data rather than samples are necessary, and no private organization could have the authority to secure without interruption this basic information. Moreover, uniformity is important, and hence it is desirable not to have the work scattered through several organizations.

## RECOMMENDATION III

**Research.**—A primary necessity is the collection and dissemination of fundamental data. Following this, we need further development of special research into economic forces, into business currents, and into broad questions of economic method. Industries generally recognize the need of research in physical science. Laboratories have been equipped with large staffs of trained workers. A similar recognition of the importance of economic research and the interpretation of economic facts would be the beginning of better control of business conditions by business men.

Although more constructive and thorough research should be carried on by individual companies with reference to their own individual business and to the industry of which they are a part, and more extensive research information should be disseminated by the Government, there is need for investigations by financially disinterested and impartial research organizations through whose work the individual manager can "check" the results presented to him by his own research department. Companies which have developed research departments for physical science have already appreciated the need for outside impartial investigation of the same problems that are being studied within their own laboratories.

The business fraternity should recognize the value of such work and encourage both outside organizations and universities to go further in the investigation of economic subjects.

The forecasting of probable business trends is difficult and can never be undertaken successfully by any kind of public institution, except in a limited field. Business men must themselves form their own fundamental judgments when adequate data are furnished. Research as to the effect of different trends and economic forces is, however, a different problem from forecasting. Such research should be carried on continuously by the Government bureaus, because the data available to these bureaus are more extensive than those available to other institutions, which must depend upon published summaries of Government data.

## RECOMMENDATION IV

**Control of Credit Expansion by Banks.**—The individuals banker, like the individual business man, may properly be asked to aliume some measure of responsibility. If only in his own interest, his policies should be determined by the general business situation as well as by the apparent soundness of the particular transactions his customers ask him to finance. The solvency of his customers is inextricably bound up with that of other business firms. The soundness of their transactions often depends upon whether or not the expansion of business is outrunning the purchasing power of consumers. To guide his policies the banker, like the business man, needs access to a large fund of knowledge about the general trend of business activities, and because he is a specialist in finance the banker has a peculiar obligation to give sound advice to his customers. One suggestion is that when prices are rising and business is expanding bankers should ask borrowers to maintain an increasing ratio of quick assets to current liabilities.

Before the establishment of the Federal Reserve System the banks often expanded their loans until their reserves were reduced to a dangerous point. Forced then to curtail credit drastically, their action had made more severe the reaction following a period of prosperity. It is generally recognized that in 1920 the resources of the Federal Reserve System enabled the banks to carry their customers through a difficult period and thus very likely prevented a panic. Much would have been gained if more of the banks had warned their customers of the impending financial stress.

The individual banks can render another service in the depression. Both the Reserve System and the banks protected customers to ar extraordinary extent during the period of falling prices.   But borrowing by individual banks from the Federal Reserve Banks during the last depression was new to the banks of this country, and many such banks had an uncomfortable feeling of inefficiency and weakness until their loans at the Reserve Banks were reduced to small amounts or were entirely eliminated.   In many specific instances this undoubtedly resulted in their bringing pressure on customers to liquidate loans as early in the period of recovery as such liquidation was possible.   And while in some ways liquidation was helpful, undoubtedly it sometimes resulted in complete or practically complete liquidation of businesses which with a little more time could have regained their feet.   Fortunately a reasonably liberal policy in the depression stage of the last cycle was the general practice on the part of banks and of the Reserve System.

### Recommendation V

**Possible Control of Inflation by the Federal Reserve System.**—A close parallel is usually observable between the cycle of business and the cycle of credit.   While the relationship between the volume of credit and the volume of business and the movement of prices is not always simple to interpret it appears to be sufficiently close to make it a matter of first importance that the volume and the flow of credit should at all times be tested by the contribution which additions to the volume of credit make to the total of economic production.   Additions to credits which cannot be economically validated by a commensurate effect in actual production are speculative, and as such should be subjected to control, so that business and industry can be maintained in a healthy state.   Such control is primarily the responsibility of the banker and secondarily of our agencies of banking supervision.

Credit conditions are of major importance in the upward movement of the cycle and in precipitating the decline, so that the first and most important method of controlling the cycle and preventing excessive expansion should be found in the fundamentals of our banking situation. Control of expansion so that production is allowed to increase and business is actively stimulated to a proper degree, while expansion is checked at the stage when it becomes dangerous, is a fundamental principle already accepted by bankers.

The only automatic check upon the expansion of bank loans in a period of prosperity is the requirement of the law that the banks shall always maintain a certain specified minimum legal reserve against their current liabilities.   But there should be an additional limitation due to the banker's own realization of his responsibility to the community in the issuance of additional credits.   This is particularly important because under the Federal Reserve System the so-called automatic check upon the banker can be rendered ineffective through the replenishment of his reserve by borrowing from Federal Reserve Banks.

With the Federal Reserve as the chief agency for the supply of credit beyond the ordinary supply of the banks of the community, the problem requires wise and sagacious administration on the part of the Federal Reserve System, so that this most important function of the Federal Reserve System can be effectively performed. From the point of view of the economic welfare of the country the Federal Reserve authorities should be given every encouragement and support in the administration of the credit facilities of the System.

The Federal Reserve Banks now hold, as a result of the War, a much larger amount of gold than would suffice to support all of the credit which American industry and agriculture can possibly need on anything like present price levels. Much of this gold we are holding only temporarily—virtually as trustees for the world. With the return of more prosperous conditions in Europe a considerable part of this gold will naturally leave us. Meanwhile this excess gold might become the basis of a disastrous inflation of our domestic credit, which would be followed by an even more disastrous collapse when the gold goes out. It has been suggested that the Federal Reserve System should, if possible, set aside or earmark as a special reserve against future foreign demands that portion of their gold holdings which is considered by them now in excess of the proportion of the world's gold which this country should normally be expected to hold. Although it is important that credit should be available at the time of a crisis, it is also important for the general public to realize that the expansion of credit in times of "prosperity" should be guarded by the voluntary action of business men cautioned and advised by bankers, to the end that "prosperity" may be preserved and not destroyed by inflation, which in due course must precipitate depression and deflation, with their inevitable consequences of social and economic distress.

Our banking system represents a common pool of both investment and commercial capital, and for that reason the devices of European systems for the control of speculation are not applicable here to the same extent as they are abroad. A finer distinction between the two broad groups is desirable but is largely impracticable in the United States. The subject, however, warrants research and study. In any event the determination of the time when business passes from the area of economically legitimate hazard to the area of economically illegitimate hazard or when the proper use of capital for the expansion of production passes into the improper use for the pyramiding of prices requires a large development of economic statistical information and agencies for its interpretation.

In a government such as ours the most difficult question to solve from the very beginning has been how to centralize in individuals sufficient power to enable the Government machinery to function wisely and promptly and at the same time to impose such restraints and balances as to guard against autocratic or arbitrary exercise of such power. This is the problem which faces us in the development of the Federal Reserve System to its maximum usefulness, and it is a problem worthy of most careful and thorough study by bankers and associations of bankers.

## RECOMMENDATION VI

**Control by Business Men of the Expansion of Their Own Industries.**—The Committee has seen numerous instances in which the individual business man, by conducting his business with reference to the business cycle, has avoided dangerous overextension of inventories and fixed capital which in many other instances resulted in unemployment and business failure during the cycle just past. It therefore believes that while the individual cannot in any large way influence the general situation or entirely avoid the losses incurred in periods of depression he can in most cases by foresight keep his business fundamentally sound.*

Few subjects in recent years have attracted more attention from business men than the stabilization of business operations. Various devices have been employed with varying success. Many of these have been ineffective because of failure to base the plans upon the fundamental fact that business policies should be determined with full recognition of their relation to the business cycle.

Planning production in advance and with reference to the business cycle, laying out extensions of plant and equipment ahead of immediate requirements with the object of carrying them out in periods of depression and carrying through such construction plans during periods of low prices in conformity with the long-time trend, the accumulation of financial reserves in prosperity in order to mark down inventories at the peak, and the maintenance of a long view of business problems rather than a short view will enable firms to make headway toward stabilization.

The firm which approaches a period of business depression in the strongest financial condition is most likely to be able to give its workers steady employment.

## RECOMMENDATION VII

**Control of Private and Public Construction at the Peak.**—One method by which periods of expansion might in part be controlled is through the cessation and postponement of construction by the Government, railroads, public utilities, and private owners in boom periods when prices are high. Cessation or postponement of construction work is obviously wise in any such period and will tend to level the cycle.

* So far as construction is concerned, this topic is treated in the next section in connection with similar governmental projects.

Individual business men and corporations should consider the business cycle far more than they do in planning their construction work. The results for the farsighted firms that exercise this type of business judgment are most satisfactory. Reserves built up in periods of high earnings and expansion are then spent for construction during periods of depression. When this policy is more generally followed it will be of peculiar value, as it will tend to keep low the ratio of fixed investment to productive capacity, to the great advantage of industry.

There are difficulties, however, in the way of a widespread extension of this practice on the part of business men. In the first place, the tax situation even now naturally tends to make companies extravagant in maintenance charges in good times. Moreover, the business man whose business has developed to a point where the demand for his finished product is in excess of his capacity to produce is always beset by the arguments of his sales organization desiring to see plant capacity balanced with apparent selling capacity, and on the other hand by the arguments of the salesmen of construction companies who, like his own salesmen, assure him that construction costs in future will inevitably be higher than they are at present. While it is desirable, therefore, to postpone as many types of permanent construction work as possible until periods of depression, the real hope that this can be accomplished as a matter of wide policy is dependent on the possession by business men of data showing fundamental conditions with reference to periodic fluctuations.

Systematic accumulation of reserves by business men in times of prosperity for use in plant expansion and improvement in times of depression would, if widely adopted, be an excellent method of controlling the crest of the boom and ameliorating the depression. It has the advantage that it is a method which any business man may adopt to his individual advantage.

Holding back public works and private construction for periods of depression not only gives employment to large numbers of workers when it is most needed but creates a demand for raw materials for construction which in turn stimulates other industries to offer employment. It maintains the buying power of those directly or indirectly employed, it creates a market for goods, and it enables the workers directly or indirectly employed to buy the products of other industries. Finally, construction work in a period of industrial depression, when costs are lower, is economical.

The essential steps in any general program are to plan construction work, private or public, long in advance with reference to the cyclical movement of business, and in the case of public works to pass the necessary legislative appropriations when facts about the trend of business show that it is sound policy to spend money for such purposes.

If it were possible for a smaller percentage of public works projects to be undertaken in periods when private industry is active, so that more work might be done during periods when private industry is slack, the Government would not compete with private industry to so great an extent in times of prosperity and thus would not be a factor in the inflation of money rates, prices of materials, and employment.

The Committee calls attention to the need for careful drafting of laws to insure a policy of reserving public works projects, if this is to be done effectively. The need for fixing the responsibility for the preparation of such plans in advance, the importance of securing the release of the projects at the right time by legislation, and the provisions for financing should be considered with special relation to the obstacles, legal and others, which the particular public authority would have to overcome. While the difficulties are great, everything which can be accomplished in this way is valuable.

## RECOMMENDATION VIII

**Public Utilities.**—The controlling factors in the management of public utilities and railroads differ obviously from private business, because of Government regulation of earnings and rates. So far as railroads and public utilities are concerned, both are likely to find their net earnings reduced in a period of high prices and high wages. This tends naturally to bring about a construction policy similar to the one which we have recommended above.

With reduced earnings and the high interest rates which are customary at the peak of inflation, the natural tendency of public utilities is to postpone improvements until net earnings are better and interest rates are lower. This is typically true in periods of low general prices.

In the interest both of the utilities and of the buying public it is obvious that the normal time to finance new construction or improvements in public utilities is in periods of depression, when interest charges are reasonable and costs of construction low, but the delays encountered at such times in obtaining the necessary authorizations by public regulating bodies may in many cases be such that the favorable money market is lost. This is a problem to be studied by public-service commissions and similar bodies, which can by prompt action meet this difficulty.

In so far as the managers of utilities and public-service commissioners can regulate construction in order to fill up the valleys and lower the peaks of the business cycle, they will aid in alleviating the extremes of the cycle, and by means of their economies they will keep their capital investment from unnecessary expansion, to the advantage both of the utilities and of the public.

## Recommendation IX

**Unemployment Reserve Funds.**—Nothing is more demoralizing for wage-earners than the feeling of insecurity of employment. Unemployment and the fear of unemployment are powerful causes of discontent. Wage-earning men and women must meet responsibilities for the support of themselves and their families wholly from their earnings. Loss of employment not only eliminates income but lessens the ability of wage-earning men and women and their families to make purchases, thus intensifying the period of depression.

To provide reserve funds or savings during periods of prosperity from which the worker may draw during periods of compulsory unemployment is one of the important methods advocated as tending toward relieving the fluctuations of business. Such plans of cooperative provision for relief against unemployment are not primarily designed to decrease the amount of unemployment but to alleviate its evil effects.

The idea of employer, employee, or both contributing during periods of employment to a reserve fund under separate or joint control to help sustain the worker when unemployed in periods of depression, and to equalize and stabilize his purchasing capacity, merits consideration. It attacks one of the most vital of our industrial problems. The establishment of funds by the employer or by associated workers to take care of foreseen or unforeseen contingencies has proved advantageous in the past. Neither reserves against decline of inventory value set up by manufacturers nor unemployment benefits of trade unions are new things to American industrial life. The principle may well be extended.

In considering the principle upon which unemployment reserves should be based, the Committee finds that American experience with cooperative unemployment reserve funds is very scanty. The experimentation which has been carried on in this country is confined largely to trade unions and to the individual efforts of a few firms.

Experiments here and abroad in this important field serve principally to suggest interesting questions for discussion. Certain inherent difficulties immediately become apparent; one of them, as the Committee has already pointed out, is the lack of essential data to determine the amount of unemployment, not to mention the unemployment specifically due to the business cycle. Among the plans considered or tried are various forms of unemployment reserve funds organized by individual companies for their workers, or by whole industries for the entire group of workers engaged in them, or by groups of workers, or state or nation. Each has obvious difficulties.

Because of the large expense involved it appears fundamental to the success of such experiments that cyclical unemployment be reduced to its minimum before any general relief measures are attempted. Moreover, effective plans for accumulating general funds against periods of cyclical unemployment require large-scale organization and the solution of many complex problems of administration. On these accounts the Committee feels that it must wait upon the experience to be gained from varied experimentation in the organization of such plans before attempting to recommend a definite program.

The Committee cannot emphasize too strongly the importance of preventing undue expansion of the business cycle as brought out in earlier sections of this report, and this will also add to the possibility of securing a sound actuarial basis for unemployment reserves.

## RECOMMENDATION X

**Employment Bureaus.**—A national system of employment bureaus was recommended by the President's Conference on Unemployment, and the Committee gives hearty approval to that recommendation. We do not regard an employment service as having a direct and immediate effect upon the business cycle. We do believe that if such employment bureaus are organized throughout the country their reports will show the demand for labor and the number of workers seeking positions and will therefore be another measure of business conditions. If employment bureaus are organized effectively enough to insure transfer from one position to another with the least possible loss of time, they will make labor more immediately available and thus prevent loss of production for the employer and loss of income for the wage-earners, thus helping to maintain the level of purchasing power. It is obvious that any measure which tends to maintain the level of purchasing power tends to stability in business.

In conclusion the Committee would reiterate its conviction that unless business men, bankers, and others who are responsible for policies and practices in industry begin without delay to study and to act in order to meet the problems of unemployment and business cycles, solutions which may prove to be fundamentally unsound will be attempted without the benefit of practical experience. No problem before the business world today offers a more inspiring challenge to sound industrial leadership.

OWEN D. YOUNG, *Chairman.*
CLARENCE M. WOOLLEY.
JOSEPH H. DEFREES.
MATTHEW WOLL.
MARY VAN KLEECK.
EDWARD EYRE HUNT, *Secretary.*

## QUESTIONS FOR DISCUSSION

By way of summarizing the main problems which the Committee has had under consideration the following general questions are set forth for discussion and comment by such groups as may desire to cooperate with the Committee in a program of study and experiment.

**1. To Business Men** (including all managers of industries and wholesale and retail distributors):

Would you regard as practicable and effective for your industry the program suggested by the Committee, including more comprehensive periodic statistics of employment and business conditions; a more adequate plan of research, possibly developed by each industry as a whole in cooperation with universities or other research agencies; revision of banking practice to conform to business policies gradually built up on the basis of more facts developed through research; a cooperative plan throughout the industry for unemployment reserve funds; and the development of a nation-wide system of public employment bureaus? What other statistics do you require in the conduct of your business and from what other industries should they be secured to be of most value to you? What problems for economic research or special study is your industry concerned with?

What would you add to this outline and how would you modify it? What facilities for putting it into effect already exist in your own industry? What obstacles do you see in carrying it out, and how could they be removed?

**2. To Bankers:**

To what extent can the business cycle be affected or its consequences averted by bankers? How far is the possibility of action by bankers dependent upon a change in laws, and how far is it dependent upon the individual action of bankers upon the basis of a sound interpretation of statistics?

**3. To Managers of Public Utilities and Public Service Commissioners:**

To what extent can public utilities now plan their operations so as to finance construction when costs are low and resist the demands for extension when costs are high? What would be the effect of such a policy upon rates, and how can the obstacles in the way of carrying it out be removed?

**4. To Wage-Earners:**

Would the bad effects of unemployment be lessened by unemployment reserve funds? How can such reserve funds be best established? How are such funds best administered? Do you favor a nation-wide system of employment bureaus, and how can the public employment bureaus best serve the workers in your trade?

**5. To Engineers:**

To what extent can improvements in methods of production and organization of marketing in each industry relieve the business cycle? What are the difficulties now in the way of making these improvements and how can the difficulties be removed?

**6. To Citizens' Organizations:**

How can the influence of citizens be most effectively enlisted in backing the proposed program for the establishment of more adequate statistical services in state and federal bureaus and the planning and timing of public works; in support of policies in public utilities which will influence the business cycle; in encouraging the cooperative action of industries to provide unemployment reserve funds and in supporting permissive legislation for this purpose if it be necessary; in support of bankers, wage-earners, and business men in their efforts to adopt a sounder policy?

## NOTE ON THE REPORT OF THE NATIONAL BUREAU OF ECONOMIC RESEARCH

The first act of the Committee after its appointment by Secretary Hoover was to ask the National Bureau of Economic Research to map out an investigation which would formulate present experience with unemployment and business cycles and so would assist the Committee in beginning its inquiry into these complex subjects. But the Committee desires to point out that it is in no way responsible as a Committee for the findings in the Bureau's report and that, in accordance with provisions in the Bureau's constitution, that organization in turn does not make itself responsible for the statements and recommendations of this Committee.

The report of the National Bureau of Economic Research is intended to furnish the Committee on Unemployment and Business Cycles and the public which the Committee seeks to interest, a statement showing—

1. Such explanations concerning the nature of business cycles and the fluctuations in employment as are necessary for understanding the problem.

2. The character and bearing of the leading devices which have been tried or proposed for mitigating unemployment through control over the fluctuations of business activity.

3. The conditions which must be considered in judging the probable effectiveness of these devices.

## ACKNOWLEDGMENTS

The Committee is indebted for valuable advice and assistance to a number of organizations and individuals:

To the Carnegie Corporation for the funds which have made the investigation possible; to the National Bureau of Economic Research

Inc. for the report prepared for the use of the Committee under the direction of Wesley C. Mitchell, who is a pioneer in the scientific study of business cycles; to the Russell Sage Foundation, the American Association for Labor Legislation, the Bureau of Railway Economics, the Federated American Engineering Societies, the American Federation of Labor, the United States Chamber of Commerce, the American Statistical Association, the American Economic Association, the federal Departments of Agriculture, Commerce, and Labor; and also to those named in the following list:

Thomas S. Adams, Professor of Political Economy, Yale University, New Haven, Connecticut.

John B. Andrews, Secretary, American Association for Labor Legislation, New York.

George E. Barnett, Professor of Statistics, Johns Hopkins University, Baltimore, Maryland.

David Beecroft, Directing Editor, Class Journal.Company, New York.

W. A. Berridge, Assistant Professor of Economics, Brown University, Providence, Rhode Island.

Anne Bezanson, Assistant Director, Department of Industrial Research, University of Pennsylvania, Philadelphia, Pennsylvania.

C. P. Biddle, Assistant Dean, Harvard School of Business Administration, Cambridge, Massachusetts.

Charles F. Boots, Legislative Drafting Fund, Columbia University, New York.

Ernest S. Bradford, Vice President, American Statistical Association, New York.

Paul F. Brissenden, Assistant Professor of Business Administration in Extension Teaching, Columbia University, New York.

Charles J. Bullock, Professor of Economics, Chairman of the Committee of Economic Research, Harvard University, Cambridge, Massachusetts.

V. E. Carroll, Editor, *Textile World*, New York.

Joseph P. Chamberlain, Director, Legislative Drafting Bureau, Columbia University, New York.

Wilson Compton, Secretary and Manager, National Lumber Manufacturers' Association, Washington, D. C.

Clifford B. Connelley, Pennsylvania State Commissioner of Labor and Industry, Harrisburg, Pennsylvania.

Melvin T. Copeland, Professor of Marketing and Director, Harvard Bureau of Business Research, Cambridge, Massachusetts.

Stuart M. Crocker, Assistant to Owen D. Young, Chairman of the Board, General Electric Company, New York.

Herbert J. Davenport, Professor of Economics, Cornell University, Ithaca, New York.

Donald K. David, Assistant Dean and Professor, Harvard School of Business Administration, Cambridge, Massachusetts.

Henry S. Dennison, President, Dennison Manufacturing Company, Framingham, Massachusetts.

Wallace B. Donham, Dean, Harvard School of Business Administration, Cambridge, Massachusetts.

John Donnan, Secretary, Southern Hardware Jobbers, Richmond, Virginia.

E. F. DuBrul, General Manager, National Machine Tool Builders' Association, Cincinnati, Ohio.

Richard T. Ely, Professor of Political Economy, University of Wisconsin, Madison, Wisconsin.

F. M. Feiker, Assistant to the President, McGraw-Hill Company, New York.

Frank A. Fetter, Professor of Political Economy, Princeton University, Princeton, New Jersey.

A. I. Findley, Editor, *Iron Age*, New York.

Irving Fisher, Professor of Political Economy, Yale University, New Haven, Connecticut.

Reginald L. Foster, Major, Quartermaster Corps, United States Army, Washington, D. C.

Edwin F. Gay, President, *New York Evening Post*, New York.

Elliott Goodwin, Vice President, United States Chamber of Commerce, Washington, D. C.

M. B. Hammond, Associate Professor of Economics, Ohio State University, Columbus, Ohio.

Alvin Hansen, Professor of Economics, University of Minnesota, Minneapolis, Minnesota.

Shelby M. Harrison, Director, Department of Surveys and Exhibits, Russell Sage Foundation, New York.

Ralph E. Heilman, Professor of Economics and Social Science, Northwestern University, Evanston, Illinois.

Jacob H. Hollander, Professor of Political Economy, Baltimore, Maryland.

Pierre Jay, Chairman Board of Directors, Federal Reserve Bank, New York.

Emory Johnson, Dean, Wharton School of Finance and Commerce, University of Pennsylvania, Philadelphia, Pennsylvania.

Vernon Kellogg, Secretary, National Reserach Council, Washington, D. C.

Willford I. King, National Bureau of Economic Research, New York.

Oswald W. Knauth, National Bureau of Economic Research, New York.

Mortimer Lane, Assistant Editor, *Survey of Current Business*, Bureau of the Census, Washington, D. C.

Frederick P. Lee, Legislative Draftsman, United States Senate, Washington, D. C.

Richard Lennihan, Assistant Director of the Harvard Bureau of Business Research, Cambridge, Massachusetts.

C. E. Lesher, Editor, *Coal Age*, New York City, New York.

Samuel McCune Lindsay, Professor of Social Legislation, Columbia University, New York.

Otto T. Mallery, Member, Pennsylvania State Industrial Board, Harrisburg, Pennsylvania.

L. C. Marshall, Professor of Economics, University of Chicago, Chicago, Illinois.

R. C. Marshall, Jr., General, Associated General Contractors of America, Washington, D. C.

Frederick R. Macaulay, National Bureau of Economic Research, New York.

E. W. McCullough, Manager, Fabricated Production Department, United States Chamber of Commerce, Washington, D. C.

M. P. McNair, Bureau of Business Research, Harvard University, Cambridge, Massachusetts.

John C. Merriam, President, Carnegie Institution, Washington, D. C.

Adolph C. Miller, Member Federal Reserve Board, Washington, D. C.

Harry A. Millis, Economist, University of Chicago, Chicago, Illinois.

Wesley C. Mitchell, National Bureau of Economic Research, New York.

Gilbert H. Montague, Member of the Bar, New York City.

Harold G. Moulton, Director, Institute of Economics, Washington, D. C.

Seaman F. Northrup, Director, Bureau of Industrial Relations, New York.

Julius H. Parmelee, Director, Bureau of Railway Economics, Washington, D. C.

Warren M. Persons, Professor of Business Economics, Editor of The Harvard Economic Service, Cambridge, Massachusetts.

Arthur L. Rice, Editor, *Power Plant Engineering*, Chicago, Illinois.

Stuart A. Rice, Department of Sociology, Columbia University, New York.

W. Z. Ripley, Professor of Political Economy, Harvard University, Cambridge, Massachusetts.

William A. Scott, Director, School of Commerce, University of Wisconsin, Madison, Wisconsin.

Henry R. Seager, Professor of Political Economy, Columbia University, New York.

Horace Secrist, Professor of Economics, Northwestern University, Evanston, Illinois.

Edwin R. A. Seligman, Professor of Political Economy, Columbia University, New York.

William M. Steuart, Director, Bureau of the Census, Washington, D. C.

Ethelbert Stewart, Director, Bureau of Labor Statistics, Washington, D. C.

Walter W. Stewart, Director, Division of Analysis and Research, Federal Reserve Board, Washington, D. C.

N. I. Stone, General Manager, Hickey-Freeman Company, Rochester, New York.

Frank W. Taussig, Professor of Political Economy, Harvard University, Cambridge, Massachusetts.

Sanford E. Thompson, The Thompson & Lichtner Company, Engineers, Boston, Massachusetts.

Homer B. Vanderblue, Professor of Business Economics, The Harvard Economic Service, Cambridge, Massachusetts.

Alexander Wall, Robert Morris Associates, Lansdowne, Pennsylvania.

L. W. Wallace, Executive Secretary, The Federated American Engineering Societies, Washington, D. C.

Joseph H. Willits, Head of Department of Geography and Industry, Wharton School of Finance and Commerce, University of Pennsylvania, Philadelphia, Pennsylvania.

Colonel Arthur Woods, New York.

Leo Wolman, Lecturer, New School for Social Research, New York.

Allyn A. Young, Professor of Economics, Harvard University, Cambridge, Massachusetts.

INVESTIGATION
MADE UNDER THE AUSPICES OF THE
NATIONAL BUREAU OF ECONOMIC RESEARCH

# PREFATORY NOTE

" Business Cycles and Unemployment" is a special investigation made under the direction of the National Bureau of Economic Research. It was undertaken under circumstances of peculiar urgency which are explained in the Introduction, and which differentiate it rather sharply from the normal type of work which the Bureau is undertaking to do. But the general procedure established in the By-laws of the Bureau has been followed, in that the manuscript of each chapter has been submitted to the Directors for their approval. Many changes in the text have been made as a result of their suggestions and constructive criticisms. Such criticisms and remarks as it was found impossible to incorporate in the text are shown in footnotes.

Two general comments by directors are appended:

I have not been able to read nearly all of the manuscript, but have looked it over in a cursory way and read a good deal. I think the work is well conceived and well done, and will be a valuable contribution to the subject.

GEORGE E. ROBERTS.

As one of the directors of the National Bureau of Economic Research I approve the publication of the report on "Business Cycles and Unemployment" as it has been submitted to me in manuscript, in common with other directors of the Bureau. I feel constrained, however, to append a note to the effect that the study of conditions and events that has been made does not give adequate attention to fundamental economic motivations that are beyond control. I refer to such things as broad national enterprises that may prove to be mistakes, to deep rooted and widely extending alterations in the conditions of production and consumption, to general wars, and to changes in social conditions.

In illustration of my meaning I cite too premature building of railways in the West of the United States, the greatly increased production of silver by fortuitous discovery and improvements in the arts of mining and metallurgy that led eventually to the demonetization of silver, the Great War of 1914–18 with its consequential economic dislocations spreading all over the world, and the social disturbances and changes which confront us now. It is important not to confuse ordinary business cycles with the irregular undulations following some great upheaval of such nature.

The Great War of 1914–18 produced an economic cataclysm that enmeshed almost every human being in the civilized world. There will be no dissent from the statement that the world has not yet passed out of its shadow. It seems to me to be highly dangerous to convey any impression that the United States in 1921 simply passed through the depression of an ordinary business cycle.

WALTER R. INGALLS.

With these amendments, the report is approved by the Board of Directors, who are as follows:

Directors-at-Large:

T. S. Adams,
    Advisor to the U. S. Treasury Department.
John R. Commons,
    Professor of Political Economy, University of Wisconsin.
John P. Frey,
    Editor of the International Molders' Journal.
Edwin F. Gay,
    President of the New York Evening Post.
Harry W. Laidler,
    Secretary of the League for Industrial Democracy.
Elwood Mead,
    Professor of Rural Institutions, University of California.
Wesley C. Mitchell,
    Professor of Economics, Columbia University.
J. E. Sterrett,
    Member of the firm of Price, Waterhouse and Company.
N. I. Stone,
    General Manager, Hickey-Freeman Company.
Allyn A. Young.
    Professor of Economics, Harvard University.

Directors-by-Appointment, Nominated by Organizations:

Hugh Frayne,
    The American Federation of Labor.
David Friday,
    The American Economic Association.
W. R. Ingalls,
    American Engineering Council.
J. M. Larkin,
    National Personnel Association.
George E. Roberts,
    The American Bankers' Association.
Malcolm C. Rorty,
    The American Statistical Association.
A. W. Shaw,
    The Periodical Publisher's Association.
Gray Silver,
    The American Federation of Farm Bureaus.

NEW YORK, N. Y.
*January,* 1923.

# PART I
# THE RELATION OF BUSINESS CYCLES
# TO UNEMPLOYMENT

# BUSINESS CYCLES AND UNEMPLOYMENT

## INTRODUCTION

By Wesley C. Mitchell

National Bureau of Economic Research

### I. HOW THIS REPORT CAME TO BE PREPARED

In his foreword to the report of the Committee on Unemployment and Business Cycles, Secretary Herbert Hoover has explained the circumstances under which he asked the National Bureau of Economic Research to investigate the feasibility of various plans which had been suggested for mitigating or preventing the widespread unemployment which accompanies business depression.

The National Bureau of Economic Research was chartered in 1920 to conduct quantitative investigations into subjects that affect public welfare. Its aim is to ascertain fundamental facts within its field as accurately as may be and to make these facts widely known. The form of organization is designed to ensure not only scientific and impartial work on the part of its staff, but also a review of their results by men who represent all the important angles from which economic problems are viewed. Control is vested in a board of twenty-one directors of widely divergent training, experience, and opinions. All reports made by the staff are submitted to this board before publication, and any director who dissents from a finding approved by the majority may have his dissenting opinion published if he so desires. It is believed that this critical scrutiny of results by such a board safeguards the Bureau's reports against bias.

In preparing the present report upon Business Cycles and Unemployment, the Bureau sought the help of various experts not connected with its staff. The field to be covered was wide, and the time allowed for completing the report was strictly limited to six months from February 20, 1922, when funds became available for starting the work. Only by securing the cooperation of those most familiar with the various detailed problems was it possible to accomplish the task within the time. A glance at the table of contents where the names of these associated workers are given will show how large a share they and the organizations with which several of them are connected have taken in the investigation.

1

## II. THE SCOPE OF THE REPORT

Three other limits were imposed upon the report. It was not to exceed 400 pages in length. It was to distinguish between the problems of "cyclical" and of "seasonal" unemployment and so far as feasible to treat only the former. It was to present, not recommendations concerning what ought to be done, but facts which ought to be considered by those who have the responsibility of formulating policies—specifically the Committee on Unemployment and Business Cycles appointed by Secretary Hoover, and more at large all citizens who participate in the discussion, enactment, or administration of practical measures for reducing unemployment.

Because of these limitations of time, size, and scope, this report is very far from being an exhaustive treatise. It is rather a reconnaissance survey, run quickly through a wide territory, in the hope of enabling the social engineers to locate the most promising routes for the construction of new highways. Books thicker than the present volume have been written upon at least half the topics here treated in a single chapter or a single section and with good reason. Indeed, it is hoped that several of the contributors to this report will soon publish the results of their investigations in fuller form than is here possible. Similar investigation and discussion on the part of many other public-spirited citizens is eminently desirable; for it is only by the cumulation of contributions from many minds that a social problem so difficult as the prevention of cyclical unemployment can be solved.

It is also hoped that the closely related problem of seasonal unemployment, which is here set aside, will be taken up by a distinct set of agencies technically qualified to deal with its endless intricacies. The attempt to segregate cyclical and seasonal unemployment has serious disadvantages, which will be clear to the reader of the following chapters. But the attempt to treat both problems with the means at hand would have been futile. Anyone who works even a little way into the problem of seasonal unemployment realizes that it breaks down under analysis into as many separate problems as there are seasonal trades, and that to treat any of these problems intelligently it is necessary to master a host of details concerning the materials and products, the technical processes and personnel, the commercial organization and the markets of the trade in question. Obviously the agencies that are to deal with these problems must have qualifications of a special sort. We have had to choose between two evils in deciding whether to treat both cyclical and seasonal unemployment or to treat one problem in artificial separation from the other. The evil of separation is decidedly less than the other evil would have been.

## III. PLAN OF THE REPORT

The table of contents shows the general plan of this report. Interest centers in the third and largest part which deals with the leading proposals for preventing or at least reducing cyclical unemployment. But the way in which these proposals operate and their prospects of success cannot be made clear without some analysis of business cycles, since periods of widespread unemployment are only one among many manifestations of the periodically recurring seasons of business depression. Hence the necessity for Part I, "The Relation of Unemployment to Business Cycles." And clearly the discussion of remedies should be prefaced, as it is, by a brief diagnosis of the disorder—the fluctuations of unemployment as shown by present statistics, the reliability of these data, and the way in which unemployment affects the worker's body and mind, his home life, and the development of his children. Any reader familiar with the phenomena of business cycles and the facts of unemployment can skip Parts I and II without much loss, and plunge at once into the practical details of Part III.

## IV. ACKNOWLEDGMENTS

The Committee on Unemployment and Business Cycles unites with the National Bureau of Economic Research in returning hearty thanks to the many organizations, business establishments, and individuals who have aided in the preparation of this report. The correspondents who have answered requests for information—often very troublesome requests—number several thousands, so that it is not feasible to publish their names. But certain organizations have made contributions on a scale so generous as to require special mention.

This list may begin with the Carnegie Corporation which provided funds enabling the National Bureau of Economic Research to secure the cooperation of workers not connected with its regular staff. The Russell Sage Foundation bore the expenses of the field work done by Miss Van Kleeck and permitted us to profit by Shelby M. Harrison's long study of employment offices. The Bureau of Railway Economics and the American Association for Labor Legislation have been similarly generous with respect to the chapters written by Julius H. Parmelee and John B. Andrews. T. S. Adams, Otto T. Mallery, and Gilbert H. Montague generously contributed the services of themselves and their assistants. We are also indebted to the Hickey-Freeman Company for letting us obtain the cooperation of N. I. Stone.

Invaluable assistance in circulating questionnaires was given by the National Conference of Business Paper Editors through a committee of which F. M. Feiker was chairman, by the Federated American Engineering Societies through L. W. Wallace, by the Taylor Society through

H. S. Person, by the Bureau of Crop Estimates through Nat C. Murray and Virgil A. Sanders, by the Bureau of Business Research of Northwestern University through Horace Secrist, by the National Association of Credit Men through John Whyte, by the Chamber of Commerce of the United States through numerous local secretaries, and by many professors of economics and statistics in the universities.   Alexander Wall of the Robert Morris Associates has put at our disposal a valuable collection of credit analyses.   The statistical data from several thousand questionnaires were compiled by the Bureau of the Census under the direction of W. M. Steuart.   Many other obligations are mentioned in the several chapters of the report.

The National Bureau of Economic Research takes this opportunity to thank Edward Eyre Hunt, Secretary of the President's Conference on Unemployment and of the Committee on Unemployment and Business Cycles, for his cordial cooperation in conducting the investigation and in editing the report.

# CHAPTER I

## BUSINESS CYCLES

### By Wesley C. Mitchell

NATIONAL BUREAU OF ECONOMIC RESEARCH

The great mass of the unemployed in periods like that which led President Harding to call the Conference on Unemployment are workers who have been "laid off" because of business depression. The reason why millions of men lose their jobs at such times is that employers are losing money. Hence it is best to begin a study of methods of stabilizing employment by looking into the processes which every few years throw business into confusion.

### I. THE NATURE OF BUSINESS CYCLES

Fifteen times within the past one hundred and ten years, American business has passed through a "crisis." The list of crisis years (1812, 1818, 1825, 1837, 1847, 1857, 1873, 1884, 1890, 1893, 1903, 1907, 1910, 1913, 1920) shows that the periods between successive crises have varied considerably in length. Further, no two crises have been precisely alike and the differences between some crises have been more conspicuous than the similarities. It is not surprising, therefore, that business men long thought of crises as "abnormal" events brought on by some foolish blunder made by the public or the government. On this view each crisis has a special cause which is often summed up by the newspapers in a picturesque phrase "the Jay Cooke panic" of 1873, "the railroad panic" of 1884, "the Cleveland panic" of 1893, "the rich man's panic" of 1903, " the Roosevelt panic" of 1907.

Longer experience, wider knowledge of business in other countries, and better statistical data have gradually discredited the view that crises are "abnormal" events, each due to a special cause. The modern view is that crises are but one feature of recurrent "business cycles." Instead of a "normal" state of business interrupted by occasional crises, men look for a continually changing state of business—continually changing in a fairly regular way. A crisis is expected to be followed by a depression, the depression by a revival, the revival by prosperity, and prosperity by a new crisis. Cycles of this sort can be traced for at least one century in America, perhaps for two centuries in the Netherlands, England, and France, and for shorter periods in Austria, Germany, Italy, Spain, and

5

the Scandinavian countries. Within a generation or two similar cycles have begun to run their courses in Canada and Australia, South America, Russia, British India, and Japan.

At present it is less likely that the existence of business cycles will be denied than that their regularity will be exaggerated. In fact, successive cycles differ not only in length, but also in violence, and in the relative prominence of their various manifestations. Sometimes the crisis is a mild recession of business activity as in 1910 and 1913; sometimes it degenerates into a panic as in 1873, 1893, and 1907. Sometimes the depression is interrupted by an abortive revival as in 1895, sometimes it is intensified by financial pressure as in 1896 and 1914. Sometimes the depression is brief and severe as in 1908, sometimes it is brief and mild as in 1911, sometimes it is both long and severe as in 1874–1878. Revivals usually develop into full-fledged prosperity, but there are exceptions like that of 1895. Prosperity may reach a high pitch as in 1906–1907 and 1916–1917, or may remain moderate until overtaken by a mild crisis as in 1913, or by a severe panic as in 1893.

These differences among business cycles arise from the fact that the business situation at any given moment is the net resultant of a complex of forces among which the rhythm of business activity is only one. Harvest conditions, domestic politics, changes in monetary and banking systems, international relations, the making of war or of peace, the discovery of new industrial methods or resources, and a thousand other matters all affect the prospects of profits favorably or adversely and therefore tend to quicken or to slacken the pace of business. The fact that the rhythm of business activity can be traced in the net resultants produced by these many factors argues that it is one of the most constantly acting, and probably one of the most powerful, factors among them.

To give a sketch of the business cycle which will be applicable to future cases, it is necessary of course to put aside the complicating effects of the various special conditions which at any given time are influencing profits, and to concentrate attention upon the tendency of the modern business system to develop alternate periods of activity and sluggishness.

Even when the problem is simplified in this way, it remains exceedingly complex. To keep from getting lost in a maze of complications, it is necessary to follow constantly the chief clue to business transactions. Every business establishment is supposed to aim primarily at making money. When the prospects of profits improve, business becomes more active. When these prospects grow darker, business becomes dull. Everything from rainfall to politics which affects business exerts its influence by affecting this crucial factor—the prospects of profits. The profits clue will not only prevent one from going astray, but will also enable one to thread the business maze slowly, if he chooses, taking time to examine all details, or to traverse the maze rapidly with an eye only for the conspicuous features. Needless to say, in this chapter we shall have to move rapidly.[1]

## II. PLAN OF DISCUSSION

Since business cycles run an unceasing round, each cycle growing out of its predecessor and merging into its successor, our analysis can start with any phase of the cycle we choose. With whatever phase of the cycle we start, we shall have to plunge into the middle of things, taking the business situation as it then stands for granted. But once this start has been made, the course of the subsequent discussion is fixed by the succession of phases through which the cycle passes. By following these phases around the full cycle we shall come back to the starting point and end the discussion by accounting for the situation of business which we took for granted at the beginning.

With full liberty of choice, it is well to start with the phase of the cycle through which American business is passing at present—the phase of revival after a depression. The first task will be to see how such a revival gathers momentum and produces prosperity. Then in order will come a discussion of how prosperity produces conditions which lead to crises, how crises run out into depressions, and finally how depressions after a time produce conditions which lead to new revivals.

This whole analysis will be a brief account of the cycle in general business. But it is important to note that different industries are affected by business cycles in different ways. Some industries, for example, are hit early and hit hard by a decline in business activity, while other industries are affected but slightly. This aspect of the subject has received scant attention from investigators so far, and it cannot be adequately treated until the various industries have collected far more systematic records of their changing fortunes than are now available outside a narrow field. But with the cooperation of trade associations and certain business men we have collected some data that show how important and how promising is further work along similar lines. This material concerning the effect of business cycles upon particular industries will be presented in the next chapter after the cycle in general business has been traced.

---

[1] The literature of business cycles is large and rather controversial. The differences among recent writers, however, are mainly differences in the distribution of emphasis. Among the best of the recent books upon the subject are the following: AFTALION, A., "Les Crises Périodiques de Surproduction," 2 vols., Paris, 1913; HANSEN, A. H., "Cycles of Prosperity and Depression," Madison, Wisconsin, 1921; HAWTREY, R. G., "Good and Bad Trade," London, 1913; HULL, G. H., "Industrial Depressions," New York, 1911; MITCHELL, W. C., "Business Cycles," Berkeley, California, 1913; MOORE, H. L., "Economic Cycles," New York, 1914; ROBERTSON, D. H., "A Study of Industrial Fluctuation," London, 1915.

### III. REVIVALS AND THE CUMULATION OF PROSPERITY [1]

A period of depression produces after a time certain conditions which favor an increase of business activity. Among these conditions are a level of prices low in comparison with the prices of prosperous times, drastic reductions in the cost of doing business, narrow margins of profit, ample bank reserves, and a conservative policy in capitalizing business enterprises and in granting credits.

These conditions are accompanied sooner or later by an increase in the physical volume of purchases. When a depression begins, business enterprises of most sorts have in stock or on order liberal supplies of merchandise. During the earlier months of dullness they fill such orders as they can get mainly from these supplies already on hand, and in turn they buy or manufacture new supplies but sparingly. Similarly, families and business concerns at the end of a period of prosperity usually have a liberal stock of clothing, household furnishings, and equipment. For a while they buy little except the perishable goods which must be continuously consumed, like food and transportation. But after depression has lasted for months, the semi-durable goods wear out and must be replaced or repaired. As that time comes there is a gradual increase of buying, and as the seller's stocks are gradually reduced, there is also a slow increase of manufacturing.

Experience indicates that, once begun, a recovery of this sort tends to grow cumulatively. An increase in the amount of business that a merchant gets will make him a little readier to renew his shabby equipment and order merchandise in advance of immediate needs. An increase in the number of men employed by factories will lead to larger family purchases and so to more manufacturing. The improving state of trade will produce a more cheerful state of mind among business men, and the more cheerful state of mind will give fresh impetus to the improvement in trade. It is only a question of time when such an increase in the volume of business will turn dullness into activity. Sometimes the change is accelerated by some propitious event arising from other than business sources, for example, good harvests, or is retarded by some influence, such as political uncertainties. Left to itself, the transformation proceeds slowly but surely.

While the price level is often sagging slowly when a revival begins, the cumulative expansion in the physical volume of trade presently stops the fall and starts a rise. For, when enterprises have in sight as much business as they can handle with their existing facilities of standard efficiency, they stand out for higher prices on additional orders. This policy prevails even in the most keenly competitive trades, because addi-

---

[1] In this and the three following sections free use has been made of material from the writer's book, "Business Cycles," published in 1913.

tional orders can be executed only by breaking in new hands, starting old machinery, buying new equipment, or making some other change which involves increased expense. The expectation of its coming hastens the advance. Buyers are anxious to secure or to contract for large supplies while the low level of quotations continues, and the first definite signs of an upward trend of quotations brings out a sudden rush of orders.

Like the increase in the physical volume of business, the rise of prices spreads rapidly; for every advance of quotations puts pressure upon some-one to recoup himself by making a compensatory advance in the prices of what he has to sell. The resulting changes in prices are far from even, not only as between different commodities, but also as between different parts of the system of prices. In most but not all cases, retail prices lag behind wholesale, the prices of staple consumers' behind the prices of staple producers' goods, and the prices of finished products behind the prices of raw materials. Among raw materials, the prices of mineral products reflect the changed business conditions more regularly than do the prices of raw animal, farm, or forest products. Wages rise sometimes more promptly, but nearly always in less degree than wholesale prices; discount rates rise sometimes more slowly than commodities and some-times more rapidly; interest rates on long loans move sluggishly in the early stages of revival, while the prices of stocks—particularly of common stocks—generally precede and exceed commodity prices on the rise. The causes of these differences in the promptness and the energy with which various classes of prices respond to the stimulus of business activity are found partly in differences of organization among the markets for com-modities, labor, loans, and securities; partly in the technical circumstances affecting the relative demand for and supply of these several classes of goods; and partly in the adjusting of selling prices to changes in the aggre-gate of buying prices which a business enterprise pays, rather than to changes in the prices of the particular goods bought for resale.

In the great majority of enterprises, larger profits result from these divergent price fluctuations coupled with the greater physical volume of sales. For, while the prices of raw materials and of wares bought for resale usually, and the prices of bank loans often, rise faster than selling prices, the prices of labor lag far behind, and the prices which make up overhead costs are mainly stereotyped for a time by old agreements regarding salaries, leases, and bonds.

This increase of profits, combined with the prevalence of business optimism, leads to a marked expansion of investments. Of course the heavy orders for machinery, the large contracts for new construction, etc., which result, swell still further the physical volume of business and render yet stronger the forces which are driving prices upward.

Indeed, the salient characteristic of this phase of the business cycle is the cumulative working of the various processes which are converting a revival of trade into intense prosperity.   Not only does every increase in the physical volume of trade cause other increases, every convert to optimism make new converts, and every advance of prices furnish an incentive for fresh advances, but the growth of trade helps to spread optimism and to raise prices, while optimism and rising prices both support each other and stimulate the growth of trade.   Finally, as has just been said, the changes going forward in these three factors swell profits and encourage investments, while high profits and heavy investments react by augmenting trade  justifying optimism, and raising prices.

### IV. HOW PROSPERITY BREEDS A CRISIS

While the processes just sketched work cumulatively for a time to enhance prosperity, they also cause a slow accumulation of stresses within the balanced system of business—stresses which ultimately undermine the conditions upon which prosperity rests.

Among these stresses is the gradual increase in the costs of doing business.   The decline in overhead costs per unit of output ceases when enterprises have once secured all the business they can handle with their standard equipment, and a slow increase of these costs begins when the expiration of old contracts makes necessary renewals at the high rates of interest, rent, and salaries which prevail in prosperity.   Meanwhile the operating costs rise at a relatively rapid rate.   Equipment which is antiquated and plants which are ill located or otherwise work at some disadvantage are brought again into operation.   The price of labor rises, not only because the standard rates of wages go up, but also because of the prevalence of higher pay for overtime.   More serious still is the fact that the efficiency of labor declines, because overtime brings weariness, because of the employment of "undesirables," and because crews cannot be driven at top speed when jobs are more numerous than men to fill them.[1]   The prices of raw materials continue to rise faster on

---

[1] Compare the discussion of fluctuations of production and of numbers employed in Section V of Chap. IV, below.   Mr. Berridge there shows that physical output rises more in booms and declines more in depressions than do numbers of employees. But he agrees with the view here expressed regarding changes in efficiency of labor, thinking that these changes are more than offset by other factors—notably the prevalence of overtime in booms and of part time in depressions.   Nevertheless, as George Soule of The Labor Bureau, Inc. who has kindly read this manuscript points out, the changes in efficiency of labor here referred to have never been statistically proved on a large scale.   There are factors which tend to decrease efficiency in dull times, such as the desire to spread out slack work as long as possible, and inability to keep men on the processes for which they are best fitted.   Mr. Soule knows personally some cases in which these causes have caused a decline of production in depression. He adds that if production does show a decline during booms per hours worked, "management or some other factor may be partly or even wholly responsible."

For  evidence supporting the text, see the writer's" Business Cycles," pp. 476–80.

the average than the selling prices of products. Finally, the numerous small wastes, incident to the conduct of business enterprises, creep up when managers are hurried by a press of orders demanding prompt delivery.

A second stress is the accumulating tension of the investment and money markets. The supply of funds available at the old rates of interest for the purchase of bonds, for lending on mortgages, and the like, fails to keep pace with the rapidly swelling demand. It becomes difficult to negotiate new issues of securities except on onerous terms, and men of affairs complain of the "scarcity of capital." Nor does the supply of bank loans grow fast enough to keep up with the demand. For the supply is limited by the reserves which bankers hold against their expanding liabilities. Full employment and active retail trade cause such a large amount of money to remain suspended in active circulation that the cash left in the banks increases rather slowly, even when the gold supply is rising most rapidly. On the other hand, the demand for bank loans grows not only with the physical volume of trade, but also with the rise of prices, and with the desire of men of affairs to use their own funds for controlling as many business ventures as possible. Moreover, this demand is relatively inelastic, since many borrowers think they can pay high rates of discount for a few months and still make profits on their turnover, and since the corporations which are unwilling to sell long-time bonds at the hard terms which have come to prevail try to raise part of the funds they require by discounting notes running only a few years.

Tension in the bond and money markets is unfavorable to the continuance of prosperity, not only because high rates of interest reduce the prospective margins of profit, but also because they check the expansion in the volume of trade out of which prosperity developed. Many projected ventures are relinquished or postponed, either because borrowers conclude that the interest would absorb too much of their profits, or because lenders refuse to extend their commitments farther.

The credit expansion, which is one of the most regular concomitants of an intense boom, gives an appearance of enhanced prosperity to business. But this appearance is delusive. For when the industrial army is already working its equipment at full capacity, further borrowings by men who wish to increase their own businesses cannot increase appreciably the total output of goods. The borrowers bid up still higher the prices of commodities and services, and so cause a further expansion in the pecuniary volume of trade. But they produce no corresponding increase in the physical volume of things men can consume. On the contrary, their borrowings augment that mass of debts, many protected by insufficient margins, which at the first breath of suspicion leads to the demands for liquidation presently to be discussed.

The difficulty of financing new projects intensifies the check which one important group of industries has already begun to suffer from an earlier-acting cause. The industries in question are those which produce industrial equipment—tools, machines, plant—and the materials of which this equipment is made, from lumber and cement to copper and steel.

The demand for industrial equipment is partly a replacement demand and partly a demand for betterments and extensions. The replacement demand for equipment doubtless varies with the physical quantity of demand for products; since, as a rule, the more rapidly machines and rolling stock are run, the more rapidly they wear out. The demand for betterments and extensions, on the other hand, varies not with the physical quantity of the products demanded, but with the fluctuations in this quantity.

To illustrate the peculiar changes in demand for industrial equipment which follow from this situation, suppose that the physical quantity of a certain product varied in five successive years as follows:

First year............................100,000 tons
Second year.......................... 95,000 tons
Third year............................100,000 tons
Fourth year..........................110,000 tons
Fifth year............................115,000 tons

This product is turned out by machines each of which will produce one hundred tons per year. Thus the number of machines in operation each year was:

First year............................1,000 machines
Second year.......................... 950 machines
Third year............................1,000 machines
Fourth year..........................1,100 machines
Fifth year............................1,150 machines

Each year one-tenth of the machines in operation wears out. The replacement demand for machines was therefore:

First year............................100 machines
Second year.......................... 95 machines
Third year............................100 machines
Fourth year..........................110 machines
Fifth year............................115 machines

The demand for additional machines was far more variable. Neglecting the first year, for which our illustration does not supply data, it is plain that no additions to equipment were required the second year when fifty of the machines in existence stood idle, and also none the third year. But after all the existing machines had been utilized new machines had to be bought at the rate of one machine for each one hundred tons added to the product. Hence the demand for additions to equipment shown by the number of machines in operation was:

First year............................... no data
Second year............................. none
Third year.............................. none
Fourth year............................100 machines
Fifth year............................. 50 machines

Adding the replacement demand and the demand for additions to equipment, we find the total demand for industrial equipment of this type to be:

First year............................... no data
Second year............................. 95 machines
Third year.............................100 machines
Fourth year............................210 machines
Fifth year.............................165 machines

Of course the figures in this example are fanciful. But they illustrate genuine characteristics of the demand for industrial equipment. During depression and early revival the equipment-building trades get little business except what is provided by the replacement demand. When the demand for products has reached the stage where it promises soon to exceed the capacity of existing facilities, however, the equipment trades experience a sudden and intense boom. But their business falls off again before prosperity has reached its maximum, provided the *increase* in the physical quantity of products slackens before it stops. Hence the seeming anomalies pointed out by J. Maurice Clark:

The demand for equipment may decrease . . . even though the demand for the finished product is still growing. The total demand for [equipment] tends to vary more sharply than the demand for finished products. . . . The maximum and minimum points in the demand for [equipment] tend to precede the maximum and minimum points in the demand for the finished products, the effect being that the change may appear to precede its own cause.[1]

When we add to the check in the orders for new equipment arising from any slackening in the increase of demand for products, the further check which arises from stringency in the bond market and the high cost of construction, we have no difficulty in understanding why contracts for this kind of work become less numerous as the climax of prosperity approaches. Then the steel mills, foundries, machine factories, copper smelters, quarries, lumber mills, cement plants, construction companies,

[1] Business Acceleration and the Law of Demand, *Journal of Political Economy*, March, 1917. Also see GEORGE H. HULL, "Industrial Depressions," 1911. Some materials concerning the sharp fluctuations in the activity of the equipment trades are given in Chap. II.

general contractors, and the like find their orders for future delivery falling off. While for the present they may be working at high pressure to complete old contracts within the stipulated time, they face a serious restriction of trade in the near future.

The imposing fabric of prosperity is built with a liberal factor of safety; but the larger grows the structure, the more severe become these internal stresses. The only effective means of preventing disaster while continuing to build is to raise selling prices time after time high enough to offset the encroachments of costs upon profits, to cancel the advancing rates of interest, and to keep producers willing to contract for fresh industrial equipment.

But it is impossible to keep selling prices rising for an indefinite time. In default of other checks, the inadequacy of cash reserves would ultimately compel the banks to refuse a further expansion of loans upon any terms. But before this stage has been reached, the rise of prices may be stopped by the consequences of its own inevitable inequalities. These inequalities become more glaring the higher the general level is forced; after a time they threaten serious reduction of profits to certain business enterprises, and the troubles of these victims dissolve that confidence in the security of credits with which the whole towering structure of prosperity has been cemented.

What, then, are the lines of business in which selling prices cannot be raised sufficiently to prevent a reduction of profits? There are certain lines in which selling prices are stereotyped by law, by public commissions, by contracts of long term, by custom, or by business policy, and in which no advance, or but meager advances can be made. There are other lines in which prices are always subject to the incalculable chances of the harvests, and in which the market value of all accumulated stocks of materials and finished goods wavers with the crop reports. There are always some lines in which the recent construction of new equipment has increased the capacity for production faster than the demand for their wares has expanded under the repressing influence of the high prices which must be charged to prevent a reduction of profits. The unwillingness of producers to let fresh contracts threatens loss not only to contracting firms of all sorts, but also to all the enterprises from whom they buy materials and supplies. The high rates of interest not only check the current demand for wares of various kinds, but also clog the effort to maintain prices by keeping large stocks of goods off the market until they can be sold to better advantage. Finally, the very success of other enterprises in raising selling prices fast enough to defend their profits aggravates the difficulties of the men who are in trouble; for to the latter every further rise of prices for products which they buy means a further strain upon their already stretched resources.

As prosperity approaches its height, then, a sharp contrast develops between the business prospects of different enterprises. Many, probably the majority, are making more money than at any previous stage of the business cycle. But an important minority, at least, face the prospect of declining profits. The more intense prosperity becomes, the larger grows this threatened group. It is only a question of time when these conditions, bred by prosperity, will force some radical readjustment.

Now such a decline of profits threatens worse consequences than the failure to realize expected dividends, for it arouses doubt concerning the security of outstanding credits. Business credit is based primarily upon the capitalized value of present and prospective profits, and the volume of credits outstanding at the zenith of prosperity is adjusted to the great expectations which prevail when the volume of trade is enormous, when prices are high, and when men of affairs are optimistic. The rise of interest rates has already narrowed the margins of security behind credits by reducing the capitalized value of given profits. When profits themselves begin to waver, the case becomes worse. Cautious creditors fear lest the shrinkage in the market rating of the business enterprises which owe them money will leave no adequate security for repayment; hence they begin to refuse renewals of old loans to the enterprises which cannot stave off a decline of profits, and to press for a settlement of outstanding accounts.

Thus prosperity ultimately brings on conditions which start a liquidation of the huge credits which it has piled up. And in the course of this liquidation, prosperity merges into crisis.

### V. CRISES

Once begun, the process of liquidation extends very rapidly, partly because most enterprises which are called upon to settle their maturing obligations in turn put similar pressure upon their own debtors, and partly because, despite all efforts to keep secret what is going forward, news presently leaks out and other creditors take alarm.

While this financial readjustment is under way, the problem of making profits on current transactions is subordinated to the more vital problem of maintaining solvency. Business managers concentrate their energies upon providing for their outstanding liabilities and upon nursing their financial resources, instead of upon pushing their sales. In consequence, the volume of new orders falls off rapidly; that is, the factors which were already dimming the prospects of profits in certain lines of business are reinforced and extended. Even when the overwhelming majority of enterprises meet the demand for payment with success, the tenor of business developments undergoes a change. Expansion gives place to contraction, though without a violent wrench. Discount rates rise higher than usual, securities and commodities fall in price, and as old orders are completed, working forces are reduced; but there is no epidemic of bankruptcies, no run upon banks, and no spasmodic interruption of the ordinary business processes.

At the opposite extreme from crises of this mild order stand the crises which degenerate into panics. When the process of liquidation reaches a weak link in the chain of interlocking credits and the bankruptcy of some conspicuous enterprise spreads unreasoning alarm among the business public, then the banks are suddenly forced to meet a double strain—a sharp increase in the demand for loans, and a sharp increase in the demand for repayment of deposits. If the banks prove able to honor both demands without flinching, the alarm quickly subsides. But if, as in 1873, 1893, and 1907, many solvent business men are refused accommodation at any price, and if depositors are refused payment in full, the alarm turns into panic. A restriction of payments by the banks gives rise to a premium upon currency, to the hoarding of cash, and to the use of various unlawful substitutes for money. A refusal by the banks to expand their loans, still more a policy of contraction, sends interest rates up to three or four times their usual figures, and causes forced suspensions and bankruptcies. Collections fall into arrears, domestic exchange rates are dislocated, workmen are discharged because employers cannot get money for pay-rolls or fear lest they cannot collect pay for goods when delivered, stocks fall to extremely low levels, even the best bonds decline somewhat in price, commodity markets are disorganized by sacrifice sales, and the volume of business is violently contracted.

## VI. DEPRESSIONS

The period of severe financial pressure is often followed by the reopening of numerous enterprises which had been shut for a time. But this prompt revival of activity is partial and short-lived. It is based chiefly upon the finishing of orders received but not completely executed in the preceding period of prosperity, or upon the effort to work up and market large stocks of materials already on hand or contracted for. It comes to an end as this work is gradually finished, because new orders are not forthcoming in sufficient volume to keep the mills and factories busy.

There follows a period during which depression spreads over the whole field of business and grows more severe. Consumers' demand declines in consequence of wholesale discharges of wage-earners, the gradual exhaustion of past savings, and the reduction of other classes of family incomes. With consumers' demand falls the business demand for raw materials, current supplies, and equipment used in making consumers' goods. Still more severe is the shrinkage of producers' demand for construction work of all kinds, since few individuals or enterprises care to sink money in new business ventures so long as trade remains depressed and the price level is declining. The contraction in the physical volume of business which results from these several shrinkages in demand is cumulative, since every reduction of employment causes a reduction of consumers' demand, and every decline in consumers' demand depresses current business demand and discourages investment, thereby causing further discharges of employees and reducing consumers' demand once more.

With the contraction in the physical volume of trade goes a fall of prices; for, when current orders are insufficient to employ the existing industrial equipment, competition for what business is to be had becomes keener. This decline spreads through the regular commercial channels which connect one enterprise with another, and is cumulative, since every reduction in price facilitates, if it does not force, reductions in other prices, and the latter reductions react in their turn to cause fresh reductions at the starting point.

As the rise of prices which accompanies revival, so the fall which accompanies depression is characterized by marked differences in degree. Wholesale prices usually fall faster than retail, the prices of producers' goods faster than those of consumer's goods, and the prices of raw materials faster than those of manufactured products. The prices of raw mineral products follow a more regular course than those of raw forest, farm, or animal products. As compared with the general index numbers of commodity prices at wholesale, index numbers of wages and interest on long-time loans decline in less degree, while index numbers of discount rates and of stocks decline in greater degree. The only important group of prices to rise in the face of depression is that of high-grade bonds.

Of course, the contraction in the physical volume of trade and the fall of prices reduce the margin of present and prospective profits, spread discouragement among business men, and check enterprise. But they also set in motion certain processes of readjustment by which depression is gradually overcome.

The operating costs of doing business are reduced by the rapid fall in the prices of raw materials and of bank loans, by the increase in the efficiency of labor which comes when employment is scarce and men are anxious to hold their jobs, by closer economy on the part of managers, and by the adoption of improved methods. Overhead costs, also, are reduced by reorganizing enterprises which have actually become or which threaten to become insolvent, by the sale of other enterprises at low figures, by reduction of rentals and refunding of loans, by charging off bad debts and writing down depreciated properties, and by admitting that a recapitalization of business enterprises—corresponding to the lower prices of stocks—has been effected on the basis of lower profits.[1]

[1] George Soule comments: "I should like to see a specific warning against the theory —so often resorted to by banks and employers in efforts to 'deflate' wages—that business cannot revive unless all levels of wages and prices bear exactly the same relation to each other as before the depression—a sort of 'normal' or mathematically

While these reductions in costs are still being made, the demand for goods ceases to shrink and begins slowly to expand—a change which usually comes after one or two years of depression.  Accumulated stocks left over from prosperity are gradually exhausted, and current consumption requires current production.  Clothing, furniture, machinery, and other moderately durable articles which have been used as long as possible are finally discarded and replaced.  Population continues to increase at a fairly uniform rate; the new mouths must be fed and new backs clothed. New tastes appear among consumers and new methods among producers, giving rise to demand for novel products.  Most important of all, the investment demand for industrial equipment revives; for, though saving slackens it does not cease, with the cessation of foreclosure sales and corporate reorganizations the opportunities to buy into old enterprises at bargain prices become fewer, capitalists become less timid as the crisis recedes into the past, the low rates of interest on long-term bonds encourage borrowing, the accumulated technical improvements of several years may be utilized, and contracts can be let on most favorable conditions as to cost and prompt execution.

Once these various forces have set the physical volume of trade to expanding again, the increase proves cumulative, though for a time the pace of growth is kept slow by the continued sagging of prices.  But while the latter maintains the pressure upon business men and prevents the increased volume of orders from producing a rapid rise of profits, still business prospects become gradually brighter.  Old debts have been paid, accumulated stocks of commodities have been absorbed, weak enterprises have been reorganized, the banks are strong—all the clouds upon the financial horizon have disappeared.  Everything is ready for a revival of activity, which will begin whenever some fortunate circumstance gives a sudden fillip to demand, or, in the absence of such an event, when the slow growth of the volume of business has filled order books and paved the way for a new rise of prices.

Such is the stage of the business cycle with which the analysis began, and, having accounted for its own beginning, the analysis ends.

---

balanced relation.  I do not believe the existence of such a normal relationship has ever been proved.  Certainly, it has not been proved that there can be no permanent changes in price and wage relationships."

# CHAPTER II

## INDIVIDUAL INDUSTRIES AND ENTERPRISES IN THE BUSINESS CYCLE

### By Frederick R. Macaulay

NATIONAL BUREAU OF ECONOMIC RESEARCH

### I. INTRODUCTION

Knowledge of the business cycle and close attention to its current phases is important to the business man, because general prosperity and depression affect his own particular affairs. But the manner, degree, and intensity with which changes in general business conditions affect different industries in the same cycle and the same industry in different cycles are by no means uniform. Probably there are a few industries in which profits rise during depressions and fall in booms. Such anomalous results may be produced if prices are fixed and demand steady, but costs highly variable (for example, many public utilities); or they may occur in industries providing cheap wares which people substitute for better grades when they must economize. Certainly there are industries which feel the effects of depression slowly and in slight degree, presenting a sharp contrast to other industries in which the effects are sudden and severe.

Furthermore, there is evidence that certain crises and certain revivals have started in one district and spread gradually over the rest of the country. For example, the panic of 1907 appears to have begun in New York City and to have radiated from there to other financial centers. Soon the financial difficulties affected the industrial districts, and within a few months checked business of almost all kinds in almost every section. Similarly, the sudden revival in the autumn of 1891 was first noted in the wheat-growing areas. The "granger" railroads reported an increase of profits some months before the lines in other districts experienced a revival.

Finally, there is a wide diversity of fortunes at the same time and in the same trade among different business enterprises. In every year of deep depression an occasional concern reports that it has had "the best season in its history." And it is notorious that there is never a year, no matter how prosperous, when hundreds of business men do not go bankrupt.

A sketch of the typical business cycle, adequately established upon summaries of general experience is both valid and useful; but the sketch would be more useful if it showed not merely the general run of affairs but also the diversities. The fortunes of individual industries, districts and enterprises are part of the business cycle, and the business executive, in adapting his policy to his opportunities and requirements, needs to know as much as possible about their peculiarities.

This is a field where the professional economist works at a disadvantage, if he works at all. It is a field which is likely to remain neglected until taken up by statisticians connected with business corporations. Such figures as exist are often difficult for an outsider, who is not intimately familiar with both the technique and history of the business from which they came, to interpret intelligently. To analyze these data in the ways most likely to extract their secrets is generally, moreover, too expensive for anyone to undertake who stands no chance of profiting by the results.

By way of indicating the need of such work we have collected some materials bearing upon the fortunes of different industries in the dramatic business years from 1919 to 1922. There are statistical records of monthly fluctuations of prices, production, and number of employees in various industries. Horace Secrist of the Bureau of Business Research of Northwestern University and John Whyte of the National Association of Credit Men have aided us by collecting a considerable number of questionnaires from business men interested in the problem. We have applied to the secretaries of numerous trade associations for their views, and have received suggestive letters from the executives and statisticians of various corporations.

What follows is an attempt to present a few of the results from these inquiries. None of them must be taken as more than a tentative statement of what seems to have happened to a particular business in a single business cycle. Though these statements possess considerable interest to the trades from which they come, they form only a beginning of work which must cover a far wider range of information and time before generalizations can be made, let alone regarded as proved. The broad general impression left by a study of the problem is one of great diversity among the fortunes not only of different industries but also of different enterprises within the same industry.

## II. DIFFERENT ENTERPRISES IN THE SAME INDUSTRY

The questionnaire which Mr. Secrist used in getting information from various groups of business men in the Chicago district included inquiries concerning the date at which enterprises were most unfavorably affected during the recent depression, when the signs of trouble were first noted, and whether the industry in question recovered from the depression relatively early or relatively late.

The following schedule presents the material he collected for all industries from which six or more answers were received. The diver-

TABLE I.—EXPERIENCES OF DIFFERENT ENTERPRISES IN THE SAME INDUSTRIES DURING THE CRISIS OF 1920 AND THE FOLLOWING DEPRESSION [a]

(Based upon answers to questionnaires sent out by Horace Secrist)

| Industry | Number of answers | Dates at which most unfavorably affected | Signs of trouble first noted | Revival early or late |
|---|---|---|---|---|
| Clothing, men's, manufacturing. | 7 | May, 1920 (3); June, 1920; Oct., 1920; Sept. to Dec., 1920; Jan., 1922. | Cancellation of orders (2); falling off of orders (4); buyers' strike (1). | Early (3) Late (4) |
| Clothing, women's, manufacturing. | 6 | June, 1920 (2); Oct., 1920; early, 1921; fall, 1921. | Cancellations (1); falling off of sales (3). | Early (3) Late (1) |
| Food for persons | 10 | Aug., 1920; Sept., 1920; fall, 1920; Jan., 1921; Aug. to Nov., 1921; Sept., 1921; Dec., 1921. | Cancellations (1); falling prices (4); falling off of sales (2). | Early (4) Late (4) |
| Household furniture | 7 | June, 1920; Aug., 1920; Sept., 1920; Oct., 1920; first half, 1921; July, 1921. | Cancellations (5); slow collections (2). | Late (7) |
| General building material including lumber, terra cotta, and structural steel. | 6 | July, 1920 to Nov., 1921; Aug., 1920; Dec., 1920; April, 1921; May, 1921. | Credit unavailable (1); lowering of prices (1); slump in construction (1); falling off of orders (3). | Late (6) |
| Paints, varnish, glass, doors, builders' hardware, etc. | 9 | Oct., 1920; Nov., 1920; Dec., 1920; spring, 1921; March, 1921; June, 1921; July to Aug., 1921; Oct. and Nov., 1921. | Falling off of sales (6); labor agitation (1); falling off of building permits (1). | Early (3) Late (5) |
| Printing, etc. | 8 | Oct., 1920; Nov., 1920 to May, 1921; early, 1921; June, 1921; May, 1922. | Cancellations (1); falling off of orders (4); collections bad (1). | Early (4) Late (1) |
| Publishing and printing, books and magazines. | 10 | July, 1920 (2); Sept., 1920; fall, 1920 (2); Dec., 1920; June, 1921; 1921. | Cancellation of advertising space (3); falling off of sales (2); falling off of advertising (2). | Early (2) Late (4) |
| Stationery, pens, etc. | 8 | Jan., 1920; Sept., 1920; Oct., 1920 (2); Nov., 1920; Dec., 1920; Feb., 1921; summer, 1921. | Cancellations (2); falling off of orders (4); collections slow (1); decrease in prices (1). | Early (2) Late (3) |
| Boxes, containers, twine, etc. | 6 | April, 1920; Nov., 1920 (2); 1920; spring and fall, 1921; Nov., 1921. | Falling off of orders (4); labor trouble; price cutting. | Early (3) Late (2) |
| Tires and rubber goods | 6 | May, 1920; July, 1920 (3); March, 1921; 1921. | Cancellations (4); falling off of sales (1). | Early (1) Late (5) |

[a] Numbers in parentheses indicate the number of establishments affected. Not all of the questions were answered on some of the questionnaires.

TABLE I.—(*Continued*)

| Industry | Number of answers | Dates at which most unfavorably affected | Signs of trouble first noted | Revival early or late |
|---|---|---|---|---|
| Machinery | 7 | July, 1920; Nov., 1920; 1921; March, 1921; June, 1921; July, 1921; fall, 1921. | Cancellations (2); falling off of orders (4); collections poor (1). | Early (1) Late (6) |
| Telephone equipment | 6 | Jan., 1921; Oct., 1921 to Jan., 1922; May, 1922. | Cancellations (2); falling off of orders (1). | Late (3) |
| Industrial engineering | 6 | April, 1920; Jan., 1921; March, 1921; Jan., 1922. | Cancellations (2); falling off of orders (2); collections bad (1). | Medium (1) Late (3) |
| Advertising | 18 | July, 1920; Aug., 1920; Sept., 1920 (2); fall, 1920; Jan., 1921; spring, 1921; June, 1921; Sept., 1921; Oct., 1921; Nov., 1921. | Cancellations (2); falling off of orders (8); collections difficult (3); lack of credit (2). | Early (8) Late (7) |
| Insurance | 9 | July, 1920; Oct., 1920; Nov., 1920; March, 1921; Oct., 1921; Oct. to Dec., 1921; 1921; Jan, 1922; Nov., 1921 to Feb., 1922. | Cancellations (1); falling off of sales (2); labor trouble (1); decline in wages (2). | Early (1) Late (7) |
| Educational service | 10 | 1920; Nov., 1920 to April, 1921; June, 1921; Jan., 1922, March, 1922. | Cancellations (1); falling off of sales (2); collections difficult (4). | Early (2) Late (4) |

sity of these answers is an emphatic demonstration of the differences of opinion among business men on these points—differences presumably arising largely[1] from differences of experience.

Mr. Whyte used a somewhat similar questionnaire at the Indianapolis Convention of the National Association of Credit Men and received equally diverse answers. The following excerpts from his tabulation suffice for the present purpose.

[1] A few answers suggest that Mr. Secrist's first question was interpreted in different ways.

Table II.—Experiences of Different Enterprises in the Same Industries During the Crisis of 1920 and the Following Depression [a]

(Based upon answers to questionnaires used by John Whyte)

| Industry | Number of answers | Dates when depression began | | Dates when sales increased again | |
|---|---|---|---|---|---|
| | | Range covered by answers | Commonest dates among the answers | Range covered by answers | Commonest dates among the answers |
| Automobile | 6 | March, 1920 to June, 1921. | March,1920 (2); Oct., 1920 (2). | March, 1921 to April, 1922. | April, 1922 (2). |
| Building, plumbing, etc. | 10 | May, 1920 to Jan., 1922. | Dec., 1920 (2); Jan., 1921 (2). | Dec., 1921 to April, 1922. | March, 1922 (4). |
| Clothing | 13 | Feb., 1920 to Nov., 1920. | May and June, 1920 (5); Aug. to Oct., 1920 (6). | July, 1921 to May, 1922. | April and May, 1922 (4); fall, 1921 (3). |
| Dry goods | 8 | May, 1920 to June, 1921. | Nov., 1920. | Jan., 1921 to May, 1922. | Jan., 1922 (2). |
| Electrical supplies | 6 | June, 1920 to Jan., 1921. | Dec., 1920 and Jan., 1921 (3). | Sept., 1921 to May, 1922. | April, 1922 (3). |
| Furniture | 10 | July, 1920 to Feb., 1922. | Oct., 1920 (3). | Nov., 1921 to May, 1922. | March, 1922 (4). |
| Groceries | 28 | Oct., 1919 to June, 1921. | July to Nov., 1920 (15). | Jan., 1921 to May, 1922. | March, 1922 (6); April, 1922 (5); May, 1922 (6). |
| Hardware | 13 | Jan., 1920 to June, 1921. | Sept., 1920 to Jan., 1921 (13). | Aug., 1921 to May, 1922. | March, 1922 (5); May, 1922 (4). |
| Agricultural implements. | 6 | June, 1920 to Nov., 1920. | June, 1920 (3). | Sept., 1921 to May, 1922. | March, 1922 (2); May, 1922 (2). |
| Metals | 21 | Aug., 1919 to April, 1921. | Sept., 1920 (3); Oct., 1920 (5); Nov., 1920 (4). | Feb., 1921 to April, 1922. | Jan., 1922 (5); Feb., 1922 (5); April, 1922 (5). |
| Paper | 12 | Oct., 1920 to June, 1921. | Oct., 1920 (4); Nov., 1920 (3). | Sept., 1921 to April, 1922. | April, 1922 (3); March, 1922 (2). |
| Shoes | 8 | March, 1920 to April, 1921. | March to July, 1920 (6). | Sept., 1920 to March, 1922. | Feb., 1922 (2); March, 1922 (2). |

[a] Numbers in parentheses indicate the number of establishments affected.

## III. VARIATIONS IN DIFFERENT INDUSTRIES—FLUCTUATIONS IN INDIVIDUAL COMMODITY PRICES

To make a rough presentation of the diversity of fluctuations among the prices of basic materials handled by different industries, we have computed for the commodities which are quoted by the Bureau of Labor Statistics in 1913 and the *Survey of Current Business* from 1919 to 1922 the

TABLE III.—PERCENTAGE RISE OF PRICES FROM 1913 TO THE POST-WAR PEAKS AND
PERCENTAGE DROP FROM THE PEAKS TO THE LOWEST LEVELS REACHED BY JUNE 1, 1922
(Commodities Arranged in Order of Percentage Declines. Data from U. S. Bureau of Labor
Statistics, *Bulletin* 269, and U. S. Department of Commerce, *Survey of Current Business*, May
and July, 1922.)

| Commodity | Percentage rises from 1913 to high | Percentage declines from high to low | Number of months between high and low points |
|---|---|---|---|
| Hides, calfskins country No. 1.................... | 390.5 | 86.5 | 19 |
| Sugar, raw, 96° centrifugal, N. Y................ | 498.0 | 82.8 | 20 |
| Coke, Connellsville............................ | 537.0 | 82.3 | 16 |
| Sheep, ewes, Chicago........................... | 204.0 | 81.1 | 14 |
| Pine, yellow, flooring........................... | 258.8 | 80.8 | 9 |
| Hides, green, salted, packers' heavy native steers.... | 182.8 | 80.6 | 20 |
| Sugar, granulated, in bbls., N. Y............... | 426.0 | 78.7 | 20 |
| Cottonseed oil, summer, yellow, prime............ | 274.2 | 78.2 | 21 |
| Oak, white, plain............................... | 279.6 | 77.2 | 15 |
| Corn, cash, contract, grades No. 2............... | 219.0 | 76.5 | 17 |
| Cotton, price to producer (weighted average of all grades)........................................ | 214.1 | 75.1 | 11 |
| Cotton print cloth, 27″, Boston.................. | 378.3 | 73.9 | 12 |
| Raw silk, Japanese, Kansai, No. 1, N. Y.......... | 366.4 | 72.9 | 6 |
| Cotton sheetings, ¾ Ware shoals, LL, N. Y...... | 327.0 | 72.9 | 13 |
| Cotton, middling upland, N. Y... .............. | 231.4 | 72.2 | 11 |
| Douglas, fir, No. 1............................. | 307.3 | 72.0 | 15 |
| Crude petroleum, Kansas-Oklahoma.............. | 275.0 | 71.4 | 7 |
| Oats, cash, Chicago............................ | 196.0 | 68.9 | 16 |
| Barley, by sample, fair to good, malting, Chicago.... | 176.0 | 68.2 | 19 |
| Cotton yarn, carded, white, Northern, mule spun, 2¾ cones, Boston............................ | 248.4 | 67.7 | 11 |
| Leather, chrome calf, "B" grades, Boston.. ........ | 373.0 | 67.5 | 25 |
| India rubber, Para Island, N. Y.............ᵥ... | −40.2 | 66.7 | 28 |
| Newsprint, spot market, domestic................ | 145.0 | 66.2 | 21 |
| Pork, loins, fresh, Chicago...................... | 171.0 | 65.0 | 15 |
| Shingles, red cedar............................. | 247.7 | 64.8 | 13 |
| Rye, No. 2, cash, Chicago...................... | 251.0 | 64.0 | 16 |
| Wool, Ohio, fine unwashed, Boston.............. | 250.0 | 63.6 | 17 |
| Wheat, No. 1 northern spring, Chicago........... | 254.0 | 62.0 | 18 |
| Beef, steer rounds No. 2, Chicago............... | 111.0 | 60.9 | 17 |
| Composite pig iron (*American Metal Market* index).. | 218.0 | 60.7 | 18 |
| Wheat, No. 2 red winter, Chicago............... | 202.0 | 60.5 | 18 |
| Pig iron, foundry No. 2 northern................. | 220.0 | 59.3 | 17 |
| Hogs, heavy, Chicago......,................... | 98.0 | 59.1 | 15 |
| Sheep, lambs, Chicago......................... | 163.0 | 58.7 | 20 |
| Tin, pig, N. Y................................ | 42.0 | 58.2 | 19 |
| Pig iron, Bessemer............................. | 195.0 | 57.5 | 17 |
| Structural steel beams, etc., Pittsburgh........... | 114.0 | 56.3 | 21 |
| Wheat flour, winter straights, Kansas City........ | 249.0 | 56.3 | 19 |
| Lead, pig, desilverized, N. Y.................... | 110.0 | 55.4 | 12 |
| Steel billets, Bessemer, Pittsburgh............... | 142.0 | 55.2 | 18 |
| Wheat flour, standard patents, Minneapolis....... | 228.0 | 54.2 | 19 |
| Iron and steel (*Iron Trade Review* index).......... | 162.0 | 52.3 | 18 |
| Zinc, prime western, N. Y...................... | 66.0 | 51.5 | 19 |
| Worsted yarn, ⅜₂'s crossbred stock, Philadelphia... | 189.7 | 51.1 | 10 |
| Composite finished steel (*Iron Age* index).......... | 139.0 | 49.4 | 18 |
| Bituminous coal............................... | 223.0 | 49.3 | 14 |
| Hemlock...................................... | 135.3 | 49.1 | 8 |
| Copper ingots, electrolytic, N. Y................ | 45.0 | 48.7 | 24 |
| Cattle, steers, good to choice, corn fed, Chicago...... | 81.0 | 47.4 | 11 |
| Newsprint, contract, Canadian................... | 77.0 | 46.3 | 11 |
| Composite steel (*American Metal Market* index).... | 121.0 | 45.0 | 18 |
| Beef, good native steers, Chicago................ | 101.0 | 44.2 | 17 |

TABLE III.—(Continued)

| Commodity | Percentage rises from 1913 high | Percentage declines from high to low | Number of months between high and low points |
|---|---|---|---|
| Women's dress goods, storm serge, all wool, double warp 50″, N. Y. | 152.6 | 42.6 | 15 |
| Common brick, red, N. Y. | 281.0 | 42.0 | 10 |
| Newsprint, contract domestic | 63.0 | 41.7 | 16 |
| Leather, sole hemlock, middle No. 1, Boston | 102.0 | 40.4 | 13 |
| Suitings, wool-dyed, blue, 5⅚6″, Middlesex, Boston | 191.3 | 37.0 | 14 |
| Sulphuric acid, 66°, N. Y. | 20.0 | 33.3 | 19 |
| Common brick, salmon, run of kiln, Chicago | 151.0 | 32.4 | 14 |
| Boots and shoes, men's black calf, blucher, Boston | 208.0 | 32.3 | 22 |
| Tobacco, Burley, good leaf, dark red, Louisville | 195.0 | 29.5 | 17 |
| Portland cement, net, without bags, Chicago | 95.0 | 23.1 | 10 |

percentage rise from the pre-war levels to the highest peaks attained after the war and the percentage drop from those peaks to the lowest points yet reached.[1] Table III shows these results and also the number of months during which the decline from the peak lasted in each case.

Once more, the outstanding result is an array of wide differences. One observes, however, that the commodities which fell most in price were generally articles that had risen violently since 1913, and conversely the articles which fell slightly were generally those which had risen but slightly. The coefficient of correlation between the percentages of rise and fall is −0.67 on a scale where perfect agreement between rise and fall would be expressed as −1.0.[2]

Another way of presenting these facts, and one which is at least as significant from the viewpoint of business cycles, is shown by the following schedules giving the months in which each commodity attained its highest price and its lowest price from January, 1919 to June, 1922. The peak months for different commodities run all the way from July, 1919 to March, 1921, and the lowest points from July, 1920 to June, 1922. Thus the highest months for some commodities overlapped the lowest months for others. Of the whole list of sixty-two commodities eighteen reached their peaks after one article (raw silk) has touched bottom.

[1] It will be noted that the two sets of percentages are computed on different bases. A commodity that quadrupled in price and then receded to its pre-war level would show a 300 per cent rise and a 75 per cent drop.

[2] The coefficient of correlation was calculated from the logarithms of the percentages that the highs were of the 1913 averages and the logarithms of the percentages that the recent lows were of the preceding highs. As the regression is more nearly linear on a logarithmic than on a natural scale and as sound theory would lead us to expect a logarithmic rather than a natural relationship between such percentages, the above procedure seems defensible. Rubber was omitted from the calculations.

TABLE IV.—Months in Which Sixty-two Important Commodities Touched
Their Highest and Lowest Prices January, 1919 to June, 1922

| Months | Commodities reaching highest prices | Months | Commodities reaching lowest prices |
|---|---|---|---|
| 1919 | | | |
| July | Cottonseed oil, summer, yellow, prime | | |
| Aug. | Hides, green, salted, packers' heavy native steers | | |
| | Hides, calf skins, country No. 1 | | |
| | Copper ingots, electrolytic, N. Y. | | |
| Nov. | India rubber, Para Island, N. Y. | | |
| 1920 | | 1920 | |
| Jan. | Tobacco, Burley, good leaf, dark red, Louisville | | |
| | Raw silk, Japanese, Kansai, No. 1, N. Y. | | |
| | Tin, pig, N. Y. | | |
| | Zinc, prime western, N. Y. | | |
| Feb. | Worsted yarn, 3⁄₂'s crossbred stock, Philadelphia | | |
| | Sheep, lambs, Chicago | | |
| | Shingle, red cedar | | |
| Mar. | Wool, Ohio, fine, unwashed, Boston | | |
| | Leather, chrome calf, "B" grades, Boston | | |
| | Lead, pig, desilverized, N. Y | | |
| Apr. | Cotton, middling upland, N. Y. | | |
| | Cotton print cloth, 27″, Boston | | |
| | Sheep, ewes, Chicago | | |
| May | Cotton, price to producer | | |
| | Cotton yarn, carded, white, northern, mule spun, 2 3⁄₄ cones, Boston | | |
| | Cotton sheetings, 5⁄₄ Ware shoals, L L, N. Y. | | |
| | Boots and shoes, men's black calf, blucher, Boston | | |
| | Corn, cash, contract, grades No. 2 | | |
| | Sugar, raw, 96° centrifugal, N. Y. | | |
| | Sugar, granulated, in bbls., N. Y. | | |
| | Douglas fir, No. 1 | | |
| | Oak, white, plain | | |
| | Wheat, No. 1, northern spring, Chicago | | |
| | Wheat, No. 2, red winter, Chicago | | |
| | Wheat flour, standard patents, Minneapolis | | |
| | Wheat flour, winter straights, Kansas City | | |
| | Barley, by sample, fair to good, malting, Chicago | | |
| June | Suitings, wool-dyed, blue 5 5⁄₆₆″, Middlesex, Boston | | |
| | Oats, cash Chicago | | |
| | Sulphuric acid, 66°, N. Y. | | |
| | Structural steel beams, etc., Pittsburgh | | |
| July | Cattle, steers, good to choice, corn fed, Chicago | July | Raw silk, Japanese, Kansai, No. 1, N. Y |
| | Beef, steer rounds, No. 2, Chicago | | |
| | Rye, No. 2, cash, Chicago | | |
| | Leather, sole hemlock, middle No. 1, Boston | | |
| | Pine, yellow, flooring | | |
| | Newsprint, spot market, domestic | | |
| | Common brick, red, N. Y. | | |
| | Steel billets, Bessemer, Pittsburgh | | |
| Aug. | Women's dress goods, storm serge, all wool, double warp 50″, N. Y. | | |
| | Iron and steel (*Iron Trade Review* index) | | |
| | Composite finished steel (*Iron Age* index) | | |
| | Coke, Connellsville | | |
| Sept. | Hogs, heavy, Chicago | | |
| | Beef, good native steers, Chicago | | |
| | Pork, loins, fresh, Chicago | | |
| | Pig iron, foundry No. 2, northern | | |
| | Pig iron, Bessemer | | |
| | Composite pig iron (*American Metal Market* index) | | |
| | Composite steel (*American Metal Market* index) | | |
| Dec. | Hemlock | Dec. | Worsted yarn, 3⁄₂'s, crossbred stock, Philadelphia |
| | Common brick, salmon, run of kiln, Chicago | | |
| | Portland cement, net, without bags, Chicago | | |

TABLE IV.—(*Continued*)

| Months | Commodities reaching highest prices | Months | Commodities reaching lowest prices |
|---|---|---|---|
| 1921 Jan. Mar. | Bituminous coal Crude petroleum, Kansas—Oklahoma Newsprint, contract domestic Newsprint, contract Canadian | 1921 Mar. | Lead, pig, desilverized, N. Y. Cotton, middling upland, N. Y. Hides, calfskins country, No. 1. Shingles, red cedar |
| | | Apr. | Cotton, price to producer Cotton yarn, carded, white, northern, mule spun, 2¾ cones, Boston Cotton print cloth, 27″, Boston Cottonseed oil, summer, yellow, prime Hides, green, salted, packers' heavy native steers Pine, yellow, flooring |
| | | May June | Common brick, red, N. Y. Cattle, steers, good to choice, corn fed, Chicago Sheep, ewes, Chicago Cotton sheetings, ⁴⁄₄ Wareshoals,LL,N.Y. Tobacco, Burley, good leaf, dark red, Louisville |
| | | July Aug. | Crude petroleum, Kansas—Oklahoma Copper ingots, electrolytic, N. Y. Tin, pig, N. Y. Zinc, prime western, N. Y. Wool, Ohio, fine, unwashed, Boston Suitings, wool-dyed, blue, ⁵⅚₆″, Middlesex, Boston Leather, sole hemlock, middle No. 1, Boston Douglas fir, No. 1 Hemlock Oak, white, plain |
| | | Oct. | Oats, cash, Chicago Corn, cash, contract, grades No. 2 Sheep, lambs, Chicago Portland cement, net, without bags, Chicago |
| | | Nov. | Wheat, No. 1, northern spring, Chicago Wheat, No. 2, red winter, Chicago Rye, No. 2, cash, Chicago Women's dress goods, storm serge, all wool, double warp 50″, N. Y. |
| | | Dec. | Barley, by sample, fair to good, malting, Chicago Wheat flour, standard patents, Minneapolis Wheat flour, winter straight, Kansas City Beef, steer rounds, No. 2, Chicago Hogs, heavy, Chicago Pork, loins, fresh, Chicago Coke, Connellsville |
| | | 1922 Jan. | Sugar, raw, 96° centrifugal, N. Y. Sugar, granulated in bbls., N. Y. Sulphuric acid, 66°, N. Y. Steel billets, Bessemer, Pittsburgh |
| | | Feb. | ·Beef, good native steers, Chicago Common brick, salmon, run of kiln, Chicago Pig iron, foundry No. 2, northern Pig iron, Bessemer Iron and steel (*Iron Trade Review* index) Composite finished steel (*Iron Age* index) Newsprint, contract Canadian Bituminous coal |
| | | Mar. | India Rubber, Para Island, N. Y. Composite pig iron (*American Metal Market* index) Composite steel (*American Metal Market* index) Structural steel beams, etc., Pittsburgh |
| | | Apr. | Newsprint, spot market, domestic Boots and shoes, men's black calf, blucher, Boston Leather, chrome calf, "B" grades Boston |
| | | May | Newsprint, contract domestic |

### IV. VARIATIONS IN DIFFERENT INDUSTRIES—FLUCTUATIONS IN PRODUCTION

The fluctuations in physical production among different industries have been nearly as varied as the fluctuations among prices.[1]

One difference between these fluctuations of production and the price fluctuations may be pointed out.  The dates of the high points of production are less scattered than the dates of peak prices, and they do not overlap upon the dates of lowest production in the way that the price quotations do.[2]  It is also interesting to note that fourteen out of the eighteen industries covered had passed their highest points of production before the Bureau of Labor Statistics wholesale-price index attained its peak (May, 1920) and that fourteen of the eighteen had passed their lowest points by July, 1921 (when the wholesale-price index of the Bureau of Labor Statistics touched its lowest point for the time being) and were on the up-grade once more.

[1] The production data given in Tables V and VI are based on more refined figures than the raw price quotations already presented.  These production data are from the "adjusted relatives indicative of the volume of manufacture" prepared by the Harvard University Committee on Economic Research.  Secular trends and seasonal fluctuations, both important factors in the physical output of many industries, were eliminated before the relatives on which these percentages are based were computed.

[2] Practically all commodities seem to have reached points of maximum production in the year 1920.

TABLE V.—MONTHS IN WHICH EIGHTEEN COMMODITIES INDICATIVE OF THE VOLUME
OF MANUFACTURE REACHED THEIR HIGHEST AND LOWEST PRODUCTION
JANUARY, 1919 TO FEBRUARY, 1922[a]

(Secular trend and seasonal variations both eliminated)

| Dates | Commodities reaching highest output | Dates | Commodities reaching lowest output |
|---|---|---|---|
| **1919** | | | |
| June | Leather, sole | | |
| Nov. | Cattle, slaughtered | | |
| Dec. | Small cigarettes | | |
| **1920** | | | |
| Jan. | Paper board | | |
| | Cotton, consumed | | |
| | Wool, consumed | | |
| | Wheat flour | | |
| | Hogs, slaughtered | | |
| Feb. | Lumber, cut, total three varieties | | |
| Mar. | Tobacco and snuff | | |
| | Large cigars | | |
| | Pig iron | | |
| | Steel ingots | | |
| | Sugar, meltings | | |
| July | Book paper | | |
| | Fine paper | | |
| | Wrapping paper | | |
| Aug. | Newsprint paper | | |
| | | **1920** | |
| | | Oct. | Sugar, meltings |
| | | Nov. | Tobacco and snuff |
| | | | Wheat flour |
| | | Dec. | Cotton, consumed |
| | | | Wool, consumed |
| | | **1921** | |
| | | Jan. | Wrapping paper |
| | | Feb. | Leather, sole |
| | | April | Fine paper |
| | | May | Newsprint paper |
| | | | Book paper |
| | | July | Lumber, cut, total three varieties |
| | | | Paper board |
| | | | Pig iron |
| | | | Steel ingots |
| | | Dec. | Cattle, slaughtered |
| | | | Large cigars |
| | | **1922** | |
| | | Jan. | Hogs, slaughtered |
| | | Feb. | Small cigarettes |

[a] Based upon "adjusted relatives indicative of the volume of manufacture,"
Harvard University Committee on Economic Research. *The Review of Economic
Statistics*, prel. vol. 4, April, 1922, supplement 1, pp. 133 ff.

TABLE VI.—PERCENTAGE DECLINES IN THE PHYSICAL OUTPUT OF THE EIGHTEEN COMMODITIES FROM THE HIGHEST POINTS TO THE LOWEST POINTS IN THE PERIODS JANUARY, 1919 TO FEBRUARY, 1922

(Commodities arranged in order of percentage declines)

| Commodity | Percentage decline | Number of months declining |
|---|---|---|
| Steel ingots.......................... | 74.5 | 16 |
| Pig iron.............................. | 72.7 | 16 |
| Wool, consumed....................... | 64.8 | 11 |
| Paper board.......................... | 61.1 | 18 |
| Sugar, meltings....................... | 60.3 | 7 |
| Fine paper............................ | 58.2 | 9 |
| Small cigarettes...................... | 54.6 | 26 |
| Book paper........................... | 52.8 | 10 |
| Tobacco and snuff.................... | 46.1 | 9 |
| Cattle, slaughtered.................. | 44.3 | 25 |
| Wrapping paper...................... | 43.2 | 6 |
| Cotton, consumed.................... | 42.9 | 11 |
| Sole leather......................... | 42.2 | 20 |
| Newsprint paper..................... | 41.0 | 9 |
| Lumber, cut, three varieties........ | 37.5 | 17 |
| Wheat flour......................... | 37.4 | 10 |
| Large cigars........................ | 35.6 | 21 |
| Hogs, slaughtered................... | 34.9 | 24 |

## V. TERRITORIAL DIFFERENCES IN BUSINESS

One bit of evidence is available concerning the fluctuations in volume of retail business in different parts of the country from 1919 to 1922.

Lawrence B. Mann has analyzed the sales of department stores as reported by seven of the twelve Federal Reserve Banks, eliminating seasonal fluctuations.[1]   His results are summarized in Table VII below.

TABLE VII.—ANALYSIS OF DEPARTMENT STORE SALES

| Federal Reserve District | Peak month of department store sales in dollars |
|---|---|
| Atlanta.............................. | November, 1920 |
| Dallas............................... | November, 1920 |
| Minneapolis.......................... | November, 1920 |
| Richmond............................ | February, 1921 |
| San Francisco........................ | February, 1921 |
| New York............................ | March, 1921 |
| Boston............................... | March, 1921 |

[1] Seasonal Trends in Department Store Trade, *Journal of the American Statistical Association*, June, 1922, pp. 255–8.

According to these figures retail business, among department stores at least, did not pass its peak in any district until six months after wholesale prices had culminated, and until after physical production had begun to decline in all of the manufacturing industries for which we have good data. When the decline in retail sales did begin, it started in the southern sections affected by the fall in cotton prices and in the northwest wheat growing area where another group of farmers had been hard hit by a price drop. Not until four months later did the great cities of the northeast see a similar decline in retail buying.

# CHAPTER III

## THE ECONOMIC LOSSES CAUSED BY BUSINESS CYCLES

By Wesley C. Mitchell and Willford I. King

National Bureau of Economic Research

### I. THE PROBLEM

The amount of energy it is wise to spend on efforts to control the business cycle depends upon the gains in national welfare which can be secured. The most definite of these prospective gains consists in diminishing the economic losses we now suffer from the wastes of booms, the forced liquidations of crises, and the involuntary idleness of depressions.

To measure these losses accurately is impossible. The chief difficulty is not lack of statistical data, though the data leave much to be desired, but the difficulty of deciding what effect the diminution of the present violent fluctuations would have upon the level about which the national income now oscillates. This problem must be faced before we can decide how to use what statistics we have.

First, it is clear that crises and depressions produce some salutary effects at present. They check foolish speculation, weed out incompetent business managers, give both employers and employees an incentive to greater efficiency, and stimulate the adoption of more economical methods of production.[1] Further, as Edwin F. Gay has recently pointed out, hard times have led to many transformations in economic organization.

The crises of 1857 and 1860 gave birth to the clearing-house [loan certificate] system. The reaction to the inflationist doctrine springing from the crises of '73 and '93 soundly educated the country to the need of a gold basis for our currency. The banking crisis of 1907 definitely brought to a head the movement for the development of central banking, which resulted in the Federal Reserve System. . . . The movement of population from the industrial East to the agricultural West has been stimulated in the past by each period of economic depression. . . . Mergers of industrial corporations, the cooperation of trade

---

[1] I think you admit too much. If business were kept running on an even keel, the incompetent would in time be weeded out and foolish speculations would be checked. Severe illnesses resulting from over eating have led many people to adopt salutary dietary rules. But the latter do not represent "improvements" or "advances." The people in question would be better off and more efficient if the excesses in question had not made remedies necessary.—Note by T. S. Adams.

32

associations and of trade unions have all grown through learning the need of closer cohesion from the lesson of adversity.[1]

While the specific changes here mentioned may be deemed either good or bad, it is evident that such remodeling of our social fabric is likely often to result in marked improvements.

Of course, all this does not mean that crises and depressions are blessings in disguise which we should be foolish to stop if we could. The economic changes cited by Mr. Gay mean rather that our predecessors have felt crises and depressions to be misfortunes and have taken measures which they hoped would prevent their recurrence. So far as these measures have succeeded, their success is an encouragement to further effort, and so far as they have failed, their failure means that the problem is still to be solved.

But the question remains whether the elimination of crises and depressions, could it be accomplished, might not leave the ill results of *prosperity* unchecked. Would not losses from rash investments, the indefinite survival of incompetent business managers, the relaxing of effort by employers and employees, and slowness in adopting technical improvements—would not these losses continue if production were stabilized, and would they not in the long run offset all the gains?

One answer to this query is that if the analysis in Chapter I is sound, the ill effects of prosperity just mentioned are among the factors which put an end to prosperity by breeding crises. In other words, methods of combatting crises and depressions which leave the wastes of prosperity unchecked will not prevent crises and depression from occurring. This answer is conclusive in a formal sense, though it serves to show how difficult it is to devise a plan of stabilizing business activity that will accomplish its aim. To succeed, the plan must be effective in preventing the wastes that now characterize booms as well as effective in relieving the sufferings of depressions.

A second problem that must be faced before the costs of business cycles can be estimated is suggested by what has just been said. If a successful plan of avoiding crises and depressions must avoid also the wastes of booms, would not that plan prevent production from reaching such high levels as have marked our busiest years? Would not the level of stabilized production be merely the level of a fairly prosperous year— the level of 1912, for example, rather than the level of 1916? Therefore, in estimating the gains theoretically attainable from perfect control over the business cycle, is it proper to use differences between production in the trough and production at the peak? Rather should not the production of every year be compared with the production attained in years of full employment without much overtime work, after this level

---

[1] The Next Great Inflation *Credit Monthly*, June, 1922.

3

has been adjusted to allow for the factor of growth?  Indeed, should not the excess production of our busiest years above this "normal" level be subtracted from the deficient production of poor years to estimate the net loss from business cycles?  And do not men unemployed in years of depression turn out many goods not represented in the statistics of production—garden products, home improvements, and the like?

No conclusive answer can be given to these questions, because we do not know what would happen if things were not as they are.  But an offsetting series of questions comes to mind.  Is the additional output of material goods produced by the intense exertion of boom years a national gain?  Is it full compensation for the haste, the worry, and strain to which workers on overtime and harried business men are subject?  Does not efficiency suffer in the long run from these strains and would not the general level of production rise if they were removed?  Similarly, are not the ill effects of crises and depressions felt long after the hard times are over?  Are not many adults made permanently less capable workers by the distress suffered and bad physiological or bad mental habits formed when out of their jobs for months at a time?  And are not many children prevented from becoming as useful citizens as they might have become, had family incomes been regular?

To repeat, the central difficulty of estimating the economic costs of business cycles is that we do not know with certainty what effect the removal of wide fluctuations in production would have upon national efficiency in the long run.  Lacking such knowledge, all we can do is to show how far production in periods of depression falls below the records of boom years and how far it falls below the records of active but unhurried years.  That is a technical problem in statistics for which the two solutions can be roughly approximated.  But when the solutions have been found, we cannot prove that the higher or the lower figures are the better.  Indeed, anyone who thinks that greater regularity of work and income would diminish efficiency may discount the lower figures, and the majority who hold the opposite opinion may add to the higher.

## II. ESTIMATES OF THE LOSSES BASED UPON INDEX NUMBERS OF PRODUCTION

At first thought, the easiest way of attacking the statistical problem seems to be to deal with it piecemeal, taking one industry at a time and analyzing the losses which are borne by property owners and employees or saddled by the industry upon the consumers of its products.  Careful consideration, however, shows that this mode of attack is impracticable.  It leads to insoluble problems of what profits and wages might have been in particular trades under conditions which have never prevailed; it involves interminable details and calls for data not to be had.

The only feasible method of approximating roughly the economic losses caused by business cycles is to deal with variations from year to year in the production or the income of the nation as a whole. These variations have been investigated of late by two groups of workers—those who have made index numbers of physical production, and those who have estimated the income of the nation in dollars. By using both sets of results it is possible to make two rough estimates of the differences

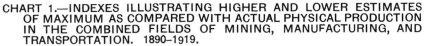

CHART 1.—INDEXES ILLUSTRATING HIGHER AND LOWER ESTIMATES OF MAXIMUM AS COMPARED WITH ACTUAL PHYSICAL PRODUCTION IN THE COMBINED FIELDS OF MINING, MANUFACTURING, AND TRANSPORTATION. 1890–1919.

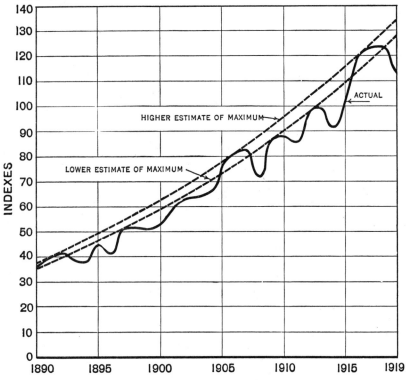

between the economic yields of good and bad years and to check the results against each other.

Of the available index numbers of production, those made by Edmund E. Day and Walter W. Stewart are best adapted to the present purpose, in that they differentiate between the output of the farms, mines, factories, and railroads. This matter is important because agricultural production is affected more by the weather than by the business cycle; for example, 1914 was a year of large harvests and 1916 a year of poor yields. To include these erratic variations of the product of farms in an estimate of the economic losses caused by business cycles would obscure what we wish to see clearly.  Hence the following estimate is based upon an average of Stewart's and Day's index numbers for the

TABLE VIII.—POSSIBLE COMPARED WITH ACTUAL PHYSICAL PRODUCTION IN THE COMBINED FIELDS OF MINING, MANUFACTURING, AND TRANSPORTATION ACCORDING TO TWO DIFFERENT HYPOTHESES

| A | B | C | D | E | F | G | H |
|---|---|---|---|---|---|---|---|
| | | | Higher estimate of loss occasioned by instability of production | | | Lower estimate of loss occasioned by instability of production | |
| Year | Actual physical production [a] | Higher estimate of maximum possible production | Amount $C - B$ | Percentage of possible maximum $(D \div C) \times 100$ | Lower estimate of maximum probable production | Amount $F - B$ | Percentage of probable maximum $(G \div F) \times 100$ |
| 1890 | 36.4 | 37.3 | 0.9 | 2.4 | 35.1 | −1.3 | −3.7 |
| 1891 | 39.6 | 39.6 | 0.0 | 0.0 | 37.3 | −2.3 | −6.2 |
| 1892 | 41.1 | 41.9 | 0.8 | 2.0 | 39.4 | −1.7 | −4.3 |
| 1893 | 38.1 | 44.3 | 6.2 | 14.0 | 41.7 | 3.6 | 8.6 |
| 1894 | 37.9 | 46.8 | 8.9 | 19.0 | 44.0 | 6.1 | 13.9 |
| 1895 | 45.0 | 49.3 | 4.3 | 8.8 | 46.4 | 1.4 | 3.0 |
| 1896 | 41.1 | 51.8 | 10.7 | 20.7 | 48.7 | 7.6 | 15.6 |
| 1897 | 51.2 | 54.4 | 3.2 | 6.0 | 51.2 | 0.0 | 0.0 |
| 1898 | 51.9 | 57.1 | 5.2 | 9.1 | 53.7 | 1.8 | 3.3 |
| 1899 | 51.0 | 59.8 | 8.8 | 14.8 | 56.3 | 5.3 | 9.4 |
| 1900 | 52.5 | 62.6 | 10.1 | 16.2 | 58.9 | 6.4 | 10.9 |
| 1901 | 59.3 | 65.5 | 6.2 | 9.4 | 61.6 | 2.3 | 3.7 |
| 1902 | 63.3 | 68.5 | 5.2 | 7.6 | 64.5 | 1.2 | 1.9 |
| 1903 | 64.1 | 71.6 | 7.5 | 10.5 | 67.4 | 3.3 | 4.9 |
| 1904 | 66.0 | 74.8 | 8.8 | 11.7 | 70.4 | 4.4 | 6.2 |
| 1905 | 76.2 | 78.1 | 1.9 | 2.5 | 73.5 | −2.7 | −3.7 |
| 1906 | 81.5 | 81.5 | 0.0 | 0.0 | 76.7 | −4.8 | −6.3 |
| 1907 | 83.6 | 85.0 | 1.4 | 1.6 | 80.0 | −3.6 | −4.5 |
| 1908 | 72.8 | 88.6 | 15.8 | 17.8 | 83.4 | 10.6 | 12.7 |
| 1909 | 87.2 | 92.3 | 5.1 | 5.5 | 86.9 | −0.3 | −0.3 |
| 1910 | 88.8 | 96.1 | 7.3 | 7.6 | 90.4 | 1.6 | 1.8 |
| 1911 | 86.7 | 100.0 | 13.3 | 13.3 | 94.1 | 7.4 | 7.9 |
| 1912 | 97.5 | 104.0 | 6.5 | 6.2 | 97.9 | 0.4 | 0.4 |
| 1913 | 100.0 | 108.0 | 8.0 | 7.4 | 101.6 | 1.6 | 1.6 |
| 1914 | 92.2 | 112.1 | 19.9 | 17.8 | 105.5 | 13.3 | 12.6 |
| 1915 | 103.0 | 116.3 | 13.3 | 11.5 | 109.4 | 6.4 | 5.8 |
| 1916 | 120.6 | 120.0 | 0.0 | 0.0 | 113.5 | −7.1 | −6.3 |
| 1917 | 124.1 | 125.0 | 0.9 | 0.7 | 117.6 | −6.5 | −5.5 |
| 1918 | 125.4 | 129.5 | 4.1 | 3.1 | 121.9 | −3.5 | −2.9 |
| 1919 | 114.6 | 134.1 | 19.5 | 14.5 | 126.2 | 11.6 | 9.2 |
| Total | 2,192.7 | 2,396.5 | 203.8 | 8.5 | 2,255.2 | 62.5 | 2.8 |

[a] Combination of indexes derived by Edmund E. Day and Walter W. Stewart, see *An Index of Physical Volume of Production* (reprint from *The Review of Economic Statistics*, Sept., 1920–Jan., 1921), p. 65; and An Index Number of Production, *American Economic Review*, March, 1921, p. 68. Weights used, the same for the indexes in each study: mining 1, factories 7, and railways 2.

physical product turned out by mines, factories, and railroads. In averaging, these industrial groups have been assigned weights of one, seven, and two respectively. For the years preceding 1899 Stewart's index alone has been used, since Day's investigation does not extend back of that year. Column *B* of Table VIII presents the index of "actual physical production" made in this way.

To compare the actual output of each year with the output of the best years, a smoothed curve has been run through the peaks attained in 1891, 1906, and 1916. Had figures been available for the late '80's, a starting point for this curve might have been obtained higher than that given by 1891, which was not a boom year. Chart 1 shows the smoothed curve as well as the fluctuating line of actual performance. Readings from the smoothed curve on the chart supply the "higher estimate of maximum possible production" shown in Column *C* of the table.

When this estimate of the level that production might attain if business cycles were controlled is used as the basis for comparison, it appears that in one year (1896) the actual output was curtailed by more than 20 per cent. In twelve years out of the thirty the deficiency of production exceeded 10 per cent of what might have been attained. Taking the whole period, good and bad years together, actual production was 8.5 per cent less than the hypothetical maximum.

Next, to compare actual production with a hypothetical level based upon the output of active but unhurried years, a free hand curve has been run roughly through the records of 1897, 1909, and 1912. This curve also appears on the chart, and readings from it give the "lower estimate of maximum probable production" in Column *F* of the table.

In ten out of the thirty years covered, the actual output exceeded the "maximum probable production" estimated in this way, and these excesses appear as minus quantities in the "loss" Columns *G* and *H*. But in two-thirds of the years, production did not attain the level of such seasons of revival as are here made the standard of comparison. In five years the deficiency exceeded 10 per cent. Nor does the excess production of the good times balance the deficient production of the dull times; for, after subtracting the gains from the losses, there remains a net loss of nearly 3 per cent of the output of a whole generation of effort.

### III. ESTIMATE OF THE LOSSES BASED UPON THE TOTAL INCOME OF THE NATION

Figures showing annual fluctuations in the national income are better for the present purpose than index numbers of production in that they are not confined to a restricted field of industries. Furthermore, it seems probable that the production indexes fail to take sufficient account of approximately stable industries such as merchandising and the hand trades, and that they stress the irregular output of raw materials too much and the relatively steady production of finished products too little. If these premises are true, the oscillations in industry as a whole may be somewhat less marked than the estimate based upon production indexes would lead us to believe. On the other hand, when we attempt to measure the variability in national productivity by the use of income statistics, we are confronted by other difficulties. The income of farmers, which is of course included, does not vary in harmony with the fluctuations in other industries. Data are available for ten years only—a period too brief to permit of measuring industrial trends with accuracy. And the necessity of reducing amounts expressed in dollars to a hypothetical money of constant purchasing power opens the door to new errors. Hence, the estimates about to be given are, perhaps, not superior to those already presented.

Table IX shows in Column B the estimates of the aggregate incomes of the people of the United States, prepared by the National Bureau of Economic Research, after the wild price fluctuations have been eliminated as well as may be. Since the period covered includes only one boom year (1916), it would be going very far to draw from these data a line showing production stabilized at the peak. But a line representing years of considerable activity is suggested by 1910 and 1913 though both were years of slowly receding business. Comparisons made between the amounts indicated by this line and the actual income, as estimated, give results corresponding to the smaller percentage losses obtained from the index numbers of production. The two sets of percentage losses differ somewhat, as is to be expected from the inclusion of farmers in one case and their exclusion in the other, yet the percentages run on about the same level, so that the one investigation confirms the other in a broad sense. The most marked differences in results occur in 1909 and 1918.

According to Table IX, the loss of income from depression in the one really bad year covered (1914), amounts to nearly 3,500,000,000 of pre-war dollars—or not quite a tenth of the national income. In seven years out of the ten the national income was below the level attained in periods of moderate activity. Could these figures be extended through 1921, they would probably show losses of greater magnitude.[1]

[1] To draw the line of "active production" through two years so close together as 1910 and 1913 seems to me too doubtful even for "rough estimates." That it results in erroneous conclusions is suggested to my mind by the loss of 5 per cent assigned to the year 1918. I can hardly believe that the latter year was so far below what might be called the "lower maximum." Contrast the percentage in Column H of Table X. Neither do I believe that 1915 was 7.4 per cent below the "lower maximum."—Note by T. S. ADAMS.

TABLE IX.—ROUGH ESTIMATE OF THE LOSS IN THE INCOME OF THE PEOPLE OF THE
UNITED STATES FROM IRREGULARITY OF PRODUCTION IN THE YEARS 1909–1918
(Based upon a comparison of the income of each year, expressed in pre-war dollars, with the level of
income attained in moderately active periods)

| A | B | C | D | E |
|---|---|---|---|---|
| | | | Estimated losses from irregular production | |
| Year | Total income in millions of 1913 dollars $^a$ | Income assumed under stabilized conditions, in millions of 1913 dollars | In millions of 1913 dollars $C - B$ | In percentages of assumed stabilized income $(D \div C) \times 100$ |
| 1909 | $ 30,101 | $ 31,365 | $1,264 | 4.0 |
| 1910 | 32,477 | 32,477 | | |
| 1911 | 31,685 | 33,561 | 1,876 | 5.6 |
| 1912 | 33,730 | 34,584 | 854 | 2.5 |
| 1913 | 35,580 | 35,871 | 291 | 0.8 |
| 1914 | 33,595 | 37,064 | 3,469 | 9.4 |
| 1915 | 35,335 | 38,146 | 2,811 | 7.4 |
| 1916 | 41,265 | 39,132 | −2,133 | −5.5 |
| 1917 | 41,910 | 40,263 | −1,647 | −4.1 |
| 1918 | 39,112 | 41,192 | 2,080 | 5.0 |
| Total | $354,790 | $363,655 | $8,865 | 2.4 |

$^a$ "Income in the United States," vol. II, Table 20G (Publications of the
National Bureau of Economic Research).

## IV. CONCLUSION

All that the preceding tables are meant to show, and that in a very
rough approximation, is the difference between the production of goods
or income in years of depression and production in years of moderate and
of intense activity.  The broad result is that the worst years run something like 15 to 20 per cent behind the best, and something like 8 to 12
per cent behind the moderately good years.  Even 10 per cent of the
national income represents several billions of dollars.

Whether these figures indicate the order of magnitude of the material
losses imposed on the country by business depressions is open to argument.  Quite apart from objections based upon the imperfections of the
statistical data that must be used in any estimate, it may be contended
that a reduction of economic uncertainty would lead to a decline of
efficiency.  It may also be contended that both the strains of booms and

the sufferings of depressions impair efficiency more than uncertainty stimulates it. The latter is probably the commoner opinion. Those who accept this view will regard even the higher of the estimates here presented as understating the losses which plans for stabilizing production aim to check.

Finally, it is obvious that certain intangibles of grave concern to social welfare are omitted from our estimates and cannot be inserted later by any process of correction. Privation, anxiety, loss of self-respect —the concomitants of unemployment—are evils not measurable in dollars or percentages of physical production. To say that these evils reduce the amount of wealth produced in future years may be proper. But even so, that correction leaves out the saddest part of the reckoning— the part that cannot be put into figures.

# PART II
## CYCLICAL FLUCTUATIONS IN EMPLOYMENT

# CHAPTER IV

## WHAT THE PRESENT STATISTICS OF EMPLOYMENT SHOW[1]

### By WILLIAM A. BERRIDGE

#### BROWN UNIVERSITY

### I. THE DATA SHOW NOT TOTAL NUMBERS UNEMPLOYED, BUT FLUCTUATIONS IN EMPLOYMENT

What do the American figures on employment and unemployment show? A general answer to this question may be given in a nutshell. The unemployment figures fail to tell us the number of the unemployed.[2] But these figures, in conjunction with the data representing the number employed according to pay-rolls, enable us to construct a barometer or index of employment cycles.[3]

Such an index has a very definite bearing on at least four important matters, relating partly to the course of employment and unemployment cycles as such and partly to the relation between employment and the business cycle. First and most directly, employment registers the *labor market;* that is, it shows relatively how "easy," or how "tight," the labor market is at any given time, much as bank reserves reflect the state of the money market. Secondly, employment shows something as to the general course of *production,* since the hiring and the firing of labor are largely resorted to by employers when they wish to increase or curtail output. A third use is to show the relation of employment to *buying power.* The total fund of purchasing power flowing into the hands of wage-earners at a given time is conditioned directly by the state of employment. A fourth and equally important feature, shown indirectly by an employment index, is the cycle of *social welfare.* Largely as a

---

[1] In preparing the present chapter the writer has drawn freely upon materials contributed to the Pollak Foundation for Economic Research, the Harvard University Committee on Economic Research, and the American Statistical Association; and cordially acknowledges their courtesy in authorizing him to do so.

[2] In this connection the reader may recall the wide variety of unemployment estimates in circulation at the time of the President's Conference on Unemployment. These estimates ranged at least from 2,000,000 to 6,000,000 persons.

[3] The employment figures also yield other useful information, but in this study the question at issue is simply employment *cycles.* This leaves out of consideration the important seasonal aspect of the unemployment problem. The effects of labor disputes, sickness, old age, disability, vacations, "loafing," and the gradual decay or removal of industries are also ignored.

result of fluctuations in the economic prosperity of wage-earners, there are pronounced cycles of suicide, crime, prostitution, pauperism, marriages, migration, and other social phenomena.

In other words, the problem of cyclical employment (or unemployment) stands in a position midway between the economic and the social phases of the business cycle; it is a connecting link. Consequently a reliable index of employment may be expected to prove of more general interest than would an index for almost any purely economic or purely social phenomenon. This analysis, therefore, concerns not only the public-spirited citizen, but even more tangibly and directly the social student and worker, and likewise the business man, whether interested chiefly in employment management, in production, or in sales.

An index of employment is a series of figures so constructed that its fluctuations will reflect changes in the *relative intensity* of unemployment between two points of time, without necessarily measuring the total *volume* of unemployment—or even the number of totally unemployed.[1] In other words, the index yields a continuous curve of employment, the high points of which represent active employment, the low points severe unemployment, and intermediate points various grades of seriousness of the unemployment problem.

By adopting this simple device we avoid several difficult problems. If we were seeking to measure the absolute volume of unemployment, we should have to allow for the amount of part-time employment in depression—a problem on which we have so little data that it is virtually insoluble. For our purpose it is sufficient to assume that part-time employment becomes more prevalent during a depression, and overtime more prevalent during prosperity, so that an index based on full-time employment alone should show correctly the relative fluctuations.[2]

## II. THE DATA AVAILABLE FOR AN INDEX OF EMPLOYMENT

Before presenting a general index of employment in the United States, it is well to consider the economic importance of the leading states for which data on employment have been or now are available, in order to judge the adequacy of our samples; then to pass in review the leading evidence upon which a general employment index may be based. This review is presented for convenience in two parts, for the periods prior to June, 1914, and since June, 1914.

---

[1] For the writer's view on the use of the index method for measuring unemployment, see Harvard Economic Service, *Special Letter*, Oct. 8, 1921, p. 6, and *Journal of American Statistical Association*, March, 1922, vol. XVIII, p. 55. For a somewhat different view see ERNEST S. BRADFORD, Methods Used in Measuring Unemployment, *Quarterly Publication of the American Statistical Association*, December, 1921, vol. XVII, especially pp. 986–9.

[2] The validity of this assumption is confirmed in Chap. V on Under-employment.

Table X shows the proportion of factory wage-earners in the leading states for which employment data are available, or have been available within recent years. New York, which heads the list, contains between one-sixth and one-seventh of all the wage-earners in the country employed in manufacturing industries. This is equivalent to Massachusetts and Illinois taken together. Compared with the lesser states, New York is equivalent to three New Jerseys, and five Connecticuts or Wisconsins. Of all the states in the country, New York is exceeded in manufacturing only by Pennsylvania, which has had no employment data in recent years except for a short time early in the war. Further economic considerations confirm the key position of New York in a study of employment,[1]— such is its industrial diversification, its ready access to the immigrant labor supply, and its central geographical position with reference to other great industrial states. In short, New York forms a large and representative sample of the country's manufacturing activity.

TABLE X.—GEOGRAPHICAL DISTRIBUTION OF WAGE-EARNERS EMPLOYED IN MANUFACTURING INDUSTRIES IN SELECTED STATES[a]

(Unit: one per cent)

|  | 1904 | 1909 | 1914 | 1919 |
|---|---|---|---|---|
| New York........................... | 15.7 | 15.2 | 15.0 | 13.5 |
| Massachusetts....................... | 8.9 | 8.8 | 8.6 | 7.9 |
| Illinois............................ | 6.9 | 7.0 | 7.2 | 7.2 |
| New Jersey......................... | 4.9 | 4.9 | 5.3 | 5.6 |
| Connecticut........................ | 3.3 | 3.2 | 3.2 | 3.2 |
| Wisconsin.......................... | 2.8 | 2.8 | 2.8 | 2.9 |
| United States...................... | 100.0 | 100.0 | 100.0 | 100.0 |

[a] *Abstract of Census of Manufactures*, 1914, p. 272, and (for 1919) the Census reports on Manufactures in the U. S. The decennial Censuses of Occupations disclose a similar relationship among the states for the manufacturing and mechanical pursuits.

Bearing in mind the differences among the states in industrial importance and position, we may review in succession employment indexes constructed from the available data.

### III. INDEXES OF EMPLOYMENT, 1903–1914

**Employment in Massachusetts and New Jersey.**—Chart 2 shows two indexes of employment derived from the pay-roll data of the manufacturing establishments in New Jersey and Massachusetts. The seasonal variation and the long-time trend have been eliminated from each of these

[1] For further consideration of the economic and statistical considerations involved, see *The Review of Economic Statistics*, January, 1922, prel. vol. 1, pp. 25, 26.

series, so that the horizontal base line measures normal employment. One may therefore read from the scale at the right the net deviation from normal attributable in any given month to the cycle of business conditions. The upper part (positive deviation) of these curves represents good employment; the lower part (negative deviation) shows the prevalence of unemployment.

CHART 2.—EMPLOYMENT IN MANUFACTURING ESTABLISHMENTS, 1903–1914.

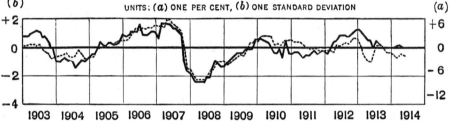

The scale at the right is in percentages. At the left of Chart 2 one may read the fluctuations in terms of the typical percentage deviation from the base line, rather than in units of 1 per cent. The typical or "standard" deviation for both of these curves happens to be the same (3.4 per cent). By using for a vertical unit the standard deviation rather than the percentage, we gain an important advantage. Comparison is made easier between curves having unequal standard deviations;

CHART 3.—UNEMPLOYMENT IN TRADE UNIONS.

for instance, compare the curves in Chart 2 with those in Chart 3. In view of this advantage, the standard deviation is used as the vertical unit for most of the curves shown in this chapter.

The Massachusetts curve is derived from data collected early in each year since 1889 by the Massachusetts Bureau of Statistics. These data show the number of wage-earners on pay-rolls at the middle of each month during the preceding year in the most important manufacturing establishments of the state.[1] The number of wage-earners covered by these reports has formed a large part of the total number employed in manufacturing within the state, having ranged from 150,000 to 800,000 or from 80 per cent upward.[2]

An important peculiarity of manufacturing in Massachusetts is the degree of industrial specialization. Cotton manufacturing, the boot and shoe industry, woolen and worsted goods, and foundry and machine-shop products comprise 40 to 55 per cent of all manufacturing in Massachusetts. This specialization is one factor which renders the Massachusetts returns imperfectly representative of general industrial conditions. Moreover, cotton manufacture, the most important of all, is wholly dependent upon agriculture for its raw material, and an especially large or small cotton crop seriously affects the response of the industry to the business cycle. Moreover, in several of the leading industries women and juveniles are heavily employed.[3] As disconnected local censuses of manufactures, year by year, these Massachusetts data are excellent, but as a continuous record of employment fluctuation they cannot be safely accepted without reservations.

From 1895 through 1918, the New Jersey Bureau of Industrial Statistics collected data similar to those for Massachusetts. The scope of the

---

[1] The data have been regularly published in the Bureau's *Annual Reports on the Statistics of Manufactures.*

[2] Although the data are comprehensive, they have not remained equally so throughout the period; for instance, in 1899 about 360,000, or 82 per cent of the 438,000 wage-earners shown by the U. S. Census for Massachusetts, were covered by the reports of the state bureau; by 1904 the number had risen to 430,000 or 88 per cent. It is impossible to determine precisely the degree of inclusiveness after 1904, because in the subsequent census years the bureau adopted outright the federal bureau's figures for Massachusetts; but the percentage appears to have risen decisively, probably to 95 per cent or more.

[3] Another important objection, statistical in its nature, lies in the discontinuity of the Massachusetts data during the past sixteen years. Prior to 1906, the data published yearly covered identical establishments over a period of twenty-four months, so that the actual degree of change between each December and the following January in these establishments can be readily ascertained. This policy of "overlapping" the yearly reports was not maintained after 1906, and consequently the problem of building up a reliable, continuous series for an extended period is not an easy one. After 1906 the data do not form a true statistical series at all, but a series of floating fragments connected with each other in a very loose and uncertain manner.

For a discussion of the method by which the fragments were welded into a continuous series, see *Journal of American Statistical Association*, June, 1922, vol. XVII, pp. 233–4. Throughout the present investigation the methods employed for elimination of seasonal variation, secular trend, etc., are based upon those devised by WARREN M. PERSONS, see *The Review of Economic Statistics*, prel. vol. 1, January and April, 1919, pp. 3–205. Variations were introduced by the writer only where necessitated by the peculiar nature of some of the employment data.

material, limited to about 50,000 wage-earners in 1895–1997,[1] was considerably enlarged in subsequent years, ranging from 140,000 in 1898 to more than 500,000 in 1918. Here as in Massachusetts the canvass did not cover a fixed proportion of establishments or even a steadily increasing proportion,[2] but 75 to 90 per cent were generally included. New Jersey is industrially more diversified than Massachusetts The machinery and metal-working industries are fairly strong; wool, silk, tobacco, and several others also rank comparatively high. It is noteworthy that cotton ranks eleventh, representing only about 2 per cent of all New Jersey's manufacturing, as contrasted with 15 to 25 per cent in Massachusetts.

**Unemployment in New York and Massachusetts.**—One can also obtain highly valuable evidence as to employment fluctuations by examining the fluctuations in unemployment—"the other side of the shield." Before the war two useful unemployment series were available; one for Massachusetts and one for New York. Each was reported in fairly consistent form, without sudden changes from year to year as in the pay-roll data; consequently the two unemployment series have in common the advantage of continuity. They have a second advantage in greater breadth of industrial scope, comprising not only manufacturing but also building, transportation, etc. Both of the unemployment series are valuable. Each has its own advantages, but that for New York has a net advantage, being reported monthly instead of quarterly, extending over a pre-war period twice as long as that for Massachusetts, and covering a much more important, diversified and favorably situated industrial state.

It is of course impossible to utilize these figures in their original form owing to the effect of disputes, seasonal variation, and long-time trend, as well as more subtle factors such as changes in industrial composition. A suitable method of analysis has eliminated these difficulties,[3] yielding the two unemployment indexes shown in Chart 3.

By comparing with each other the two curves in Chart 3, and contrasting these with the pair shown in Chart 2 , one may see a high order of agreement as to the course of employment cycles in the dozen years before the war. Only minor disagreements are to be found. Thus after the depression of 1903, and again after the prolonged boom of 1905–

---

[1] The data for the years 1895–1916 were obtained from the Bureau's *Annual Reports*. Those for 1917 and 1918 were made available through the courtesy of J. A. T. Gribbin of the Bureau. The series was discontinued in 1918.

[2] Thus in 1899 an average of 175,000 wage-earners was represented, *i.e.*, 82 per cent of the number shown by the federal Census of Manufactures. In 1904 the ratio fell to 77 per cent, then rose to 87 in 1909 and 88 per cent in 1914.

[3] For a detailed discussion of the methods employed, see *The Review of Economic Statistics*, prel. vol. 4, January, 1922, pp. 26–34.

1907, a turn appeared in the New York curve slightly earlier than in the others.[1]

The degree of the similarity, or "excellence of fit," among these curves may be measured numerically by noting the coefficients of agreement or correlation coefficients. These coefficients are simply numbers derived from a mathematical formula, so contrived that +100 per cent represents perfect agreement and 0 per cent nonagreement.[2] The correlation coefficients are as follows: between the two unemployment indexes +72 per cent, between New York unemployment and New Jersey employment −73 per cent, between New York unemployment and Massachusetts employment −80 per cent, between Massachusetts employment and unemployment −88 per cent.

**A General Index of Employment Cycles, 1903–1914.**—We now have before us all the materials necessary for constructing a monthly general index of employment cycles for the United States from 1903 to 1914. The three states represented in Charts 2 and 3 comprise a fairly large sample, more than one-fourth of all the industrial wage-earners in the United States.[3] The indexes appear to represent adequately the course of employment cycles in the respective states, and they support each other so thoroughly as to justify beyond any reasonable doubt a combination of the three.

Two such combinations are presented in Chart 4. Both are based upon the two employment indexes and the inverted unemployment index for New York.[4] In the weighted index (full line), the three components are assigned weights of five points (New York), three (Massachusetts), and two (New Jersey) in proportion to the actual industrial

---

[1] The discrepancy in 1904 seems due to the peculiar effect of a "tandem revival" from the depression caused by the rich man's panic in 1903. One revival, an abortive one, took place early in 1904. It was followed by a distinct slump, then by a more pronounced recovery lasting into 1907. This "reflex action," indicated also by other industrial barometers such as pig iron production, and by notes in the trade journals of the time, stands almost unparalleled in American experience. With such sudden reversals of the industrial machine, it is not unnatural that dissimilarities should be found in different states during that year.

The slightly earlier increase of unemployment in New York in 1907 is also attributable to business conditions, not to any peculiarity in the unemployment curve as such. Upon analysis the bank clearings of cities in New York State outside the metropolis are found to follow the same course as the inverted unemployment curve.

[2] By nonagreement is meant complete *lack* of correspondence. This is different from *inverse* correspondence, which is represented by negative percentages, running between 0 and −100 per cent. A correspondence or correlation of −80 per cent means the same thing as an inverse correlation of +80 per cent.

[3] New York 15 per cent, Massachusetts 8 per cent, and New Jersey 5 per cent—a total of 28 per cent. Compare Table X.

[4] The Massachusetts unemployment index, being quarterly, could not well be utilized in a monthly composite.

4

importance of the three states[1] on the assumption that each of the indexes properly represents employment in the corresponding state. An unweighted average was also constructed, allowing equal influence to each of the three state indexes. The result shown by the dotted line in Chart 4 nearly coincides with the weighted index.[2] The correlation coefficient is 99 per cent. The close agreement between the weighted and unweighted composites shows that accuracy in weighting is of only slight importance, owing to the similarity of the three components.

At this point some valuable supporting evidence from the federal Censuses of Manufactures may be introduced. These are monthly data covering practically all industrial wage-earners in the United States, in the census years 1904, 1909, and 1914.[2] They form by far the most comprehensive employment data we have, covering in 1904, 5,000,000

CHART 4.—GENERAL INDEXES OF EMPLOYMENT, 1903–1914.

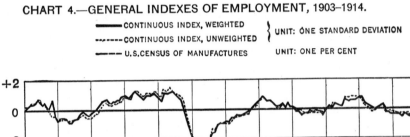

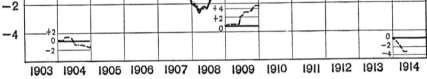

and in 1914, 7,000,000 wage-earners. It should be noted that each of the leading manufacturing industries has maintained its quota of the total throughout the period in such a stable manner that the data may be regarded as industrially homogeneous.[3]

Although no similar data are available for intercensal years, it has been possible with the aid of a special technique[4] to eliminate most of the seasonal variation and long-run trend present in these data, and get a fragmentary idea as to the course of the employment cycle during

[1] Compare Table X.

[2] For the 1919 data see section IV, below, especially Chart 6.

[3] In not more than two or three cases (vehicles for land transportation, railroad repair shops, and the miscellaneous group) has there been any decisive increase, while in only two cases (lumber and its products, and leather and its products) has there been a decline. Compare, *Abstract of Census of Manufactures*, 1914, p. 435. In all the other groups, quotas have remained constant.

[4] For the method utilized, see *Journal of American Statistical Association*, June, 1922, pp. 230–2.

these three years. The results are shown by the segments at the bottom of Chart 4. Inspection shows that on the whole these Census data strongly confirm the continuous index based on the three-state sample, when allowance is made for differences of scale.[1]

## IV. INDEXES OF EMPLOYMENT, 1914-1922

Beside the obvious economic reasons, there are statistical grounds for breaking our study into two parts, that before and that since the outbreak of the war. The best of the current employment indexes were not begun until the early part of the war. One of these is the index representing employment in manufacturing establishments of New York State, which was begun in June, 1914. Similar to this is the series of the United States Bureau of Labor Statistics, begun in October, 1915. Early in 1915 the Wisconsin Industrial Commission began to collect employment data at quarterly (later monthly) intervals, and under the stress of business depression similar series have been inaugurated, in 1921 and 1922, by several other states—notably Illinois and Connecticut. In January, 1921 the United States Employment Service also began a series collected, like that of the Bureau of Labor Statistics, from manufacturing establishments in a large number of states.

**Five State and Federal Indexes.**—In Chart 5 are shown three semi-adjusted indexes,[2] and two wholly unadjusted series. The first curve represents in semi-adjusted form the employment index of the New York State Industrial Commission. This index includes on the average about 500,000 wage-earners. Although restricted geographically, it is well planned in industrial composition. Especially significant is the fact that machinery, iron, and steel form an influential component of this index, since (as has been shown elsewhere[3]) employment fluctuations in the metal industries register very accurately fluctuations in other lines of industrial activity. Overweighting the metal group is therefore more advantageous than otherwise.

The second curve represents the semi-adjusted indexes based upon the month to month link relatives reported by the United States Bureau of Labor Statistics. These data have been compounded into chain relatives, which in turn have been combined for the several industries, using weights proportional to the importance of the industries according to the

---

[1] In 1904, for the reason already indicated, the agreement is much less close. The fairly decisive lag at the turning points of the Census fragment seems to represent a more sluggish response to the industrial reversal by the country as a whole than by the three states represented in the continuous index.

[2] Based on the average for 1919 as 100 per cent, but not corrected for seasonal variation.

[3] *The Review of Economic Statistics*, prel. vol. 4, January, 1922, pp. 23, 24, 32, 33.

CHART 5.—UNADJUSTED INDEXES OF EMPLOYMENT, 1914–1922.

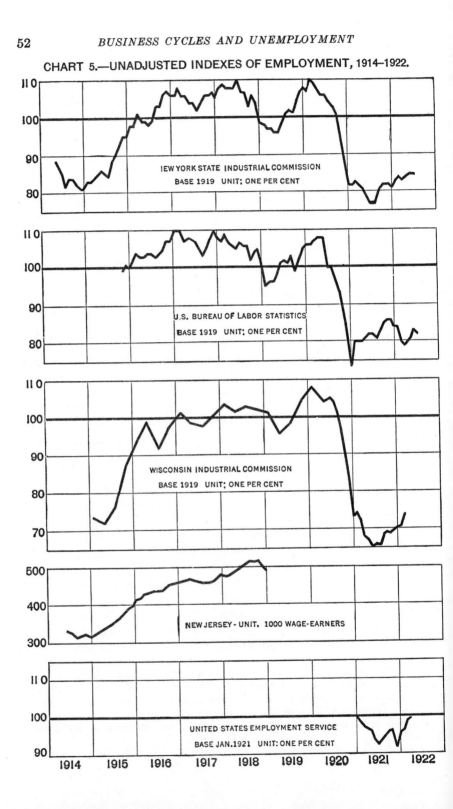

NEW YORK STATE INDUSTRIAL COMMISSION
BASE 1919   UNIT: ONE PER CENT

U.S. BUREAU OF LABOR STATISTICS
BASE 1919   UNIT: ONE PER CENT

WISCONSIN INDUSTRIAL COMMISSION
BASE 1919   UNIT: ONE PER CENT

NEW JERSEY - UNIT. 1000 WAGE-EARNERS

UNITED STATES EMPLOYMENT SERVICE
BASE JAN.1921   UNIT: ONE PER CENT

1914 Census of Manufactures. Finally, the weighted chain relatives[1] have been reduced to the average for the Census year 1919 as a base. The series has several points of merit. Although planned with prime reference to industries rather than states, its geographical composition is in point of fact fairly broad, covering the largest manufacturing states.

In industrial make-up the series is somewhat peculiar. In the distribution of the 600,000 to 800,000 wage-earners actually embodied in the returns, the automobile, iron, and steel industries are represented strongly, textiles and others lightly; but the process of weighting indicated by the Census of Manufactures turns the tables, greatly reducing the emphasis on metal industries and stressing the textiles. The groups have been so selected that those falling under "textiles" have a weight of about 45 per cent, and those falling under metals about 35 per cent. This selection gives a much stronger representation to the textile industry than is apparently justified by the Census of Manufactures, in which the textile industry amounts only to 21 per cent of all manufacturing. Such weighting is not well suited to the list of industries used, owing to the considerable difference between cotton-crop cycles and business cycles.

The first two curves in Chart 5 show a remarkably close agreement in both timing and amplitude. Each of the discrepancies noted is wholly attributable to differences in the industrial distribution: textiles are represented very strongly in the Bureau of Labor index, less strongly in the New York index, in which metals, machinery, etc., outweigh textiles and their products.

The employment curve for Wisconsin fluctuates in nearly the same manner as the others shown in Chart 5, except that the amplitude of its movement in the recent depression is somewhat greater. In form, the Wisconsin index more closely resembles the index for New York than that for the United States, chiefly because in Wisconsin as in New York the metal industries are heavily represented.[2]

[1] These figures have been kindly supplied by Ethelbert Stewart, U. S. Commissioner of Labor Statistics.

[2] The Wisconsin curve in Chart 5 really represents not one series but two, which though not wholly alike in nature have been grafted together by the Industrial Commission of Wisconsin. The figures reported monthly since July, 1920, are based on establishments representing one-fourth to one-third of the wage-earners engaged in manufacturing industries in Wisconsin. The quarterly figures extending from the first quarter of 1915 to the second quarter of 1920 covered a much smaller proportion, probably 15 to 20 per cent. Differences in the inclusiveness, the industrial composition, and the purpose of the two series of reports may account for the peculiarity in the form of the curve. The purpose of the earlier reports was simply to obtain data on the incidence of industrial accidents, in order to check up the rates provisionally assumed in the workmen's compensation act. Until July, 1920, reports were made to the Commission only by self-insured employers, but after July, 1921, many employers insuring with the liability companies began to report. It is especially

The two curves of original items at the foot of Chart 5 merit only passing attention. So far as may be judged by the chart, employment in New Jersey increased during the war in much the same manner as in other states, although this state was more affected relatively by the expansion of war industries—munitions, chemicals, explosives, etc.—than were most states. The New Jersey data are, of course, not continuous between calendar years, and furthermore, they were discontinued altogether in 1918,[1] so that the available fragments are not useful in setting up a current index of employment.

The index established in January, 1921 by the United States Employment Service has not yet covered a period long enough to enable us to test its merit empirically. In general it followed a course not unlike the New York and Wisconsin indexes during 1921, except at the beginning and the end of the year. Theoretically at least the series seems promising. It covers about 1,500,000 wage-earners, a larger number than any other index now being reported currently. Its industrial composition, though imperfect, is on the whole well planned, being fairly representative of manufacturing in the United States.[2] This series also has the advantage that current data are published earlier than those for other series, being telegraphically reported by the district directors of the Service and announced shortly afterward by the central office at Washington. It must, however, be admitted that corresponding to this advantage is a correlative disadvantage; that is, some of the basic reports seem to be gathered by the district directors from the employers by such methods, and in such haste, as to cast doubt upon the results.

**Four Adjusted Indexes.**—In Chart 6 are shown some fully corrected indexes of employment and unemployment available during and since the war. The first curve represents the adjusted employment cycles in Massachusetts. The second represents the employment cycles obtained by analysis and inversion of the quarterly unemployment data for Massachusetts. The third curve represents the index that is probably

---

probable that a standardization of the industrial weights in the two periods will make the composite series more trustworthy as a continuous record for the years since 1915.

The writer's surmise on this point is confirmed by the independent study of the problem by A. J. Altmeyer, Secretary of the Commission, whose intention is now to standardize the weights.

For further facts on the nature of this series, see Industrial Commission of Wisconsin, *Biennial Report*, 1918–1920, esp. p. 81; also the Commission's monthly *Bulletins*.

[1] According to a recent communication from J. A. T. Gribbin, who also kindly placed at the writer's disposal the unpublished data for 1917 and 1918. Of course the year 1919 was covered by the U. S. Census canvass.

[2] The chief objections to its industrial composition are that (1) the iron and steel group is somewhat overweighted (21.3 vs. 15.8 per cent of the aggregate); (2) textiles are underweighted (16.7 vs. 21.3 per cent); vehicles are greatly overweighted (11.3 vs. 3.7 per cent); and lumber greatly underweighted (1.4 vs. 11 9 per cent).

CHART 6.—ADJUSTED INDEXES OF EMPLOYMENT, 1914–1922.

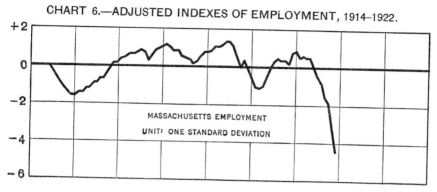

MASSACHUSETTS EMPLOYMENT
UNIT: ONE STANDARD DEVIATION

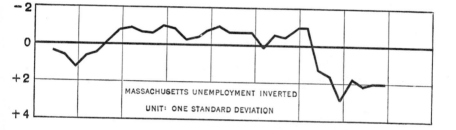

MASSACHUSETTS UNEMPLOYMENT INVERTED
UNIT: ONE STANDARD DEVIATION

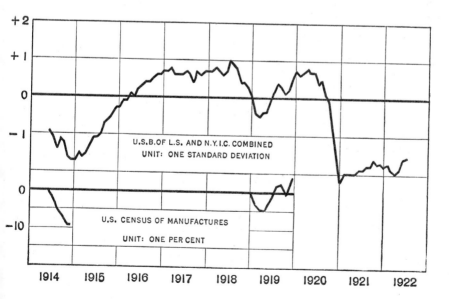

U.S.B. OF L.S. AND N.Y.I.C. COMBINED
UNIT: ONE STANDARD DEVIATION

U.S. CENSUS OF MANUFACTURES
UNIT: ONE PER CENT

the most reliable current measure of the general employment cycle in the United States which can readily be constructed in the present state of knowledge. It is an average of the employment indexes of the United States Bureau of Labor Statistics and the New York Industrial Commission, corrected for seasonal variation, etc., like the other curves on Chart 6. At the foot of Chart 6 are shown the fragments representing the United States Censuses of Manufactures in 1914 and 1919, corrected for seasonal variation in the same manner as those at the foot of Chart 4.

The high order of correspondence among these curves is indicated by the following coefficients of correlation: United States Bureau of Labor Statistics with New York Industrial Commission (1915–1921) 95 per cent; combination of these two, with Wisconsin series (1915–1921) 98 per cent; adjusted combination, with Massachusetts employment series (1914–1920) 80 per cent; adjusted Massachusetts employment and unemployment series inverted (1914–1920) 89 per cent. Perhaps most important of all is the support indicated by the Census data, which agree with the combination of the two series with coefficients of 79 per cent for June–December 1914 and 97 per cent for the twelve months of 1919. Here as in the pre-war comparison the agreement is close in amplitude as well as in direction and form.

Why should the proposed current index be made up of the Bureau of Labor and the New York data but no others? The choice hinges on the purpose in view. The present purpose is to construct an index with the following properties; (a) its components must have been reported in a comparable form for a sufficiently long period to establish a basis for empirical test, comparison, and appraisal; (b) it must be reasonably representative, industrially and geographically; and (c) its components must be reported currently, in monthly form, with reasonable promptness, and with accuracy.

Among all these series only the above-mentioned combination meets the three tests. The Massachusetts employment series lacks the third property, since the monthly figures for each year are not known until long after the end of the year. The unemployment data for Massachusetts are reported quarterly, not monthly. The New Jersey series is defunct. The Employment Service data fail to meet test (a).

Considering the indexes of the New York Industrial Commission and of the United States Bureau of Labor Statistics, we find that each meets test (a) better than do any others now being reported. The latter meets admirably the second half of test (b) concerning geographical representation, and judging by the industrial position of New York and the findings concerning employment in the pre-war period, the New York index must also be highly representative of the industrial states.

Each of these indexes fails, when taken alone, to meet the first half of test (b), since the former has been shown to overstress metals, and the latter textiles. This failure is largely remedied by the mere process of combination; the textile and the iron industries are thereby restored more nearly to their true relationship. The groups including textiles and those including iron and steel and their products both enjoy a weight somewhat (though only moderately) in excess of their true importance.

In the light of all these facts, there is a very strong probability that the average of these two series shows the consensus of monthly employment fluctuations in the United States in recent years better than any other readily constituted index. The homogeneous and continuous nature of this combination forms an important Advantage. In support of its validity, it is worth noting that even if we did include in the average other series covering parts of the period 1914–1922, only slight differences from the average here shown would result.

**Cycles of Employment since 1914.**—According to the corrected index based on these two series, employment has passed through some interesting phases during the past eight years. These fluctuations may be attributed in part to the business cycle and in part to other factors, notably the changing situation as to immigration and the military demand for men. The depression of 1914–1915, the war boom of 1916–1918, the relapse during the half year after the Armistice, the boom of 1919–1920, the acute depression of 1920–1921, and the incipient recovery in recent months are in a measure reflections of the change in the demand for production, and therefore in one sense simply a passive factor in the business cycle. But during the war employment became a potent limiting factor.

Our entry into the war introduced a tremendous new force into the industrial situation: in addition to war demands by our own government for goods, a direct call for man-power to be used in actual military operations. Military need for men affected the labor market enormously for a period of twenty months. During that time the labor supply became one of the factors which drastically limited economic activity. Enlistments, which increased immediately after our entry into the war, were supplemented by the first increment of the draft in the late summer of 1917 and in 1918 by several additional increments amounting to about 2,500,000 more men. The rapidly increasing drain of man-power from civil life is shown by Chart 7, representing the total army personnel by months.[1] The number increased from 200,000 to more than 1,000,000 before the end of 1917, and to 3,600,000 at the time of the Armistice, finally attaining a rate of increase of 400,000 men a month. These figures of course fail to tell the absolute magnitude of the loss of industrial wage-earners from civil life, partly because many were engaged in war work outside of the army and navy. They do, however, show fairly well the increasingly rapid rate of change in the supply of available man-

[1] AYRES, LEONARD P. "The War with Germany, a Statistical Summary," p. 15.

power, and consequently account for some of the dents in the employment curve. Undoubtedly, these dents would have been much deeper but for the heavy influx of women, youths, and young girls from home and school into industry, as well as that of adult male labor transferred from normal occupations in office or farm work to certain lines of manufacturing, under the double attraction of high wages and a deferred classification in the draft.

Demobilization shows an illuminating but quite different relation to the employment index. During the first six months after the Armistice, discharges took place at twice the average monthly rate of mobilization, reducing the strength of the army from 3,600,000 to 2,000,000 by April,

CHART 7.—UNITED STATES ARMY PERSONNEL,
APRIL, 1917 TO AUGUST, 1919.
UNIT: 1,000,000 MEN

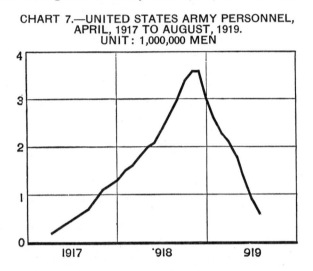

and to 1,000,000 before July, 1919. The discharge of enlisted men alone averaged 400,000 a month during the first half of 1919.[1] It is evident from a comparison of Charts 6 and 7 that most of this huge labor supply was being dumped on a falling market. At the time when employers were rapidly dismissing their employees in the post-armistice slump,[2] soldiers were being discharged from the army. At the bottom of the slump in midsummer of 1919, 2,000,000 soldiers had been discharged, several hundred thousand of whom must have remained unemployed for months before being reabsorbed in industry.[3] If the relapse of 1919 had not been fairly brief, there would have arisen still more urgently the

[1] Secretary of War, *Annual Report*, 1919, p. 17.

[2] This statement refers, of course, to the general index of employment. Employment had begun to improve earlier in the summer in some industries, notably textiles. See *The Review* of *Economic Statistics*, prel. vol. 4, January, 1922, p. 20, Chart 3.

[3] The situation disclosed by the two curves probably accounts in part for the prevalent impression that the soldiers returning in 1919 "did not want to work." Apparently lack of the opportunity to work was also a potent factor.

question as to whether the demobilization policy allowed a rate of discharge so high that it hampered proper industrial reabsorption and precipitated a needless unemployment crisis.[1] In either event, the labor supply previously withdrawn from the market by military demands was restored so soon after the war that, when the recovery came in 1919–1920, industry could proceed unchecked by such potent limitations as had prevailed in the two preceding years and without need of resorting so widely to inexpert labor from other fields.

The severity of unemployment in 1920–1921 may be compared with that in earlier periods of the sort by noting the relative amounts by which employment falls off between a boom and the succeeding depression within each business cycle. The accompanying list shows that the available indexes of employment in manufacturing industries responded more violently to the recent depression than to earlier ones.

TABLE XI.—INDEXES OF EMPLOYMENT IN INDUSTRIES MOST EFFECTED BY DEPRESSION

| Between the peak of the boom | And the bottom of the depression | Employment declined approximately |
| --- | --- | --- |
| Middle of 1903 | Middle of 1904 | 5% |
| Middle of 1907 | First quarter of 1908 | 15 |
| Early in 1910 | Middle of 1911 | 5 |
| Early in 1913 | End of 1914 and early in 1915 | 10 |
| Third quarter of 1918 | Second quarter of 1919 | 15 |
| Early in 1920 | First half of 1921 | 25–30 |

It is possible, but unlikely, that much of this difference is due to differences in composition between the current and the earlier indexes. There seems good ground for believing that, in actual diminution of employment, the depression of 1921 was almost twice as acute as that of 1908 and at least twice as acute as that of 1914–1915.

### V. CYCLES OF EMPLOYMENT AND PRODUCTION

One of the possible functions of an employment index mentioned at the beginning of this chapter is its use as a barometer of industrial activity. This may be demonstrated by comparing the employment index with an index of production.

Unfortunately production data for only a few manufacturing lines were available in monthly form until recent years. One of the most comprehensive studies of these monthly production data is that of

[1] It may be observed that approximately the last million men were returned to civil life in more moderate installments, much better timed with reference to the business cycle.

Edmund E. Day. Chart 8 shows his unadjusted index for the period since January, 1919, covering production in a large number of lines of manufacture, and compared with it is the writer's employment index, likewise uncorrected for seasonal variation, etc.

Throughout the three years covered, the curves representing employment and production show change of direction at nearly the same time. Every critical movement is shown with almost equal clearness in both curves; the relapse after the Armistice, the recovery in the second, third, and fourth quarters of 1919, the culmination of the boom early in 1920, the ebb of prosperity, at first slow then precipitate, until the middle of 1921, and the gradual improvement since August. The correlation coefficient is +96 per cent, even higher than that between the two series entering the index of employment.

:CHART 8.—UNADJUSTED INDEXES OF INDUSTRIAL EMPLOYMENT AND PRODUCTION, 1919–1922.

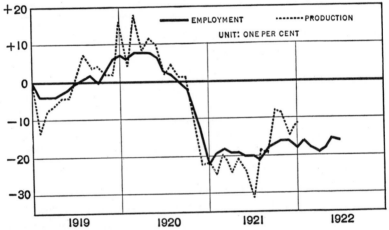

Three significant differences between the curves appear. (1) Unlike production, the employment index was unaffected by the varying lengths of the months. For instance, in each February, production slumped owing primarily to the 10 per cent difference in the number of days included. Until corrected for seasonal variation, the production index therefore represents less well than employment the varying *intensity* of industrial activity. (2) The employment curve was much less disturbed than the production curve by the various strikes of September to December, 1919 and the winter of 1921. Partial explanation for this may be found in the fact that the supply of basic materials, which are the chief constituents of the production index, was affected much more by these disturbances than was the manufacture of semi-finished and finished goods, which could maintain itself during the interval presumably on a carry-over of raw materials. Moreover, employers doubtless hold their labor force over a temporary shortage of raw materials incident to labor disputes in key industries; at least this is very likely at a time of prosperity such as the autumn and winter of 1919–1920. (3) The production curve, if the temporary effect of these labor disputes be smoothed out, clearly rose to a greater height in the boom of 1919–1920, and recently fell to a greater depth, than did the employment curve. Employment rose only about 8 per cent above its 1919 average, but production increased twice as much; in the recent depression, employment fell only about 20 per cent, production about 30 per cent, below the average for 1919. In other words, the production index fluctuates over a wider range than the employment index.

This difference in the amplitude of the two indexes is extremely important. To what is it due? It is impossible to get conclusive evidence on the point, but three considerations bear upon it. First of all, employment data are based on the number of employees on pay-rolls, and therefore *understate* the real extent of labor activity in *prosperity*, since overtime work does not increase the number reported; they also *overstate* the extent of activity in *depression*, since part-time work does not decrease the number. In other words, no distinction is made in the employment figures between workers who are engaged part time, full time and overtime. To a certain extent this tendency is counterbalanced by a second consideration—fluctuations in the efficiency of labor. During prosperity labor efficiency is likely to diminish, partly because of industrial fatigue due to speeding and working overtime, partly because of indifference to duty in the face of plentiful opportunities for work in other establishments, and partly because of the hiring of untrained or inferior workers; in a depression the reverse is the case.[1] A third consideration is the fact that the production index is necessarily derived, in large measure, from data on the production of basic materials, such as sole leather and steel ingots, more than finished goods, such as shoes and machinery. The reason is that, in more advanced stages of manufacture, units of output are so varied and complex that few reliable data on production at these stages can readily be obtained. The employment data, on the other hand, relate to industrial groups at all stages of fabrication. If, as seems probable, the production of basic materials responds more decisively to the course of the business cycle than does that of finished goods,[2] the production curve must swing through a greater range of variation than the employment curve.

[1] There are also forces which tend to decrease rather than increase efficiency during depression—such as the greater desire of workmen to "stretch out" their work as far as possible. But in the view of the writer this group of psychological forces is subordinate to that outlined above.

[2] DAY, EDMUND E. The Measurement of Variations in the National Real Income, *Quarterly Publication of the American Statistical Association*, March, 1921, vol. XVII p. 559.

Changes in labor efficiency would thus lead probably to *wider* fluctuations in the employment curve than in the production curve. On the other hand the existence of overtime or part-time work, and the probably greater sensitiveness of the production of basic materials would lead to *narrower* fluctuations in the employment curve, such as Chart 8 actually shows.[1] Although little can be said as to the relative importance of

CHART 9.—ADJUSTED INDEXES OF INDUSTRIAL EMPLOYMENT AND PRODUCTION, 1919–1922.

these factors, probably the failure of employment data to take account of overtime or part time is the main reason for the narrower range of fluctuations.

Chart 9 shows the employment and production indexes fully corrected for seasonal variation, etc. Here as in certain earlier charts the inequalities in amplitude of the two curves have been lessened by using the

CHART 10.—EMPLOYMENT AND PRODUCTION OF ALL MANUFACTURES, 1899–1913.

standard deviation as the vertical unit. Again the correlation coefficient is 96 per cent.

[1] Incomplete allowance for "mushroom establishments" also tends to reduce the amplitude of the employment boom. The New York Industrial Commission definitely excludes these by covering only establishments which reported in June, 1914; the U. S. Bureau of Labor Statistics does not.

Chart 10 shows the employment index thrown into annual form and extended back to 1899. It is constructed by weighting the New York, Massachusetts, and New Jersey data on the 5-3-2 basis.[1] The curve is shown for comparison with Day's annual production index for all manufacture.[2] The correlation is very high, being represented by a coefficient of 86 per cent.

These two agreements—in annual form before the war and monthly form since the war—are very close despite the differences in the source and nature of the two groups of data. The high order of the agreements suggests the possibility of utilizing employment as an index of monthly production cycles prior to the war. Since very few other production series than that for pig iron were available in monthly form prior to the

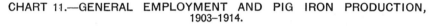

CHART 11.—GENERAL EMPLOYMENT AND PIG IRON PRODUCTION, 1903–1914.

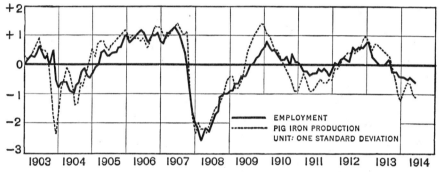

war, employment provides a much more comprehensive basis for picturing the monthly pre-war cycles of industrial activity than can be obtained from evidence as to production. The employment index covers not only a much wider variety of lines, but many more advanced stages of fabrication than could be represented in an index based on monthly production data.

Chart 11 shows the monthly index of employment, compared with pig iron production. Here again the agreement is very close (89 per cent). Further substantiation of the validity of employment as an

[1] Here the Massachusetts component was obtained by taking the average of the employment and the reversed unemployment figures. To center the average of the quarterly unemployment cycles in the middle of the calendar year, a five-quarter rather than a four-quarter average was used: December 31 of the previous year, and March 31, June 30, September 30, and December 31 of the current year.

The New York unemployment data are based upon the reports of all the unions in the state, rather than the representative selection (one-fourth to one-third as great) embodied in the monthly data.

[2] DAY, EDMUND E., *An Index of the Physical Volume of Production*, pp. 62–3.

index of industrial activity is found in the relation[1] of employment to other series representing the volume of activity, such as bank clearings outside New York City. These relationships afford conclusive evidence that employment forms a highly satisfactory index of industrial activity both before and since the war.

### VI. CYLES OF EMPLOYMENT AND BUYING POWER

The employment index is useful not only as a guide to the labor market and to the course of industrial activity, but also to fluctuations in buying power. Any shrinkage of employment tends to curtail the earnings, and therefore the effective demand, of the working group involved; this curtailment of demand may lead to further shrinkage of employment in other lines, then to further curtailment of demand, and so on. In every depression this vicious circle rapidly spreads until it involves, directly or indirectly, a very large part of the urban population.

CHART 12.—EMPLOYMENT AND WAGE RATES, 1899–1913.

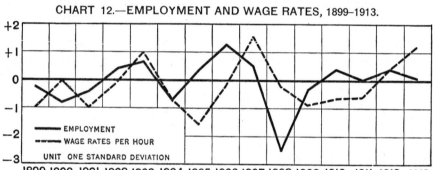

Employment affects buying power not only through its direct influence on the volume of earnings, but also indirectly through its influence on the rise and fall of rates of wages. Chart 12 shows the relation between cycles of employment and of wage rates[2] from 1899 to 1913. At several turning-points in both depressions and booms, wage-rates lag decisively after employment. Whether this lag is a full year or not is uncertain, as no reliable data on wages were available before the war except in annual form. If the pre-war lag was only six to ten months,[3]

[1] Described in *The Review of Economic Statistics*, prel. vol. 4, January, 1922, pp. 36–9.

[2] This series represents wage rates per hour, according to the investigations of Messrs. Rubinow and Douglas and Miss Lamberson, based on U. S. Bureau of Labor data. Compare PAUL H. DOUGLAS and FRANCES LAMBERSON, The Movement of Real Wages, 1890-1918, *American Economic Review*, September, 1921, vol. XI, p. 417.

[3] This is approximately the lag of recently constructed quarterly and monthly wage indexes after the employment index, for the period 1914-1922. See W. RANDOLPH BURGESS, Index numbers for the wages of common labor, *Journal of American Statistical Association*, vol. XVIII, p. 103.

the annual data might well appear as in Chart 12. How much the lag is between employment and the composite purchasing power is still more problematical. In amplitude employment appears to be much more sensitive to the business cycle than wage rates, perhaps more. than twice as sensitive.[1] This means that the composite product representing pecuniary buying power probably lags less than half as long after employment as do wage rates. It seems clear that the employment index forecasts by a few months the commercial buying power of those large numbers of our people whose earnings are in the form of industrial wages. Indirectly, of course, this fact is quite as full of meaning to the social worker as to the business man.

## VII. FORECASTING EMPLOYMENT CYCLES FROM OTHER STATISTICAL SERIES

This naturally raises the question whether unemployment itself can be forecasted from the fluctuations of other economic indexes. Warren M. Persons has clearly demonstrated the possibility of forecasting general business conditions on the objective basis of statistical and economic

CHART 13.—EMPLOYMENT AND A BUSINESS FORECASTER, 1903–1914.

analysis.[2] Although Persons gave no attention to data representing employment or unemployment in constructing his barometer and his forecaster of business, the forecaster does very effectively forecast unemployment, as is shown in Chart 13. The writer's analysis of employment, though conducted as an independent research without reference to any other economic indexes, "ties in" so well with several members of

[1] As measured by the standard deviation of the employment and wage indexes, which were approximately 3.5 and 1.5 per cent, respectively, between 1899 and 1913. Since the employment index does not take into account either overtime or part time, 3.5 per cent is really a *lower limit* of the elasticity of employment fluctuations.

[2] *The Review of Economic Statistics*, prel. vol. 1, January and April, 1919, pp. 3–205. For a more compact and non-technical treatment see WARREN M. PERSONS *Interpretation of the Index of General Business Conditions*, 1922.

5

Persons' business group ("Group *B*") that his general business fore-caster proves satisfactory for our purpose also. The problem of fore-casting cyclical unemployment is essentially that of forecasting business conditions.

The close linkage shown to exist between cyclical employment and its economic correlatives should lead everyone who is interested in employment—whether for commercial or industrial or social purposes—to keep in touch with the measurements and forecasts.[1] Eventually, perhaps we shall achieve positive control over some of the more harmful phases of the business cycle, but until this is done the ability to trace current fluctuations of employment, and to forecast its future fluctuations a few months in advance, may go far to alleviate the evils due to the intimate relation of unemployment to business cycles.

[1] For a description of various business forecasting services see Chap. XX, below.

# CHAPTER V

## UNDER-EMPLOYMENT

By Paul F. Brissenden

Columbia University

### I. RELATION BETWEEN UNDER-EMPLOYMENT AND UNEMPLOYMENT

Most of the known facts about the amount of employment are "yes and no" facts reported by employers or trade union secretaries to show how many are, or how many are not, on a pay-roll. These facts do not throw any light upon the question: How many workers are partially employed or under-employed? If a wage-earner's name is on the pay-roll he is among the employed; if, and when, it is dropped from the pay-roll he is among the unemployed. But though on the pay-roll the employee may be working only three days a week, while, on the other hand, his absence from one pay-roll does not necessarily mean absence from other pay-rolls.

### II. PHASES OF UNDER-EMPLOYMENT

The employer may meet a serious slump in the demand for his product in several ways. (1) He may run the plant at less than capacity but at normal or customary full-time schedule. This reduced capacity operation may be brought about through the lay-off of a sufficient number of hands or through the rotation of hands by employing, say, half of them on Mondays, Wednesdays, and Fridays and the other half on the other three working-days of the week. (2) He may reduce the operating time of the plant. This part-time operation may be managed by reducing the length of the work day, by cutting down the number of days worked per week, or where more than one shift per day is worked, by reducing the number of shifts. (3) He may close the plant entirely for a longer or shorter period of time.

Manifestly, these several alternatives mean somewhat different predicaments for the workers involved. Under-capacity operation at full-time schedule means total unemployment for the workers in so far as it is attained by the laying off of hands. In so far as it is accomplished by rotation of hands, or "division of work," it means under-employment. The worker is also under-employed when the operating time of the whole plant is reduced either in hours per day or days per week.[1] The effect

[1] This may not be the case when the shorter operating schedule is accomplished by reduction in the number of shifts per day. The result in this case is unemployment.

of closing down the plant may be unemployment or it may be under-employment, depending upon the circumstances.   If the worker who is thrown out as a result of a shut-down remains unemployed and continues in the community anticipating a resumption of operation, and particularly if he is somewhat relied upon by his old employer as an available hand when business picks up, it would seem to be under-employment.

### III. CHARACTER OF THE DATA ON UNDER-EMPLOYMENT

In this country we have no continuous "time data" showing directly either the extent or the trend of under-employment.[1]   Foreign employ-ment statistics contain a good deal more direct information on under-employment than do our own, possibly because the alternative devices of short-time operation and division of work are more widely resorted to in Europe.   In default of direct time data on under-employment, resort must be had to fragmentary statistical data on (1) relative numbers unemployed and employed on part time, (2) yearly operating time in factories and mines, (3) time actually worked compared with normal full time, (4) time lost "on the job," and (5) overtime.

### IV. WHAT THE PRESENT DATA SHOW

**Relative Numbers Unemployed and Employed on Short Time.**— Although not continuous data, the results of three recent investigations possibly deserve a passing reference because they represent important official estimates of the amount of under-employment.[2]   The first inquiry was that made by the United States Bureau of Labor Statistics in 1915. The figures tell us nothing about cyclical under-employment.   They do reveal, however, the great importance of under-employment in relation to the general problem of unemployment.   This inquiry indicated that in 1915 in the specified cities, 16.6 per cent of the 647,394 wage-earners covered were under-employed while only 11.5 per cent were totally unemployed.[3]

The other two investigations are much more recent.   The Mayor's Unemployment Committee of Columbus, Ohio, in October and November, 1921, found that 13.6 per cent of the 9,000 men and 7.0 per cent of the 2,000 women reported were entirely idle, while 10.4 per cent of the men and 9.3 per cent of the women were employed part time.[4]   In December,

---

[1] An exception should be made of the figures collected by W. I. King and inter-preted by him in the following chapter.

[2] What was probably the first detailed and comprehensive investigation of the extent of under-employment was the work of Carroll D. Wright in the Massachusetts Census of 1885.   Mr. Wright's figures showed exact proportions of part time worked and classified them so as to show what part of the under-employment in that year was due to slack work.   *Massachusetts Census of 1885*, vol. II, pp. 1163–89.

[3] U. S. Bureau of Labor Statistics, *Bulletin* 195, p. 6.

[4] MARK, MARY L., and CROXTON, F. E., Unemployment survey in Columbus, Ohio, *Monthly Labor Review*, April, 1922, p. 17.

1921, the New York State Department of Labor found that of more than 300,000 workers in 1,320 factories 75.9 per cent worked at least full time, including 8.1 per cent who worked overtime while 24.1 per cent worked part time.[1]

**Statistics Showing Days in Operation.**—The extent of under-employment is not by any means accurately measured by reporting the number of days a plant is not in operation. None the less a large and probably a major part of this lost time represents under-employment. This is particularly true in industries like coal mining, where closing down of the works is unlikely to result in the men's abandoning their position as potential employees.

Records of this type running back to 1890 are available in summary form for bituminous coal mines, Massachusetts cotton mills, and for all manufacturing industries in Massachusetts.[2] All three series show pronounced cyclical fluctuations. For example the number of days bituminous coal mines were in operation was 48 days less in the dull year, 1894 than in the good year, 1892. The corresponding decline in working time was 32 days in the cotton mills and 21 days in all Massachusetts factories. At the next great change from boom to depression, 1906-1908, the decline in working time for these three groups was 20, 34, and 22 days respectively. Between 1913, not an active year, and 1914 the drops were 37, 1, and 9 days. For the post-war years we have figures for coal mines only. They worked 220 days in 1920 and according to the latest official estimate, 155 days in 1921—a decline of 65 days.[3] In general, bituminous coal miners lose about one-fourth of their possible working time through non-operation of the mines—a loss attributed to over-development and to seasonal factors as well as to business depression.

It is to be remembered that these figures represent probably minimum under-employment, since what they reflect is the number of days the employees have opportunity to work. Under-employment due to absenteeism and under-employment on the job due to waiting for work, for cars, etc., must be added to that caused by suspension of operation.

**Normal or Basic Full Time Compared with Actual Time Worked.** To report merely the *number* of workers who are employed on part

[1] *The Industrial Bulletin,* January and February, 1922, p. 67. The figures reported are for the week including December 15, in most cases the week ended December 17. For distribution of those working part time see below, p. 71.

[2] Reports of the U. S. Geological Survey, Massachusetts *Annual Report on the Statistics of Manufactures,* and HOWARD, S. E., *Unemployment in the Massachusetts Cotton Industry,* p. 89. Other data on yearly operating time have been published by the U. S. Bureau of the Census, the U. S. Bureau of Labor Statistics, and by several states besides Massachusetts, but the figures are not continuous.

[3] TRYON, F. G., and McKENNEY, W. F., The Broken Year of the Bituminous Miner, *The Survey Graphic,* April, 1922, p. 1009. The figures given in this article are 222 days worked in 1920 and 169 in 1921. The revised figure for 1920 is 220 and recent official reports indicate that 155 is close to the truth for 1921.

time is to get only the vaguest notion concerning the precise amount of under-employment suffered by them. Such a report does not inform us whether the part-time workers were reduced from a full-time 6-day week to a 5-day week or whether they were cut to a 3-day week. There is, manifestly, three times as much under-employment in the latter case as there is in the former. ·

Some conception of the width of the margin between theoretically possible full-time employment and the time actually worked as well as the cyclical fluctuations in the width of this margin may be had from figures showing the total number of days or hours actually worked during specified periods as compared with normal full-time.[1]

In the report of an investigation of unemployment in Philadelphia, made in 1915 by Joseph H. Willits, a chart is given showing the total number of man-days actually worked each week by piece workers in an Axminster carpet mill and the total days which would have been worked by the same employees if they had had full-time employment.[2] Data for the time actually worked include only time lost outside of the mill and do not include time lost on the job waiting in the mill for dye or other material. Nor, of course, do the figures include employees who are laid off and consequently put in a situation which means total unemployment. The data refer almost entirely to time lost on account of irregularity or lack of orders. For the whole period covered, April, 1911–March, 1915, the proportion of full time actually worked was not quite 75 per cent. The maximum proportion in any quarter was 93 per cent (April–June, 1914) and the minimum 44 per cent (January–March, 1915).

The record of this carpet mill is significant, but it is, after all, only one establishment. More comprehensive is the comparison between actual and full-time records in the iron and steel industry made by the United States Bureau of Labor Statistics. The record shows by months from July, 1913 to June, 1915, for 59,752 iron and steel employees in 227 plants, the per cent of the turns (shifts) customarily worked which were not worked because of slack work. This is equivalent to the per cent of full time lost because of slack work. The figures run from a minimum

---

[1] A similar indirect clue to the extent of part-time employment may be had by an examination of such time data on earnings as include comparison between actual weekly earnings and nominal full-time earnings. The U. S. Bureau of Labor Statistics and a few of the state bureaus have published statistics of this sort. Also, as pointed out in Chapter XIX, figures showing for the same groups of establishments the number of employees and amounts paid in wages may reflect part-time and overtime employment. The value of such statistics as a measure of part time may be almost entirely destroyed, however, because of the disturbing effect of changes in rates.

[2] WILLITS, JOSEPH H., "Philadelphia Unemployment," Philadelphia Department of Public Works, 1915, opp. p. 125. Published also in *The Annals*, May, 1916, Supplement, opp. p. 60.

loss of 10 per cent of full time in July, 1913 to a maximum loss of 47 per cent in December, 1914.[1]

A more exact idea of the relation between time worked and nominal full time is given by figures showing the distribution of the total number on short time according to the percentage of nominal full time worked by them. Of such figures one sample must suffice.[2] In its series of reports on wages and hours of labor in different industries the Bureau of Labor Statistics has published certain tables giving the number and per cent of employees working different percentages of full time. Some of these figures are brought together in Table XII. As would be expected a larger proportion of the employees worked less than 100 per cent of full time in 1914 than in either 1916 or 1918. It is not entirely clear from

[1] *Bulletin* 218, pp. 28, 30–55. The figures given are obtained by combining the Bureau's figures for the separate divisions of the iron and steel industry. Unfortunately the Bureau's recently published bulletin (305) on wages and hours in the iron and steel industry does not continue this valuable series.

[2] The New York State report already mentioned showed that in December, 1921, a time of depression, 13.9 per cent of the 313,167 factory employees reported 5 days worked a week, 5.4 per cent 4 days, and 4.8 per cent 3 days or less. *The Industrial Bulletin*, January and February, 1922, p. 67. Figures for different industries are as follows:

| Industry (December, 1921) | Number of establishments | Number of employees | Percentage working | | | | |
|---|---|---|---|---|---|---|---|
| | | | Over-time | Full time | Five days | Four days | Three days or less |
| Boots and shoes.......... | 29 | 8,013 | 0.6 | 54.5 | 31.9 | 7.6 | 5.4 |
| Men's clothing............ | 59 | 14,145 | 5.7 | 85.7 | 3.3 | 1.8 | 3.5 |
| Cotton goods............. | 5 | 4,640 | 5.2 | 91.6 | 2.3 | 0.7 | 0.2 |
| Hosiery and knit goods..... | 56 | 13,817 | 6.8 | 72.1 | 12.4 | 4.4 | 4.3 |
| Wool manufactures........ | 19 | 12,343 | 2.5 | 90.1 | 1.8 | 2.8 | 2.8 |
| Saw and planing mill products............... | 39 | 4,096 | 8.0 | 69.5 | 14.4 | 3.9 | 4.2 |
| Furniture and cabinet work. | 42 | 6,070 | 9.6 | 66.3 | 13.4 | 1.3 | 9.4 |

A short series of time data revealing the extent of under-employment in the bituminous coal mining industry in a period of depression has been computed by the U. S. Bureau of Labor Statistics on the basis of reports made to the U. S. Geological Survey. The figures show for each week from Oct. 8, 1921, to Mar. 18, 1922, the number of mines closed the entire week and the number operating specified lengths of time during each week. For the original data by weeks see *Monthly Labor Review*, April, 1922, p. 13 and May, 1922, p. 144. The record from October to February first appeared in *Hearings before House Committee on Labor* on H. R. Bill No. 11022, Sixty-seventh Congress, Second Session, 1922, p. 37.

these figures, however, that a smaller proportion worked overtime in 1914. The figures are inconclusive.

TABLE XII.—PERCENTAGES OF EMPLOYEES WORKING SPECIFIED PROPORTIONS OF FULL TIME IN CERTAIN INDUSTRIES: 1914, 1915, 1916, 1918, AND 1920[a]

| Year and industry | Number of establishments | Number of employees | Percentage of employees working specified proportions of full time | | | | |
|---|---|---|---|---|---|---|---|
| | | | 100 per cent and over | Under 100 per cent | Under 75 per cent | Under 50 per cent | Under 25 per cent |
| 1914 Boots and shoes [b] | 85 | 50,662 | 39 | 61 | 18 | 5 | 1 |
| Mens clothing [c] | 153 | 22,386 | 59 | 41 | 13 | 4 | 1 |
| Cotton goods, manufacturing [d] | 62 | 38,558 | 63 | 37 | 19 | 9 | 4 |
| Cotton goods, finishing [d] | 25 | 11,178 | 63 | 37 | 9 | 3 | 1 |
| Knit goods [e] | 47 | 18,548 | 52 | 48 | 16 | 4 | 1 |
| Woolen and worsted, manufacturing [f] | 44 | 26,976 | 55 | 45 | 14 | 5 | 2 |
| 1915 Lumber [g] | 88 | 11,285 | 62 | 38 | 15 | 6 | 3 |
| Millwork [g] | 229 | 12,917 | 63 | 37 | 10 | 4 | 2 |
| Furniture [g] | 163 | 16,573 | 32 | 68 | 17 | 4 | 1 |
| 1916 Boots and shoes [h] | 130 | 61,127 | 44 | 56 | 13 | 4 | 1 |
| Cotton goods, manufacturing [i] | 85 | 46,479 | 66 | 34 | 18 | 9 | 4 |
| Cotton goods, finishing [i] | 30 | 11,821 | 74 | 26 | 9 | 4 | 2 |
| 1918 Boots and shoes [j] | 136 | 60,779 | 52 | 48 | 11 | 4 | 1 |
| Cotton goods, manufacturing [k] | 89 | 47,099 | 69 | 31 | 17 | 8 | 3 |
| Cotton goods, finishing [k] | 30 | 13,148 | 73 | 27 | 8 | 4 | 1 |
| Woolen and worsted, manufacturing [l] | 57 | 34,351 | 69 | 31 | 11 | 4 | 1 |
| 1920 Boots and shoes [m] | 112 | 49,480 | 47 | 53 | 12 | 4 | 1 |

[a] Based on pay-roll records for one week in each of the years indicated. Only one-week pay-rolls are included.
[b] U. S. Bureau of Labor Statistics *Bulletin* 178, p. 20.
[c] *Bulletin* 187, p. 23.
[d] *Bulletin* 190, p. 32.
[e] *Bulletin* 177, p. 21.
[f] *Bulletin* 190, p. 135.
[g] *Bulletin* 225, pp. 23, 258, 286.
[h] *Bulletin* 232, p. 19.
[i] *Bulletin* 239, p. 26
[j] *Bulletin* 260, p. 16.
[k] *Bulletin* 262, pp. 22, 23.
[l] *Bulletin* 261, p. 18.
[m] *Bulletin* 278, p. 27. In *Bulletin* 288 figures are given for cotton goods manufacturing for 1920, but they are not presented in a comparable form.

The reason that such figures as those given in Table XII are inconclusive is that they contain items which have no reference to underemployment. Figures making comparisons between time actually worked and normal full time or, what foots up to the same thing, between full-time earnings and actual earnings, should be used very cautiously. At the best, they are significant only in reference to changing relations. They have no value as measures of the absolute amount of under-employment. These data, for example, nearly always cover labor turnover as well as part-time service. On the pay-roll a man who is hired midway between Saturday pay-days will in all probability have his first or last week's service record reflected in the figures as half-time employment. The degree of this padding varies directly with the rate of turnover and with the length of the pay-roll period. Since the one-week pay-roll periods are likely to be most free from the turnover items, only the one-week pay-rolls have been utilized here. Finally, it is to be observed that turnover varies inversely with unemployment,[1] whereas part-time employment, of course, fluctuates roughly parallel to total unemployment. The result is that the figures purporting to show the proportions of full time worked are more or less blurred by the turnover figures included in them.[2]

**"Unemployment on the Job."**—So far as workers who are paid on the time basis are concerned, it is the time lost outside of the plant, off the job, which measures the amount of under-employment to which they are subject. For piece workers, however, even though they remain at the work place, there is likely to be a considerable amount of "unemployment on the job." A distinction should be noted: "Unemployment within employment" refers to time lost outside of the plant or mine when the employee remains attached to the enterprise and is considered one of the work force, although not actually working, say, more than three days a week, while "unemployment on the job" refers to the additional time which may be lost by piece workers while they are in the factory or mine. Here belong the daily and hourly interruptions which result from break-

---

[1] An investigation of labor turnover by the U. S. Bureau of Labor Statistics, covering 244,814 employees in 84 establishments in the fiscal year 1913–1914 and 305,901 employees in 176 establishments in 1917–1918 showed that in the earlier period the rate of labor change (the sum of the hiring rate and the separation rate) was 1.9 per full-year (3,000-hour) worker in the earlier and 4.1 in the later period. *Monthly Labor Review*, June, 1920, p. 41. The rates are given in the *Review* as rates "per 10,000 labor hours."

[2] While it seems highly undesirable to have under-employment data tainted with turnover data, the latter could be made to serve a highly useful purpose in connection with employment and under-employment statistics. It was shown in the last chapter that figures reporting the number employed (or unemployed) constitute a sensitive index to general business conditions. For many purposes their value would be greatly enhanced, if, along with the number employed, there could be reported from month to month the numbers hired and leaving. The accession and separation rates derived from these absolute numbers could then be thrown alongside the employment figures. This would make possible, for instance, the detection of any industries, occupations or plants where, say, inordinately high turnover appeared at a time of low employment. The collection of such figures by the Bureau of Labor Statistics and by such states as New York, as a part of the returns now made on employment, would seem to be feasible.

down of machinery, waiting for work, waiting for dye (in carpet mills), waiting for cars (in coal mines), and so forth.[1]

While most loss of time on the job is occasioned by the necessity of waiting for work, waiting for parts, and by machine breakdowns, not all of it is due to such shortcomings. Some is unquestionably due to inefficient methods of work, not to mention downright "soldiering" on the part of employees. Thus, the Committee on Waste in Industry made a careful study of the methods and performances of eleven workers in the men's ready-made-clothing industry. These workers were on week work and, consequently, lacked certain incentives which they would have had on piece work. The investigation showed that 45 per cent of the time spent on the work was unnecessary.[2] Part of this waste was due to unnecessary slowness and part of it to unnecessary time spent in doing the job in a roundabout way. Obviously in these circumstances, there is no under-employment, inasmuch as the time workers are getting paid for all of the time.[3] Such time-wasting methods would mean virtually unemployment on the job in the case of piece workers, and for that very reason, there is among them little unnecessary slowness.

**Statistics of Overtime.**—To some extent, naturally, the loss incurred by an employee because of short-time employment in periods of depression may be compensated for by overtime employment which he may secure in periods of business prosperity. The statistical evidence

[1] For example, in "one of the best run plants in the country" in the boot and shoe industry the total working time, represented as 100 per cent, is divided up as follows:

| | | |
|---|---|---|
| Actual productive time | 76 | per cent |
| Lost time | 24 | per cent |

This 24 per cent of lost time is divided up as follows:

| | |
|---|---|
| Variation in style | 7.2 per cent |
| Poor deliveries | 4.5 per cent |
| Lack of machine parts | 3.5 per cent |
| Poor control flow work | 2.8 per cent |
| Machine breakdowns | 2.6 per cent |
| Findings | 2.4 per cent |
| Equipment failure | 1.0 per cent |

This record is reported by the Committee on Elimination of Waste in Industry of the Federated American Engineering Societies, "Waste in Industry," p. 148. The Committee found that the average loss in productive time in other shops in the same industry is between 30 and 35 per cent. Unfortunately there appear to be no time data in existence to throw light upon the relation between "unemployment on the job" and the business cycle. It is not likely, however, that the relation between the two is at all the same as that which holds between the business cycle and other phases of under-employment. In periods of prosperity, both management and men are less efficient and, consequently, less time is probably lost within the shop in periods in depression than in boom periods.

[2] "Waste in Industry," p. 109.

[3] It is to be noted that in such circumstances the employer is the one who must shoulder the loss.

of the extent of overtime is discontinuous and fragmentary, but a few samples may be presented.

1. The extent of overtime in a key industry in May, 1910 was shown in a report made by the Department of Commerce and Labor on *Conditions of Employment in the Iron and Steel Industry*. For 17,170 productive employees in various divisions of the steel industry, the per cent of overtime to regular full time was 8.0 per cent, while for 20,811 nonproductive employees this percentage was 8.7 per cent.[1] The report states, in connection with these figures that "conditions shown here may . . . be regarded as those normally existing in large plants during periods of full activity."[2]

2. The amount of overtime among the employees in the lumber, mill work, and furniture industries is reported for the year 1915 by the Bureau of Labor Statistics.[3] These figures show that of 40,775 employees on one-week pay-rolls in more than four hundred establishments, 3,125, or 7.7 per cent worked overtime and that of 31,080 employees on two-week or semi-monthly pay-rolls in more than two hundred and fifty establishments, 2,877 or 9.3 per cent worked overtime.

3. Of 12,156 telephoue operators employed in New York State during the week ending Dec. 13, 1919, 30 per cent worked overtime.[4]

4. Among workers in the metal trades in Massachusetts the percentage of actual hours worked weekly which were overtime hours increased continuously each year from 1914–1918 and dropped considerably between 1918–1919. The figures are given in the following table:

TABLE XIII.—OVERTIME AMONG METAL TRADES WORKERS IN MASSACHUSETTS[a]

| Year | Number of male time workers | Average hours actually worked | Percentage weekly hours worked in overtime | Percentage of time workers working over-time |
|------|------|------|------|------|
| 1914 | 3,875 | 46.4 | 0.6 | 5.8 |
| 1915 | 4,430 | 54.5 | 3.9 | 25.6 |
| 1916 | 8,151 | 53.4 | 6.3 | 39.7 |
| 1917 | 8,433 | 53.7 | 8.6 | 44.7 |
| 1918 | 9,115 | 51.9 | 14.2 | 65.3 |
| 1919 | 7,310 | 49.3 | 4.2 | 39.5 |

[a] *Annual Report on the Statistics of Labor* for year ending Nov. 30, 1920, Part III, p. 22.
[1] Report on Conditions of Employment in the Iron and Steel Industry in the United States, Sixty-second Congress, First Session, *Senate Doc.*, No. 110, vol. III, pp. 196, 197.
[2] *Ibid.*, p. 195.
[3] U. S. Bureau of Labor Statistics, *Bulletin* 225, pp. 54–61, 270–3, 308–14.
[4] New York State Department of Labor, *Special Bulletin* 100, The Telephone Industry, July, 1920, p. 31.

5. Comprehensive figures on wages and hours of steam railroad employees became available in July, 1921, when the Interstate Commerce Commission began the publication of a revised series of railway wage statistics. The Commission's reports show that the average overtime per employee per month from July, 1921–April, 1922 inclusive, was 9.2 hours.[1]

6. The Annual Reports of the New Jersey Bureau of Statistics of Labor and Industries furnish, for the period 1905–1916, important time data on both overtime and days in operation. A comparison of the two series is made in Table XIV. The inverse cyclical relation between overtime and short-time operation is obvious.

TABLE XIV.—OVERTIME AND TIME LOST IN NEW JERSEY MANUFACTURING
ESTALISHMENTS, 1905–1916[a]

| Year | Number of establishments | Average number of workers employed | Average days in operation | Number of working days lost[b] | Number of establishments in which overtime was worked | Average hours overtime per worker employed |
|------|------|------|------|------|------|------|
| 1905 | 2,018 | 239,113 | 290 | 16 | 367 | 7.3 |
| 1906 | 2,120 | 260,072 | 289 | 17 | 434 | 7.6 |
| 1907 | 2,152 | 280,280 | 286 | 20 | 348 | 8.5 |
| 1908 | 2,127 | 245,712 | 279 | 27 | 254 | 3.3 |
| 1909 | 2,291 | 279,351 | 287 | 19 | 341 | 4.7 |
| 1910 | 2,423 | 302,265 | 288 | 18 | 388 | 7.1 |
| 1911 | 2,475 | 305,295 | 287 | 19 | 373 | 5.7 |
| 1912 | 2,556 | 323,390 | 288 | 18 | 428 | 5.6 |
| 1913 | 2,638 | 333,018 | 284 | 22 | 399 | 4.0 |
| 1914 | 2,624 | 325,634 | 280 | 26 | 269 | 3.1 |
| 1915 | 2,817 | 353,848 | 286 | 20 | 423 | 5.2 |
| 1916 | 2,950 | 437,657 | 292 | 14 | 607 | 15.7 |

[a] N. J. Bureau of Statistics of Labor and Industry, *Annual Reports.*
[b] On the basis of 306 possible working days.

## V. CONCLUSIONS

The foregoing recital of the odds and ends of statistical evidence concerning the extent and character of cyclical under-employment shows the inadequacy of the data. We have little enough information on cyclical unemployment. On under-employment there is even less. What fragmentary data do exist are almost entirely discontinuous—the by-

[1] Interstate Commerce Commission, *Wage Statistics, Class I Steam Roads in the U.S.* This figure is based upon employees reported on an hourly basis. These constituted during the period covered about 94 per cent of all employees on Class I roads.

products of surveys. Yet it seems a simple enough matter, along with returns for the number employed or unemployed, to get continuing monthy reports giving the number partially employed. Several European countries have within a year or two begun the continuous reporting of data of this character.

The figures which we have been able to present suffice, however, to show (1) that there is a good deal of under-employment of a cyclical character (2) that under-employment fluctuates with the peaks and depressions of the business cycle in much the same manner as unemployment, and (3) that overtime employment rises when under-employment falls. Further, it seems probable that overtime does not fluctuate as widely as under-employment, that is, overtime probably does not even in the long run compensate for short time. European evidence suggests that at the beginning of depression there are likely to be more persons partially employed than are totally unemployed. How that matter stands in this country we have still to learn. But it is clear that even the best figures which show merely the number of men unemployed, or the shrinking numbers on pay-rolls, are an inadequate measure of unemployment.

# CHAPTER VI

## CHANGES IN EMPLOYMENT IN THE PRINCIPAL INDUSTRIAL FIELDS

### JANUARY 1, 1920 TO MARCH 31, 1922

By Willford I. King

National Bureau of Economic Research

### I. THE COMPARATIVE MEASURABILITY OF EMPLOYMENT AND UNEMPLOYMENT

How important was the reduction in the volume of employment brought about by the decline in business activity occurring between 1920 and 1922? The object of this chapter is to answer the above question.[1]

In Chapter IV, W. A. Berridge has derived an index number showing the fluctuations in employment which have occurred in recent years, but he makes no attempt to measure the absolute amount of unemployment at any time. In taking this course, he is following the precedent accepted by most statisticians. The fact is that unemployment is so difficult to define that there are likely to be as many definitions as there are writers on the subject. There may, however, be some points on which accord is possible. Most persons, presumably, would say that only those desiring gainful employment can be subject to unemployment. But who are those that seek gainful employment? Experience shows that thousands of persons are on the border line. Many women work intermittently. The same holds true of many old men and boys. The number seeking gainful work is then, at best, subject only to approximation and not to accurate measurement.

Furthermore, even if the number seeking employment could be ascertained, how could we determine when an individual was involuntarily idle? Is the man who is sick unemployed? Granted that he is, if he remains disabled for years, does he still continue in this status? Shall we count an aged man whose health permits him to work only occasionally as unemployed for the remainder of the time? How shall we class the striker? What about the man who is eager for work at $1.00 an hour but refuses work at half the pay?

[1] More detailed information concerning this query and also regarding earnings and hours worked is to be found in the report of the National Bureau of Economic Research entitled, "Employment, Hours, and Earnings in Prosperity and Depression."

True, arbitrary rules can be made to fit all of these cases, but the fact should not be overlooked that these rules must be empirical and may represent the exact views of few but the framers. As Mr. Wolman shows in a later chapter, the British have worked out elaborate definitions for use in the administration of unemployment insurance. These definitions are, however, exceedingly complex and require constant interpretation and expansion.

Since it is so difficult to obtain a definite measure of unemployment, it is desirable to attack the problem from another angle. For a long time Massachusetts has furnished monthly records of the number of persons on the pay-rolls of part or all of the factories in that state. There has been a marked growth during recent years in the available supply of this type of statistics.

Owing to the difficulty of defining unemployment, we may hesitate to attempt a statistical measurement, but in these pay-roll records have we not a source of accurate information concerning employment?

One can safely say that pay-roll records represent perfectly definite facts and that their use eliminates most of the difficulties connected with definitions and subjective opinions. If pay-roll statistics are available in complete form, one can ascertain not only the fluctuations in the number of persons on the pay-roll but also the changes occurring in the number of employee-hours worked. With complete data of this sort at hand, it would certainly be possible to answer the query made at the beginning of this chapter and show the magnitude of the cyclical variations in employment.

However, until very recent years, as Miss Van Kleeck points out in Chapter XIX, the data of this sort available have been decidedly scanty. Recent statistics from other states have proved that records for Massachusetts factories indicate reasonably well the course of factory employment in the country as a whole, and hence we can estimate with some confidence the course of factory employment for several decades;[1] but can we assume that fluctuations in factory pay-rolls are representative of the oscillations occurring in agriculture, in merchandising, in banks, or in public utilities? Such an assumption takes too much for granted. Is it not equally probable that every decline in the combined factory pay-roll is met by an increase in the pay-roll of some other industrial field? Further, are we sure that changes in the numbers on the pay-rolls are reasonably good indications of changes in the volume of employment, even in the manufacturing field, when we remember that Mr. Brissenden's figures, recorded in the preceding chapter, indicate that part-time employment plays an important role?

[1] Perhaps estimates for years previous to 1920 might also be successfully made upon the basis of Edmund E. Day's indexes of physical production.

With so many queries unanswered, it is not surprising that, even among experts, there has been great divergence of opinion concerning the volume of unemployment in any period of depression. Estimates of the number idle in 1921 have varied by several millions. The need for a quantitative measurement is illustrated well by Mr. Wolman's description of the experience of the British Government in financing its unemployment insurance fund, and by the difficulty that Mr. Mallery found in securing data suitable for measuring the wage diminutions during a depression so that he could compare this quantity with the size of the potential public works reserve fund.[1]

## II.   THE SCOPE AND METHOD OF THE PRESENT INVESTIGATION

The need of more complete knowledge along this line seemed so great that, in planning the present report, a nation-wide inquiry was undertaken with the purpose of securing the requisite information. The leading results of this investigation appear in the following pages. The specific questions which this inquiry was designed to answer are as follows:

1. Do the high wages characterizing boom times lead many women and others not normally engaged in gainful occupations temporarily to work for wages or salaries?

2. Are fluctuations in different industries complementary, so that the total amount of employment in all fields remains approximately constant? For example, do agricultural laborers or the sons and daughters of farmers or other small employers become employees in factories during boom times and return to their former callings when the depression sets in?

3. Are the fluctuations in factory employment—the only field for which we have records—characteristic of the fluctuations in the entire industrial field including agriculture, merchandising, finance, transportation, and the hand trades?

4. Are changes in the number of persons on the pay-rolls good indicators of the variations occurring in the total volume of employment, or are such variations materially affected by the existence of part-time and overtime employment?

5. Is the existence of much part time or overtime widespread or is it mainly confined to a few industries?

6 Are large and small scale enterprises affected by unemployment to about the same relative extent?

Three questionnaires were devised in the hope of obtaining the material necessary to answer the above queries. The first schedule was designed to secure directly from employees information showing the time they lost through various causes, their hours of work, pay, and family

[1] See Chaps. XVIII and XIV.

income. The effort to secure an adequate number of voluntary enumerators who would canvass employees and obtain records of their employment was not a success. Since the funds available did not permit of the hiring of any considerable number of enumerators, this inquiry was not pushed and the results obtained have but slight value.

The second questionnaire was distributed through the courtesy of the Federal Bureau of Markets and Crop Estimates to their Township Crop Reporters. It asked for the occupations followed during the last two years by members of farmers' families and also for the number of employees hired by each farmer, the hours they worked, and the wages[1] they received. Some 8,500 schedules were returned, most of which were found to contain usable information.

The third questionnaire asked employers in other industries to furnish information similar to that requested of farmers. The United States Census Bureau assisted materially in distributing these schedules. Numerous teachers of economics and a few other teachers and their students, a considerable number of secretaries of Chambers of Commerce, and a large number of individual business men devoted much time, effort, and expense to assisting in the collection of the data.

The Bureau of Railway Economics furnished practically complete data for the railways. The United States Chamber of Commerce circularized its members in behalf of the study. In addition to such voluntary efforts, paid enumerators obtained numerous records from employers in the cities of New York, Chicago, and St. Louis. In all, nearly 3,000 satisfactory records were obtained, covering all sections of the United States and most of the important fields of industry. The schedules were edited and verified by the National Bureau of Economic Research, but the Bureau of the Census assumed the burden of tabulating the data.

Manifestly, a large proportion of all the records received, especially in the case of smaller concerns, rest upon estimates rather than upon actual accounts. The estimates, however, relate to things concerning which the employer, as a rule, is far from ignorant; hence there is little reason to suppose that accidental errors in the estimates have materially affected the accuracy of the averages. The belief that the estimates are substantially accurate is supported by the fact that, in almost every industry, the reported data show but a small scatter.

It is highly probable that the changes shown by the data are more typical than are the absolute sizes of some of the quantities. In many instances, for example, an employer cannot estimate very accurately the absolute number of hours worked per week by his employees, but he is likely to know approximately how much the average working day has increased or diminished in a given period.

[1] For wage records see the detailed report entitled, "Employment, Hours, and Earnings in Prosperity and Depression."

6

Another question of moment is whether enough reports have been deliberately falsified to vitiate the averages. We have no guarantee of course that some such cases have not occurred, but it is believed that the fact that the schedules were obtained under the auspices of the Bureau of the Census and that assurance was given to informants that all information would be considered confidential has minimized any tendency to falsification which might otherwise have existed. The similarity of the items in the reports received from different employers in the same business leads one to believe that the results are reasonably dependable.

It also is worthy of mention that schedules collected from similar establishments by hired enumerators and those collected by mail lead to identical conclusions regarding tendencies within any given field of employment. The pay-roll data secured from factories show the same general trend that appears in similar records published by governmental departments, both state and federal. On the whole, then, the evidence seems to be sufficient to warrant the belief that the results of this inquiry are for the most part reliable.

### III. RESULTS

Records were secured from employers who hire about one-tenth of all the employees in the United States. However, the proportion differs radically in different industries, a fact that is illustrated by the entries in Table XV. Under these circumstances, a total or average of all the samples would be highly misleading. To secure significant results, it has been necessary to reweight all of the items according to the number of workers employed in the industry in question. The process followed has been first to estimate the ratio of the total number of employees in the United States falling in the given category on August 15, 1920 to the number who on the same date were working for the reporting employers, and then to multiply all items of earnings or hours by these ratios. In this manner, a record is obtained which portrays, as accurately as the data will permit, the results for the Continental United States. Owing to the paucity of existing information concerning the number of employees working for large and for small scale enterprises in such fields as the hand trades, public, domestic, and professional service, or commerce and trade, the weights used may sometimes be very faulty, but, fortunately, the nature of the data is such that it is almost certain that errors arising from this source will not invalidate any of the major conclusions of the study.

Fortunately, answers have been secured for all six of the questions previously cited as the goal of this study.

Tables XVI and XVII show no indication that there has been any noticeable migration from one industry to another of the sons and daughters either of farmers or of other employers. All that is apparent is

TABLE XV.—AN ESTIMATE OF THE PER CENTS OF ALL EMPLOYEES IN THE VARIOUS INDUSTRIAL FIELDS WHO WERE WORKING ON AUGUST 15, 1920 FOR THE EMPLOYERS FROM WHOM REPORTS WERE RECEIVED

| Industry | Size of enterprise as measured by the number of employees | Estimated thousands of employees actually working in entire U.S. | Number employed by employers responding to this inquiry | Estimated per cent of all employees working for reporting employers |
|---|---|---|---|---|
| All industries | Any number | 29,180 | 3,146,682 | 10.784 |
| | Less than 21 | 10,110 | 25,113 | 0.248 |
| | 21 to 100 | 4,630 | 36,521 | 0.789 |
| | Over 100 | 14,440 | 3,085,048 | 21.364 |
| Agriculture | Any number | 2,300a | 14,705 | 0.639 |
| | Less than 21 | 2,120 | 14,171 | 0.668 |
| | 21 to 100 | 130 | 272 | 0.209 |
| | Over 100 | 50 | 262 | 0.524 |
| Extraction of minerals | Any number | 1,120a | 56,771 | 5.068 |
| | Less than 21 | 60 | 26 | 0.0433 |
| | 21 to 100 | 140 | 320 | 0.228 |
| | Over 100 | 920 | 56,425 | 6.133 |
| Factory work | Any number | 11,370a | 581,879 | 5.118 |
| | Less than 21 | 1,360 | 2,672 | 0.196 |
| | 21 to 100 | 1,950 | 16,902 | 0.867 |
| | Over 100 | 8,060 | 562,305 | 6.976 |
| Building and construction | Any number | 1,600a | 1,400 | 0.0875 |
| | Less than 21 | 570 | 497 | 0.0872 |
| | 21 to 100 | 530 | 462 | 0.0871 |
| | Over 100 | 500 | 441 | 0.0882 |
| Other hand trades | Any number | 550a | 1,370 | 0.249 |
| | Less than 21 | 280 | 439 | 0.156 |
| | 21 to 100 | 160 | 630 | 0.393 |
| | Over 100 | 110 | 301 | 0.273 |
| Transportation | Any number | 3,420a | 2,301,636 | 67.299 |
| | Less than 21 | 400 | 549 | 0.137 |
| | 21 to 100 | 220 | 3,361 | 0.153 |
| | Over 100 | 2,800 | 2,297,726 | 82.062 |
| Commerce and trade | Any number | 2,600b | 137,202 | 5.277 |
| | Less than 21 | 1,650 | 5,558 | 0.337 |
| | 21 to 100 | 400 | 11,256 | 2.814 |
| | Over 100 | 550 | 120,388 | 21.889 |
| Finance | Any number | 400b | 29,758 | 7.439 |
| | Less than 21 | 150 | 483 | 0.322 |
| | 21 to 100 | 100 | 2,061 | 2.061 |
| | Over 100 | 150 | 27,214 | 18.142 |
| Public and professional service | Any number | 3,000c | 2,454 | 0.0818 |
| | Less than 21 | 1,600 | 87 | 0.00544 |
| | 21 to 100 | 400 | 188 | 0.047 |
| | Over 100 | 1,000 | 2,179 | 0.2179 |
| Domestic and personal service | Any number | 2,820b | 19,507 | 0.691 |
| | Less than 21 | 1,920 | 631 | 0.0328 |
| | 21 to 100 | 600 | 1,069 | 0.178 |
| | Over 100 | 300 | 17,807 | 5.936 |

a Estimates of number of employees and their apportionment probably close to the truth

b Total number of employees approximately correct, but apportionment may be widely in error.

c Estimates very rough.

TABLE XVI.—DISTRIBUTION BY INDUSTRIES IN 1920–1922 OF PERSONS WHO IN 1922 WERE MEMBERS OF THE FAMILIES OF REPORTING ENTREPRENEURS (EXCLUDING FARMERS) AND WHO WERE 16 YEARS OF AGE OR OVER IN 1922 [a]

| Sex | Industry | 1920 | | | | 1921 | | | | 1922 |
|---|---|---|---|---|---|---|---|---|---|---|
| | | First quarter | Second quarter | Third quarter | Fourth quarter | First quarter | Second quarter | Third quarter | Fourth quarter | First quarter |
| Male | All industries | 1,415 | 1,415 | 1,415 | 1,414 | 1,414 | 1,414 | 1,415 | 1,415 | 1,415 |
| | Agriculture | 163 | 175 | 219 | 168 | 165 | 177 | 220 | 172 | 169 |
| | Extraction of minerals | 4 | 6 | 4 | 4 | 4 | 6 | 5 | 5 | 5 |
| | Factory work | 147 | 145 | 147 | 145 | 148 | 148 | 150 | 148 | 149 |
| | Building and construction | 70 | 73 | 74 | 70 | 68 | 69 | 72 | 68 | 68 |
| | Other hand trades | 92 | 90 | 92 | 89 | 91 | 92 | 93 | 90 | 90 |
| | Transportation | 14 | 15 | 16 | 16 | 15 | 16 | 17 | 16 | 16 |
| | Commerce and trade | 615 | 615 | 626 | 616 | 616 | 616 | 629 | 622 | 621 |
| | Finance | 19 | 19 | 19 | 18 | 20 | 19 | 19 | 20 | 18 |
| | Public and professional service | 22 | 22 | 24 | 23 | 22 | 21 | 22 | 17 | 17 |
| | Domestic and personal service | 86 | 87 | 91 | 89 | 87 | 89 | 92 | 89 | 88 |
| | Not gainfully occupied | 163 | 148 | 82 | 157 | 159 | 143 | 74 | 148 | 152 |
| | Industry unknown | 20 | 20 | 21 | 19 | 19 | 18 | 22 | 20 | 22 |
| Female | All industries | 487 | 487 | 487 | 487 | 487 | 487 | 487 | 487 | 487 |
| | Agriculture | 1 | 1 | 3 | 2 | 1 | 1 | 3 | 2 | 1 |
| | Factory work | 17 | 16 | 18 | 16 | 16 | 16 | 18 | 16 | 16 |
| | Other hand trades | 12 | 12 | 12 | 12 | 12 | 12 | 13 | 13 | 13 |
| | Transportation | 2 | 2 | 2 | 2 | 2 | 2 | 2 | 2 | 2 |
| | Commerce and trade | 70 | 70 | 72 | 70 | 71 | 71 | 72 | 70 | 72 |
| | Finance | 3 | 3 | 3 | 5 | 3 | 3 | 5 | 2 | 3 |
| | Public and professional service | 37 | 37 | 36 | 39 | 39 | 39 | 36 | 41 | 40 |
| | Domestic and personal service | 29 | 31 | 34 | 32 | 31 | 33 | 35 | 32 | 31 |
| | Not gainfully occupied | 290 | 289 | 283 | 284 | 288 | 287 | 282 | 285 | 286 |
| | Industry unknown | 26 | 26 | 24 | 25 | 24 | 23 | 21 | 23 | 23 |

[a] Females working on the home farm are classed as "Not Gainfully Occupied."

TABLE XVII.—THE NUMBER OF MEMBERS OF 8,477 REPRESENTATIVE[a] FARMERS' FAMILIES WHO WERE 16 YEARS OF AGE OR OVER IN 1922 AND THE INDUSTRIES IN WHICH THEY HAD BEEN EMPLOYED

| Sex | Industry | 1920 | | | | 1921 | | | | 1922 |
|---|---|---|---|---|---|---|---|---|---|---|
| | | First quarter | Second quarter | Third quarter | Fourth quarter | First quarter | Second quarter | Third quarter | Fourth quarter | First quarter |
| Male | All industries | 14,643 | 14,643 | 14,643 | 14,643 | 14,642 | 14,641 | 14,639 | 14,637 | 14,637 |
| | Agriculture | 11,671 | 12,312 | 12,993 | 11,810 | 11,717 | 12,324 | 12,909 | 11,786 | 11,739 |
| | Extraction of minerals | 30 | 24 | 28 | 37 | 38 | 32 | 44 | 46 | 51 |
| | Factory production | 100 | 90 | 93 | 107 | 100 | 73 | 83 | 94 | 88 |
| | Construction | 102 | 99 | 113 | 104 | 85 | 113 | 134 | 124 | 98 |
| | Other hand trades | 161 | 125 | 134 | 152 | 163 | 131 | 125 | 138 | 165 |
| | Transportation | 197 | 174 | 192 | 198 | 201 | 182 | 191 | 197 | 198 |
| | Commerce and trade | 273 | 220 | 232 | 277 | 295 | 249 | 265 | 311 | 325 |
| | Finance | 64 | 58 | 60 | 69 | 67 | 63 | 66 | 75 | 70 |
| | Public and professional service | 406 | 278 | 221 | 380 | 405 | 287 | 225 | 423 | 420 |
| | Domestic and personal service | 22 | 16 | 29 | 23 | 24 | 22 | 31 | 26 | 26 |
| | Not gainfully occupied | 1,484 | 1,126 | 423 | 1,371 | 1,423 | 1,057 | 444 | 1,290 | 1,336 |
| | Industry unknown | 133 | 121 | 125 | 115 | 124 | 108 | 122 | 127 | 121 |
| Female | All industries | 6,614 | 6,614 | 6,612 | 6,612 | 6,611 | 6,611 | 6,611 | 6,609 | 6,609 |
| | Agriculture | 26 | 29 | 43 | 29 | 28 | 32 | 48 | 32 | 34 |
| | Extraction of minerals | | | | | | | | | |
| | Factory production | 15 | 15 | 12 | 15 | 15 | 16 | 13 | 19 | 18 |
| | Construction | | | | | | | | | |
| | Other hand trades | 25 | 27 | 27 | 27 | 27 | 26 | 28 | 27 | 27 |
| | Transportation | 26 | 26 | 30 | 29 | 29 | 31 | 31 | 31 | 31 |
| | Commerce and trade | 126 | 128 | 145 | 134 | 130 | 134 | 152 | 145 | 137 |
| | Finance | 9 | 8 | 9 | 10 | 11 | 10 | 8 | 8 | 8 |
| | Public and professional service | 603 | 553 | 228 | 650 | 664 | 604 | 245 | 716 | 722 |
| | Domestic and personal service | 64 | 67 | 79 | 71 | 75 | 74 | 88 | 81 | 84 |
| | Not gainfully occupied | 5,683 | 5,723 | 6,004 | 5,610 | 5,596 | 5,651 | 5,965 | 5,513 | 5,508 |
| | Industry unknown | 37 | 38 | 35 | 37 | 36 | 33 | 33 | 37 | 40 |

[a] Information obtained from the *Crop Reporters* of the U. S. Department of Agriculture. All sections of the Continental United States represented in approximately correct proportions.

a growth in numbers in almost every industry, the growth doubtless being due to the fact that many of the younger boys and girls working in 1922 finished school during the period under consideration. The records received furnish, then, no evidence whatever that any material part of the additional force of employees recruited in boom times by manufacturers or other large scale employers is drawn from the households of small employers, farmers, or others working on their own account.

Table XVIII measures the estimated changes in the total number of hours worked by different classes of farm employees in the different sections of the United States. Though one is impressed by the very great seasonal fluctuations in agricultural employment, there is no evidence of any startling change brought about by the business cycle. There was apparently a slight tendency for farmers to hire fewer employees during the depression. There is certainly no evidence that the farmers took on any considerable number of the workers whom the factories, mines, and railways laid off. Since the sample of farms secured is large enough to be representative this conclusion seems to rest on a firm foundation and strengthens the indications given by the figures pertaining to business men's families that the depression was accompanied by a striking decline in the total volume of employment in the United States.

Table XIX records the estimated numbers of employees who were on the pay-rolls of the various industries in each quarter. The last column of the table shows the per cent of change in this number taking place between the peak and trough of the cycle. Allowance has been made for the seasonal variations in many industries.[1] The figures show that the business depression brought about a reduction in the number employed in every industry except the hand trades and the trivial increase in that one field is scarcely sufficient to keep pace with the growth of population. The reduction in all industries amounted to about 4,000,000 workers or nearly one-seventh of all persons employed at the crest of the 1920 boom. There is, however, a striking difference between industries in the degree to which they were affected. Mines, steam railways, and factories dealing in metals, metallic, and miscellaneous products lost very large fractions of their employees, while the construction industry and factories in general, with the exception of paper and printing establishments, also had a notable falling off in the numbers employed. On the other hand, the records for agriculture, finance, public utilities,[2] and wholesale

[1] In such industries, (namely agriculture, building and construction, other hand trades, public, professional and domestic service, transportation, wholesale trade, and establishments manufacturing food, drink, tobacco, lumber, paper, and derived products) the per cents stated represent the maximum declines between corresponding quarters of 1920 and 1921 or of 1920 and 1922. This same procedure is followed in other tables of this chapter.

[2] See sub-title "Other Transportation" in all tables. This item includes telephones and telegraphs.

TABLE XVIII.—EMPLOYEE-HOURS WORKED PER WEEK ON A GROUP OF REPRESENTATIVE FARMS OF THE CONTINENTAL UNITED STATES

| Sex | Employees working by | Number of farms enumerated | Section of the United States | 1920 | | | | 1921 | | | | 1922 |
|---|---|---|---|---|---|---|---|---|---|---|---|---|
| | | | | First quarter | Second quarter | Third quarter | Fourth quarter | First quarter | Second quarter | Third quarter | Fourth quarter | First quarter |
| Male | Month | 6,348 | Entire U. S. | 222,582 | 306,022 | 336,664 | 260,342 | 218,639 | 301,533 | 329,119 | 255,650 | 220,421 |
| | | 988 | Northeast | 51,700 | 64,126 | 74,929 | 60,485 | 52,467 | 66,901 | 76,449 | 61,987 | 53,663 |
| | | 2,557 | North Central | 59,142 | 96,542 | 107,793 | 75,542 | 56,244 | 91,360 | 100,717 | 71,846 | 55,851 |
| | | 2,136 | South | 88,075 | 109,101 | 109,336 | 96,640 | 86,713 | 106,869 | 106,824 | 94,443 | 87,252 |
| | | 667 | West | 23,665 | 36,253 | 44,606 | 27,675 | 23,215 | 36,403 | 45,129 | 27,374 | 23,655 |
| | Day | 5,978 | Entire U. S. | 128,176 | 189,078 | 303,803 | 189,105 | 121,269 | 195,994 | 300,839 | 185,794 | 129,931 |
| | | 905 | Northeast | 22,890 | 38,211 | 65,945 | 38,564 | 23,412 | 39,870 | 66,606 | 39,469 | 23,316 |
| | | 2,417 | North Central | 15,126 | 34,216 | 79,051 | 35,108 | 15,720 | 37,142 | 75,995 | 32,613 | 17,309 |
| | | 2,000 | South | 76,237 | 91,205 | 103,163 | 88,922 | 68,407 | 92,827 | 103,681 | 86,680 | 75,342 |
| | | 656 | West | 13,923 | 25,446 | 55,644 | 26,511 | 13,730 | 26,155 | 54,557 | 27,032 | 13,964 |
| | Week | 5,687 | Entire U. S. | 26,836 | 32,804 | 37,100 | 28,756 | 25,996 | 32,100 | 36,444 | 28,131 | 28,337 |
| | | 833 | Northeast | 6,700 | 7,818 | 10,505 | 7,716 | 6,427 | 7,889 | 10,040 | 7,734 | 6,705 |
| | | 2,258 | North Central | 7,051 | 9,235 | 11,245 | 7,503 | 6,162 | 8,849 | 10,327 | 6,779 | 6,741 |
| | | 1,960 | South | 11,450 | 13,417 | 12,358 | 12,003 | 11,874 | 13,211 | 13,083 | 12,012 | 13,141 |
| | | 636 | West | 1,635 | 2,334 | 2,992 | 1,534 | 1,533 | 2,151 | 2,994 | 1,606 | 1,750 |
| Female | Day | 5,629 | Entire U. S. | 31,528 | 43,365 | 56,815 | 41,663 | 25,261 | 42,409 | 52,338 | 36,659 | 27,134 |
| | | 835 | Northeast | 4,864 | 7,071 | 14,294 | 7,642 | 4,433 | 7,018 | 14,840 | 6,936 | 3,610 |
| | | 2,218 | North Central | 3,527 | 5,426 | 7,199 | 4,135 | 3,421 | 4,793 | 7,376 | 4,095 | 3,406 |
| | | 1,940 | South | 21,803 | 28,643 | 29,573 | 25,999 | 16,021 | 27,953 | 25,024 | 22,694 | 18,628 |
| | | 636 | West | 1,334 | 2,225 | 5,749 | 3,887 | 1,386 | 2,645 | 5,098 | 2,934 | 1,490 |

TABLE XIX.—AN ESTIMATE FOR THE CONTINENTAL UNITED STATES OF THE TOTAL NUMBER OF EMPLOYEES ON THE PAY-ROLLS OF ALL ENTERPRISES OF WHATEVER SIZE

| Industry | 1920 | | | | 1921 | | | | 1922 | Maximum cyclical decline (per cent) |
|---|---|---|---|---|---|---|---|---|---|---|
| | First quarter | Second quarter | Third quarter | Fourth quarter | First quarter | Second quarter | Third quarter | Fourth quarter | First quarter | |
| | Thousands of employees on the pay-rolls | | | | | | | | | |
| All industries | 27,232 | 28,352 | 29,180 | 27,416 | 24,828 | 24,600 | 25,078 | 24,774 | 24,147 | 14 |
| Agriculture | 1,370 | 1,871 | 2,300 | 1,724 | 1,355 | 1,823 | 2,204 | 1,666 | 1,372 | 4 |
| Extraction of minerals | 1,047 | 1,072 | 1,120 | 1,077 | 1,011 | 960 | 944 | 862 | 819 | 27 |
| Building and construction | 1,240 | 1,492 | 1,600 | 1,307 | 1,104 | 1,211 | 1,415 | 1,404 | 1,320 | 19 |
| Other hand trades | 548 | 575 | 550 | 568 | 554 | 581 | 565 | 572 | 561 | 0.7[d] |
| Finance | 390 | 399 | 400 | 396 | 398 | 384 | 380 | 373 | 374 | 7 |
| Public and professional service | 3,075 | 3,022 | 3,000 | 3,047 | 3,120 | 2,973 | 2,940 | 3,161 | 3,269 | 2 |
| Domestic and personal service | 2,683 | 2,763 | 2,820 | 2,781 | 2,741 | 2,753 | 2,786 | 2,701 | 2,661 | 3 |
| All transportation | 3,169 | 3,243 | 3,420 | 3,352 | 2,847 | 2,739 | 2,865 | 2,922 | 2,674 | 16 |
| Steam railways | 2,032 | 2,044 | 2,200 | 2,101 | 1,724 | 1,599 | 1,710 | 1,741 | 1,586 | 22 |
| Other transportation | 1,136 | 1,199 | 1,220 | 1,251 | 1,123 | 1,140 | 1,155 | 1,181 | 1,088 | 6 |
| Commerce and trade | 2,562 | 2,580 | 2,600 | 2,656 | 2,507 | 2,527 | 2,520 | 2,582 | 2,477 | 3 |
| Wholesale | 288 | 303 | 300 | 286 | 274 | 284 | 284 | 273 | 265 | 6 |
| Retail | 2,274 | 2,277 | 2,300 | 2,370 | 2,233 | 2,242 | 2,236 | 2,309 | 2,212 | 3 |
| All factories | 11,149 | 11,334 | 11,370 | 10,507 | 9,189 | 8,648 | 8,460 | 8,532 | 8,621 | 26 |
| Food, drink, and tobacco | 1,048 | 1,015 | 1,120 | 1,075 | 881 | 858 | 959 | 952 | 861 | 16 |
| Lumber and its products | 985 | 1,062 | 1,050 | 912 | 839 | 928 | 915 | 852 | 855 | 15 |
| Metals and metal products[a] | 5,104 | 5,213 | 5,200 | 4,743 | 3,901 | 3,305 | 2,979 | 3,020 | 3,238 | 43 |
| Paper and printing | 639 | 636 | 640 | 666 | 619 | 602 | 599 | 623 | 620 | 6 |
| Mineral products[b] | 878 | 881 | 910 | 892 | 793 | 748 | 750 | 763 | 760 | 18 |
| Textile and leather products[c] | 2,495 | 2,525 | 2,450 | 2,220 | 2,155 | 2,206 | 2,257 | 2,322 | 2,287 | 15 |

[a] Vehicles, railroad cars, and all products not elsewhere recorded are included here.
[b] Includes chemical, stone, glass, and clay products.
[c] Includes clothing of all kinds.
[d] Increase—minimum for corresponding quarters.

dealers, show very moderate decreases, while public, professional, domestic, and personal service, and retail trade gave approximately the same amount of employment throughout the period.

CHART 14.—DIFFERENCES IN THE TOTAL HOURS OF EMPLOYMENT GIVEN QUARTERLY AT THE PEAK AND AT THE TROUGH OF THE BUSINESS CYCLE BY ENTERPRISES EMPLOYING FEWER THAN 21 PERSONS EACH IN THE FIRST QUARTER OF 1920.

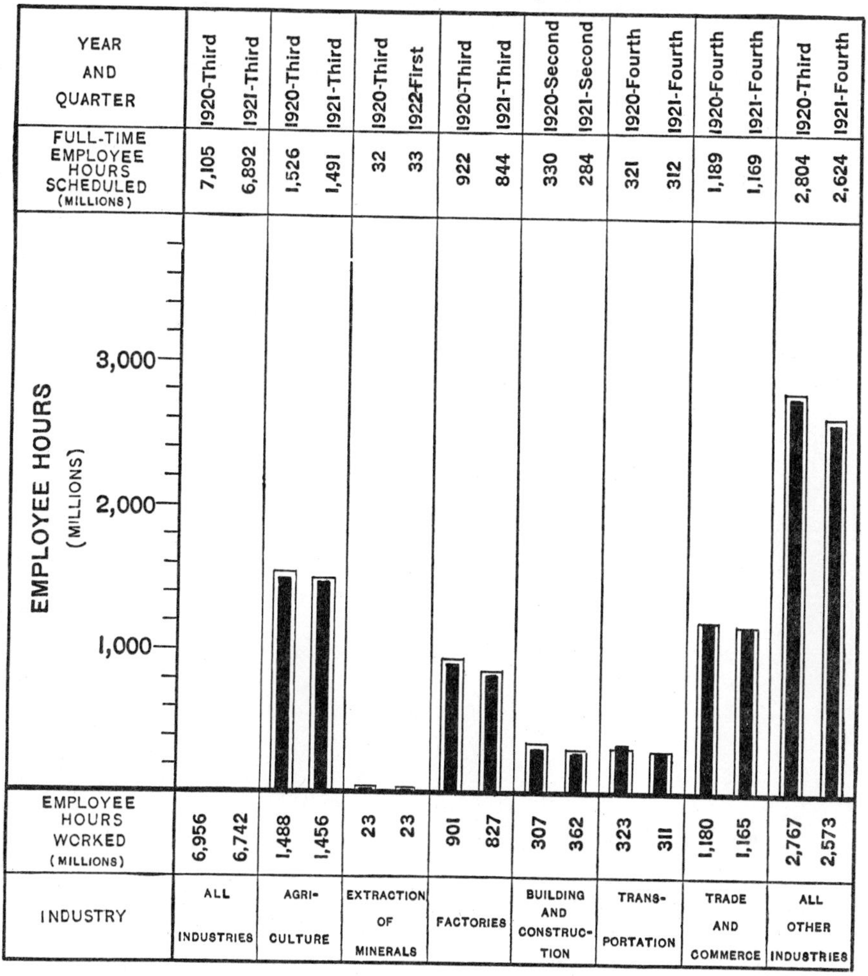

| YEAR AND QUARTER | 1920-Third | 1921-Third | 1920-Third | 1921-Third | 1920-Third | 1922-First | 1920-Third | 1921-Third | 1920-Second | 1921-Second | 1920-Fourth | 1921-Fourth | 1920-Fourth | 1921-Fourth | 1920-Third | 1921-Fourth |
|---|---|---|---|---|---|---|---|---|---|---|---|---|---|---|---|---|
| FULL-TIME EMPLOYEE HOURS SCHEDULED (MILLIONS) | 7,105 | 6,892 | 1,526 | 1,491 | 32 | 33 | 922 | 844 | 330 | 284 | 321 | 312 | 1,189 | 1,169 | 2,804 | 2,624 |
| EMPLOYEE HOURS WORKED (MILLIONS) | 6,956 | 6,742 | 1,488 | 1,456 | 23 | 23 | 901 | 827 | 307 | 362 | 323 | 311 | 1,180 | 1,165 | 2,767 | 2,573 |
| INDUSTRY | ALL INDUSTRIES | | AGRICULTURE | | EXTRACTION OF MINERALS | | FACTORIES | | BUILDING AND CONSTRUCTION | | TRANS-PORTATION | | TRADE AND COMMERCE | | ALL OTHER INDUSTRIES | |

EMPLOYEE HOURS (MILLIONS): 3,000 — 2,000 — 1,000 —

Table XX furnishes the best available measure of the fluctuations of the actual volume of employment, for it records the numbers of employee-hours worked rather than the numbers of persons on the pay-rolls. The falling off for all industries amounted to about one-sixth of the hours of work put in at the peak of activity in most lines of business. However, this decrease was far from uniform, the hand trades even showing a very small increase. Mining, construction work, steam railways, and factories were the industries which felt the cycle most severely.

CHART 15.—DIFFERENCES IN THE TOTAL HOURS OF EMPLOYMENT GIVEN QUARTERLY AT THE PEAK AND AT THE TROUGH OF THE BUSINESS CYCLE BY ENTERPRISES EMPLOYING FROM 21 TO 100 PERSONS EACH IN THE FIRST QUARTER OF 1920.

| YEAR AND QUARTER | 1920-Third | 1922-First | 1920-Second | 1921-Second | 1920-Fourth | 1922-First | 1920-Third | 1921-Third | 1920-Third | 1921-Third | 1920-Fourth | 1921-Fourth | 1920-Third | 1921-Third | 1920-First | 1922-First |
|---|---|---|---|---|---|---|---|---|---|---|---|---|---|---|---|---|
| FULL-TIME EMPLOYEE HOURS SCHEDULED (MILLIONS) | 3,132 | 2,640 | 117 | 89 | 99 | 59 | 1,313 | 1,010 | 322 | 278 | 156 | 140 | 270 | 255 | 904 | 851 |
| EMPLOYEE HOURS WORKED (MILLIONS) | 2,926 | 2,521 | 98 | 81 | 92 | 54 | 1,171 | 946 | 311 | 264 | 153 | 138 | 258 | 243 | 894 | 836 |
| INDUSTRY | ALL INDUSTRIES | | AGRICULTURE | | EXTRACTION OF MINERALS | | FACTORIES | | BUILDING AND CONSTRUCTION | | TRANSPORTATION | | TRADE AND COMMERCE | | ALL OTHER INDUSTRIES | |

(Chart axis: EMPLOYEE HOURS (MILLIONS) — 1500, 1000, 500)

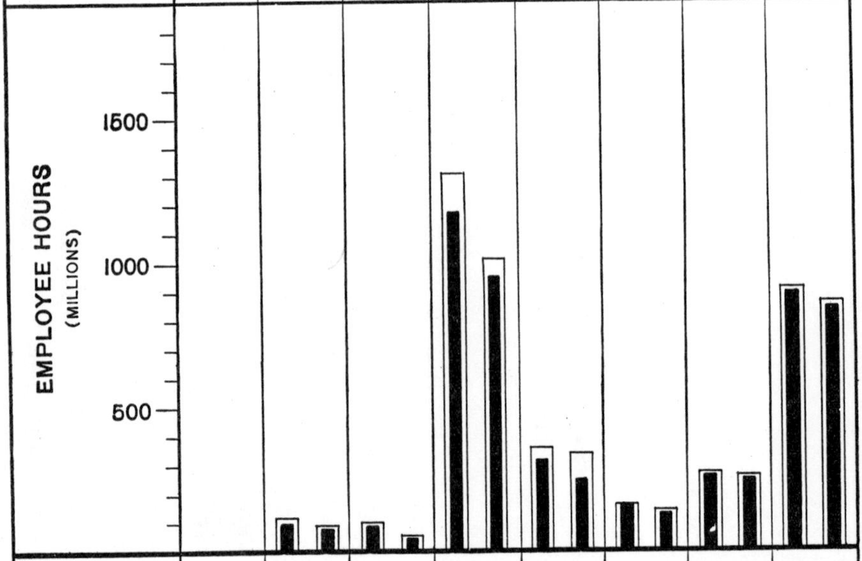

The totals of time worked declined somewhat more than did the numbers of workers on the respective pay-rolls. The reason for this is mainly that there was a tendency in some fields during the depression to retain the employees on the pay-rolls but to have them work part time. This fact is brought out in Charts 14, 15, 16 and Table XX. On these charts the hollow bars represent the number of hours that would have been put in if all employees on the pay-rolls had worked full time.   The

CHART 16.—DIFFERENCES IN THE TOTAL HOURS OF EMPLOYMENT GIVEN QUARTERLY AT THE PEAK AND AT THE TROUGH OF THE BUSINESS CYCLE BY ENTERPRISES EMPLOYING MORE THAN 100 PERSONS EACH IN THE FIRST QUARTER OF 1920.

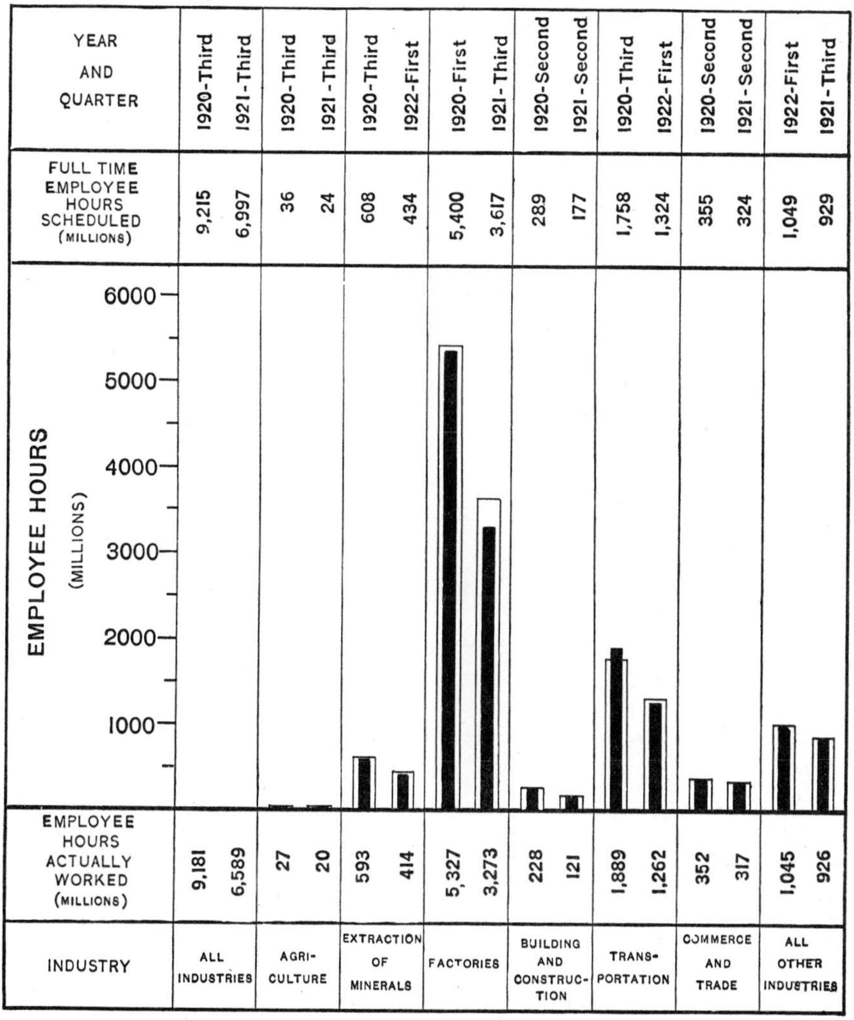

| YEAR AND QUARTER | 1920-Third | 1921-Third | 1920-Third | 1921-Third | 1920-Third | 1922-First | 1920-First | 1921-Third | 1920-Second | 1921-Second | 1920-Third | 1922-First | 1920-Second | 1921-Second | 1922-First | 1921-Third |
|---|---|---|---|---|---|---|---|---|---|---|---|---|---|---|---|---|
| FULL TIME EMPLOYEE HOURS SCHEDULED (MILLIONS) | 9,215 | 6,997 | 36 | 24 | 608 | 434 | 5,400 | 3,617 | 289 | 177 | 1,758 | 1,324 | 355 | 324 | 1,049 | 929 |
| EMPLOYEE HOURS ACTUALLY WORKED (MILLIONS) | 9,181 | 6,589 | 27 | 20 | 593 | 414 | 5,327 | 3,273 | 228 | 121 | 1,889 | 1,262 | 352 | 317 | 1,045 | 926 |
| INDUSTRY | ALL INDUSTRIES | | AGRICULTURE | | EXTRACTION OF MINERALS | | FACTORIES | | BUILDING AND CONSTRUCTION | | TRANSPORTATION | | COMMERCE AND TRADE | | ALL OTHER INDUSTRIES | |

EMPLOYEE HOURS (MILLIONS) — vertical axis: 6000, 5000, 4000, 3000, 2000, 1000

solid black bars indicate the hours actually worked.   The difference in the lengths of the bars of each pair represents the change in employment taking place between the crest and the trough of the employment cycle in the given industry.   It is clear that when measured in absolute terms the important declines in employment were those occurring in factories,

TABLE XX.—AN ESTIMATE FOR THE CONTINENTAL UNITED STATES OF THE TOTAL HOURS ACTUALLY WORKED PER QUARTER BY ALL EMPLOYEES IN ENTERPRISES OF ALL SIZES

| Industry | Millions of hours worked per quarter | | | | | | | | | Maximum cyclical decline (per cent) |
| --- | --- | --- | --- | --- | --- | --- | --- | --- | --- | --- |
| | 1920 | | | | 1921 | | | | 1922 | |
| | First quarter | Second quarter | Third quarter | Fourth quarter | First quarter | Second quarter | Third quarter | Fourth quarter | First quarter | |
| All industries | 17,747 | 18,395 | 19,063 | 17,611 | 15,515 | 15,548 | 15,918 | 15,655 | 15,180 | 16 |
| Agriculture | 911 | 1,265 | 1,603 | 1,148 | 882 | 1,250 | 1,552 | 1,112 | 898 | 3 |
| Extraction of minerals | 648 | 654 | 698 | 672 | 590 | 549 | 534 | 509 | 491 | 30 |
| Building and construction | 702 | 851 | 914 | 751 | 619 | 690 | 805 | 796 | 751 | 19 |
| Other hand trades | 353 | 377 | 357 | 370 | 355 | 379 | 367 | 370 | 361 | 0.5[d] |
| Finance | 231 | 234 | 238 | 234 | 235 | 225 | 224 | 221 | 221 | 7 |
| Public and professional service | 1,961 | 1,928 | 1,922 | 1,905 | 1,952 | 1,841 | 1,834 | 1,939 | 2,032 | 5 |
| Domestic and personal service | 1,956 | 1,991 | 2,037 | 2,019 | 1,973 | 1,985 | 2,022 | 1,936 | 1,920 | 4 |
| All transportation | 2,104 | 2,163 | 2,323 | 2,231 | 1,800 | 1,755 | 1,824 | 1,866 | 1,639 | 21 |
| Steam railways | 1,359 | 1,374 | 1,513 | 1,388 | 1,068 | 1,004 | 1,064 | 1,080 | 936 | 30 |
| Other transportation | 745 | 789 | 810 | 842 | 731 | 750 | 759 | 785 | 703 | 7 |
| Commerce and trade | 1,733 | 1,772 | 1,762 | 1,799 | 1,698 | 1,723 | 1,707 | 1,749 | 1,671 | 3 |
| Wholesale | 185 | 197 | 195 | 186 | 178 | 187 | 184 | 176 | 171 | 6 |
| Retail | 1,548 | 1,574 | 1,566 | 1,612 | 1,519 | 1,535 | 1,523 | 1,573 | 1,500 | 3 |
| All factories | 7,143 | 7,154 | 7,204 | 6,478 | 5,406 | 5,148 | 5,045 | 5,152 | 5,191 | 30 |
| Food, drink and tobacco | 678 | 664 | 740 | 710 | 573 | 564 | 628 | 627 | 557 | 15 |
| Lumber and its products | 648 | 704 | 699 | 591 | 530 | 608 | 594 | 551 | 555 | 18 |
| Metals and metal products[a] | 3,375 | 3,331 | 3,354 | 2,953 | 2,244 | 1,857 | 1,679 | 1,736 | 1,954 | 50 |
| Paper and printing | 396 | 394 | 394 | 412 | 375 | 359 | 352 | 379 | 368 | 11 |
| Mineral products[b] | 565 | 571 | 583 | 570 | 492 | 474 | 474 | 488 | 477 | 19 |
| Textile and leather products[c] | 1,479 | 1,488 | 1,431 | 1,240 | 1,189 | 1,284 | 1,315 | 1,368 | 1,277 | 20 |

[a] Vehicles, railroad cars, and all products not elsewhere recorded are included here.
[b] Includes chemical, stone, glass, and clay products.
[c] Includes clothing of all kinds.
[d] Increase—minimum for corresponding quarters.

especially in the larger plants. There were also shrinkages of some moment in mining, in building and construction, and in miscellaneous industries.

CHART 17.—RELATIVE CHANGES IN THE NUMBER OF EMPLOYEES ON PAY-ROLLS, TOTAL EMPLOYEE HOURS WORKED, AND COMBINED SALARY AND WAGE PAYMENTS IN THE CONTINENTAL UNITED STATES.

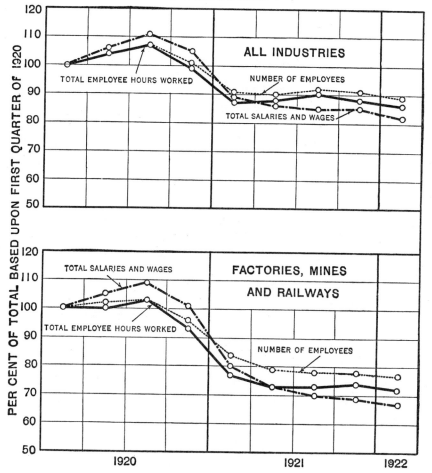

Part time appears to have been resorted to mainly by the railways, by the mining industry, and by certain classes of manufacturers. The figures for agriculture are based upon only a few records and therefore cannot be considered dependable. It is clear that, during a depression, part-time work is in general responsible for a far smaller proportion of the decline in total employment than is the laying off of employees.

That total payments in the form of wages and salaries declined to even a greater degree than did the total hours worked is apparent from a comparison of the right hand columns of Tables XX and XXII. Chart 17 brings out the interesting point that the records neither of the numbers of persons on the pay-rolls nor of the total wage and salary payments are accurate criteria of changes in the volume of work done.

CHART 18.—EMPLOYMENT AT THE TROUGH OF THE 1921 DEPRESSION EXPRESSED AS A PERCENTAGE OF THE MAXIMUM IN THE 1920 BOOM, MEASURED IN TOTAL HOURS WORKED BY ALL EMPLOYEES.

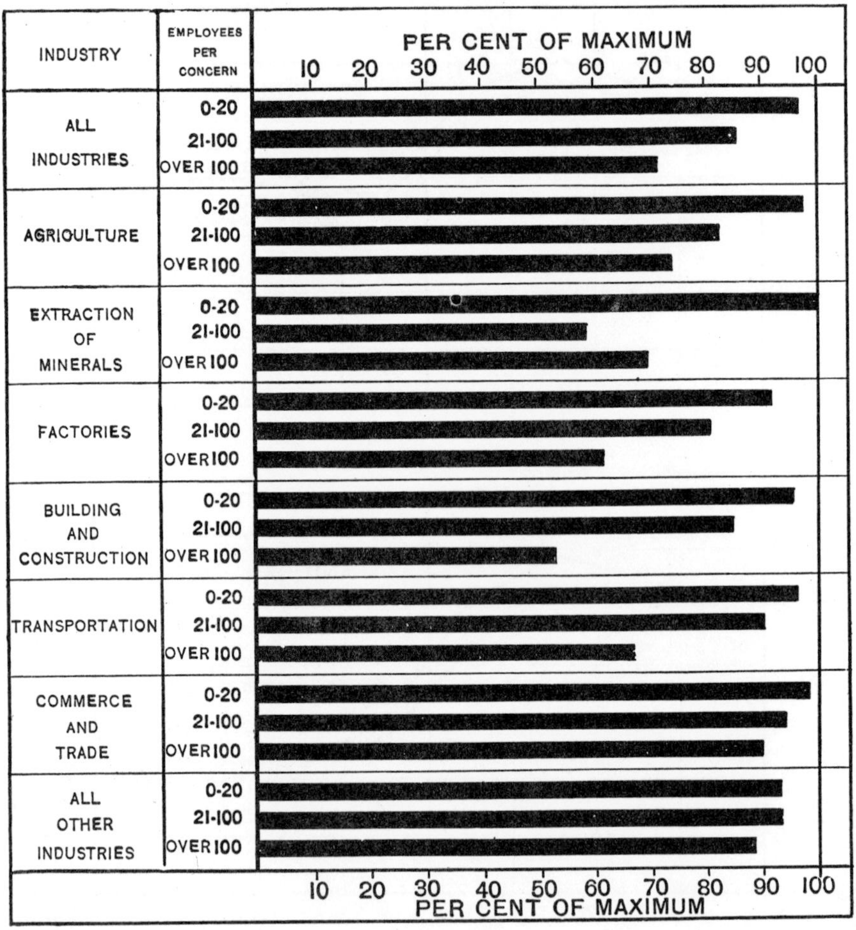

During the boom, salaries and wages rose faster than did total employee-hours, and in the following depression they fell further. On the other hand, the total number of hours worked during the period of decline in industrial activity diminished distinctly faster than did the number of employees on all pay-rolls. Evidently, then, adequate statistics of employment must include a record of the total employee-hours worked as well as records of the numbers on the pay-rolls and totals of wage and salary payments.

TABLE XXI.—AN ESTIMATE FOR THE CONTINENTAL UNITED STATES OF THE PER CENT OF FULL TIME WORKED BY THE AVERAGE EMPLOYEE WHILE ON THE PAY-ROLL IN ENTERPRISES OF ALL SIZES

| Industry | Per cent of full time worked | | | | | | | | | | Decline from highest to lowest recorded |
| --- | --- | --- | --- | --- | --- | --- | --- | --- | --- | --- | --- |
| | 1920 | | | | 1921 | | | | 1922 | | |
| | First quarter | Second quarter | Third quarter | Fourth quarter | First quarter | Second quarter | Third quarter | Fourth quarter | First quarter | | |
| All industries | 98.5 | 97.5 | 98.0 | 97.4 | 95.3 | 95.8 | 95.8 | 96.4 | 96.2 | | 3.2 |
| Agriculture | 95.1 | 93.2 | 96.9 | 98.9 | 92.4 | 95.1 | 97.4 | 99.6 | 94.1 | | 6.5 |
| Extraction of minerals | 94.3 | 93.1 | 95.1 | 94.8 | 90.7 | 90.2 | 88.8 | 92.8 | 93.4 | | 6.7 |
| Building and construction | 94.1 | 94.6 | 94.6 | 94.9 | 92.9 | 94.3 | 94.4 | 94.5 | 102.1 | | 2.0 |
| Other hand trades | 96.9 | 98.3 | 97.1 | 97.6 | 95.8 | 97.7 | 97.2 | 97.0 | 96.2 | | 2.5 |
| Finance | 99.5 | 100.1 | 100.1 | 99.3 | 99.4 | 98.9 | 99.7 | 99.4 | 99.5 | | 1.2 |
| Public and professional service | 100.6 | 100.1 | 100.0 | 100.3 | 101.4 | 100.3 | 99.9 | 99.9 | 100.5 | | 1.5 |
| Domestic and personal service | 98.2 | 97.8 | 97.9 | 98.5 | 97.8 | 98.0 | 97.9 | 97.0 | 97.9 | | 1.5 |
| All transportation | 103.6 | 103.8 | 105.7 | 103.1 | 98.6 | 99.7 | 99.0 | 99.0 | 95.9 | | 9.8 |
| Steam railways | 106.8 | 107.4 | 109.9 | 105.6 | 99.0 | 100.4 | 99.5 | 99.1 | 94.2 | | 15.7 |
| Other transportation | 98.2 | 98.1 | 98.7 | 99.3 | 97.9 | 98.9 | 98.5 | 98.8 | 98.1 | | 1.4 |
| Commerce and trade | 97.9 | 98.1 | 98.1 | 98.7 | 98.1 | 98.1 | 97.7 | 98.7 | 98.2 | | 1.0 |
| Wholesale | 98.9 | 99.0 | 99.0 | 100.3 | 99.9 | 99.4 | 98.6 | 99.0 | 98.8 | | 1.7 |
| Retail | 97.8 | 97.9 | 98.0 | 98.5 | 97.9 | 97.9 | 97.6 | 98.7 | 98.1 | | 0.9 |
| All factories | 98.1 | 96.3 | 96.2 | 94.4 | 91.6 | 92.3 | 92.2 | 93.3 | 93.3 | | 6.5 |
| Food, drink, and tobacco | 97.4 | 97.9 | 95.8 | 96.3 | 97.6 | 98.1 | 95.7 | 96.8 | 96.6 | | 2.4 |
| Lumber and its products | 94.7 | 94.9 | 95.6 | 95.0 | 94.0 | 94.7 | 95.2 | 95.5 | 95.5 | | 1.6 |
| Metals and metal products[a] | 99.7 | 96.0 | 96.6 | 93.9 | 88.5 | 87.0 | 87.0 | 88.5 | 92.5 | | 12.7 |
| Paper and printing | 98.7 | 98.6 | 98.0 | 98.5 | 96.8 | 95.9 | 95.8 | 98.2 | 95.7 | | 3.0 |
| Mineral products[b] | 98.4 | 99.0 | 98.5 | 97.4 | 94.1 | 96.0 | 95.6 | 96.4 | 95.2 | | 4.9 |
| Textile and leather products[c] | 96.0 | 95.4 | 94.3 | 91.6 | 91.3 | 94.7 | 94.4 | 94.9 | 91.0 | | 5.0 |

[a] Vehicles, railroad cars, and all products not elsewhere recorded are included here.
[b] Includes chemical, stone, glass, and clay products.
[c] Includes clothing of all kinds.

TABLE XXII.—AN ESTIMATE FOR THE CONTINENTAL UNITED STATES OF THE TOTAL QUARTERLY WAGES AND SALARIES PAID TO ALL EMPLOYEES BY ALL ENTERPRISES OF WHATEVER SIZE

| Industry | Millions of dollars paid to employees | | | | | | | | | Maximum cyclical decline (per cent) |
|---|---|---|---|---|---|---|---|---|---|---|
| | 1920 | | | | 1921 | | | | 1922 | |
| | First quarter | Second quarter | Third quarter | Fourth quarter | First quarter | Second quarter | Third quarter | Fourth quarter | First quarter | |
| All industries | 9,463 | 10,048 | 10,472 | 9,905 | 8,380 | 8,114 | 8,047 | 8,055 | 7,743 | 23 |
| Agriculture | 216 | 323 | 483 | 316 | 201 | 279 | 390 | 250 | 181 | 19 |
| Extraction of minerals | 477 | 488 | 548 | 540 | 465 | 423 | 396 | 364 | 349 | 36 |
| Building and construction | 528 | 656 | 684 | 553 | 446 | 495 | 573 | 575 | 549 | 25 |
| Other hand trades | 180 | 193 | 190 | 195 | 183 | 192 | 189 | 193 | 186 | 1 |
| Finance | 156 | 161 | 168 | 173 | 169 | 165 | 164 | 169 | 165 | 5 |
| Public and professional service | 964 | 960 | 912 | 1,046 | 1,062 | 1,002 | 951 | 1,124 | 1,117 | 4[d] |
| Domestic and personal service | 666 | 690 | 700 | 695 | 678 | 678 | 672 | 661 | 643 | 8 |
| All transportation | 1,197 | 1,341 | 1,512 | 1,458 | 1,170 | 1,119 | 1,087 | 1,111 | 1,005 | 28 |
| Steam railways | 811 | 921 | 1,073 | 1,002 | 772 | 713 | 679 | 691 | 628 | 37 |
| Other transportation | 386 | 420 | 440 | 456 | 398 | 406 | 408 | 420 | 377 | 7 |
| Commerce and trade | 828 | 854 | 862 | 887 | 829 | 830 | 823 | 839 | 795 | 5 |
| Wholesale | 100 | 105 | 107 | 106 | 96 | 99 | 98 | 95 | 88 | 18 |
| Retail | 728 | 749 | 756 | 781 | 734 | 731 | 725 | 744 | 707 | 5 |
| All factories | 4,252 | 4,382 | 4,410 | 4,042 | 3,176 | 2,929 | 2,802 | 2,769 | 2,752 | 38 |
| Food, drink, and tobacco | 343 | 343 | 359 | 368 | 297 | 279 | 299 | 288 | 257 | 30 |
| Lumber and its products | 331 | 364 | 361 | 321 | 275 | 296 | 290 | 273 | 267 | 20 |
| Metals and metal products[a] | 2,176 | 2,223 | 2,246 | 2,004 | 1,405 | 1,142 | 988 | 970 | 1,060 | 57 |
| Paper and printing | 240 | 249 | 254 | 272 | 244 | 238 | 232 | 248 | 237 | 9 |
| Mineral products[b] | 303 | 317 | 334 | 335 | 283 | 265 | 260 | 254 | 248 | 26 |
| Textile and leather products[c] | 859 | 887 | 856 | 742 | 673 | 708 | 733 | 737 | 683 | 24 |

[a] Vehicles, railroad cars, and all products not elsewhere recorded are included here.
[b] Includes chemical, stone, glass, and clay products.
[c] Includes clothing of all kinds.
[d] Increase—minimum for corresponding quarters.

Perhaps the most surprising discovery made in the course of this investigation is the fact brought out by Table XXIII and by Chart 18, that the reduction in employment during the depression of 1921 was a phenomenon affecting most severely the establishments of the larger sizes. While there are a few exceptions to this rule, it nevertheless holds for the great majority of industries. The reason for this state of affairs is not made clear by the figures. It may be due to the more intimate personal relationships existing between small scale employers and their employees; it may arise from the fact that the small producer is in closer touch with the ultimate consumer of his products and can, therefore, better gage the demand; it may be the result of differences in the nature of the large and small establishments or it may arise from some unsuspected cause.[1] The fact remains that the difference exists and is large enough to be important.

TABLE XXIII.—A COMPARISON OF THE VOLUME OF EMPLOYMENT AT THE PEAK AND IN THE TROUGH FOR LEADING INDUSTRIAL GROUPS

| Industry | Employees per concern | Full-time hours (Millions) | | | Hours actually worked (Millions) | | |
|---|---|---|---|---|---|---|---|
| | | Peak | Trough | Per cent decline | Peak | Trough | Per cent change |
| All industries............. { | 0– 20 | 7,105 | 6,892 | 3.00 | 6,956 | 6,742 | 3.08 |
| | 21–100 | 3,132 | 2,640 | 15.71 | 2,926 | 2,521 | 13.84 |
| | Over 100 | 9,215 | 6,997 | 24.07 | 9,181 | 6,589 | 28.23 |
| Agriculture............... { | 0– 20 | 1,526 | 1,491 | 2.29 | 1,488 | 1,456 | 2.15 |
| | 21–100 | 117 | 89 | 23.93 | 98 | 81 | 17.35 |
| | Over 100 | 36 | 24 | 33.33 | 27 | 20 | 25.93 |
| Extraction of minerals...... { | 0– 20 | 32 | 33 | 3.13 | 23 | 23 | 0.00 |
| | 21–100 | 99 | 59 | 40.40 | 92 | 54 | 41.31 |
| | Over 100 | 608 | 434 | 28 62 | 593 | 414 | 30.18 |
| Factories................ { | 0– 20 | 922 | 844 | 8.46 | 901 | 827 | 8.21 |
| | 21–100 | 1,313 | 1,010 | 23.07 | 1,171 | 946 | 19.21 |
| | Over 100 | 5,400 | 3,617 | 33.02 | 5,327 | 3,273 | 38.56 |
| Building and construction... { | 0– 20 | 330 | 284 | 13.94 | 307 | 262 | 14.66 |
| | 21–100 | 322 | 278 | 13 66 | 311 | 264 | 15.11 |
| | Over 100 | 289 | 177 | 38.75 | 228 | 121 | 46.93 |
| Transportation ........... { | 0– 20 | 321 | 312 | 2 80 | 323 | 311 | 3.72 |
| | 21–100 | 156 | 140 | 10.26 | 153 | 138 | 9.80 |
| | Over 100 | 1,758 | 1,324 | 24 69 | 1,889 | 1,262 | 33.19 |
| Commerce and trade........ { | 0– 20 | 1,189 | 1,169 | 1.68 | 1,180 | 1,165 | 1.27 |
| | 21–100 | 270 | 255 | 5.56 | 258 | 243 | 5.81 |
| | Over 100 | 355 | 324 | 8.73 | 352 | 317 | 9.94 |
| All other industries......... { | 0– 20 | 2,804 | 2,624 | 6.42 | 2,767 | 2,573 | 7.01 |
| | 21–100 | 904 | 851 | 5 86 | 894 | 836 | 6.49 |
| | Over 100 | 1,049 | 929 | 11.44 | 1,045 | 926 | 11.39 |

[1] I am inclined to believe that one reason why small enterprises show a lower percentage of unemployment during depressions is that in such enterprises there is a prompter liquidation of costs, perhaps even of wage rates.—Note by M. C. RORTY.

7

## IV. SUMMARY

The results of this investigation may be summarized briefly as follows:

1. The depression of 1921 caused a diminution of approximately one-sixth in the total volume of employment in the United States.

2. The reduction due to part-time work was confined mainly to a few fields and was relatively of slight importance when considered for industry as a whole.

3. The shift of workers from one industrial field to another was small in extent.

4. Workers in mining, transportation, and manufacturing were the principal sufferers from the decline in employment.

5. Small employers in general gave more steady employment than did large employers in the same industries.

6. To get an accurate picture of changes in total employment, it is not sufficient to collect data concerning numbers on the pay-rolls or total wages and salaries paid. The only data that give the precise measurement needed are those showing the numbers of employee-hours worked.

# CHAPTER VII

## THE EFFECT OF UNEMPLOYMENT UPON THE WORKER AND HIS FAMILY

### By Stuart A. Rice

Columbia University

#### I. UNEMPLOYMENT SELECTIVE

A pioneer in the field of social inquiry has written in a memorable work, "The unemployed are, as a class, a selection of the unfit and on the whole, those most in want are the most unfit."[1]

There is both truth and error in this generalization. In "good" and "bad" times alike, employers who reduce their working forces will release, on the whole, those who are less efficient. Employers who take on men will select, on the whole, those applicants who are more efficient. There is thus a constant tendency for the unemployed to be those who are less useful to industry. These again will tend to be the less "fit" from the standpoint of society.

This constant tendency is largely counterbalanced during a business depression. Cyclical unemployment is undiscriminating. Whole industries, occupations, or professions become idle simultaneously, throwing out of work not only the inefficient, but the efficient and highly skilled as well. Groups of employees in processes requiring specialized skill may be "turned off" first of all. Since these specialized workers are normally more useful to society than less skilled or "all-around" men, the selective process noted by Booth is even reversed at the outset of a business depression. That is, the unemployed may be *more* "fit" than those left at work.[2]

---

[1] Booth, Charles, "Life and Labor of the People in London," vol. I, p. 149. See also, vol. IX, Chap. IX, summary and conclusions on "Irregularity of Earnings."

[2] The Children's Bureau of the U. S. Department of Labor, during the winter of 1921–1922, made an intensive study of the effects of unemployment upon the welfare of children in two American cities. Prior to publication, in June, 1922, an abstract from its report was supplied the writer by Grace Abbott, Bureau Chief.

Three hundred sixty-six families in the two cities were visited. Families were chosen in which there were two or more dependent children, and in which the wage-earner's unemployment was of long duration. In other respects, the Bureau believes that "the families selected for visitation comprised in each city a group fairly representative of those affected by unemployment."

Eighty-three per cent of the wage-earners visited in one city and 74 per cent in the other "had previously been skilled workers in regular trades."

99

"Hard times" dislocate the affairs of a great many persons who are unaffected by seasonal trade fluctuations. The steady "year-'round" employee forms all of his plans upon the expectation of a reasonably regular income. Those with whom he has personal or business relationships have the same expectation. Family, friends, and tradesmen as well as himself will be "hard hit" when his income stops. The seasonal worker, on the other hand, is more likely to accept unemployment as a recurring phenomenon and to become inured to its hardships and makeshifts. Its effects will be discounted, more or less, by all concerned.

## II. THE SELECTIVE RESULTS

While "fitness" has relatively little to do with determining *who* shall be idle at times of business depression, it has much to do with determining the *results* of unemployment. Any human deficiency, whether of organic or nervous mechanism or of moral stamina, tends to disclose itself under the stress of protracted idleness. Those who deteriorate the more quickly and the more completely are, on the whole, a selection of the weaker members of society. Every increase in the severity or duration of business depression will extend the demoralization higher and higher into society along the scale of social value.

Nevertheless, other things than "fitness" will influence the weight of the load and the ability to bear it. Sex, age, temperament, and family responsibilities will be factors in the results. The man with a large family, for example, may "give out" sooner than the irresponsible single man, although he may be more valuable to society and more useful to industry. Here again we have an adverse selection in which the less "fit" are favored.

Misfortune is not always to be appraised at face value. It drags down one person to ruin and despair. It serves another as a whetstone to point ambition and sharpen latent powers. The young, the irresponsible, those whose lives are "on the make," may be sobered and disciplined in character by the misfortune of unemployment.[1] Those who are bearing a heavy load of life's responsibilities may be demoralized and wrecked by it.

Unemployment, then, is sometimes good, is generally bad, and is frequently disastrous beyond repair for those concerned. The exact consequence will depend upon all of the particular circumstances surrounding each of these persons and upon the kind of individual that

[1] "The period of unemployment has been the making of a great many persons, who during the period of the war and immediately following were the roving, shiftless sort and were out after the most money they could get. Many of these have right-about-faced and, when given an opportunity for work, are making some of the best people who are securing employment today."—M. E. Luethi, Personnel Director, The Acme Wire Co., New Haven, Conn.

each may be. Many of these consequences recur with sufficient frequency to constitute typical occurrences, and it is these that this chapter attempts to describe.

## III. A COMPOSITE PICTURE

The writer has sought to eliminate from this description any bias originating in his own experience. He has endeavored to describe those consequences of unemployment upon which there is agreement among those best situated to know them. To this end, he has had the cooperation of approximately forty competent and careful observers, including employment managers of industrial establishments, executives and workers in social agencies, Catholic and Protestant clergymen, labor leaders and men from the ranks of labor. The long contacts of these persons with wage-earners of many differing industries and occupations provide a wide and representative foundation for the generalizations drawn.[1]

## IV. OPPOSING OPINIONS

Two opposing types of opinion have been disclosed among these observers. To a minority, the *benefits* of unemployment loom large. To the greater number, unemployment is a thing of unmitigated evil. Between these are those who see both good and evil and those who feel that unemployment is overrated in its evil effects.

The first of these positions is taken by the employment manager of a firm that has made striking progress toward the establishment of cordial and democratic relationships with its employees.[2]  His statement is made

[1] In addition to those from whom he has quoted, the writer wishes to express cordial appreciation for opinions and "case histories" supplied by the following: Nell Alexander, Charity Organization Society, Bridgeport; F. J. Bruno, Associated Charities, Minneapolis; John Calder, Swift & Co., Chicago; Doris M. Cangney and Miss Kellar, Social Service Federation, Toledo; Rev. John J. Cloonan, C. M., St. John's College, Brooklyn; Mary J. R. Condon, The Associated Charities, Pittsburgh; Ethel M. Cotter, Social Welfare League, Seattle; John P. Coughlin, Metal Trades Council, Brooklyn; Karl de Schweinitz, Society for Organizing Charity, Philadelphia; E. H. Fish, Rehabilitation Division, Veterans' Bureau, Needham, Mass.; W. P. Johnson, Taylor Instrument Companies, Rochester; William H. Mathews, and S. E. Parlato, A. I. C. P., New York; Eddison Mosiman, Social Service Bureau, Newark; Earl B. Morgan, Curtis Publishing Co., Philadelphia; E. S. McClelland, Westinghouse Electric & Manufacturing Co., East Pittsburgh; Justin W. Nixon, Rochester Theological Seminary; Wesley A. O'Leary, Department of Public Instruction, State of New Jersey, Trenton; Lawson Purdy, Charity Organization Society, New York; Stockton Raymond, Family Welfare Society, Boston; Alice E. Richard, The Associated Charities, Cincinnati; W. C. Roberts, American Federation of Labor, Washington; Amelia Sears, United Charities, Chicago; Patrick J. Shelley, Family Court, New York; Jane C. Williams, The Plimpton Press, Norwood, Mass.; Joseph H. Willits, The Wharton School, University of Pennsylvania, Philadelphia.

[2] RECTANUS, S. R., Director of Employment, The American Rolling Mill Co., Middletown, Ohio.

after "very serious and thoughtful consideration" and discussion with his associates:

Our conclusions have been that the "morale" of our group has been strengthened, not broken down. We find that during periods of excessive employment there is much greater weakening of morale than during periods of unemployment. We find that the spirit of extravagance grows rapidly with very little stimulation so that individuals and groups quite readily try to spend more than they earn. We are not suggesting that unemployment is desirable nor that the expenditure of savings for living expenses is a happy experience. . . . Within our experience there are no specific outstanding cases of disaster as the result of unemployment nor can we say that this individual or that was particularly benefited, but our general impression gained through rather close observation is that the moral fiber of our community was strengthened during the past fifteen months.

At the other end of the scale is another employment manager[1] who says:

I have witnessed real suffering as the result of the industrial depression. Unemployment is deadly in its effects. It breaks down morale, destroys courage, confidence and ambition, and finally produces poverty, than which there is no greater evil.

The secretary of a family case-working agency has found both evil and good in a period of industrial depression. As evidence of good, he states that "a considerable number of men have profited by their idleness in having taken general educational courses or vocational training." It seems obvious that these advantages must have been confined to a limited number of younger and superior men, without family responsibilities. The secretary[2] adds:

The Director of the Bureau of Domestic Relations says there are fewer domestic difficulties than before, that people seem really happier when there is not so much money to quarrel over. Now there is little desertion and on the whole perhaps the bonds of family life have been strengthened. This corroborates the dominant opinion of the Associated Charities staff.

Directly contrary to the foregoing experience is that of the Family Courts in the city of New York. According to the Chief Probation Officer of the city,[3] the Family Courts "act almost as barometers" with reference to employment conditions. He says:

When there is plenty of employment and wages are high there is a lesser number of cases in the Court. When unemployment is prevalent there is a decided increase in the number of arraignments.

---

[1] M. HARRISON, Director of Personnel, Hammermill Paper Co., Erie, Pa.

[2] JACKSON, JAMES F., General Secretary, the Associated Charities, Cleveland, in a letter, April, 1922.

[3] COOLEY, EDWIN J., in a letter, May, 1922.

A settlement worker[1] has reached the same conclusions. She says:

In many families domestic unhappiness is greatly increased by unemployment. The man is discouraged, irritable, and hopeless. The wife, tied to her home, and faced each moment with the necessity of providing for the children, is apt to nag and to feel that the man might be making more effort to secure work than he is. If there has been any source of irritation before, it becomes greatly aggravated. On the other hand many families weather the crisis with remarkable fortitude and courage and trust in each other.

Suffering and wrong inflicted upon a group from without often build up the spirit of sympathy and solidarity within. In accordance with this fact, the "bonds of family life" must sometimes be strengthened during unemployment. When this occurs, how will the attitudes of such a family toward society at large be affected? Particularly, how will it feel toward employers, the government, or whomever it holds responsible for its miseries?

A western clergyman[2] writes:

I used to imagine that unemployment would stimulate radicalism. In my practical experience this winter with hundreds of cases it has made the unemployed cautious . . . While this is the effect (at least the surface effect on individuals) I believe there is a deeper social resentment smouldering beneath the surface. Some outrageous act of repression would instantly crystallize this.

Enough has been said to indicate the main differences of opinion on the subject. The preponderance of judgment regards unemployment as one of the most fatal evils of civilization.

Let us now attempt a closer analysis of our problem. The effects of unemployment upon individuals are both material and mental. In most cases, the mental consequences are the more serious.

### V. IMMEDIATE MATERIAL RESULTS

First of all, the family income is reduced, or cut off entirely. This means, inevitably, the expenditure of whatever savings exist. Debts are almost equally inevitable; the family borrows from friends or relatives; dealers for a time extend credit; the rent falls into arrears; insurance policies lapse.[3]

If unemployment is protracted, the physical disintegration of the home soon begins. The piano or phonograph, and later the household necessities—sewing machine, chairs, and carpets—go back to the installment firm or into the hands of the second-hand dealer. Dispossession

---

[1] TAYLOR, LEA D., Chicago Commons, in a letter, May, 1922.

[2] LACKLAND, REV. G. S., D.D., pastor, Grace Community Church, Denver, Colo.

[3] The Children's Bureau found that 10 per cent of the 366 unemployed families visited had received aid from relatives, 32 per cent were the recipients of loans, 66 per cent had gone into debt for food, 69 per cent had contracted other debts, 43 per cent had savings which helped them to tide over the period of depression.

may conclude this series of amputations, together with the loss of payments already made if the family has been trying to buy its home.

I could cite many instances of fine men, good citizens—husbands and fathers, in semi-skilled lines, who had purchased homes with small cash payments down, and were paying the balance on monthly installments. . . . In spite of all they were eventually forced to see their homes lost, with what little money they had scraped together to put into them originally.[1]

### VI. A LOWER PLANE OF LIVING

Long before these more obvious sacrifices occur, unfortunate economies have been lowering the family plane of living, and ultimately reducing its living standards.

The problem of rent is perhaps the first attacked; families "double up," rent out rooms, take in boarders, or move into cheaper, less sanitary, and more congested quarters.[2]

Clothing becomes shabby and is not replaced. Since fuel is reserved for cooking, the house in winter becomes damp and unventilated. Expenditures for recreation cease.

Almost universally, the family curtails its expenditures for food.[3] "Undernourishment" and "malnutrition" are the consequences.[4]

[1] HARRISON, M., Hammermill Paper Co.

[2] "A part of the family income during unemployment was derived from boarders and lodgers in sixty-one cases; thirty-eight of these families had kept lodgers previously." Children's Bureau findings.

[3] The colored residents of a northern industrial district are said by an intimate observer to resist this curtailment of food to a greater degree than the white workers in the same locality. "Among colored people, during the first six months of recent business depression, there was no considerable change" in the quality and quantity of the food eaten. "During the last four months the colored people have largely eliminated meat from their diet even where the families are employed."—Excerpt from a statement prepared by a social worker in a northern industrial district, April, 1922.

[4] The Children's Bureau has compared for 90 unemployed families the monthly income from all sources (including credits, loans, charitable aid, and savings used, as well as earnings) with a budget estimate, "made by a large manufacturing firm," of the actual cost of the necessities of food, clothing, rent, fuel, and sundries. The percentage which the monthly receipts constituted of the estimated budget for each family, in accordance with the number and ages of its members, and the number of families in each group, were as follows:

| RATIO OF MONTHLY INCOME TO ESTIMATED BUDGET OF NECESSITIES | NUMBER OF FAMILIES |
|---|---|
| Less than 15 | 1 |
| 15 and under 25 | 6 |
| 25 and under 50 | 38 |
| 50 and under 75 | 34 |
| 75 and under 100 | 11 |
| | 90 |

ROWNTREE and LASKER in their English study "Unemployment, a Social Study," Chap. VIII, ascertained the food actually consumed by eight unemployed families

Coincidently, attention to physical defects, such as decayed teeth, diseased tonsils, and adenoids, is neglected.

## VII. HEALTH AND VITALITY

A lowered plane of living results directly in bad health and lowered physical vitality.[1] Like machinery abandoned to disuse and rust, the wage-earner himself deteriorates. He loses industrial efficiency. He will return to work less competent and less skilled. His output per unit of overhead investment in the plant will be less than before.[2]

Impairment of health and vitality is notably occurrent in the case of children and of mothers already carrying a full share of domestic burdens. Approaching motherhood is rendered terrifying by the grim reality of an empty purse, exhausted credit, and depleted vitality.

Grace Abbott, Chief of the federal Children's Bureau at Washington states: "The ill effects of a lowered standard in the care of the growing children of this generation because of unemployment means physically a permanent loss to them and to the world."[3]

## VIII. THE FUTURE

Along with its economies, the unemployed family discounts its future. Fortunately or unfortunately, there is generally paid employ-

---

over a period of four weeks. The amounts varied in calories from 31 per cent to 68 per cent of those required for physical efficiency. The supply of protein varied from 32 per cent to 60 per cent of the amounts required. These budgets "do not represent the lowest level of want; rather they represent the level at which underfeeding can continue week after week and month after month."

[1] "In addition to the other hardships coincident with or caused by unemployment, 880 children—almost two-thirds of those included in this study—were affected by illness of some member or members of their family. Illnesses or disabilities during the time of unemployment were reported by 231 families—63 per cent of the entire number." Children's Bureau study.

[2] Hugh Fullerton of the H. Black Co. of Cleveland states that in the ladies' garment trade, workers almost always lose efficiency during periods of unemployment. It takes three or four weeks after an extended idle period to get back to a high rate of production. Mr. Fullerton attributes this effect to psychological causes. He holds that people get to thinking about other things than production while they are idle and do not concentrate vigorously upon their work until they have become readjusted to it. There is much opinion and considerable evidence behind our contention that the same result is frequently caused by the lowered physical vitality of those who have been unemployed.

[3] From a letter. The Children's Bureau study above referred to found that 60 per cent of the children who were under seven years of age were in families in which unemployment of the father had cut the average monthly income from all sources to less than half of the amount available to the family previously.

ment still available for women when the work for men has ceased. The homekeeper goes out to toil.[1]

It is the children who suffer most from this expedient. In many cases they remain alone. If very young, they are placed in day nurseries, in other families, or are left in the none too skilful charge of the husband and father. Very often they are placed in institutions.

> With unemployment there is an increase in the commitment of children to institutions. As times improve many of these children are again returned to their homes.[2]

Educators agree that the foundations of moral character are completed in early childhood. What will the foundations be when the master mason is away?

It is probable that more children of older years are retained in school in dull times than in prosperous periods. When jobs are unobtainable, the education of many boys and girls is allowed to continue. This must be counted among the incidental benefits of unemployment. On the other hand, among the older children who are able to secure jobs, the tendency is accentuated to begin work prematurely and to enter street trades and "blind alley" occupations of the most unwholesome sort. The advantages of added "schooling" for some are offset by the bad occupational start given to others.[3]

The majority of wage-earners will ask for charitable aid only with the greatest reluctance and mental anguish. The evidence seems clear that trade-union members and skilled men generally comprise only a very small proportion of those applying to social agencies. Dependence upon charity signifies to them the final step in degradation and humiliation.

---

[1] Of one hundred and fifteen mothers who were working in homes visited by the Children's Bureau, ninety had secured employment after their husbands had been thrown out of work. Only twenty-five had worked previously. Almost three-fourths of the working mothers were employed away from home.

The fact is further illustrated by the experience of the state employment offices in New Jersey. In several of the larger cities, placements of men began to fall off sharply in October, 1920. The placements of women were maintained at the previously existing level and have since exceeded the placements of men. Since industrial employment had declined for both sexes, the inference is drawn by R. J. Eldridge, State Director, that the wives and daughters of unemployed men were supporting their families by domestic employment and "work by the day." The inference is strongly supported by the personal and statistical experience of the offices.

[2] COOLEY, EDWIN J., Chief Probation Officer, City Magistrates' Courts, New York.

[3] "Of the one hundred and forty-eight children between fourteen and eighteen years in the families of unemployed men in the two cities, a total of thiry-nine children were regularly employed, of whom thirteen were under sixteen years. More than half of the working children left school to go to work after their fathers lost their regular employment." Children's Bureau study.

Once the stigma of dependence has been acquired, it is not easily thrown off.[1]

The ill effects of unemployment are not confined to the period during which the worker is out of a job. They keep unfolding indefinitely, after the wage-earner has returned to work. Likewise, they long precede the actual "lay-off."

A western coal miner[2] has described the anticipatory evils of unemployment in the following simple and incisive language:

In my opinion, the worst thing about unemployment is the uncertainty of the future. When a man is fortunate enough to hold a job for a while, he is still handicapped with this future outlook. He is unable to make his savings work for him because he may be unemployed the next day. . . . To buy his necessities at seasonable times is about the only investing that a worker should undertake. Why can't he do it? Potatoes are going to be $60 per ton in the winter, it is digging time, I can buy a ton for $25. I have this much saved but I dare not make this good investment because I might lose out on the job and *need* the $25.

A working man has sort of a treadmill existence. The treadmill sets on the edge of a cliff. You work for a while, pay your debts, unemployment comes, back you go into debt, each time a little farther. When work comes again it finds one a little weaker, and the battle against the mill is not as successful as before. Your creditors become alarmed; possibly a garnishment of your next earnings. The mill has got you over the cliff.

### IX. PERMANENT MENTAL RESULTS

It is the fear and worry, about the future as well as the present, that are chief among the mental responses produced by unemployment.

The fear that his job may end any day, with a cutting of his income, without any notice or warning, dominates the worker long before actual unemployment begins. It is a force that is of much longer duration than actual unemployment; and one can almost imagine a feeling of relief when the worst happens and the uncertainty becomes a certainty.[3]

Worry over the outcome, worry over bills, how to make ends meet, how to get the children's food and clothing—these worries are no less a cause of physical breakdown than the physical deprivations previously mentioned.

Discouragement and melancholy impair the initiative of many families. "Morale" may sink so low that self-help becomes almost an impossibility. Among persons of other temperament, a virulent, unrea-

---

[1] Of the 366 families visited during the Children's Bureau study, 185 or 51 per cent had been compelled to apply for charitable aid. Only twenty-two of these had previously needed such assistance.

[2] MITCHELL, DAVID, JR., a worker from boyhood in the mines at Renton, Wash.

[3] ODENCRANTZ, LOUISE C., author of "Italian Women in Industry," from letter written in May, 1922.

soning bitterness develops and directs itself toward other members of the family, employers, government, or society at large.

The individual forced upon the streets without choice, not only degenerates as far as standards are concerned, but also engenders a bitterness against governments and capitalistic institutions which is dangerous to our commonwealth. . . . [This danger] cannot with safety be ignored.[1]

Far from being temporary, these mental reactions are fixed indelibly on the character and personality of the victims. *Habituation* to bitterness, to dependency, to lowered standards of living, to lowered vitality and physical efficiency, will normally long outlast the conditions responsible for their formation.

## X. EFFECTS ON SELF-RESPECT

Beneath the emotions we have named, definite injury to the pride and self-respect of the unemployed wage-earner is concealed.

Vivid recollection of a personal unemployment experience, supplemented by contacts with thousands of men who had reached the lower levels of respectability,[2] has given the writer firm convictions on this point. In his opinion, the largest single factor in the physical and moral deterioration so often observed in an unemployed man is the damage done to his sense of up-standing self-importance within the group in which he moves.

"The job's the thing," says Whiting Williams. "Wages are interesting but the *job* is the axis on which the whole world turns for the working man."[3] Unless he is unusual in instincts or intelligence, the man who loses his job feels himself without "status;" he is an outcast from the herd. He is "not wanted" by society. The overpowering human impulse to be one among his fellows—the fellows who are at work— finds no satisfaction. A "man without a job" is in the same psychological setting as a "man without a country."

When society refuses participation in its organized activities of production, the pariah of industry, as he regards himself, usually responds in one of two ways. If his personality be weak, he accepts the social verdict of his uselessness to the world. He sinks into a hopeless and listless indifference to his own future and the needs of industry. He becomes one of those drifting individuals who are the despair of every social agency and employment manager. If his personality be strong, on the other hand, he seeks mental compensation for his wounded pride and the incessant rebuffs of job-hunting. He finds it in refusing to accept society's codes of conduct. He becomes a rebel.

[1] DUNCAN, JAMES A., Secretary, Central Labor Council, Seattle.

[2] We refer to the applicants of the New York City Municipal Lodging House, from December, 1915 to February, 1918.

[3] "What's on the Worker's Mind," Chap. III.

A similar, though less explicit, injury is wrought upon the personality of the wife and mother. Humiliation at the family fortunes and the shabbiness they entail, the realization of her husband's failure, the indignity of tasks and make-shifts regarded as beneath her—these things are not soon to be wiped off her account with the world.

Can the children escape infection in such an atmosphere? Many life-long attitudes are formed in childhood. If bitterness, fear, and humiliation surround the early years of the coming generation of workers, we cannot expect industrial relations in the future to be orderly and kind.

# PART III
# PROPOSED REMEDIES FOR CYCLICAL
# UNEMPLOYMENT

# CHAPTER VIII

# THE VARIOUS KINDS OF REMEDIES PROPOSED

By Wesley C. Mitchell

National Bureau of Economic Research

## I. THE AIM OF PART III

Proposals for preventing business crises and depressions are as old and as numerous as theories concerning their cause. Almost every diagnosis of the disorder has suggested a course of treatment, and the diagnoses have ranged from speculation to "capitalism," from competition or over-saving, from sun spots to morbidity rates. There have been writers who held that nothing can be done to avert the calamities of business cycles, writers who believed that no remedy will suffice short of a reorganization of society or a regeneration of human nature, and writers who found a panacea in some trifling reform.

In this book no effort is made to consider the whole range of these remedies. The aim is to select those proposals current today which seem most practicable and to present the leading facts pertinent to each which must be considered by men who wish to form an intelligent judgment concerning their promise. In accordance with the general plan of the investigation, none of the proposals are advocated in this part of the report, except the proposal to improve the statistics of unemployment. No program of action is offered, though the practical steps necessary to apply some of the remedies are sketched. The various contributors seek to supply, not conclusions, but materials which will help readers to reach their own conclusions. Needless to say, most of the contributors have definite views concerning the merits of the proposals which they discuss. These views will be clear to the attentive reader. It may be added explicitly that the National Bureau of Economic Research neither endorses nor opposes any of the measures treated.

## II. DEVICES FOR STABILIZING PRODUCTION

Crises and depressions are national misfortunes because they bring losses upon individual businesses and individual workers or investors. While most of the remedies proposed call for action by government agencies, a considerable number of enterprising business men have sought to help themselves out of these troubles. To this end they have experimented with various devices suited to the particular needs and opportunities of their several concerns. Mr. Stone and Mr. Thompson have made a brief but diligent canvass of numerous industries to learn what devices have been tried and how they have worked in practice. Their results are set forth in Chapters IX and X.

## III. THE PROPOSAL TO TREAT ORDERS AS LEGAL CONTRACTS

In 1920 the cancellation of orders attracted more attention than in any earlier crisis. Not only does cancellation make the confusion of a liquidation worse confounded, but the possibility of cancelling orders later on also incites buyers to give inflated orders during the preceding boom and so increases the blunders which help to bring on the crisis. Hence the suggestion that orders for goods of all sorts be treated strictly as enforceable contracts. The legal and economic aspects of this proposal are treated by Mr. Montague in Chapter XI.

## IV. THE PROPOSAL TO USE CONSTRUCTION WORK AS A BALANCE WHEEL

Next to be discussed is the proposal to use construction work as a balance wheel of the business machine. In the chapter on Business Cycles it was shown that the intensity of booms is increased at present by an exceptionally rapid increase in the demand for new construction, that the checking of this demand helps to bring on the crisis, and that its rapid further decline intensifies depression. Since in a rapidly developing country like the United States construction work of all kinds, from the building of houses and ships to the building of machinery and rolling stock, is a factor of considerable magnitude even when set against the imposing figures for total business transactions, and since construction work can be done most cheaply in dull times, several men have suggested that the peaks and valleys of the business cycle can be partially levelled by shifting some construction now done during booms into the subsequent depressions. This proposal is discussed by Mr. Bradford with reference to the building trades at large in Chapter XII, by Mr. Parmelee with reference to railways in Chapter XIII and by Mr. Mallery in reference to public works in Chapter XIV.

## V. PROPOSALS TOUCHING CURRENCY AND CREDIT

Many writers have held that the chief cause of crises lies in the misuse of credit and, therefore, that the chief remedy lies in improving our banking or monetary systems. This range of suggestions falls outside the province of a Conference on Unemployment. To treat it adequately would require a separate report larger than the present volume. But not to pass by in silence so important a part of the field, Mr. Adams outlines briefly in Chapter XV the outstanding devices of a financial sort now under discussion for controlling the business cycle.

## VI. IMPROVING THE MECHANISM OF THE LABOR MARKET AND PROVIDING UNEMPLOYMENT INSURANCE

Most direct in their reference to unemployment are the proposals to improve the mechanism of the labor market by setting up a system of employment offices under public supervision, and to pay men out-of-work allowances. The first measure is intended to reduce the "reserve army of labor" in good times and bad. It is treated by Mr. Harrison in Chapter XVI. The second measure is intended primarily to reduce the sufferings endured by the unemployed. But it is also expected to prevent the purchasing power of wage-earners from shrinking as much as it does now in depressions and, therefore, to contribute toward mitigating the business difficulties. Further, it is believed by some publicists that unemployment measures can be developed into a powerful agency for preventing unemployment or at least reducing the number of men laid off by employers. Mr. Andrews treats the out-of-work benefits given by trade unions in Chapter XVII and Mr. Wolman the unemployment insurance schemes of governments and business concerns in Chapter XVIII.

## VII. BUSINESS STATISTICS AS A MEANS OF CONTROL

There remains the suggestion that, if business men had better information about business conditions and made more effective use of the data, the number of mistakes which contribute toward the breeding of crises would be vastly diminished. In Chapter XX Mr. Knauth reviews the materials now available for business forecasting and sketches the way in which they can be used. Among these materials an index of employment holds high rank as a "business barometer." Since the improvement of this index is a matter of grave importance on other grounds as well, it is given a Chapter (XIX) to itself written by Miss Van Kleeck.

By way of summary a Committee of the Federated American Engineering Societies presents in Chapter XXI a review of the extent to which various devices for stabilizing business throughout the cycle are now applied in practice.

# CHAPTER IX

## METHODS OF STABILIZING PRODUCTION OF TEXTILES, CLOTHING, AND NOVELTIES

### By N. I. Stone

General Manager, Hickey-Freeman Company

### I. PREVENTION OR REDUCTION OF SEASONAL FLUCTUATIONS

Our investigation has shown that no manufacturing concern has been able to grapple effectively with the problem of cyclical disturbance of business which has not first learned how to deal successfully with seasonal fluctuations in the demand for its products.

Several of the methods used for overcoming cyclical fluctuations are an outgrowth of, or are supplementary to, the policies developed for the purpose of securing steady production from one end of the year to the other in spite of seasonal ups and downs in consumers' demand. Seasonal fluctuations recur with fair regularity from year to year and the statistical and other information required to guide the business executive is less complex and more easily secured than that needed in connection with cyclical fluctuations. For the same reasons, the business technique which must be gradually built up and adjusted to the many phases of a manufacturing enterprise—labor, production, buying, financing, merchandising, and selling—in order to secure continuous production, cannot be made equal to the task of coping with the comparatively uncertain, irregular, and less easily foreseen cyclical fluctuations unless it has first mastered the fairly regular and frequently recurring seasonal fluctuations.

For these reasons an analysis of the successful methods in vogue for preventing losses and hardships caused by cyclical fluctuations of business must include and indeed begin with a presentation of the means developed for preventing or minimizing seasonal fluctuations in production.

**Causes of Seasonal Fluctuations.**—Seasonal variations in demand are caused chiefly by climatic conditions which on the one hand determine a great many of the consumers' demands such as for warm or light clothing, fuel, ice, etc., and on the other, influence directly a great many processes of production such as agriculture, building construction, water transportation on rivers or harbors subject to freezing, etc. They are also caused by custom, such as the demand for flowers at Easter, for jewelry, toys, and other "holiday goods" at Christmas, for fire works on July 4, etc.

Each of these trades, which is directly influenced by seasonal demand, in turn affects other industries from which it derives its raw materials, and the intermittent flow of the earnings of the millions of workers who are engaged in all of these industries lends a seasonal aspect to all industries which supply the personal wants of these workers.

**Wastefulness of Intermittent Production.**—The intermittent consumers' demand causes seasonal ordering of goods on the part of the distributor—retail and wholesale; in turn the manufacturer, in his anxiety to attain the maximum rate of turnover for his current investment, concentrates his production within the shortest possible period of time preceding date of delivery. The presence of a reserve of unemployed workers in "normal" times permits of an intermittent system of production under which weeks and months of involuntary idleness are succeeded by periods of intensive work with long hours and overtime.

That the effect of such a method of production is hurtful to the human factor in industry and injurious to society is obvious. It destroys regular habits of industry; it impairs the health of workers who are driven for part of the year to the extremes of intensive effort during long hours succeeded by periods of idleness and frequently of dissipation. It undermines good citizenship on the part of a large element of the electorate. It results in large loss of potential wealth to the country as a whole through failure to use labor power and industrial equipment.

Apart from the social injury which intermittent production causes, a broad view of the ultimate interests of the individual manufacturing concern discloses the disadvantages of intermittent production and the gains that would flow from continuous operation. This is especially true of plants having a large overhead expense, a considerable part of which is in the nature of fixed charges which cannot be eliminated while the plant is temporarily shut down. These overhead charges are a total loss. Business men now recognize the wastefulness of a large labor turnover, the expensiveness of training new help, and their inefficiency and resultant high cost, even when hired at comparatively low wages. The increased cost of production during the period of "tuning up" a plant to its state of efficiency, is an item familiar to every industrial engineer and plant manager. Added to these is the loss of the more capable and ambitious workers who drift away during periods of idleness to more steady occupations unless held by the inducement of higher rates of wages than would be necessary to satisfy them under steady employment. Finally there is the lowering of the morale on the part of the labor force under conditions of uncertainty.

These considerations have prompted a small but growing number of concerns to devise means for keeping plants in continuous operation despite the intermittent consumers' demand. The methods described below have been developed in one or more of the plants of the following concerns within the industrial field covered by this chapter:

| | | |
|---|---|---|
| Dennison Manufacturing Company | Framingham, Mass. | Manufacturers of paper products and stationery supplies |
| Joseph & Feiss Company | Cleveland, Ohio | Manufacturers of men's clothing |
| Printz-Biederman Company | Cleveland, Ohio | Manufacturers of women's suits and coats |
| Hickey-Freeman Company | Rochester, N. Y. | Manufacturers of men's clothing |
| Brown & Bigelow | St. Paul, Minn. | Manufacturers of advertising novelties |
| Guiterman Brothers | St. Paul, Minn. | Manufacturers of men's wear |
| Cooper Wells Company | St. Joseph, Mich. and Albany, Ala. | Manufacturers of hosiery |
| Fort Wayne Corrugated Paper Company | Fort Wayne, Ind. | Manufacturers of paper products |
| Waldorf Paper Products | St. Paul, Minn. | Manufacturers of paper products |

**Methods of Reducing Seasonal Fluctuations of Production.**—The methods which have been devised to secure greater continuity of production are:

1. Spreading delivery of orders over a large part of the season instead of delivering the entire order at the opening of the season. This has been found feasible by the clothing houses mentioned above. In the case of "holiday goods" such as the Dennison Manufacturing Company is producing, which must be delivered complete because of the shortness of the selling season, success has been achieved by

2. Inducing retailers to place their orders long in advance of delivery. To quote the Dennison Company:

Originally paper box production was exceedingly seasonal. Orders would not come in in any large number until late in the summer, and then there would be a painful rush of work until Christmas. As a result of modified sales policies, however, we now secure a considerable number of our holiday orders in January, and even get a fairly large proportion of orders for Christmas delivery in November and December of the preceding year. Similar results have been accomplished in the crepe line.

The same is true of the other "Christmas goods" manufactured by the company such as cards, seals, etc.

3. Inducing retailers to accept deliveries well in advance of the season, through deferred dating or special discounts. The certainty of having the goods on hand when they will be needed is in itself a considerable inducement to the retailer in complying with this plan.

4. Interdepartmental orders. Where the nature of the goods manufactured is such that the products of one department are used by another, the planning of interdepartmental orders a long time in advance of

actual need, enables the producing department to schedule its production in such a way as to do most, if not all of the work, when there are no outside or seasonal orders on hand.

5. Developing one or more staple products on which the plant can be kept busy between seasons. A minimum amount of such staples may have to be manufactured at all times. But their chief advantage is that they make possible

6. Manufacturing to stock. This can be done with a fair degree of safety only if the conditions called for under (5) have been developed. The practice has its obvious limitations in the financial resources of the manufacturing concern. The more the staples manufactured to stock approach the ideal combination of a high labor and low material value, the better they will lend themselves to the purpose of keeping the plant busy when orders are low.

Conspicuous instances of the policy described under (5) and (6) are to be found in the case of the Dennison Manufacturing Company, the Hickey-Freeman Company, and the Joseph and Feiss Company. These three companies are cited because of the variety of products they represent. The Dennison Company manufactures tags and other paper products. The Hickey-Freeman Company manufactures the highest grade of ready-made men's clothing. The Joseph and Feiss Company manufactures one of the lowest-priced lines of men's clothing. Yet each has been able to follow this policy successfully.

7. Developing a standard of excellence in the grade of product manufactured and educating the retailer and the consuming public to a realization of this excellence through proper coordination of production, merchandizing, advertising, and selling.

A good illustration of this policy is to be found in the case of the Printz-Biederman Company of Cleveland, Ohio. Although manufacturing an article in which style is the determining factor, this company follows the rule of "selling what it makes" as against the ordinary opportunistic policy known in the trade as "making what you sell."

Months in advance of the selling season this company selects and orders its cloths, determining the number and kind of garments it wants to make the following season in order to keep its plant at capacity production. Then it instructs its designers to make the necessary models. As soon as these are approved by the firm, quantity manufacture is begun before any orders have been solicited from customers. Through years of consistent maintenance of this policy the company has inspired its retailers with confidence in its judgment, the reliability of its promises, and the value of its merchandise. Its salesmen in different territories are given their respective quotas which they are expected to dispose of and which they usually do sell. In this they are helped not a little by the act that the goods of the company are sold under a trade mark which is known among the consuming public through national advertising. While occasionally the firm may lose on a model and be obliged to sell at a loss, in the long run it has been eminently successful in maintaining production for fifty-one weeks in the year, one week being devoted to plant repair during which the workers enjoy a vacation with pay.

The only serious setback the company has experienced was in connection with the great cyclical depression of 1920–1921. How such difficulties can be guarded against is shown below in discussing the prevention of cyclical fluctuations of business.

8. The transfer of surplus help from one operation to another or from one department to another. This practice presupposes adequate training of the working force to enable employees to do more than one operation.

Such are the principal means which have been successfully employed by concerns like those mentioned, engaged in highly seasonal business. Their chief value apart from the immediate gain of steady operation of the plant is that they develop the habit and the capacity for planning ahead. This is what constitutes the bed-rock foundation on which rests the entire technique of eliminating or reducing cyclical fluctuations in individual business enterprises.

## II. PREVENTION OR REDUCTION OF CYCLICAL FLUCTUATIONS

Two sets of remedies are open to private business for mitigating the effects of cyclical disturbances: one, constructive, aims at finding a market for its products in spite of the general depression; the other, preventive, seeks to avoid the pitfalls of over-expansion and to minimize the consequent losses of depression. The first set includes proper merchandizing and selling policies; the second, proper purchasing, construction, financing, and credit policies. These policies have been developed by the Dennison Manufacturing Company to a greater extent than by any of the concerns investigated in the textile, clothing, and novelty industries.

**Merchandizing.**—Merchandizing may be regarded as the pivotal activity in securing the continuous operation of a manufacturing plant. Its function is to study the needs of the consumer and to adapt the products of the company to those needs; it seeks to find new uses for these products and directs the publicity efforts of the advertising department to the task of educating the consumer in those uses; it inspires the selling force to follow up the gains won by this publicity work and to consolidate the newly won positions in the public favor by pushing the distribution of these products; it conducts research work which frequently results in the creation of new products and plans and directs the activities necessary to develop a consumer's demand for a product which he has never known before. It is the supreme coordinating factor among the production, selling, and advertising departments. It helps to remind the production department that it is not a self-sufficing entity, and that it can only survive if it serves the wants of the consumer. It artfully guides those wants to maintain the production of the plant at full capacity.

*Elasticity of Demand.*—All products may be divided into two classes: Those intended for the direct use of the consuming public, and those used in productive processes. The marketing of the former is governed as a rule by conditions of elastic demand, that of the latter by conditions of inelastic demand. To illustrate: When prices of clothing rose to an unheard of extent at the height of prosperity in 1920, the consumer stopped buying; when the depression which began in the fall of 1920 caused the flooding of all markets with clothing at retail prices which did not cover the cost of production, the clothing was absorbed by a public suffering from the effects of that depression. Even in staple foods, the demand for which is the least elastic of all articles of consumption, an unusually high price will lead to the use of substitutes and a correspondingly low price will cause a marked increase in sales. In the case of articles of apparel and personal adornment or household furniture or ornamental objects, the demand is extremely elastic and as the saying in the trade goes, "any amount can be sold at a price."

On the other hand with articles used in production the demand is generally inelastic, except within narrow limits. For example, when industry was booming, manufacturers of machine tools could not supply the demand at any price; when the industrial depression set in, "you could not give them away," to quote Mr. Du Brul, Secretary of the Machine Tool Manufacturers' Association.

The reason for this is not far to seek. When a concern is busy and behind with its deliveries, it will add new machinery even at a high price because the element of machine depreciation entering into the cost of a manufactured article is insignificant; on the other hand, the owners of an idle plant, who are suffering a daily loss in fixed charges, can not be tempted to add to their idle machinery, no matter how' attractive the price of the new machinery may be. It is obvious that the policies of marketing to be followed in these groups of products must be different, and that the manufacturer of an article subject to inelastic demand has a more difficult problem on his hands.

*Creation of New Products.*—We have noted the successful application of the policy of selling at cost or thereabout in the case of an elastic-demand article like clothing as a means of keeping a plant busy in off seasons. This policy degenerates into a stampede of price slaughter at a time of general depression such as set in during the latter part of 1920. Such price cutting can be used as a desperate makeshift to "get out from under" accumulated stocks, but not as a means of keeping a plant busy. When there is no demand or an insufficient demand for the products of the company to keep its plant busy, the only alternative to a shut-down is the placing of new articles on the market.   When faced by such conditions, the concerns engaged in the manufacture of articles subject to inelastic demand are at a disadvantage.   Their recourse is to turn to a machine or tool which will greatly reduce production costs as compared with the old machine or tool, or to turn to an article of personal consumption, to the manufacture of which their plant can be easily adapted.

In any event the development of the new product should not be deferred until the moment when the depression has set in.   It is at this point that a well organized merchandizing department conducting aggressive researches will demonstrate its usefulness.

Most concerns make the error of placing their new products on the market as soon as they have been developed.   This policy is justified only if the demand for the existing product is inadequate to keep the plant busy.   Even then care should be taken to ascertain whether the appropriation for publicity necessary to introduce the new product would not result in an equal volume of business if spent in additional sales promotion of the old product.   The latter course has its obvious advantages: if successful, it means manufacture on a larger scale and, therefore, as a rule, at a reduced cost of production; it presents fewer and simpler problems of distribution and selling and for these reasons is preferable.

Quite different is the case when a depression sets in and the old consuming constituency is no longer able to absorb the customary quantity of the existing product.   That is the psychological moment for placing the new product on the market.   To be ready for prompt action, all work of preparation must be done in advance; that is to say, during the period of prosperity, when the existing plant facilities may be strained to the utmost to meet the current demand for the old products.   In other words the research department must always be working and scheming ahead of the plant and must have its own facilities for work which may seem superfluous in the eyes of the production department.

The product having been perfected on its technical side, the merchandizing department must seek to develop all possible uses for it in an experimental way.   Then a plan of publicity including advertising, demonstration, and any other means found appropriate must be worked out ready to be launched at a moment's notice.

To illustrate: While the Dennison Manufacturing Company was turning away orders for their products at the height of prosperity in 1919–1920, the company developed two new products, one a crepe paper hat for festive parties, the other the use of sealing wax as a plastic material for objects of art and adornment.   At the time these products were developed, the company was the largest producer of sealing wax in the country and one of the largest makers of crepe paper, which it had originated.   To have put the new products on the market would have required new buildings and machinery. Nearly everybody at the time was making such extensions, competing for the labor, materials, and equipment of the building industry and causing prices already inflated to soar still higher. Not so the Dennison Company. A study of statistical reports on the state of business in the United States, convinced the management that the industrial and financial structure of the country was top-heavy and that expansion at prohibitive cost at that time would be dangerous. The new products were quietly put away for a rainy day. In January, 1920, the entire selling force was called together and told that prosperity was at its peak, that a break was expected within four to eight months, and means were discussed for meeting the coming emergency. One of the steps decided upon was the placing of these new products on the market as soon as the break should come. All arrangements were made to expedite the production, marketing, advertising, and selling of the new products. Seventy-five thousand letters to customers were written, signed, and required only the insertion of the date to be ready for mailing. When the break came, the plans went through without a hitch, with the result that the company sold more crepe paper and sealing wax in 1921 than ever before.

In the case of articles prepared for trade use, which have an inelastic demand, appropriate steps were likewise taken to get new orders. Thus, to quote Henry S. Dennison:

We have found, for example, that customers who would not buy ordinary tags were willing to buy when we made up some new, attractive design which especially appealed to them.

*Advertising.*[1]—When business depression sets in, the cry goes out to "reduce your overhead." Business experts counsel it, trade papers admonishingly repeat it, banks insist on it, company presidents order it, and plant executives ruthlessly apply the pruning knife. One of the first items of overhead to go by the board is advertising.

The following charts show the variations in the volume of advertising during the course of the last business cycle. Chart 19 shows the monthly fluctuation of newspaper and magazine advertising.[2] It shows a striking

---

[1] For information on the subject of advertising, the writer is indebted to James O'Shaughnessy, Executive Secretary of the American Association of Advertising Agencies; Stewart L. Mimms of the J. Walter Thompson Co., and H. L. Roth of Hoyt's Service, Inc.

[2] The newspaper data cover the monthly volume of advertising from 1914 to 1922 in one hundred and nine newspapers published in twenty-three leading cities. The original figures were obtained from *Editor and Publisher*, Jan. 28, 1922. The magazine data have been compiled by *Printers' Ink* since June, 1911, and cover the principal weeklies and monthlies having a national circulation. Both forms of advertising are measured in agate lines.

seasonal fluctuation occurring with great regularity year after year.  Each
year shows no less than two peaks and two depressions: first, a slight

CHART 19.—MONTHLY VOLUME OF NEWSPAPER ADVERTISING[1] IN 23
    CITIES AND OF MAGAZINE ADVERTISING IN THE UNITED STATES.

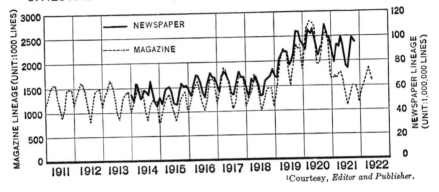

[1]Courtesy, *Editor and Publisher.*

depression in the early winter months followed by a recovery in the spring;
the midsummer months invariably show a great falling off in advertising

CHART 20.—ANNUAL VOLUME OF NEWSPAPER ADVERTISING[1] IN 23
    CITIES AND MAGAZINE ADVERTISING IN THE UNITED STATES.

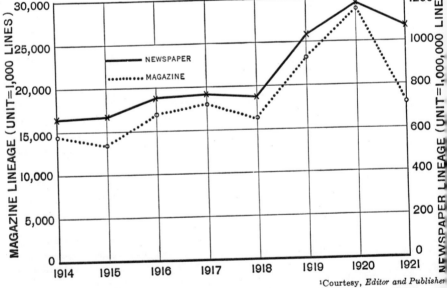

[1]Courtesy, *Editor and Publisher*

and the autumn months a recovery.  As will be seen from the chart,
magazine and newspaper advertising have the same seasonal character.
   Chart 20 shows the changes in the annual volume of newspaper and
magazine advertising with the changing phases of the business cycle.

The falling off in the volume of advertising in 1914 and 1915, its rise during the war years, the check in 1918, the phenomenal rise in the prosperous period of 1919 and 1920, and the serious decline in the depression of 1921, are clearly shown by the chart.[1]

A tabulation of all advertisers spending more than $10,000 per annum on magazine advertising, prepared annually by the Statistical Bureau of the Curtis Publishing Company, shows that in 1921, when the volume of magazine advertising fell off 37 per cent from that of the previous year, out of 2,247 such advertisers, 1,507 or about two-thirds reduced their advertising expenditure, while 740 or about one-third maintained the same appropriation or even exceeded their appropriation for the preceding year.

A questionnaire sent out to those who increased their advertising in 1921 in the face of a falling market, designed to bring out the results of such a policy, brought replies from 265 firms. Only 146 of the replies, however, were sufficiently definite to lend themselves to tabulation on the first and most important question as to whether the volume of sales increased or declined in 1921 as compared with 1920. Of these 146 firms, 67 reported a falling off in the volume of sales ranging from 6 to 82 per cent, while 68 reported an increase in sales ranging from 5 to 100 per cent over 1920, and 11 maintained the same volume of sales.

These figures, while interesting, cannot be regarded as conclusive. In the first place, there was a great increase in advertising rates in 1921, some of the firms reporting increases of as much as 100 and 200 per cent. Mr. O'Shaughnessy, Executive Secretary of the American Association of Advertising Agencies, estimates the average increase in the cost of magazine advertising at 20 per cent. The increased appropriation by most of the firms in question did not, therefore, mean an increased amount of advertising space. In some cases the additional appropriation was sufficient to maintain the same space, in others it did not suffice to do so. In only a minority of instances was the appropriation sufficiently increased to result in increased advertising.

[1] It is interesting to observe that newspaper advertising declined only 9 per cent from 1920 to 1921 as against 37 per cent for magazine advertising. This is due to the different character of advertising in the two fields. Merchandise advertising in magazines emanates chiefly from manufacturers, while that in newspapers comes chiefly from local stores. The store is in a different position from the factory. The latter depends for its sales on its salesmen, the advertising being regarded merely as a means of creating a favorable atmosphere for the salesman's efforts, while the store depends chiefly upon advertising to "move" its merchandise in volume. Newspapers moreover carry a much larger proportion of advertising other than that of merchandise than magazines. Help and situations wanted, amusements, real estate, and similar items of advertising are less affected by industrial depression than manufacturers' merchandise advertising.

In the second place, 1920 was an unusually favorable year, when orders were placed on an inflated basis in the expectation that only a part of the orders would be delivered. Few concerns could hope to maintain the same volume of sales in 1921. A falling off in sales in all such cases does not, therefore, indicate a failure to be charged to advertising. In many cases the reduced sales in 1921 as compared with 1920 actually represent an increase over the last normal year preceding 1920. Third, lines catering to the farmer as a producer could not possibly maintain their volume of sales, with the farmer's purchasing power cut to a fraction of what it was in 1920. Fourth, many of the replies to the questionnaire refer to the fact that merchants were overstocked in 1920, carried their surplus stocks over into 1921, and bought less freely for a time—a decline in orders which advertising could not prevent. These advertisers report a gratifying increase in 1922, which they credit to the increased amount of advertising done in 1921.

On the other hand, the reports of increases in sales cannot all be credited to increased advertising in 1921, since other important factors affected the results. For example, certain lines of business were benefited by the incipient revival of the building industry and the consequent increased demand for building materials.

Bearing in mind the recurring phases of the business cycle, what should be the policy of a manufacturing concern which normally sets aside a certain amount of money for advertising? To this, as to many other questions which have been discussed here, the Dennison Manufacturing Company contributes the most considered judgment. It advocates a normal annual appropriation for advertising. Instead of expending the appropriation actually year by year, however, this company believes in spending it sparingly in good years, when orders are plentiful, and accumulating the savings from the appropriations of the preceding years to be spent during the depression, when increased selling efforts must be made to maintain the volume of business.

This policy seems not only sound and in harmony with the general policy of trying to flatten out the curve of the business cycle, but it seems also to be within the means of most of the concerns which do national advertising.

*Selling.*—What has been said about advertising applies with equal force to other items of selling expense, including salaries of salesmen. Instead of following the usual course of maintaining the selling force at its highest point in times of prosperity and reducing it to the limit during depression, the Dennison Company again reverses the process. One of the steps taken to meet the coming depression, when the company foresaw it months in advance, was the hiring and training of new salesmen, whose number had been allowed to run down during the prosperous period through not filling vacancies. By the time the depression was on, the sales force had been raised about 60 per cent. The company's business had amounted to $10,475,000 in 1919 and increased to $15,-195,000 in 1920. In 1921 it declined to $12,800,000, but when the reduction in the average price per unit is taken into account, the net decline in volume of business was only 5 per cent.

**Regulating Inventories.**—*Losses through Depreciation of Inventories.*— One of the largest items of loss sustained by manufacturing concerns in the break in 1920 was the shrinkage in the values of inventories. The continuous rise in prices for a long time preceding the break, which forced conservative buyers to pay higher and higher prices each time they came into the market for additional supplies, coupled with slow and uncertain deliveries of supplies on the one hand and with pressure from customers for deliveries of finished goods on the other, swept nearly everybody into a mad scramble of buying. When the break finally did come, the depreciation of inventories shook the foundations of many a strong house and seriously affected nearly every house.

It is at this point that constant study of the course of the business cycle becomes imperative for any house which prefers intelligent guidance to blind and dangerous guessing. By familiarizing himself with the course of cycles in the past and following the current reports, the business man can gage with a fair degree of accuracy what phase of the cycle general business conditions of the country are in at any given time.[1]

*The Cycle as a Guide to Buying.*—The business man who watches the cycle will become extremely cautious when a boom develops and buy only enough to keep his plant busy. In fact, he will begin to put on the brakes before activity becomes intense, reduce his volume of purchases, and some time before the peak has been reached gradually work off his inventory until it is reduced to the absolute minimum necessary to operate his plant. When the break finally occurs it will find him with practically no inventory to write down, as the supplies he has on hand can be worked off in a very short time on the remaining unfilled orders. After business is on the downward grade the well-informed executive will continue to be conservative in his purchases, first, because of his smaller requirements and secondly, because of the expectation of still lower prices. As the bottom is neared he will become more liberal in his purchases, increasing still more on the upward grade after the turning point has been passed while prices are still below normal.

The theoretical presentation of such a policy is of course simpler than its practical application. In practice, questions will arise as to whether the critical points marking off the ebb and flow of business have

[1] See Chap. XX.

actually been reached. Hindsight is clearer than foresight and the rule can not work to perfection. A practical working rule has been developed by the Dennison Manufacturing Company which is illustrated in Chart 21. The actual purchases of the company vary "according to the position of actual prices relative to the three lines" in the chart. To quote Mr. Dennison:

The minimum purchase line represents the smallest we dare carry for current needs and the maximum purchase line represents the most that we consider it wise to invest in inventories. Suppose, for instance, on a certain material that

### CHART 21.—JUTE PRICES.

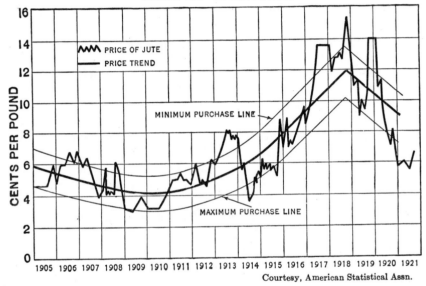

Courtesy, American Statistical Assn.

our standard quantity to order is six weeks' supply. If prices are below the line of secular trend we may buy up to twelve weeks' supply, but if prices are above the line of secular trend we may buy not more than two weeks' supply. We make no attempt to gauge the actual turning point, because we believe that it is impossible to hit it exactly.

As a matter of fact, when the price of copper was very low, the company put in a two years' supply of the metal at a large saving. Similar charts should be kept for every important commodity which a manufacturing concern is using in its processes.

*Watching Inventories.*—The complete utilization of price curves will be impossible without a thorough control of inventories. This implies, in the first instance, the keeping of accurate and up to date statistics of raw materials and finished stock. The inventory, however, is not affected by purchases alone. The stock of raw materials is constantly drawn upon to keep up production. The stock of finished goods is added to by production and reduced by shipments. Hence the necessity of a thorough and unified control of production and sales through the merchandizing department.

Complete control of production must be maintained at all times and it must be planned at least a season and, if possible, a year ahead. The production schedule should be laid out in conference between the merchandise manager and production executives, assisted by the planning department. The production schedule is usually based on the sales during the preceding year with such percentage of estimated increase of sales added for the ensuing year as previous experience justifies. In this connection, charts of sales by the company in previous years showing the effect of the general business cycle on the volume of business of the company taken in conjunction with charts of current general business showing probable trend of business in the near future, should be utilized.

If sales fail to keep up with the production schedule, it is the business of the merchandise manager to go after the sales department. The only alternative to increased sales is a downward revision of the monthly or weekly production schedule before the stock of finished goods has accumulated beyond the limits of safety. If sales exceed production, the schedule must be revised upward, provided manufacturing facilities are available for the purpose. The only other alternative is to refuse new orders.

These adjustments of production schedules up or down must, of course, be made in conference with all the department heads concerned and with a view to avoiding changes in production schedules which would result in idle machinery and unemployment on the one hand or excessive overtime or serious delay in deliveries on orders on the other hand.

*Cancellation of Orders.*—In industries in which cancellation of orders is permitted, this factor must be constantly borne in mind in gaging the size of the inventory at different phases of the cycle. This is another point at which it is especially important to watch the cycle. A chart should be constructed covering the history of the company as far back as available data will permit and showing the cyclical fluctuations in the volume of business and the amount of cancellations each year. The percentage of cancellations at different phases of the cycle should then be ascertained and used as a guide in placing orders for materials from year to year.

*Goods on Order.*—It goes without saying that in estimating inventories, goods on order and en route must be added to goods on hand. The relation between these items varies with each passing phase of the cycle. In busy times, there is always more or less freight congestion on railways and steamship lines, and the execution of orders is comparatively slow, the two factors combining to cause delay in deliveries. There is,

9

therefore, a tendency to order a larger supply than would be necessary with prompt deliveries.

As business begins to slacken, freight congestion disappears and the execution of orders becomes more prompt, with the result that there is a very marked rise of inventories on hand. If to that be added a slower consumption of supplies because of diminished orders, the overstocked condition of the plant becomes still more aggravated.

The factor of variable rates of delivery at different points of the business cycle must therefore be taken into account when placing orders for supplies.

**Plant Extension.**—The rules which guide the buying of supplies can be made to apply with equal success to the problem of when to build plant extensions and add new machinery. The call for more facilities usually comes after the period of prosperity has been well under way or has largely spent itself. As it takes time to plan new buildings and still more time to execute the plans when there is scarcity of labor and materials, and since there is additional delay in equipping the new buildings with machinery, the extension is apt to be completed when the need for it has largely passed owing to a downward swing in the cycle. A new source of loss is then added in the form of increased fixed charges on buildings and equipment acquired at top-notch prices.

Chart 22 illustrates the method followed by the Dennison Manufacturing Company to guide it in its plant construction. This chart of past accomplishment, taken in conjunction with the charts of current business to gauge the outlook for the near future, furnishes a guide which has enabled the company to avoid the pitfalls of building at the crest of the wave on the one hand and waiting too long for new buildings and thereby being forced to turn away business on the other. The future requirements are estimated for several years in advance to cover the period of an entire cycle as shown by past experience. Then, when cost of construction and prices of machinery are below the secular trend, the company anticipates its requirements by building a little beyond the line of normal growth, thus avoiding the necessity of building more than a minimum when costs are above normal.

**Financing.**—The financial difficulties which a business gets into when the slump sets in are due to two causes: First, the losses caused by depreciated inventories, unremunerative prices, and idle plant; second, the lack of ready cash due to the tying up of funds through over-extension at the crest of the cycle. The means of preventing the former set of difficulties have been already discussed. The cash problem will be largely eliminated as a consequence of meeting the other difficulties. The point to be made here is the same that has been made in discussing goods on order: Namely, that neither the absolute amount of cash and other quick assets nor its ratio to current liabilities can be regarded as fixed, as is the usual

custom with business men as well as banks. The ratio will differ with
the phase of the cycle. On the upswing expenses will increase and this
increase will precede the increase in income by many weeks, sometimes

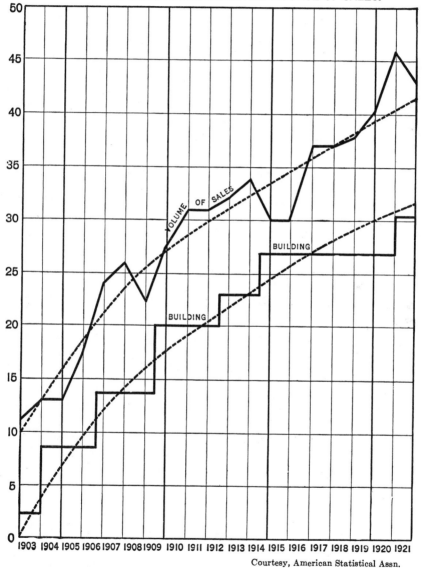

CHART 22.—BUILDING PROGRAM AND COURSE OF SALES.

Courtesy, American Statistical Assn.

months. The ratio of cash to liabilities required to do business properly
is, therefore, much greater at that time than in the downward course of
the cycle. While bank loans are more readily available in the prosperous

phase of the cycle, rates of interest are much higher and add to the already high cost of doing business. The Dennison Manufacturing Company estimates its cash requirements over a period of years covering the probable duration of a cycle in order to guide it in its dividend and reserve policies as well as in other matters affecting the cash position of the company.

**Credit Policy.**—The usual attitude of business concerns is to scrutinize very closely in bad times the credit rating of customers and to be more liberal when business is good. The policy has logic behind it. When business is poor and collections slow there are more failures than usual and the weaker concerns are the first to go to the wall; on the other hand, in good times there are fewer failures, the risk is smaller and the credit department can afford to be lenient. This logic is sound from a short-range point of view.

The Dennison Manufacturing Company looks at this question as on all others from the long-range viewpoint of the cycle as a whole. In flush times when orders begin to tax the capacity of the plant and it is realized that some business has to be unavoidably lost through slow deliveries, the company feels it is in a better position to scrutinize the credit standing of its customers and weed out those who will probably be among the first to feel the pinch of bad times when the turn in the cycle comes. On the other hand, when times are poor and the plant is hungry for orders, the company, without relaxing its scrutiny of the customer's credit standing, is willing to take greater chances. As Mr. Dennison says,

> We expect, of course, a bigger ratio of loss in depressions, but so far as possible we want that loss to result from orders taken when they are needed, rather than from orders taken months before, manufactured on overtime pay, and in conflict with orders for good pay customers.

Mr. Dennison points to the results obtained from following this policy since the last period of prosperity. During the depression from September, 1914 to August, 1915 the company's ratio of losses to sales was 0.52 per cent. In the prosperous year of 1920 they were 0.04 per cent. During the year of depression in 1921 they were only 0.14 per cent. The company was thus able to keep its losses very low though following its novel policy.

### III. PRIVATE VERSUS GOVERNMENT EFFORTS TO COPE WITH THE BUSINESS CYCLE

Such are the main features of a constructive policy which private business has evolved in an attempt to adapt itself to the fluctuations of the business cycle. In the chapters of this book which are devoted to the discussion of government policies and financial devices, these policies are described as policies intended to control the business cycle. Their adoption would undoubtedly have the effect of modifying the business cycle by reducing the extremes of its alternate swings toward inflation and depression.

No such claim is made for the individual business policy outlined in this chapter. All that the individual business firm, no matter how large it may be, can hope to accomplish is to *adapt itself* to the course of the business cycle, so as to take advantage of the variations in prices and in volume of business, instead of being a helpless victim of what have seemed until now blind, unfathomable, and uncontrollable economic forces.

While the complete utilization of the policies outlined may not be feasible for any but the large industrial corporations, at least a partial realization of the program is open even to concerns of moderate size. The study of reports of business forecasting agencies and the compilation of the price tables and charts does not call for an elaborate staff.

While it is true that a single business corporation cannot materially affect the course of the business cycle, a fairly general adoption of the program outlined in this chapter, by concerns of medium and large size would tend to have that effect. When it is remembered that out of a total of 290,105 concerns engaged in manufacturing and mining, 1,019 concerns or 0.4 per cent employing 1,000 or more workers each, give employment to more than 26 per cent of all the wage-earners employed in these industries and that 2 per cent of the plants employ more than 53 per cent of all the workers in these industries, the tremendous aggregate power which this comparatively small number of concerns could exert in modifying the business cycle will become apparent. Apart from the direct effect which they would exert as producers, their immense purchasing power as users of the products of other industries, coupled with the purchasing power of their employees as consumers, would have a great steadying influence on the demand for the products of industries and concerns which might not be taking any initiative or making any conscious efforts to adapt themselves to the business cycle. The cumulative power of private initiative can thus be made a powerful factor in seconding governmental efforts to control the business cycle.

# CHAPTER X

## METHODS OF STABILIZING PRODUCTION AND DISTRIBUTION

### By Sanford E. Thompson

The Thompson and Lichtner Company, Engineers—Boston

### I. INTRODUCTION

During the recent depression, a few manufacturing concerns in nearly all industries maintained almost normal production and employment. This exceptional position in a few cases may have been due to fortunate conditions, but in general the avoidance of appreciable losses and the maintenance of nearly constant employment can be traced to a definite policy adhered to on the rising, as well as on the falling market—a policy based on keen study of the situation and, in a few cases, on scientific analysis of production and of market and banking conditions. Coupled with this, and as an essential feature of it, we find good financial and plant and labor management making for economical production and extensive sales.

Comparatively few establishments found themselves with excessive quantities of raw materials—although there were certain widely advertised exceptions to this rule. On the other hand, the insatiable demand for merchandise late in 1919 and early in 1920, together with the congestion of business channels, especially the railroads, had produced advanced orders of extraordinary volume. These orders led manufacturers to operate at maximum capacity even when the demand suddenly dropped off, so that they had dangerously large stocks of finished products on their hands.

In merchandising the difficulties were similar to those in manufacturing, but the remedies were somewhat different. Excessive purchase orders resulted in surplus stocks and made mark-downs necessary. The saving factor was that the volume of retail sales was maintained throughout the depression with remarkable steadiness. The losses of retailers were therefore confined almost entirely to losses on inventory.

The investigation which is the basis of this chapter took the form not merely of interviewing business executives but particularly of collecting intimate statistical records of purchases, inventories, production, sales, and employment. Of 253 firms approached, confidential statistical data covering a part or all of these divisions were received from 110 concerns, while 94 contributed by correspondence or interviews. Eighty-

134

six concerns were called upon personally. Use was made of all this information in study and comparison, although only a small part even of the exceptionally good material was used directly.

The data have been drawn from concerns that are skilfully managed by keen executives, and also from those concerns representing the forward movement in industry whose results were attained through a scientific analysis of fundamental business conditions within the industry and within the company itself, and who recorded these facts and analyses for future use.

The successful company of both these types approached the decline knowingly and liquidated at the peak, thus conserving its gains from the period of prosperity. The less skilfully managed concerns were forced, step by step, to liquidate and reduce prices with an accompanying restriction of activities and with substantial losses in proportion to their failure to recognize the trend and inaugurate concordant policies. The progressive companies aided in shortening the period of depression by obliging the reactionary establishments to fall into line.

From an economic viewpoint the methods of stabilization resolve themselves into clear cut rules to avoid excess purchases and other expenditures on the rising wave and to entice sales in the trough. In practice, however, the manufacturer must formulate guides to govern the extent of his curtailment of expenditures, must develop administrative policies to cover all phases of the situation, must work out his sales plans in detail for each phase of the cycle, and must control his production with a view to making the right products by methods that will permit attractive selling prices and satisfy his employees. It is necessary, therefore, in the treatment of the subject to take notice of many minor factors which indirectly tend toward stabilization.

## II. MANUFACTURING

*Essentials of Stabilization of Production.*—Methods of mitigating the extremes both of booms and depressions are considered in two divisions, methods of prevention and methods of relief. For prevention the attack must be made during the period of increasing business. Essentials are:

Knowledge by chief executives of principles of economics and of underlying principles governing business fluctuations.

Accumulation of facts and presentation of data thoroughly analyzed to guide business policies and permit planning and budgeting.

Conservation of assets in prosperity, avoiding undue increase in plant and equipment and in dividends.

Management of plant to (a) avoid decrease in unit production, (b) avoid increase in unit overhead, and (c) maintain satisfactory labor conditions and steady employment throughout the year.

Avoidance of excess of inventories of raw materials, material in process, and finished stock.

Avoidance of purchase commitments in excess of financial resources and of reasonably quick use.

Avoidance of excessive sales which result in cancellations.

Service to customers.

To mitigate the effects of depression are needed:

Quick liquidation of inventories and adjustment of prices to replacement values.

Reduction of costs of manufacture, both direct and indirect.

Improvement of quality to enhance demand.

Adoption of selling methods based on accurate analysis of the situation of lines of product that will create demand.

Development of plant and organization for future business.

Part-time operation.

Utilization of profits gained in good times for payments to out-of-work employees.

*Relation of Cyclical to Seasonal Movements.*—Seasonal depressions are not treated in this report but it may be remarked that the remedies for them are in many cases similar to those applied to cyclical depressions. Among these remedies are planning production well in advance, making for stock, developing proper proportion of staples, reducing selling prices, inducing dealers to order early, developing different lines of products for different seasons, introducing new or improved lines, training operatives in several jobs, and making finished parts—especially those involving low material but high labor costs.

**Preventive Measures.**—The avoidance of extremes of inflation as well as the forecasting of events to come is essential for the successful manufacturer. There must be a close determination of broad policies, the recording and study of facts, and the practical application of the conclusions to purchases, manufacturing, and sales.

*Use and Value of Statistics.*—Internal statistics are used as a basis for formulating plans of future activities, to measure the conduct of the business, to forecast sales, production, and purchases, and to coordinate the efforts of the organization. They are generally sent to chief executives and department heads, but many establishments fail to supply these at regular intervals, and again, executives too often give them scant attention. The value of these statistics is in proportion to the amount of study given them. Some establishments give department heads only such statistics as immediately concern them, but the best managed plants give their executives charts showing the activities of the major divisions. In order to draw correct conclusions, detailed data are needed. Many executives demand condensed statistics owing to the pressure of time, but these often conceal valuable information.

The following tabulation gives the subjects analyzed and studied by successful concerns before establishing new policies. The subjects are listed in the order of the percentage of concerns using them.

Graphic charts are best for presenting data.—

| Statistical subjects | Percentage of selected establishments using |
|---|---|
| Production............................................... | 74 |
| New orders............................................. | 71 |
| Costs.................................................. | 60 |
| Markets of raw materials and product..................... | 21 |
| Unfilled orders......................................... | 18 |
| Finance................................................ | 18 |
| Employment............................................ | 18 |
| Purchases.............................................. | 16 |
| Departmental output.................................... | 11 |
| Stock of finished goods ................................. | 9 |
| Consumption of materials in manufacture.................. | 9 |
| Cost of living.......................................... | 9 |
| Shipments.............................................. | 9 |

On these, along with the curves, should be noted any causes of deviation from normal. Charts most commonly used are those comparing production, new orders, shipments, stocks, and unfilled orders. Cancellations should be included. Another chart commonly used compares purchases of materials used in manufacture with consumption of the same materials and inventory by months. This shows whether or not the purchases are running close to the consumption of essential materials and shows pointedly any sharp or extended increases in inventories. Another chart of the financial situation can be prepared from a record of billings, cash receipts, cash disbursements, and bank balances. It shows the trend of the financial status of the company and helps to control credits.

Use of Statistics in Forecasting Business.—The best managed concerns consult and study continually not only internal but also external data. The character and uses of general statistics for guiding business policy, however, are treated in Chapter XX below, so that no more than this brief mention of the practice need be inserted here.

*Organization Needed to Forecast and Carry Out Programs Intelligently.—* The concerns which have succeeded in smoothing out the irregularities in distribution and production attribute their success for the most part to their auxiliary departments, which tend to insure the carrying out of plans, forestalling false moves, and lessening the cyclical depression. The concerns investigated, which as a whole are well organized, maintained auxiliary departments, and in many cases are improving their personnel and planning to carry their development work further. Departments were of the following classes:

| Department | Percentage of selected establishments maintaining |
|---|---|
| Cost............................................. | 100 |
| Statistical........................................ | 80 |
| Employment and service or welfare.................. | 75 |
| Time study....................................... | 70 |
| Planning and control.............................. | 60 |
| Laboratory....................................... | 50 |

The majority of the concerns have developed methods of cost finding which are tied in with their general books. Cost departments have pointed out where economies can be effected, waste eliminated—which in turn permits reduction in selling prices—and further have enabled their companies to know whether they could profitably take business offered.

Statistical data have provided a basis for the formulation of the administrative policies and a better view of the activities of the different divisions of the organization, and have generally increased the efficiency of the organization as a whole.

The employment department and its related sections has proved valuable because of its skill in dealing with the employees on difficult problems, particularly in handling wage adjustments. Certain establishments included in this study have found it unnecessary to make any cuts in wages because of the proficiency of their operating force.

When properly handled, the time study section has provided for fair compensation to employees, and has given the management and men accurate knowledge of the skill and effort required to do a fair day's work. It effects economies in manufacture through development of improved methods and tends to maintain costs at the lowest point even through periods when labor is scarce.

The planning department furnishes material of substantial value to the statistical department in its compilation of data pertaining to the internal activities of the various organizations. Directly or indirectly because of this department, piling up of work in process, raw materials in stores, or finished goods in stock has been avoided. It has assisted in establishing and maintaining low unit costs of production through providing a constant flow of work, has maintained quality, and has made it possible to order more intelligently and closer to actual requirements. Waste and inefficiency have been immediately brought to the attention of the management.

Laboratories have insured maintenance of quality and standards in both raw materials and product.

*Responsibility for Formulation of Policies.*—Concerns which have been conspicuously successful in overcoming the effect of the recent depression followed the policy of charging their directors alone with responsibility for formulating policies on production, sales, and finances. The success with which policies have been carried out is in proportion to the extent to which they were formulated upon a basis of fact, without influence of mental reservation or hopes. In varying degrees department heads have been consulted, but in final decisions the directors have taken action. In no cases noted have the employees been represented. The majorities of the boards of successful establishments have been drawn from the active administrative personnel of the establishment.

In several establishments which had suffered severely, the executives criticised directorates composed of a majority of prominent or moneyed men without detailed knowledge of the business. They said that men of this type, being extremely busy, had not time to consider in detail the problems which the company had to meet. These men determine, in a few minutes, immediately before or at the meeting, the status of the company's affairs and form policies on scant or superficial information. The opinion of such men is recognized as valuable in so far as it reflects the trend in general business, provided it does not dominate the situation.

Where committees of employees have been formed to deal with the management on problems of working conditions, including hours and wages, cooperation has proved advantageous to both parties. This is especially true where facts pertaining to the problems of management have been presented to the employees and their help has been obtained in reducing costs without controversy.

*Value of Budget.*—Practically every business has at least a crude plan of operations. Some establish certain anticipations as to volume of sales desired, volume of production based on estimated sales, amount of stock they will carry, departmental expenses and relation of indirect to direct expense. These are all good so far as they go. Budgets are used in many highly organized establishments, especially those which manufacture for stock. These companies are enthusiastic about this method. The budget basis of operation has coordinated the plans and efforts of the various divisions and financial policies with the resources of the business, requiring thorough analysis of all phases, and forestalling any serious financial errors and miscalculations. There are two classes of budgets, those made for the information of the financial managers, and those which serve as binding appropriations.

Budgets are usually prepared for at least a year and then broken down by months. Use of monthly figures serves to increase accuracy. The results of each month's activities are compared with the budget estimate. Actual transactions may show necessity for adjustment from time to time, but advance plans prevent a drifting policy. The budget restricts purchases and leads the entire organization to consider carefully before requisitioning an article.   Advance planning, and checking results against plans, effect economies not otherwise possible.

The objection has been commonly made that sales cannot be estimated. The fallacy of this objection has been proved in a number of establishments.   Once the estimated volume to be manufactured is pro-rated, the expense necessary to handle it is comparatively easy to figure.

*Production Held Close to Orders.*—Concerns conspicuously successful in the recent depression are about equally divided between those making

CHART 23.—AVERAGE NUMBER OF EMPLOYEES IN CONFECTIONERY INDUSTRY AND NUMBER OF EMPLOYEES IN A WELL MANAGED CONFECTIONERY ESTABLISHMENT.

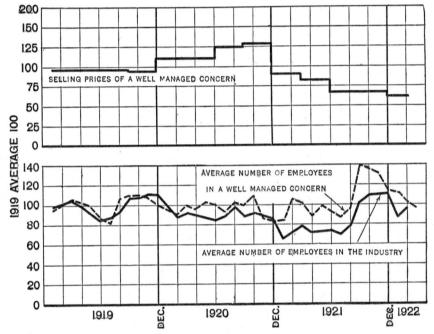

a regularly manufactured product and those which manufacture on special orders.   The majority of the companies keep the volume produced in close relation to the new orders received.

Only three of the companies investigated manufactured for stock; their aim was to maintain balance in their manufacturing by making up a conservative amount of product which analyses of past sales indicated could be sold.   Careful studies are made of market conditions for the sale of the product and the purchase price of essential materials, before embarking upon any extensive manufacturing campaign.

The effect on employment of producing close to orders and pursuing a conservative policy throughout the recent period of inflation is contrasted with the employment situation in the industry at large in Chart 23. This concern which makes confectionery has maintained a relatively more uniform and higher average number of employees than the industry. Even in 1921, the worst year, this establishment found it possible to maintain its standing of 1919. A run-away market had existed in the essential materials used in manufacturing, and many in the industry contracted near the top for their requirements for many months ahead. This concern bought on spot market and, whereas their paper profits were not as great as those of certain other establishments for a time, the net result of the policy has been more profitable in the end. They manufactured two classes of articles, one which they controlled to the time it reached the consumer, and another which they sold in bulk to the retailers. They made substantial reductions in the selling price of the bulk materials and increased the quantity sold for the same price on the other class when the depression started. The volume of business done in the class within their control was maintained. The volume of business in the bulk goods fell off sharply. An investigation showed that many retailers handling their bulk goods had not reduced the selling price, but were maintaining it at the peak, and consequently not selling.

*Purchasing.*—Pyramiding of purchasing is generally conceded to be an important cause of the recent depression. A sudden surge of buying in 1919 was soon reflected in increased orders to the wholesalers and manufacturers. The sudden demand could not be met and buyers received only partial shipments. Buyers became panicky, bought on spot market, doubled and trebled orders, thereby causing a fictitious market. All this time prices soared. The consuming demand was soon satisfied and early in 1920 further increase of prices was accompanied by a declining volume of sales. Producers found orders falling off and cancellations started in a flood.

Many manufacturers condemned severely the practice of cancellation and blame it for most of their losses. Many have only themselves to blame, for cases have been brought to light in which manufacturers accepted orders from their customers for five times the volume ordinarily placed or accepted. Had credits been properly approved they would have had less cause for complaint. Many ordered blindly, at no time realizing fully the extent of their unfilled purchase commitments, and going far beyond what they could possibly use within a reasonable time.

Too few companies have any tangible record of the amount of money involved in their purchase commitments outstanding. Public accountants in conducting examinations in the boom period found necessary a study of unfilled purchase orders outstanding to establish the extent of contingent liabilities and profit or loss. A running balance of purchase commitments has served to put a brake on over-ordering.

The relation of purchases of raw materials to volume actually used is shown in Chart 24.   A study of the fundamental conditions at the time orders were placed in 1920 and the relation of purchases to consumption would have shown the need for conservatism.   A chart of this type, with purchase commitments added, will prove a valuable adjunct to the statistical department.

CHART 24.—MATERIALS USED IN MANUFACTURE, MATERIALS PURCHASED, AND INVENTORY OF RAW MATERIALS.

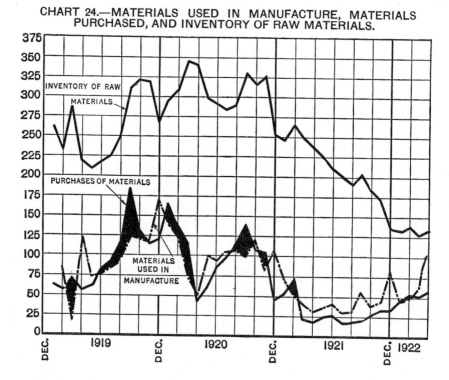

Concerns investigated have variously consulted the following indexes before making purchase commitments:

New orders
Market condition of essential materials
Previous consumption
Reported supply available
Production plans
Normal supply maintained regardless of condition
Present prices
Prices in past
Quality
Salesmen's reports

Whatever indexes have been consulted, the majority of the successful concerns have bought close to actual requirements.   Many of these had opportunity to speculate, for some are required to order from four to six months ahead. They have not done so, being satisfied to make a conservative manufacturing profit rather than gamble on market fluctuations. The purchasing policy of a conservative and conspicuously successful concern from the point of view of earnings is shown by Chart 25. This house buys on the basis of orders in hand. Four months must be allowed

CHART 25.—PURCHASES AND UNFILLED BUSINESS.

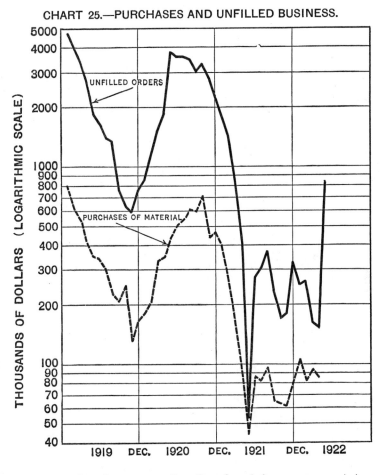

for delivery and orders are ordinarily placed for an amount to carry them approximately sixty days after receipt. Beyond extending rather liberal credits this company is handicapped in stimulating sales in a period of depression because of the nature of the product. Cautious buying in 1920 prevented serious liquidation. A normal sixty days' supply would suffice for two years on the basis of 1921 production.

*Selling Prices.*—Due weight given quality, nothing so affects demand as does the proper fixing of selling prices. It played its important

part in the period of inflation and the following depression.   The bases
used in establishing prices by the concerns investigated are:

>                Market conditions
>                Costs
>                Competition
>                Cost plus basis
>                Material costs
>                Prime costs
>                Labor markets

Market conditions (meaning the available supply of the commodity
being priced, its existing market price, and anticipated cost of replacement) have been given first consideration in the setting of prices to
maintain sales.   The price situation is well within the control of the
consumer-goods manufacturer, while on the other hand, the producer-goods
manufacturer must prevail upon his customers to establish policies that
will be in line with the economic trend.

CHART 26.—AVERAGE NUMBER OF EMPLOYEES IN AUTOMOBILE INDUS-
TRY AND NUMBER EMPLOYED BY A PROGRESSIVE MANUFACTURER.

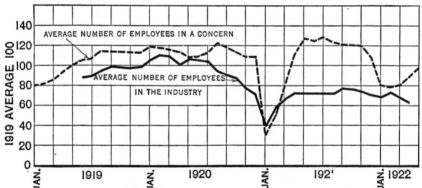

The effect of establishing proper selling prices on the employment
situation of an individual concern is shown in Chart 26.   This manufacturer has led the way in reducing selling prices in the industry and
he has fared better than the other establishments whose reductions have
been made piecemeal and much slower.   Every economy in the conduct
of this conspicuously successful company is passed on to the consumer.

Relation of Selling Price to Cost.—A manufacturer whose name is
known to almost everybody says in a recent issue of *System:*

> Manufacturing is not buying low and selling high.   It is the process of buying
> materials fairly, and by the smallest possible addition to cost, transforming those
> articles into a consumable product and giving it to the consumer.   Gambling,
> speculating, and sharp dealing tend only to clog this progression.   Any economy
> of production will result in a glut of goods if the price advantages of the economy

in manufacture are retained by the producer instead of being passed on to the consumer. Every price has been a challenge to ourselves. It has always been below the lowest cost we could figure out in advance. We have then gone ahead with this new price hanging over us and have found so many new and better ways and less expensive ways of doing things, that the price which once—under the ordinary method of calculation—would have been considered impossible, became very profitable. Competition is disregarded.

The notion persists that prices should be kept up. On the contrary, good business, large consumption, depends upon their going down. The price of our product is roughly 33 per cent of what it was eighteen years ago. That price to the consumer is only 33 per cent of what it was, but we pay higher wages, higher prices for material, and have a better product than we had eighteen years ago, and in consequence, our volume of business has increased some thousands of fold. This increase is in proportion as we better serve our customers and for no other reason.

To be a leader in his industry, especially in times of prosperity, a manufacturer must think less of his competitors' prices and more of the consumer. In periods of depression, he must think in terms of replacement values.

*Profit-sharing Plan for Executives.*—Several cases have come to light of establishments in which officials receive comparatively low salaries, not in excess, for example of $7,000 to $10,000 per year, but which have a contingent arrangement to participate in the net earnings of the business, such that staff men may receive even greater earnings than they might reasonably expect on a straight salary basis. In a period of prosperity these corporations can well afford to compensate their executive staff from earnings more generously than can be profitably done in lean years. On the other hand, in periods when strictest economies must be effected, this low salary arrangement makes a substantial reduction in the total overhead charges and affects the unit overhead costs.

There has been in vogue for years in England an arrangement in many corporations by which "management shares" are reserved for the directors and active chief administratives. Provision is made in the by-laws for setting aside a certain proportion of the net earnings after the dividend requirements of other classes of stock issued have been provided for. The income credited to management shares is distributed at regular intervals to the holders of the management securities. This serves to attract the most competent administrators.

This plan is gaining favor in this country, as is witnessed by the provision for management shares in the articles of incorporation of certain of the new and large corporate enterprises.

**Relief from Effect of Depressions.**—Once the change from the upward trend in prices and volume is definitely recognized and the period of downward revision of prices is certain, the sooner the policies of any establishment can be changed to meet the new conditions, the better.

10

Stimulation of sales by a reduction in prices is shown in Chart 27. This automobile manufacturer led the way in reductions, making the first in September, 1920.   The immediate effect was an increase in sales.   The volume dropped off during the usual dull season in the industry, but in the spring of 1921 buying at the same price level substantiated the wisdom of the policy.   Further reductions helped to create a volume of sales not enjoyed by any other establishment in the industry.   This policy was made possible by increased production per employee and reduction in manufacturing cost.

CHART 27.—EFFECT OF SELLING PRICE ON SALE OF AUTOMOBILES.

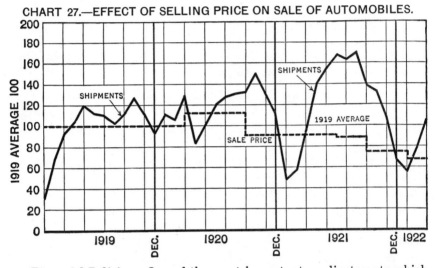

*Financial Policies.*—One of the most important readjustments which must be made is in financial policies.   During times of prosperity, profits are easily made and credits in many instances are extended too liberally, as shown by the increased volume of orders which were placed in many cases without regard to how payment could be made.   Many concerns are without any means of knowing at any time the extent of their commitments, though it behooves all establishments to maintain a close control of both credits and commitments.

The policies of finance which are effective in stabilizing business are:

Conservation of assets when prosperous
Close watching of credits
Liberal extensions of time of payments
Thorough and prompt liquidation
Marking prices down to replacement
Smaller margins of profit

*Conservation of Assets.*—Manufacturers have been prompted in periods of prosperity to expand their plants and commitments on the basis of seemingly unlimited demand for their product.   The fixed charges which accompany the construction of increased capacity in boom periods

at high cost are a factor not given proper consideration. Such additions
with proper study of fundamental conditions to forecast the demand,

CHART 28.—TOTAL YEARLY EARNINGS AND NUMBER OF EMPLOYEES IN
A PROGRESSIVE BOOT AND SHOE ESTABLISHMENT.

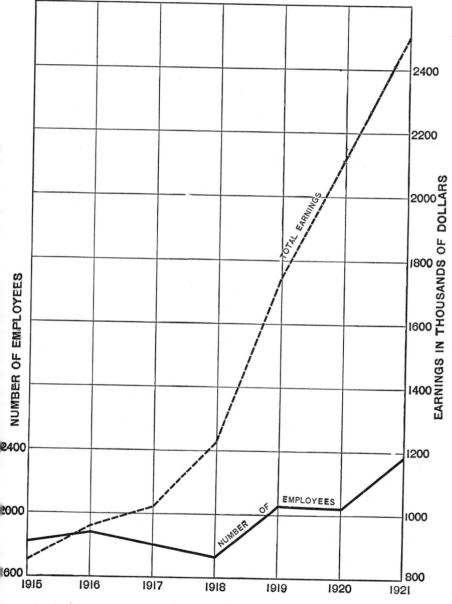

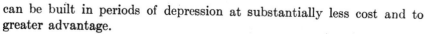

can be built in periods of depression at substantially less cost and to
greater advantage.

The large profits piled up in boom times tempt many to distribute large dividends with frequent extras. Depleting current assets in this manner is as injurious to the financial status of a business as any excessive expenditures for additional plant facilities or speculative investments in essential materials.

Liquidation.—When the time of deflation comes, liquidation must be prompt and thorough. The effect of this is shown by Chart 28, giving the number of employees on the pay-roll of a boot and shoe manufacturer and their total earnings by years from 1915 to 1921 inclusive. When this

CHART 29.—COMPARISON OF UNIT COST OF MANUFACTURING, UNIT SELLING PRICE, AND SHIPMENTS.

(ILLUSTRATION FROM THE METAL TRADES INDUSTRY)

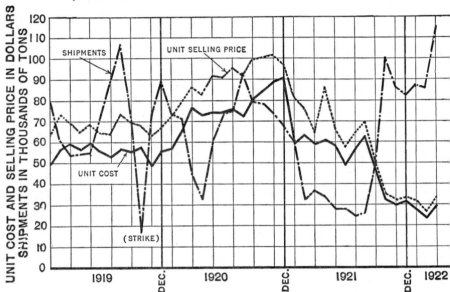

organization faced the depression, it liquidated promptly. Selling price of product was reduced not only to the basis of the liquidated market price of their basic materials at the time but to the anticipated further liquidation within a reasonable period as indicated by hide values, this latter basis of value having been determined after consultation with and getting advice from leading tanners. Their activities were confined increasingly to production and sale of staples in greater volume. Sales efforts were renewed, and when orders fell off, the company continued manufacturing for stock. This policy attracted sales in sufficient volume to permit the factories to be operated at capacity, and losses from inventory adjustment were more than offset by profits from operations.

Smaller Margin of Profit.—Chart 29 shows the relation of the unit selling price to unit cost of manufacture and the effect of selling price upon sales.  This illustration drawn from the metal trades is conspicuous as it shows markedly the effect of the policy of closer margins of profits and the early recovery.  Reductions in cost of manufacture have been passed on to the manufacturers using the output of this company as their basic material.

Another concern which operated overtime during the period of depression, liquidated promptly and thoroughly, brought prices to rock bottom, made reductions in their selling prices, improved the quality of their product, and substantially reduced their margin of profit.  The employees were called together and informed that costs must be cut and production jammed through as orders were received.  Reductions of 25 per cent were made in wages.  The president of the company called upon his customers and told them that he would sell his output at substantially lower prices which he quoted definitely.  He prevailed upon his customers to obtain reductions from other manufacturers whose product was necessary in manufacturing and urged them to pass on to their consumers these reductions in cost of products.  The company applied the same rules to the executives as to the machine operators.  All worked the same hours and operated under the same conditions.  Economy is the watch-word in the plant and talks are frequently given to the force on this subject. A complete system of costs enables the executives to obtain weekly reports of departmental expenses and small items are carefully observed to see that there are no wastes.

*Administrative Policies.*—The administrative policies which have served to smooth out the irregularities of production and sales during periods of depression are:

> Introducing improved machinery
> Adding new products
> Reducing number of products
> Giving more for money than competitors
> Selling short
> Increasing auxiliary departments
> Increasing efficiency of individual
> Improving morale of organization
> Improving plant facilities
> Dovetailing seasonal articles

**Improved Machinery Boomed.**—Manufacturers of producer-goods have found the introduction of improved machinery or introduction of new products of great value in stimulating sales and manufacture.  The accomplishments of one manufacturer of producer-goods are shown in contrast to general conditions in his industry by Chart 30.  This establishment retained a higher percentage of its employees than the average in the trade.  Success was won through the introduction of improved machinery which they developed in periods of prosperity and used as a means of inducing new orders in periods of depression. Their customers are more disposed to try improved articles at that time. Reductions amounting to 15 to 30 per cent in selling prices have been made. They have manufactured for stock certain articles which are known to be good sellers. Their warehouse has been filled with standard lines, especially machine parts, and they have repaired machinery, jigs, and general equipment to retain their organization. The introduction of new lines has generally stimulated the sale of the regularly manufactured product.

Short Selling.—Short selling has been successfully employed by manufacturers who use crops as a basic material. This practice has also been adopted by certain producer-goods manufacturers who have an opportunity of taking long-term contracts. One concern took an order at substantially less than market, after it had made a careful study of

CHART 30.—NUMBER OF EMPLOYEES IN MACHINE MANUFACTURING INDUSTRY AND THE NUMBER OF EMPLOYEES IN A SINGLE PLANT.

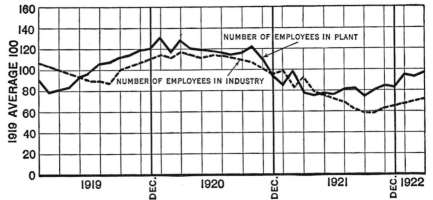

the trend. The chief executives firmly believed that the trend of prices was downward, and whereas the contract as drawn up would require delivery of a certain portion of the product in the near future, and would cause a loss, they felt prices would be so much lower when the contract was terminated that the ultimate result would be a large profit. Their prediction based upon careful study was correct.[1]

Internal Development.—Many establishments, even those highly organized, have found it advisable to increase the individual proficiency of their employees through the development of improved methods which are brought about through the auxiliary departments.

[1] The method of short-selling described above is a form of speculation which may result in losses unless protected by some kind of covering contract such as that used by cotton cloth manufacturers.

Low overhead has been over-emphasized. It is low unit cost that makes for profit. As the cases cited show, a proper increase of total overhead expenses by additions to auxiliary departments lowers direct cost at all periods and in prosperous periods actually reduces unit overhead by increasing production. But overhead expenses at all times should be confined to such things as increase the production or sales per man.

*Manufacturing Policies.*—One of the most substantial losses sustained by manufacturers during the recent depression arose from closing the factory. The successful manufacturers have not found it necessary to shut down their plants and have avoided the resulting impairment of liquid assets. The policies which have been pursued successfully are:

> Improvements in methods of manufacture
> Reductions in cost of manufacture
> Manufacture of improved quality
> Manufacture for stock
> Assembling of parts
> Best quality for price
> Increasing flexibility of workmen

The staff of employees retained by a conspicuously successful manufacturer of producer-goods is shown in Chart 31. This company before the depression manufactured small lots for a few customers on a specialty

CHART 31.—AVERAGE NUMBER OF EMPLOYEES IN A GROWING ESTABLISHMENT.

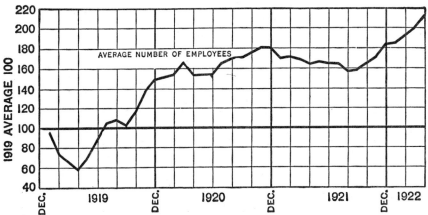

basis. Everything was done to please and hold customers, but nothing to obtain new business. These policies were changed to meet the requirements of new conditions when the depression started. The introduction of improved methods has resulted in better quality, increased output per man, substantial reductions in unit costs, and increased volume of business.

The steps taken which contributed to the volume of business handled by this company were:

Improvement of quality of product
Introduction of automatic machinery for production of small parts
Explanation of situation to employees, who accepted a wage reduction of 28 per cent
Development of greater production per man, so that total earnings were not decreased
Introduction of: Time Study
                Planning and Control
                Modern System of Accounting
                Perpetual Inventories
                Cost System
                Budget Plan of Control
Change in sales policy from narrow distribution of many products to wide distribution of products best suited for quantity production
Increase in advertising, pushing home the fact that their basic materials were a certified and guaranteed product. Samples of certificates with catalogue were sent out by registered mail. Advertising was concentrated on the dealer.
Increase in sales force
Reduction of selling prices 45 per cent
Opening an export department
Improvement of plant facilities for manufacturing
Purchasing close to requirements
Organization of Joint Conference Committee consisting of six representatives of workmen and same number of executives to decide all questions of hours, wages, and working conditions
Improvement in morale of organization.

On January 15, 1922, the company had four months' unfilled orders ahead, and advanced prices about 10 per cent for future business. This increase in price represents the extent to which prices now exceed those in the trade. Despite this, orders continue to be received in large volume, substantially because of improved quality.

Manufacturing for Stock.—The most commonly used policy in overcoming depression has been to manufacture for stock. Numerous cases were found however where companies had followed this policy with success in the past, but failed during the latest depression. Data from the books of companies investigated show that manufacturing for stock is a dangerous policy to pursue. It not only means piling up inventories of high-cost materials, but also, unless most efficient methods of manufacture are used, it is likely to mean excessive costs due to high wages and waste. Only those companies were successful in their plan which made a thorough study of past performances, determined the grade and classes of product which had a stable market, and manufactured only the quantity which they knew with reasonable certainty from analysis of their records could be disposed of within a reasonable period.

Selling Policies.—Maintenance of uniform production is dependent upon continuity of sales. The sales policies that have been employed successfully are:

Price guarantee
Staples pushed
Specialties pushed
Following up inquiries
Free deals
Premiums
Concentration on best sellers
Bonus to salesmen on heavily stocked lines
Renewed sales effort
Obsolete lines pushed
Assistance to dealers
Demonstrations
Increased advertising

CHART 32.—INFLUENCE OF SELLING PRICE ON VOLUME OF NEW ORDERS.

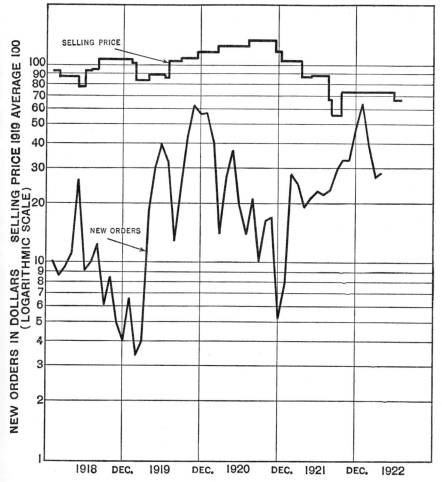

**Effect of Selling Policies on Sales.**—A manufacturer of producer-goods by reductions in selling price of nearly 50 per cent has been able to increase his volume of business in the depression as shown in Chart 32. Advertising and development of improved methods of manufacturing which reduced cost and improved quality have contributed to this.

Chart 33 shows what one boot and shoe manufacturer has accomplished through marking down inventories and selling prices to replacement value and liquidating thoroughly. This company pushed specialties, disposed of obsolete lines, and watched credits carefully.

CHART 33.—EMPLOYEES AND EARNINGS IN A BOOT AND SHOE MANUFACTURING PLANT.

Concentration on Best Sellers.—Concentration on best sellers is in effect the same as reducing the number of products manufactured. This plan has operated successfully in numerous instances. A metal working concern has added new lines having the same distribution as the old, which can be produced with existing equipment. They have concentrated their advertising and display on fifteen best sellers of the regularly manufactured products. They have tried to advertise in a manner to reach distributors and point out the profits which can be made by handling their goods.

Bonuses on Heavily Stocked Lines.—A manufacturer of producer-goods whose business has been built up on earnings, has stimulated all division heads and gives bonuses to the salesmen on heavily stocked lines.

Service to Customers.—Far too many concerns adopt an independent attitude when business is booming knowing that at the time they can readily dispose of their output. Quality is frequently sacrificed to quantity in such periods. When readjustment comes, these same companies find old friends gone and must incur large expense to overcome their reputation in the trade for high-handed dealings.

One successful establishment has as its watchword "service." Its sales force and advertising were increased to stimulate sales during the depression, but it relied mostly upon the service given its customers.

Eighty per cent of the business done by this company is for special orders. Prompt deliveries are urged by customers, and the company

CHART 34.—COMPARISON OF PURCHASES, SALES, EMPLOYEES, AND EARNINGS IN A CERTAIN ESTABLISHMENT.

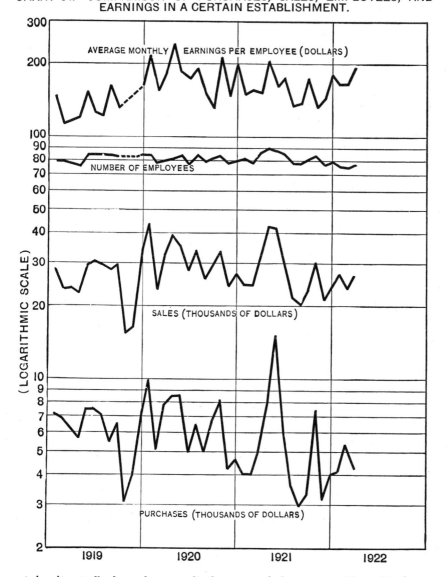

retains its staff of employees whether occupied or not. Chart 34 shows the effect of this company's policy upon its force of employees which has remained practically uniform throughout the years of prosperity and depression. The fluctuations in earnings are due to income from overtime in addition to their regular guaranteed weekly rate.

**Reputation for Technical Knowledge.**—A company manufacturing machinery ascribed its success in overcoming the depression largely to its reputation for technical knowledge of the industry in which the equipment is used. They are continually consulted on problems of manufacture and requested to furnish suggestions for means of removing certain defects in existing methods.

**Additional Information Desired to Forecast Trend.**—Business men have expressed a desire for additional information promptly compiled which will enable them to determine with greater accuracy the probable volume of business in the future. Listed in the order of the number of establishments requesting each item, the desired information is:

> Unfilled orders in the industry
> Current volume of business in the industry
> Production in the industry
> Information as to position in business cycle
> New orders in the industry
> Hours operated in the various establishments
> Wages of employees in the industry
> Shipments in the industry
> Supply of raw materials available
> Experience of other establishments in industry in periods of depression
> Volume of purchases of raw material
> Prosperity of the country
> Railroad construction
> Data on foreign business
> Proportion of indirect workers to direct.

**Labor.**—It is noticeable in our examination that the establishments maintaining definite standards of production with the cooperation of the workers were able to keep their manufacturing costs at a minimum even during the expansion.

Another important factor in the situation is the basic wage rate. The fluctuation in money values necessitates wage changes in both directions. While the general trend of wages through the years has been and must continue to be upward, reductions may be inevitable at times of extreme deflation in business.

*Methods of Providing Relief in Depression.*—Few concerns were found which provided a careful well-thought-out labor policy during the depression. There was a general tendency to make for stock as long as possible. As has been noted, however, this plan while of great value in meeting seasonal fluctuations, is of doubtful expediency in cyclical depressions. The policies followed by various firms may be summarized as follows:

> Operate a few days per week
> Operate part time per day
> Rotate employment in alternate weeks with half the force each week

Some firms have given vacations with pay. Others have encouraged bank deposits through the company by employees. Assistance in obtaining employment elsewhere has been given, although with small results. Most companies keep in touch with their people out of work and assist in cases of illness. Few concerns, however, are yet giving attention to definite plans for stabilizing the income of the worker by remuneration during periods of forced unemployment.

Relief funds have been developed to a small extent. Under one plan the workers contribute 1 per cent of their weekly earnings for thirteen weeks, or until a sufficient amount is laid aside for estimated requirements.

*Repairs and Maintenance.*—Many successful companies have found it advantageous to make physical improvements and changes that will avoid shut-downs and reduce manufacturing cost when business improves. This policy provides employment to labor when other jobs are difficult to obtain.

### III. MERCHANDISING

**Scope of Retail Study.**—Just as in the study of manufacturing activities, special attention has been paid in the examination of merchandising to methods that have proved successful in stabilizing sales and profits. As it was impossible to cover more than a small fraction of 1,000,000 or more retail shops in the United States, the search for successful methods was confined largely to the more successful stores.

In addition to specialty and department stores, several chain-store systems have been included. Their figures differ from those of individual stores in reflecting general rather than local conditions.

**Essentials of Stabilizing Retail Trade.**—Studies of merchandising indicate:

That, in most lines, seasonal fluctuations in volume of business are more pronounced than cyclical fluctuations.

That retail stores suffered more in the recent depression from shrinkage of inventory values than from falling off in business.

That there is a lack of effective contact and team work between the manufacturer, the wholesaler or jobber, and the retailer.

That there is a lack of appreciation of the value of external statistics in forecasting changes in conditions.

That there is a need for comprehensive information regarding the statistical position of all important commodities.

That there is a need for greater development of methods of laying out buying schedules and of coordinating the three main functions of merchandising, *i.e.*, management, buying, and selling.

During 1918 and 1919 the retail merchant made more money than ever before. When the break came in 1920 much of this profit was in the form of large inventories bought at high prices.

It soon became apparent to the more farsighted dealers that there was small chance of disposing of these stocks except at greatly reduced prices. Some promptly accepted this way out, marked prices down, cleaned their shelves, and bought such goods as they needed at bargain prices.

It was soon demonstrated that this was the part of wisdom. Many merchants, however, failed to appreciate this fact for many months, and as a result suffered much more severely than those who acted with greater promptness.

**Fluctuations in Retail Trade.**—Retail stores reported a surprisingly constant volume of sales from 1919 to 1921. Whereas most factories shut down or ran short time with reduced force, retail stores reported

CHART 35.—INDEX NUMBERS OF AVERAGE MONTHLY SALES OF 159 DEPARTMENT STORES AND OF 4 LARGE MAIL ORDER HOUSES.

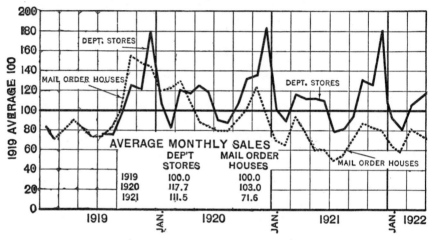

comparatively slight reductions in volume of sales or of employment. This is true in spite of the fact that sales are usually stated in terms of dollars. When prices are falling, sales in dollars will tend to decrease even though no falling off occurs in the physical volume of merchandise sold. Sales figures of retail stores are presented in Charts 35, 36, and 37. These charts bring out forcibly the surprising maintenance of retail business (excepting that of mail order houses which reflects less purchasing in farming districts) during the recent depression.

*Luxury Stores Hit.*—Certain lines of retail stores, however, experienced a falling off in trade. These are mainly "luxury" stores, jewelry and music stores being notable examples. Such stores also are affected severely by seasonal fluctuations.

*Losses Due to Shrinkage of Inventory Values.*—While the average retail store did not suffer as much as might have been expected from lack of business, most retailers did take very severe losses as a result of the shrinkage in inventory values due to the general process of deflation.

*Effect of Mark-downs on Sales and Profits.*—To illustrate the serious losses in 1920 caused by shrinkage in inventory values, figures covering

CHART 36.—INDEX NUMBERS OF AVERAGE MONTHLY SALES OF 16 CHAINS OF GROCERY STORES, 4 FIVE- AND TEN-CENT STORE CHAINS, AND 6 CHAINS OF DRUG STORES.

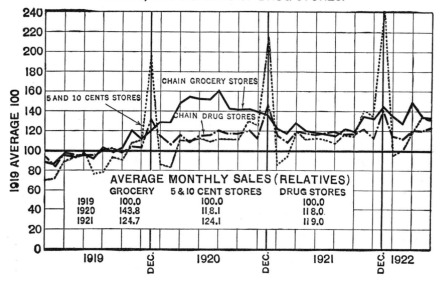

the operations of a group of thirty-six department stores are given.[1]   These stores range from $250,000 to $5,000,000 total sales per year.   Compara-

CHART 37.—INDEX NUMBERS OF AVERAGE MONTHLY SALES OF 5 CHAINS OF SHOE STORES AND 4 MUSIC STORES.

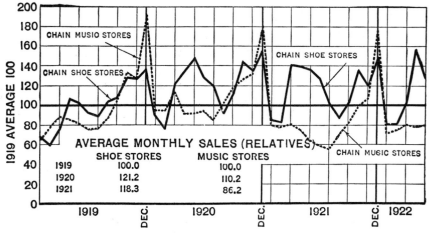

tive figures are exchanged by these stores and their methods are probably somewhat better than the average store of the same class.   Figures taken

[1] **By courtesy of Mr. James W. Eadie, Jr.**

from a group of this size tend to eliminate individual peculiarities and therefore show general tendencies.

MERCHANDISE CONSUMED

|  | 1919 | 1920 | 1921 |
|---|---|---|---|
| Sales.............................. | $28,529,000 | $33,381,000 | $30,523,000 |
| Mark-downs....................... | 1,768,000 | 4,210,000 | 2,462,000 |
| Merchandise shortages............. | 584,000 | 837,000 | 710,000 |
|  | $30,881,000 | $38,428,000 | $33,695,000 |

In 1919 these stores received 92.4 cents for every dollar's worth of goods disposed of, they marked down merchandise 5.7 cents and had merchandise shortages due to losses, theft, and waste of 1.9 cents. In 1920 they received only 86.9 cents for each dollar's worth disposed of, took mark-downs of 10.9 cents, and suffered shortages of 2.2 cents.

CHART 38.—SALES AND PRICES OF SHOES SOLD BY 202 CHAIN SHOE STORES.

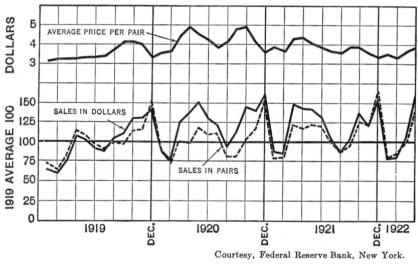

Courtesy, Federal Reserve Bank, New York.

Expenditures were 86.8 cents per dollar of merchandise disposed of in 1919 and 87.1 cents in 1920, a difference of only 0.3 cents. Yet because of the shrinkage in values represented by the increase in mark-downs and the increase in merchandise shortages, these stores show a drop from a net profit of 5.6 cents per dollar of sales in 1919 (one of the highest averages of recent years) to a loss of 0.2 cents per dollar of sales in 1920.

While total expenditures rose from 86.8 cents per dollar of sales in 1919 to 87.1 in 1920, this rise was caused by an increase of 1 cent in amount paid for goods, while other expenses, such as salaries, wages, rent, light, heat, power, advertising, interest, depreciation, taxes, etc., decreased 0.7 cents per dollar of sales, leaving a net increase of 0.3 cents.

*Physical Volume of Sales.*—Figures showing the physical volume of shoes sold by several chains operating a total of 202 retail shoe stores are presented in Chart 38. It will be noted that sales for this large group showed an increase over 1919 in succeeding years, whether expressed in dollars or in pairs.

*Effects of Seasonal Fluctuations.*—In general the seasonal fluctuations have proved more important than cyclical variations as will be noted in the charts presented above. In addition to the wide differences from month to month which are indicated on the charts, there are also daily and even hourly fluctuations. These are of considerable importance; in most cases they are regular and can be predicted with considerable accuracy.

Dealers must provide stores large enough to take care of the peak loads, and in lines where trained and experienced clerks are necessary, a larger force than is required by the normal demand must be employed. Extra delivery costs are incurred and larger stocks must be maintained than would be needed if these variations could be reduced.

**Methods of Minimizing Effects of Business Depressions.**—Reports show three principles which form a basis for the most effective course of action for the retail store before and during periods of depression.

Study of conditions and prompt action which make it possible to anticipate and provide against the decline in values, before the actual break occurs.

Avoidance of heavy inventories at all times.

Prompt reductions of price to reflect lower replacement costs in time of falling markets.

*Forecasting and Business Barometers.*—Individual retail stores are affected more severely by local than by general conditions. For this reason many business barometers are less serviceable to the merchant than they are to the manufacturer who has a national field of distribution. Independent research work on the part of the retail store is needed to tie in local conditions with the general trends. Another important factor for the local merchant to consider is that all parts of the country are not affected at the same time by changes in business. He must study the geographical path followed by changing conditions.

*Need of Statistics of Production and Stocks on Hand.*—There is a widespread demand among retail merchants for statistical information regarding stocks of commodities on hand and for figures showing production. Many dealers feel that they were the victims of misrepresentation regarding the situation in the spring of 1920. Statements from dealers

11

in all parts of the country agree that they were strongly advised by manufacturers to place large orders, on the ground that there was a shortage of goods, and that only those who were prompt in placing orders could expect to have them filled.[1]  In certain instances, retailers say they were urged to order more than they actually needed, to allow for scaling down. The manufacturer then promptly and most unexpectedly filled orders completely, and having reduced his stocks announced price reductions. Many retailers claim that they were thus caught with large inventories and forced to take heavy losses in mark-downs based upon replacement costs.[2] In one case noted, a manufacturer who claimed inability to make deliveries on contracts was found to have his warehouses piled high with goods which he was holding back for further price increases.

*Accumulation of Stocks Important Cause of Break in Prices.*—In view of the maintenance of retail sales during the period of depression, the question arises: Why with the outlet running nearly full, should there be a surplus of stock in the country?

In the first place the growth of retail trade from 1919 to 1920 demanded some 17 per cent more in value of merchandise in 1920 than in 1919 while retail prices rose about 11 per cent. This demand of itself suddenly thrown on the manufacturer in the latter part of 1919 might well suffice to congest production and to speed the rise in prices. Increase in orders and transportation delays necessitated longer time for delivery and the piling up in the factories of some raw materials with shortages in others. Long-time deliveries necessitated abnormally large orders by distributors as well as manufacturers. There was also occasional speculation by manufacturers and retailers who continued to buy surplus because of the rising prices.

Stocks produced at abnormally high intrinsic costs became a drug in the market. During 1921 and the early months of 1922 there was a considerable reduction in the quantity of new materials produced and as a result much of this surplus stock was consumed.

These various facts are of great importance for both the manufacturer and the retailer, because with the continuation of the business cycle the same ill conditions will be produced unless counteracted by sound policies and economical production and distribution.

These things bring out forcibly the need for closer contact all along the line from the producer of raw materials to the seller of finished products.

[1] What is needed is a further development and extension of the excellent statistical information now published by the Federal Reserve Banks, the Department of Commerce, and a number of public and private agencies.

[2] Needless to say, this presentation of cancellation from the retailers' viewpoint is far from a complete discussion of an extremely complicated subject. Compare the discussion of cancellation from the manufacturers' viewpoint earlier in this chapter, and the discussion from the legal viewpoint in Chap. XI, below.

*Practical Value of Production Statistics.*—One way in which retail stores may use production statistics is illustrated by a large department store in the East. Its statistical department made arrangements to obtain regularly current figures showing production of silk goods and shoes in a number of large factories. They plotted for each of these two commodities: (*a*) normal (estimated) sales, (*b*) actual sales, (*c*) production figures from factories. Early in 1920 an inspection of these curves showed that production figures were increasing at a greater rate than normal estimated retail sales, while actual sales (retail) were falling behind. Soon they began to get reports of cancelled orders for silk; but production figures continued to climb while sales fell further behind expectations. The store then decided to liquidate its stock of silk goods and had practically completed the process before other stores had any idea of what was coming. A similar situation soon developed in the shoe department, and again the store was able to reduce its inventories without much loss. When this series of events had occurred in silk goods, closely followed by shoes, the management foresaw what was in prospect all along the line and made preparations to meet conditions in all departments. As a result comparatively slight losses were suffered. The management, in fact, was actually in a position to recoup itself, taking advantage of "distress sales," so-called, to buy cheap and offer bargains to customers, while their competitors were taking severe mark-downs on goods bought at boom prices.

*Importance of Statistical Position of Commodities.*—This topic has been emphasized because it brings out one of the most effective methods of stabilizing business during cyclical depressions (that is, forecasting events, and guiding policies by the statistical position of commodities), and because reports from stores, trade associations, banks, and statistical organizations show forcibly the need of more complete figures of production and sales.

Buying must necessarily be more or less in the dark without some such foundation, and close contact between manufacturer and retail dealer can be satisfactorily developed only in some such way. Figures of this kind afford a quick corrective to tendencies to over-increase productive capacities, and would do much towards eliminating periodic unemployment.

**Merchandising Methods and Store Management.**—In the inquiry into methods of combating and overcoming the effects of cyclical business depressions, we were often met by the statement that not much had been done by retail stores mainly because they had not felt an appreciable falling off in business.

During periods of depression when competition is most keen and when there is an increasing tendency to buy closely and to compare values, it becomes of the greatest importance to reduce the cost of merchandizing to a minimum.   This means an intensification and development of efficient methods of management including methods of buying, selling, and financing as well as store management.

*Methods and Policies of Purchasing.*—Coordination of purchases to sales is particularly important during a time of depression as the basis for securing frequent stock turnover coupled with a sufficiently complete line to avoid loss of sales resulting from an inability to meet customers' requirements.   This coordination is being effected in many of the larger stores by an executive known as the merchandise manager.   Each buyer then is no longer independently responsible for his department.

One large department store in the East which is noted for its management methods reports:

The quantity of stock carried depends on market conditions.   We carry low stocks on falling market.   Records are kept of calls for merchandise not in stock and sales lost.   Over-buying is guarded against by departmental budget, layout plan of purchases, sales, stock on hand at beginning of the period, also mark-up, mark-down, and gross profit.   For some departments we have a model stock plan, showing distribution of budget over various lines by styles, price, size, etc.   This plan is complete about six months before buying season.   There is a definite app opriation for each depa tment and line which limits the amount which a buye  may spend.   A study of sales from month to month is made in order to determine minimum stock.   Normal growth is provided for in making budgets and appropriations.

*Sales Analyses and Buying Schedules.*—Close analysis will bring out the comparative sales of various sizes, colors, and types of articles, thus furnishing an accurate guide to purchasing.   For example, an analysis of sales of shoes by sizes and widths made in one department store recently yielded figures regarding the proportion of sales among the different lengths, widths, colors, heights, and styles which differed considerably from the usual schedule.   As a result of this analysis, the buyer reduced his stock and at the same time gave appreciably better service to his customers.   Such analyses afford one of the best methods of reducing the cost of doing business and at the same time increasing the quality of service.

*Stock Turnover.*—The importance of frequent stock turnover can hardly be exaggerated.   This has proved an almost unfailing gage of good management.   In the early stages of a depression when falling markets are the rule this is of unusual importance.   The fact already brought out that retail stores suffered far more from shrinkages in inventory values than from loss of business is vital.

An expert accountant who specializes in department store accounting states to us these advantages of low stock and frequent turnover:

Facts prove conclusively that the securing of a proper turnover—that is, keeping the stocks at a figure where they belong—is one of the major elements of merchandising in any period of the business cycle, whether it be in what are termed normal times or in the times we have just been experiencing. Heavy stocks mean to the merchant heavy markdowns and shortages, and the inability to catch the market on the turn and, what is of the greatest importance, in many departments, the failure to catch the customer's ever changing fancy.

A large New England department store confirms this principle in the following words:

Periods of depression did not hurt business because we turned stock every sixty days. At the beginning of the depression we turned stock on an average of forty-three days. We had low inventories when the recent depression began.

Many stores which had low stocks and large cash reserves bought materials after the break at attractive prices and found the liquidation and depression periods of the last cycle an opportunity rather than a set-back. Several reported the best business in the history of the store at a time when others were staggering under losses.

Avoidance of heavy inventories and conservation of liquid resources also makes it possible to take advantage of purchase discounts. The importance of purchase discounts in reducing costs of doing business is very generally under-estimated. Reports received have shown case after case where the savings from this source actually exceeded the total net profits for the year. It has been found that the better stores almost invariably take their discounts, and consider this a matter of prime importance. This policy is not nearly so universal among the smaller and less progressive establishments.

Reports received show great differences in the skill with which purchases have been timed to arrive just before they are required. Many stores have increases of inventory just in time for heavy buying periods; while others have accumulation of stock several months ahead of requirements.[1]

*Effect of Improved Management Methods during Depressions.*—While much thought has been given to retail store problems, most of the development has been in the direction of improving selling methods. The improvements in management have been made with this object in view. Much can be done by the application to the problems of retail store management of the principles that have proved so effective in reducing factory costs.

Analyses and standardization of methods of checking and handling incoming stock, of deliveries, of office management, of store upkeep, of methods of replacing stock, and of utilization of sales clerks' spare time will result in large reductions of cost.

*Exchange of Statistics.*—A recent development which promises much is the exchange of operating statistics and cost figures between stores.

[1] Chart 39, necessary Christmas purchases but also large purchases in March, 1920 just before the break in prices.

Each store knows exactly how its expenses for salaries, advertising, deliveries, merchandise losses, etc., agree with similar figures for the other stores in the group.  To utilize this information, however, each store must set up standards of accomplishment adapted to its own conditions.  This can be done only by thorough and detailed analysis.  There is a large and inviting field for development through some independent agency, trade association, or special expert service.  Reports received from stores which exchange statistical data show them to be considerably better managed generally than those which have not availed themselves of this service.

CHART 39.—COMPARISON BETWEEN SALES, PURCHASES, AND
INVENTORIES IN A DEPARTMENT STORE.

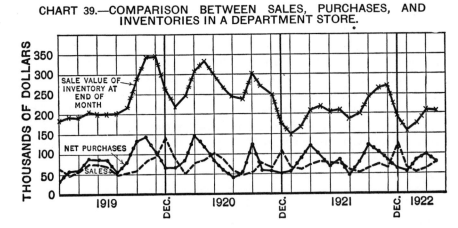

**Methods of Stabilizing Sales.**—The methods used to meet falling off in sales due to cyclical business depressions may be grouped under the following heads:

> Reducing price to reflect reduced replacement costs.
> Advertising.
> Special sales.
> Increasing sales efficiency through incentive to salesmen.
> Featuring special lines adapted to prevailing conditions.

*Prompt Mark-downs to Reflect Lower Replacement Values.*—It has been a general belief that the retail merchant has retarded liquidation by delays in reducing prices.  Reports received show that many, perhaps most, of the larger stores did begin to liquidate promptly.  Evidence of this fact is the review of the group of department stores referred to near the beginning of this section, in which it is shown that during the year 1920 mark-downs of $4,210,000 were taken—almost 11 per cent of total sales.  This mark-down is approximately one-third of the retailer's margin above cost to him, and appreciably greater than average profit.

In our contact with stores in various parts of the country we find this policy of prompt price reduction emphasized over and over again by the successful managers as a prime essential at the beginning of a falling market. On the other hand, the characteristic of the majority, who were severely caught, was their failure promptly to follow this policy.

*Piecemeal Reductions Not Effective.*—The practice of reducing prices by degrees has been shown to defeat its own purpose, because it gives the impression that prices will be lower still. It is not until they feel that the bottom has been reached and expect prices to rise that buyers will come into the market. Sharp cutting and then maintaining the price stimulates buying, while several smaller cuts which total as much or more than the decided reduction may fail to attract business.

CHART 40.—EARNINGS AND NUMBER OF EMPLOYEES ON SELLING AND NON-SELLING FORCE IN RETAIL STORES.

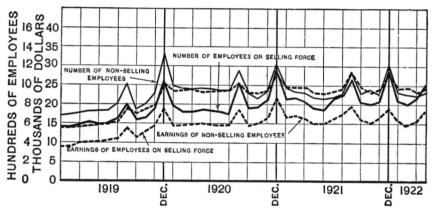

*Advertising.*—The following question was put to retail merchants in all parts of the country:

Do you increase or decrease your advertising expenditure, during business depressions?

In answer to this question only 12 per cent of the stores stated that they increased expenditure for advertising during business depressions, about 25 per cent reported decrease of advertising, and 62 per cent answered that conditions of increasing or decreasing business did not govern advertising expenditure.

Reports and interviews brought out the fact that very few stores felt that they could determine at all accurately the effects of their advertising. Nearly all believe that advertising is necessary—practically none had any records which prove the relative effectiveness of different mediums and displays.[1]

[1] Compare the fuller discussion of this topic in the preceding chapter.

**Employment in Retail Stores.**—The conditions of employment in retail stores are much more stable than in the manufacturing processes. It is a general policy among dealers to maintain a regular force the year round, adding temporary clerks at Christmas and other rush times. Many of the smaller stores have arrangements whereby they are able

CHART 41.—RELATIVE EMPLOYMENT IN MISCELLANEOUS MANUFAC-
TURING INDUSTRIES AND IN 40 DEPARTMENT STORES.

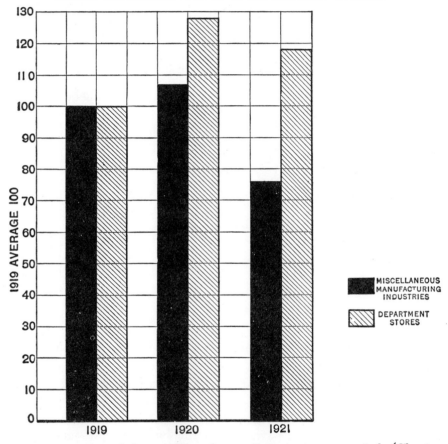

to secure extra help on Saturdays. Curves are presented (Charts 40 and 41) showing conditions of employment in typical retail stores. It will be noted that there is but slight monthly fluctuation in these figures and a rising trend in the number of employees. Advertising costs in these stores rose from an average of $4,000 per month in 1919 to about $8,000 in 1921.

### ACKNOWLEDGMENT

Appreciation is extended to the various executives of the many manufacturing plants and retail stores who have cooperated so cordially by replying in person or by correspondence to questions. Particular thanks are due for the tabulations of plant statistics which were necessary to present a comprehensive view of the facts.

Valuable assistance has been rendered by the United States Labor Commissioner, Ethelbert Stewart, the United States Department of Commerce, James W. Eadie, Jr. of Boston, Harvard University Committee on Economic Research, Babson's Statistical Organization, Federal Reserve Banks, and various trade associations.

For the detail work of the investigation appreciation is expressed to our engineers, Edward H. Hansen for conducting the major part of the manufacturing investigation, and James Forrestal, Jr. in the merchandising studies. Miss C. J. Griffith also assisted in developing the merchandising analysis.

# CHAPTER XI

## THE PROBLEM OF "CANCELLATION"

### By Gilbert H. Montague

of the New York Bar

#### I. "CANCELLATION" FROM THE LEGAL VIEWPOINT

Between September, 1919 and April, 1920, while prices generally were rising, more orders and larger orders were the rule. This was natural, because ordinarily prices rise only when demand increases, and increased demand expresses itself in more orders and larger orders.

Between May, 1920 and May, 1921, while prices generally were falling, fewer orders and smaller orders were the habit. This alone would have brought about the general price decline. But the decline was accelerated, and throughout almost the entire period assumed the velocity and steepness of a drop, because of the widespread prevalence of "cancellation."

"Cancellation," colloquially and in the sense here used, means notification by the buyer before delivery that he cancels, wholly or in part, the order which he has previously placed with the seller. If the seller has accepted the order when it was placed—and this happens almost always—what is then called the order is really a legal contract. This contract obligates the seller to deliver to the buyer the merchandise specified in the accepted order and obligates the buyer to pay to the seller the price specified in that order. When, therefore, the buyer "cancels" the order, in effect he notifies the seller that he considers himself relieved, in whole or in part, of his legal obligation to take and pay for the merchandise which he has contracted to buy.

If the seller acquiesces, the "cancellation" wipes out the contract and all its legal rights and obligations. If the seller does not acquiesce, the "cancellation" constitutes a repudiation and breach of the contract. The seller then has ground for a lawsuit against the buyer, in which the seller only occasionally can compel the buyer to take and pay for the merchandise; and usually can only obtain judgment against the buyer for the difference between the price specified in the accepted order and the "open market" price (as determined by the jury) of merchandise of the same general class at the time and place of delivery specified in the order.

## II. THE PREVALENCE OF "CANCELLATIONS" IN 1920–1921

Manufacturers, producers, and sellers, between June, 1920 and May, 1921, were everywhere complaining of "cancellation." If contemporary testimony may be believed, the prevalence of "cancellation"—"cancellitis" as it was humorously called—exceeded anything that had been experienced for years. No commercial country escaped it, though British merchants professed that it was less common in Great Britain than in other countries. American merchants, on the other hand, declared that it was less common in American domestic trade than in export trade. No line of business escaped, though perhaps it was most noticeable in those in which the period is longest between the time of placing the order and the time for delivery. Trade associations, in conventions and committees, adopted resolutions against "cancellation," exhorted their members to sue all customers who attempted to "cancel orders," and in several instances proposed agreements binding their members to such action. "Cancellation" nevertheless continued and was one of the chief phenomena, and perhaps one of the chief accelerants, of the price decline throughout that period.

Since "cancellation" is legally nothing but repudiation and breach of contract, the question may be asked: Why does any commercial community tolerate it?

In some lines of business, "cancellation" is practically unknown. A banker, who would attempt the "cancellation" of his commitment to purchase and pay for the securities of a tire manufacturer whom he had undertaken to finance would promptly find himself ostracized. If a member of a Stock Exchange, after selling on the floor some securities to another member and receiving the latter's confirmation, should later receive a "cancellation" of it, he would promptly sell the securities for the latter's account and hold the latter liable for any deficiency. No financial stringency or trade condition would justify failure by the banker or the Stock Exchange member to fulfill his legal obligations under these transactions.

But if a dealer had ordered $10,000 worth of tires from this same tire manufacturer, or if the tire manufacturer had ordered $25,000 worth of fabric from a textile manufacturer, and a price decline had followed, the dealer and the tire manufacturer might at any time before delivery attempt "cancellation" of their respective orders with relatively little danger of moral opprobrium. And if their respective sellers should resist "cancellation," without offering some reduction in price, or some "adjustment" to "absorb" or "split" part of the loss, trade sympathy would largely favor the buyer as against the unyielding seller.

In some sections of the business community, accepted orders for merchandise seem to lack most of the sanctity that belongs to contracts generally.

In certain lines of business, in normal times, an accepted order, in spite of its legal status as a contract, may before delivery be cancelled by the buyer almost at will without objection by the seller. So long as buyers and sellers, in normal times, commonly disregard the legal significance of accepted orders, it is not surprising that their legal enforcement in abnormal times seems to the buyer wholly unjust.

### III. TYPES OF SELLERS' CONTRACTS WHICH TEMPT BUYERS TO CANCEL ORDERS

In some lines of business an accepted order, in the form which the sellers have succeeded in imposing upon the trade, binds the buyer so tightly, while permitting the seller such latitude as to time and quantity to be delivered, that the buyer's situation, according to his own opinion at least, is almost intolerable, unless he be allowed by custom considerable latitude in "cancellation."

In the textile industry, orders frequently are accepted "subject to release for all or part of same in case of fires, strikes, lock-outs or other unavoidable delay caused by casualities or occurrences over which we have no control," or on condition that in event of "unavoidable casuality, the deliveries shall only be made proportionate to the production."

In the canning industry, orders frequently are accepted on condition that the seller guarantee delivery only "of the pro rata amount of each item on this order, such as the total quantity ordered from all sources of said item bears to the seller's total season's pack thereof," and that the buyer "shall accept delivery of any portion of this order at such times as seller is able to deliver."

Whoever has collected sales contract forms adopted or recommended by trade associations must be impressed by the frequency with which clauses like these are imposed by sellers upon buyers.

Under such clauses sellers may, in the events specified, which necessarily are for the most part solely within the sellers' knowledge, deliver only a part, or none, of the quantity ordered.

During the period of rising prices, between the summer of 1919 and the spring of 1920, court calendars, which frequently are a significant index of disturbed business conditions, abounded in cases in which buyers charged sellers with unscrupulous conduct under contracts containing clauses similar to these, and the Federal Trade Commission was flooded with complaints against sellers who, it was charged, were utilizing these and similar clauses to withhold deliveries on orders that had been accepted at low prices many months before, and were selling surreptitiously the quantities so withheld to new purchasers at greatly increased prices.

Just as excessive harshness in criminal statutes breeds laxity in their observance and enforcement, so excessive harshness in sales contracts breeds the spirit that leads to "cancellation."

## IV. ECONOMIC CONSEQUENCES OF THE PRACTICE

But even if harsh sales contracts were abolished, "cancellation" would still exist.

So long as eager sellers, competing with one another to obtain more and larger orders, encourage buyers to order too much rather than too little, and so long as eager sellers, competing with one another to obtain the good-will of buyers, dare not offend buyers by resisting "cancellation," "cancellation" will continue. As prosperity approaches high tide and the probability of turning over merchandise at a profit diminishes, buyers are thus induced to continue ordering, knowing that "cancellation" will be tolerated and that at any time before delivery they can avoid their losses and throw them back upon the sellers. This is the real evil of "cancellation."

In extreme cases, buyers at the peak of the boom, expecting that they will receive only a moderate quota of what they order, place orders for two or three times the quantity of goods they need, or order the full bill from two or three different houses. Such practices would be exceedingly risky were orders generally treated as contracts. As matters stand, the practice is not only common, but also has been encouraged in some cases by over-zealous salesmen who wish to book the business. These inflated orders may deceive the wholesale merchants and manufacturers regarding the extent of the demand and lead them in turn to place larger orders for goods or materials than they can use. Thus the practice of "cancellation" aggravates the business errors committed in boom periods.

The other side of the practice becomes obvious after the tide has turned. "Cancellation" then wipes out the demand expressed in the order, and destroys the support which the order gave to the price level. And since "cancellation," like any other repudiation or breach of contract is always a disappointment and frustration of hope, "cancellation" accelerates the general price decline much more than refusal originally to place the order could possibly have done.

If accepted orders for merchandise had everywhere the same sanctity that belongs to contracts generally, and if "cancellation" were wholly abolished, prices would nevertheless rise and fall, and speculation would continue. Our Stock Exchanges prove that speculation exists even when contracts are strictly enforced. But imagine what speculation on the Stock Exchange would be if repudiation and breach of contracts were tolerated! Here is simply another proof that speculation in industry is undoubtedly more excessive than speculation on any Stock Exchange. If by trade association action, or by trade education, or by recommendation from individual banks and from the Federal Reserve Banks, the practice of "cancellation" could be diminished, speculation in industry would be kept within narrower bounds.

CHAPTER XII

## METHODS OF STABILIZING WORK IN THE BUILDING INDUSTRIES

By Ernest S. Bradford

Vice-president of the American Statistical Association

### I. THE BUILDING INDUSTRY

Introduction.—The purpose of this chapter is to state how private building is affected by the business cycle, how much unemployment results, and what can be or is being done to reduce such unemployment.[1]

The importance of the building industry may be judged from the fact that private building in the United States amounted in 1919 to over $3,500,000,000 and employed probably 1,500,000 wage-earners.

Volume-of-building Curve since 1900.—The volume-of-building curve which follows (Chart 42), based on the estimated value of buildings for

CHART 42.—VALUE OF BUILDING PERMITS ISSUED IN 40 CITIES, 1901–1921.

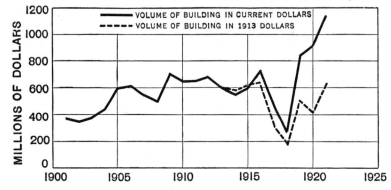

which permits were granted annually from 1900 to 1921 in forty cities of the United States representing a population of about 21,000,000 in 1920, shows the high and low period of building. For the years since 1914 which are affected to an unusual extent by inflated prices, these money figures have been reduced to the basis of 1913 prices by means of an index of building costs for the years 1913–1921.

[1] The term "building" as here used does not include construction work connected with road-making and paving, bridges, dams, canals, irrigation works and similar projects, primarily because no authentic record of such construction exists over a long enough period.

This chart, which is typical of building in the country as a whole, shows clearly the depression of 1908, the beginning of the depression of 1914 and 1915, the boom of 1916, the enormous slump in building during 1917–1918 due to war conditions, the drop in 1920 after the partial recovery of 1919, and the recent upward trend.

TABLE XXIV.—VALUE OF BUILDINGS FOR WHICH PERMITS WERE GRANTED IN REPRESENTATIVE AMERICAN CITIES (1901–1921)

| Year | Value of buildings in forty cities (millions of dollars) | Index number of building costs[a] | Value of buildings in forty cities in terms of 1913 prices (millions of dollars) |
|---|---|---|---|
| 1901 | $369 | | |
| 1902 | 347 | | |
| 1903 | 375 | | |
| 1904 | 435 | | |
| 1905 | 597 | | |
| 1906 | 613 | | |
| 1907 | 547 | | |
| 1908 | 497 | | |
| 1909 | 700 | | |
| 1910 | 653 | | |
| 1911 | 656 | | |
| 1912 | 680 | | |
| 1913 | 606 | 100 | $606 |
| 1914 | 553 | 96 | 576 |
| 1915 | 601 | 98 | 613 |
| 1916 | 734 | 114 | 644 |
| 1917 | 461 | 139 | 331 |
| 1918 | 272 | 153 | 177 |
| 1919 | 846 | 167 | 506 |
| 1920 | 914 | 224 | 408 |
| 1921 | 1,143 | 179 | 638 |

[a] Based on index numbers of building material costs and building labor costs of the U. S. Bureau of Labor Statistics, weighted by the author 60 and 40 respectively, following the weighting used by the Federal Reserve Bank, New York District.

**Relation of Increase in Population to Volume of Building.—** Increase in population, rather than number of inhabitants, determines the need for building. Although existing houses and factories require repairs and additions, which accounts for some construction work, "we build primarily because our population grows." Increase in population being the main factor, it is of interest to compare the building curve with the trend of population year by year, as in Chart 43. The volume of building does not always follow the increase of population. At times it fails to keep up with new population, particularly when the prices of building materials and labor are high; or again, some kind of building falls behind, as in 1915–1916, when the demand for industrial buildings was greatly stimulated by the expanding requirements of munition and other war factories, while the construction of dwellings remained normal or sub-normal. In general, the two curves have the same trend over a series of years.

CHART 43.—VALUE OF BUILDING OPERATIONS IN 40 CITIES COMPARED WITH THE ESTIMATED ANNUAL INCREASES IN THE POPULATION OF THE UNITED STATES.

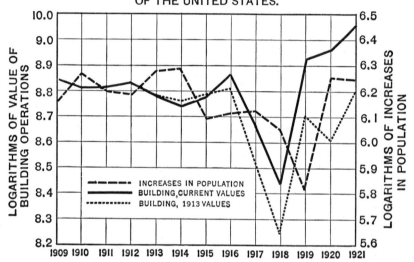

**Additions, Alterations, and Repairs.**—Additions, alterations, and repairs average about one-seventh of the total annual volume of building, measured in dollars. This is shown by the estimated costs of buildings covered by permits issued in a varying number of leading cities, as reported by their building departments to the United States Geological Survey for the years 1910–1919, and to the United States Bureau of Labor Statistics for 1920. The lowest percentage of alterations and repairs in any of these years is 10 per cent of the total in 1910; and the highest figure is 23 per cent in 1918.

These additions, alterations, and repairs are made necessary by fires, depreciation, obsolescence and the shifting of local needs from dwellings to stores or factories, and demand for better and more convenient houses.

During the past five years, losses from fire amounted to $1,338,178,142 in the United States, according to the Actuarial Bureau of the National Board of Fire Underwriters, or an average of over $260,000,000 a year. If to this amount is added 25 per cent additional for unreported fires, as recommended in the publication of the National Board of Fire Under-writers,[1] the total is $1,672,722,677 or over $300,000,000 a year.

Sources of Building Information.—A comparison of the figures for identical years indicates that the estimated cost of buildings, for which permits were granted in cities, suitably increased to make allowance for under-reporting of building costs[2] represents the volume of building in the years before the war more closely than the figures for contracts awarded. Since 1919, however, the latter figures reported monthly by the F. W. Dodge Company have closely approximated the volume of building permits as reported by cities. Chart 44 compares the estimated cost of projects contemplated, and contracts awarded as supplied by the Dodge Company with building permits in fifty identical cities.

CHART 44.—COMPARISON OF VALUE OF BUILDING PERMITS, CONTRACTS AWARDED, AND PROJECTS CONTEMPLATED IN 50 LARGE CITIES BY MONTHS, 1919–1921. (UNIT: $1,000,000)

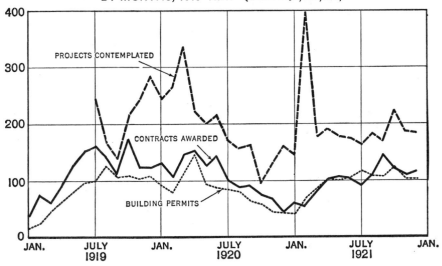

Volume of Building in the United States.—An estimate of the volume of building in the United States may now be built up on the value of the permits granted in one hundred thirty-one cities in the years 1910–1920. (1) The new construction in these cities can be separated from the repairs. (2) Twenty per cent is added to correct underestimates of cost. (3) Building in other cities is estimated on the basis of popula-tion. (4) Building in rural districts is estimated from the city figures

---

[1] *Safeguarding America against Fire*, New York City, pp. 4, 5. Some buildings destroyed by fire are not rebuilt.

[2] Twenty per cent increase was adopted, as recommended by a large number of architects, engineers, and contractors.

12

on the basis of additions to population.   (5) Alterations and repairs are then added to the new construction, the same figure being used for cities and for rural districts.   The results of this process, of course, are rather rough approximations.

TABLE XXV.—VALUE OF BUILDING IN UNITED STATES, 1910–1921

| A | B | C | D | E | F | G | H |
|---|---|---|---|---|---|---|---|
| Year | Value of building permits issued in one hundred and thirty-one cities (millions of dollars)$^a$ | Value of new construction in one hundred and thirty-one cities (millions of $^b$ dollars) | Estimated cost of new private construction in | | | Estimated cost of new private construction and alterations, additions and repairs, in total United States (millions of dollars)$^e$ | Total estimated cost in terms of 1913 prices (millions of dollars)$^f$ |
| | | | Urban United States (millions of dollars)$^e$ | Rural United States (millions of dollars)$^d$ | Total United States (millions of dollars) D + E | | |
| 1910 | $   914 | $   822.6 | $1,707.2 | $225.7 | $1,932.9 | $2,277.5 | $ |
| 1911 | 918 | 807.8 | 1,689.6 | 223.4 | 1,913.0 | 2,326.4 | |
| 1912 | 952 | 841.6 | 1,766.3 | 233.6 | 1,999.9 | 2,409.9 | |
| 1913 | 853 | 742.1 | 1,568.7 | 207.4 | 1,776.1 | 2,186.0 | 2,186.0 |
| 1914 | 749 | 656.1 | 1,391.1 | 381.9 | 1,575.0 | 1,915.1 | 1,994.9 |
| 1915 | 776 | 689.1 | 1,470.7 | 194.5 | 1,665.2 | 1,982.1 | 2,022.6 |
| 1916 | 982 | 854.3 | 1,828.3 | 241.8 | 2,070.1 | 2,532.0 | 2,221.1 |
| 1917 | 650 | 559.0 | 1,206.0 | 159.5 | 1,365.5 | 1,693.4 | 1,218.3 |
| 1918 | 401 | 308.8 | 667.9 | 88.3 | 756.2 | 1,086.0 | 709.8 |
| 1919 | 1,259 | 1,070.1 | 2,327.2 | 307.7 | 2,634.9 | 3,307.3 | 1,980.4 |
| 1920 | 1,343 | 1,077.1 | 2,347.2 | 310.4 | 2,657.6 | 3,597.6 | 1,606.1 |
| 1921 | 1,602 | 1,364.9 | 2,985.9 | 394.1 | 3,380.0 | 4,213.6 | 2,353.9 |

$^a$ U. S. Geological Survey, *Mineral Resources of the U. S.*, Clay Working Industries . . . and Building Operations in the Larger Cities, 1910–1919; U. S. Bureau of Labor Statistics, *Bulletin* 295, 1920.

$^b$ The fraction of total construction accounted for by new construction is assumed to be the same as that shown for recorded cities in corresponding years by the Geological Survey 1910–1919 and the Bureau of Labor Statistics 1920.

$^c$ Represents value of new construction in one hundred and thirty-one cities first increased one fifth to cover underestimates of values of buildings and then multiplied by the ratio of the total urban population of the United States to the population of the one hundred and thirty-one cities, which was about 29,900,000 in 1920.

$^d$ Since the increase in rural population in the United States during the decade was 0.132 as great as the increase in urban population, the items in Column D have been multiplied by this ratio to obtain the figures here given—increase in population being the main factor in building, as explained on p. 175.

$^e$ Estimate made as follows: the value of new construction in the one hundred and thirty-one sample cities was multiplied by the ratio of repairs, etc., to new construction as shown by the Geological Survey and Bureau of Labor Statistics reports.   The cost of repairs, etc., for the one hundred and thirty-one cities was then multiplied by the ratio of the whole population of the United States to the population of the one hundred and thirty-one cities.   This product, representing the assumed cost of alterations additions, and repairs was then added to the corresponding item in Column F.

$^f$ Derived from Column G, by dividing the items therein by the index of building costs described on p. 175.

**Purposes for Which Buildings are Erected.**—From data for 1920 covering over 200 cities with a population of about one-third of the United States,[1] it appears that housing constituted 37.2 per cent of the value of all new construction during the year.   If to this is added the value

[1] U. S. Bureau of Labor Statistics, *Bull.* 295, 1920, p. 5, giving detailed data for 196 cities, with a population of about 34,400,000.

of private garages, which under present conditions are closely related to residences, construction for dwelling purposes constituted somewhat over 42 per cent of the volume of building.[1]

Sixteen per cent of the value of construction in 1920 was for factories and workshops, 14.6 per cent for stores and other mercantile buildings, including commercial garages, and about 11 per cent for office buildings.

These three classes account for approximately 42 per cent more of all construction work, leaving a balance of about 16 per cent to cover buildings of a public, semi-public, or miscellaneous character of which schools constitute 4 per cent; amusement places, 3.4 per cent; hospitals, 1.8 per cent; churches, 1.5 per cent; sheds, stables, and barns about 0.4 per cent; public buildings, 1.4 per cent; and the balance, miscellaneous, about 3.9 per cent.

It is believed that the figures for schools and public buildings reported, which together constitute only about 5 per cent of the total annual building (if 1920 is typical of other years), cover only a small portion of the public buildings erected in cities, in a large number of which municipal structures and those of the federal government and states are not required to have a building permit and hence are not included in the summary.

## II. THE BUILDING MATERIAL INDUSTRIES

**Material and Labor Costs.**—Fluctuations in the volume of construction tend to produce like fluctuations in the demand for lumber, brick, structural steel, cement, glass, paint, lime, lath, shingles, sand, plumbing and heating apparatus, and electrical supplies. There are other uses for some of the products of building material manufacturers which tend to stabilize these fluctuations; the lumber turned out by sawmills is in demand for furniture, packing boxes, and other industrial purposes; cement is used for paving, road-making, dams, piers and other construction work not classed here as building; structural steel goes into bridges and ships. Nevertheless, the building curve and the curve for these products, which enter so largely into building, influence one another to a marked degree. High prices of materials tend to reduce the volume of building and to produce unemployment in the building trades. A stoppage of building lessens the demand for materials, leads to depressed material prices, and tends to produce unemployment in the mills manufacturing building materials; and similar seasonal factors and cyclical swings are found in both.

**Relative Importance of the Various Kinds of Buildings.**—In the cities for which data are available, the most important building material is wood, and the value of the annual consumption of lumber is much

---

[1] This is on the assumption that about two-thirds the value of the garages constructed, or 5 per cent of all buildings, are private garages. In 1921, private garages constituted two-thirds of the total value of garages.

greater than that of any other one building material.    While brick dwellings have largely superseded frame structures in large cities, these so-called brick dwellings require a vast amount of lumber, and in hundreds of small cities and villages wood still holds first place in the construction of new dwellings.    Concrete and steel are an increasing factor in the erection of stores, offices, apartments, and factories.

Table XXVI shows the relative proportion of buildings classed as wood or brick since 1910 in over 100 large cities:

TABLE XXVI.—RELATIVE IMPORTANCE OF KINDS OF BUILDINGS ERECTED
1910–1921[a]

| Year | Number of cities reporting | Per cent of total value constituted by | | |
|---|---|---|---|---|
| | | Wooden buildings | Brick[b] buildings | Buildings of other materials |
| 1910 | 127 | 26 | 56 | 16 |
| 1911 | 108 | 30 | 47 | 26 |
| 1912 | 105 | 29 | 59 | 12 |
| 1913 | 108 | 34 | 44 | 22 |
| 1914 | 113 | 38 | 40 | 23 |
| 1915 | 123 | 33 | 51 | 16 |
| 1916 | 129 | 27 | 44 | 29 |
| 1917 | 129 | 27 | 51 | 22 [c] |
| 1918 | 132 | 32 | 50 | 16 [c] |
| 1919 | 128 | 32 | 44 | 24 [c] |
| 1920 | 207 | 24 | 45 | 31 |

[a] Includes both new building and additions, alterations and repairs.  Data from U. S. Geological Survey except those for 1920, which are from U. S. Bureau of Labor Statistics.  (See Table XXV note a).

[b] Includes hollow tile, 1920.

[c] Of this 9 to 11 per cent represented buildings of concrete, 4 to 9 per cent steel skeleton, 1 to 2 per cent buildings of stone, and the balance buildings of other materials.

**Production of Building Material and Number of Wage-earners Employed.**—Table XXVII shows the production in 1914 and 1919, according to the Census of Manufactures, of the leading materials that enter into building.

These industries account for about 900,000 wage-earners in 1919. If those who are engaged in other building material industries, such as the electrical industries,[1] are included, between 950,000 and 1,000,000 employees are represented.    Not all of the employees in these industries are engaged exclusively in producing building materials or equipment;

[1] As the proportion engaged in building lines is unavailable, no figures are given in Table XXVII for electrical industries.

TABLE XXVII.—PRODUCTION OF BUILDING MATERIALS[a]
1914 AND 1919

| Material | Value of products (millions of dollars) | | Number of wage-earners (thousands) | | Per cent of product used for building[b] |
|---|---|---|---|---|---|
| | 1914 | 1919 | 1914 | 1919 | |
| Lumber and timber products | $716 | $1,387 | 480 | 480 | 60[c] |
| Planing mill products[d] | 308 | 500 | 96 | 87 | |
| Building brick | | 95[e] | | 36 | 100 |
| Structural iron work | 159[f] | 295 | 47 | 44 | |
| Cement | 102 | 175 | 28 | 25 | |
| Glass | 123 | 262 | 74 | 77 | 30 |
| Paints | 112 | 257 | 13 | 17 | |
| Varnishes | 33 | 84 | 3 | 4 | |
| Building sand | 8[e] | 12[e] | | | |
| Lime | 18 | 34 | 12 | 11 | 36[e] |
| Building stone | 18[e] | 11[e] | ... | | 100 |
| Cast-iron pipe | 27 | 50 | 12 | | |
| Plumbers' supplies | 43 | 60 | 18 | 13 | |
| Roofing materials | 28 | 86 | 4 | 9 | |
| Stoves and hot air furnaces | 68 | 146 | 29 | 33 | |
| Steam fittings, and steam and hot-water heating apparatus | 64 | 160 | 26 | 37 | |

[a] U. S. Bureau of the Census, Manufactures, 1919, prel. totals for U. S. Big Industries and Geographic Divisions and States.
[b] Includes building, repair, and maintenance work but not paving or construction work other than building.
[c] Rough estimate of Secretary of National Lumber Manufacturers' Association.
[d] Exclusive of planing mills connected with sawmills.
[e] U. S. Geological Survey, Mineral Resources of U. S., 1914, 1919.
[f] Not made in steel works or rolling mills. This figure covers iron and steel, structural and ornamental work for buildings, bridges, and subways.

possibly three-fourths of them is a fair approximation. Those employed in the building industries and in the building material industries together number between 2,250,000 and 2,500,000.

**Relation of Material and Labor Costs.**—The costs of building are divided between materials, labor, other expenses, and profits. Material costs and labor costs in the aggregate are commonly believed to be nearly equal, as items entering into the cost of buildings, though the exact ratio may vary considerably from year to year. This ratio appears to be between 50–50 and 60–40.

The National Federation of Construction Industries completed a composite building cost index in November, 1921 on the basis of Philadelphia cost figures from seven different types of buildings. The distribution of building costs in 1913 and 1921[1] according to this study was as follows:

|  | 1913 | 1921 |
|---|---|---|
| Material | 42.88 | 70.74 |
| Labor | 44.00 | 70.40 |
| Overhead | 5.80 | 8.70 |
| Compensation |  |  |
| Sub-contractors | 3.90 | 5.85 |
| General contractors | 3.42 | 5.13 |
| Total | 100.00 | 160.82 |

Labor costs in this index include: (1) all skilled labor and supervision on the building, including stone cutting, shop work on sheet metal, and mill work, but no other manufacturing costs, (2) unskilled labor, (3) general supervision, including office work, estimating, and engineering salaries, (4) liability insurance.

The percentages which each of these items constitute of the total labor cost in 1913 for the Philadelphia district according to the National Federation of Construction Industries were as follows: skilled labor 27.6 per cent; unskilled labor 9.4 per cent; supervision, etc., 5.6 per cent; liability insurance 1.4 per cent; total 44.0 per cent.

The ratio used currently by the Federal Reserve Bank of the New York district is 60–40, which ratio is also used by Leonard C. Ayres in a monograph prepared June, 1922 for the Cleveland Trust Company, entitled "The Prospect for Building Construction in American Cities."

**Course of Building Material, Prices, and Labor Costs since 1913: Index of Bureau of Labor Statistics.**—The index of the Bureau of Labor Statistics, revised in May, 1922 to include structural steel, re-enforcing bars, and nails, with weightings based on the 1919 Census, shows the course of prices of materials and wage rates since 1912. The wage-rates curve is based on rates covering over 420,000 wage-earners, and the union rates of carpenters and brick-layers represent 135,000 carpenters and 30,000 bricklayers. While there is always a difference of opinion as to just what weights to give each item in a composite index, this curve is one of several which are believed to indicate closely enough for present purposes the course of material prices and wage rates in the building trades for several years past.

Regarding these figures, the Bureau of Labor Statistics[2] makes the following statement:

Wholesale prices are available month by month, but union wage rates are available only as of May 15 each year, consequently their change from month to month can not be shown. However, the building trades wage rates have experienced no such wide fluctuation as have building material prices. So far as the

[1] The 1921 figures represent percentages of the 1913 total.
[2] *Monthly Labor Review*, May, 1922, p. 100.

large cities are concerned the union wage rate is the prevailing rate, if not the only rate, for the city.

Beginning with 1917 it will be seen that building material prices constantly advanced above building wage rates until 1920, in the spring of which year building material as a whole had reached triple the prices of 1913 and wage rates as a whole had doubled the level of 1913. Beginning with the spring of 1920 and continuing through into 1921 there was a heavy fall in building material prices. Building wage rates, however, held their position between 1920 and 1921. . .

With a decline in prices there was a decline in the volume of building material sold; statistics on this subject, however, are not available. During the same period while wage rates did not drop, there was a great reduction in earnings due to unemployment.

CHART 45.—PRICES OF BUILDING MATERIAL AND BUILDING WAGE RATES SINCE 1916.

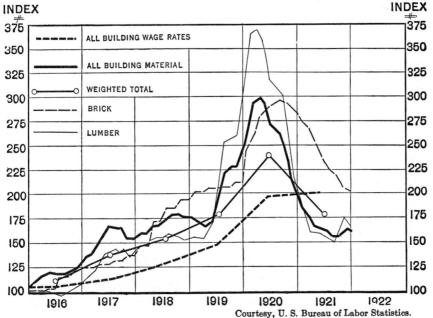

Courtesy, U. S. Bureau of Labor Statistics.

**Relation of Construction Costs to Housing and Rents.**—The costs of building materials, which rose higher in proportion to 1913 figures than the prices of other commodities, tended to discourage building and alter the ratio between the supply of houses and the demand. With increased demand for housing came an increase in rents, which gradually rose until at the end of 1921 they had reached a level between one and two-thirds and one and three-fourths times the rate in 1914. By this time falling construction costs were beginning to stimulate building and the increasing number of houses and apartments prevented a further advance in rents. While there are other elements such as taxes, interest rates, and legal exemptions or restrictions, all of which enter into the final figure of rent, construction costs are a primary factor in producing a shortage or surplus of housing.

Table XXVIII shows the relation according to different indexes, between the rent curves in New York City[1] and the United States,[2] and costs of building in New York City[3] and the United States since 1914.

TABLE XXVIII.—INDEX OF RENTS AND CONSTRUCTION COSTS IN NEW YORK CITY
AND THE UNITED STATES, 1914–1922
(1914 = 100)

| Year | Rents | | | Building Costs | |
|---|---|---|---|---|---|
| | New York City apartments, type A [a] | New York City apartments, type B [b] | United States [c] | New York City [c] | United States [d] |
| 1914 | 100 | 100 | 100 | 100 | 100 |
| 1915 | 101 | 101 | 102 | 112 | 102 |
| 1916 | 102 | 102 | 102 | 143 | 119 |
| 1917 | 102 | 107 | 100 | 164 | 145 |
| 1918 | 110 | 112 | 109 | 168 | 159 |
| 1919 | 121 | 127 | 114 | 168 | 174 |
| 1920 | 144 | 145 | 135 | 230 | 233 |
| 1921 (May) | 160 | 166 | 159 | 193 | 186 |
| 1921 (Oct.) | 167 | 175 | 160 | 177 | |
| 1922 (Jan.) | 167 | 175 | 161 | 173 | |

[a] Renting under $15 per room in 1920.
[b] Renting $15 to $30 per room in 1920.
[c] See text.
[d] Index of building costs (see Table XXIV) on 1914 base.

**Other Factors: Costs of Financing.**—In addition to materials and labor, the costs of financing constitute an important factor in building. The amounts paid in order to secure funds for the building of apartments, office buildings, department stores, factories, and other large structures during the period immediately following the war were in many instances excessive. Large bonuses or commissions charged in addition to interest by some of the concerns which supplied the money raised the cost of

[1] Federal Reserve Bank, New York District *Monthly Review*, March 1, 1922, p. 11; an average of typical buildings reported by twenty-one owners and operators of apartments.

[2] *Monthly Labor Review*, May, 1922, p. 76.

[3] Computed by the Geo. A. Fuller Co., New York City. Cost of typical hotel building used in lieu of apartment house costs, the two having fluctuated closely together.

construction and resulted in increased rents. In some cases the proposed charges for money became so high as virtually to prevent building.

### III. UNEMPLOYMENT IN THE BUILDING TRADES

**New York.**—In states such as New York and Massachusetts where there exist records of the unemployment of considerable numbers of wage-earners, collected for a series of years by an established public bureau, it appears that unemployment in the building trades is greater than in most other lines of industry.

The average percentage of union building-trade workers unemployed in New York State, where figures are available showing the percentage out of work at the end of each month from 1904 to 1916, is 26.5 per cent. This is to be compared with 19.87 per cent in all industries, 13.77 per cent in metals and machinery, and 10 per cent in printing. In clothing the percentage is also high—26 per cent. Building, therefore, has been one of the worst two industries in New York as regards unemployment. There is no reason to believe that the ratio among non-union building workmen is particularly different from that among union building workmen.

Chart 46[1] shows in four trades in New York State the percentages of union wage-earners unemployed at the end of each month from 1904 to 1916. The depressions of 1908 and 1914–1915 are evident in all four; together with the dull period of 1911, they are especially marked in the metal trades and very evident in the building trades, though the seasonal factor is also strongly marked. The winter peak in unemployment is an outstanding feature of building. In clothing, the cyclical movement is obscured somewhat by the presence of unemployment due to strikes; the seasonal swing is wide. Printing has an unusually even curve of employment.

**Massachusetts.**—A similar chart is available for Massachusetts union workers, data for which cover the years 1908 to date,[2] whereas the New York figures of union unemployment were not collected after the middle of 1916. The Massachusetts figures are quarterly, and unemployment due to strikes has been eliminated as far as separate records were available, namely, for the years 1917–1921.[3] They show an average for 1908–1921 (excluding strikes for the five years mentioned) of 13.8 per cent unemployment in the building trades, as compared with 10.5 per cent in the metal trades, 10.8 per cent in textiles, 6.5 per cent in printing, and 10.8 per cent in all industries.

[1] From N. Y. State and Department of Labor, *Special Bulletin* 85, July, 1917.

[2] Data for Chart 47 supplied by Roswell F. Phelps, Director of the Division of Statistics, Massachusetts Department of Labor and Industries.

[3] See also Mass. Department of Labor and Industries, *Labor Bulletin* 135, November, 1921, which includes unemployment due to strikes.

CHART 46.—PERCENTAGES OF ORGANIZED WAGE-EARNERS UNEM-
PLOYED IN NEW YORK STATE BY MONTHS, 1916–1904.

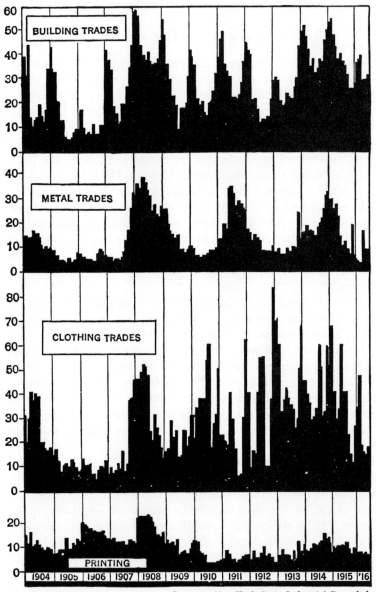

Courtesy, New York State Industrial Commission.

CHART 47.—PERCENTAGES OF ORGANIZED WAGE-EARNERS UNEM-
PLOYED IN MASSACHUSETTS BY QUARTERS, 1908–1921.

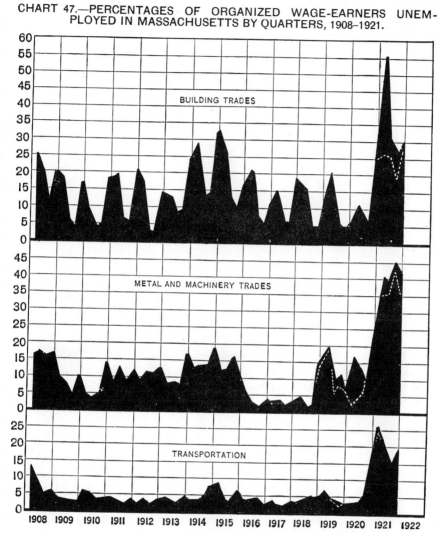

(CHART 47 CONTINUED)

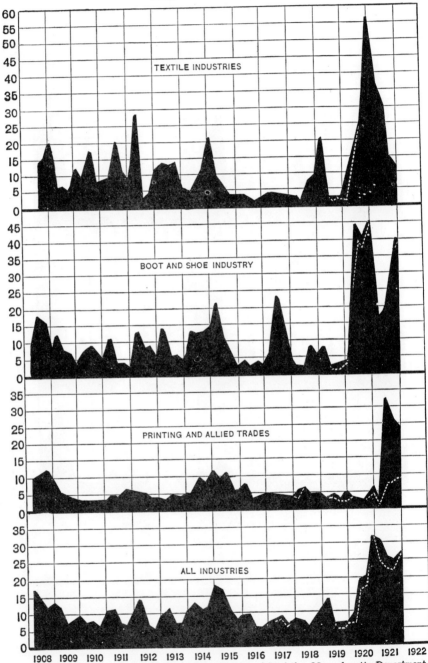

**Wage Loss Due to Cyclical Unemployment.**—Assuming that the average unemployment in the building trades in the United States as a whole lies somewhere between the 26.5 per cent of the union unemployed in New York State, 1904–1915, and the 13.8 per cent of those similarly unemployed in Massachusetts, 1908–1921, we may take, say, 20 per cent (or about sixty days per year) as a very conservative average of the time lost by the building trade workman.[1,2]

The average wage of the union workman in the building trades, according to the table prepared by the Bureau of Labor Statistics, covering over 400,000 union workers in the building trades, was about $1.00 per hour in May, 1921 and has not materially decreased since. While many carpenters and bricklayers are receiving more than $10 a day, unskilled labor is getting very much less. Assuming that the average building wages run about $6 per day and that there are 1,500,000 wage-earners,[3] a loss of sixty days each means an annual loss of $540,000,000. While it is true that a large but undetermined part of this is due to seasonal factors, strikes and disability, a glance at the charts for New York and Massachusetts shows that a great part must be cyclical in character.

## V. METHODS ACTUALLY IN USE AND PROPOSED FOR STABILIZING BUILDING WORK

**Methods Used by Manufacturers: Planning Work Ahead: Repair Work.**—The Charles Warner Company of Wilmington, Delaware, manufacturers and dealers in lime and dredgers of sand and gravel, who employ about five hundred men normally, used the following plan of meeting the depression:

About three years ago, we submitted to our Board of Directors a five-year program, the items of which were to be carried out in whatever order proved most practicable. In the fall and winter of 1920 after our business had fallen off and we began to really feel the depression, we undertook the building of eight barges for use in dredging sand and gravel. At 1920 prices these would have cost us about $25,000; they actually cost us about $18,000, a saving of $7,000. This was not only good business for the company, but kept many of our men

---

[1] The report on, "Waste in Industry," found more rather than less, than the above amount, as the time lost, reporting that the average wage-earner in the building trades worked only 190 days in the year. "Waste in Industry," Chap. V, The Building Industry, p. 53.

[2] In the trade-union figures for unemployment, there is, I believe, a certain fictitious element, due to men who are superannuated or are otherwise unable to work, being reported as unemployed. This error in the figures may be suspected from the fact that practically none of them hit the zero point of unemployment with any regularity. —Note by M. C. RORTY.

[3] The Committee on Construction of the President's Conference on Unemployment put this number at 2,000,000; others have placed it only slightly above 1,000,000. The U. S. Census of Occupations (Press release, July 29, 1922) places it at 1,878,000. Willford I. King estimates it at 1,600,000.

employed who would otherwise have been out of work and without funds.  Then we built a new stone-crushing plant, which we had in mind for some time previously.  In the fall and winter of 1921, when times were bad, we rebuilt and enlarged two of our dredges, and did a lot of renewal work on the steel cars at our limestone quarries.  There is always a lot of such work and renewals which need to be done to keep a plant in condition, and the time to do it is when business is slack; repairs and reconstruction always interfere with operations and can be done best when orders are not pressing.  We were also able to increase somewhat our sales of lime to farmers during the depression, by pointing out the advantage to them of existing low prices.

Of course, the ability to carry on improvement work during times when little money is coming in presupposes either a financial reserve or good credit.  It is not well to wait until a depression is on before jumping in with improvement projects; there should be a plan worked out beforehand.

A large management corporation says:[1]

As public utilities, our companies have to plan well ahead and it is necessary to anticipate extensions and do new construction work before conditions force us so do so.  Our engineering investigations, in particular, we make long in advance, so that when the need arises, it is not necessary to delay construction until after the requisite preliminary work has been done.  A case in point is Seattle where we planned out a five-year development of dams and power houses.

Another large engineering management firm, which directs an extensive line of properties by keeping in constant touch with the executive officials of utilities using its management and engineering service, is able to formulate construction programs for some of them considerably in advance of immediate needs.  The fact that the company has a large number of properties under its management makes it possible to keep its engineering department constantly busy in connection with one or another, and helps to iron out any high or low spots in its own staff.  This makes it possible to keep specialists employed even during times of depression.

An electrical railway company in northern Ohio planned its tie renewals ahead:

We knew that each year on a certain section of track about six hundred ties had to be put in and that the men in the regular renewal gang were not able to put in that number.  At times, therefore, when the steel mills in our town were shut down, we made a practice of hiring idle steel workers and putting them on the job of renewing ties along the line.  The putting in of new steel was similarly done at slack periods.  The steel mills producing special railroad work, urged street railways to contract for their crossing switches, inter-locking plants, etc., in the fall and winter, to be delivered along in the spring.  These orders kept the steel men going all winter, and enabled the mill company to plan its work some months ahead.

[1] STONE & WEBSTER, Boston, letter of May 12, 1922.

A boiler manufacturer[1] states:

We have endeavored to overhaul machinery, make any necessary repairs to buildings, and do whatever construction work is possible on the plant during slack periods, thus keeping as many men employed as we could, while at the same time putting everything in first-class condition to be ready to operate when the business depression ceases.

A glass manufacturer[2] of Toledo, Ohio, says:

The construction work which we have done during the period of depression has been largely in the nature of alterations and repairs, giving that portion of our organization, which would not otherwise be busy, work during these dull periods.

The Flour State Baking Company[3] of St. Paul, Minnesota, states that it is their settled policy to make renewals during depressions. "This work is partly new construction and partly repairs. It has kept our house engineering and maintenance crew busy during the slack season."

One of the most comprehensive systems of planning ahead is that used by the Bell Telephone Companies. In many territories the telephone company makes a very thorough survey of every large city and semi-urban districts as well, for the purpose of determining what the probable population will be in twenty years and its character. With this as a basis, it estimates how many new central offices will be required and how many telephones will be in use in the city or district at the end of this period. This thorough sort of forecasting is a complex process involving the close study of a considerable number of factors, such as growth, character and nationality of population, immigration, income as indicated by rents paid, telephone using habits, etc. The result gives a very comprehensive view of the future needs of the business and makes it possible for the company to go confidently ahead, in periods of poor business, getting ready for the business which is coming when times are better. It is also valuable in preventing the placing of telephone exchanges in wrong locations, where future business might not warrant.

**Stabilizing Methods Used by Contractors and Builders.**—The effect of the long-range planning of the manufacturer may be either to provide work for large numbers of those engaged regularly in building or to keep his own employees busy—the latter being the case when repair and maintenance work is utilized to provide employment. The problem of the contractor-builder is narrower—that of getting enough business for his own concern to hold his working force intact.

*Educating Customers to Build during Low Cost Periods.*—One of the methods used by building contractors to stabilize their business during

[1] Abstract of letter from Duluth Boiler Works, Duluth, Minnesota, May 10, 1922.
[2] Letter, June 6, 1922 from Libbey Glass Manufacturing Co.
[3] Letter, May 10, 1922.

depressions is to call the attention of customers to the advantages of building during such periods.

L. C. Wason of the Aberthaw Construction Company, Boston, says:

We study our market and seek business from concerns who, we know, are strong and far-sighted enough to plan the construction of additions to plant some time in advance. We are putting up a new factory now for a manufacturer who will not need the building until next year, but who has seized this opportunity to put up his new structure while materials are low priced and labor is plentiful. In times of activity we make a careful selection of the work offered and do not take more than we can do justice to; in times of depression all hands turn in and do an aggressive job of selling our services, thereby getting more business. We have issued a number of circulars showing concrete construction in cold weather and the ease with which it could be done, and in the fall of the year have tried thereby actively to stimulate building during the winter with some degree of success. The difference in cost between summer work and winter work is, at a maximum 5 per cent and sometimes even less.

We have not been in the habit of cutting prices in the winter, but of showing the owner that the difference in price is a good deal less than the loss he would sustain by delay if he is really in need of a building now.

William Steele & Sons Company, one of the largest contractors in Philadelphia, who specializes in the construction of commercial and industrial buildings and factories, states:

When business fell off in the fall of 1920, we began to advertise, urging people to build during this period of reduced labor cost. This had an immediate effect in increasing business, and enabled us to keep a large part of our workmen employed during the fall and winter.

It is possible to provide steadier employment when a concern is large and has a number of jobs always ahead or going on at the same time. This enables a concern like ours, for example, to shift men from one contract job to another and makes it possible to keep employees busy more continuously.

In addition we use some men in more than one occupation or job. We keep a nucleus of two to three hundred men all the time—those who are the most dependable.

Our work normally is the construction of industrial buildings of all types, but principally of concrete. Our total business runs between seven and eight million dollars a year.

Hoggson Brothers, New York City, use the following plan:

While our business is principally with a clientele with whom "high peaks" and "deep depressions" occur less frequently than in many other lines of business, still there have been times when depression has been reflected among our customers. Under such conditions we have redoubled our efforts at the selling and advertising ends of our business, and have undertaken contracts in smaller units than we would or could consider in busier times. As our work is carried on both north and south, the winter months do not present the difficulties to us that they do to others.

Kuehnle, painting contractor, Philadelphia, attempts to create steady business both in times of depression and during the winter months by the following methods:

A strong selling organization is constantly on the lookout for houses and other buildings which need painting.

1. To the owners of buildings they explain the advantages of painting during slack times when plenty of good workmen are available and costs of materials and labor are reasonable.

2. To a mailing list of 30,000 names, a letter is sent twice a year asking them to specify their painting requirements. This list consists of customers who have had this concern do painting for them, mainly home owners, or persons who have requested estimates on painting or decorating work; it includes also some hotels, railway stations, office buildings, clubs, etc. A large volume of work is secured by this means, much of it during the winter, consisting mainly of repainting jobs.

3. Advertising results in increased business. The company has a sign on every large job with their distinctive trade mark, a painter running swiftly with a brush in one hand and a pail of paint in the other.

The painting business of this concern amounts to about $700,000 a year. About 80 per cent of their painting business—as far as number of men are concerned—is repainting work; the remaining 20 per cent is work on new buildings. The company which averages about three hundred men in its employ in normal times kept about that number pretty continuously at work even in 1921.

There appears to be considerably less steady employment in cases where contractors do not use stabilizing methods. Another painting contractor in Philadelphia who employs from one hundred to one hundred and fifty men normally, and who is known to do good work, is able during the winter to keep only from fifty to seventy-five men busy, mainly on inside work. He states that he has no way of getting work for his other men during December, January, and February.

*Permanent Nucleus of Workers; Using Same Men on Several Jobs.*— A method employed by a number of concerns, already referred to, is to keep during good times and bad a nucleus of workers whose industry and loyalty are known. The result is that an amount of production per man is secured which is not equalled by that of the employee who is hired today and let go tomorrow, and who feels no particular sense of responsibility for results.

Closely related is a third device, found effective by the Aberthaw Company and others, of using the same men on several kinds of work. This is not quite the same as "dovetailing occupations," but the effect is similar giving steady employment to men who would otherwise be out of work for a time.

13

The Aberthaw Construction Company states:[1]

Most of our mechanics or riggers will work at times erecting structural steel where the connections are bolted.

Our carpenters invariably erect the steel sash, thereby giving some of them employment after the form-work is over. Some carpenters also work as painters and at glazing steel sash.

Cement finishers combine also as cement plasterers. Bricklayers also do lime plastering. Laborers start with pick and shovel, later work in the concrete gang, then at rubbing down concrete surfaces, also some of them go into the gang for laying reinforcing steel.

*Taking Contracts at or near Cost.*—A contracting and building company of Philadelphia and Pittsburgh, states:

We got business during the depression of 1921 by telling prospective customers who hesitated to build during a falling market that we would divide with them any saving in cost (due to fall in prices either of labor or materials) which might take place between the time of making the contract and the time of building. This insured the customer against loss and made it advantageous for him to place the contract at once. This method was responsible for a large share of the business that we got in 1921.

We also, when necessary, took business at a low margin of profit in order to keep the wheels going, figuring this margin at exactly the cost of overhead. This, of course, is done only in times of unusually poor business.

Our firm keeps a number of superintendents—fifteen or twenty in number—continually employed: These we rely upon to direct our workmen. We also keep one or more foremen for each superintendent. We normally employ about seven hundred and fifty men on our various jobs, keeping a small nucleus of reliable workmen and picking up other men at such times and places as we need them.

While we specialize in factory buildings, in time of depression we widen our field of activity and take any kind we can get—hotels, office buildings, large dwellings, etc.

A Southern contractor writes:[2]

Our company had a very successful year in 1921, which the writer attributes entirely to the fact that we observed plain common sense rules based on the law of supply and demand. Business was slack and we figured very low, in many cases at actual cost. Not having labor contracts that prevented, our men agreed to reduced wages which enabled us to keep them employed at practically

---

[1] Personal interview with L. C. WASON, President of Aberthaw Construction Co., 27 School Street, Boston, Mass.; letter from C. E. PATCH, Statistician, dated May 22, 1922. This company gets its business on the basis of a cost plus a fixed fee, rather than by competition on a price basis.

[2] Letter of May 19, 1922, from W. F. CREIGHTON, President, Foster & Creighton Co., Nashville, Tenn.

full time—the result was very satisfactory. In purchasing material every care was exercised to secure the lowest price.

*Repair Work.*

During periods of depression we 'put our house in order,' take inventory, repair, and build tools and equipment, either for ourselves or for others or both.[1] While this district suffered less than most others during the recent depression, we did make a definite effort to keep up our volume of business. One method of increasing business was the establishment of a remodeling and repairing department, under a separate and distinct management, which would not interfere with our regular contract work. This department handles all kinds of repair work, but most of the work is obtained on commercial buildings rather than residence work. This department has shown a good profit and we have continued it ever since.[2]

When winter comes, we endeavor to keep our regular employees busy on southern work, where field operations can be carried on during the winter months and also on repair work on equipment so that it will be in shape to put on work when the season opens in the spring.[3]

The taking of repair work and other small work, which was about the only thing that could be gotten during these depressions, at practically cost, has proved to be about the best thing to do to hold your organization together, as well as to furnish employment for what men could be used.[4]

It is our policy to encourage repair work as much as possible during the winter season and at times when big work is at a low ebb.[5]

*Turning Attention to New Kinds of Contracting Work.*—The Thomas Haverty Company,[6] California contractors, say:

It has been our policy to follow the class of work for which there has been the greatest demand. Our business is sanitary engineering, and a few years ago when the big building operations were held up on account of the war, we conceived the idea of training our men to do residence work, which at that time was very good. We also went into pipe line construction, which during the war proved to be work of considerable volume.

A factor which we consider of great value lies in the labor-saving devices which we purchase. It has been our aim to buy the best machinery obtainable, employing high grade operators to take care of it. Our equipment is kept up in every conceivable manner so that once it goes to the job it is as nearly perfect as we can make it. Considerable business is secured through advertising.

[1] Letter of May 16, 1922 from W. J. HOWARD, Engineer, The Kelly-Atkinson Construction Co., Security Building, 189 W. Madison Street, Chicago, Ill.
[2] Letter of May 22, 1922 from R. A. SMALLMAN, Smallman-Bruce Construction Co., Inc., Avenue E between 11th and 12th Streets, Birmingham, Ala.
[3] Letter of May 15, 1922 from GEORGE W. KOSS, President and General Manager, Koss Construction Co., 5th and L. U. Ry. Tracks, Des. Moines, Iowa.
[4] Letter of May 15, 1922 from W. J. QUICK, Alexandria, La.
[5] Letter of May 16, 1922 from C. E. BAXTER, Baxter Brothers, Huntsville, Ala.
[6] Letter of May 18, 1922 from GEORGE HESS, Thomas Haverty Co., Eighth and Maple Sts., Los Angeles, Cal.

An Alabama concern[1] states:

There is but little repair work done out of our office, but we have what we call the fire loss department and through this we handle, protect, and replace fire damages. And this we use as our fill-in, and taking the total work handled during the year it makes quite a nice business in this line.

Another plan is shown in the following letter:[2]

In the construction field our activities have been confined to foundation and bridge construction for railway and mining companies.

While there was a depression in all construction lines following the war period, in many cases similar to ours, the constructors' activities were so specialized that when the railways ceased construction work their construction forces practically ceased activities for months.

However, prior to the period of depression, in October 1919, realizing that our business should be spread over other lines, we started the manufacture of concrete piling and reinforced concrete pipe. From May, 1921 to December, 1921, during which time our construction department was idle, the concrete products portion of the business materially assisted in carrying our fixed expense.

Perhaps the concrete products business, on account of the fact that these products are used largely by railway companies, is not so good a medium for averting depression as some business not so closely allied with construction; still, at the same time, it does give access to a larger field—which, in principle, is the thing that the constructor perhaps needs most at such a time, and in our case required little additional capital investment.

*Assisting Customers in Financing Building.*—The C. S. Lambie Company, contractors, of Denver,[3] emphasizes a different angle:

When work is scarce, we find that we can very often go out to prospective builders and by assisting them in a financial way—that is, getting them the money with which to build and by giving them extended credit, we can very often induce them to go ahead with work which might otherwise be delayed.

Other concerns state:

We keep as many of our Class 'A' employees busy on repairs as conditions will permit so as to have machinery and equipment in shape when business resumes.

We have on several occasions continued our operations beyond the point which our clients believed conditions warranted, on a deferred payment plan, and have suggested it at other times as a means of relief to the unemployment situation.[4]

[1] Letter of May 18, 1922 from W. P. Blair, Manager, Inglenock Construction Co., 4011 First Avenue, Birmingham, Ala.

[2] Letter of May 22, 1922 from J. R. Stack, Stack Construction Co., Duluth, Minn.

[3] Letter of May 15, 1922 from C. S. Lambie, President, C. S. Lambie Co., Tramway Building, Denver, Col.

[4] Letter of May 16, 1922 from F. H. Holladay, Vice-President and General Manager, Winston-Dear Co., Hibbing, Minn.

In times past, when the sale for securities has been dull, this company has taken work and carried the securities when the investment was a safe one. This has not only helped out the unemployment, but has proved good business on our part.[1]

We make every effort to have inside work. We take a smaller profit during winter season and just now (1921) are operating at no profit at all in order to create a pay-roll.[2]

We heat the houses so the workmen can work in them.

We do quote at a lower profit, but the risk is greater in winter and this offsets the reduction a great deal.[3]

A company[4] hiring between 1,000 and 2,000 men writes as follows:

If possible, we try to enclose our buildings before cold weather, then finish interior with heat on.

Another company[5] hiring normally 200 men reports that:

We attempt to get buildings closed in before winter weather sets in. We will take work at a smaller profit any time to keep our organization intact and cover our overhead, but due to slack season in winter being the most risky season to do work we usually have to carry more profit to cover the risk involved.

The Portland Cement Association has issued several booklets describing successful ways of carrying on concrete construction during the winter. The secretary of the association estimates that there has been an increase of 15 per cent in the amount of winter concrete work in the past three or four years.

*Dovetailing of Occupations.*—The dovetailing of summer occupations with winter employment is receiving attention. An architect recently stated that about the only workmen who need to remain idle most of the winter are the masons, softstone cutters, and bricklayers. Where masons are permitted by the unions to do plastering, they are able to get a good deal of inside work during the winter. In softstone cutting, it may be necessary to provide another trade, since there is no demand for this sort of work for more than six or seven months of the year. To some extent it is possible to anticipate stone cutting jobs and to do this work under cover in the winter.

All of these represent the efforts of contractors or engineers to cope with an existing depression and are but a beginning on a part of a few of the more progressive and intelligent concerns. The more fundamental task of reducing or foreseeing and preparing to meet the depression has

[1] Letter of May 17, 1922 from S. H. HEDGES, President Puget Sound Bridge & Dredging Co., 811–821 Central Building, Seattle, Wash.

[2] Letter from The A. Bently & Sons Co., Toledo, Ohio.

[3] Letter from The W. J. Parsons Housing Co., 1616 Monadnock Building, Chicago, Ill.

[4] Letter from Walbridge-Aldinger Co., 2356 Penobscot Building, Detroit, Mich.

[5] Letter from W. A. and H. A. Root, 1 Beacon Street, Boston, Mass.

been given little attention. This involves a thorough study of the business cycle in general, its relation to building, and analysis of the methods by which a whole industry can be organized on a more continuous basis, and includes such subjects as standard sizes and shapes of building materials, the relations of contractor-employers to labor, and other fundamental problems of organization or management.

**Elimination of Unnecessary Grades, Sizes, and Shapes of Building Materials.**—The Department of Commerce suggests standardizing building materials. Present day manufacturing constantly anticipates demand. In order to manufacture to stock, the manufacturer of building materials should have a minimum of sizes and styles to make and to carry on hand. In some lines, such as common brick, the sizes are already few, to the manifest advantage of all concerned. In others, much remains to be done. In window glass, are one hundred to one hundred and fifty sizes of single strength glass necessary to satisfy the needs of our people? In window sash the wholesale sash and door dealers often advertise more than four hundred different sizes and styles. Why so many? It is a burden to the producer, wholesaler, and retailer; an extra cost which is handed on to home owner or renter, office or store owners, or other consumers.

It has been the custom in the structural slate industry for the quarryman to prepare the structural slate in accordance with the orders he receives. The architect and builder specify the sizes. Here we have another instance of production to order which does not permit the quarryman to produce for stock, for neither the size nor the design is known in advance. This results in a heavy investment to take care of the peak in production. It means not only an unnecessary investment and equipment but high seasonal employment of labor. It results in unemployment and a high labor cost.

The structural slate producers of Pennsylvania have proposed standards after very careful study, but before much good can come from this step, they must have the support of the architects and the builders.

It is possible that a smaller number of sizes of pipes, drain tile, hollow building tile, glaze tile, the fittings, doors, locks, and other items of hardware can be produced. Just how far it is advisable or advantageous to go in the direction of the elimination of variety, few manufacturers or builders are now in a position to say. It is time, however, that a study be made with the cooperation of all groups interested in construction to determine how far fewer dimensions should be produced, fewer varieties placed on the market without curtailing or without hindering the initiative of 'the individual in making intelligent progress and advancement.[1]

The owner of the building when completed would find it much more economical to be able to buy standard stocks in maintaining the structure.

[1] Address before National Assn. of Builders' Exchange at Memphis, Tenn., February, 1922 by J. M. GRIES, Chief of Division of Construction and Housing, U. S. Department of Commerce.

So also with standards of work, which need to be more definitely established, standard methods of cost keeping among contractors, and a more nearly standard form of building contract.

The adoption of a uniform building code throughout the entire country will also tend to stabilize the building industries, making it possible for contractors to buy standard materials for jobs in the different states. Simplification in all these lines means more stable business and steadier employment.

**Building Statistics: Study of the Market for Construction Work.—** The preparation and use of adequate building statistics, showing the annual volume of construction of dwellings, stores, mills, theatres, etc., will call attention to temporary overbuilding in one line or in general, and warn the contractor or engineer against a coming condition of stagnation. It may lead the manufacturer to hasten his building expansion or to postpone it to a time of lower costs.

Study of the market for a contractor's service may prevent his entrance into a field already over-crowded with competitors and lead him to seek expansion in less occupied territory. It may also disclose possibilities in respect to repair work, building management or special kinds of new construction which promise active and continuous business. What has already been done in these respects by those who have given the subject even cursory attention, suggests how much more can be done when a thorough study is made.

**Builders' Exchanges as Clearing Houses of Information.—**The more complete organization of the industry into local builders' exchanges with provision for workmen's participation when feasible, as in the Philadelphia plan, proposed by the Building Trades Council of that city under the leadership of D. Knickerbacker Boyd, is another fertile field for consideration.

A clearing bureau of building activities for an entire city or district, as proposed, would supply materials and employees to all as required, and the exchange of information would tend to prevent over-building. There is a considerable group of functions, including the direction of building-trades schools to be performed by this sort of trade association.

**Education of the Public.—**The public should be educated to do its repair work in the dull times of mid-winter or other off seasons. Here a large home-owning population is an advantage. It is the owner of his own house who is in a position to defer his carpenters' alterations, painting, or electrical and plumbing changes until the building rush is over; the landlord or leasing agent, who has to prepare in August and September for the next tenant, is almost compelled to crowd his repair demands into sixty or ninety days, which come at a time when other construction is in full swing.

So all parts of the problem dovetail together; the rental season and the extent of home ownership affect the possibility of the shifting of a part of the peak of building work.

**Job Scheduling and Planning.**—Each building job should be studied in detail and planned ahead, in order to have materials and men on the job as required.[1]

This scheduling, together with proper cost-keeping, should in time enable contractors and engineers to estimate closely the cost of any proposed job, and thus bid more intelligently on contracts.

## V. SUMMARY

The planning of work ahead by manufacturers and public utilities has proved to be an effective factor in stabilizing business and employment in a number of instances, though practiced as yet by few manufacturers. Repairs and renewals, undertaken during depressions, have given employment to considerable numbers of wage-earners in particular companies. Contractors and engineers have been able to keep employees busy by the various methods cited, one of the most important of which has been the cutting of building costs. These have been entered upon principally in an effort to meet the depression of 1920–1921 and without any fundamental program of preparation for the next depression, or study of the means by which it may be made less severe. Most of what has been done has been by individual concerns. The fundamental economic facts of building and their bearing on one another remain yet to be collected and studied by the building industry as a whole.[2]

[1] "Waste in industry," 1921, The Building Industry, p. 73.

[2] A real stimulus to building construction during a depression can only be given by at least a temporary sharp cut in building costs. Nearly all other devices appear to relate to the regulation of seasonal fluctuations, and to the maintaining of steady activity on the part of individual firms, without any general effect on the building industry as a whole. As I see it, to start a recovery from any acute depression, it is necessary to induce someone, somewhere, to borrow money and spend it. In the field of consumption goods, this appears to be more difficult than it might be in the field of building construction. On the other hand, no prospective investor in a building is going to borrow money to build unless he thinks he is getting a bargain. Such bargains develop, unfortunately, rather late in the ordinary business cycle; and the problem, I feel, is rather clearly that of presenting such bargains at a much earlier date in the cycle than they have hitherto been presented.—Note by M. C. RORTY.

# CHAPTER XIII

## THE STABILITY OF RAILWAY OPERATIONS

### By Julius H. Parmelee

Director of the Bureau of Railway Economics

Summary of Railway Activities.—Our steam railways comprise an industry with a total investment and value in excess of $20,000,000,000. They employ in normal times 2,000,000 men and women, expend $3,000,000,000 for wages and more than $1,500,000,000 for materials and supplies each year out of operating expenses alone. In addition to operating expenditures, there are spent annually large sums on capital account for additions, betterments, and improvements to the physical plant.

According to the latest governmental study of the national wealth of the United States, the value of the physical property of the steam railway industry was about one-tenth of the total wealth of the country. The railway industry represents the largest, most valuable, and most important concentrated industry in the United States. The only industry with anything like a comparable aggregate value is the agricultural industry, which is not concentrated but is composed of a vast number of individual and uncoordinated plants.

In 1920 the Interstate Commerce Commission fixed a tentative valuation of $18,900,000,000 on the steam railway properties of the carriers. This tentative valuation was solely for rate-making purposes and covered only the property owned by the railways which was used in the service of transportation. The present value of railway transportation property, including new investment since 1920, plus the value of railway-owned physical property not devoted to transportation, plus the value of materials and supplies on hand and the amount of necessary working capital, represents a sum far in excess of this tentative valuation. In fact, the grand total has been variously estimated at from twenty-one to twenty-five and one-half billions of dollars.

Railway activities may be considered in three aspects: The railways are manufacturers of transportation. They are employers. They are purchasers. In each of these aspects the railways play an important role, and their activities are closely intertwined with those of industry in general.

In 1921 the operating revenues of the railways of Class I[1] amounted to $5,517,000,000. Operating expenses totaled $4,563,000,000. Of this last sum, $2,590,000,000 or 56.8 per cent was expended directly for labor, and $1,656,000,000 or 36.3 per cent, for materials and supplies, including fuel and miscellaneous items. The balance of $317,000,000, or 6.9 per cent, was spent for loss and damage payments, for injuries to persons, for insurance, and for depreciation and retirements. Much of this latter figure is eventually spent for materials.

**The Railways as Manufacturers.**—The steam railway industry is a manufacturing industry. What a railway produces and has for sale is service, an intangible product, at prices strictly controlled and regulated by state and federal authorities.

The amount of freight and passenger service rendered by the railways each year is usually measured in terms of ton-miles and passenger-miles, namely, the equivalent of a certain number of tons carried one mile, and the equivalent of a certain number of passengers carried one mile. In addition to the transportation of freight and passengers, the railways also perform an important service in carrying mail and express. There is, however, no exact physical unit in terms of which the amount of this traffic may be measured, and while the service is vital to the country, its physical volume and the financial returns to the railways are relatively small in comparison with the freight and passenger business.

By far the most important part of railway transportation is the freight service. Second in importance only to the freight traffic is the passenger transportation service provided by the railways. The amount of the freight and passenger service, for each year from 1911 to 1922, Class I railways, is shown below:

---

[1] Carriers are, for statistical purposes, separated into classes based on the amount of their annual operating revenues, as follows: Class I—above $1,000,000. Class II—from $100,000 to $1,000,000. Class III—below $100,000. Class I carriers operate about 90 per cent of the total operated steam railway mileage, and handle more than 95 per cent of the traffic.

TABLE XXIX.—REVENUE TON-MILES AND REVENUE PASSENGER-MILES, 1911 to 1922

| Year | Ton-miles (millions) | Passenger-miles (millions) |
|---|---|---|
| 1911 (fiscal) | 249,843 | 32,371 |
| 1912 | 259,982 | 32,316 |
| 1913 | 297,723 | 33,875 |
| 1914 | 284,925 | 34,567 |
| 1915 | 273,913 | 31,790 |
| 1916 (calendar) | 362,444 | 34,586 |
| 1917 | 394,465 | 39,477 |
| 1918 | 405,379 | 42,677 |
| 1919 | 364,293 | 46,358 |
| 1920 | 410,306 | 46,849 |
| 1921 | 306,737 | 37,313 |
| 1922 | 339,811 | 35,439 |

In return for their services rendered—in receipt for the sale of their sole product, transportation—the Class I railways have received since 1910 annual sums varying from $2,752,000,000 in 1911 to $6,178,000,000 in 1920. These "gross receipts from sales" suffice to show the importance of the railways as manufacturers, without considering the fact that their product is essential to individual and national existence.

The manufacturing expenses of the railways in producing transportation service are a second indication of the railways' importance. In the eleven years 1911–1921 inclusive, the Class I railways spent more than $34,-000,000,000 in producing transportation and maintaining their properties alone. From 90 to 95 per cent of this total, which includes operating expenses only, was expended directly for labor and materials.

**The Railways as Employers.**—The steam railway industry is one of the largest direct employers of labor in the United States. In the past ten years Class I railways alone have paid out more than $20,000,-000,000 in direct wages to labor. The total number directly employed at any one time by these roads has risen (August, 1920) as high as 2,198,-000. The average number in 1920 was 2,012,706, which was 4.8 per cent of the total number of persons reported by the Census Bureau as gainfully employed in that year.

The following table gives the number of railway employees as summarized by the Interstate Commerce Commission every five years from

1889 to 1914. The number is as of June 30 of each year. Total compensation was first reported in 1895.[1]

TABLE XXX.—NUMBER OF RAILWAY EMPLOYEES AND THEIR COMPENSATION AT
FIVE-YEAR INTERVALS, 1889–1914
(Railways of Class I, II, and III)

| Year | Employees on June 30 | Total compensation |
|------|---------------------|-------------------|
| 1889 | 704,743 | not given |
| 1894 | 779,608 | not given |
| 1899 | 928,924 | $ 522,967,896 |
| 1904 | 1,296,121 | 817,598,810 |
| 1909 | 1,502,823 | 988,323,694 |
| 1914 | 1,710,296 | 1,381,117,292 |

Beginning with 1915, the number of employees has been shown as a yearly average. The statistics for the years 1915–1922, Class I railways, are given below:

TABLE XXXI.—RAILWAY EMPLOYEES AND COMPENSATION, 1915–1922
(Railways of Class I)

| Year | Average number | Total compensation |
|------|---------------|-------------------|
| 1915 [a] | 1,491,849 | $1,236,305,000 |
| 1916 (fiscal) | 1,599,158 | 1,366,101,000 |
| 1916 (calendar) | 1,647,097 | 1,468,576,000 |
| 1917 | 1,732,876 | 1,739,482,000 |
| 1918 | 1,841,575 | 2,613,813,000 |
| 1919 | 1,913,422 | 2,843,128,000 |
| 1920 | 2,022,832 | 3,681,801,000 |
| 1921 | 1,660,617 | 2,765,236,000 |
| 1922 | 1,579,000 | 2,634,717,000 |

[a] Partially estimated to include certain Class I roads not reporting these data to the Interstate Commerce Commission.

The statistics by months from January, 1920 to December, 1922 are given below. These cover railways of Class I, including large switching and terminal companies.

[1] Because of the rather gradual development of employee and wage statistics, it is impracticable to set up a tabulation for any extended period that is comparable throughout. The statistical tables accompanying the following textual discussion are therefore general, and deal merely with total number of employees and total compensation.

TABLE XXXII.—RAILWAY EMPLOYEES AND COMPENSATION, BY MONTHS, 1920–1922
(Class I railways and large switching and terminal companies)

| Month | Number of employees | Compensation |
|---|---|---|
| January, 1920................... | 2,000,105 ⎫ | |
| February....................... | 1,970,525 ⎬ | $ 795,616,000 |
| March.......................... | 2,009,948 ⎭ | |
| April.......................... | 1,952,446 ⎫ | |
| May............................ | 2,005,483 ⎬ | 903,484,000 |
| June........................... | 2,056,381 ⎭ | |
| July........................... | 2,111,280 ⎫ | |
| August......................... | 2,197,824 ⎬ | 1,052,109,000 |
| September...................... | 2,164,880 ⎭ | |
| October........................ | 2,136,259 ⎫ | |
| November....................... | 2,068,454 ⎬ | 982,607,000 |
| December....................... | 1,976,429 ⎭ | |
| January, 1921.................. | 1,804,822 ⎫ | |
| February....................... | 1,676,543 ⎬ | 757,325,000 |
| March.......................... | 1,593,068 ⎭ | |
| April.......................... | 1,542,716 ⎫ | |
| May............................ | 1,575,599 ⎬ | 699,685,000 |
| June........................... | 1,586,143 ⎭ | |
| July........................... | 1,634,872 | 214,339,000 |
| August......................... | 1,679,927 | 227,746,000 |
| September...................... | 1,718,330 | 223,973,000 |
| October........................ | 1,754,136 | 237,603,000 |
| November....................... | 1,732,353 | 225,304,000 |
| December....................... | 1,637,151 | 214,921,000 |
| January, 1922.................. | 1,552,014 | 205,179,000 |
| February....................... | 1,545,040 | 194,523,000 |
| March.......................... | 1,570,158 | 216,704,000 |
| April.......................... | 1,578,133 | 203,413,000 |
| May............................ | 1,628,228 | 216,672,000 |
| June........................... | 1,685,414 | 222,933,000 |
| July........................... | 1,467,824 | 193,571,000 |
| August......................... | 1,594,074 | 224,977,000 |
| September...................... | 1,708,591 | 238,735,000 |
| October........................ | 1,804,315 | 255,514,000 |
| November....................... | 1,820,463 | 249,287,000 |
| December....................... | 1,787,000 | 247,268,000 |

Not only do the railways directly employ many men and women, but they are indirectly responsible for the employment of a large number through the purchase of articles produced by other industries.

The number of men employed in the manufacture and distribution of goods purchased and utilized by the railways has been variously estimated. How closely these estimates run with actual facts it is impossible to say, but they have been made by men intimately connected with the railway supply industry, and represent the careful judgment of those best qualified to know the facts.

A bulletin issued in 1921 by the Railway Business Association, which described itself as a "national organization of concerns making or selling railway equipment, materials and supplies," estimated that 2,000,000 men are normally employed "in the manufacture, repair and reconstruction of railway rolling stock, track, and structures, and the fabrication of all the parts and materials used therein." This estimate does not include the men engaged in the production of the basic materials used indirectly by the 2,000,000 men cited above, as, for example, the coal miners employed in furnishing coal to iron and steel mills producing railway steel, whose employment is due, although indirectly, to railway purchases. The inclusion of these workers would increase this estimate of the total number of men indirectly employed by the railways by at least 10 per cent. Although at best little more than a rough estimate, an analysis of the occupational census statistics for 1920 lends some strength to this approximation. In passing, it may be noted that this total does not include the indirect employment ascribable to the railways through the expenditure by railway employees of their wages.

Adding together the 2,000,000 men employed by the railways under normal conditions and the more than 2,000,000 men estimated as engaged in supplying equipment and materials to the railways, we have a total of over 4,000,000 men directly or indirectly depending for their livelihood on the railway industry. This is approximately 10 per cent of the total number of persons reported by the Census Bureau as gainfully employed in the United States in 1920.

**The Railways as Purchasers.**—In discussing the railways as purchasers, the purchase of new equipment is the logical starting point, for the reason that equipment represents the most complicated product bought by the railways, and the direct purchase of equipment means the indirect purchase of iron, steel, lumber, copper, brass, and countless other raw and semi-manufactured materials.

The following table shows the number of locomotives, passenger-train cars, freight-train cars, and company service cars installed by Class I roads during each year from 1912–1921. Some of this equipment—a relatively small percentage—was built in company shops, but this fact has little bearing upon the status of the railways as purchasers.

TABLE XXXIII.—SUMMARY OF EQUIPMENT INSTALLED, CLASS I CARRIERS
(July 1, 1911–December 31, 1921)

| Period | Locomotives | Passenger-train cars | Freight-train cars | Company service cars |
|---|---|---|---|---|
| July 1, 1911–June 30, 1912......... | 2,861 | 3,060 | 97,972 | 10,630 |
| July 1, 1912–June 30, 1913......... | 4,381 | 2,823 | 162,670 | 13,014 |
| July 1, 1913–June 30, 1914......... | 3,245 | 3,629 | 150,813 | 12,354 |
| July 1, 1914–June 30, 1915......... | 1,114 | 2,664 | 86,012 | 10,228 |
| July 1 1915–June 30, 1916......... | 1,475 | 1,261 | 88,254 | 13,086 |
| July 1, 1916–Dec. 31, 1916ᵃ........ | 993ᵃ | 897ᵃ | 63,426ᵃ | 6,986ᵃ |
| Jan. 1, 1917–Dec. 31, 1917......... | 2,148 | 2,535 | 117,210 | 9,445 |
| Jan. 1, 1918–Dec. 31, 1918......... | 2,803 | 1,817 | 65,249 | 9,310 |
| Jan. 1, 1919–Dec. 31, 1919......... | 2,062 | 435 | 76,019 | 5,925 |
| Jan. 1, 1920–Dec. 31, 1920......... | 1,017 | 621 | 36,044 | 6,608 |
| Jan. 1, 1921–Dec. 31, 1921......... | 1,330 | 1,629 | 62,351 | 4,273 |
| Total........................ | 23,429 | 21,371 | 1,006,020 | 101,859 |

ᵃ Estimated.

These statistics give only numbers. An important development during this period has been in the direction of larger or more powerful locomotives and cars, and a gradual shifting with respect to cars from wooden to steel construction. The table on the following page shows that between 1911 and 1921 the number of locomotives increased only 12 per cent, whereas their aggregate tractive power increased 45 per cent; that the number of freight cars increased only 9 per cent, whereas their aggregate capacity increased 26 per cent. Comparative statistics of passenger-car capacity are not available, but the average size, length, and carrying capacity of passenger equipment have been increasing, as well as their safety and comfort through the installation of steam heat, electric light, and safety devices. Complicated safety devices are also being installed on locomotives and freight cars. These developments mean that more material is required per unit of equipment built, and consequently, that a falling off in number of units bought does not necessarily cause a corresponding decrease in indirect purchases of the basic materials.

A comparison of these two tables vividly illustrates the necessity of large annual railway purchases, because of the wearing out and retirement of equipment. From July 1, 1911 to December 31, 1921, 23,429 locomotives were installed, yet because of retirements, there was a net increase of only 6,860 locomotives in service. Similarly, a gross installation of 1,006,020 freight cars and of 21,371 passenger cars meant only the net addition of 198,056 freight and 7,426 passenger cars.

TABLE XXXIV.—EQUIPMENT IN SERVICE, CLASS I RAILWAYS.

| Item | June 30, 1911 | Dec. 31, 1921 | Increase | |
|---|---|---|---|---|
| | | | Amount | Per cent |
| Number of locomotives.... | 58,071 | 64,931 | 6,860 | 11.8 |
| Aggregate tractive power (lbs.).................. | 1,643,700,000 | 2,376,176,000 | 732,476,000 | 44.6 |
| Average tractive power (lbs.) | 28,305 | 36,803 | 8,498 | 30.0 |
| Number of freight carrying cars................... | 2,117,644 | 2,315,700 | 198,056 | 9.4 |
| Aggregate capacity (tons).. | 78,100,000 | 98,020,000 | 20,432,000 | 26.2 |
| Average capacity (tons).... | 36.9 | 42.5 | 5.6 | 15.2 |
| Number of passenger cars.. | 46,905 | 54,331 | 7,426 | 15.8 |

A second important field of railway purchases lies in the construction of new trackage—main line, secondary and passing tracks, yard tracks, and sidings. Rails, ties, ballast, tie plates, spikes, joints, all these and many other materials are fundamental essentials for the construction of a mile of track. The following figures[1] show the amounts of the more important materials required to build one mile of certain types of single track, and with these figures in mind some idea may be formed of what the appended figures of railway mileage construction mean when converted into terms of purchases.

TABLE XXXV.—AMOUNTS OF MATERIAL TO ONE MILE OF SINGLE TRACK

Cross ties (24" center to center)...................................2,640
Spikes (5½" × $\frac{9}{16}$", 4 per tie) (lbs.)........................... 5,632
Rock ballast (cu. yds.) Class A track........................... 3,488
Rock ballast (cu. yds.) Class B track........................... 2,692
Cementing gravel (cu. yds.) Class A track....................... 2,747
Cementing gravel (cu. yds.) Class B track....................... 2,291
Rail (gross tons), 80 lbs. per yd................................ 125.7
Rail (gross tons), 90 lbs. per yd................................ 141.4
Rail (gross tons), 100 lbs. per yd.............................. 157.1
Rail (gross tons), 110 lbs. per yd.............................. 172.9
Rail (gross tons), 120 lbs. per yd.............................. 188.6

There appear below the number of miles of railway track constructed in the United States by decades from 1850 to 1910 and by years from 1910 to date. Consibered in connection with the foregoing figures, they help to illustrate the great importance of the railways as purchasers.

[1] Prior, F. J., "Construction and Maintenance of Railway Roadbed and Track," 1908, pp. 256-7, 287, 293.

TABLE XXXVI.—MILES OF LINE CONSTRUCTED IN THE UNITED STATES[a]

| Period | Miles | Period | Miles |
|--------|-------|--------|-------|
| 1851-1860 | 21,605 | 1914 | 1,532 |
| 1861-1870 | 22,096 | 1915 | 933 |
| 1871-1880 | 40,382 | 1916 | 1,098 |
| 1881-1890 | 75,724 | 1917 | 979 |
| 1891-1900 | 32,001 | 1918 | 721 |
| 1901-1910 | 47,185 | 1919 | 686 |
| 1911 | 3,066 | 1920 | 314 |
| 1912 | 2,997 | 1921 | 475 |
| 1913 | 3,071 | 1922 | 324 |

[a] Prior to 1881, figures represent net increase in mileage.

Railway growth during the past ten years has proceeded along a line somewhat different from new construction. This line has been the intensive development of existing facilities, representing additions to equipment, construction of second, third, fourth, fifth, and sixth main tracks, and increases in such subsidiary tracks as yard tracks, industrial tracks, passing tracks, and the like. The relative increase since 1900 in mainline mileage operated, and in the other forms of operated trackage, is indicated in the following table:

TABLE XXXVII.—INCREASE IN OPERATED TRACKAGE,
1900-1920

|  | Miles | Per cent |
|--|-------|----------|
| Main line. . . . . . . . . . . . . . . . . . . . . . . . . . . . . . . . . . . | 67,026 | 35 |
| Other main tracks. . . . . . . . . . . . . . . . . . . . . . . . . . . . . | 22,582 | 160 |
| Yard track and sidings . . . . . . . . . . . . . . . . . . . . . . . . . | 57,439 | 110 |
| All tracks. . . . . . . . . . . . . . . . . . . . . . . . . . . . . . . . . . | 147,047 | 57 |

Still a third general field of railway purchases is the construction of new bridges, station and office buildings, terminals and the like. In this field lie also the improvement of such facilities as large terminals, both freight and passenger, and of large shops equipped with better tools and better working facilities for employees; the electrification of tunnels, terminals, and many miles of suburban and main lines; the reduction of grades, elimination of curves, introduction of signals and safety devices.

A large part of the work of new construction and improvement is done by outside companies under contracts for which statistics are not

14

available; but indirectly the railways are the motivating force—the "ultimate purchasers."

An approach from a slightly different angle serves to emphasize even more strongly the magnitude of the railways in the buying field. Exact statistics of consumption do not exist for most of the articles purchased directly by the railways, but an effort has been made to arrive at more accurate figures for the present report than have heretofore been ascertained. The larger railways of the United States have been requested to report the total number of physical units of various commodities purchased by them during each year from 1910 to 1915, a fairly normal prewar period. The reports made by thirty-nine of the principal railways have been consolidated, and the totals so derived have been increased in the ratio which the trackage or operating expenses of these thirty-nine railways bear to the total trackage or operating expenses, respectively, of all steam railways. The average operating expenses and trackage of these thirty-nine railways were approximately 51 per cent of the totals of all railroads. Ties and rails have been increased in the ratio of trackage, and the other commodities in the ratio of operating expenses. In the case of coal and fuel oil, official statistics are available for all railways. The railway aggregates thus ascertained have been compared on a percentage basis with the total production or output of the several commodities in the United States.

This method omits, it is plain, the considerable amounts of materials used indirectly by the railways and directly and indirectly by railway employees. On the basis of the best information available, estimates have been made of the quantities of various materials used indirectly "at first hand" by the roads, and these estimates are included below. But due to endless ramifications, no attempt has been made to include either the goods used indirectly by the railways "at second hand"—the coal, for example, used by the iron and steel mills in producing railway steel— or the goods used directly or indirectly by railway employees. The results which appear below are thus incomplete, nor are they held out as exact, for they are based on certain assumptions admittedly open to question. However, they are offered as the result of a more nearly accurate investigation into the subject than has heretofore been made.[1]

[1] The leading details of this investigation are as follows:

**Coal.**—Not only is the transportation of coal the most important factor in railway freight traffic, about one-third of the total tonnage handled each year, but the railways are also the largest single group of coal purchasers in the United States. According to the United States Geological Survey, the average production of bituminous coal during the six calendar years 1915–1920 was 515,158,000 net tons of 2,000 pounds. Of this total production, the steam railways of the United States consumed an annual average of 143,290,000 net tons. The average annual production of anthracite coal during the same period was 92,034,000 net tons, of which the railways consumed 5,428,000 net tons annually. The percentage of total output consumed by

It appears that the railways purchase directly one-quarter of the total output of coal in the United States and one-ninth of the total petroleum production. Directly and indirectly they purchase approximately 30 per cent of the iron and steel output, at least 25 per cent of the lumber produced, a considerable but indeterminable percentage of the copper and brass output, and smaller percentages of many other products.

## II. RELATIVE STABILITY OF RAILWAY EMPLOYMENT

Census returns show a gradual increase in the proportion of the population and of those gainfully occupied who were in railway employ. For example, the percentage of the gainfully occupied who were in railway service rose from 3.2 per cent in 1890 to 4.8 per cent in 1920.

It is a generally accepted theory that railway service, compared with other industries, offers fairly steady employment. It is true that in the

---

the railways was 27.8 per cent with respect to bituminous coal, 5.9 per cent with respect to anthracite coal, and 24.5 per cent with respect to bituminous and anthracite coal combined. In other words, the railways purchase and consume a quarter of the total output of coal in the United States.

**Fuel Oil.**—According to the Geological Survey, the average annual output of petroleum from 1910 to 1920 was 305,183,000 barrels. The amount of fuel oil consumed by oil-burning railway locomotives during that decade was 36,064,000 barrels per year, or 11.8 per cent of the total output of petroleum. Of fuel oil alone, the Geological Survey estimates the annual average consumption in the years 1910, 1911, 1914, and 1915 at 62,750,000 barrels, of which railway consumption was 30,327,000, or 48.3 per cent. That is, the railways use almost as much fuel oil as all other industries and individuals combined.

**Iron and Steel.**—The average production of pig iron during the years 1910–1915, as reported by the American Iron and Steel Institute, was 30,780,000 net tons annually. Of this production, the railways purchased and utilized 2,580,000 net tons in steel rails each year and 2,565,000 net tons of other iron and steel products. The total iron and steel product, including steel rails, utilized by the railways was 5,145,000 net tons. Allowing for the use of scrap steel in production, the railways purchase directly from 12 to 15 per cent of the annual iron and steel output of the country. (An indeterminable amount of steel is produced from scrap, which does not appear in the annual pig iron production figure.)

These figures take no account of the iron and steel products that go into locomotives, passenger cars, and freight cars built for the railways in outside shops, or of iron and steel used in new construction work which is handled under contract. Into this class falls such construction work as the building of new railway line, of bridges and other large structures, of large stations, office buildings and the like, and many other forms of improvement work handled through outside contractors for a fixed sum. In cases of this kind, of course, the materials involved are purchased by the contractor, not by the railways, and do not enter into the supply records of the railway companies.

It seems reasonable to assume that at least as much iron and steel is used for the railways by outside contractors and construction companies as is purchased directly by the railways. It has been estimated, for example, that nearly 10 per cent of the iron and steel production goes into locomotives and cars alone. This would make summer extra section hands and other laborers are taken on and that at times of heavy business, all forces are somewhat increased. But the railway employee who has a year or two of continuous service, and thus gains a seniority standing, generally escapes a lay-off except in times of unusual depression.

Although the relative stability of employment in railway service is generally regarded as greater than in other lines of industry, little information exists on the subject.

The United States Employment Service has compiled since January, 1921, monthly data concerning the number of employees in 1,428 indus-

---

the total percentage of the iron and steel output consumed directly or indirectly by railways not less than 30 per cent.

**Lumber.**—It is impossible to ascertain exactly the proportion of lumber output used by the railways, because so much lumber goes into new equipment, large structures, and buildings constructed by outside contracts.

It appears from a careful study of lumber purchases reported by the larger railway companies for 1910–1915 that the total number of cross ties purchased by the railways was 130,000,000 per year, equivalent to 4,814,000 M feet; also 345,000 M feet of bridge and switch ties, and 2,141,000 M feet of other lumber. The aggregate lumber purchased by the railways is thus 7,300,000 M feet per year, which is equivalent to 17.5 per cent of the total saw-mill lumber output during that period.

How much additional lumber goes into railway equipment and structures of various kinds built under contract it is difficult to say, but assuming that it is only one-half the amount purchased directly by the railways for their own use, the percentage of lumber output utilized directly or indirectly by the railways would be at least 25 per cent.

**Other Products.**—Of copper and brass products of various kinds the railways during the period 1910–1915 purchased an average of 74,000 net tons per annum. The copper production of the mines of the United States during the same period averaged 598,600 net tons, while the output of the refineries was 767,250 net tons annually. A correct percentage of the railway use of copper cannot be computed from these figures, for the purchases reported by the railways include the zinc and tin in the brass and bronze they bought, but it is clear that the railways of the United States play an important part in the copper business. Also it is certain that the data reported by the railways fall short of the full magnitude of their demand for this metal, inasmuch as equipment bought by the railways, such as locomotives and cars, contains a large amount of copper.

Other metals, chiefly aluminum, lead, zinc, and tinplate, are purchased directly by the railways in amounts averaging less than 1 per cent of the total output each year. Including the quantities used to build equipment and manufacture tools, implements, and machinery for the railways, the total percentages are much higher. Cotton is bought by the railways in the form of cotton waste and other articles. Their average purchases compared with the total production are somewhat less than 1 per cent.

For cement, figures are available in a rather small way for the years 1911–1915. During this period the railways purchased directly about 3 per cent of the total output. Including cement used by contractors in railway construction, the total percentage consumed directly or indirectly by the railways must run well above 5 per cent, and the percentage is probably increasing with the development of concrete work in railway construction.

trial establishments, with a total of approximately 1,600,000 men. A comparison of the results of this compilation with the number of railway employees month by month during the same period seems to indicate greater fluctuation in railway than in other employments. On the other hand for a number of years, Massachusetts has summarized the unemployment situation within the state. The results from 1917 to 1921 show a lower and more constant percentage of unemployment among transportation employees than in other industries, throughout almost the whole of the period. But neither this study, nor that of the Department of Labor, is conclusive. The periods covered are short, and the conditions pictured were abnormal.

### III. FLUCTUATIONS IN RAILWAY ACTIVITIES

Railway activity fluctuates in three distinct ways: seasonally, secularly, and cyclically. The four principal factors of traffic, revenues, expenses, employees, are all subject to these definite variations. Traffic may be taken as the most reliable measure of railway activity and the most sensitive barometer of change; first, because it is a controlling factor—because it is a prerequisite for that continued activity—and second, because its unit of measure remains constant.

Seasonally, there is a normal month to month variation in the amount of traffic offered to and transported by the railways. Revenues, expenses, and employees vary accordingly, the latter two being affected, in addition, by the fact that much of railway maintenance work can be performed only at certain seasons of the year.

Secularly, there is a continual upward trend in traffic caused by the increase in population, the increased demands of industry for transportation, and finally, by the trend toward a generally higher standard of living, and toward centralization of population, both of which are continually requiring more and more transportation service per individual. The number of employees has the same general trend as traffic; revenues and expenses are complicated by rate, wage, and price levels.

Cyclically, there are peaks and valleys in all four factors, following closely the fluctuations of general business.

**Seasonal Fluctuations.**—Railway activity is in a sense the reflex action of all other industries. Certain industries are highly seasonal in nature, and their traffic comes onto the railway lines at well defined periods of the year. The ruling seasons, however, vary from industry to industry. Railway traffic, therefore, reflects in a composite way the seasonal characteristics of all industries served by the railways. In addition railway traffic has some seasonal features of its own. The passenger business, for example, is greatest in the summer months.

As a result the changes in railway traffic, revenues, expenses, and number of employees are markedly seasonal in character.

Chart 48 shows the monthly fluctuations in railway traffic, revenues, expenses, and employment. In each case the average month of the

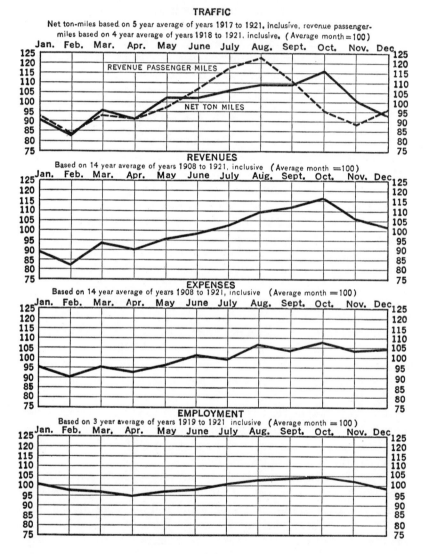

CHART 48.—SEASONAL FLUCTUATIONS IN RAILWAY TRAFFIC, REVENUES, EXPENSES, AND EMPLOYMENT.

period covered is regarded as equivalent to 100 and the individual months are related to that average on an index number or percentage basis. As noted on the chart, the periods for which data are available differ from item to item.

It appears that the low month for both freight and passenger traffic is February, that there is a fairly constant upward trend to August for passenger traffic, and to October for freight traffic; the curves then turn downward until February, except that holiday travel raises the passenger traffic temporarily in December and January.

Railway revenues naturally follow the traffic. They vary from a low point in February to a high point in October, and the trend is almost consistently up or down between the extremes. The curve for expenses also runs from February to October and back again, but is influenced by the seasonal nature of maintenance expenses, which will be shown in some detail in a later chart.

The number of railway employees fluctuates seasonally and in sympathy with the traffic fluctuations but to a much less degree. Thus the low point comes in April, and the peak in October, after which the curve declines again to April. It should be noted that the three-year period on which this curve is based was unusual in many ways, and that the employee curve is not fully representative of normal conditions. The number of employees in January, 1921 was unusually large, because the full effect of the decline in traffic had not yet been realized. The three-year average shown for January is above 100, whereas it is normally several points below. April, on the other hand, is unusually depressed because of the yardmen's strike of April, 1920. The principal use of the chart is to show that there is a definite relationship between seasonal fluctuations in railway traffic and in the number of railway employees.

Some light on this subject may be had from another source. A tabulation covering approximately three-quarters of the employees of Class I roads shows the following seasonal fluctuation for each of the years 1916–1918. In this table, the average for each year is taken as 100.

TABLE XXXVIII.—SEASONAL FLUCTUATION IN RAILWAY EMPLOYMENT, 1916–1918

|  | 1916 | 1917 | 1918 | Three-year average |
|---|---|---|---|---|
| Average for year.............. | 100.0 | 100.0 | 100.0 | 100.0 |
| January..................... | 93.0 | 96.1 | 97.2 | 95.5 |
| April....................... | 100.4 | 98.6 | 98.4 | 99.1 |
| July........................ | 102.4 | 103.3 | 101.0 | 102.2 |
| October..................... | 104.1 | 102.1 | 103.4 | 103.2 |

The upward trend from the earlier to the later months of the year is clearly discernible in the average figures.

Chart 49 shows the monthly maintenance, transportation, and other operating expenses of railways of Class I, averaged over the fourteen-year period 1908–1921. Again the average month is taken in each

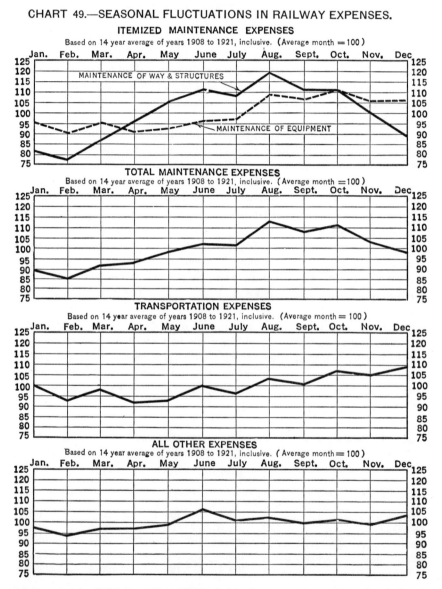

CHART 49.—SEASONAL FLUCTUATIONS IN RAILWAY EXPENSES.

ITEMIZED MAINTENANCE EXPENSES

Based on 14 year average of years 1908 to 1921, inclusive. (Average month = 100)

TOTAL MAINTENANCE EXPENSES

Based on 14 year average of years 1908 to 1921, inclusive. (Average month = 100)

TRANSPORTATION EXPENSES

Based on 14 year average of years 1908 to 1921, inclusive. (Average month = 100)

ALL OTHER EXPENSES

Based on 14 year average of years 1908 to 1921, inclusive. (Average month = 100)

case as equivalent to 100. This chart shows a more sharply defined, seasonal fluctuation in maintenance of way expenses than in any other class. The high months are June to October, when the bulk of outdoor maintenance work is done. This fluctuation is the more marked, because many railway companies, in accordance with the prescribed accounting rules of the Interstate Commerce Commission, charge their maintenance expenses to the appropriate accounts on a program basis, regardless of the actual work done each month.

Maintenance of equipment expenses have their peak in August, September, and October, but in general closely follow the curve for total expenses. When the two maintenance accounts are combined, the fluctuations are less marked.

Secular Fluctuations.—The secular trend in railway activities, while ever present and as marked as the seasonal fluctuation, differs from

CHART 50.—GROWTH OF RAILWAY TRAFFIC.

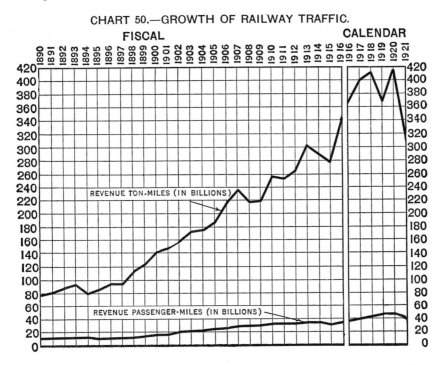

it in a fundamental aspect. The seasonal fluctuation is rhythmical; that is, in any year, it has consistent and well defined crests and troughs, and the monthly figures for a number of years appear as a fairly regular succession of waves when charted. The secular trend, however, is a straight line or a regular curve continually moving in an upward direction.

The secular trend represents the normal growth of railway activity caused by the economic and social development of the country. It may best be illustrated, perhaps, by the growth of railway traffic. On Chart 50 there are shown the revenue ton- and passenger-miles, by years, from 1890 to 1921. No attempt has been made to draw the smoothed line of the secular trend as the continual rising tendency is clear despite a few minor drops.   There is a similar general upward trend in railway revenues and expenses and in the number of men employed.   This trend appears in the following figures showing the growth of railway revenues, expenses, and employment.

TABLE XXXIX.—RAILWAY REVENUES, EXPENSES, AND EMPLOYMENT

| Year | Operating revenues (millions) | Operating expenses (millions) | Number of employees (thousands) |
|---|---|---|---|
| 1890 (fiscal) | $1,052 | $   692 | 749 |
| 1895 | 1,075 | 726 | 785 |
| 1900 | 1,487 | 961 | 1,018 |
| 1905 | 2,082 | 1,291 | 1,382 |
| 1910 | 2,812 | 1,882 | 1,699 |
| 1915 | 2,956 | 2,089 | 1,525[b] |
| 1916 (calendar) | 3,691 | 2,426 | 1,701 |
| 1917 | 4,115 | 2,906 | 1,733[a] |
| 1918 | 4,985 | 4,072 | 1,842[a] |
| 1919 | 5,250 | 4,499 | 1,913[a] |
| 1920 | 6,310 | 5,957 | 2,023[a] |
| 1921 | 5,517[a] | 4,563[a] | 1,661[a] |
| 1922 | 5,558[a] | 4,417[a] | 1,579[a] |

[a] Class I roads only.
[b] Partially estimated to include certain roads not reporting these data to the Interstate Commerce Commission.

**Cyclical Fluctuations.**—The cyclical feature of railway traffic is very marked, following automatically from the fact that the railway business, as already indicated, is a composite reflection of business in general.

The oscillations of railway activity over a period of years may be shown by means of the four factors already enumerated: number of employees, traffic, revenues, and expenses.

During the years 1890–1921, it will be recalled, there were four periods of severe financial and business depression: 1893–1896, 1907–1908, 1914–1915, and 1921.   Charts 51 and 52 present the factors of traffic and employees, and of revenues and expenses, for each year since 1890. As before, the actual amounts are reduced to a relative basis, the annual average of the whole period being taken as equivalent to 100.

In 1921, the final year of the period, the relatives were as follows:

Number of employees..............................................  124
Passenger-miles....................................................  147
Ton-miles .........................................................  145
Railway revenues...................................................  219
Railway expenses...................................................  249

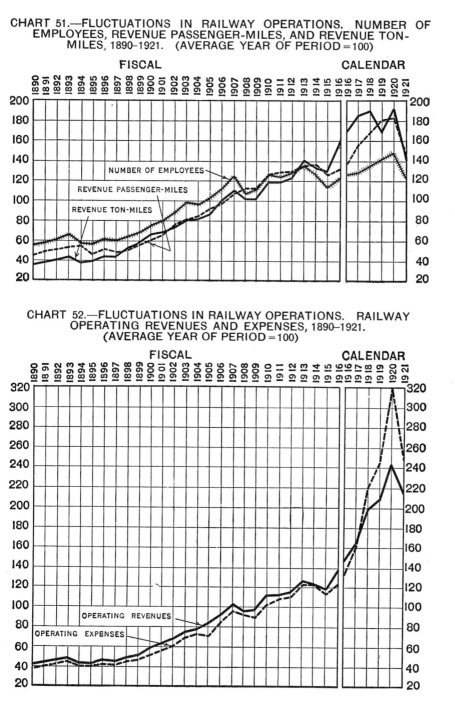

CHART 51.—FLUCTUATIONS IN RAILWAY OPERATIONS. NUMBER OF EMPLOYEES, REVENUE PASSENGER-MILES, AND REVENUE TON-MILES, 1890-1921. (AVERAGE YEAR OF PERIOD=100)

CHART 52.—FLUCTUATIONS IN RAILWAY OPERATIONS. RAILWAY OPERATING REVENUES AND EXPENSES, 1890-1921. (AVERAGE YEAR OF PERIOD=100)

Thus the several factors showed widely varying rates of increase, and it is a significant comment on the railway problem that operating expenses show the highest relative.

The charts bring out clearly the cyclical fluctuations about the secular trend of each factor. Generally speaking, the curves rise from 1890 to 1893, show a decline in 1894 and to some extent in 1895, then rise almost steadily to 1907. The sharp drop in 1908 was the result of the financial panic of 1907. The year 1909 showed a slight improvement over 1908, and there was a further gain in 1910, which with a slight recession in 1911 continued to 1913. The drop in 1914 to some extent foreshadowed, while the further drop in 1915 clearly reflected, the European war. The sharp turn upward in 1916 was also due to war conditions, while the continued rise to 1918 grew out of our own war activities. Ton-miles broke sharply in 1919, but all the curves reached their peak in 1920. Then came the unprecedented decline of 1921.

The principal conclusion to be drawn from the charts is that railway activity, however measured, is in fact cyclical, and that it closely follows the trend of business in general. This was to be expected from the nature of the railway industry, but the charts establish the relationship beyond question.

#### IV. THE RELATION OF RAILWAY PURCHASES TO BUSINESS

That there exists a relationship between railway purchases and general business has been emphasized many times and by many observers.

In 1908, for example, W. R. Taylor, Vice-President of the Reading Company, made the following statement:

An examination of the statistics would seem to justify the opinion that if the influence of the railroad companies did not predominate (in industrial activity) it, at least, set in motion the means that produced that activity. This conclusion would seem to be negatively proved by the fact that the industrial depression began immediately upon the suspension by the railroad companies of their construction work and the completion or withdrawal of their orders for equipment late in 1907.

Judge A. C. Spencer, General Attorney of the Oregon-Washington Railroad and Navigation Company in 1914 expressed the same thought as follows:[1]

Railway purchases are the initial impetus, or force, in starting and sustaining the current of general business.

The statistics already presented, showing how large a proportion of the output of the more important industrial products is used by the railway industry, serve to emphasize the statement (and others which might

[1] *Oregon Manufacturer*, February, 1914, p. 21.

be quoted to the same effect), that the steam railway as a purchaser is a factor to be dealt with in any survey of market conditions.

The claim is sometimes made that purchases by the railways measure business prosperity. Some go farther, and argue that prosperity actually depends on railway purchases.

Statement of this doctrine is usually coupled with the plea that the railways should come into the market in times of depression, so as to encourage manufacturing and construction companies, and furnish labor to men who need employment most at that time. It is pointed out that railway orders for equipment, for example, will mean business for locomotive and car companies, which in turn will spell orders for steel companies, for machine and implement manufacturers, for lumber men, and so on back to the producers of raw material. Railway orders create business activity, and activity provides employment.

Perhaps the best statement of the case is contained in an open letter written by E. B. Leigh, President of the Chicago Railway Equipment Company, to Secretary Hoover in September, 1921, at the time of the President's Unemployment Conference. This letter read in part as follows:

> Restoration of national prosperity can be started on its way by just one factor—purchasing power. All substitutes are bootstraps or phantoms.
>
> Among the sources of purchasing power the largest and most definitely available is the power of the railroads to buy material and labor for maintenance, additions, and betterments. In normal years, the railways directly and indirectly have consumed from 40 to 50 per cent of the iron and steel production, admittedly the 'barometer of business.'
>
> It is the history of depressions that recovery is always accompanied by resumption of large railroad buying, and never comes without it, the only exception being the war period. The business so initiated flushes the channels of all industry and trade, including agriculture, and favorably affects every inhabitant of every community.
>
> However it starts, a resumption of general business is strengthened and hastened by railroad buying and cannot be permanent without it.

It has been pointed out furthermore that there is usually either a feast or a famine in the railway supply industry.

The railways are themselves poor in times of depression. They are forced because of this to stay out of the supply market at the very time when that market needs help. Then when they do begin to buy after the volume of business increases, prices have begun to rise and deliveries are slow. The very fact that railways begin to buy tends to increase the price; in other words the financial condition of the railways, brought about by the limitation of their earnings, forces them to stay out of the market when it would be helpful for them to go in and then when they do go in, it sometimes causes excessive increases in price.

## V. STABILIZATION OF RAILWAY ACTIVITIES

In their role of manufacturers of transportation the railways have little opportunity to control the amount of their product. Unlike other manufacturing industries, when business falls off, the railways are not able to stabilize their operations by the manufacture of their commodity —transportation service—for stock, or by attempting to develop a subordinate by-product. Transportation is a "current" commodity, produced only when demanded and there are no stabilizing by-products. Individual railway companies maintain traffic bureaus, outside agencies, and advertising organizations to attract traffic to their own lines, which in a degree may affect the amount of traffic offered to them. To some extent, however, what new traffic is secured by one railway is at the expense of other railways. In the aggregate, the railways themselves create only such traffic as represents the transportation of their own supplies, or of the equipment and other items they purchase. This is not the bulk of their traffic considered as a whole. They handle the traffic that is offered them by other industries the amount of which is controlled in turn by the business situation and by circumstances generally beyond railway control.

It appears therefore that the transportation service of the railways is controlled in large measure by the demand of the general public for freight and passenger service. There is a fixed minimum demand below which the service will not go, and there is also a maximum demand which is frequently affected by temporary circumstances. During the past five years, the largest number of revenue and non-revenue ton-miles handled by the railways in any one month was 42,734,000,000 in the month of August, 1920, while the smallest number was 24,723,000,000 ton-miles, in the month of April, 1922. The difference between these two extremes is very great, the maximum being 73 per cent above the minimum.[1]

With reference to the passenger service, there has also been a wide variation, indicated by the fact that the largest number of passenger-miles handled in any one month during the past five years was 5,004,000,-000, in the month of August, 1920, while the smallest number was 2,396,000,000, in the month of February, 1922. The high mark was here more than 109 per cent above the low mark.

Seasonal variations of traffic, such as have been described, produce some variations in railway employment, particularly among those groups of employees whose service is directly related to transportation. Little

---

[1] One reason why the month of August, 1920 was the largest freight traffic month in the history of the railways is that the increased freight rates put into effect by the Interstate Commerce Commission on August 26 of that year were known to shippers thirty days in advance, and a great amount of traffic was rushed onto the rails in advance of the increase. On the other hand, the low freight traffic of April, 1922 was largely due to the coal strike.

constructive planning is possible with respect to this form of railway service, which is dependent almost entirely on business and public demands. Traffic frequently increases with but little warning, with the result that the number of employees does not immediately increase in proportion to the increase of traffic. Freight and passenger trains may be loaded to greater capacity, and more frequent schedules may be inaugurated, bringing heavier duties onto the shoulders of the train employees and giving them more compensation on account of overtime, but perhaps adding little to the number of men on the pay-roll.

On the other hand, it frequently happens that traffic falls off almost over night. This was the case in the early part of 1921 when traffic declined rapidly after several months of the heaviest movement of freight and passengers on record. It took time for the railways to adjust themselves to this change, with the result that several months were consumed in getting the number of men on their pay-rolls and the compensation paid to them onto a lower level in sympathy with the decline in traffic. The relative decreases in the number of employees in service, and in revenue ton-miles each month from August, 1920, the month with the heaviest traffic and the greatest number of employees ever recorded, to April, 1921, when the tide finally turned, appear below. It will be noticed that the reduction in the number of employees lagged decidedly behind the falling off in traffic.

TABLE XL.—PERCENTAGE DECLINE IN RAILWAY EMPLOYMENT AND REVENUE TON-MILES

| Month | Percentage decline from August, 1920 | |
|---|---|---|
| | Employees in service | Revenue ton-miles |
| September, 1920 | 1.5 | 3.4 |
| October | 2.8 | 0.2 |
| November | 5.9 | 11.5 |
| December | 10.1 | 19.3 |
| January, 1921 | 17.9 | 32.0 |
| February | 23.7 | 43.3 |
| March | 27.5 | 38.2 |
| April | 29.8 | 41.1 |

If the railways have only partial control over their traffic, it follows that they have only partial control over the number of employees engaged in transportation. This assumption is borne out by Chart 53 which shows the relationship between ton-miles, passenger-miles, and number of transportation employees from 1890 to 1921. For comparison a curve is also included for maintenance employees. The annual average of the period is taken in each case as 100, and every year in the period is related to that average on a percentage basis.

The number of employees engaged in transportation shows a close relationship to the amount of traffic. The number of maintenance employees increased more rapidly than those engaged in transportation, but showed a tendency to decline more sharply in times of depression. This is noticeable in 1894, 1908, 1914, and 1921. While the basic employment figures supplied by the Interstate Commerce Commission for the

CHART 53.—RAILWAY TRAFFIC AND RAILWAY EMPLOYEES. REVENUE TON-MILES, REVENUE PASSENGER-MILES, AND NUMBER OF MAINTENANCE AND TRANSPORTATION EMPLOYEES, 1890–1921. (AVERAGE YEAR OF PERIOD = 100)

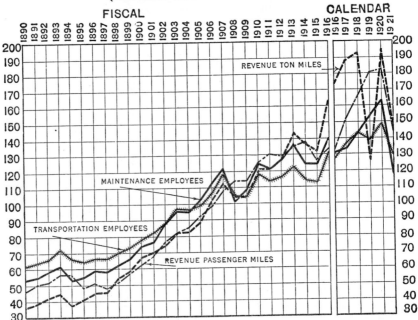

years prior to 1915 are none too reliable, whatever conclusion can be drawn from Chart 53 indicates that the number of maintenance employees has been controllable to a greater extent than the number engaged in transportation. This tallies with the prevailing impression with respect to railway maintenance—that there is a margin within which railway managements have some opportunity to exercise discretionary powers.

In their capacity as purchasers, which brings in the influence exerted on employment in other industries, the railways have somewhat greater freedom of action than they have as manufacturers of transportation. It is for the boards of directors of individual railways to decide whether or not their traffic needs call for more equipment, for enlargement of their shops, or for additions to trackage facilities and other parts of the railway plant. In times of low traffic and reduced earnings, everything tends toward the cutting down of new construction and improvement work, as well as maintenance of way and of equipment. How far the maintenance of railway property can be postponed or deferred with safety, and to what extent omissions must be made up at some future time with perhaps added expense and difficulty, is a much mooted question. In particular, it has been the subject of debate between the United States Railroad Administration and many railway companies, because the Railroad Administration during the period of federal control reduced the amount of railway maintenance below the normal level.

**Construction and New Equipment.**—In times of low earnings, the railways are naturally forced to retire very largely from the equipment market. The reasons are two: In the first place, low earnings do not furnish a sufficient margin of return to warrant the railways in seeking enlarged credits for new equipment, and they may even find their cash in hand inadequate to make the necessary first payments on equipment trust obligations. In the second place, their traffic is low and the equipment in service at the time may be more than sufficient to meet current demands. Under such conditions it is not strange that the need for new equipment does not press for attention. With hundreds of thousands of idle freight cars on hand, and with no prophetic knowledge of the future, it is not surprising that the railways hesitate to invest their scanty funds in new equipment for which there is no immediate need, and which may not yield any return for an indefinite period upon the money invested.

During the year 1921 there was a continuing condition of car surplusage, or idle cars, and the number idle at the close of the year was much larger than at the beginning. In the face of a discouraging situation of this sort, it was to be expected that orders for new freight cars would be at a low point in 1921. During that year orders were placed by the railways for only 23,346 freight-cars, with one exception the lowest number on record. Since the beginning of 1922, however, railway managements have thought they foresaw a period of slowly returning prosperity, and during that year orders were placed for more than seven times the number of new freight cars that were ordered during the year 1921. A large measure of faith entered into their policy, for the idle-car situation during the first six months of the year was far from satisfactory, even though it exhibited some improvement over 1921. But with the belief that better traffic conditions were bound to come, the railways took a leaf out of their own past record, and prepared for the future. This indicates the extent to which the psychological element in the railway situation tends to guide the policy of the railways as to new equipment and other improvements in plant.

15

With respect to new locomotives and passenger cars, the situation was much the same. The number of new locomotives ordered in 1921 was 239, and the number of passenger cars ordered 246. In each case this was the lowest in more than twenty years with but a single exception. During 1922, however, orders were placed for more than ten times as many locomotives as during the year 1921, and for more than nine times as many passenger cars.

With respect to improvements other than new equipment, such as enlargement of terminal facilities, provision of additional trackage, and the like, exact statistics are more difficult to secure. The same principles apply here, however, as in the case of equipment. A period of low traffic and reduced earnings keeps the railways out of the market for new facilities and improvements, both because their treasuries and their credit are restricted, and because the traffic needs do not at the time call for additional facilities.

**Railway Maintenance.**—Maintenance work, like new construction or equipment purchase, is regulated to some extent by policies of management, although to a much less degree than in the case of new construction. The railway plant must be kept up to a certain level of physical condition, regardless of traffic or revenue. This is the minimum below which no management dare go. Traffic conditions are also a factor in maintenance; the more train-miles produced upon a given section of track, the greater the wear and tear on roadway, rails, and ties. The more locomotive-miles and car-miles, the greater the need for repairs to those classes of equipment.

Above these requirements of safety and of traffic, there is, however, some margin for the play of discretion on the part of the managements.

As to maintenance of way, carefully outlined programs are adopted by many railway companies at the beginning of each year. These programs are determined in part by the maintenance requirements and in part by the best estimate that can then be made as to the probable earnings of the year.[1] Programs are frequently modified as the year draws on, being sometimes increased and sometimes decreased, in sympathy with traffic and revenue changes. During 1921, largely because of the unfavorable financial results of operation, there was some tendency to reduce maintenance programs as the year went on.

Expenditures for maintenance of equipment are also controllable to some extent, for there is no call immediately to repair locomotives and cars classified as in need of repairs, unless there is urgent demand for them. Here again, while safety and traffic conditions set the minimum standard, there is also a margin for the play of policy.

---

[1] For a detailed discussion of this subject, see WM. C. WILLARD, "Maintenance of Way and Structures," 1915, Chap. XXI, pp. 417–424, entitled, Annual Program for Maintenance of Way and Structures.

There is a field for long-range planning with respect to maintenance work, and a larger field with respect to construction of new equipment and other facilities. The control over maintenance is exercised directly through the medium of the employment of greater or lesser forces of maintenance workers, while the control over new construction operates indirectly, and tends to increase or decrease employment in other industries.

### VI. PROPOSALS LOOKING TOWARD GREATER STABILIZATION

While the subject of stabilization of railway employment has been discussed for years, but few definite proposals have been made looking toward any program or policy that would increase stability.

The Committee on Economics of Railway Labor of the American Railway Engineering Association in 1920 made the following comment on seasonal fluctuations in railway employment:

There appears to be an almost universal appreciation by the roads of the serious effect that intermittent labor has on their organization and efficiency in maintaining the railways of the country. There is also a general feeling on the part of a majority of the roads that this can only be corrected, or at least minimized, by working out a more scientific method of arranging the maintenance of way program whereby large armies of workers will not be made idle during a very considerable part of the year. The annual man-hours remain about the same, but due to the fact that it is not scientifically arranged, a great many excess workers remain frequently on furlough, creating an economic condition that is hurtful to all concerned.

In 1921 the same committee set forth the difficulties of a definite labor program in the following words:

The problem of furnishing labor for railway service is complicated by fluctuations in the available supply in labor markets, by the seasonal nature of track work, and especially by that class of extensive improvements usually termed construction work.

Weather conditions determine the months in which outside work can most economically be done for practically all railroads in the United States. In the northern states, both east and west, this work is difficult and expensive if undertaken during the months December to March inclusive, while the ground is frozen or covered with snow. In the southern states it is expensive if done during the rainy season.

For this reason, it seems impracticable to recommend a country-wide plan for the permanent employment of laborers in the maintenance of way department, but consideration is recommended for a much broader, all-year program of maintenance work and permanent force wherever conditions permit.

With respect to long-range planning by railway companies, the subject has received but little treatment. Alba B. Johnson, formerly president of the Baldwin Locomotive Works, appeared before the House Committee on Interstate and Foreign Commerce on August 25, 1919 and, speaking for the Railway Business Association, made the following comment on railway practice:

The greatest railroad genius America has produced, the late E. H. Harriman, pursued the well-settled policy of liberal buying in depressions with the two-fold motive of relieving the depression and of obtaining goods at bargain prices. A similar policy has been characteristic of the Pennsylvania system. The principle was coming to be understood and gradually brought into application in the period before 1906.

Proposals for railway construction budgets on a wide scale have been made in other countries than the United States, notably in France. There was published in 1907 a document[1] prepared by Georges Villain, Director of Commercial Control of Railroads in the French Ministry of Public Works, recommending such procedure on the French railways as would avoid the effects of recurring business crises.  Two proposals were made: (a) establishment of a yearly budget by the railway companies, instead of making additions and betterments in years when receipts are heavy, and curtailing them in years when finances are low, and (b) establishment of a five-year program of expenditures for rolling stock, terminal improvements, and other forms of extensions and improvements.

In recommending the establishment of a long-term program of orders for rolling stock and material, M. Villain observed that periods of industrial activity generally found the railroads unable to handle the shipments offered them, because of lack of cars and tractive power, or because of insufficient terminal facilities.  The companies at such times immediately placed large orders, necessarily paying peak prices not only for manufactured articles but also for the raw materials and for labor, and deliveries were not usually made before depressions had set in.  French factories, M. Villain pointed out, were unable to increase their production suddenly, and many of the rush orders went to foreign countries at greater prices, increased delay, and loss to French trade.  If the proposed long-term program were adopted, French factories would have the benefit of the orders, their labor the benefit of steady employment, and the railroad companies the benefit of lower prices.

This French doctrine has striking similarities to that laid down by some American observers.

That there is planning on the American railways with respect to their maintenance work and their construction work (including equipment orders) is unquestionable.  The number of transportation employees

[1] *Notice sur la périodicité des crises economiques et ses rapports avec l'exploitation des chemins de fer français.  Paris, Ministry of Public Works, 1907.*

needed at any time depends almost wholly on the state of traffic. Maintenance work follows the traffic to some extent, but there is a margin above the level fixed by traffic requirements that must be, and usually is, governed by the current situation as to railway revenue. If traffic is heavy and receipts are large, there is every incentive for conscientious and efficient managements to keep up the plant, and even to improve its condition wherever possible. If revenues are low, then it is a matter of necessity—not choice—that maintenance expenditures be reduced. There is more play for fluctuation here than in the case of transportation expenses.

Much of the maintenance work is necessarily seasonal in character, and little of it can be handled in a long-range program. Even so, if the farms, mines, and mills keep their production and shipments uniform and on a steady scale, and the railways can avoid labor difficulties, they could measurably be assured of giving steady employment even on road maintenance, for notwithstanding seasonal variations, railway expenses follow the trend of revenues very closely.

As to improvements, orders for new equipment, and new construction, the prime question is that of adequate and continuous credit. This credit depends in part on the state of current railway earnings, but it rests basically on the history of each railway company, which in turn is a composite of many factors, some dependent on the efficiency and foresight of management, some on the psychology of the current business situation, and many on the result of conditions beyond railway control. These conditions are the policy of public regulation—the control of rates by the Interstate Commerce Commission, of wages, rules and working conditions by the Railroad Labor Board, and of many other features of railway operation by state and local authorities—the state of business in general, the concentration or decentralization of industry, shifts in the currents of traffic, and many others.

But behind all these factors lies the question of railway finances. The small return upon the value of their property which the railways have had for years has had a depressing effect on the credit of nearly all companies, and has made it difficult either to lay down or to carry out a long-range program. The railways have earned as much as 6 per cent on their investment in only one year of recent history. Under federal control they were assured slightly over 5 per cent, and during the guaranty period of 1920, a little over 4 per cent. From the close of the guaranty period through December, 1922, their net income averaged 3.6 per cent per annum.

A railway executive has recently expressed this idea of the relationship between railway credit and stabilization in the following words:

Railroad managers are anxious to make money for their companies and naturally desire to buy material and equipment and make repairs under the most economical conditions, but when, as in recent years, the railroads have been obliged to make every possible economy in order to get through and maintain their interest and dividend payments—and many have failed to maintain dividend payments—they have not been able because of their financial condition to take advantage at all times of periods of depression in order to build up and extend their plant. Everyone recognizes the desirability of such a policy. Mr. Harriman was able to do it with his system because in the first place the financial condition of his properties was so strong that he was able to take advantage of the situation, while other managers equally anxious to do so were prevented because of their financial circumstances.

There are other obstacles to the establishment of long-range programs. Changes in accounting practice would become necessary, the attitude of regulatory commissions toward the policy of building up maintenance or other reserves would become a factor, and the relation between such a policy and the working of the "recapture" clause of the Transportation Act would be a matter for public consideration. But these obstacles, important as they are, are subordinate to the outstanding factor of railway net income. Its adequacy is what must underlie any consistent effort, on the part either of individual railways or the railways as a whole, to carry out a consistent policy or program of railway maintenance and railway improvement.

Elimination of waste in railway operation, wherever such waste may exist, is one step toward an increase in net income. Driven by the necessities of their financial situation, stimulated by the provisions of the Transportation Act that railway operation shall be "efficient and economical," and influenced by other social forces, the railways individually and collectively are giving much consideration to this problem. Their efforts are bearing, and will continue to bear, fruit. But, assuming the continuance of private operation of the railroads, only the establishment of a stable policy of public regulation will furnish the railways with a financial basis that will enable them to plan for the future, and thus to stabilize railway employment and railway purchases.

# CHAPTER XIV

## THE LONG-RANGE PLANNING OF PUBLIC WORKS

### By Otto T. Mallery

Member of the Pennsylvania State Industrial Board

### I. THE PROBLEM

Our problem is to examine public works in order to determine whether through their timely prosecution cyclical unemployment periods may be diminished or prevented. Can public works, by forethought, advance planning, and financial prevision, be expanded in periods of cyclical unemployment? To what extent? How far can public works be prevented from adding to the height of a boom wave through competition with private industry during periods of industrial activity? How far can the resulting fall into a trough of depression be lessened? With what economic effect on industry in general?

### II. ECONOMIC BASIS

**Flexible Public Works and Regularized Private Industry.**—There are two kinds of business, private and public. The object of most private business is profit; of public business, service.[1] Regularization of production is profitable for private business; on the other hand there is no commercial value in regularizing the annual execution of public works, though of course governments can keep down the taxpayers' burden by executing public works economically. After every private plant and industry has made every effort to stabilize production, a considerable fluctuation will remain. Government—federal, state, and municipal— would obviously increase the value of its services to the public, could it absorb a part of this fluctuation by conscious expansion and contraction of its public works at specific times and in reverse direction to the flow of private industry. On the other hand, a government which competes with private industry for the same men and materials by executing public works during periods of industrial activity does a positive injury

[1] I take exception to this distinction. The legally required purpose of the business of regulated public utilities is service. Profits are permitted only as an incident to the rendering of service. Furthermore, many private businesses such as mutual life insurance companies, savings banks, building and loan associations, etc., are operated primarily for service. Some professional men, manufacturers and merchants would say, with a measure of truth, that they aim at service rather than profit. On the other hand, the service motive is frequently subordinated in public business to the profit of office-holders and political machines.—Note by M. C. Rorty.

231

to the economic structure and brings on the evils it might prevent.[1] Prices of materials and rates of wages are sky-rocketed; labor turnover is increased; transportation facilities are overtaxed; interest rates on commercial and other credits are lifted and the costs and selling prices of all commodities raised.

**Total Cost Decreased by Expansion in Bad Times.**—One obvious benefit of the reverse policy is that the total cost of public works would be less over a ten-year period containing both prosperous and depressed years. Whatever percentage is executed during depressions may be contracted for at lower prices for materials and labor. Since unemployment of capital coincides with, or closely follows, unemployment of labor, the interest paid on municipal bonds sold during and immediately after depressions will in the long run be less.[2]

**The Social Cost of Dependents.**—The informed taxpayer and voter has a pecuniary motive in putting this policy into practice. A decrease in unemployment, however accomplished, decreases the local appropriation for poor relief and the more remote by-products of poverty, including the costs of the institutional support of dependents.

**Taxpayers' Motives.**—In many New England towns it has long been the practice to employ mill operatives on wood cutting and the building of stone walls—primitive forms of public work—when the mills are closed. The town obtains a return for funds which would otherwise be dispersed as charity. What is true in a small town is equally true in a large city, though it may be less obvious to the taxpayer. The mere size and complexity of the city often conceal from the citizen his true relationship to the costs of unemployment.

**Purchasing Power of Wages.**—The effect of public works upon unemployment does not stop with the employment of the man upon the particular job. The manufacture of the materials requires the employment of as many or more additional men. The purchasing power of the wages is an equally important consideration. For example, wages are partly spent upon shirts. The demand for shirts causes unemployed cotton and wool operatives to go back to their looms, moves cotton bales from the South and wool from the West, liquefies frozen credits

---

[1] I do not agree with Mr. Mallery that governmental competition in the execution of public works during periods of prosperity is necessarily an injury to the economic structure. I feel that governmental competition during both periods of depression and periods of prosperity may have a very salutary effect in raising the standard of living of the workers, their consequent purchasing power and the health of industry. I realize, however, the very great value of extensive public operations during periods of depression.—Note by H. W. LAIDLER.

[2] Taking the years 1878–1912 in England, grouping them into cycles of seven years, we find that in the years when unemployment is above the average, interest rates are below the average and *vice versa*. British Board of Trade figures quoted in the *Report of the Ontario Commission on Unemployment* (Canada), 1916, p. 144.

in cotton and wool, increases freight receipts of the railroads, etc. The purchase of clothes, shoes, food, and countless other commodities from the proceeds of public works' wages exerts a cumulative effect upon general industry and employment.

**A Small Variation in Public Works Affects All Industry.**—Public works need give direct employment to only a small percentage of the unemployed in order to improve the situation. Between a year of boom and a year of depression there is a difference of only 10 to 20 per cent in the weight or quantity of production.[1] This means that prosperity can be destroyed by making only nine sales where ten were made before, or it can be created by making eleven sales where ten were made before.[2] Just as it is the last few hundreds of millions of orders which raise the boom wave to the breaking point, so it is the first few hundred millions of orders that check the depression and begin the reconstruction of the industrial structure. Can public works supply such a check and such a forward impulse?

**III. POWER OF CONCENTRATED PUBLIC WORKS TO CHECK CYCLICAL UNEMPLOYMENT[3]**

Obviously the long-range planning of public works is no panacea for the ills of cyclical unemployment. But is its contribution toward control trifling or substantial? To answer that question some rough statistical estimates are necessary.

**Average Expenditure for Public Works.**—The best data for estimating the aggregate expenditure on public works are the "outlays" reported by the Census in its reports on *Wealth, Debt and Taxation* and in *The Financial Statistics of States* and *Cities.* "Outlays" is an accounting term which covers permanent improvements. From these sources Table XLI has been made:

TABLE XLI.—OUTLAYS UPON PUBLIC WORKS.

| Branch of government | Period covered | Average "outlays" |
|---|---|---|
| Federal government.................. | 1913 | $ 64,380,000 |
| States............................. | 1915–19 | 77,000,000 |
| Cities over 30,000.................... | 1909–19 | 300,000,000 |
| Smaller cities, villages, and counties...... | 1913 | 163,000,000 |

[1] See the estimates in Chap. III, above.
[2] Moody's Investors Service *Weekly Review of Financial Conditions,* Jan. 12, 1922, p. 2.
[3] This section is the net resultant of work by T. W. Mitchell, W. I. King, E. E. Hunt, and W. C. Mitchell.

Aggregate public expenditures of this sort in 1913 were $586,000,000; but the total from the above schedule (some $600,000,000) may be nearer the pre-war average.

At present prices, government "outlays" are probably running in the neighborhood of $900,000,000 per annum. The F. W. Dodge Company reports an average expenditure on public works in 1919–1921 of about $700,000,000—an amount consistent with a total of $900,000,000 for the whole country, when an estimate is added for the territory not included by the Dodge Service.

**Size of a Possible Public Works Reserve Fund.**—To determine what fraction of the expenditure could be postponed to, or advanced to coincide with, a period of depression would require an elaborate investigation. If, however, we assume that one-third of the work could be assigned to the long-range program, $300,000,000 a year might go into the public works reserve fund.

Probably two-thirds of the money spent for goods goes directly or indirectly to pay wages and salaries.[1]  On this basis the annual addition to the public works reserve fund would provide some $200,000,000 for pay-rolls.[2]

The size which this reserve would reach depends, of course, upon the number of years during which accumulations continued. Here is a difficult problem. Within the last thirty-three years the United States has suffered five severe depressions which began in 1893, 1903, 1908, 1914, and 1920—say one in every six or seven years. Can we then count on a five- or six-year period for building up the reserve? Scarcely, because the depressions have lasted from about thirteen months (1908) to about four years (1893–1897, with a brief and partial revival in 1895). An administrative board might spend all its accumulated reserve in the first year of a long depression, and would scarcely stint public expenditures in the second or third year in order to start accumulating new reserves to meet a future emergency. It is doubtful whether five years' accumulations would have been made before the panic of 1893 because of the brief period of dullness in 1890–1891. Not more than four or five years' accumulations would have been available in 1903; and three years' accumulation in 1908. The next case is harder to guess because 1911 was a dull time; but certainly not more than five years' accumulations would have been in the reserve fund by 1914, and not more than five

---

[1] See the report of the National Bureau of Economic Research on "Income in the United States," New York, 1921 and Sir J. C. Stamp, "Wealth and Taxable Capacity," London, 1922.

[2] The reserve fund would depend only in small part upon accumulated cash and postponements. Its chief strength would consist of authorized bond issues, of engineering plans ready for specific works, and of the formulated determination of federal, state, and municipal governments to catch up with existing needs and to anticipate needs of the near future when unemployment is greatest.

years' accumulations by 1920. On the basis of this experience, we may take four years as a rough average attainable by a board capable of withstanding pressure, determined to stimulate public works only in times of severe depression, and insisting upon continuing its accumulations during periods of moderately heavy unemployment. Four years would provide a reserve of $1,200,000,000 or a pay-roll fund of $800,000,000. Whatever the size of the reserve, it is clear gain if the time of its expenditure is based upon unemployment statistics.

**Adequacy of the Possible Reserve Fund.**—How far would such a reserve, plus the increase of public "outlays" from $600,000,000 to $900,000,000 per annum, offset the wage losses of a single year of depression?

The only class of workers whose wage losses we can approximate from available data are factory employees, but it seems probable that workers in most other lines are much less affected by cyclical unemployment.[1]

From the Census of Occupations and the employment figures of the Bureau of Labor Statistics we estimate that factory employees numbered not far from 11,500,000 in 1920 before the crisis. Other statistics in the *Monthly Labor Review* indicate that these workers were earning about $100 per month on the average, and that the number on factory pay-rolls dropped 2,200,000 between May, 1920 and May, 1922.[2] All these rough figures indicate a loss of wages exceeding $2,600,000,000 per year among factory workers—a sum far larger than any public works reserve fund we can regard as likely.

But should we take the number of employees and the rate of wages at the peak of the boom as the basis for estimating the burden of unemployment relief to be carried? Are there not many women and youths of school age who are attracted into factories only when unusual inducements are offered and who are not properly included among the "unemployed?" And is it proper to count the decline in number of employees over so long a period? May not that number be the result of a cumulation of misfortune, among which the earlier discharges counted as an important factor? Even a partial remedy quickly applied might have prevented unemployment from becoming so great.

Would a Board of Public Works be expected to pay top prices for labor and materials in a depression? If the Board did pay top prices, would not the tendency be merely to delay the depression until the reserve fund was exhausted? Would not the reduction of public works during prosperity do something toward lessening the intensity of the boom, and the severity of the crisis? Would not the prompt letting of public contracts exceeding a billion dollars mitigate the depression? And again

---

[1] The statistics in Chap. VI above show that this was the case in 1920–1922.

[2] Table XIX in Chap. VI indicates a maximum decline between the third quarter of 1920 and the third quarter of 1921 of 2,910,000 employees on factory pay-rolls.

must we not take account of the psychological effect of this action upon business men? Would the effects be limited to the direct disbursements upon public works? Is it not necessary to consider the cumulative effects started by the spending of the wages and profits of the men employed on public works?

Experience alone can answer these questions. Much doubtless would depend on the length of the preceding period of good times, the length of the depression, and the wisdom of the administrators of federal, state and city reserve funds. Probably the plan would be more effective in some cycles than in others. But under favorable circumstances it seems reasonable to believe that the public-works reserve fund would make a substantial contribution toward the mitigation of general unemployment.

## IV. EXPERIENCE IN RELIEF WORKS

**Relief Works Unlike Commercial Works.**—Relief works are improvised to afford emergency employment and are performed by necessitous persons often without consideration of their fitness and usually at wages below the market rate. Quantity and quality of production are secondary matters.

Commercial public works on the other hand are executed by any available workers, hired and discharged under the usual commercial conditions. Commercial public works may be suddenly expanded in an emergency or planned at long range.

**No Federal Relief Works.**—In the United States relief works have never been undertaken or assisted by the federal government. Each city and town has struggled alone with its unemployment problem without national recognition of the existence of successive periods of unemployment, until after the Armistice of 1918. Then, and again following the President's Conference on Unemployment, 1921, a stimulation of local public works was undertaken under the leadership of the federal government but without its financial assistance except in the building of public roads.

**Local Relief Works.**—Mayor Wood of New York in 1857 suggested employing on public works everybody who would work, payment to be made one-quarter in cash and the balance in cornmeal and potatoes. During the successive unemployment periods previous to 1893 no general record was made of the character and interrelationship of the relief works of scattered towns or of the combined effect upon unemployment. The Massachusetts Report of 1895 on the Unemployed [1] showed that 21 of the 30 cities of Massachusetts and 13 of the 41 larger towns gave emergency employment on public works. Wages of from one to two dollars per day were paid; only simple kinds of work were undertaken; not enough work

[1] *Report of the Mass. Board to Investigate the Subject of the Unemployed* (Boston, 1895) Part I, pp. xxv–xxxiii, 58–107.

could be extemporized for the applicants; workers were rotated; the total expenditure was inadequate; from a business point of view the results were not economical. Some consider, however, that "public work has paid if it has made men anew, restored their self-respect, prevented their losing their self-control and becoming permanent charges against the community as unemployables."[1] Many cities tried relief works in the depression of the middle nineties with results similar to those in Massachusetts. Work of any kind was regarded as better than none and some examples were regarded as wholly successful.

In 1914 over 100 cities succeeded in expanding their public works to some degree and employed several thousands of persons for periods of from one to six months in two-day to two-week shifts. These works were largely on a commercial basis with hours and wages as usual. Many officials in charge stated that they had secured full efficiency from workmen, while a few said the work had been done at a distinct saving.[2]

**Result of Experience in Relief Works.**—General experience in relief works shows their inadequacy to relieve national unemployment, the pitfalls to be avoided, and points toward long-range planning as a more economical and potent method.

### V. EXPERIENCE IN FLEXIBLE DISTRIBUTION OF PUBLIC WORKS

**England.** *Bowley's Estimates.*—The distinguished British statistician, Bowley,[3] estimated that if for ten years between 3 and 4 per cent of the ordinary annual appropriations for public works and services had been set aside in normal years and the accumulation expended in times of depression, the amount would have been sufficient to offset the wage loss during the decade due to industrial depressions.

*British Legislation, 1909 and 1914.*—Bowley's proposal gained legislative recognition in the Development and Road Funds Act of Great Britain in 1909. The act provides that national public works and Parliamentary grants to local authorities for local public works "must be expended having in mind the general state and prospects of employment." Early in 1914 the Development Commission set aside a reserve for use in depression years, and when war broke out, drew upon it for works in localities where unemployment prevailed. Arrangements were perfected for $10,000,000 of additional road work in case unemployment should require it, but the latter reserve was not drawn upon because war activities soon changed the situation.

---

[1] SNOWDEN, PHILIP M. P., "Labour and the New World," London, 1921.

[2] For description of local public works in 1914 see "Out of Work," by FRANCES KELLOR, New York, 1915; and *American Labor Legislation Review*, November, 1915.

[3] A. L. BOWLEY, Professor in the London School of Economics, in *Report of the Royal Commission on the Poor Laws and Relief of Distress*, 1909, Cd. 4499, p. 1195.

*British Results in* 1921.—War acted as a check upon local public works in England as in the United States. A peace control instead of a war check is needed. The possibility of advance planning contained in the act of 1909 was utilized by the British government after the Armistice. Large sums were appropriated for public works while demobilization was in progress. During the unemployment period of 1920–1921 over 3,500 local public works were assisted by the British government at a total cost to the combined authorities of about $125,000,000. The work provided amounted to about 1,000,000 man-months of direct employment.[1] In afforestation 559 schemes were subsidized. Government purchases of supplies were made earlier in order to exert their purchasing power when most needed, but on a small scale only. These policies were the result of activities in and out of Parliament during the previous decade carried on by men who had popularized and pressed the long-range planning of public works. Although the concrete results are greater than those so far attained elsewhere, only the surface possibilities have been touched.

**France.**—The French government evolved a more comprehensive solution, but the World War interrupted its development beyond the theoretical stage.

In 1896 the French Minister of Commerce, through the Bureau of Labor, reported the most successful methods of the various municipalities in alleviating unemployment through public works but no new administrative methods of control were advanced.

The Commission on Industrial Crises recommended in 1909 far-reaching financial reforms; the inclusion in annual budgets of specific appropriations for public works not to be executed in a budget year; the creation of special reserve funds for various city industrial services, such reserve fund to be expended during depression years; the use of trust funds placed under state control by public and private bodies with the same principle in mind; and the possible creation of a general reserve fund for public works in bad times.[2]

**Germany.** *City Reserves.*—In German cities it has long been the practice to accumulate a special reserve for the building of high schools and public baths, broadening of streets, and for nearly every form of civic development.[3] These reserves are not necessarily intended to be spent in bad times but such improvements are accelerated when prices are low and labor plentiful.

[1] Great Britain *Parliamentary Debates:* Feb. 9, 1922, vol. 150, col. 363; Mar. 8, 1922, vol. 151, col. 1261; Mar. 16, 1922, vol. 151, col. 2376.

[2] International Association on Unemployment, *Bulletin,* January to March, 1914, p. 263.

[3] SHILLADY, JOHN R., *Planning Public Expenditures, to Compensate for Decreased Private Employment during Business Depressions.* (Mayor's Committee on Unemployment, New York City, November, 1916.)

*Policy of* 1920–1921.—Since early in 1920 a large public works program has been under way. The Ministry of Labor subsidizes local works to the extent of three-sixths, and the state two-sixths, while the municipality pays the remaining one-sixth. Felix Morley states that "during the first five months of 1921 an average of 230,000 formerly unemployed men were continuously engaged. This cut down directly the number dependent on unemployment relief by 35 per cent and later by 50 per cent. Over 9,000 contracts were let, including those for flood regulation in Leipsig, subways in Berlin, immense highway projects over the Jura Mountains to connect Bavaria with northern Germany, irrigation, afforestation, electrification, etc."[1]

The municipality as the applicant for the subsidy submits full particulars. The Ministry of Labor decides whether the project is of economic value, the estimate reasonable, and the local unemployment situation compelling. After approval, the municipality, either directly or through a private contractor, picks the necessary key-men of proved ability. The remaining five-sixths of the workers, who in ordinary operations would be hired by the private contractor at the gate, must be taken on through the public labor exchange. The labor so obtained is not an unknown quantity but consists of registered men with every incentive for keeping their industrial record good. If familiar with the work, they receive standard wages, and if not, are assured a living while being given special opportunity to learn. The contractor is of the usual type who must bid low to get the contract and manage it efficiently to keep it. Consequently the work is free from the deteriorating influences associated with relief works and is developing successfully as part of a permanent national policy of flexible public works.

**Italy.**—In Italy 130,000,000 lira have been expended since 1919 upon public works to combat unemployment. Recent appropriations give a total of over 900,000,000 lira still available. In addition a permanent fund of 50,000,000 lira has been placed in the hands of the central unemployment office to be advanced to cooperative societies, companies which have obtained municipal contracts, land-reclaiming societies, etc., in order to enable them to begin work at once or to overcome temporary obstacles. This permanent fund is to be used only where unemployment in a particular district constitutes a menace to the peace.[2]

**Other European Nations.**—Since the Armistice there has been purposeful expansion of public works throughout Europe. As a whole the movement bears few of the characteristics of old-time relief works. The central government stimulates, frequently subsidizes, and sometimes pays in full. Because the World War checked customary public works, a

---

[1] *London Nation and Athenaeum,* Nov. 26, 1921.

[2] Special report of American Commercial Attaché H. C. Maclean to the Bureau of Foreign and Domestic Commerce, U. S. Department of Commerce.

reserve of useful public works was ready for the subsequent unemployment period. Large public works have been executed in Belgium, Switzerland, Czecho-slovakia, etc.[1]

**Canada.**—The Ontario Commission on Unemployment (1916) found that

> During the period of development of a new country no group of employers controls so large an expenditure of capital as the Dominion, Provincial and Municipal authorities. Of even greater importance is the fact that no other group controls to an equal extent employment which may be postponed with a view to supplementing the business activity of lean years. To plan public works and expenditures for the lean years, in order that public employment may compensate as far as possible for lessened private employment, is one of the most effective methods of dealing with the problem of periodic unemployment.

These principles have been sought to be applied by various governmental agencies. A most useful result has been the stimulation of public work in winter. Public work undertaken by municipalities specially for the relief of unemployment have been subsidized by the Dominion government to the extent of one-half the difference between the normal cost and the cost incurred by reason of the winter. As the province pays an additional third of the excess cost, the municipality is assured that winter costs to it will not be a deterrent, and many have therefore increased the volume of winter work.

Where work can not be provided, the Dominion government refunds to the municipality one-third of its expenditures for direct unemployment relief conditional upon an equal participation by the province.[2]

**United States.**—After the Armistice, the War Labor Policies Board, anticipating widespread unemployment during demobilization, sought to stimulate local public works. The board was dissolved before its plans were consummated. The War Department, under Arthur Woods, Assistant to the Secretary, successfully expedited the resumption of local public works. By June, 1919 it was clear that industry was on the eve of a post-war boom, and stimulation was therefore discontinued.

*Proposed United States Emergency Public Works Board.*—In order to make flexible expansion a permanent policy, early in 1919 Senator Kenyon of Iowa introduced a bill creating a United States Emergency Public Works Board to aid the states, and through the states, the municipalities, to execute public works during periods of unemployment.[3] A favorable committee report was not obtained.

[1] Report of International Labor Office, quoted in *Report of the President's Conference on Unemployment*, 1921, pp. 104–5.

[2] Canadian Government Orders-in-Council of Oct. 7, 1921 and Jan. 25, 1922, see *The Canada Gazette*, Oct. 15, 1921, p. 1597, and Feb. 4, 1922, p. 3187.

[3] *Hearings before Senate Committee on Education and Labor*, Feb. 7, 1919, pp. 75 ff. on S-5397 introduced Jan. 21, 1919.

*President's Conference on Unemployment,* 1921.—The President's Conference on Unemployment of September, 1921 marks an epoch. Previous to its sessions unemployment and long-range planning had been subjects left largely to groups outside the government—to local committees, charitable associations, social workers, and labor unions. In the public works field the conference produced results of immediate as well as far-reaching influence.

*Municipal Bonds for Public Works Break All Records.*—The sale of municipal bonds for local public works broke all records during the months immediately following the Conference on Unemployment.[1] The term "municipal bonds" includes bonds of counties, school districts, road districts, states, etc. The total for the year 1921 was $1,383,000,000 or nearly double that of any previous year and over three times the sixteen-year average.[2] The amount of work executed was, however, much less than the amount of bonds sold. The F. W. Dodge Company statistics for twenty-seven northeastern states show that about the same amount of public works was contracted for in that section in 1920 and 1921. The *Engineering News-Record's* figures for the whole country show a gain of 13 per cent in 1921 over 1920.[3] Neither of these sources account for more than one-third of the municipal bonds issued in 1921 or for more than one-half to three-fifths of those issued in 1920. After making allowances for bonds issued for non-productive purposes such as refunding, soldiers, bonus, etc., the expenditure of a large percentage of the proceeds remains unaccounted for. Aside from the obvious lack of inclusiveness of existing statistics of public works contracted for, two other important factors explain the discrepancy. First, the letting of the contract often lags many months behind the bond sale. Second, large sales of bonds are often made for projects requiring several years to complete.

Thus an appreciable "reserve" for public works is lying in municipal treasuries at all times. This practice supplies the financial foundation for expanding construction during unemployment periods. The effect of the President's Unemployment Conference was to increase this "reserve" by the unprecedented bond sales already noted and also to

[1] From *Bond Buyer:* Municipal bond sales in the last quarter of 1921 were $560,-000,000 against $209,000,000 and $253,000,000 in the last quarters of 1920 and 1919, which in turn exceeded previous years. In the first half of 1922 sales were $725,000,-000 against $518,000,000 and $349,000,000 for the first half of 1920 and 1919 respectively.

[2] During the sixteen years ending 1920, $6,500,000,000 of municipal bonds were issued for the following purposes: streets, roads and bridges 25.96 per cent, schools 14.10 per cent, water 13.04 per cent, general buildings 8 per cent, sewers and drainage 7.24 per cent, parks and museums 2.75 per cent, electric light and gas 1.05 per cent, refunding 5.03 per cent, funding and improvements 5.61 per cent, and miscellaneous 17.12 per cent.

[3] The *Engineering News-Record* figures exclude all public buildings and the smaller projects under certain minimum costs.

16

expedite construction already financed. The mayors of one hundred and twenty-five cities with a total population of 25,500,000 reported to the Conference that public works construction was being energetically pressed.

*Experience of American Cities.*—An unprecedented amount of winter work was undertaken. In one city (Baltimore) about half of the registered unemployed were given jobs by city departments; the volume of public works exceeded any year since 1914 in paving, sewers, and school buildings; in the laying of water pipes all records were broken; work was done as economically as heretofore by regular forces. In another city (Philadelphia) public works expenditures exceeded any previous year. In another city (Fitchburg, Mass.) more sewers were built than in any year since the bad times of 1893, more paving was laid than for twenty years with the exception of 1914—also a depression year. In all lines public works of 1921 were double those of 1920. In Lynchburg, Va., more public work was done than in five years preceding. In Middletown, Ohio, a spring meeting of the Chamber of Commerce laid plans for winter public works and the starting of street paving early the following spring "so that employment would be given in the slack season and the work finished in time to release men and teams for harvesting and private work in general." In Buffalo, a special appropriation was made for the repair of all municipal buildings. In Dayton concrete coverts over the river were finished in April; sewer excavations in addition to the usual program were continued throughout the winter with stops of two or three days at a time in severe weather. In Columbus public works and other municipal measures gave aid to many and "no person passed a night without shelter." In Gloucester, Mass., more new buildings were under way than in ten years. In another city (Bridgeport, Conn.) the Department of Public Charities provided work for over 1,000 men, on the streets, wall building, and improving playgrounds, parks, and hospital grounds. In still another city (Toledo) a bond issue, "especially authorized to relieve unemployment," afforded work for 3,000 different men in two working shifts during the fall and winter at thirty-five cents per hour. In another (Wilmington) one-half the total public works appropriation was expended during the winter. In Richmond, Va., the City Council authorized work which had been waiting several years, and pressed it throughout the winter. In Peoria every asphalt and brick street was repaired between October, 1921 and May, 1922. In Rochester the interior finishing of five new schools and six additions was undertaken during the winter. In Detroit extra forces kept the streets "disgracefully clean," and an extraordinary expansion of public works was promptly executed. On the other hand, some large cities, notably New York and Chicago, executed much less public works in 1921 than in 1920.

The stimulus of the President's Conference on Unemployment was not felt until late fall of 1921 and the effect of large bond sales then could not be fully operative until the open season of 1922. The F. W. Dodge Company's statistics confirm this remark by showing that contracts awarded during the first half of 1922 were more than half the total of any previous full year. The time of maximum execution coincided with the end of the depression and the turning of the tide.

*Conclusions as to Cities.*—In general, American cities in 1921–1922 made the greatest effort on record to expand public works during an unemployment period. The effect of the nation-wide program, executed because of a national emergency under national leadership, was a powerful one. Organized national determination, locally expressed, galvanized our industrial and civic forces to fight depression and unemployment as never before. Where two forces in a given town were arrayed against one another, one for, and the other against some immediate public-works project, the positive force was strengthened. The proposal to anticipate public works, which would have waited ordinarily until "a more convenient season," came from the Conference to several hundred local emergency committees. The spirit of helplessness and inaction noted in other periods of unemployment was conspicuously absent. Without national leadership it is possible that public works would have diminished as private business slumped and general confidence fell.

Successful execution of public works assisted the resumption of private construction on the large scale noted in 1922. The total probably shortened the depression, but is only a partial index to what may be accomplished in the next unemployment period if the states, counties, and towns incorporate their experience into administrative methods of long-range planning.

*Federal Aid Appropriation for Roads.*—Road building was given a national impetus by the passage of a $75,000,000 Federal Aid appropriation to the states in the autumn of 1921. While the appropriation was hanging fire in Congress, the Chairman of the Conference on Unemployment, Herbert Hoover, asked the governor of each state how much road building he could have under way within ninety days if the appropriation were passed. The governors made substantial promises, which the highway commissions undertook to fulfill after the passage of the appropriation. The appropriation was passed earlier because of the direct urge of the Conference and of the home districts. The Chief of the Bureau of Public Roads, Thomas H. MacDonald, under whose supervision the appropriation was made available to the states, was alert to facilitate the national policy by arranging for rapid federal approval of local projects.

*Orders Given in Winter instead of Spring.*—Manufacturers of road-building machinery reported that they received orders in December instead of in April, as in previous years. Thus men were employed in making the machinery during the winter who would otherwise have been idle until spring, and orders for the constituent steel and other materials advanced employment in those industries. The movement extended to industry in general for "the spring trade [of 1922 showed unusual] gains over [the trade of] the winter months. . . . Indeed the spring business began about six weeks [ahead of time] and then proceeded rapidly.[1]"

*Other Federal Works.*—Aside from roads, Congress did not increase public works appropriations. The Reclamation Service expended for construction in 1921 less than the ten-year average and less than one-half of the fund available. River and harbor and other public works appropriations were not increased and the normal appropriations were not made available earlier for use in the winter and early spring.

Federal "economy" was held to preclude an increase of productive public work during the depression and to require postponement of new undertakings no matter how necessary or economical their immediate execution might be. With the exception of large appropriations for army hospitals, Congress made no provision for public buildings, post offices, etc., although many important cities urgently required additional space and no comprehensive building program had been authorized since 1913. The Federal Reserve Bank buildings in various districts were actively prosecuted, this agency being independent of Congressional appropriations and able to utilize its own surplus reserves.

*President's Letter to Heads of Departments.*—President Harding's letter to the heads of Federal departments, under date of January 26, 1922, asked them to anticipate by a few months any necessary public works for which appropriations were available.[2] This proposal produced no results because the available funds were insignificant. The President's request, however, sanctioned the policy and constitutes an important precedent. After long-range planning has been administratively established a similar request will have far-reaching results.

### VI. ADMINISTRATIVE MEASURES

**Federal.** *Roads and "Reserve" Clause.*—Although the public works of the states and cities are about five times those of the federal government, the federal one-fifth is a convenient key to unlock many doors. An important part of federal public works appropriations is given in aid or subsidy to the states on a fifty-fifty basis for road building. In 1916 road appropriations were outlined for five years ahead, and in 1922 a similar program was adopted for three years In the latter case the appropriations totalled $540,000,000 and if met by the states, they will provide for over a billion dollars' worth of road building. This is an intrenched policy likely to continue to command the necessary votes in Congress and to reach a great total in the next two decades.

---

[1] Moody's Investors Service *Weekly Review of Financial Conditions*, April 27, 1922.

[2] *Congressional Record*, Feb. 15, 1922. p. 2898.

All that is required to assure the building of more roads in bad times than in good times is that a clause be attached to each federal appropriation for roads, reserving a certain part, say 20 per cent for expenditure only when the President shall find a period of national unemployment and industrial depression to exist. In exercising control of the time of construction the President would follow the precedent of the Governor of Pennsylvania, whose duty it is to decide when extraordinary unemployment is present and then release a reserve for general public works, as he did in March, 1922.[1] In practice the President would mean the Secretary of Agriculture acting through the Chief of the Bureau of Public Roads, or after the creation of a Department of Public Works, the secretary of that department. Such Congressional action would impel state legislatures to appropriate like funds contingent upon the availability to them of the reserved percentage. Otherwise the state not appropriating would lose its federal aid.

*More Roads for the Same Money.*—At present there is no motive for a State Highway Department to plan roads long in advance because no one can tell what amounts will be appropriated by succeeding legislatures. It is known that many hundreds of miles of roads will be built in each state within the next ten years but nobody knows how much will be built in any year of the ten. The federal "reserve" clause would put all legislatures on notice that funds would be available for a given number of miles in the next year of industrial depression. The greatest value of federal aid would be this creation of a unified, nation-wide policy. The "reserve" clause should result in more roads being built because a greater proportion than otherwise would be built at the lower prices prevailing during depression.[2]

An alternative suggestion is the use of comparative statistics compiled by the Department of Commerce in the *Survey of Current Business* as a guide to the President in recommending larger road appropriations when a trend toward business depression is indicated.

*Advance Authorization of Bond Issues for Roads.*—If political obstacles prove serious, a possible alternative which has been proposed is the authorization of a federal bond issue of a given total, say $100,000,000-$200,000,000, to be sold by the Secretary of the Treasury only when a period of unemployment shall exist, the proceeds to be appropriated and expended according to existing federal aid practice. The authorization of such a bond issue, although of course not the sale of the bonds, must

[1] Minutes of Industrial Board of Pennsylvania, May 9, 1922, p. 25; Emergency Public Works Act, July 25, 1917, Pennsylvania, *Pamphlet Laws*, p. 1193.

[2] The Lighthouse Service asked for an appropriation during the boom of 1920 estimated to be sufficient to build three light ships. By the time the appropriation was available, the same sum built five ships during the depression instead of three during the boom.

take place in good times, several years before the depression arrives. Otherwise the state legislatures which meet infrequently would not have time to make like appropriations in order to obtain their full share of federal aid.

*Road Building by the Federal Government.*—A more doubtful suggestion is that the federal "reserve," or proceeds of the contingent road bond issue, should be expended under the direction of the Chief of Engineers of the Army or through other federal agencies upon national highways to whatever extent the states may fail to match the federal appropriation reserved for the period of unemployment. This might, if enacted, prove effective. On the other hand it would probably increase resistance to any "reserve" legislation whatever because the states might oppose in Congress the diversion of any funds from their control.[1]

The detailed study and recommendation of a "reserve" clause or "contingent bond issue" would seem to be the function of the Bureau of the Budget or of a Congressional committee.

*Classes of Public Works Appropriations.*—Federal public works appropriations fall into the following classification:[2]

1. Annual: such as federal aid to road building, rivers and harbors, lighthouses, forestry, roads and trails in national forests, national and military parks, flood control, Indian schools, irrigation works on Indian reserves, Panama Canal Zone construction and equipment.

2. Spasmodic: such as public buildings, post offices, court houses, customs houses, quarantine immigration· stations, hospitals, monuments and memorials, departmental buildings, etc.

3. Revolving funds for works such as reclamation and irrigation.

4. Unusual projects dependent upon the solution of difficult questions of technique or policy before authorization for construction or appropriation will be made: for example, the Boulder Canyon power dam in Arizona, large scale drainage and flood prevention projects, the Muscle Shoals proposal, the Alaskan Railroad, etc.

5. Municipal: such as carrying out the city plan of Washington and the ordinary public works of the District of Columbia.

*Centralization of Federal Public Works.*—These public works are performed by thirty-nine federal agencies, four of which are independent and unattached and the remaining thirty-five are each a part of some one of nine of the ten national departments. Sixteen federal agencies are authorized to build roads, nineteen to do hydraulic construction, sixteen

---

[1] I have always been impressed with the advisability of long-range planning of public works; but I would not approve the suggestion that the Chief Engineer of the Army or any federal agency be authorized to expend the proceeds of a suggested bond issue to whatever extent the states may fail to match the federal appropriation reserved for periods of unemployment, until I had given this suggestion further consideration.—Note by A. W. SHAW.

[2] Military and naval works are omitted.

to work on rivers, and twenty-two on engineering and research.[1] No one would have designed such cumbersome confusion. It is the unpruned, rank growth of a century and a half. The President, Congress, and public opinion combined are helpless to make all of these agencies do any one thing in any one way. To establish natural relations among the members of the public-works family is a necessary part of the policy of long-range planning. Expression of this need is found in the bill to create a department of public works.[2] The Public Works Department Association has popularized the case for administrative reform and the chance of some unification of public-works agencies is regarded as good. A department of public works should be able to give better effect to a national policy of expanding public works in bad times.

*Legislation for Future Cyclical Depressions.*—Senator Kenyon of Iowa, in a bill introduced November 16, 1921, sought to carry out the recommendations of the President's Conference on Unemployment and to cover all federal public-works agencies by stating one policy for all. This bill to "prepare for future cyclical periods of depression and unemployment by systems of public works" was reported favorably by the Senate Committee on Education and Labor.[3] It authorized all federal public works agencies to make advance engineering plans and to keep them up to date so that when an unemployment period arises a Congressional appropriation would result in immediate construction. These plans would afford a diversified and comprehensive list ready to hand from which Congress could quickly choose. In order to decide when a period of cyclical unemployment is at hand, the bill authorized the development of the monthly *Survey of Current Business*, already published by the Department of Commerce, to include available statistical data upon production, trade, and commerce. The aim was to afford at any moment a comparative picture of the past and the present state of business. Such a picture is needed as a guide for federal, state, and city governments in determining when public works should be expanded or contracted. A few large corporations at their own expense have successfully marshalled the meager statistics now available and made money by planning long-range adjustments of purchases of raw materials to contemplated output. The proposed publication would place small business men on the same information footing with these few large corporations and give to both more complete facts.

---

[1] WILHELM, DONALD, Unscrambling the Departments, *Saturday Evening Post*, May 22, 1920.

[2] U. S. Sixty-sixth Congress, Third Session, S-4542, bill introduced Dec. 7, 1920.

[3] U. S. Sixty-seventh Congress, Second Session, S-2749 introduced Nov. 16, 1921; Hearings before Senate Committee on Education and Labor, Dec. 21 and 22, 1921; *Congressional Record*, Feb. 16, 1922, pp. 2948–53, 2957–60.

The final clause of the Kenyon bill provided that when Congress has not stipulated the beginning or completion of a specific public work within a given time, the President may order such work to be expedited or retarded in accordance with general business conditions. General support of this bill developed at the hearings before the Senate committee but on the floor of the Senate opposition was encountered. Some Senators stated that past and present throw no light on future business conditions; that information might bring on the very panic it sought to prevent; that federal public works are too trifling in volume to make any difference; that unemployment periods are acts of God, which "not even the Congress of the United States can control;" that too great power would be given to the President if he could retard public works authorized by Congress; that such a measure is paternalistic and invades a field where government has no place; that it is a measure fathered by big business to insure profits in bad times.[1] A fear apparently existed that a president of one party might postpone public works in the territory of the opposite party while forwarding public works in the territory of his own party. The Democratic Senators voted almost solidly for an amendment to withdraw the types of public work more prevalent in the South and West, such as rivers and harbors and reclamation, from the scope of the bill. An emasculating amendment prevailed by the narrow margin of three votes and the bill was recommitted to committee.

Among the advocates of the Kenyon bill were the President's Conference on Unemployment, the Federated American Engineering Societies, the American Federation of Labor, the Associated General Contractors of America, the Industrial Board of Pennsylvania, the American Association for Labor Legislation, members of the United States and local Chambers of Commerce, and many economists and industical leaders. The advocates of the bill hold that there is need of a better organization and marshalling of public opinion of the kind which effectively demanded the national budget.[2]

*Possible Changes in Appropriation Policy.*—Long-range planning requires consideration of the various prevailing methods of appropriating for different kinds of public work.

Annual Appropriations.—Annual appropriations are made for such public works as federal aid to road building, rivers and harbors, lighthouses, etc. These show wide variations from year to year. The larger appropriations have often been made in years of greatest industrial activity and the smaller appropriations in years of depression.

---

[1] *Congressional Record*, Feb. 16, 1922, pp. 2957 ff.

[2] Steps in this direction are proposed for 1923 through a Public Works Committee composed of various national organizations. Those interested may communicate with the American Association for Labor Legislation, 131 East 23d Street, New York City.

However, nearly all public works appropriation are available until expended. Hence it makes no difference to the plan under discussion how much may be appropriated in years of active industry provided a clause is inserted reserving some part, say 20 per cent, for expenditure during a year of depression.

Spasmodic Appropriations.—The latest bill for federal public buildings, chiefly post offices, was passed in 1913. Construction under it and under previous bills was actively prosecuted during the succeeding four years until the war intervened. More work was done in good years than in bad years because the program happened not to get under full headway during the unemployment period of 1914 and gained its momentum thereafter.[1] The next public buildings bill will be a large one because the accumulated needs are great. Contrary to general belief, there has been little waste in public buildings appropriations. When a post office has been built too large for a town, it has commonly proved less wasteful than fitting the town to its measurement and ten years later tearing down the building to replace it with a larger one. The United States is still renting post office buildings in hundreds of towns and in many buildings mail clerks are crowded under unhygienic conditions. A comprehensive program to give every town an adequate and well designed post office seems probable in the near future.

This prospect may be used to illustrate the arguments of those who advocate long-range planning. What means, they ask, can be devised to prevent the throwing of such additional fuel under the pot at the boiling point of a building boom? They answer, the plans can not be prepared in time to start all the buildings in two or three years. Some will be automatically postponed. Few Congressmen will wish those in their district to be delayed. Many ought undoubtedly to be built as soon as possible. Who will decide which? Administrative discretion rests in the Secretary of the Treasury and the Supervising Architect. Under the Kenyon bill the Supervising Architect would be instructed to use that discretion by increasing operations during periods of unemployment and *vice versa*. Without the Kenyon bill the Supervising Architect, whoever he may be, will be tempted to make excuses to those Congressmen whose political pressure is least compelling. The easiest way out of his dilemma is to accommodate all as far as possible and do the whole program at one swoop, forgetting those absent parties, "unemployment" and "industrial depression," who have no official representation. With the Kenyon bill the President may request the Secretary of the Treasury or the heads of departments to speed or delay construction. This is now his privilege rather than his duty—a doubtful privilege with unknown political consequences. A President may cheerfully and safely expand public works during bad times, if he can, but to contract them at any time will require courage and the support inherent in an accepted policy.

[1] The program is not yet completed (1922) because of price changes since 1913.

Revolving Funds.—The Reclamation Service, one of our greatest federal engineering agencies, receives no appropriations, but is given loans to its revolving fund to be returned to the Treasury from future payments by settlers. The scope of its operations therefore usually depends not on the Congress in session, but on the current amounts paid by settlers. These current payments are likely to decrease in bad agricultural years and automatically to restrict construction. In 1921 the settlers' difficulties caused by the fall in agricultural prices delayed their payments. In order to remedy this situation the Conference on Unemployment recommended a loan by Congress to complete projects under way. The House Committee on Irrigation of Arid Lands approved such a course but Congress remained inactive.[1] In 1921 funds were obtained from a new source: leases from oil, phosphate, and other mineral lands. These, added to other receipts, made available a larger construction fund than the average for the preceding ten years. Thus accidentally a fund for construction expansion in a year of depression was had. Its use was postponed by the lag of departmental, public, and Congressional opinion and the absence of a conscious policy. The opposition of farm organizations was a contributing factor. These apparently believed that any increase in farm land would decrease the selling price of existing farms and farm products.

Chart 54 shows that expansion of construction in years of depression is feasible and occurred in 1908 and in 1914. Expenditures were sharply curtailed during the years of high cost and of active industry (1916–1920), but quick expansion did not occur during the period of falling costs and industrial depression (1921).

The Reclamation Service seems well adapted to long-range planning. Its engineering plans are made long in advance and its operations scattered over wide areas. Its work creates a demand for innumerable products manufactured in states other than those where the lands are under development. A reclamation project in Arizona makes itself felt immediately in A-ville, Ill., in an order for wheel-barrows; in B-burg, Mich., for motor trucks; in C-wood, Pa. for steel, etc.

The potential activities of the Reclamation Service in the next two decades are very great. Vast areas of the South require drainage. Deforested areas need development. Arid regions await irrigation. Most of this work will be done some day. Meanwhile the choice of projects, their planning, and preparation for financing might readily proceed in advance of the next depression.[2]

Advocates of long-range planning hold that reclamation interests will best accomplish their purpose by obtaining assurance of a Congressional loan contingent upon the existence of unemployment and by the

[1] Hearings before the House Committee on Irrigation of Arid Lands, Oct. 26, 1921.
[2] U. S. Reclamation Service, *Annual Reports*.

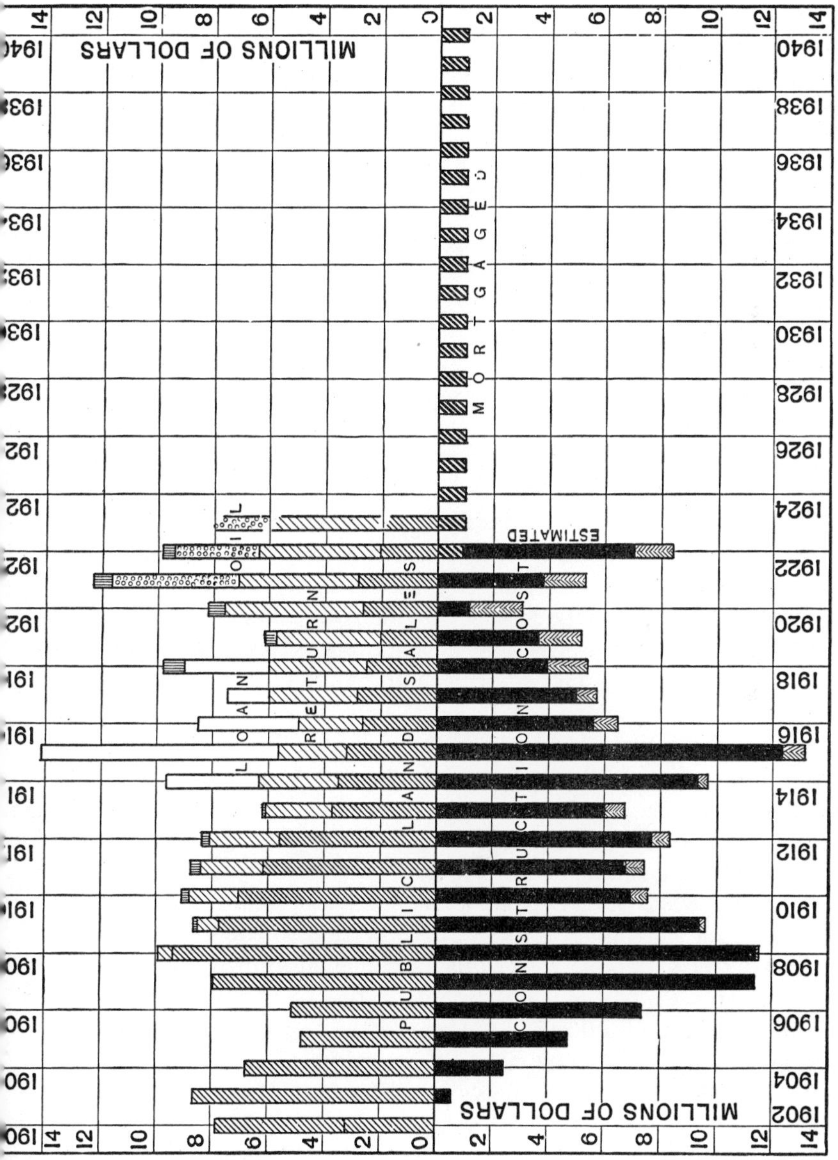


Courtesy, U. S. Reclamation Service.

adoption of a policy of putting all available funds under contract during a period of depression.

Extraordinary Projects.—The federal government has under consideration several great exceptional undertakings. During the unemployment period of 1921 none had reached a stage where sufficient information was at hand upon which to make a decision. If a positive decision had been made, it could not have resulted in prompt construction. Examples of these extraordinary projects are the Colorado River power and irrigation undertaking, known as the Boulder Canyon dam of Arizona, for large scale irrigation and power development; the Muscle Shoals fertilizer project; and several great flood prevention and drainage proposals. In all these cases political action must wait upon the study of engineering facts. If a central public works agency were established, it would be easier to pursue a continuous policy of obtaining engineering facts as a preliminary basis for Congressional decision. If the preliminary plans and rough estimates were ready for a number of such projects, it would be possible, indeed natural, to start some of them during a period of depression.

Municipal Work Done by the Federal Government.—Congress is also the city council of Washington, D. C. Visitors who admire the city's beauty may not be aware that this beauty is the result of a city plan prepared in 1901 as a public service by men of standing in the professions of architecture, sculpture, and landscape architecture. The plan enjoys such general approval and understanding that nothing has been done contrary to its provisions. A proposal now before Congress includes an annual appropriation of $5,000,000 to the Public Buildings Commission.[1] If this appropriation is made continuing and the portion unexpended one year remains available until spent, long-range planning under perfect conditions will be possible. After catching up with immediate needs it will be natural for the Public Buildings Commission to proceed more slowly when costs are high. A similar principle might be incorporated in the customary annual appropriation to the Commissioner of the District of Columbia for ordinary municipal improvements.

For many years the Department of Justice has occupied a rented building. The landlord raised the rent in the happy confidence that the government would not build during a period of unemployment even though it had bought a site long ago. The Department of Commerce is renting several buildings scattered widely over Washington to the detriment of efficiency. The Treasury Department needs large additional space. An opportunity for long-range planning of these and many other structures might readily be given to the Public Buildings Commission.

[1] Composed of senators, congressmen, architects, and appropriate government executives.

*Federal Reserve Funds and Contingent Bond Issues.*—Public works reserves require merely the making of a present appropriation available for future use; not the setting up and withdrawal from use of a separate treasury fund of non-interest yielding cash. The political objection to any reserve is that it makes the appropriations of the party in power appear, at first blush, unduly extravagant. Upon analysis these reserve appropriations are to be spent not by the Congress in power but by succeeding Congresses, and are therefore a husbanding of present resources. Although setting aside any reserve is contrary to the government bookkeeping custom of making yearly appropriations balance with yearly expenditures, it is regarded as sound practice by important private industrial corporations, whose reserves are a source of great strength not only to them but also to the general business and employment fabric in time of need.

The "contingent bond issue," to be sold only during periods of extraordinary unemployment, avoids these objections and resembles closely existing practice under the law authorizing the Secretary of the Treasury to issue short-term certificates of indebtedness in order to make available the monies appropriated when revenues are temporarily insufficient. Although the Secretary of the Treasury may be already technically authorized to issue such certificates for emergency public works, he is unlikely to do so without specific authority and the existence of an unmistakable legislative policy. Hence, if a policy of long-range planning is adopted, authorization by Congress of contingent bond issues for emergency public works will be desirable and will lessen the delay inherent in securing legislation and starting work after an emergency is at hand.

**State.** *Placing Responsibility.*—In the state the first step in long-range planning would be to place the definite responsibility upon some one state agency. Everybody's business is nobody's business. Should an existing agency be chosen or a special one created? As the long-range public-works agency is intended to overlook all the state departments participating in public works, the agency should include general officials responsible for the financial and administrative conduct of the state. This intention led to the membership of the governor, the treasurer, the auditor-general, and the commissioner of labor and industry in the Pennsylvania Emergency Public Works Commission.[1] A request from such officials carries authority. As they have many other irons in the fire, an executive secretary is needed on the job part time, preferably an official employed elsewhere in the state government or one who knows its ins and outs. The Pennsylvania Commission is custodian of a reserve fund accumulated during good years for expenditure in bad times through the usual state agencies. The activities of such a commission may gradually influence the policy of state departments, and also the

[1] Act of July 25, 1917, Pennsylvania, *Pamphlet Laws*, p. 1193.

legislature's method of appropriating for public works. In some states an existing agency may better exert this influence—for example, the industrial commission, the highway department, the commissioner of public institutions, etc. In any case the introduction of legislation instructing some specific official or commission to cause advance planning to be done by all agencies should have educational value.

California attacks the problem in a way similar to Pennsylvania by requiring the Board of Control[1] to secure tentative public works plans from various departments; by placing upon this board the responsibility for reporting to the governor when a period of unemployment exists; and by authorizing the governor then to release the accumulated public works. The effect of the Pennsylvania and California acts has been wider than their content implies. In both states public works by the cities and towns were stimulated during the unemployment period of 1921–1922. The California Board of Control and the Pennsylvania Emergency Public Works Commission are influencing public opinion and public action throughout the political subdivisions of the state.

*Ten-year Program for State Institutions.*—State institutions for dependents, feeble-minded, insane, and criminals are chronically inadequate. In many states each institution is managed by a separate commission or board. A comprehensive building policy or the central purchasing of supplies is then impracticable. The resulting waste and confusion suggest remedy through one central agency such as the New Jersey State Board of Control of Institutions and Agencies.[2]

The New Jersey Board after checking building during the war and post-war high prices, promulgated a ten-year building program and asked for successive regular appropriations. New Jersey has here proposed an administrative solution of the long-range planning of state institutions, if these appropriations are made available until spent, thus enabling it to go ahead full speed in certain years and to hold back in others. Execution would depend very largely upon employment or unemployment. "The plans will be ready for fifteen institutions, each consisting of several buildings. It will be easier to concentrate construction during unemployment periods than to spread it out equally."[3]

*Increasing Production of Governmental Supplies in Depression Years.*—The New York State law of Feb. 10, 1922, provided for the creation of a state department for the centralized purchase, control, and distribu-

[1] Act to Provide for the Extension of Public Works of the State of California during Periods of Extraordinary Unemployment, approved May 26, 1921, cited in *Commonwealth Review* of the University of Oregon, January, 1922, p. 58.

[2] *The Ten-year Construction Program* for 1922–1933, with graphic charts.

[3] Statement of Burdette C. Lewis, Commissioner of Institutions and Agencies of New Jersey.

tion of all supplies required by the state. Another law passed at the same time established a bureau of standards. A modern supply system is being installed similar to those used by large private corporations. The exact knowledge of current needs and the accurate estimate of future requirements afforded by such a system enables large corporations to make service agreements with large producers. These service agreements not only give price protection in boom times but may result in increased orders for production during periods of depression. A manufacturer can readily finance such orders during a depression either for immediate or future delivery, whereas he could not as easily finance manufacture for stock even if he were willing to take the risk. Under its new system there is nothing to prevent the State of New York from making such service agreements covering at least the period of time for which appropriations are customarily made. No obstacle prevents buying from hand to mouth during boom times or placing larger orders during periods of depression. A director of supplies might also develop the practice of giving timely orders to certain industries during their slack seasons.[1] Thus the purchasing power of the state would be controlled for the mutual advantage of the state, the manufacturer, and the worker. In most states appropriations are for two years and service agreements could be made for that period. When a depression coincides with the year in which the appropriation is made the orders would presumably call for the immediate manufacture of the major part of the known requirements of staple non-perishable commodities for the two years. The service agreement would cover dates of delivery.

Eight states now have laws which permit central purchasing of supplies, but practically all of them lack the business organization to make them effective. The supply requirements of all the states and of thirty-one large cities involve a purchasing power of about $650,000,000 per annum.[2] The Associates for Government Service, Inc., a semi-public, non-profit taking corporation, proposes to combine the supply purchases of state and municipal governments which have similar specifications for the same commodities by bidding in contracts and securing advance options from producers at prices based upon the combined requirements. This plan may harness purchasing power to pull against a depression.

The Federal Purchasing Board has recently been established at the suggestion of the Director of the Bureau of the Budget. It is making the

---

[1] Memorandum of Employment Service of Canada, *Government Employment as a Factor in the Prevention of Unemployment;* Department of Labour (Canada), *Proceedings of the Eighth Annual Meeting of the International Assn. of Public Employment Services,* 1921, pp. 29, 30.

[2] Estimate of Associates for Government, Service Inc., 60 Trinity Place, New York City. This estimate excludes all supplies purchased through bond issues.

first approach toward coordinating the purchases of the various federal departments, but is not a central purchasing agency. Before any federal establishment could buy two years' supplies during a depression, Congressional appropriations would have to be made for longer than one year. The Navy Department and, to a less extent, the Post Office Department are now the only ones so financed as to buy beyond the needs of a current year. This policy might be extended to other departments, and centralized purchasing and storekeeping authorized in places like the District of Columbia where many branches of the government are contiguously located.

In road building the policy of the national government, as incorporated in federal aid appropriations, will largely determine the degree of long-range planning by the states. Nevertheless the state highway commissioner and the governor will have a large voice in determining whether more roads are ready to be built in bad times.

**Municipal.** *Breaking up the City Plan.*—The city plan is the entering wedge in long-range planning by municipalities. It shows the city's future growth and needs. Its major proposals cannot be reached in one jump but can best be obtained by systematic approach over a period of years. Parts will be halted for one reason or another until some unusual impetus propels them. An unemployment period may be such an energizing impulse which breaks through obstacles. The program, then, is to develop the city plan, to gain general understanding and approval of it, and to break it into parts. While it need not have the force of law, it must have the support of public opinion and rest upon detailed plans constantly under preparation and revision.

An examination of several city plans reveals an especial value in dividing the plan into parts somewhat as follows:

*Vitally Needed.*—Work which should, and will be, done as soon as financial provision can be made. Examples: schools, fire protection, street improvement and extension, etc.

*Periodic.*—Works requiring a long period, which gain in usefulness and economy if planned as a whole and executed in conformity with a long-range plan. Example: sewage disposal, sewerage system, increased water supply, outer park system.

*Delayed.*—Works which are likely to be delayed by the greater pressure of others. Example: civic center, municipal buildings, etc.

*Desired.*—Works long desired but never authorized whose best chance of getting done rests upon an unusual impulse. Examples: boulevards, park extension, complete recreation facilities, golf course, terminal rearrangement.

*Left-overs.*—Examples: renovation of jails, police stations, and court houses; adequate housing for welfare institutions, municipal lodging house; street marking and repairing; destruction of condemned or antiquated structures, etc.

The practicability of some such breaking up of the city plan has been approved by representative city planners and city engineers. It is generally agreed to be practicable from an engineering standpoint to consider the needs of a city over a ten-year period, to list these needs, and to double public work in a year of unemployment.[1] Advocacy and accomplishment rest with such organizations as the National Conference on City Planning, National Municipal League, American Civic Association, Federated American Engineering Societies, American Institute of Architects, American Society for Municipal Improvements, City Managers' Association, and local Rotary, Civic, City, and Women's clubs.[2]

*Financing.*—After the city plan has been conveniently subdivided the chief remaining provision needed for a flexible construction program is a financial one. The advance authorization of a bond issue for certain projects is desirable, the bonds to be sold only during bad times. The legal proceedings required to authorize and validate a bond issue, if begun during an unemployment period, may delay construction until too late to relieve unemployment. The unconsidered sale of large successive bond issues during boom times may leave a city with small borrowing power for use during bad times. A good market exists for municipal bonds when business is bad because at that time capital unemployed in private industry is seeking investment elsewhere and because conservative investors turn from industrial investments to those backed by the credit of the community.[3] The unprecedented volume of municipal bonds sold in 1921 did not prevent a sharp decline in interest rates on this class of bonds in the last half of the year. This decline, to be sure, was contemporaneous with a similar decline in the rate of interest on corporation bonds; but was in the face of a steadily growing volume of municipal issues as the year progressed, whereas corporate financing was distinctly less heavy in the second half than in the first of that year. The marketability of municipal bonds has, especially since the

---

[1] Among those who have given valuable suggestions are: Ivan E. Houk, City Engineer, Dayton. Morris L. Cooke, Ex-Director of Public Works, Philadelphia. Allen J. Saville, Director of Public Works, Richmond. Robert Whitten, City Planning, Cleveland. Harland Bartholomew, City Plan Engineer, St. Louis. L. W. Wallace, Secretary, Federated American Engineering Societies, Washington, D. C. Philip W. Foster, City Planning, Cambridge, Massachusetts. Fred B. Williams, Chairman City Planning Committee, City Club, New York. Nelson P. Lewis, City Club, New York. Kenyon Riddle, City Manager, Middletown, Ohio. Frederick Bigger, Member City Plan Committee, Pittsburgh.

[2] Those interested may correspond with the Federated American Engineering Societies, 719 Fifteenth Street, Washington, D. C.

[3] *Report of President's Conference on Unemployment,* 1921, p. 96.

17

war, been enhanced by the exemption of the income therefrom from the federal income tax; but even before this tax was enacted, municipal bonds had probably been more readily marketable in bad times than any but the highest grade of corporation bonds and the fluctuations in the interest yields on the former had probably been less from year to year than was the case with a great majority of corporation bonds. The conclusion would seem to be fair that the obstacles in the way of municipal financing of public works in bad times are less than those which check corporate financing for plant extension during such periods.

The creation of reserve funds from annual taxation for specific work is possible but more difficult. Alameda, California, accumulated such a reserve through a tax of one one-hundredth of 1 per cent on real estate. Milwaukee has an emergency fund for any emergency purpose, which was used for public works in 1921.

*Political Considerations.*—Where there is an able city manager a reserve fund is practicable. Where the city council is elected by wards, the serious obstacle is presented of inter-ward competition for improvements, which prevents consideration of the needs of the city as a whole. Where the city government swings from one rival administration to another, each is likely to spend everything in sight, including the reserve funds of its predecessor. Outside of the larger cities such chaotic changes are no longer the general practice.

Yet the flexible policy of construction seems not impracticable from the political standpoint. The unemployed in bad times comprise steady and substantial citizens and therefore reliable political support. Storekeepers and merchants trace the connection of the public works done in bad times with their trade and the payments of their customers' bills. Consequently the political objection to deferring work may be counterbalanced by political advantages to those politicians who can afford to wait to reap them.

A semi-permanent public-works official will be found in many cities, usually a subordinate, whose accumulated knowledge of every inch of the city has made him indispensable.[1] This man is also indispensable to long-range planning of public works. He knows what is feasible and what is not. His city is his life work and he responds to whatever he believes to be for its ultimate good.

American cities grow so rapidly that they are chronically behind in necessary public improvements. Over half our streets and alleys are still unpaved. Only a small percentage of water supply is filtered. Few sewage disposal plants exist.[2] Consequently the problem is more largely

---

[1] A committee of contractors touring the country recently reported that the public-works officials of the cities of middle size and below were in general efficient and honest.

[2] *Engineering and Contracting*, Sept. 7, 1921, p. 225.

one of supplying accumulated needs in an unemployment period than of postponing specific works. Experience shows that financial and administrative machinery cannot be set up quickly enough after the exigency is at hand. The crucial point is the development of the method during good times.

The purchase of supplies for city welfare institutions and departments is enormous in volume and is farther along the road to centralization than that of the states. Although the first step has been taken toward the administrative possibility of more flexible and larger purchases during bad times, the practice remains to be developed.

**County, District, Etc.**—Geographic subdivisions with taxing power are so manifold and various that no policy can be made to fit all of them. The county is an important unit in some states and negligible in others. The New England "town," and Louisiana "parish," etc., are of consequence. In addition there are numerous types of road, drainage, metropolitan, and school districts—"Carey Act" irrigation districts, conservancy districts, etc. Although each furnishes a mere drop in the bucket, the aggregate public works of these units is important. Similar principles of long-range planning are adaptable to most of them in varying degrees.

**Summary of Practical Measures That Would be Required for Efficient Long-range Planning of Public Works.**—The following are among the steps which would have to be taken to secure efficient long-range planning of public works. In dealing with federal public works it would be necessary to:

1. Continue to outline federal aid road appropriations for five year periods; include a "reserve" clause in annual appropriations; authorize in advance a "contingent bond issue" to be sold only during a period of unemployment and industrial depression; use the large potential power of federal aid appropriations to increase state road construction during bad times.

2. Create a federal Department of Public Works or centralize all public works in one existing department, for instance Department of the Interior.

3. Enact the Kenyon bill or equivalent legislation requiring advance planning.

4. Develop the *Survey of Current Business* of the Department of Commerce as a guide to the expansion and contraction of public works—federal, state, and municipal.

5. Have the Bureau of the Budget devise improved methods of Congressional appropriation for public works.

6. Use in public buildings appropriations a "reserve" clause, "contingent bond issue," and advance planning.

7. In reclamation and irrigation make advance authorization of a loan to the reclamation revolving fund for expenditure during the next period of depression.

8. In extraordinary projects authorize preliminary engineering plans and estimates.

9. In the prosecution of the Washington city plan and of departmental buildings make regular annual appropriations to the Public Buildings Commission which shall be available until spent.

In dealing with state public works it would be necessary to:

1. Place the responsibility in a commission, like that of Pennsylvania or California, or utilize some appropriate existing agency.

2. Develop a ten-year plan for state institutions of welfare and correction like that of New Jersey.

3. Create an agency for central purchasing of supplies like that of New York, with provision for buying larger supplies of staple commodities in a year of unemployment.

In dealing with municipal public works it would be necessary to:

1. Develop a city plan.

2. Break up the city plan into parts.

3. Authorize a "contingent bond issue" and "reserve fund."

4. Conduct educational campaigns by national and local civic organizations.

### VII. CONCLUSION[1]

The long-range planning of public works and of the purchase of supplies seems to be one of the simplest and most promising devices for stabilizing industry and employment. Its principles appear economically sound. The obstacles in the way of practical trial are chiefly political and administrative. The tools are popular knowledge and appropriate administrative measures. After a careful canvass of various proposals, the British Commission on the Poor Laws concluded that "It is now administratively possible . . . to remedy most of the evils of unemployment to the same extent, at least, as we have in the past century dimin-

---

[1] BIBLIOGRAPHY.—The first complete bibliography of the subject has been compiled for this study by the Library of Congress and is available to libraries on request.

An excellent popular presentation is that of William Hard, "Big Jobs for Bad Times" in *Everybody's Magazine*, August, 1919. A careful technical study is that of John R. Shillady, *Planning Public Expenditures to Compensate for Decreased Private Employment During Business Depressions*, Mayor's Committee on Unemployment, New York, N. Y., November, 1916.

ished the death rate from fever and lessened the industrial slavery of young children."[1]

The flexible distribution of public works merits careful consideration as a factor in limiting the swing of the industrial pendulum and in lessening the shocks of unemployment.[2]

[1] National Conference of Charities and Correction, *Report*, 1916, p. 174, quoting the Majority Report of the British Royal Commission on the Poor Laws and Relief of Distress of 1909.

[2] A draft of a Federal Act embodying some of these recommendations can be obtained from the American Association for Labor Legislation, 131 East 23d Street, New York City.

## CHAPTER XV

## FINANCIAL DEVICES FOR CONTROLLING OR MITIGATING THE SEVERITY OF BUSINESS CYCLES

By Thomas Sewall Adams

Yale University

The distinctive evil of the business cycle is due to the abuse or misuse of credit. At some point in the cycle, borrowers and buyers ask for credit which in their own and the public interest should be refused. To do this it is necessary (*a*) to find some practical test or index by which to determine when the time for credit restriction has arrived; (*b*) to devise some process or mechanism by which restriction can be exercised; and (*c*) to select the men or agency of control upon which the responsibility for initiating action may properly be placed. It is primarily to these questions that the proposals discussed in this chapter are addressed.

### I. PROPOSALS RELATING TO THE CONTROL OF BANK CREDIT

A considerable measure of responsibility for the regulation or regularization of credit obviously rests upon the banks. Here fortunately the discussion may start with an established principle. It has long been an accepted rule of banking practice that interest rates should be increased when there is danger of a panic; and this rule is commonly interpreted to mean, under existing conditions in the United States, that the Federal Reserve Banks should raise their discount rates sharply when the reserve ratios established by law (35 per cent in lawful money against deposits and 40 per cent in gold against federal reserve notes in circulation) are threatened.

Recent experience seems to show that this rule is inadequate and should, if possible, be amended or supplemented.

As a matter of business experience since the Armistice, the country has passed through a brief period of falling prices; a boom in 1919 and early 1920 which was characterized—to use the descriptive phrases applied by the Federal Reserve Board[1]— by "over-extended business," a "mania for speculation," "unprecedented orgy of extravagance," and a period of painful prostration and reaction. But, it is significant to note, we have passed through the crisis without a panic, without recourse

[1] *Annual Report* of the Federal Reserve Board covering operations for the year 1920, p. 1.

to the emergency note provisions of the Federal Reserve Act, and without material reduction of bank reserves below the legal minima. We have stayed within the established limits, and yet we have suffered. New limits, new rules are obviously desirable.

Investigation seems to show that the introduction and amendment of the Federal Reserve System has resulted in an enormous increase of the amount of bank credit which may be based upon the given reserve of gold, and that the stock of gold in this country has been abnormally swollen as a result of the war. O. M. W. Sprague estimates that "the available supply of credit was more than doubled as a result of the establishment and operation of the reserve banks," and that "all future additions to the stock of gold in this country will provide the basis for at least twice as great an increment to the volume of credit as was possible in the later years of the national banking system."[1]

It is impracticable, within the space assigned to this chapter, to follow in detail either the recent business and banking history of this country, or the analysis which links that experience with the subject here under discussion. They establish, however, in the opinion of the writer, two facts of controlling importance for this chapter:

First, that as prevention is better than cure, any action which may properly be taken to avert over-expansion of credit, should be taken before the legal reserve ratios of the banks are actually threatened; that is, in the boom period or prosperity phase of the cycle.

Second, that under existing conditions in this country, bank credit may become harmfully over-extended while the reserves are still well above the legal minima. Expressed concretely, the present reserve ratios of 35 and 40 per cent are ineffective and misleading indicators of the time or condition at which further extensions of credit should be discontinued.

The proposals to remedy this situation are as follows:

**Adjusting discount rates in accordance with index numbers of production, employment, prices, and profits.**

The starting point of the recent discussion of this subject is found in O. M. W. Sprague's initial proposal that the discount rates of the Federal Reserve Banks should be sharply raised, regardless of reserve ratios when the capital and labor of the country are fully employed and when, therefore, there can be little or no increase of output in response to the stimulus of additional credit and rising prices. The proposal is based on the thought that credit is over-extended, not when the reserve ratios are threatened, but when production has reached its peak and further credit results principally in fruitless speculation. The suggested method or mechanism is, not that discount rates should be based in any definite mechanical way upon index numbers, but that the Federal

[1] The Discount Policy of the Federal Reserve Banks, *The American Economic Review*, March, 1921, p. 16.

Reserve Banks in the formulation of their credit policies should make greater use than they have made in the past of those statistics which indicate the development and probable culmination of a boom.

It is true that those statistics are imperfect and that our knowledge of cyclical cartography is in dire need of improvement. It is also true that many factors other than index numbers must be taken into account in formulating a sound credit policy. But we should not use these facts as a smoke screen behind which to dodge a question of principle. The country knew with sufficient certainty in 1919 that it was in the midst of an inflationistic boom. We shall probably recognize the next boom when we meet it. When it arrives, will those who control the actions of the Federal Reserve Banks act to restrict credit when credit expansion begins to do its destructive work, or will they wait until the credit of the Federal Reserve Banks shows signs of exhaustion?

The proposal here under consideration has the great merit of stating that issue in an unescapable way, and in emphasizing the responsibility of the Federal Reserve Banks for cooperating actively in the development of what has been called above "cyclical cartography." The proposal, however, is essentially a graphic statement rather than a solution of the problem, and Mr. Sprague now regards it "as a matter of secondary importance, and in peace-time cycles probably, only of cautionary value."[1] As a solution it is not only subject to the limitations noted above, but it exaggerates the power of an increase in discount rates to restrict credit, and suggests a method of regulation which would possibly encounter grave political opposition.

**Raising the legal reserve requirements against federal reserve notes and deposits.**

If the present reserve ratios are misleading guides to a sound credit policy, because under existing conditions they make possible an over-expansion of bank credit, an obvious suggestion is to raise the ratios. Such a suggestion has been made by Mr. Sprague.

A reserve ratio of 50 per cent or even 60 per cent would permit much more additional credit expansion than was possible under the national banking system, and quite as much as could be advantageously employed.[2]

This, however, proposes to limit rather than to regulate or control credit expansion, and is only to be considered in the event that more elastic and adaptable measures of regulation are found to be impracticable. Devices which would in effect raise the note-reserve ratio, however, have been suggested by many authorities, and must be regarded as important possible means of restricting credit expansion. Thus, R. C. Leffingwell proposes to restore gold and gold certificates to circulation

[1] From a letter to the writer.
[2] *The American Economic Review*, March, 1921, p. 29.

and thus recreate the "greatly depleted secondary reserve." A similar idea forms an integral part of the important proposal of A. C. Miller, next to be considered.

## Increasing the sensitiveness of the deposit-reserve ratios of the Federal Reserve Banks.

A. C. Miller of the Federal Reserve Board proposes not to abandon the reserve ratio, but to make it a safer and more sensitive guide to a sound credit policy. He suggests not a device but a detailed plan of procedure which can be best explained in his own words:

> The main change in the published weekly statement of the Federal Reserve Banks that would be necessary would be to report the specific note reserve, held by the Federal Reserve Agent, and the specific deposit reserve, held by the bank. . . .
>
> The existing gold holdings of the reserve banks should be reapportioned between the deposit reserve and the note reserve. To the deposit reserve might be allocated an amount of reserve money equivalent, say, to 45 per cent of their deposit liabilities as of the date when the new form of accounting would become effective. To the note reserve should be allocated all the remaining reserve, and, as the law requires, be in the form of gold.
>
> The reserve thus allocated to the deposit reserve *should be regarded* as the working reserve of the banking or discount department of the Federal Reserve Bank. The banks *should be expected* to conduct their discount operations on the basis of this reserve. Until conditions justified, the amount of this reserve *should not be changed.* Fresh accessions of gold received by the banking department *should be transferred* to the note reserve by way of substitution for other collateral held by the Federal Reserve Agent, or in exchange for federal reserve notes. Withdrawals of gold from Federal Reserve Banks for foreign shipment *should, for the present at least, be taken out of the note reserve* by the presentation of federal reserve notes for redemption in gold or by the substitution of commercial collateral for gold in the security held by the Federal Reserve Agent. . . .
>
> While the deposit reserve under the arrangement proposed above would be constant, the deposit reserve ratio would not be constant, but would fluctuate. Any expansion of the loan account of the Federal Reserve Banks would quickly reflect itself in the diminution of the reserve ratio below 45 per cent; any diminution of their loan account would quickly reflect itself in an increase of the reserve ratio above 45 per cent. In brief, fluctuations in the reserve ratio would reflect quickly and accurately changes in the volume of the reserve banks' discounts.
>
> *From time to time the situation of the reserve banks as a whole, and of the several reserve banks individually, should be reviewed in the light of current credit conditions and needs in order to determine whether any reapportionment of reserves should be made; whether, e.g., any given bank should enlarge its deposit reserve at the expense of its note reserve.* . . .
>
> As a result, the reserve ratios of the Federal Reserve Banks would have a meaning not now possessed by them. As the banking and business community came to be educated to the new method of stating the position of the reserve banks, primary attention would be paid to the movements of the deposit reserve

ratio; that ratio would be the immediate gage of the banking and credit situation. As credit expansion was in process, that reserve ratio would decline much more rapidly than it now does. It would be a faithful indicator of what was going on. It would rise only in reaction to a decline in the rate of expansion or as liquidation was in process. Moreover, as the community came to appreciate the significance of changes in the deposit ratio, that ratio would come to be regarded with heightened interest because of the evident bearing in the logic of reserve banking, of changes in the reserve ratio upon credit and discount policy. And thus would the problem of credit administration also be simplified and its solution be aided by anticipatory action, both on the part of the banks and on the part of the borrowing community.

The note reserve ratio, under the scheme of operation here under consideration, would have real significance as indicating the extent of the gold cover against federal reserve notes. Fluctuations in the note reserve ratio would indicate the increase or decrease of federal reserve notes outstanding, movements of gold into and out of the Federal Reserve System, and reapportionment of existing gold holdings between the deposit reserve and the note reserve.[1]

Mr. Miller's proposal is largely educational in purpose. It eschews mechanical controls and trusts that the deposit reserve, having been disentangled from its present misalliance with the note reserve, public opinion, and the "live judgment" of the federal reserve banker, will do their appointed work of "regulating the flow and volume of credit with regard to the trend of business and the volume of banking."

There is something disappointingly vague about regulation *"with regard to."* Does it look towards preventing the over-extension of credit or merely preventing the exhaustion of credit? Doubtless we must renounce all hope of finding a neat little clockwork device which will automatically raise discount rates as we approach the crest of a boom, but men, particularly public officials, need the help of rule-of-thumb devices which, like alarm clocks, announce the hour when they ought to wake up. Political exigency may make it impracticable to get up at that moment but the clock is nevertheless serviceable. Mr. Miller shows how the clock, which has not been keeping time accurately, may be repaired. But he does not give it an alarm bell.

The management of the reserves, under Mr. Miller's plan, would involve the exercise of a large degree of discretionary control. Certain aspects of the procedure (italicized by the writer in the quotation) have an air of unreality. A temporary fixity is to be imparted to the deposit reserve, but at indefinite times by indefinite authorities (possibly on the initiative of the Federal Reserve Banks with the approval of the Board), the deposit reserve might be increased by transfers from the note reserve "in order to give the bank an enlarged basis of lending." This feature, if its weakness may fairly be tested by a touch of caricature, seems a little

[1] Federal Reserve Policy, *The American Economic Review*, June, 1921, pp. 203–5.

like play—let us play that the deposit reserve is fixed, it being understood that when the ratio approaches the legal minimum, new reserves will be brought up from the note department. There is virtue in some forms of play (as in discretionary control), but it is doubtful whether this particular device or procedure could secure the legislative sanction which its introduction would probably require. And a similar verdict must be reached with respect to the proposed management of the note reserve. It is avowedly an attempt to approximate the machinery and procedure employed by the Bank of England before the war. Whatever the merits of that procedure, and they are great, the Federal Reserve System has been constructed on a different theory and it is highly improbable that the system could be revised in the approximate future with the purpose of so handling withdrawals of gold that they would exercise the maximum restrictive effect upon the supply of bank credit.

Great importance attaches to Mr. Miller's simple proposal that the specific deposit reserve and ratio be separately stated, particularly in view of his opinion that this is contemplated by the Federal Reserve Act. In addition, it would probably be comparatively easy for the Federal Reserve Banks to compute and publish nearly all the significant figures and ratios which would result if Mr. Miller's plan were adopted. The gold holdings of the banks could be constructively or statistically reapportioned. Thereafter figures could be prepared on this basis and the resulting ratios published with such comment or action as they seemed to require. To the extent that we are to put our trust in the philosophy that to be free we only need to know the truth, the problem would seem to be soluble without fundamental changes in the banking law.

## II. PROPOSALS RELATING TO GRANTING OR ASKING FOR CREDITS— SELECTIVE CREDIT CONTROL

While the discount rate of the Federal Reserve Banks "is an indispensable factor in the regulation and control of credit . . . the conditions that make this traditional control effective do not all exist at the present time."[1] And the limitations upon its efficiency are not all temporary. A general elevation of the level of discount rates—even when control by a central banking system is sufficient to accomplish that—is too undiscriminating to serve as a complete or perfect method of regulation. In boom periods, its blanket quality, or its wet-blanket quality, serves properly to discourage or postpone the financing of many projects which under other conditions would be plainly entitled to credit assistance. But it fails to repress the speculator feverishly bent on anticipating an expected jump in prices. Consideration of these serious limitations upon the rediscount rate as an instrument of control has led naturally to

[1] *Annual Report* of the Federal Reserve Board covering operations for the year 1919, p. 70.

proposals for decentralized control or what has been called above "selective credit."

**Raising credit tests by commercial banks in periods of business expansion.**

This proposal, which also comes from the suggestive pen of O. M. W. Sprague, is that:

> Commercial banks generally in analyzing credit should insist upon an improving ratio between current assets and current liabilities during periods of active business and large profits. In general, the opposite condition has characterized past practice. The average quality of both inventory and receivables deteriorates under the influence of a seller's market and rising prices. If those for whom a ratio of two to one was adequate in 1916 had been required to show a higher ratio, say, three to one, in 1919, it is certain that much of the credit expansion of that year would not have occurred, and the cyclical fluctuations of the last few years would have been less extreme. On account of the large number of banks, this proposal may seem at first sight rather utopian, but it involves nothing more than an extension of familiar practice, attacking the problem concretely and from an angle with which both business men and bankers are familiar.[1]

Interpreted not as a method of external or compulsory control, but as an educational device appealing both to the public spirit and the self-interest of the banks, this proposal appears to have considerable merit. Competing banks operated for profit could hardly be expected to curtail loans in the earlier part of a boom. But it is in the latter part of the boom period that credit restriction is most needed, and at that time it becomes a profitable policy for the banks, or what is the same thing, a policy which looks to the avoidance of loss. The efficacy of the proposal, however, depends upon the success which the economists of the country achieve in demarcating the prosperity phase of the cycle and determining its approximate duration. If the banks can be convinced that within a reasonably definite period a sharp shrinkage of business and values is to be expected, credit expansion will be checked almost automatically.

**Adjusting banking to the phases of the business cycle.**

In the opinion of the writer practically all of the proposals which have been made to regulate bank credit by a specific financial device or mechanism err through over-simplification of the problem. Specific devices have their value and function, for much the same reason that the wise merchant does not omit to dress the windows of his store even though he realizes that only a small fraction of his wares can be represented there. But the larger view, particularly in view of our imperfect knowledge of the phases of the cycle, is to take not one test, but many tests, of the time to act, and many lines, not one, of remedial action. A more comprehensive description of the tests and remedies (which it may

---

[1] From a letter to the writer. Compare O. M. W. Sprague, *Bank Management and the Business Cycle, Harvard Business Review,* October, 1922.

be noted are usually implicit in the minds of those who propose specific devices) is given in the following statement by E. W. Kemmerer:[1]

Assume for example, that the evidence at a particular time shows we are several years along on the rising curve of a business cycle, that there has been no substantial liquidation for two or three years, that speculative activity is running high on the exchanges, that prices of the more speculative stocks are rising, that bank clearings are large, that reserve ratios at Federal Reserve Banks and commercial banks are tending downward, call and short-time interest rates and Federal Reserve discount rates rising, the ratios of bank loans to deposits increasing, credit becoming more and more extended, and that commercial failures for some time have been running abnormally low, showing that little dead wood has of late been cut out of the business structure. This, for example, is a substantially correct picture of the year 1906, and of the latter part of 1919, and the early part of 1920.

He adds that a prudent and far-sighted banker in these circumstances would

probably try to get his assets in a more liquid condition. He would sell his less gilt-edged securities while the selling was good, and place the proceeds either in the most gilt-edged securities on the market—the kind that ordinarily suffers least in a period of crisis and that usually alone advances during the early part of the ensuing depression—or he might purchase with the proceeds prime commercial paper of short maturities, scattering well his risks. He would place a larger proportion of his resources in the best commercial paper of concerns outside of his own community whose businesses were of the kinds least affected by crises—concerns whose paper he would have no responsibility to renew at maturity. He would clean up his loan accounts with his Federal Reserve Bank and with his correspondent banks, and strengthen his reserve position. He would get a larger proportion of his paper into short maturities and would bring pressure to reduce his "capital loans," the kind that have formed the "renewal habit."

The general plan of action that he adopted for himself he would suggest to many of his customers. He might be premature in his action; if so, he could console himself with the thought that it is better to be safe than to be sorry, that he moved in the right direction, and that the very prematurity of himself and of others who acted like him contributed towards stabilizing the situation.

**Adjusting the commitments and financial activities of business concerns to the phases of the cycles.**
The conditions which make it expedient for banks to restrict credit, make it equally expedient in general for business concerns to refrain from seeking or using credit. This obvious aspect of the subject is noted only to record the fact that some American business concerns have found it both practical and profitable to adjust their financial operations to the phases of the cycle. But that topic is covered in other chapters.

---

[1] *The Business Cycle* (published by the *New York Evening Post*), 1921, pp. 14–15.

### III. PROPOSALS TO STABILIZE THE DOLLAR

A complete survey of the devices suggested for mitigating the severity of business cycles would include an examination of various plans proposed for stabilizing the purchasing power of the dollar, particularly Irving Fisher's carefully elaborated plan to adjust the amount or weight of the gold bullion in the dollar in accordance with the deviations from par of an index number of representative commodity prices. These proposals, despite weighty opinion to the contrary, seem to be entirely relevant to the subject here under discussion. If introduced and successfully operated the price level would remain approximately constant; *i.e.*, the range and significance of price fluctuations would be greatly reduced, and in any future period of time the number of rising prices would be substantially balanced by an equal number of falling prices. One of the principal causes of business cycles, the contemporaneous rise of most prices (and the expectancy thereof) would therefore be removed or essentially modified.

A discussion of these plans would carry the present chapter beyond the limits assigned to it. Most of them are described in Mr. Fisher's book "Stabilizing the Dollar" (particularly in Appendices III and VI), and more recent plans will be found in Carl Strover's "Monetary Reconstruction" and in Representative T. Alan Goldsborough's bill to stabilize prices "by controlling the quantity of money and credits in relation to the volume of trade by increasing or diminishing that quantity as the average price level goes down or up."[1] These plans, Mr. Fisher's plan in particular, deserve thorough examination by every person whose mind is practical enough to entertain the belief that some of the deeper sources of cyclical disturbances may by time and thought be removed. But they are impracticable at this time, because people believe them impracticable—if for no other reason. They propose to lay hands upon the economic holy-of-holies, and before they can be acted upon they will require an amount of critical discussion commensurate with that which should be given, say, to a proposal fundamentally to alter the marriage relation.

\*    \*    \*

A review of the financial devices for controlling or mitigating the severity of business cycles which have been proposed, leads to the conclusion that there is no simple device which it is reasonable to insist shall be employed by business men or by bankers for the purpose in view. As we approach the crest of a boom in any particular trade or industry, it is desirable that buying and commitments should be reduced, and that to this end credit accommodation to that trade or industry should be restricted. Such action, to business man and banker, represents not

[1] From a speech by Representative Goldsborough in the House of Representatives, May 23, 1922, *Congressional Record*, vol. 62, no. 135, p. 8149.

only their self-interest, but their public obligation. But they must first know, with that degree of precision and certainty required for business action, that the trade or industry in question is actually approaching the crest of a boom. The ways and means of controlling credit—financial devices, in short—are thus subordinate to knowledge of the cycle. The clearest duty of business man and banker is to assist in the development of more accurate cyclical statistics. Plot the phases of the cycle, and a combination of self-interest and vitalized public opinion will force the application of the many remedies—not one remedy—which common sense will show to be appropriate. To anticipate the cycle is to neutralize it.

# CHAPTER XVI

## PUBLIC EMPLOYMENT OFFICES AND UNEMPLOYMENT[1]

### By Shelby M. Harrison

Director of Department of Surveys and Exhibits, Russell Sage Foundation

### I. INTRODUCTION

Between 1910 and 1916, seven important studies were made in the United States into the causes of unemployment, and accompanying programs of remedial procedure were put forward. Each recommended the establishment of public employment offices as one of the immediate steps to be taken. The Wainwright Commission of New York, whose recommendation is typical, after an exhaustive study here and abroad, urged the establishment of "a system of public employment offices. . . covering all sections of the state," giving as its reason that "much of that unemployment which is due to maladjustment—to the failure of demand and supply to find each other—can be eliminated by such a system."[2] Even before 1910, when the first of these commissions was appointed, sentiment favorable to this step had developed, and several state systems of public employment exchanges had their beginnings in that period.

In the two years following the Armistice, the President urged Congress to continue, during the demobilization period, the United States Public Employment Service which had been developed as a war measure aimed primarily to help employers to secure labor. Although this service was practically discontinued, the demand for some national employment service continued to be voiced in responsible quarters, and a number of the states appropriated more money for their own public employment work than they had ever supplied before, conservative estimates placing the total for 1919 at upwards of $785,254, and at more than $1,000,000 in 1920.[3] Among other representative groups the Second Industrial Conference, called by President Wilson in 1920, recommended "a national system of

---

[1] The material here presented is drawn mainly from Part I of a forthcoming report on Public Employment Offices. The study was made under the direction of Shelby M. Harrison for the Department of Surveys and Exhibits and the Department of Industrial Studies of the Russell Sage Foundation, New York. Part I reports the findings of the section of the investigation covered by J. B. Buell.

[2] New York State Employers' Liability Commission *Reports*, 1910–1911, No. 3, Unemployment and Lack of Farm Labor, p. 13.

[3] "Waste in Industry," pp. 279–80.

employment exchanges, municipal, state, and federal, which shall in effect create a national employment service." More recently, the Conference on Unemployment called by President Harding, also favored the establishment and coordination of "an adequate permanent system of public employment offices;" and Governor Smith's Reconstruction Commission, New York, in its Report on a Permanent Unemployment Program in 1919 recommended the continued development of "the state employment service looking toward an ultimate state monopoly in this field, excepting possibly a small number of union agencies and private agencies supplying service of a personal and professional character." Beginning with the Murdock bill in 1914 resulting from a period of unemployment, and extending to the recent Kenyon-Nolan bill, there has been continuous and strongly backed agitation in Congress for legislative provision for some kind of national employment service.

These are only a few of the many significant and impressive indications of the growing popular interest in public employment work as a means of reducing unemployment in this country. There was, to be sure, a certain amount of organized opposition to the Federal Employment Service, but the greater part of this was opposition to *the* service as set up and administered during the war rather than to *a* national system of public employment offices or to public employment bureaus as such. On the other hand much vigorous and widespread approval and support was found. Indeed, except for the type of opposition referred to, a high percentage of the various civic and industrial organizations consulted, favored the continuation and development of some type of nation-wide public employment system.

## II. WHAT EMPLOYMENT BUREAU WORK IS

What is the nature of this organized employment work, in support of which sentiment has been growing?

The seventy or more public employment offices which were visited in the course of the investigation by the Russell Sage Foundation may be divided into three large groups: (1) the "two-man" office, the smallest staffed bureau which is able to render effective service; (2) the middle-sized bureau where the volume of work requires a larger staff and some division of function; and (3) the largest and most highly organized of the public bureaus.

Similarly the fee-charging employment agencies, the chief competitors of the public bureaus, fall into three main types. The small agency making a specialty of placing unskilled men is the most common type. Observation indicates that something like half of all the commercial bureaus are of this type. Then there are agencies dealing almost exclusively with domestics and women day-workers carried on by small staffs in small

18

offices, and the larger offices serving clerical and office workers, both men and women.

Whatever the routine, however general or specialized the experience of bureau staffs, however simple or highly organized the work of the different offices, however well or poorly the work was being done, in the last analysis all the bureaus visited were engaged in doing the same essential things. They were, first, giving information about jobs to workers, and information about available workers to employers; second, they were helping to bring together the worker wanting a job and the employer wanting workers. Thus the primary function of the employment bureau work is seen to be the collection and making available of information on work openings and on workers in search of them, and through the use of this information, the making of contacts between workers wanting jobs and employers wanting workers.

**The Different Agencies and Mediums Performing This Service.—** Besides the public and commercial labor exchanges, a considerable number of other agencies and mediums were found performing somewhat similar services.

All of these group themselves into two main divisions. The first are the direct, or informal, or unorganized methods or agencies through which this service is performed. A new job may be secured through (1) more or less promiscuous application at the employer's gate; (2) the help of a friend or mutual acquaintance; (3) a waiting list kept by the employer; or (4) miscellaneous methods.

The second, the indirect, or more formal, or organized methods and agencies will be treated after the direct methods and agencies have been discussed.

### III. THE DIRECT AND UNORGANIZED METHODS

**Application at the Gates.—**Many employers rely mainly if not entirely upon men who apply directly at the factory gates. A number of reasons were found for this. Only a minimum of effort is required on the employer's part, and employment managers take a certain pride in the fact that men continually come to their factories without solicitation.

When numbers of men are available at the gate, there is also more likelihood that employers will get some worker and perhaps a worker well fitted for the job. The employment manager of an electric light and power company wanted "to have just as many people coming to us as possible. We interview everyone that comes and if we haven't a job, we encourage him to come back again and to keep at us until we do have something." And a fourth reason was akin to the last; the larger the number of men who come asking for work, the greater the bargaining power of the employer in agreeing on wages and terms of work. The competition of workmen against each other puts the employer in a position of advantage; he can be more confident that he can get what he wants; and conversely, the men asking work become less confident—particularly if, as sometimes happens, they are forced to wait long periods before being interviewed or are treated with a good deal of gruffness.

The reasons given by workers as to why they follow the method of applying for work at the gate came down to two chief and obvious facts. First, very often necessity forces them to it. Many workers have no sources of information on jobs, they have no affiliations or friends who can make contacts for them, or they do not know about or have not become accustomed to using organized employment agencies.

Second, even where men do not feel impelled by necessity to call at the factory gate, there are some who see or think they see an advantage in going directly to the factory and getting there first. There might be an unexpected opening which in this way can be secured before the employer calls the outside employment bureau or has time to advertise.

**Contact Made by Acquaintances.**—Sometimes the employer recruits workers through his own employees, and workers learn of jobs through friends or acquaintances. Among the more highly trained professional workers this method is one of the common means of effecting changes. Some employers of skilled and unskilled labor rely upon their foremen for this assistance, and others occasionally find workers who seem to have special facility in keeping in touch with available people. This is especially true of plants employing immigrant labor and negro workers.

The more important reasons given by employers and workers as to why this method has proved satisfactory are four:

In the first place, it is much easier for the employer's representative to step into the factory and talk with an employee for two or three minutes than either to write a newspaper "ad," continue it for several days, and then select from numerous candidates, or to call up an employment agency and explain the character of the job to someone not entirely familiar with it.

The method is easy for the worker also. One employer states that his men "generally know that a job is going to be vacant before I do." To pass on to some friend the news of a job is a friendly act not limited to any walk of life.

Second, this method puts a more personal element into the contact of employer with worker. The worker's desire for personal recognition and self-development is to some extent satisfied. It was, in fact, in the plants which emphasized the value of good personnel relations that we found a systematic cultivation of their own workers as a source of labor supply in greatest favor.

A third reason was that this method usually provides full and accurate information on both men and jobs. The information which a worker gets from his friends is usually of an accurate and intimate kind. They can pass on what they know of the characteristics of the boss, the firm's general attitude toward labor, transportation facilities, the congeniality of the other workmen, and other items which are of importance to the man looking for a job.

Fourth, in recruiting large numbers of workers, this method has advantages. Employers find that frequently a worker represents a coterie of acquaintances on which they may draw when necessary. For the worker, there is advantage in having many avenues through which to learn of jobs. Each of his friends represents a nucleus of information which may possibly result in an employment contact.

**Waiting List or Application File.**—Many of the employers interviewed used a waiting list or application file as a means of making employment contacts.

The opinions of employers as to the usefulness of these lists varied greatly. A few placed a good deal of emphasis on them. One very large concern hiring all types of workers was "keeping an application file of all the people coming in for jobs." The file was kept active, and the officers turned to it first. Another firm in New England claimed that "aside from people whom our own workers bring in, we fill all our jobs from our waiting lists."

Other employers, however, were less enthusiastic. For common laborers few employers thought it worth while to keep applications for more than a few days, and many paid no attention to such registrations.

Workers as a rule had little faith in these lists. "I went up for a job, but they didn't have anything. Just took my name and address. You know what that means." This comment expressed the common attitude.

**Miscellaneous Direct and Unorganized Employment Contacts.**— In one city a group of employment managers through their local associations had become more or less intimately acquainted with each other. They met regularly to exchange ideas, and much of the suspicion which sometimes exists between competing concerns had been dispelled. It became a common practice to call on each other for help when they needed a special kind of worker, and when a good man came in whom they could not use to call up "Bill" or "Charlie"— they knew each other by their first names—and ask whether he could use such a man.

Still another kind of contact-making point was described by a marine steward on the Great Lakes. "The best way to land something, outside of your friends amongst the captains, is to hang around the marine stores. There are several of them on the lakes, and they are general loafing places for lake people. When his boat docks, a captain always comes up for supplies and to talk; and if he needs a steward, he usually says so."

In one town the boss baker in a large baking establishment was a common source both of jobs and of men. He had been in the business for a long time, knew most of the men in the trade, and became in a natural and informal way the medium through which many of the changes occurred.

These three instances are typical and indicate how naturally employment contact-making takes place whenever people for one purpose or another come together.

## IV. INADEQUACY OF UNORGANIZED METHODS AND THE NEED OF ORGANIZED SERVICE

The question which immediately arises, after reviewing these direct methods and after noting the reasons for their use, is *whether they alone are equal to the demand which has been growing for an efficient means of securing jobs for men, and men for jobs.* If they are not adequate then the problem of establishing additional mediums or agencies for employment contact-making needs to be pursued further.

**Resort to Other Methods as Evidence of Inadequacy.**—One of the first and most important pieces of evidence bearing on the question of adequacy is the fact that other agencies for making employment contacts have been set up and that some of them have done and are still doing a great amount of business. In other words, that employers' associations, trade unions, philanthropic societies, private fee-charging agencies, not to mention various government agencies, federal, state, and city, have found it expedient to operate formally organized employment bureaus, and that these have been patronized in large volume by both employers and workers, we may take as *prima facie* evidence that the unorganized means of recruiting and job-getting have not been sufficient to meet the needs of either employers or workers.

**Numbers and Types of Workers Placed.**—Our field work included a study of the different types of employment agencies which have grown up in recent years and the number of workers placed by some of them. Consideration of the facts back of these figures shows some of the reasons why such agencies as the public bureaus and the private fee-charging offices have been resorted to, and at the same time sheds further light upon the inadequacy of the direct methods.

Unfortunately, the statistics kept by many public bureaus are not altogether satisfactory for our purpose: in some cases they are compiled in such a fashion as to have little significance. There were, however, a few noteworthy exceptions, and from these several conclusions appeared obvious. In the first place it was seen from the data collected that among men applicants numerically the largest group handled by all of the bureaus was common labor.[1]  Nearly 23,000 out of 48,000 in San Francisco in the year 1917–1918, and some 60,000 out of about 109,000 in Ohio in the year 1916–1917, and 6,000 out of 17,000 in New York State in the nine months ending with June, 1916 or 50 per cent of the male workers placed in the large occupation groups, were found in the general class of unskilled and common labor.  Moreover, some acquaintance with the work of the private fee-charging agencies tends to the conclusion that the fifty-eight labor agencies specializing in unskilled workers in Illinois in 1919 and the equal number in the city of New York a few years earlier were doing a much larger gross business than the larger number placing other types of workers.

Another important group for whom positions were secured through public bureaus and private agencies was found in the service occupations, such as bell boys, choremen, elevator boys, flunkeys, horsemen, janitors, porters; among women, they were domestics, day workers, and chambermaids.  With these also may be classed the hotel and restaurant workers.

A third general class, covering a number of miscellaneous occupations of a more skilled nature, such as clerical and mercantile workers, nurses, teachers, barbers, machinists, carpenters, painters, and the like, is much smaller numerically, especially in the figures for the public bureaus.

It is evident, therefore, that of the fields which are being occupied by the two main types of employment bureaus, public and private, the first, that of common labor, has special significance; the second or service field is also important, while for the skilled worker there is relatively little activity.

The reason why floating, unskilled laborers, and the employers who hire them need the assistance of an employment bureau is fairly obvious. Such workers for the most part are unfamiliar with local conditions, many of them having come from distant places.  They are in general a homeless and often a friendless lot; and the rumors of jobs which pass around among them are likely to be vague and inaccurate.  Likewise the jobs which come to these agencies are in comparatively isolated places, such as railroad construction and lumber camps, farms or fruit ranches. And distance itself, in the main, precludes the use of direct methods or agencies, such as application at the gate or the aid of acquaintances, in making the employment contacts.  As a result many employers and workers have been forced to enlist organized assistance.

Wherever, therefore, there is much of this in-and-out-of-town shifting, an employment bureau is usually found or the need of it is evident.

A second fact, less evident perhaps but of equal importance, is seen from a further analysis of the semi-skilled group of elevator men, servants,

---

[1] For a fuller presentation of the statistical material and other data upon which conclusions here reached are based, the reader is referred to the full report of the Russell Sage Foundation here summarized in part.

porters, hotel and restaurant workers, and the like. With domestics it is perhaps most obvious. Here the possible positions are scattered all over the city, with one or two workers to each employer. In a locality offering employment in homes to, say, one thousand domestic servants, an applicant who tried to cover the whole field in all probability would have to apply to nine hundred or more scattered employers. This is in marked contrast to the applicant at a department store who, to cover an equal number of possibilities, would have to go only to two or three stores located near each other in the center of the city.

Thus when jobs are widely distributed in any locality the opportunity for employers and workers to come together is lessened, and both have found it expedient to seek the assistance of some organized employment agency.

Third, as our investigation showed, the worker who changes his job frequently and the employer who has a large labor turnover will need organized assistance and will resort to it more often than workers who hold jobs for long periods and employers whose labor turnover is low.

In the fourth place, the relatively less able workmen in a trade require organized assistance. One important reason is because they are more frequently called upon to find employment for themselves than are the efficient workmen.

The same thing was found true of employers who offered less desirable jobs. There were numerous instances of firms trying to get men at a little lower than the average rate of wages, who tried to enlist all the outside assistance they could; and many employment bureaus had on file a quantity of calls for boys or clerks at wages just a little below the usual rate—calls, incidentally, which they neither could fill nor found it desirable to try very seriously to fill.

A fifth reason found was that many workers used the organized agencies not because of inferior ability as workers but because of inferior ability as job-getters. In other words our findings agree in part at least with the contention of the Webbs that there is a distinction to be drawn between "the faculty of finding work and the faculty of doing work."[1]

There may be still other reasons why employers and workers find it desirable at times to turn to the organized agencies in making employment contacts; but whether there are or not, the reasons given suffice to show the inadequacy of the direct methods. If, then, the direct methods are inadequate, and modern industry requires an organized service for bringing employers and workers together to talk about jobs, the question immediately arises as to the kind of organized service which is needed.

[1] WEBB, SIDNEY and BEATRICE, "Public Organization of the Labor Market," p. 169.

## V. ORGANIZED EMPLOYMENT METHODS AND AGENCIES

Seven important organized methods or agencies are used by employers and workers in getting together to talk about employment.

**"Want-Ad" Employment Service Advantages and Disadvantages.—** The newspaper "want-ad" column is one of the most common means by which employers and workers get in touch with each other. While this is an organized service, it differs from the employment bureaus in that it is concerned only with the distribution of information. For the large majority of job openings there is little or nothing selective about the distribution, and the newspaper assumes no responsibility for seeing that the worker and employer come in contact with each other, as does the employment bureau.

The use of the want-ad column was found practically universal. Only one or two employers claimed never to have resorted to it, although a larger number of workers stated that they never answered advertisements. "Somebody always gets there before you" was the reason given.

From the employer's standpoint the "want-ad" offers certain advantages: in the instances where the job requires a worker of special ability it may be possible through "ads" calling for written replies to eliminate a considerable number of applicants obviously unqualified for the work in question, and to spend time in interviewing only the most promising; it is often an easy means of keeping a steady supply of applicants coming to the gate of the plant; it often proves useful in cases of emergency when workers are wanted quickly; and this method, by bringing applicants into competition with each other at the gate, tends to increase the employer's bargaining power.

The advantages of this method seem to accrue almost entirely to the employer. There are disadvantages to him, however, as well as to the workers. One is the tendency of this kind of advertising to cause people to change jobs and thus increase the general labor turnover of the district. Another disadvantage is its cost.

This method usually means also a serious waste of time to the worker. For him to answer an "ad" is often only slightly better than going around from gate to gate. Moreover, the more general abuses of newspaper advertisements which have been given much publicity in the past are continually cropping up. The "fake" advertisement, the "ad" which grossly misrepresents, and the "ad" which is inserted for evil or immoral purposes, are extremely difficult to control.

**Bureaus Operated by Employers' Associations, Boards of Trade, Etc.—**Organized employment work is also carried on by a number of employment bureaus. Important among these is the type of bureau operated by employers' associations, boards of trade, and similar organizations. Some of these are run with the interests of the employer chiefly if not exclusively in mind; others are operated on a less partisan basis.

In general the reason found for the operation of employment bureaus by employers was the feeling that if circumstances make organized employment work necessary at all, it is desirable that the employers get what benefit they can from the method used. Employers felt that bureaus maintained by employers' associations had their interests at heart—not only those immediately concerned with efforts to get workers, but often other important related interests.

**Trade Union Bureaus.**—For much the same reason the trade unions have set up and are operating employment bureaus or exchanges; they too wish to exercise as much control as possible over the making of employment contacts. In addition to keeping its own members employed, the trade-union bureau may be of service also in placing men in plants where they can help the cause of unionism as opportunity permits.

Only a few trade unions operate organized employment bureaus in the accepted sense. Nevertheless, every union office and every union secretary is a center of information about jobs. As one observer puts it, "the trade unionist thinks it only natural that his business agent should secure work for him when he is unemployed. This he considers, is one of the principal benefits of the union."

A very few local unions have men who do nothing but employment work, as was the case in Cleveland, where a number of the organizations housed in the central labor headquarters, cooperated in using one man as office secretary and placement secretary. Even here, however, no records were kept and his work was largely through personal contacts and by word of mouth.

From the standpoint of the worker, there are several reasons why the employment work of the trade-union secretary is likely to be satisfactory. For union members the employment contact made at union headquarters is natural, easy, in the line of least resistance. The office is a loafing place out of hours or when men are out of work. They go there also to pay their dues. Again, the worker usually gets his job without bargaining for it. The information which the worker gets, moreover, usually covers other matters of interest to him than are commonly covered by other agencies; he is asked to pay no fee; and finally the number of jobs about which the union secures information through its members is often considerable.

**Bureaus Operated by Fraternal, Professional, and Other Organizations.**—Still another type of organized contact-making is that accomplished through certain organizations in which both employers and workers have some interest outside of the employment service itself. Examples are employment bureaus of fraternal organizations; employment bureaus of professional societies, such as those of the chemists, and the engineers; agencies operated by state teachers associations; and perhaps college appointment bureaus.

In a sense also employment bureaus run by trade unions which have a closed shop agreement with employers and where relations are in the main friendly belong in this class. Examples from the photo-engraving, printing, and clothing trades can be found where employers recognize the seeming permanence of the union and the possibilities of cooperating with it for the benefit of the trade.

Most of the large fraternal orders, such as the I.O.O.F., and the Masons, run employment bureaus; but the total of their business is small. The advantages of employment bureaus of this kind are that both employer and applicant are members of the same association and so have a mutual interest apart from the job which they are discussing.

The obvious limitation of both the lodge and professional bureaus is that they serve mainly their own membership. This is not as serious a handicap in the professional bureaus where engineers or chemists or social workers look only for jobs in their own fields and where the societies embrace a large part of the qualified workers.

**Bureaus Maintained by Philanthropic and Social Welfare Organizations.**—The fifth type of agency embraces those organized by philanthropic societies, churches, settlements, immigrant societies, prison associations, day nurseries, and other welfare associations. The older bureaus of this kind were started to care for families and individuals in distress. One of the important causes of such distress was unemployment; and the charitable societies decided that the constructive way of helping families and individuals suffering under this disability was not only to give them food, clothing, fuel, and other material relief temporarily, but also to assist the breadwinner in the family to obtain employment.

In looking over the work of the philanthropic bureaus as a whole, several characteristics were noted. First, while it was recognized that the employer might benefit from having some place to go for workers, these bureaus labored almost entirely in the interests of the worker. This meant in general that these bureaus were active chiefly in periods of depression and of unemployment, and that they did very little during times of labor shortage. Second, most of these agencies were serving groups of workers who were handicapped in securing positions. There were two main groups of these—those against whom as workers in their plants, employers held some prejudice or regarding whose abilities employers entertained doubts, as, for example, ex-convicts, aged persons, the physically handicapped, or negroes; and those who were unskilled in the technique of securing jobs. Juveniles are perhaps the best example of the latter.

In the third place, as their names and supporting organizations indicate, these bureaus do not receive support from fees nor from public taxation. This fact limits the chance of extending their service. Hence the possibility of any large part of employment contact-making being done through the philanthropic bureaus is not great.

**Fee-charging Employment Agencies.**—The commercial or fee-charging bureaus are agencies which have been called into existence because employers and workers need organized employment assistance enough to be willing to pay for it, and thus far no other sufficient means for securing the needed assistance have been available. The best known bureaus of this kind are those placing professional workers, especially teachers, clerical and office workers, workers in domestic service, and casual and unskilled labor. The last named type so outnumbers the others that the fee-charging agencies as a class are usually thought of as general labor agencies.

Toward private agencies as a class employers are either indifferent or suspicious; while workers, both organized and unorganized, are definitely hostile. Very few employers interviewed had confidence in the private agencies or regarded them as anything but a last resort for getting workmen; and where their experience had been satisfactory it was practically always with the higher class technical bureaus. Organized labor has of course, long been opposed to the private bureaus, charging that they are used as strike-breaking agencies, that they inevitably favor the employer, that their sole purpose is to exploit the worker.

**The Public Employment Bureau.**—Finally, organized employment work is also carried on by governmental agencies, national, state, or municipal, either separately or in combination. These bureaus are supported by public funds, and the bureau workers are public officials.

In some respects the public exchanges are similar to the private fee-charging agencies. In general, neither is controlled by one side, employer or worker (to the extent at least that control is exercised in employers' and union bureaus). Thus neither provides the assistance in bargaining power which usually inheres in employers' bureaus for employers or in union bureaus for workers. They are moreover open to all employers and all workmen and in the main, open to all employers on equal terms and all workers on equal terms. There are however important differences between the public and the commercial bureaus which have influenced the attitude of both parties toward them: (1) the service of the public bureau is borne by taxpayers, not by the applicants; (2) public bureaus although intended to be non-partisan can be controlled in the interests of either employers or workers; and (3), if controlled by one side or the other, the government organization can be used for partisan purposes much more effectively than can the small private organization.[1]

[1] I doubt whether a public employment bureau could be used for partisan labor purposes more effectively than can a small private bureau be used for the partisan purposes of employers. The employer can bring in many communities a very great pressure to bear on the private bureau.—Note by HARRY W. LAIDLER.

The fact that the public bureau offers free service influences naturally the attitude of the worker toward the public bureau as opposed to a fee-charging agency. To apply there is much more in "the line of least resistance" than to go to an agency which may require a registration fee before it gives any service at all and which will certainly deduct a large portion of the first wages for whatever service it renders.

To a combination of the second and third points can be ascribed much of the employers' opposition to the continuance of the United States Employment Service, and the workers' support of it. Private agencies are very largely dependent on the patronage of employers. It was a great change in the situation to find—as they thought, whether rightly or wrongly—that the United States Employment Service, organized on a national scale and with the authority of the federal government behind it, showed more sympathy than the commercial bureaus did for the interest of the workers, particularly union workers.

While the resolutions passed by employers' associations soon after the Armistice appear to have been part of the propaganda against the United States Employment Service, as it was operated in 1918 and the early part of 1919, rather than against public employment bureaus as such, many individual employers were found who were opposed to public bureaus however organized and administered.

The fact that trade unions passed resolutions supporting the United States Employment Service with the same unanimity that employers condemned it, tends to support the contention of the employers regarding union control. All but three of the labor organizations from which replies were received in answer to our general inquiry had gone on record as favoring the Service; and the American Federation of Labor in its 1919 convention by a large majority endorsed "the Nolan Bill for the continuation of the United States Employment Service."

The attitude of the unions, however, was not entirely due to a desire to gain control. For years they had been bitter opponents of the private agencies because of alleged abuses. Even if they could not obtain the upper hand in the administration of the public bureaus the unions thought they gained something in the establishment of bureaus controlled by neither side.

The history of the United States Employment Service shows that the assurance of a strictly neutral attitude becomes one of the most serious problems which confronts any employment service. That it is not necessarily an inherent danger, nor one which cannot be eliminated is shown by the history of a number of the state employment systems, particularly those of Wisconsin, Massachusetts, Ohio, and New York, where among large numbers of employers interviewed, complaint of this kind was very seldom encountered. Experience indicates that in this as in other lesser difficulties which have arisen in the public service the weakness can be solved by proper attention to administrative methods. In the case of the United States Employment Service, set up almost over night as a war measure, there was not time to perfect methods nor did it seem possible in the rapid wartime expansion to take advantage fully of experience. The marvel was that the Service did not lay itself open to more criticism.

One other important weakness laid at the door of the public bureaus is the danger that the workers who are appointed to the bureaus will secure office through political or other influence rather than on the ground of their equipment for the duties involved. This again is not to be regarded as an insurmountable difficulty since the experience in some of the state and local public bureaus has demonstrated that it is possible to secure and retain a satisfactory grade of personnel. Moreover, in other forms of public service, particularly those like the public schools, post office, and offices carrying heavy financial responsibilities, where the public in general has become convinced of the importance of efficient service, it has been possible to secure a comparatively high grade of personnel.

## VI. THE CASE OF THOSE WHO ADVOCATE A PUBLIC EMPLOYMENT SERVICE

It has been seen that four important direct and unorganized methods have been developed to meet the needs of employers and workers in making employment contacts; and seven important organized methods or agencies. Behind each there has been a different set of reasons and motives; each has been the outgrowth of special objectives and interests which in turn have left their mark on the character of the institution. Each has a particular significance for and contribution to the further development of organized employment work.

It has also been seen that the direct or unorganized methods of making employment contacts are inadequate. For the vast majority of workmen and employers unorganized methods mean a great loss of time in securing work or workers. While use will undoubtedly be made of the unorganized instrumentalities for a long time to come, they at best can handle only a small proportion of the cases. Some type of organized service seems needed—some type which will meet the requirements of industry and the community better than they are met at present.

Which, then, of the seven forms of organized employment work, with which we have had experience, offers the greatest promise of meeting these present and future needs?

An absolute and unqualified answer to this question at this time is not possible—certainly not within the space here available. All of the organized methods, as has been seen, have various weaknesses as well as advantages. With both fully in mind, however, and with full appreciation also of the reasons why the other agencies and bureaus have come into existence and have enlisted ardent supporters, the answer, on the basis of our investigations and contact with people interested in employment from all angles, seems reasonably clear. The greatest promise seems to lie in the development and raising to a high standard of efficiency of a national system of public employment bureaus.[1] Among the more important sets of facts pointing to this conclusion are four:

**Number of Workers to be Placed.**—The first is quantitative. There were in the United States, according to the census of 1920, some 42,000,000 persons having gainful occupations, of whom about 31,000,000 were wage- and salary-earners. There were at that time probably less than 5,000,000 members of trade unions.[2] Even if we assume that the trade unions entirely fill the need for employment assistance for their own members (a fact by no means certain), this leaves 26,000,000 to be served by employers' association bureaus, fraternal and professional bureaus, philanthropic, private, and public bureaus, and the various unorganized forms of contact-making.

In practically every industrial and occupational group there is need for organized assistance in finding jobs for workers and workers for jobs. It may be limited to a small percentage of the group, or it may be spread over the entire number; but practically no trade or industry is found where the demand will not sooner or later be made for some degree of organized assistance.

The maximum limit of the annual need is not indicated simply by the 26,000,000 workers, but rather by the total number of jobs which they hold in a year. During 1918 the United States Bureau of Labor Statistics made a study of labor turnover in representative factories in Cleveland, Cincinnati, and Detroit. The turnover was above 150 per cent in 80 per cent of the factories in Cleveland, in 78 per cent of the Cincinnati factories, and in over 80 per cent of those in Detroit. In Cleveland two-thirds of the factories had a turnover that ran above 200 per cent, in Cincinnati one-third, and in Detroit three-fourths. For the industrial workers covered in these three cities each person held on the average over two jobs a year.

Again, in some of the fields where the need for organized employment work is clearest, the census figures are illuminating. There are over 2,300,000 farm laborers, not working at home, subject to the seasonal fluctuations in demand for labor and the necessity of moving from one

---

[1] Evidence gathered points to the desirability of making the state the administrative unit, with federal machinery for coordinating the system, and with local cooperation to make the bureaus function to their fullest possibilities. For a fuller discussion of the question of organization and administration of a national system of public employment bureaus, the reader is again referred to the forthcoming report, in the Russell Sage Foundation publications, parts of which are here summarized.

[2] The estimate of GEORGE E. BARNETT, American Economic Association, December, 1921, *Papers and Proceedings of the Thirty-fourth Annual Meeting*, p. 55.

place to another, which farm work for the most part entails. Over 3,000,000 men and women are reported by the census as employed in domestic and personal service, thus giving us in these two groups representing on the whole what has in the past been the maximum quantitative need for employment assistance, a little over 5,000,000 men and women whose employers need help perhaps as much as the workers themselves. There were moreover nearly 762,000 teachers, 300,000 nurses trained and not trained, 176,000 agents, canvassers and collectors, and 3,000,000 in other clerical occupations—to name only a few of the specific occupations where a pressing need for organized employment work has been generally recognized.

The non-public agencies or mediums (other than the union bureaus) which have been developed to meet this need in an organized way include; (1) "want-ads," which by causing people to change jobs tend to increase rather than lessen the labor turnover and which are objectionable on other grounds; (2) a small number of bureaus operated by employers' associations doing almost a negligible amount of placement work when the aggregate need is considered; (3) a relatively small number of bureaus maintained by philanthropic organizations in a few of the larger cities and performing also a limited service due to the fact that they are concerned only or chiefly with certain special groups of workers, in the main the handicapped; (4) a small group of agencies conducted by fraternal and professional societies and the like, which since their service is available only to members, also touched a relatively small number of people; and (5) between 2,500 and 5,000 private fee-charging bureaus, which cannot cover the vast field left after the other organized and unorganized non-public agencies have done what they can.

There are no available data upon which to form an accurate estimate of the total business done through the private bureaus. In some instances, however, reports of placements are made by these agencies to the licensing bureaus. In Illinois in the year 1917–1918, according to the Chief Inspector of Private Agencies, 593,482 people were placed by them. This figure is substantial, but there must have been at that time upwards of 2,000,000 wage-earners in Illinois, who with a general turnover of only 100 per cent, would in that year have represented four times as many potential placements as the number actually made by the private bureaus.

The private agencies in Wisconsin placed 14,950 people in the year 1916–1917 and 20,967 in 1917–1918, a number which compared to the wage-earners of the state, or even the work of the public bureaus, is insignificant. Similarly, what facts were available for other states indicate that the fee-charging bureaus in placing workers were handling only a comparatively small part of the work of this kind which needed to be done. There is no evidence that the business of this type of bureau is increasing sufficiently to cover the entire field.

**Important Fields Left Undeveloped.**—It is altogether improbable that the fee-charging bureaus, which from a quantitative standpoint offer more promise than the other non-public agencies, can cover the field because the commercial agencies are interested in rendering employment service where it is profitable. They will operate only at the places where the need for such a service reaches a point which will enable the managers to clear something for the business. These will be the localities in which the demand for jobs and for workers is greatest; localities with smaller demands will necessarily be neglected. The great concentration of fee-charging agencies in New York, Chicago, and several other centers is illustrative. Indeed, even in the larger centers there is reason to question whether the fee-charging agencies can fully meet the need for making employment contacts, as is indicated by the fact that even in localities where private agencies have been long established, the public bureaus soon find it possible to do a capacity business.

There are also certain special groups of workers who are not now adequately served because, among other things, their business is not sufficiently profitable to the bureaus. One of these groups is the juvenile workers. Because of their inexperience and need for protection, and their almost total lack of technique of finding proper jobs for themselves, perhaps more than any other group they require organized assistance; and for them comparatively little is being done. A few philanthropic agencies, a certain amount of organized work being conducted in an experimental way by the schools in some of the largest cities, a junior employment service in a very few states, do not represent even adequate pioneering. Much the same thing is to be said for the physically handicapped, and for certain racial or national groups, such as negroes and immigrants. If these are to be taken care of in a way even approaching adequacy, it seems probable that the work must be done through the public or governmental agencies.

**Need of System National in Scope.**—It became increasingly evident as our investigations proceeded, that if we are to have a system of employment contact-making which will in reality help the employer find the best workers for his kind of enterprise, aid the worker to find the work at which he can do his best, and thus increase in general our national industrial efficiency by reducing the waste due to lack of information on available openings and to workers being placed in jobs where they are misfits—if we are to have a system of employment work that will do its share toward this end, it must be large enough to see our industrial situation as a whole. It must also provide the machinery for opening up opportunities to workers in many industries and localities, and similarly it must be able to give employers wider ranges of choice than their immediate industry or locality. The only substantial hope of a system which can meet these needs adequately would seem to lie in the public bureaus working together through a certain amount of national coordinating machinery.

**Requirements of Impartiality.**—And finally, it has already been seen that the question of neutrality as between conflicting industrial interests is essential if employment work is to succeed. Here again the public bureaus offer the greatest promise among the organized agencies.

The case of those who advocate public employment bureaus, then may be summed up as follows:

The organized employment work being done through "want-ads," and by the labor unions, employers' associations, fraternal and technical associations, philanthropic societies, and the fee-charging agencies, falls far short of the needs of the country. Some industries and regions cannot be served by the fee-charging bureau because their business is not sufficiently profitable. And even in some important fields like the harvesting of wheat where it does seem profitable for the private bureaus to operate, there is lack of coordination and waste for both employers and workers. A system of employment is needed large enough to see our industrial situation as a whole and the most substantial hope of such a system lies in the public bureaus. Finally, in the important matter of neutrality in organized employment work, the public bureaus offer the greatest promise of reasonably satisfactory results.

In addition to these four main considerations, the advocate of public bureaus would add that we have had sufficient experience with such bureaus in this country to show that they may be expected to produce satisfactory results in actual practice. Notwithstanding certain weaknesses exhibited by the rapidly expanded United States Employment Service during the war, even that Service had much to its credit; and the work done in many of the state bureaus has been of sufficient quality to gain for it increasing public favor, as evidenced by the increasing financial support supplied by state legislatures.

**Gradual Development of Public Service.**—In view of the many forms and methods of employment work which are found in use, and of the reasons why some of these methods are adhered to at one place and some at another, the change from employment work as now carried on to a situation where a maximum proportion of all employment work is done through the public agencies, if it comes about, will be gradual. A gradual change will allow the public system first to handle the more urgent and as far as possible the less difficult fields of operation, and thus to build solidly upon a foundation of practical experiences for handling the more highly technical work.

### VII. PUBLIC EMPLOYMENT OFFICES AND THE PROBLEMS OF UNEMPLOYMENT

Whether the establishment of a comprehensive national system of public employment offices comes about soon or has a gradual develop-

19

ment, it is important that the influence such a system may have upon unemployment be recognized and at the same time not overestimated. That it will have a potent influence toward the reduction and prevention of unemployment is expected; but it must be admitted that the setting up of public employment bureaus is only one of several measures to be considered in framing a program to reduce unemployment.

The conclusion has too often been jumped at that, once public labor exchanges were established, the problem of unemployment would be solved; the moment we have unemployment we must establish a public employment bureau, and then the trouble will be over. The leaders in the movement however have had no illusions in the matter. Our discussions with those who have been longest at work on employment bureau questions have shown that they recognized from the beginning that public employment exchanges could not make jobs in periods of depression when or where there were no jobs, and that in periods of prosperity and labor shortage they could not discover more workers when the supply was fixed and no more were to be found.

But the advocates of public labor exchanges did have very clearly in mind certain services which would tend to reduce unemployment and labor shortage at all times, either prosperous or depressed. They thought that a well-functioning system of public labor exchanges could reduce the amount of time lost in job-getting and in the securing of labor by employers and thus reduce waste and unnecessary idleness.

The argument on this head runs as follows: Because of the changing demand and the semi-mobility of labor, each industrial center (particularly where there is considerable casual labor) tends to create an individual labor reserve, which will be drawn upon when the demand in that center is at a maximum and allowed to accumulate in slack periods. The actual situation is of course by no means simple. The reserves of a single plant are never clearly separated. A particular individual, out of work, may be a more regular workman than others then employed. The individual employment manager can seldom say, "There is our permanent force, there are our reserves." But he will admit that when business is slack, men are laid off, and when business picks up again, extra laborers will be taken on.

This tendency to build up individual reserves not only adds to the total amount of unemployment, but makes it a continuous phenomenon. The total labor force attracted to a center is not and probably never can be employed continuously.

It is this situation which has caused the advocacy of an organized labor market. If hiring at individual plants in New York means building up individual labor reserves for each plant, then a central employment office in New York through which everybody will be hired, will pool these separate reserves. In the words of Beveridge, the plan is "that all the irregular men for each group of similar employers should be taken on from a common center or exchange, and that this exchange should so far as possible concentrate employment upon the smallest number that will suffice for the work of the group as a whole."[1] This will help to decasualize these workers by releasing a certain number for other jobs. That it is usually possible for workers "squeezed out" in this way to secure jobs elsewhere has been indicated in the past by the ability of this country for considerable periods at a time to absorb large numbers of immigrants. It was pointed out further by one prominent employment bureau official that the "squeezed out" can still more certainly be taken care of if immigration is checked for a time. It is the application of this idea to all industry which will doubtless bring a reduction of unemployment, although it is fully appreciated that it will not entirely eliminate the labor reserve.

**Other Ways in Which Public Bureaus May Affect Unemployment.** Again, the effect of public bureaus upon unemployment includes a certain amount of assistance toward the long-range planning of public works. The public bureaus can supply figures regarding the general demand for and supply of labor which will help in determining the best time for engaging in public works. Bureaus are automatically collecting information on these matters, together with facts as to wages, hours and the general condition of employment. It has been urged that a centralized employment bureau could thus provide a valuable measure of unemployment. Special investigations may be and are being conducted, but the advantage of the employment bureau information would be that it is continuous, up-to-date, and if properly handled, always available. During the war the United States Employment Service not only published a bulletin for general information and propaganda, but also a weekly statistical report which carried the reports of the bureaus, and estimates as to the demand and supply of labor based on figures gathered from employers. It is true that the records in the past have not been all that they should be, but the data from the bureaus might readily be improved.

Further, the public bureaus might furnish information of value in vocational guidance, indicating dying trades, new lines of development, and other trends in the employment field. This would ultimately affect unemployment through a more precise adjustment of the supply of workers to the numbers demanded in different occupations.

Finally, in still another way public employment bureaus, it is argued, might have an important influence on this problem. Unemployment insurance is urged as providing, among other things, a financial incentive

[1] BEVERIDGE, W. H., "Unemployment: A Problem of Industry," 1919, p. 201, for further discussion of this point and for Beveridge's classic illustration of the way in which these reserves would be eliminated through the organization of the labor market.

to industry to eliminate irregular work.     If the time ever comes in this country when some system of public unemployment insurance is set up, public employment exchanges will be necessary for its administration, if for no other reason because no other organization can be so well situated as they for making accurate "work tests" as to when workers are actually unemployed.     Abuses of the insurance system may thus be controlled through the knowledge of opportunities for employment which the exchanges would have.

A national system of public employment exchanges is thus seen to be one of the proposals which merit careful consideration in any comprehensive program for the reduction of unemployment.

# CHAPTER XVII

## TRADE UNION OUT-OF-WORK BENEFITS

By John B. Andrews

Secretary of the American Association for Labor Legislation

### I. INTRODUCTION

The experience of a number of trade unions with out-of-work benefits is the earliest, and perhaps the only, example in America of prolonged organized effort toward systematic advance planning to mitigate the effects of cyclical unemployment.

While American trade unions have used this insurance method less extensively than have labor movements in some other countries, their varied experiences are difficult to present within ten pages. There is a considerable "literature" upon the subject, consisting mainly of articles and official reports. The most important of the secondary sources is the monograph by David P. Smelser,[1] which however does not carry the statistical data beyond 1915. To follow the very significant developments of the past seven years, it has been necessary to send questionnaires to all of the national trade unions and to supplement these returns in many important cases with personal letters and interviews. Earnest efforts have been made, within the brief period allotted, to glean from available trade-union sources their own conclusions as to the efficacy of their out-of-work benefits. Responses from the experienced leaders of the American labor movement have been most cordial and helpful.

Most students of the subject are now agreed that, from the viewpoint of general welfare, any system of financial relief that is to meet effectively the social problem presented by a prolonged period of unemployment, should embrace at least four principal features. In any searching inquiry into a system of cash benefits, of whatever nature, these questions are asked:

1. *Is the system inclusive*, that is, does it extend its benefits to all who need the protection and particularly to those who are likely to need it most?

2. Does the system provide with certainty for the collection year after year of *ample premiums to pay adequate benefits* during times of greatest need?

[1] "Unemployment and American Trade Unions," Johns Hopkins University Studies in History and Political Science, ser. 37, No. 1 (1919).

3. Is there provided an *efficient administration of the funds*, which, while granting prompt relief to legitimate claimants will just as effectively deny unworthy appeals?

4. Does the plan *stimulate efforts toward the prevention of the evil* for which relief is provided, particularly does it give to those most directly responsible an incentive to eliminate every removable cause?

These tests will be applied in the above order to the accumulated American experience with trade-union out-of-work benefits.

## II. ARE ALL PROTECTED?

After deducting from 41,600,000 gainfully employed people of this country such groups as those in public service, in domestic and personal service, in the professions, farmers, and those between the ages of ten and fifteen, we have still about 27,000,000 people who work for wages in normal times. Of these 27,000,000, less than 5,000,000 or less than 19 per cent are in labor organizations of any kind. Moreover, as we shall see in a moment, only a very small minority of the organized wage-earners themselves are provided in advance with any assurance of cash out-of-work benefits. No one knows exactly how many thousands are protected, but compared with the total membership of trade unions the number is small.

In earlier periods of wide-spread unemployment prominent representatives of labor have recommended the establishment of regular out-of-work cash-benefit systems. As early as 1831 the Typographical Association of New York paid $3 a week to unmarried members who were unemployed and $4 weekly to unemployed married members. But after ninety years a bare half-dozen national unions are known to be paying out-of-work benefits. Samuel Gompers as Secretary of the New York local Cigar Makers' Union in the seventies of the last century strongly urged his national organization to establish a plan. The Cigar Makers did organize a national cash-payment system in 1890 and it has been cited frequently as the chief successful example. But in 1920, after thirty years of experience, the Cigar Makers, "as a result of wide-spread unemployment among their members,"[1] gave up the effort and abandoned their national cash-benefit plan. The Jewelry Workers and the Coal Hoisting Engineers are among other unions that maintained national cash-payment systems at an earlier date, but these two unions have gone out of existence.

The four American unions which on July 1, 1922 reported national out-of-work benefits are the Deutsch-Amerikanische Typographia which has about 700 members, the Diamond Workers with 600 members, the Potters with a membership of 9,200, and the Lithographers with 7,200 members. In addition two unions of foreign origin and direction—

[1] Interview with Samuel Gompers, July 17, 1922.

the Amalgamated Carpenters and the Amalgamated Engineers—have had a limited membership in this country protected by unemployment benefit.[1]

Cash out-of-work benefits, however, have been more common among local than among national unions. The local Typographical Association of New York, mentioned above, provided unemployment benefits at various periods from 1831 to 1907, when the system, for reasons which will be made clear presently was finally abolished. A considerable number of locals of various trades—including certain locals of the Cigar Makers on an optional basis—continue to pay out-of-work benefits. As a result of his inquiry Mr. Smelser concludes that failure of the national unions to establish out-of-work benefits has led many local unions in various trades to provide systems of their own. These scattering experiments have been made from time to time in locals of nearly all trades, indicating wide recognition among local trade unionists of the need for systematic advance planning for periods of unemployment. It will be especially helpful, therefore, to inquire whether the comparatively few organized workers entitled to unemployment benefits of this kind have been able to set aside sufficient funds to make adequate payments.

## III. ARE THE BENEFITS ADEQUATE?

The problem of collecting premiums sufficient to pay adequate cash benefits where trade-union funds have been organized, brings out very strikingly the difficulties encountered by American trade unions in attempting to deal unaided with extended periods of unemployment. In exceptional instances a trade-union out-of-work fund, by making meager weekly allowances, has been able to continue payments to its unemployed membership throughout an industrial depression. But even the exceptional plan formerly operated by the national Cigar Makers, which expressly excluded members from benefit during the seasonal periods of slackness in mid-winter and early July, found its resources rapidly fading with months of general depression.

In some instances, as with the New York City branch of the Deutsch-Amerikanische Typographia, the local supplements the benefits paid through the national organization. In this particular case national cash benefits of $6 weekly for four weeks are continued if necessary for three weeks longer by the local, after which the unemployed member again becomes eligible for national benefit. The national plan of this organization, which was put into effect in 1884, continued in operation despite industrial depressions, the introduction of typesetting machinery, and finally the practical suspension of German language publications during the war. But it was necessary to decrease the weekly benefit

[1] The American division of the Amalgamated Engineers was discontinued in September, 1920.

just at the times when mounting costs of living accentuated the need of adequate financial support. Only during times of prosperity, and when backed by a large working membership, has even this union fund been able to pay unemployment benefits as high as $6 a week.

The national organization of Lithographers recently organized for its unemployed members a weekly cash benefit of $3 to be paid for not more than ten weeks in any one year. During the depression of 1920–1922 this union disregarded the ten weeks' limit and continued payment of cash benefits by transferring resources from the general funds of the organization which has had but two strikes in its history.

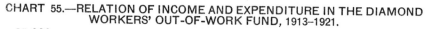

CHART 55.—RELATION OF INCOME AND EXPENDITURE IN THE DIAMOND WORKERS' OUT-OF-WORK FUND, 1913–1921.

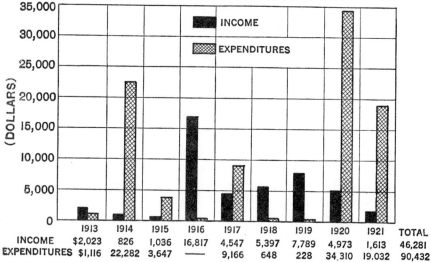

|  | 1913 | 1914 | 1915 | 1916 | 1917 | 1918 | 1919 | 1920 | 1921 | TOTAL |
|---|---|---|---|---|---|---|---|---|---|---|
| INCOME | $2,023 | 826 | 1,036 | 16,817 | 4,547 | 5,397 | 7,789 | 4,973 | 1,613 | 46,281 |
| EXPENDITURES | $1,116 | 22,282 | 3,647 | —— | 9,166 | 648 | 228 | 34,310 | 19,032 | 90,432 |

Since April, 1921 cash benefits have been paid by the National Brotherhood of Operative Potters. During its first fiscal year of 1921–1922 the fund suffered a deficit disclosed by the following figures: expenditures $143,000, receipts $52,662.

The Diamond Workers' Protective Union of America, organizea in 1902, has paid unemployment benefits since August, 1912. At that time the out-of-work fund was established by transferring to it $600 from the general fund. It was planned to maintain the fund by a weekly assessment of ten cents per capita. The expenses caused by the depression of 1914–1915 were, however, so great that from January 1, 1914 to March 31, 1915 it was necessary to transfer $22,600 more from the general fund. The deficit remained so great that no benefits could be paid in 1916, and during that year an additional assessment of $1 per week was levied on all employed members in order to revive the fund. In 1922 the assessment was twenty-five cents per week. From 1912 through 1921 the total assessed income of the fund amounted to $46,281, whereas the expenditures in cash benefits amounted to $90,432; the deficit of the fund at the end of 1921 was therefore in excess of $40,000. The inadequacy of the specific income as compared with the expenditures for unemployment benefit in this national union is shown by the accompanying Chart 55. Andries Meyer, President of the Diamond Workers, believes that on account of financial difficulties, "It is impossible, in the long run, for a trade union to maintain an adequate system of unemployment benefits."[1]

Space does not permit the inclusion of detailed statements of individual union financing of out-of-work benefits, but we may condense into comparable form in a table some additional significant items from the experience of the national organizations.

TABLE XLII.—COMPARATIVE ANALYSIS OF NATIONAL TRADE UNION OUT-OF-WORK BENEFITS.
July 1, 1922

| National union benefit funds | Weekly benefits | Maximum yearly benefit | Average annual per capita cost | Total amount expended | Number of years effective |
|---|---|---|---|---|---|
| Cigar makers (1889–1920).............. | $ 3 | $ 72 | $ 1.73 | $1,731,209 | 32 |
| Deutsch-Amerikanische Typographia (1884)... | 5–6 | 96 | 5.02 | 220,192 | 38 |
| Lithographers (1918).... | 3 | 30 | | | 4 |
| Diamond workers (1912). | 6–7.50 | 72–90 | 2.71 | 90,432 | 10 |
| Potters (1921).......... | 10 | 130 | 15 | 143,030 | 1 |
| Amalgamated carpenters (1860).............. | 2.10–4.20 | 63 | 4.80 | 16,836 [b] (in 1921 only) | 62 |

[a]The lithographers do not keep separate accounts of their sick and out-of-work funds. The total expended for these two purposes from October, 1918 through June, 1922 was $104,134, paid by a membership which numbered 6,114 in June, 1919 and 7,564 in June, 1921.

[b] This figure for 1921 was calculated by the Secretary of the union. Figures for the other years are not available as the Amalgamated Carpenters have one fund for all countries.

In general the funds have not been sufficient in amount to provide out-of-work benefits on an adequate permanent basis.[2] George Perkins,

[1] Interview with Andries Meyer, April, 1922.

[2] Striking exceptions are the cash benefits recently paid by certain locals of the Photo-engravers. Most liberal are those of the New York City local which, beginning in February, 1921, has paid the unemployed journeymen a weekly cash benefit of $25, without limitation as to period of benefit.

President of the Cigar Makers, has insisted that the wage-earners should not be expected to bear the whole burden.[1] The Chicago Mayor's Commission on Unemployment reported in 1914 that the trade-union experiments were then practically the only approach to unemployment insurance.

Since unemployment is caused by general conditions, and the evil of idleness is not confined to the wage-earners directly involved, it is both unfair and impolitic to impose the whole cost of unemployment insurance on the workmen even if their wages might possibly furnish adequate premiums.[2]

Mr. Smelser sets down his conclusion that the first of two reasons why there has been such a slight development of out-of-work benefits in American trade unions is "the unwillingness of the average union member to acquiesce in the necessary increase of dues." The second reason is now to be stated.

### IV. ADMINISTRATION OF FUNDS

It frequently has been argued by those who concern themselves with systems of cash benefits that public administration by political appointees is likely to result in lax administration, to the demoralization of the recipients, and the rapid depletion of the funds. It has been suggested therefore that there should be local administration in which those who pay premiums into the insurance fund and those who draw benefits therefrom should jointly participate. Trade-union out-of-work benefits furnish illustrations of administration where the same people are donors and recipients and handle their own funds. Has their experience demonstrated that they can administer effectively a fund sufficient to carry their membership through periods of prolonged industrial depressions?

The administrative test as applied to American trade-union experience with cash out-of-work benefits alone, is not entirely clear. It is clear that the funds have not always been organized and conducted for the sole purpose of paying cash to the unemployed. Holding members in the organization during times of individual hardship or during periods of organization stress and strain has admittedly been one outstanding motive of the administrative officials.

In the administration of the national Cigar Makers' fund "many attempts were made to break down the safeguards established for its proper management"—and yet it endured for thirty years. This is a tribute to the leadership. The German-American printers have con-

[1] *American Labor Legislation Review*, June, 1913, pp. 234–7.
[2] *Report of Mayor's Commission on Unemployment*, Chicago, 1914, p. 92.
[3] SMELSER, p. 146.

tinued to pay benefits regularly despite extraordinary extraneous obstacles. The Diamond Workers also have been fortunate in leadership which is able and above suspicion of favoritism. On the other hand some local trade organizations found their expenditures on account of unemployment mounting pretty steadily year after year regardless of years of prosperity. The printers in New York abolished their system in 1907 after paying out more than $500,000 during the fourteen years following 1894. A number of funds have been abolished because abuses became flagrant. Apparently one chief difficulty in the national administration of trade-union out-of-work funds has been "personal acquaintance of the local union officials with the applicants for benefit. . . There are always local union officials who pay benefits which should not have been paid . . . The local officials seem unable to deal strictly with a member who abandons a job on plausible grounds." And finally Mr. Smelser, from whose report the above quotations are extracted, concludes that the second of the two reasons for the slight development of the out-of-work benefit in American trade unions is "the apparent inadequacy of the administrative agencies of the union to secure a just distribution of the benefit."[1]

Various other related expedients of the trade unions to hold their membership during trying times and to offer assistance to the unemployed, throw additional light on their intimate problem of administration. For a great many years labor organizations experimented with traveling loan systems to assist unemployed members to move on to more promising employment centers. But this device has been peculiarly subject to abuse. Union after union has been compelled to give it up on account of administrative difficulties.

Perhaps more significant is the growing tendency of the most ably directed labor organizations to pay no regular cash benefits on account of unemployment, but instead to exempt their unemployed members from the payment of dues. This scheme has the advantage of retaining the member in good standing and keeping him eligible to all union privileges including sick and other benefits. One of the best examples of this type of protection is the out-of-work stamp system of the Iron Molders' Union. It was inaugurated in 1897 as a direct result of the establishment during the previous year of their sick benefit. The national union arranged to pay for a period of thirteen weeks the dues of members in six months good standing who had been unemployed two weeks. Later the executive board was empowered to extend the stamp benefits indefinitely when an exceptional degree of unemployment should be encountered. During the latest industrial depression, due stamps were kept paid up in some instances on behalf of the same individuals for more than fifteen months.

[1] SMELSER, pp. 146–7.

During 1921, 778,826 out-of-work stamps were issued to members, this amount representing a loss in dues of $467,895.[1] During the first quarter of 1922, 192,075 out-of-work stamps were issued as compared with 206,925 stamps for the same period of 1921. The out-of-work fund is raised at the rate of one cent per capita per week, this amount being absorbed from the sick benefit (under International control) which is raised at the rate of eight cents per week. In the Molders' Union the funds which would normally be kept up by a member's dues are not allowed to fall behind when he is exempted from payment through unemployment, but are maintained from the out-of-work fund.

For every out-of-work stamp placed in a member's due book, an equivalent amount of cash is drawn from the out-of-work fund, and transferred to the fund from which sick, total disability, and death benefits are paid, so that the out-of-work system represents a definite financial item in the affairs of the International Union.[1]

Admirably thought out and carefully administered plans for exemptions of dues like that of the Molders help to prevent disorganization in difficult times and represent a direct protection to the unemployed and also to employed members. At the same time such a plan conserves for the organization as a whole many of the advantages of a cash-payment plan. Just as clearly it would not adequately carry the families of unemployed members through a prolonged period of unemployment.

There remains for our consideration the influence of trade-union benefit systems upon the prevention of unemployment.

### V. UNEMPLOYMENT PREVENTION

In comparatively recent times there has come a demand for "real thinking and sincere action" in reference to the causes of cyclical depressions and the removal or mitigation of those causes. It must be here set down from an examination of American trade-union experience with out-of-work benefit funds, that there is nothing to indicate that the shouldering of the care of wage-earning families during industrial depression by labor organizations exerts any salutary pressure to prevent cyclical depressions.

### VI. CONCLUSION

The trade unions through their out-of-work benefits have provided this remedy for only a small minority even of their own unemployed members. Further, several of the few systems in operation have failed to attain the permanency desirable in plans for relieving the needs suddenly

---

[1] In June, 1922 the American Federation of Labor reported at its Cincinnati convention that during the preceding year the Molders had furnished in unemployed benefits $446,385, which was more than two-thirds of all such benefits paid by the national unions.

[2] Letter to the writer from JOHN P. FREY, July 1, 1922.

produced by cyclical depressions. The funds accumulated from wage-earners alone have been insufficient in amount and the problem of administration by fellow trade unionists has been troublesome. Placing the financial burden of relief solely upon wage-earners has not utilized effectively an economic force which in our most outstanding American success in such matters, workmen's accident insurance, has resulted in active measures of prevention.

Passing over, as we must in this study of unemployment and busines cycles, the incidental or any other advantages of trade-union out-of-work benefits, the conclusion is unescapable that they cannot be depended upon to furnish an adequate source of relief in prolonged periods of unemployment. The tendency of trade-union policy, moreover, appears to be away from systematic accumulation during years of comparatively regular employment of special reserves out of which periodical cash payments might be made to unemployed workmen during the recurring industrial depressions. Out-of-work benefits for the unorganized obviously can not be maintained through unemployment funds of the trade unions, and the unorganized constitute in this country the vast majority of wage-earners and the very ones who on account of their weaker position are likely to suffer first and longest as a result of industrial depression. The facts suggest that if the method of insurance is to be utilized in attacking the industrial tragedy of cyclical unemployment, the formulators of our social policies will do well to consider (1) additional sources for the accumulation of adequate financial reserves and perhaps (2) some kind of additional representative participation in the administration of the funds.

# CHAPTER XVIII

## UNEMPLOYMENT INSURANCE

### BY LEO WOLMAN

#### NEW SCHOOL FOR SOCIAL RESEARCH

### I. THE NATURE AND TYPES OF UNEMPLOYMENT INSURANCE

The assumption by the general community of the responsibility for unemployment is a phenomenon of comparatively recent origin. Gradually an increasing section of public opinion has come to recognize that unemployment is not a matter of personal responsibility and that as a problem it cannot be met by throwing the burden on those who happen to be unfortunate enough to be out of work. It is, of course, still a common practice to entrust the support of the unemployed to agencies of private and public charity. But in the main there is a strong and growing tendency to devise new and more substantial methods for dealing with the problem. Such methods as have been devised rest almost universally on the assumptions that the incidence of unemployment is beyond the control of the unemployed persons and that adequate measures of treatment will lead ultimately to the control and reduction of involuntary idleness.

Among the many measures proposed for the treatment of unemployment, insurance, in one form or another, has found the most general acceptance. The principles on which unemployment insurance is based are relatively simple, although in practice many real difficulties are always encountered and are not always overcome. The procedure in a system of unemployment insurance is at bottom no different from that pursued in any other form of insurance. Once the risk, against which people wish to insure, is discovered and defined, those who suffer from the risk associate themselves for the purposes of mutual protection. The form of the association and conditions for membership in it, may, vary widely according to circumstances. Since the purpose of the association is protection against losses in income due to unemployment, the first task of the enterprise is to collect an insurance fund from which unemployed members may draw during the whole or part of their periods of idleness.[1] Creation of the fund and the establishment of the right to draw from it require the determination of premiums, or rates of contribution,

---

[1] A doubtful statement.—Note by T. S. ADAMS.

and of rates of benefit. Where the risk has been studied for a long time and where a considerable body of accurate and continuous statistical material has been collected, the risk can be measured with precision and the rates of both contribution and benefit calculated with a high degree of accuracy. In this regard, as is well known, all systems of insurance are by no means alike. While, for instance, the premium on a life insurance policy can now be determined within a negligible margin of error, the premium on an unemployment insurance policy can at this time lay no such claim to precision. To what extent, therefore, unemployment has become an insurable risk, in the ordinary sense of the term, is a question which will be discussed in some detail later.

As commonly considered, however, unemployment insurance falls into the special class of insurance undertakings known as social insurance. The line of division between social insurance and the ordinary or private insurance is not a sharp one. The distinction is one that has arisen in a practice dictated by considerations of social policy. Unemployment, like industrial disease and industrial accidents, is one of the hazards of industry which attacks great masses of workers who do not set up, and probably cannot be expected on their own initiative to set up, adequate insurance against the risks involved. It is not necessary to consider here the question of whether the working out of economic laws would in the end require the cost of such insurance to be borne by the workers, the employers, or the state, or by the consumers of the goods produced. The essential fact is that, if insurance is to be provided against the recurring distress due to unemployment, the initiative in establishing such insurance must be taken either by the state or by the employers, or both, acting in cooperation with the workers. The question of how the insurance premiums are collected, or by whom and in what manner they are (directly or indirectly) finally paid, is not the determining one as to the character of the insurance. If considerations of public policy indicate that insurance should be provided, and if, furthermore, the surrounding conditions are such that voluntary action toward such provision will not naturally be taken by those immediately affected, and if the people as a whole must, in some manner take the initiative in establishing the required protection, then the insurance resulting may properly be described as social insurance.

In practice, there are many variations in the details of schemes of social insurance, notably in industrial accident insurance, or workmen's compensation. Here in many instances the insurance provides not only for the compulsory payment of benefit to those who have had their incomes interrupted by industrial accident, but imposes the payment of the entire premium upon the employer on the general theory that the cost of such insurance is a legitimate burden upon the industry. By the operation of this provision which makes large risks costly, it is hoped to supply the incentives that will lead to the study and analysis of the particular hazard and, finally, to its reduction or total elimination.

These variations in the principles of social insurance have been accompanied by changes in the form and content of systems of social insurance. Almost from the beginning of the discussion of such schemes, controversies have raged over their details. In the main the important discussion has been concerned with three issues. One is the relative desirability of compulsory as contrasted with voluntary insurance; the second, the advantages of contributory against non-contributory insurance; and the third, the merits of subsidized insurance. Later experience has proved pretty conclusively that only two of these issues are real. Both, in fact, lead to the question whether it is possible to organize a system of social insurance in which all of the people who need the insurance are included and in which the premiums they pay can yield adequate benefits, unless such a system is made compulsory by statutory enactment and provides, at least for a long time, liberal subsidies from either employers or the state or from both. However this question may be answered, the fact is that the trend in social insurance and particularly in unemployment insurance, is unmistakeably in the direction of compulsory and subsidized insurance.

To the student of all types of social insurance, unemployment insurance offers a rich field of inquiry. Throughout Europe and the United States, the problem of unemployment is met by every conceivable combination of types of unemployment insurance. In Belgium, Denmark, France, Norway, and other countries of Europe, unemployment benefits are paid by trade unions and subsidies are received from the state. Occasionally the payment of benefit stops with members of trade unions or benefit societies and at other times provision is made for subsidies to those who do not belong to such associations. In Italy, Austria, Russia, and England, unemployment benefits are provided by compulsory state insurance schemes.

In the United States, a scattering of trade unionists receive benefits from their trade unions; in one industry the payment of insurance is compulsory on the employers, and workers do not contribute at all; and in a few cases insurance is voluntarily provided for the workingmen by the employers. American experience with unemployment insurance, while of short duration and limited in its extent, has already developed features which distinguish it sharply from the forms of insurance current in Europe. Without the spur of legislation a few employers, in diverse industries, have laid aside funds from which their employees draw benefits during periods of unemployment. The level of benefits provided by these funds runs as high as from 50 to 90 per cent of the normal wages of the workers. In each case, also, the payment of unemployment benefits is coupled with serious, and in the main successful, attempts to regularize the business and thus to reduce unemployment. In the field of proposed legislation, likewise, the reduction of unemployment is the primary purpose of the suggested laws. Unlike the foreign precedents, American proposals in the states of Pennsylvania, Massachusetts, and Wisconsin are so framed as to grade insurance premiums with regard to the unemployment experience of particular firms. Features such as these, it is hoped, will encourage regularization and the reduction of unemployment, since with an improvement in his employment record an employer will be rewarded either by a refund or by a reduction in his insurance premium. The present status and the extent of American schemes are considered in some detail in the third part of this chapter.

All of these experiments in unemployment aid are naturally affected by the peculiar conditions of each country. They can be studied effectively, therefore, only on the spot, and not even then without an intimate acquaintance with the local background. A number of them, moreover, have been in existence for only short periods and have accumulated little experience. Without doubt the most illuminating experiment with unemployment insurance is that which has been conducted by England without interruption since 1911. Prior to the adoption of the Unemployment Insurance Act in that year, England had employed all the devices that were then known for helping the unemployed. Many of the English trade unions paid unemployed benefits. Local and national authorities contributed poor relief. Employment exchanges were experimented with and funds were liberally appropriated for public works. The net effect of all of these expedients fell far short of what was needed. Trade union benefits touched only a small proportion of the working population. Money subsidies that were designed to help workingmen, pauperised them. Emergency public works mounted so rapidly in cost through the inefficiency and unsteadiness of labor as to make their continuance impossible and undesirable.[1]

On this background, the government of England began in 1909 the organization of an ambitious unemployment program which has proved the most interesting of any such plans. The first step in the program was the organization in 1910 of a national system of employment exchanges. This was followed in 1911 by the enactment of a compulsory unemployment insurance scheme which in 1912 covered more than 2,000,-000 people and which in 1920 was extended to cover practically the whole industrial working population of England, or roughly 12,000,000 men and women. During the ten years of its operation, the original act has been frequently amended in many particulars. The scheme has, moreover, existed through a period which has been as rich in the variety of

---

[1] *Report of the Royal Commission on the Poor Laws and Relief of Distress*, Command 4499, 1909, Part VI, Chap. 3.

20

its political and industrial incident as probably any period of similar length in the history of the world. For almost two years the scheme met the conditions of pre-war industry. Suddenly, in 1914, it was confronted with problems of war and mobilization. Then came the growth of the munitions industries and the period of great industrial activity. In 1918, almost without warning, both the military and industrial armies were demobilized. Thousands were left without work. Soon upon this came the short post-war boom, and at last the collapse of industry in the depression of 1920.

Like all public enterprises in England, the system of employment exchanges and of unemployment insurance has been subjected to frequent and expert scrutiny. The ten years' experience of England with unemployment insurance has been laid bare in one report or another, in the testimony before an investigation committee or in the memoranda of the Government Actuary. It would seem necessary, therefore, to preface a considered estimate of the principles and practice of any type of unemployment insurance by a careful analysis of the experience of England since 1909 with its unemployment legislation.

## II. UNEMPLOYMENT INSURANCE IN ENGLAND

Although the English system of unemployment insurance has been in operation for about ten years, it cannot be said to have passed yet, for certain purposes, out of the experimental stage. The recognition of this fact by the various British governments, which have legislated for the scheme and administered it, has resulted in the trial in England of many devices peculiar to no single system of unemployment insurance. Enumeration of these features of the British system, including those that were discarded as well as those that were retained, will bring to light practically all of the elements that are essential to any well conceived and workable proposal for unemployment insurance. These elements will not, of course, always appear in the form in which they were used in the English legislation and administration, but essentially they are the elements which will be taken into account in any scheme for unemployment insurance. If, therefore, these elements can be distinguished and their course during the British experience can be understood, the road should be clear for fruitful generalization concerning the type of unemployment insurance that will most successfully meet the needs of modern communities.

The Maintenance of the Unemployed during Periods of Unemployment.—No matter what unemployment insurance may become in the future, its first purpose at present and in the past has been to support the unemployed. One primary test of the success of such a scheme of insurance is its ability to provide during unemployment an adequate income to the unemployed. It is a fact of first-rate importance that practically no extensive scheme of unemployment insurance has so far met this test. Under the British plan those who are unemployed and receive benefits are considerably better off than they were formerly, but the benefits fall far short of any reasonable standard of adequacy. During the history of the British scheme, the rates of benefit and the periods for which benefits may be received have been changed frequently. But the purpose of the change has not always been the same. When the insurance fund was solvent and had accumulated a substantial surplus, it was possible to raise rates in the attempt to keep pace with the rise in the cost of living and even to raise the standards of benefit. But when the surplus had been exhausted and the scheme faced a growing deficit, the ruling consideration was no longer the standard of benefit, but the solvency of the fund. Table XLIII shows the rates of benefit for men and women during the whole history of the scheme from 1911 to the present, under both the unemployment insurance acts and the system of out-of-work donations which practically replaced the insurance acts in the year following the Armistice.

TABLE XLIII.—RATES OF BENEFIT

| Source of benefit | Period | Rate of benefit per week | |
|---|---|---|---|
| | | Men | Women |
| Unemployment insurance. | Jan. 15, 1913–Dec. 25, 1919 | 7s. | 7s. |
| Out-of work donations.... | Nov. 25, 1918–Dec. 12, 1918 | 24s. | 20s. |
| Out-of work donations.... | Dec. 12, 1918–May 25, 1919 | 29s. | 25s. |
| Out-of work donations.... | May 25, 1919–Nov. 25, 1919 | { 29s.[a] 20s.[b] | { 25s.[a] 15s.[b] |
| Out-of work donations.... | Nov. 25, 1919–Mar. 31, 1921 | 20s.[c] | 15s.[c] |
| Unemployment insurance. | Dec. 25, 1919–Nov. 8, 1920 | 11s. | 11s. |
| Unemployment insurance. | Nov. 8, 1920–Mar. 3, 1921 | 15s. | 12s. |
| Unemployment insurance. | Mar. 3, 1921–June 30, 1921 | 20s. | 16s. |
| Unemployment insurance. | June 30, 1921– | 15s.[d] | 12s.[d] |

[a] This amount was paid in this period to soldiers.
[b] Applied to civilians receiving out-of-work donations.
[c] Payments to civilians stopped on Nov. 24, 1919 but were continued at the rate indicated for members of His Majesty's Forces until Mar. 31, 1921 when they came under the provisions of the unemployment insurance acts.
[d] Under the Unemployed Worker's Dependants (Temporary Provision) Act, 1921, an unemployed worker entitled to benefit under the principal acts receives, after Nov. 10, 1921, in addition 5s. a week in respect of a wife or housekeeper, and 1s. a week in respect of each dependent child. Under the out-of-work donation provisions, also, supplementary allowances were made in respect of dependent children under fifteen years of age at the rate of 6s. per week for the first child and 3s. for each other.

The insufficiency of these benefits, which amount to from one-fourth to one-fifth of the average weekly wages of men and women in England, has been recognized from the very beginning. All of the acts and their amendments have, accordingly, contained provisions for the purpose of encouraging other agencies to add to the rates of benefit fixed under the State schemes. Trade unions, benefit societies, individual employers, and industrial councils have at one time or another been encouraged to establish relations with the general scheme whereby the rates of benefit could be increased through additions from these various sources. The relations of trade unions and of other voluntary associations with the general scheme are complicated and merit separate attention. In two industries, however, voluntary action by individual firms, in one case, and by the industry as a whole, in the other, has resulted in substantial additions to the benefits there paid.

Of these plans the most interesting is that introduced by Rowntree & Company, Ltd. It is, first of all, the purpose of the Rowntree plan to increase the benefits to the extent that single men and women shall receive 50 per cent of their regular earnings and married persons with three children up to 75 per cent. In order to pay this benefit, the firm has set aside £10,000 to found an unemployment fund and has agreed in each year commencing with the year 1921 to set aside sums equal to 1 per cent of its wages bill in such year, until the fund reaches £50,000 or 5 per cent of the wages bill, whichever is the greater. Thereafter the company will set aside annually such sums (not exceeding 1 per cent of the wages bill) as are necessary to keep the fund up to the amount just mentioned. The plan further provides that those employed by Rowntree must contribute to their trade unions at the rate of 2d. per week, for which they receive on the average a benefit of 6s. per week. The unemployed workman under this plan, therefore, will receive his benefit from the general scheme, an additional benefit from the trade union, and a third increment, sufficient to raise his total benefit to 50 or 75 per cent of his average earnings, as the case may be, from the fund established by the company.

A scheme that follows in practically all of its details the Rowntree plan, even with regard to the rate of benefits paid, came into force in the match manufacturing industry on April 15, 1921 and applied to the whole of that industry. On December 15, 1920, Cadbury Brothers, Ltd., of Birmingham, initiated a plan of insurance, supplementary to the State scheme, wherein the firm deposited on that date a sum of £5,000 and agreed to add annually thereafter an amount based upon a flat rate payable per ton of the company's finished product. Out of the insurance fund so established, the firm will add to the benefits payable under the State scheme 22s. per week during the first six weeks of unemployment and 11s. during the second six, in the case of married men and 16s. and 8s. per week, respectively, in the case of single men and women. Plans such as these three are typical of the attempts to raise by outside funds the rates of benefit paid under the State scheme. There may be other examples of experiments of this nature, but it is reasonably certain that all such do not affect more than a very small proportion of the working population of the country. The great bulk of insured workers receive the State rates of benefit with the small benefits added by trade unions and other voluntary associations.

With some minor exceptions, the State insurance schemes have observed the principles of a flat rate of benefit. Little attempt has been made to vary benefits in accordance with the needs or the normal earnings of the beneficiary. In the out-of-work donations scheme different rates of benefit were for the first time given to men and women and this practice has been followed in the insurance acts of 1920, 1921, and 1922. The out-of-work donations scheme, also, first recognized the factor of need by providing additional allowances for dependent children. This measure was later revived in the special act of November 8, 1921, which provided for additional benefits in respect of dependent wife and children. Two of the supplementary schemes, described above, carry the principle of differentiation in benefits much further than they are carried under the State scheme. In the plans conducted by the Rowntree company and by the match industry, the benefit paid to a married man with three children is considerably greater, for persons of the same level of earnings, than that paid to unmarried men. Both plans depart, moreover, in another important respect from the practice under the State scheme. The periods, under the State scheme, for which benefits are allowed are determined by general rules applicable to all beneficiaries alike. But by the terms of these supplementary schemes, the period of benefit varies with the length of service in the firm or industry of the particular beneficiary, so that the periods of benefit run from 3 to 43 weeks as service in the firm varies from 6 months to 30½ years.[1]

**The Sources of Contributions to the Insurance Fund.**—Contributions to the insurance fund have from the outset come from three sources— the employer, the employed, and the State. As in the case of benefits, the insurance acts have always subscribed to the principle of flat rates, with no variations in the rate of contribution because of differences in the unemployment risk, either with regard to individuals, occupations, firms, or industries. At the beginning, of course, such a differentiation would have been fraught with great practical difficulties due to the lack of reliable and extensive statistics of unemployment, essential for the computation of the degree of risk. With the extension of the national scheme of insurance in 1920 and after a few years of the further collection of unem-

---

[1] Rowntree & Co., Ltd., *Unemployment Benefit Scheme, Explanatory Memorandum,* p. 2; Joint Industrial Council of the Match Manufacturing Industry, *Supplementary Voluntary Unemployment Benefit Scheme,* p. 6; Cadbury Bros., Ltd., *Unemployment Scheme,* Bournville, Dec. 9, 1920.

ployment statistics, some plan of premium rating should be not only feasible but also, on the record, highly desirable.

Although the rates of contribution, or premiums, have not been graded with reference to specific risks, the general level of the rates has been changed several times during the life of the scheme. In each case the change was made for the purpose of protecting the solvency of the fund. Experience with the rates now prevailing has shown that they have failed to serve this purpose both because of the wide incidence of unemployment and because of the increasing length of the spells of unemployment and, hence, of the periods of benefit payment. Clearly an insurance fund, not supported by a very large accumulated surplus, cannot survive a prolonged and serious industrial depression and remain solvent without the aid of additional subsidies or loans. When the rate of unemployment begins to climb and continues to do so for a long period, it is as a practical matter impossible to make, at the time, the necessary adjustments in the premiums from employers and employees. There is apparently a working level of contributions above which it would be hazardous to raise the rates.

From the outset the shares of the various contributors to the insurance scheme have not been the same. As can be seen in Table XLIV, the share of the State has varied from one-fourth to one-fifth of the total contributions. This does not, however, account for the total expenditures of the State on unemployment insurance. The cost of out-of-work donations, which largely replaced the insurance payments from November, 1918 to November, 1919 and which paid benefits to soldiers and sailors until about the middle of 1921, was completely borne by the State. The scheme was altogether non-contributory. Furthermore, the State makes annually substantial payments, in addition to its regular contributions, for the cost of administering the scheme. In the last year, also, the exhaustion of the surplus previously accumulated by the scheme has led to substantial borrowings from the State. Beyond this, the differences in the rates of contribution are slight and unimportant.

TABLE XLIV.—CONTRIBUTIONS TO INSURANCE FUND.

| Period | Weekly contributions by | | | | | |
|---|---|---|---|---|---|---|
| | Employer | | Employee | | State | |
| | Men | Women | Men | Women | Men | Women |
| July 15, 1912–Nov. 8, 1920 | 2½d. | 2½d. | 2½d. | 2½d. | 1⅔d. | 1⅔d. |
| Nov. 8, 1920–July 3, 1921 | 4d. | 3½d. | 4d. | 3d. | 2d. | 1⅔d. |
| July 4, 1921—[a,b] | 8d. | 7d. | 7d. | 6d. | 3¾d. | 3¼d. |

[a] Under the Act of 1921, (No. 1) Mar. 3, 1921, the rates fixed were lower than those given here; but the new rates of July 4, 1921 were determined upon before the old rates had become effective.

[b] Under the terms of the Unemployed Workers' Dependents (Temporary Provision) Act, effective Nov. 7, 1921, employers, employees, and the State pay additional premiums for men of 2d., 2d., and 3d., respectively, and for women, 1d., 1d., and 2d. The fund so collected is used as the source for benefits in respect of dependent wives and children.

It is, of course, not easy to weigh the relative burden of these contributions. For the workers the burden is clearly not excessive and amounts to probably less than 1 per cent of their average earnings. The contribution by the employers has been estimated to represent a bit more than 1 per cent of their wages bill.[1] The state expenditures are even more difficult to weigh in the balance because they are made to procure conditions of well-being and states of mind—intangibles not reducible to quantitative terms. So far as the contributions by employers are concerned, it is not clear that they cannot be increased so as to permit the payment of a somewhat higher rate of benefits. A few firms have already voluntarily so increased their contributions, and there is no indication that these firms enjoy peculiarly favorable conditions. It is estimated by Rowntree that, during a period in which the rate of unemployment was on the average 5 per cent, contributions by employers of 2½ per cent of their wages bill in addition to contributions by employees and the State substantially at their regular rates would yield an insurance fund able to pay benefits ranging from 50 to 75 per cent of the average earnings of the beneficiaries.[2]

**The Definition of Unemployment.**—It seems to be essential in any system of insurance to define carefully the risk and to take measures that will guard the insurance reserve against fraud, deception, or, in general, an undue increase in the incidence of the risk. So important has this factor been in the insurance business that a substantial literature has grown up concerned with the control of risks in the various branches of insurance. Even in life insurance, which rests probably on the soundest actuarial basis and where the risk would seem capable of detection and definition beyond any reasonable question, elaborate precautions are devised to ensure the payment of benefits only under appropriate conditions. Thus from the time when a prospective policyholder makes application for his insurance until he actually receives his insurance, he undergoes severe scrutiny designed to protect the company and the other policy-holders. Purchasers of life insurance, for instance, must receive a medical examination that establishes at the time their physical fitness; they must testify concerning their family history; and they must subscribe to a variety of conditions touching such diverse matters as domicile and habits of life before they can be admitted to insurance.

The temptation to establish improper claims for benefit varies markedly with conditions. Experience shows that life insurance companies must exercise much greater care with applicants for very large

---

[1] ROWNTREE, B. SEEBOHM, Prevention and Compensation of Unemployment, *International Labor Review*, December, 1921, p. 14.

[2] *Ibid.*, p. 11.

insurance than with those who wish to buy only a moderate amount. In general the greater the prize, the greater seem to be the chances of deception, deliberate or unconscious. Similarly, it is held and probably with reason, that if the rate of unemployment benefit were placed too high, people would prefer unemployment to work and the volume of insured unemployment would rise to unprecedented heights, unless effective measures of control were devised. Some risks, moreover, are intrinsically difficult to define. Unemployment is a risk of this type. The establishment of a system of unemployment insurance almost universally gives rise to a host of problems relating to the definition and control of unemployment, many of which are rarely foreseen.

When, therefore, the English government embarked on its scheme of compulsory unemployment insurance in the Act of 1911, detailed provisions were therein made for the preliminary definition of unemployment. Gradually as the system came into operation and accumulated experience, these first statutory provisions were supplemented by administrative rules and orders, by rules of procedure, and by semi-judicial interpretations which together represent the definition of unemployment under the successive acts. Analysis of these many rules and provisions shows that the definition of unemployment for insurance purposes is, to a much greater degree than with other insurable risks, an arbitrary matter, determined by prevailing industrial practices and customs in the country where the scheme operates and by the financial necessities of the particular situation. And this must necessarily be the case.

Certain of the statutory provisions, which have been retained with only minor amendments throughout the history of the scheme, are financial in character and depend in practice for their effectiveness purely on the efficiency of the accounting department of the scheme. Such provisions limit the period of benefits, fix the proportion of benefits to contributions, and establish a right to benefit only when the individual has not exhausted his quota of the insurance fund. More interesting and more difficult, however, are the statutory provisions which define the conditions under which an applicant for benefit becomes and ceases to be unemployed.

Before the Act of 1920 the number of trades to which the insurance scheme applied was limited. There was frequently, therefore, the necessity under the early acts of determining whether an applicant for insurance was working in an insured trade. If he was not, he was ineligible for benefit. The 1920 Act covered practically the whole of English industry, but, as before, insurance is limited to "employed" persons, possessing certain qualifications, working in the insured industries. Once eligibility for insurance is established in accordance with these various terms, the question of the legitimacy of the particular period of unemployment becomes important. On this matter statutory provision and administrative practice have been so framed as to protect at the same time the insurance scheme against malingering and the insured from harsh and unjust measures of disqualification.

Protection against malingering is sought by providing that a workman is disqualified for benefit if he lost employment through misconduct or voluntarily left his employment without just cause; if he lost his last employment by reason of a trade dispute; and if he refuses to accept suitable employment. The workman, on the other hand, is protected by the further provisions that he is not disqualified from benefit if he has declined an offer of employment in a situation vacant as a result of a stoppage of work due to a trade dispute; or an offer of employment in the district where he was last employed at a rate of wages lower, or on conditions less favorable, than those which he habitually obtained in his usual employment; or an offer of employment in any other district at a rate of wages, or on working conditions, below trade union standards or the standards of good employers in such district.[1]

Simple as the terms of disqualification and of protection seem to be, they have become in practice the subject of frequent controversy. Such conceptions as "misconduct," "just cause," "suitable employment," "by reason of a trade dispute," "more or less favorable conditions," prevailing and standard rates of wages, have turned out to require frequent interpretation in the light of particular conditions. To provide for the interpretation of these provisions of the law, there has been set up under the scheme an elaborate machinery of investigation, administration, and interpretation. Decision on the validity of a claim to benefit is first made by a government agent, known as the insurance officer. He decides in the first instance whether a claim shall be allowed and also later whether the payment of benefit should be discontinued. In the event that the claimant is satisfied with the decision of the insurance officer, the case stops at that point. The claimant has, however, the right of appeal to a Court of Referees, composed of representatives of the workers and of the employers and an impartial chairman, when he is dissatisfied with the decision of the insurance officer. Should the decision of the Court of Referees affirm the decision of the insurance officer, the case is closed. Where the Courts finds differently, however, the claimant receives his benefit and will continue to do so unless the insurance officer appeals from the decision of the Court to a species of appelate court, known as the Umpire. The decision of the Umpire is in all cases final, but cases may be reopened on the presentation of new facts.

In the decisions of the Umpire, a portion of which now fill more than four thick volumes, such conceptions as "suitable employment" and

---

[1] All of these provisions of the insurance acts are as follows: Act of 1911, Sec. 86 and 87; Act of 1920, Sec. 7 and 8.

the rest take on specific meaning.   There is no more illuminating source of information on the practicability of defining unemployment and on the influence of industrial practice and custom in a country on the operation of unemployment insurance, than the abstracts of the decisions of the Umpire.   Concerned at first largely with fixing the demarcation of insured trades, the Umpire has gradually constructed a body of principles and rules which give force to the provisions of the statutes.   In one case, for example, the Umpire held that a job offered eighty miles away from the workingman's home, which the workingman did not accept because he did not consider the work sufficiently attractive to warrant his leaving home and a wife and two children, was not suitable employment.[1]   A large number of decisions hold that refusal to do extra work "outside the contract of service"[2] does not constitute leaving employment without just cause and does not, therefore, disqualify the workman for benefit. Misconduct, likewise, has been the subject of frequent interpretation. Under this last subject alone there have been a very considerable number of cases classified under such heads as, absence from work without leave, disobedience to orders, personal conduct, bad time-keeping, and general questions including among others such matters as misconduct out of working hours, false representations in order to obtain employment, and discharge for making disparaging remarks to customers about employers' material.

A large number of cases have been brought before the Umpire through requests by associations, such as trade unions, for refunds where members of the associations had been disqualified from benefit for failure to take suitable employment.   In a number of interesting and important cases the association held the proffered employment not suitable because acceptance would conflict with the rules of the association.   In one such case, for instance, the Umpire held that "if the Society desire to maintain such a rule [against doing piece work] in circumstances such as these where satisfactory earnings can be obtained, they alone must bear the cost.   It is not a case for assistance from the Unemployment Fund."[3]

The determination of the loss of employment by reason of a trade dispute and of the right of a workman to decline a situation vacant as a result of a stoppage of work due to a trade dispute has occasioned considerable difficulty and has given rise to many decisions.   In a series of very early cases, the task of the Umpire was to decide whether people thrown out of work in the course of a trade dispute were engaged in

---

[1] *Decisions given by the Umpire respecting Claims to Benefit*, Unemployment Insurance, U. I. 440A, vol. 1, Case 43.

[2] See for instance, *ibid.*, Case 5.

[3] *Ibid.*, vol. 3, Case 1154.

"separate branches of work commonly carried on as separate businesses in separate premises" and were therefore qualified to receive benefit.[1]

"This workman," said the Umpire in one of these cases, "appears to have been engaged in work of a kind which is required at all tube factories as a necessary part of the working of such factories. I do not think, therefore, that he can be said to have been engaged in a separate branch of work which is commonly carried on as a separate business in separate premises."[2] Another group of cases fixes the status of people thrown out of work as the result of strikes, but not themselves on strike. Thus in two early cases, the Umpire said: "This workman lost his employment by reason of a stoppage of work which was due to a trade dispute. There was a dispute between the strikers and the non-strikers and the employer of the non-strikers in connection with employment of all persons at the factory at which this workman was employed."[3] The benefit was in these cases disallowed. A significant finding of the loss of employment through a stoppage in work due to a trade dispute is illustrated in the case of an applicant for benefit who was in arrears with his contributions to his association and was unable, on the demand of the branch secretary, to pay them. "The employer was informed that there would be a strike of the masons employed by him unless the applicant were discharged forthwith, and in order to prevent the threatened stoppage of work the employer dismissed the applicant. It was contended that the applicant did not lose his employment owing to a trade dispute, as he had no difference whatever with his employer, who merely discharged him in order to prevent unpleasantness with the other workmen. On the other hand, it was pointed out that there was a trade dispute between workmen and workmen at the premises, and that the applicant lost his employment on account of that dispute. The Court of Referees (Western Ireland District) were of opinion that there was no trade dispute within the meaning of the Act, and accordingly recommended that the claim for benefit should be allowed." The insurance officer declined to accept the recommendation and the benefit was disallowed by the Umpire.[4]

In 1913 an analysis was made of the reasons for disallowance of benefits in a certain proportion of the cases coming before the Courts of Referees and the Umpire. The results of this analysis, which are shown below, indicate the preponderance of disallowances because of misconduct and leaving employment voluntarily without just cause. While the materials for a similar analysis are not readily available subsequent to 1913, it is probable that the proportions have not varied considerably,

---

[1] Act of 1911, Sec. 87 (1).

[2] *Decisions given by the Umpire respecting Claims to Benefit*, Unemployment Insurance, U. I. 440A, vol. 1, Case 90, also Cases 54, 79, and 92.

[3] *Ibid.*, Cases 88, 89, and 94.

[4] *Ibid.*, vol. 3, Case 1309; vol. 1, Cases 304 and 370.

with the difference, however, that after the war and the demobilization of the war industries, disallowance for refusal to accept suitable employment bulked much larger in the total than before. This was particularly the case with many women applicants for unemployment insurance benefit during the latter period.

TABLE XLV.—REASONS OF DISALLOWANCE[a]

| Grounds of disallowance of claim | Percentage of appeals heard by Courts of Referees | Percentage of cases decided by Umpire |
|---|---|---|
| Section 86: | | |
| Insufficient contributions.......... | 4.7 | 4.2 |
| Not capable of work.............. | 1.2 | 1.4 |
| Failure to prove inability to obtain suitable employment............ | 4.3 | 12.7 |
| Section 87 (1): | | |
| Trade dispute................... | 3.2 | 17.0 |
| Section 87 (2): | | |
| Misconduct..................... | 28.5 | 19.7 |
| Employment left voluntarily without just cause................ | 55.7 | 36.6 |
| Other reasons................... | 2.4 | 8.4 |
| | 100.0 | 100.0 |

[a] *First Report on the Proceedings of the Board of Trade under Part II of the National Insurance Act*, 1911, Command 6965, 1913, p 33.

On the record, the task of defining unemployment and controlling it within the statutory limits has been successfully accomplished by the machinery of insurance officer, Court of Referees, and Umpire. An important factor that has contributed to the working of this machinery is the degree to which trade unionism and trade-union standards are accepted in England. The practices and standards of organized workers thus afford a measuring rod with reference to which adjustments can be generally made. In the United States, just because the trade-union practices and standards are not so completely accepted, the definition of unemployment and the determination of suitable employment or misconduct would, for a considerable period at least, encounter real obstacles.

In addition to the control exercised over unemployment by the measures just considered, the public employment exchanges, in their relation with the scheme of unemployment insurance, have played an important part in the administration of the same elements of the insurance acts. Organized in 1910, two years prior to the organization of national unemployment insurance, the national public exchanges have been constantly extended so that they might more effectively serve the needs of the system of unemployment insurance. Indirectly their service consists in facilitating the mobility of labor by finding all possible and available vacancies and by referring the applicants for jobs to such vacancies. While the employment exchanges have constantly been exposed to severe criticism for failing to perform this function satisfactorily, the evidence points to a large measure of efficiency in this regard. But beyond this the employment exchanges are essential elements in the administration of the scheme of unemployment insurance, since it is at the exchange that the applicant for benefit lodges his unemployment book, registers daily during his period of unemployment, is offered employment, and receives his benefit. However defective the employment exchanges may be in lending mobility to labor, even their critics agree that the administration of unemployment insurance is impossible without them, or at least an equally efficient substitute. For the time being no such substitute has been produced.

Since the Armistice, November, 1918, the task of controlling unemployment has been considerably more difficult than it was before. The difficulties began on November 25, 1918, with the coming into effect on that date of the out-of-work donation scheme. Prior to the Armistice, the English government foresaw the problems which would attend the demobilization of the armed forces of the country and of the civil war workers. There was no time to extend the limits of the unemployment insurance acts. So the plan was conceived of paying to members of His Majesty's Forces and to civilians weekly benefits during prescribed periods of unemployment. The scheme differed from the prevailing system of unemployment insurance in that it covered a much greater number of persons, it was non-contributory, and the level of benefits was considerably higher than ever before.[1] At the same time, also, the shutting down of war industries threw out of work many persons, particularly women, who found it difficult, if not impossible, to get work under conditions as satisfactory as those they had enjoyed during the war. This plan had been in operation only a short time before it met with extensive criticism as encouraging fraud and deception and imposing excessive burdens on the country. The reply to the criticism was an elaborate investigation of the scheme which concluded with a statement by the investigating committee that " . . . the evidence so far heard by us indicated no grounds for supposing that there had been extensive fraudulent abuse of the donation scheme . . ." The impression obtained, however, that it was easy to get the donations. Changes were, therefore, made in the administration of the scheme. Among these changes was that which gave to Local Employment Committees the right to issue

---

[1] It should be remembered, however, that the increase in benefits was accompanied, indeed preceded, by great increases in prices.

additional donation policies only when they were satisfied that the applicant was normally in employment, genuinely seeking work, and unable to obtain it. The effect of this change was indubitably to eliminate many persons not eligible for benefit.[1]

Conditions similar to those obtaining under out-of-work donations appeared also in the administration of the Acts of 1921. In these acts, because of the great and increasing volume of unemployment, benefit was made payable to large numbers of persons who had made few or no contributions to the fund. Eligibility to benefit turned largely on the applicants having been "normally in employment" and on their "genuinely seeking whole-time employment." Again as before, there was a feeling of laxity. "The view has been expressed that in some cases young men and women, not altogether dependent upon themselves for maintenance, do in fact seek to avail themselves of benefit without making any very serious effort to seek work; and have, indeed, refused offers of employment for reasons which ought to involve forfeiture of benefit."[2] The administrative machinery was, accordingly, kept in a measure in the form which it assumed during out-of-work donations by the retention of Local Employment Committees, with power to inquire into such questions as normal employment and the genuine quest for work. Instructions sent to these committees from the Ministry of Labor are evidence of the difficulty of the problem of controlling employment and of the vigorous efforts made by the administration to prevent the payment of improper claims. One instruction states, for instance, that: "The mere fact that the applicant dislikes the employment offered does not, in itself, make the employment unsuitable. There must, in addition, be some satisfactory ground for the objection. For example, if a woman who is prepared to accept day work as a domestic servant objects to becoming a resident domestic servant, this is not, in itself, a ground for holding that resident domestic service is not suitable employment in her case; there must, in addition, be—for example— some valid objection arising from her domestic ties."[3] In another place the Ministry cautions the administration against a too great liberality in allowing claims to benefit. "The funds which accrue under the act are contributed, as to four-fifths, by employers and employed persons, and as to the final fifth by the State. The Minister and those who

---

[1] *Interim Report* of the Committee of Inquiry into the Scheme of Out-of-work Donation, Command 196, 1919; *Final Report* of the same committee July 25, 1919. Command 305, 1919; *Decisions given by Umpire respecting claims to Out-of-work Donations,* U. I. 440B vol. 1, Prefatory Note, p. ii.

[2] Circular letter from the Minister of Labor to the chairmen of Local Employment Committees, Mar. 8, 1921.

[3] *General Memorandum for the Guidance of Local Employment Committees and Officers of the Ministry of Labour* (Unemployment Insurance Act, 1921) U. I. A. 505, p. 3.

assist him are in the position of trustees for the contributors to the Fund. Accordingly, however deserving an application may be in other respects, and whatever sympathy the Committee may feel in the particular circumstances, they should . . . keep always in mind the essential fact that they are not administering a compassionate allowance, but that they are administering benefit under a compulsory insurance act."[1]

It has been proposed from time to time that mobility of labor could be increased and malingering more effectively controlled if the administration of the payment of benefits and of the finding of jobs were entrusted to agencies other than the employment exchanges. In many cases trade unions already have their employment offices and vacancy registers; they are in close touch with industrial conditions in the trades in which their members work; and as a result of their knowledge of industrial conditions they can the more easily and swiftly detect malingering. From the beginning, indeed, a share of the administration of the insurance acts, in this regard, has been assumed by trade unions and other associations which met the conditions imposed first by the Board of Trade and later by the Ministry of Labor. No data exist which make possible an estimate of the relative merits of one or another system of administration. There is a widespread feeling that such a decentralization of administration in the hands of specialized industrial groups does in some cases, at least, bring superior administration. In general, however, trade unions and other associations have not worked out their placement problems so efficiently as to warrant a wholesale transfer of administration from the State to these private industrial agencies.

A plan of administration that is designed to protect the insurance fund against improper claims and that is apparently working with marked success is that embodied in the Rowntree scheme of supplementary unemployment insurance. In the Rowntree scheme, the fund is administered by a committee appointed entirely by the workers. Furthermore, while the firm guarantees the premiums under the scheme, it does not guarantee benefits. "If the scheme were abused, the premium might not suffice to pay the benefits expected. Thus all the workers have an interest in seeing that it is not abused, lest on their becoming unemployed they should find the funds so depleted that they could not obtain their full benefit."[2] This scheme has obviously much to recommend it; but it must wait for more general adoption upon the assumption by employers of a larger measure of responsibility toward the unemployed.

[1] *General Memorandum for the Guidance of Local Employment Committees* (Unemployment Insurance Act (No. 2) 1921) U. I. A. 505A, p. 4; *Suitable Employment*, Note on the Application of Sec. 96 (provisos (*b*) and (*c*), to Women applicants, U. I. 445.

[2] ROWNTREE, B. SEEBOHM: Prevention and Compensation of Unemployment, *International Labor Review*, December, 1921, p. 13.

**The Prevention of Unemployment.**—Advanced insurance practice makes provision for the substantial reduction, if not the elimination, of the risk against which persons insure themselves. These provisions as a rule go much beyond the attempt merely to control the risk by the prevention of malingering. They, in fact, consist in taking the necessary steps to effect considerable and continuous reductions in the risk. Even in life insurance, where, of course, the risk is not totally preventable, a large degree of prevention is accomplished by measures leading to the prolongation of life. Nearly every large life insurance company today spends considerable sums on the education of its policy-holders in the elementary facts of preventive medicine and personal hygiene. In other fields of insurance the chances for almost total prevention are good. The spread of fire insurance, for example, has been followed by notable reductions in the loss of property through fires. Much the same quality of record has been achieved, in a much briefer period, under the influence of accident insurance or workmen's compensation.

In the field of social insurance, prevention has come to be accomplished by two devices that are commonly used together. The premium under such schemes is paid not by the persons who suffer from the particular hazard but by those who are, at the time, deemed to be responsible for the hazard. Premiums, moreover, are not flat and equal for all insured but are graded with reference to the degree of hazard. American workmen's compensation systems are outstanding illustrations of the type of insurance that combines both features. Under our compensation legislation the premium is paid not by the workman who meets with an industrial accident but by his employer and the employer with a bad record of industrial accidents pays greater premiums than one with fewer accidents. The insurance premium is, thus, conceived as a tax or penalty which is designed to stimulate the employers to avail themselves of all possible means of prevention so that their premiums may be reduced in proportion as their "experience" proves prevention to have been successful. The application of this procedure to unemployment insurance would produce a system in which the total premiums would be paid by the employer and the premium rates would vary with the risk of unemployment.

Preventive measures, of this type, have so far played little part in the English unemployment insurance legislation. It is true that part of the cost of the present scheme is borne by the employers but the burden is in absolute amount not great and is not graded so as to penalize carelessness in the organization and use of the labor market. Prior to the Act of 1920, the English scheme contained one provision designed to regularize employment. This provision granted employers a refund of one-third of their contributions during a year in respect of each workman continuously in their service during that period and for whom not less than forty-five contributions had been paid during the period.[1] The refunds[2] paid under this provision were:

| | | | |
|---|---|---|---|
| 1913–14 | £113,106 | 1917–18 | £117,034 |
| 1914–15 | 120,475 | 1918–19 | 137,242 |
| 1915–16 | 94,034 | 1919–20 | 117,391 |
| 1916–17 | 107,404 | | |

In the Act of 1920 this provision was abandoned and has not been again enacted. Its net effect on the reduction of unemployment was negligible.

The germs of a plan of preventive unemployment insurance are to be found in the "special schemes" provisions of the Act of 1920.[3] The plan originated, however, in a purpose quite distinct from that of prevention at the time when it was contemplated to extend the Acts of 1911 and 1916 to cover the whole industrial population of England. There then developed considerable opposition to inclusion in the scheme of compulsory unemployment insurance from industries which believed that their rate of unemployment was considerably below that of the older insured trades.[4] In order to placate the representatives of these industries, those which were willing to subscribe to conditions formulated in the Act of 1920 and by the Minister of Labor were allowed to "contract out," or in other words to carry and administer their own unemployment insurance. Those industries which elected to "contract out" were to receive a State grant fixed at a maximum of 30 per cent of the normal rate, or one-tenth of the contributions of employers and employees instead of the one-third paid in respect of those remaining in the general scheme. The more important conditions which industries were required to meet before they were permitted to introduce special schemes, were that the insurance would be more satisfactorily provided than under the general scheme; benefits would be not less favorable; contributions would be regular and sufficient to cover all costs without requiring special levies in bad times; appropriate machinery of administration must be established.[5] If, therefore, it turned out that an industry really had a lower rate of unemployment, the cost of the insurance to the industry would be

---

[1] Act of 1911, Sec. 94 (1); see also for slight amendments to this provision, Act of 1914, Sec. 5, (1) and (2).

[2] *Account of the Unemployment Fund . . . with the Report of the Comptroller and Auditor General thereon,* each year.

[3] Act of 1920, sec. 18.

[4] For an interesting discussion of the attitude of these industries see Ministry of Reconstruction, *Second Interim Report* of the Civil War Workers' Committee, Report of Sub-committee on Unemployment Insurance, Feb. 12, 1918, Command 9192, 1918.

[5] *Notes on Special Schemes and Supplementary Schemes for Industries* (Unemployment Insurance Act, 1920) U. I. A. 2. Revised October, 1920.

lower than under the general scheme and the benefits at least as high.[1]
Before many "special schemes" could be organized, the growing volume of unemployment made it necessary to suspend the right to
organize such schemes, on the general ground that, during the period of
insolvency of the insurance fund, industries with low unemployment
rates would help maintain the solvency of the fund.[2] No special industry
schemes can, accordingly, be set up from July 1, 1921 until the close of
the period of insolvency. Before the suspension, however, one such
scheme had already been put into operation in the insurance industry[3]
and another is under consideration for the banking industry. Neither
industry is large, nor are the employees subject to considerable
unemployment.

The principle of the "special scheme," if it were applied throughout
the whole industry, might lead to measures for the prevention of unemployment. The defect in the plan was, however, that it encouraged
"contracting out" only among those industries whose unemployment
record was already fair and left in the general scheme the "bad risks."
Upon the bad risks the general scheme imposes only moderately large
premiums, which in turn yield inadequate benefits, and the penalty or
tax on responsibility for excessive unemployment is lacking. Ten years
experience with compulsory insurance against unemployment in England
has not yet produced measures that have substantially affected the risk
of unemployment.

**The Solvency of the Insurance Fund.**—An insurance fund, into which
contributions are paid and from which benefits are drawn, rests on actuarial estimates. Except in assessment insurance where assessments are
levied to meet current expenditure, the necessary size of the insurance
fund is estimated a considerable time ahead from more or less accurate
statistical materials. The same estimates, of course, also determine the
required rates of contribution and of benefit. The purpose of these preliminary actuarial estimates is to find the rate of contribution that over a
considerable period of time will produce an insurance fund or reserve,
sufficient to yield the desired rate of benefit. In order, therefore, to
establish an insurance fund that will possess any elements of security, it
is essential to know beforehand the magnitude of the risk, the capacity

---

[1] *Report by the Government Actuary on the Financial Provisions of the Bill* (of 1919),
Dec. 23, 1919, Command 498, 1919.

[2] Another reason for the suspension was, of course, that "all industries had had
their share of benefit and it was right that they should stay and make it good again
when employment became better." PHILLIPS, T. W., Work of the Employment and
Insurance Department of the British Ministry of Labour, *Labour Gazette* (Canada),
September, 1921, vol. XXI, p. 1179.

[3] Incorporated Insurance Industry Unemployment Insurance Board, *The Insurance Industry Unemployment Insurance Scheme and Rules*, 16 Russell Square,
London.

of the insured to pay premiums, and the volume of benefits which it is desired to draw from the insurance fund. To the extent that any insurance scheme falls short of supplying such security, the insured will be exposed to frequent changes in premiums, the beneficiaries to variations in their benefit, or the insurance fund to insolvency. Any or all of these possible contingencies may indeed, as they frequently did, happen at the same time. If, accordingly, it is desired that the insurance scheme avoid the uncertainties that are normally associated with risks, such as unemployment, the rate of benefit and the conditions of receiving it must be at the outset carefully defined, the necessary rate of contributions must be accurately estimated, and the rates and rules so decided upon must be departed from only rarely. Such precision in estimating the magnitude of risks is rarely possible. For this reason it is the common practice in many branches of insurance to include in the premiums a substantial margin of safety for the purpose of building up a surplus or contingency reserve.

By the terms of the English unemployment insurance acts, the payment of benefits has always been limited by statutory provisions and the necessary rates of contribution have been computed with reference to the influence of these provisions. Thus the first act, that of 1911, limited the payment of benefit to persons who could prove employment in the insured trade in each of not less than twenty-six separate calendar weeks in the preceding five years.[1] No benefit was paid at all during the first six months of operation in order to enable the scheme to collect a reserve. Unemployed persons under the act received no benefit during a "waiting period" of one week. Benefits were not paid, even after the "waiting period" had elapsed, during the whole period of unemployment but were restricted to a maximum of fifteen weeks of benefit during the year. And even then benefits were not paid whenever the number of weeks' benefit received exceeded the proportion of one week's benefit for every five contributions paid by the workman under the act.[2] With minor modifications, the same or similar provisions were retained until shortly after the Act of 1920 became operative when a series of new and unanticipated conditions forced radical changes in procedure and, at the same time, exerted a marked influence on the status of the insurance fund.

The Act of 1920, effective November 8, 1920, extended the application of compulsory unemployment insurance from less than 4,000,000 persons to almost 12,000,000. As in the previous acts the maximum period of benefit was placed at fifteen weeks; but the proportion of benefit to contribution was changed from one to five to one to six, the waiting period reduced to three days, and the insured was required to prove

---

[1] Sec. 86 (1).
[2] Sec. 84.

that not less than twelve contributions had been paid in respect of him under the act.[1] There were likely to be, however, a substantial number of persons thrown out of work who had not had the opportunity to make twelve contributions before their spell of unemployment began. The status of such persons was met by the further provision of the Act of 1920 that insured persons who have paid four' contributions shall receive benefits for a maximum period of eight weeks during the first year of the Act.[2] If the Act of 1920 had become effective during a period of only moderate unemployment, it would probably have been unnecessary to modify radically any of these provisions and the status of the insurance fund would have been assured. But very soon after the close of 1920 there began in England, as elsewhere, that long and severe spell of unemployment which played havoc with previous calculations and forced the adoption of new practices. As the following table shows, average unemployment of members of trade unions,[3] during the year 1921, was more than six times greater than in 1920; it rose to a peak about the middle of 1921, then receded slightly and still remains more than seven times as high as it was during the whole of 1920. While the table below does not show the percentage of unemployment among insured persons, because the available data for the latter are not strictly comparable with the trade-union figures, the course of unemployment among insured was much the same as among the trade unionists. Unemployment among the insured likewise rose from 5.8 per cent in December, 1920 to 17.8 per cent in June, 1921 and was 14.4 per cent in April, 1922.

TABLE XLVI.—AVERAGE UNEMPLOYMENT OF TRADE UNION MEMBERS

| Month | Per cent | Month | Per cent | Month | Per cent |
|-------|----------|-------|----------|-------|----------|
| **1920** | | **1921** | | **1921** | |
| Sept. | 2.2 | April | 17.6[a] | Nov | 15.9 |
| Oct. | 5.3[a] | May | 22.2[a] | Dec | 16.5 |
| Nov. | 3.7 | June | 23.1[a] | **1922** | |
| Dec. | 6.0 | July | 16.7 | Jan | 16.8 |
| **1921** | | Aug | 16.3 | Feb | 16.3 |
| Jan | 6.9 | Sept | 14.8 | Mar | 16.3 |
| Feb | 8.5 | Oct | 15.6 | April | 17.0 |
| Mar | 10.0 | | | | |

[a] Coal mining excluded owing to strike.

The effect of this prolonged spell of unemployment was, on the one hand, to makè it difficult for employed persons to pay their contributions

[1] Sec. 7, (1).
[2] Sec. 44. This section was later repealed as from June 30, 1921.
[3] Ministry of Labour, *Labour Gazette*, each month.

and, on the other, to increase seriously the need of the unemployed for benefit payments. Almost immediate action was taken, therefore, to extend the periods of benefit and to wipe away some of the restrictions on the right to receive benefits. The first of such measures was embodied in the Unemployment Insurance (Temporary Provision Amendment) Act, of 1920, which became effective December 25, 1920. This act substituted for the four contributions required in the Act of 1920, proof of previous employment. There then came a rapid series of drastic amendments of the Act of 1920 which, in order to meet the serious conditions of unemployment, made the conditions of receiving benefit on the whole considerably easier than they had been before. The one-in-six rule is practically suspended. The waiting period is raised from three to six days and the periods of maximum benefit are extended as indicated in the next table.[1]

TABLE XLVII.—PERIODS OF BENEFIT

| Act | Date when act becomes effective | Duration of special period | Maximum weeks of benefit in special period |
|---|---|---|---|
| Act of 1921 (No. 1)... | Mar. 3, 1921 | Mar. 3, 1921–Nov. 2, 1921 | 16 weeks |
| | | Nov. 3, 1921–July 2, 1922 | 16 weeks |
| Act of 1921 (No. 2) .. | June 30, 1921 | ...................... | Adds maximum of six weeks in each of the above special periods. |
| Act of 1922.......... | Apr. 6, 1922 | Apr. 6, 1922–Oct. 31, 1922 | 15 weeks[a] |
| | | Nov 1, 1922–June 30, 1923 | 12 weeks[a] |

[a] These fifteen weeks of benefit are payable in three periods of five weeks each separated by intervals of five weeks. When a person has received twenty-two weeks benefit in all since Nov. 2, 1921, he is not entitled to benefit until April 17, next. See *Report of Government Actuary on the Financial Provisions of the Bill* (of 1922), Mar. 25, 1922, Command 1620, 1922; *Memorandum on Unemployment Insurance Bill*, Mar. 24, 1922, House of Commons Bill 62, 1922.

[b] The Minister of Labor is empowered to grant two further periods of five weeks each, making twenty-two in all.

All of these factors, then, were making for progressively larger and larger drafts on the insurance fund, while the general state of business

[1] *General Memorandum for the Guidance of Local Employment Committees and Officers of the Ministry of Labour* (Unemployment Insurance Act, 1921), U. I. A. 505; *General Memorandum for the Guidance of Local Employment Committees* (Unemployment Insurance (No. 2) Act, 1921), U. I. A. 505A; Committee on National Expenditure, *First Interim Report*, Command 1581, 1922, Appendix (A), pp. 149–53; *Explanatory Memorandum* (Unemployment Insurance Acts, 1921), U. I. A., 518.

depression and unemployment would not permit substantial assessments on either employers or employed for the purpose of making good these additional withdrawals. Even in periods of relatively moderate unemployment, the suspension of the one-in-six rule and the limitation on the benefit period would add appreciably to the expenditure for insurance. The Government Actuary estimated, for instance, that the waiting week and the limitation of benefits to fifteen weeks reduced the number of "benefit days" to 71 per cent of the days of unemployment; while the further limitation under the one-in-five (in the 1911 Act) rule reduced the proportion to 64 per cent.[1] It is clear, therefore, that if such limitations are not to apply or are suspended, the contributions must be proportionately increased during the period of suspension unless the prevailing rates of benefits are also proportionately lowered.

The most serious obstacle in the way of preserving the solvency of an unemployment fund consists in the difficulty of predicting the frequency and duration of extreme business depressions with their widespread unemployment. From 1912 to early 1921 the insurance fund was in such a favorable situation that not only had it met all of its obligations but there had in addition been accumulated a surplus of more than £20,000,000. This condition of prosperity was, of course, a reflection of good business conditions and of steady employment. Table XLVIII shows how in a fairly long period of steady employment, the amount spent on unemployment benefit was so moderate as to permit the accumulation of a surplus. By the end of 1918 unemployment began to mount and continued upward through part of 1919. The effect of this rise in unemployment is hardly discernable in the expenditures for unemployment benefit in 1919 because from November, 1918 to November, 1919, the unemployment insurance acts were largely suspended,[2] while unemployed civilians drew benefits under the out-of-work donations scheme. This scheme, as said above, was entirely non-contributory. By means of it, the government paid in out-of-work donations to ex-service men £40,000,000 and to civilians

[1] *Report by the Government Actuary on the Financial Provisions of the Bill* (of 1919), Command 498, 1919, p. 7. The further important estimate is here made that "the several limitations proposed will restrict the benefit days to a figure between 60 per cent in periods of good trade when spells of unemployment are relatively short as well as relatively few, and 70 per cent in periods of bad trade when the contrary conditions prevail."

[2] "For the year 1919–1920 the Unemployment Fund was advantageously affected by the benefits granted under the Scheme for Out-of-work Donation in operation as regards ex-members of His Majesty's Forces for the whole period and as regards civilians to November 30, 1919. These benefits were greater than and not payable concurrently with, those under Unemployment Insurance; the payment of benefit normally chargeable to the Fund to a great extent ceased, and the Fund continued to accumulate during the year." Report of the Comptroller and Auditor General of Feb. 23, 1922 in *Account of the Unemployment Fund, 1919–1920*, House of Commons Paper 34, 1922.

TABLE XLVIII.—EXPENDITURES FOR UNEMPLOYMENT

| Year | Per cent of working people unemployed in trades insured under the Act of 1911 [a] | Year | Total expenditure in unemployment benefit[b] |
|---|---|---|---|
| 1913 | 3.2 | 1912–13 | £208,317 |
| 1914 | 4.2 | 1913–14 | 530,592 |
| 1915 | 1.2 | 1914–15 | 418,700 |
| 1916 | 0.6 | 1915–16 | 78,969 |
| 1917 | 0.6 | 1916–17 | 34,308 |
| 1918 | 1.15 | 1917–18 | 86,152 |
| | | 1918–19 | 152,720 |
| | | 1919–20 | 1,009,125 |

[a] Ministry of Labour, *Labour Gazette*, January, 1919, vol. XXVII, p. 2. Owing to the suspension of the Unemployment Insurance Acts, during the greater part of 1919, strictly comparable figures with the other years are not available.

[b] *Account of the Unemployment Fund . . . with the Report of the Comptroller and Auditor General thereon*, each year. Figures in this column are obtained by adding together the unemployment benefits paid to workmen and refunds to associations in lieu of unemployment benefit.

£22,000,000 making a total of £62,000,000.[1] This amount, of course, does not enter into the insurance accounting, but it represents the sum spent in bridging over the first post-war crisis of unemployment.

The crash which came in 1921, however, was even greater and, as it has turned out, more expensive. This time the insurance fund was not helped by out-of-work donations but had to stand itself the great drain from the rising tide of unemployment. In March, 1921, the surplus of £20,000,000, which had been before then treated as a capital fund, was made available to be spent currently. By the end of June, 1921 most of the £20,000,000 was gone. Under the Act of 1921 (No. 1) the fund had been empowered to borrow from the Treasury £10,000,000. This amount was increased by the Act of 1921 (No. 2) to £20,000,000 and again further increased by the Act of 1922 to £30,000,000. For the insurance year 1921–1922, it is estimated that the amount payable in unemployment benefit exceeds £46,000,000. This expenditure is covered by estimated contributions amounting to only £33,270,000, thus leaving a deficit at the close of 1921–1922 of almost £14,000,000.[2] Estimates

[1] PHILLIPS, T. W., Work of the Employment and Insurance Department of the British Ministry of Labour, *Labour Gazette* (Canada), September, 1921, vol. XXI, p. 1175.

[2] *Report by the Government Actuary on the Financial Provisions of the Bill* (No. 2 of 1921), June 8, 1921, Command 1336, 1921.

moreover, for the period of fifteen months from April 6, 1922 to July 1, 1923 place the payment for benefits in that time at £60,000,000 and the total debt to the Treasury on July 1, 1923 at £27,000,000.[1] In little more than two years, therefore, adverse conditions, largely unpredictable, have converted a surplus of £20,000,000 into a deficiency of almost £30,000,000.

Data such as these are interesting and important not only as revealing the magnitude of the charge of unemployment insurance, but also for the light they throw on the fundamental difficulty of predicting the turn in the business cycle. When, for example, the Government Actuary made his first estimate, on June 8, 1921, of the probable income and expenditure of the fund during the year 1922–1923, he concluded that contributions would yield £35,000,000, expenditures would amount to £20,000,000, and there would accordingly be on June 1, 1923 a surplus of £15,000,000. In arriving at this estimate he assumed an average unemployment in the year 1921–1922 of 1,250,000 persons and in the year 1922–1923 an approximation to normal unemployment, together with the restoration of the restrictions on the payment of benefit contained in the Act of 1920.[2] Less than a year later estimates for the same periods are based on the assumptions that up to the end of June, 1922 unemployment will not exceed on the average 1,900,000 persons and that during the twelve months following June, 1922 the average number of insured persons unemployed will not be more than 1,500,000.[3] By that time, too, it was known that the limitations on the right to benefit were not only not restored but their suspension was extended to June 30, 1923. Consequently the revised estimates show not a surplus on July 1, 1923 but a substantial deficiency and the duration of the deficiency period becomes highly uncertain. "The proposed rates of benefit," wrote the Government Actuary on March 25, 1922, "are to continue during the deficiency period and it may be presumed that with a continuous improvement in the industrial position this debt will be steadily reduced. The rate at which the debt will be repaid must, of course, depend upon the course of unemployment and the conditions governing the receipt of

[1] *Report of Government Actuary on the Financial Provisions of the Bill* (of 1922) Mar. 25, 1922, Command 1620, 1922.

[2] The comments of the Actuary on these estimates are interesting. "It is impossible," he writes, "to suggest any close figure with reference to the probable expenditure on benefits. Even under normal conditions there is a wide fluctuation in the claims from year to year as the trade cycle pursues its course, and to estimate merely on the average of a trade cycle would give a figure which is meaningless in regard to a particular year, though it may be properly used with reference to the operation to the scheme when viewed over a series of years." *Report by the Government Actuary on the Financial Provisions of the Bill* (No. 2 of 1921), Command 1336, 1921.

[3] *Memorandum on the Unemployment Insurance Bill*, Mar. 24, 1922, House of Commons Paper 62, 1922.

benefit, but so far as can be seen at present, it is unlikely that the fund will become solvent until several years after July, 1923."[1]

The evidence is overwhelming that the greatest obstacle to successful unemployment insurance, of any type, lies in our inability to forecast the length of successive phases of the business cycle. As long as this inability continues, systems of unemployment insurance will be confronted more or less frequently with sudden catastrophes, in the form of widespread and enduring unemployment, against which they will be forced to take hasty and incomplete measures. Indirectly, also, the experience of the English scheme testifies to the absolute necessity of building adequate insurance funds when business is on the up-swing. When business is in depression, the need for benefit is great and the ability to pay low. It then becomes necessary to vary the rates of contributions and of benefit, to obtain subsidies from the outside, and the insurance scheme begins to become almost as uncertain as the hazard it is designed to insure against. Greater certainty can come only from a more adequate statistical basis for the forecast of unemployment and from an insurance fund accumulated at a time when substantial contributions are not so difficult to get as they are at present.[2]

**The Encouragement of Voluntary Insurance.**—Trade unions and voluntary associations of workmen, of one type or another, have for a long time played a prominent part in English economic life. One of the functions which many such associations have exercised is the payment to their members of unemployment benefit. The passage of the Unemployment Insurance Act of 1911, therefore, found a substantial number of workmen already in receipt of unemployment benefits of greater or smaller amounts. It was deemed highly desirable, in the first place, that such associations as did pay benefits should not discontinue their payment, since the statutory rate of benefit was notoriously too low. Secondly, it seemed equally desirable to avoid any unnecessary duplication in the machinery of benefit payment. The Act of 1911, accordingly, contained provisions[3] which made it possible for associations, which met certain conditions to the satisfaction of the Board of Trade, to assume

[1] *Report of the Government Actuary on the Financial Provisions of the Bill* (of 1922), Command 1620, 1922.

[2] For an illuminating discussion of this point see *Report by Government Actuary on the Financial Provisions of the Bill* (of 1919), Command 498, 1919, p. 8. His concluding remarks on the nature of the risk of unemployment are particularly pertinent in this connection. "It is obviously impossible to predict the course of the trade cycle or to measure the extremes in the rate of unemployment which will be touched in its progress; in this respect the Fund is subject to contingencies, such as do not operate in any other sphere of insurance, and while for practical purposes the average conditions alone can be investigated, it is clear that the resulting surplus is not of the same dependable character as the surplus found on the valuation of a life assurance company or even of a friendly society."

[3] Sec. 105.

the payment of the "public" benefit as well as their own. Where this was done, the members of associations, "in lieu of being concerned with two sets of rules as to benefit, and in lieu of attending at the office of the association to draw money on account of the association and at the Local Office of the Unemployment Fund to draw state benefit, may get a single combined benefit from their association."[1] The payment of benefit in addition to that furnished by the State was, moreover, assured by the rule that associations could not recover from the unemployment fund more than three-fourths of what they had themselves paid out. This meant that, in order to recover from the State an amount equal to the State benefit of 7s., the association had to add an amount of not less than 2s. 4d. for each week of unemployment. Associations subscribing to these rules, then, assumed a share of the administration of the scheme of unemployment insurance and paid to their members something over and above their State benefits.

The Act of 1911, unlike that of 1920, covered only a relatively small proportion of the working population of England. Probably as many as 9,000,000 employed persons were excluded from the recepit of unemployment benefit. The purpose of this early limitation of the scope of the scheme was to permit experimentation in those trades which seemed at the time to need unemployment benefit most, before applying the plan universally. At the same time, however, it was deemed advisable to encourage where possible the payment of benefits in the uninsured trades and the increase of benefits, above the statutory rates, in the insured trades. There was consequently embodied in the Act of 1911 the provision[2] for a species of subsidy to all associations, whether in the insured trades[3] or not. Under these provisions, the Board of Trade was empowered to make arrangements with an association whereby the government agreed to pay part of what the association had spent in the preceding year for unemployment benefit. The share of the government was, however, in no case to exceed one-sixth of the aggregate amount so spent by the association. Where, moreover, the rate of benefit paid by the association was more than 12s. a week, the amount in excess of 12s. was excluded in computing the State's share. The moneys spent in providing this State subvention came not from the unemployment fund, but from an independent parliamentary grant.

Both of these sets of provisions were retained substantially in their original form until the Act of 1920. Since that Act extended the operation of compulsory insurance over practically the whole industrial work-

---

[1] First Report on the Proceedings of the Board of Trade under Part II of the National Insurance Act, 1911, Command 6965, 1913, p. 6, paragraph 41.

[2] Sec. 106.

[3] Where associations in the insured trades claim refund under Sec. 106, the refund is calculated on the expenditure of the association after the deduction of any sums recovered by it from the unemployment fund under the provisions of Sec. 105.

ing population, the latter section, providing partly for subventions to uninsured trades, was dropped. The provisions for administration by associations, however, and for the refund of part of their payments of benefit to their members were retained almost in the same form in which they appeared in the first act.[1]

The effects of these provisions in encouraging the growth of voluntary unemployment insurance are hard to estimate. During the first year of the operation of the scheme, 105 associations with an estimated membership of 539,775 availed themselves of the opportunity of making arrangements under section 105. Under section 106 by the end of the first year, 275 associations with an estimated membership of 1,104,223 had been admitted as satisfying the conditions of the Board of Trade. Of these 275 associations, 103 with a total membership of 728,182 and a membership in the insured trades of 538,045 had made arrangements under section 105 as well. In addition, 343 associations with an estimated membership of 1,259,846 had by July 12, 1913, given notice of intention to claim subvention under the provisions of section 106.[2] The first effect clearly of the provisions of the scheme was to stimulate the payment to voluntary insurance and to encourage associations to assume a part of the administration of the scheme. The following table, for the period in which the data are available, shows the amount of benefit paid directly, to associations under section 105, and to associations

TABLE XLIX.—BENEFITS PAID UNDER SECTIONS 105 AND 106

| Year | Benefits paid direct[a] | Refunds under section 105[a] | Refunds under section 106[b] |
|------|------|------|------|
| 1912–13 | £183,193 | £25,124 | £ |
| 1913–14 | 364,555 | 166,037 | 15,167 |
| 1914–15 | 249,532 | 169,168 | 114,593 |
| 1915–16 | 39,972 | 38,997 | 50,658 |
| 1916–17 | 24,133 | 10,175 | 13,736 |
| 1917–18 | 75,128 | 11,024 | 18,270 |
| 1918–19 | 148,881 | 3,839 | 7,586 |
| 1919–20 | 869,424 | 139,701 | 1,678 |

[a] Account of the Unemployment Fund . . . with the Report of the Comptroller and Auditor General thereon, each year.
[b] Civil Services and Revenue Departments, Appropriation Accounts, each year.

[1] See Act of 1920, sec. 17. This section provides that payment by associations to members must exceed the "public" rate of benefit by at least one-third of the amount of that benefit. In the Act of 1921 (No. 1) this provision was amended so that the payment by associations to members would exceed the "public" rate of benefit by at least 5s. per week for men, 4s. for women, 2s. 6d. for boys, and 2s. for girls.
[2] First Report on the Proceedings of the Board of Trade under Part II of the National Insurance Act, 1911, Command 6965, 1913, p. 15.

under section 106. After 1920, with the repeal of section 106, refunds to associations were made under provisions laid down in the section (17) that in the Act of 1920 replaced section 105. The continuous record of the refunds in 1920 and 1921 under this section are not available, but it is stated that in 1921, 193 associations with a membership of 2,110,000 were participating in the scheme under the section.[1]

The fear that the adoption of public insurance would discourage the payment of unemployment benefits by trade unions and the few other voluntary associations, which had been accustomed to pay such benefits in the past, was found to be apparently unwarranted. While the scheme of unemployment insurance did not have the effect of stimulating a notable increase in the volume of benefits paid by associations, it also did not lead such associations to abandon their provisions for the payment of unemployment benefits. The following statistics on the unemployment benefits[2] paid by trade unions reporting to the Registrar of Friendly Societies show that the volume of benefits has varied with changes in the membership of trade unions and in the rate of unemployment. In the past few years, as the tide of unemployment has risen so sharply, the volume of benefits paid by trade unions grew considerably and is stated to have reached in the year ending September, 1921, for 154 reporting unions, the sum of £7,500,000.[3]

TABLE L.—UNEMPLOYMENT BENEFITS PAID BY TRADE UNIONS

| Year | Benefits | Year | Benefits | Year | Benefits |
|------|----------|------|----------|------|----------|
| 1908 | £1,046,258 | 1912 | £632,389 | 1916 | £120,164 |
| 1909 | 904,104 | 1913 | 509,895 | 1917 | 270,489 |
| 1910 | 663,928 | 1914 | 885,362 | 1918 | 327,005 |
| 1911 | 482,972 | 1915 | 294,530 | | |

An important, if indirect, effect of these attempts to encourage voluntary insurance has been to draw associations, particularly trade unions, into the administration of the scheme of insurance. But this has not been accomplished without friction. In the period in which unemployment was small and the scope of the act restricted, relations were easy and peaceful. After 1920, however, there came first the enormous increase in the number of insured and later the rise in unemployment.

[1] PHILLIPS, T. W., Work of the Employment and Insurance Department of the British Ministry of Labour, *Labour Gazette* (Canada), September, 1921, p. 1177.

[2] *Annual Reports of the Chief Registrar of Friendly Societies for the Year ending, December 31st . . . Part C, Trade Unions.* Number of registered unions reporting Unemployed, Travelling and Emigration Benefits: 1911, 346; 1912, 358; 1913, 350; 1917, 294, 1918, 293; other years not available.

[1] *The New Statesman*, Dec. 24, 1921, vol. XVIII, p. 339.

The extension of the act produced at once ill feeling between the trade unions and the friendly societies. The trade unions were jealous of their position and the friendly societies feared that the unemployment scheme and its administrative machinery would swallow up the administration of health insurance and their place in that administration. They, therefore, demanded the right to exercise the same functions under the unemployment scheme as were exercised by the trade unions.[1] When, however, this right was finally granted them, most of them apparently found their duties too onerous and the drain on their finances too great, and did not avail themselves of it. The trade unions, likewise, during the period of prolonged unemployment grew restless under the burden of mounting costs of administration and were granted in addition to the normal refund a subsidy for administration of ls. for every week's benefit paid by them.[2] In spite of these manifestations, which are in some measure reactions to the severe depression and its prolonged unemployment, the influence of the system of public insurance has been wholesome both in stimulating the payment of benefits and in spreading the responsibility of administration.

**Problems of Administration.**—The employment exchange is the most important element in the machinery of administration of a system of unemployment insurance. By means of the exchange, it is designed to decrease the period of waiting between jobs, to assist the less organized workers to find jobs, to enable the government to measure the volume of unemployment, and to operate the scheme of compulsory insurance. The development of the English system of employment exchanges has been practically synchronous with the growth of the scheme of insurance. Every extension of the system of insurance, as well as unfavorable conditions of employment, have thrown additional burdens on the exchanges. From the beginning the exchanges have been subjected to severe criticism on many grounds. They were too expensive. Most jobs were found by persons independent of the exchanges. They had not earned the good will of the employers and the trade unions. They were resorted to largely by unskilled workers and were not used by the skilled.

It is doubtful, however, whether the criticism stands the test of actual performance of the English system of public employment exchanges. The system necessarily had to undergo a period of scrutiny in which the attitudes of the exchanges towards trade unions and employers were closely watched. They were forced to meet extremely difficult emergency conditions at the outbreak of the war, with the extension of insurance in

---

[1] National Federation of Employees' Approved Societies, *Report of the Special General Meeting and the Annual General Meeting*, London, Oct. 12, 1920; Association of British Chambers of Commerce, *Report of Meeting of Representatives of Chambers of Commerce*, 14 Queen Anne's Gate, Jan. 12, 1921.

[2] *The New Statesman*, Dec. 24, 1921, vol. XVIII, p. 339.

1916, in the administration of out-of-work donations in 1918 and 1919, and during the present severe crisis. From 1910 to 1920 the staff of the exchanges increased in number from 528 to roughly 13,000 persons, with a maximum on June 7, 1919 to 21,331.[1] In the interval, also, from 1911 to 1919 the number of registrations for jobs increased from 1,966,000 to 5,929,000, and the number of vacancies notified from 608,000 to 1,259,-000.[2] The coming into effect in November, 1918 of the scheme of out-of-work donations threw a heavy additional burden on the exchanges.

Both in 1919 and in 1920 the employment exchanges were made the subject of critical and competent investigations by special committees appointed for that purpose. In both cases the evidence is overwhelming that the exchanges performed their function with notable success. Most of the charges were found to have little foundation in fact. The exchanges were utilized on a very large scale by employers and by trade unions. Statistical records indicate that they were used extensively by skilled workers. While there was considerable room for greater cooperation with employers and while there was some discussion of making the notification of vacancies compulsory on employers, no change in this direction was finally recommended. In the administration of the insurance scheme, the evidence was conclusive that the exchanges played an essential part in protecting the unemployment fund by recommending to unemployed insured persons suitable employment. Through their method of local and divisional organization, their labor control section, and their machinery for notifying vacancies and applications from one district to another, they seemed to be gradually approximating as complete a control over the mobility of labor as can in practice be achieved.[3]

It is, however, on the score of excessive cost that the whole scheme of unemployment insurance has been most severely attacked. The great increase of the tax burden in England during and after the war has led there, as elsewhere, to the examination of those functions which are deemed either too wasteful in themselves or wastefully administered. No absolute standards exist, of course, by which it is feasible to measure the waste or profit involved in the cost of administering an extensive system of compulsory unemployment insurance. The table below shows the total cost of administration of the scheme and the contributions

---

[1] *Minutes of Evidence Taken before the Committee of Enquiry into the Work of the Employment Exchanges*, Command 1140, 1921, p. 11.

[2] *Ibid.*, Appendix 3, p. 434.

[3] *Minutes of Evidence Taken before the Committee of Enquiry into the Work of the Employment Exchanges*, Command 1140, 1921; *Minutes of Evidence Taken before Committee of Inquiry into the Scheme of Out-of-work Donations*, Command 407, 1919. See particularly the testimony of T. W. Phillips, Assistant Secretary, Employment Department, Ministry of Labor, and of Commander J. B. Adams, General Manager, Employment Department, Ministry of Labor.

paid by the government into the unemployment fund.[1] It does not, however, include the expenditure of more than £60,000,000 on out-of-work donations from 1918 to 1921, or the somewhat less than £30,000,000 which will have been borrowed from the government for the unemployment fund by June 30, 1923. The administrative expenses were in fact

TABLE LI — TOTAL CHARGE ON GOVERNMENT

| Year | Net charge to Exchequer on account of administration | Government contribution to fund | Total charge |
|---|---|---|---|
| 1912–13 | £489,000 | £378,000 | £867,000 |
| 1913–14 | 523,000 | 602,000 | 1,125,000 |
| 1914–15 | 537,000 | 546,000 | 1,083,000 |
| 1915–16 | 603,000 | 538,000 | 1,141,000 |
| 1916–17 | 576,000 | 746,000 | 1,322,000 |
| 1917–18 | 723,000 | 1,007,000 | 1,730,000 |
| 1918–19 | 1,495,000 | 994,000 | 2,489,000 |
| 1919–20 | 3,154,000 | 912,000 | 4,066,000 |
| 1920–21 | 3,478,000 | 2,200,000 | 5,678,000 |
| 1921–22 | 2,789,000 | 6,720,000 | 9,509,000 |
| 1922–23 | 870,000 | 8,231,000 | 9,101,000 |

larger than are indicated in the table, but a substantial proportion of them was borne by segregating from the government contribution to the unemployment fund a percentage for use in meeting the cost of administration. This percentage is included in the figures in the third column of the table, so that the total charge of the unemployment scheme on the government is properly represented in the final column.

With a view to suggesting savings in the cost of administration, the Government Actuary made in December, 1921 a report on the expenses of administration and recommendations for their reduction.[2] The most important of his recommendations was that there be substituted a single contribution card for the two cards now held by persons insured in the schemes both of health and of unemployment insurance. This practice, it is pointed out, means that the contribution record of each of 12,000,000 people under unemployment insurance is practically duplicated under health insurance. The suggestion is one that has been made before, but it has always been rejected, probably because it is still considered the sounder public policy to permit each scheme, for the time at least, to retain its identity. An Interdepartmental Committee appointed "to consider the relations of Health Insurance and Unemploy-

[1] Committee on National Expenditure, *First Interim Report*, Command 1581, 1922, p. 145.

[2] *Ibid.*, Appendix (B), pp. 153–60.

ment Insurance" reported on March 17, 1922 that "whatever may be our ultimate recommendation, it is not possible to bring a combined card into use so soon as next July."[1] when the unemployment books and the health insurance cards now in use expire.

In addition to this duplication in administration between the schemes of health and unemployment insurance, the system of unemployment insurance has used an administrative and accounting procedure that has been often regarded as too cumbersome and expensive. This procedure has originated not in any peculiar principles of administration but in what have seemed to be the requirements of sound insurance practice. Thus the rule restricting the payment of benefits to one week's benefit for every six contributions, or the "one-in-six rule," has imposed on the administration of the system the necessity of keeping a vast number of individual records of the payment of contributions and of benefits. The expense of maintaining these records is undeniably great. But the method by which the administration may be simplified is not clear. A suggestion by the Government Actuary that the claims of individuals for benefits be controlled by reference to their "general employment records" seems to raise more serious difficulties than it settles. Other proposals for drastic administrative simplification seem, likewise, to create new problems where old ones existed before.[2] Reform in administration, when it does come, will come slowly and experimentally and will be made with due regard, not only for cost, but also for the purposes of the scheme.

### III. AMERICAN EXPERIMENTS WITH UNEMPLOYMENT INSURANCE

American experience with unemployment insurance is more important for its promise than for its accomplishment. As in many other fields of social legislation, in this, too, the United States has followed slowly and reluctantly the steps of other countries. Until rather recently, this country treated unemployment and the unemployed with measures that are known to have outlived their usefulness. There were the hastily improvised schemes designed to solve the problem of depression unemployment. Contracts were let hurriedly for public work. Charity facilities were extended. Employers were encouraged to divide the work among all their employees. At about that point the activities of the community stopped. Within less than a decade, however, there have been carried on a few experiments in unemployment insurance in the United States that command consideration. While these experiments affect only an insignificant proportion of the whole working force of the

[1] Interdepartmental Committee on Health and Unemployment Insurance, *First and Second Interim Reports*, Mar. 17, 1922, Command 1644, 1922, p. 10.

[2] Committee on National Expenditure, *First Interim Report*, Command 1581, 1922, pp. 145, 153 ff.

country, they have in them the germs of effective measures for attacking unemployment through the medium of insurance. Unemployment insurance or compensation, as it has been called in this country, has developed in the form of establishment funds, of an industrial fund confined to one city, and of proposed legislation by three American commonwealths.

The best known examples of the establishment fund are those organized under the auspices of Deering, Milliken Company in the Rockland Finishing Company at West Haverstraw, New York, and in the Dutchess Bleachery, Inc. at Wappinger Falls, New York, and by the Dennison Manufacturing Company at Framingham, Mass. In the three instances, the fund is set aside by the companies out of their profits. Once established, the funds are administered either by a committee of workers, as in the first two cases or by a joint committee of workers' and employers' representatives as in the last. What constitutes unemployment, under the administration of the fund, is in each case defined with precision and detail and benefits range from 50 to 90 per cent of their normal wages.[1] In their main features, although not in their details, these provisions for unemployment insurance are quite similar to those made by the Rowntree and Cadbury firms in England to supplement for their employees the benefits from the State fund.

A sum of $20,000, set aside by the directors of the company in 1916, was the beginning of the unemployment fund maintained by the Dennison Manufacturing Company. Additional sums were appropriated for the same purpose in 1917, 1918, and 1919. The articles governing the control and use of the fund were drafted in 1920. The accounts of expenditures from the fund in the past few years bear testimony to the degree to which this firm has been able to reduce the volume of unemployment. In 1920 the amount of unemployment compensation was $4,490; in 1921 it was $22,989; and in the first six months of 1922 only $95. For both 1920 and 1921 the amount of unemployment compensation represented less than 1 per cent of its total pay-roll. At the Dutchess Bleachery and at the Rockland Finishing Company the volume of unemployment compensation seems to have run relatively higher than at the Dennison Manufacturing Company. The expenditures of the first establishment were $15,875 in 1920 and $11,973 in 1921, or on the average 2 per cent of the total pay-roll; and those of the second establishment were $59,512 and $27,660 in 1920 and 1921, respectively, or on the average about 3.75 per cent of the total pay-roll.

While these experiments in unemployment compensation have not been generally and extensively adopted, they have been received with con-

---

[1] For the details of these schemes see *Experience of American Employers Favorable to Unemployment Compensation* (reprint from *American Labor Legislation Review*, March, 1921, vol. XI, No. 1), pp. 3, 9.

22

siderable interest.   Only in the past few months a group of manufacturers in Philadelphia, engaged in the manufacture of box-making machinery, locks and hardware, leather belting, and electric measuring instruments, has been studying proposals for the initiation of similar unemployment compensation funds.   The tentative plan on which this group is working provides for the establishment of an unemployment compensation fund by the firm; it limits the liability of the firm for the payment of compensation to the fund itself; after the manner of the British scheme it proposes safeguards to protect the fund against malingering; the rate of benefits it proposes is 50 per cent of normal wages in the case of unmarried persons and 75 per cent for a married man with a wife and three children.   At this writing the proposal is still in the state of discussion.[1]

An unemployment insurance fund which has quite a different origin was created in Cleveland in June, 1921 as a part of a collective agreement between the local branch of the International Ladies Garment Workers' Union and the manufacturers of women's clothes in that city.   This agreement requires each manufacturer to guarantee his regular workers twenty weeks of employment in each six months.   If the employer fails to provide this amount of unemployment, he must pay his employees during the unemployed part of the period, two-thirds of their minimum wages.   Since this agreement became effective when employment was particularly low in the industry, the liability of the manufacturers for unemployment pay was limited to 7½ per cent of their total direct labor pay-roll during each period of six months.   These funds laid aside by each employer, and deposited weekly at the office of the impartial chairman of the industry, are not thrown into a common pool but are kept separate.   At the end of each six months, therefore, such employers as have not had their complete fund drawn receive refunds of their balances.[2]

[1] On Jan. 1, 1922 the Delaware and Hudson Co. put into effect a comprehensive scheme of insurance, insuring their employees against death, accident and sickness, dismemberment or death by accident, old age and unemployment.   The terms under which an employee receives unemployment insurance are as follows: "Provided he applies for and keeps in force at least two of the three classes of insurance (Life, Health, and Accident)—the Delaware and Hudson Co. will undertake to insure the employee against unemployment resulting from dismissal for any cause—the entire cost to be borne by the company.   The amount of such insurance shall be $15 per week for a period not to exceed six weeks, or for so much of that time as the employee is unable to find employment except that employees whose average annual wages during the preceding two years of continuous service have not been more than $1,000 will be paid $10 per week for the same period."

[2] MACK, W. J., Safeguarding Employment: The "Cleveland Plan" of Unemployment Compensation: *American Labor Legislation Review*, March, 1922, vol. XII, No. 1, p. 25.   In a decision of the Board of Arbitration, May 16, 1922, the manufacturers who avail themselves of a reduction in wages are required to raise their minimum weekly guaranty fund payment from 7½ to 25 per cent of their total pay-roll and to pay benefits at the rate of the full minimum wage instead of two-thirds the minimum, as before.

An incentive is thus presumably given to employers to regularize their business and to save the payment of unemployment benefit. The interpretation of the experience of the first six months, from June to December, 1921, with this system of unemployment insurance in Cleveland is made difficult by the character of the ladies' garment industry. In Cleveland, as elsewhere, the industry is divided into two branches, the inside shops, generally of substantial size, and the outside shops of small size operated by contractors. An analysis of contributions to and expenditures from the insurance fund indicate a much greater regularity of employment in the inside shops and consequently the receipt of larger refunds by the inside manufacturers, and the more rapid exhaustion of the unemployment funds of the outside shops. From June to December, 1921 inside manufacturers paid into the fund $93,274 and received back $60,747; the outside employers paid in the same period $9,609 and had refunded to them $3,293. Of the thirty-three inside manufacturers, four received back their total contributions; three used up all of their contributions, and thirty received refunds of smaller or greater amounts. Of the forty outside employers, on the other hand, thirty-three used up all their contributions and only seven received refunds.

Not until 1921 has there been any promising attempt to establish by statutory enactment compulsory unemployment insurance for large numbers of persons. On February 4, 1921 such a bill was introduced in the Wisconsin[1] legislature by Senator Huber; on March 21, 1921 a bill of the same character was introduced in the house of representatives of the Pennsylvania legislature by Christian Miller;[2] and about a year later a similar bill was introduced in the legislature of Massachusetts[3] by Representative Shattuck. In many of their important features the three bills bear a close resemblance to the various English acts. The statutory definition of unemployment follows closely the English provisions, restrictions are placed on the benefit periods, waiting periods are provided, and the administration of the insurance scheme is connected intimately with the conduct of a system of public employment exchanges. In other respects, however, the English legislation and that proposed in the United States show striking differences. Under both the Wisconsin and Massachusetts bills, the burden of raising the necessary unemployment fund is not apportioned among the state, employer, and employed, but is imposed entirely on the employer. The amount of contribution, likewise, does not vary alone in proportion to the number of employees but is graded with reference to the unemployment risk of particular employers. The insurance carrier is no longer the state, as in England, but a liability insurance company or a mutual insurance company. Elaborate provi-

---

[1] 1921 Wisconsin Senate Bill No. 122.

[2] 1921 Pennsylvania House Bill No. 1100.

[3] 1922 Massachusetts House Bill No. 278.

sions are embodied in the bills for the organization of agencies qualified to study the employment experience of the insured employers, to fix and supervise the fixing of the proper premiums, and to establish the proper charges and credits. None of the bills have yet become law. But if and when they do, they will in all probability represent the first serious experiments in preventing unemployment through the medium of a scheme of unemployment insurance.

## IV. CONCLUSIONS

The experience of England with compulsory unemployment insurance, under conditions both favorable and highly adverse, has not supported the argument of those who had predicted it would be unworkable. By the creation of adequate machinery and by coupling the insurance scheme with a comprehensive system of employment exchanges, unemployment can for practical purposes be defined and fraud and evasion largely eliminated. Rules can be laid down and enforced which define unemployment in consonance with the customs and practices of the country in which the scheme operates. The whole history of the functions of the insurance officer, the Courts of Referees, and the Umpire make it entirely clear that the interpretation of statutory rules can proceed along lines that commend themselves to the common sense of the community.

So far as unemployment insurance is designed to afford relief to the unemployed, the English system has also revealed the possibilities of compulsory insurance. The benefits, to be sure, have been small; Englishmen and foreigners have complained of this mere pittance; but conditions in England doubtless have been considerably better than they would have been in the absence of the insurance.[1] Workmen, moreover, who have received unemployment benefit have been made aware of the difference between benefits and doles. The opposition to compulsory state insurance that characterized the debates preceding the adoption of the Act of 1911 has in large measure subsided. Little is now said of paternalism and of unwarranted state interference with private enterprise. Criticism of the scheme of unemployment insurance is, to be sure, as widespread and as vigorous as it ever was. But the terms of the criticism are not to any considerable extent concerned with general opposition to state insurance but rather with opposition to particular features of the system. Employers find the cost of administration too high. They condemn what seems to them an undue laxity in the payment of benefits. The employment exchanges are not as efficient as they might be. The trade unions and workingmen's groups, on the other hand, find the benefits too little to be satisfactory. They would

[1] This conclusion may be valid; but where is the evidence to convince a sceptic?— Note by T. S. ADAMS.

like industries to assume a greater share of the responsibility for unemployment and, in some instances, they recommend a differentiation in the rates of contributions. After the manner of the proposed American legislation, they would impose the total cost of unemployment benefits on the industry and would require no contributions from workingmen. Thus the experience of ten years in England has shifted discussion from opposition to a principle to scrutiny of specific administrative devices. With all of its possible shortcomings, it is probably no exaggeration to conclude that compulsory insurance against unemployment has become a permanent feature of English economic life.

It is with regard to the problem of unemployment prevention that the English scheme has made its smallest contribution. Yet it is just at this point that progress is most necessary. Once or twice timid steps in the direction of prevention were made through the British scheme, but, for one reason or another, they soon came to naught. Bills introduced in American legislatures have put their emphasis on penalizing unemployment to the extent of promoting prevention, and if these should be passed in the near future, as their supporters hope, America will be the first to have this type of legislation. The bills pending in Wisconsin, Pennsylvania, and Massachusetts represent the outlines of measures that stress prevention. In them, as in our workmen's compensation legislation, the compulsory payment of benefit is coupled with a premium rate structure that penalizes unfavorable experience and rewards the favorable. In theory, at least, the incentive to prevention is provided. It will not do, however, to become too sanguine over the probable effects of this type of insurance, sound as it seems in principle. An insurance premium does not exercise its full preventive influence just because there are differentials advantageous to some insurers and disadvantageous to others. No matter what the differentials, prevention will probably not be accomplished until the premiums are in absolute amount at a very high level. As E. H. Downey has pointed out in his discussion of workmen's compensation legislation, prevention is achieved when the cost of non-prevention becomes greater than that of prevention. Unemployment, likewise, will probably not be reduced substantially through insurance if it is cheaper to pay the insurance premium than to take the measures necessary to reduce unemployment.[1]

[1] "We have given much lip service to the principle of industrial responsibility but our practice has fallen far short of our professions . . . prevention is much short of what would be attained under an adequate scale of benefits. . . . Effective safety engineering costs much money. . . .. To reduce the fatality rate from three to two per million tons of coal is perfectly feasible, but when the saving represents only one-quarter cent per ton it does not pay. If the average cost per death were raised from $2,500 to $10,000 much would become practical which is now deemed visionary." DOWNEY, E. H., American Compensation Laws, *American Labor Legislation Review*, March, 1922, vol. XII, No. 1, p. 55.

# CHAPTER XIX

## CHARTING THE COURSE OF EMPLOYMENT

### BY MARY VAN KLEECK

DIRECTOR OF THE DEPARTMENT OF INDUSTRIAL STUDIES, RUSSELL SAGE FOUNDATION

"To inquire into the volume and distribution of unemployment" was the first object of the Conference on Unemployment as defined by President Harding in his telegram of invitation in the autumn of 1921. How inadequate was the information then available has been set forth in earlier chapters. Even after a thorough examination of all the facts in the possession of state or federal bureaus of labor statistics, the official estimate of the government had to be a guess "that there are variously estimated from three and one-half to five and one-half millions unemployed." The Committee on Unemployment Statistics of the Conference included in its work, therefore, the consideration of a program for improving and extending statistics of employment and unemployment.

### I. THE LACK OF SATISFACTORY EMPLOYMENT STATISTICS

The Committee found that facts were available showing the number on the pay-roll and the total earnings in manufacturing industries in New York State and Wisconsin, and that for a limited number of industries the same information was being secured monthly by the federal Bureau of Labor Statistics. The United States Employment Service was making monthly surveys based on local estimates in various cities in the country. Through the Interstate Commerce Commission facts regarding employment on the railroads were collected monthly. Only in Massachusetts, through quarterly reports from trade unions, was information about unemployment secured. No facts were obtainable regarding the state of employment on the farms, and only an estimate could be made for the mining industry. Even the information available was less useful than it might have been because it was not brought together promptly from all sources and published in a single report for the use of those groups in the community who must be counted upon to act in the prevention or the relief of unemployment.

It was clear to the Committee from a study of past experience that it would be impossible to make a count of the number of unemployed throughout the country with sufficient regularity to be a guide for action.

The most satisfactory data which could be collected at a reasonable expense seemed to be the kind gathered by the federal Bureau of Labor Statistics and by the New York and Wisconsin bureaus, showing for a sample list of establishments in typical manufacturing industries the number employed and the total pay-roll each month. From this information, if it were sufficiently inclusive, an estimate could be made, showing whether employment was decreasing or increasing, and from this could be inferred the increase or decrease of unemployment.

## II. RECOMMENDATIONS OF THE CONFERENCE ON UNEMPLOYMENT

It was with this purpose in view, to secure not statistics of unemployment, but information necessary for charting the course of employment, that the Committee on Unemployment Statistics made the following recommendations which were adopted by the Conference on October 13, 1921:

1. That the present practice of the federal Bureau of Labor Statistics of collecting from manufacturing concerns as of the fifteenth of each month data concerning the number of employees on pay-rolls and the amount of their earnings and of publishing monthly indexes of the changes therein be extended to cover transportation, trade, mining, and quarrying.

2. That in getting the data concerning the state of employment in mining and quarrying, the Bureau of Labor Statistics collaborate with the Geological Survey.

3. That in getting data concerning the state of employment in railroad transportation the Bureau of Labor Statistics collaborate with the Interstate Commerce Commission.

4. That where competent, reliable state bureaus of labor statistics exist or become established, like the Massachusetts and New York bureaus, the Bureau of Labor Statistics collect through such bureaus within such states instead of collecting directly from the establishments.

It was recognized that these recommendations would not be put into effect without further study which would result in a comprehensive plan for extending and strengthening the statistics. It was, therefore, urged by the Conference that "an Interdepartmental Committee be constituted to consider means of extending and improving employment and unemployment statistics and of coordinating the informational service of local, state, and federal agencies."

The organization of this committee was made unnecessary for the moment because the program of work undertaken by the Committee on the Business Cycle, which followed the President's Conference on Unemployment, included employment statistics as one of the subjects to be covered in its report. This was necessary because, in the view of the Committee on the Business Cycle, no adequate program for mitigating the extreme fluctuations from a business boom to the depths of depression could be successfully put into effect without the basic facts currently available to show the condition of business. Employment statistics constitute one of the most important of the indexes of business conditions.

### III. THE USES OF EMPLOYMENT STATISTICS

To devise and apply remedies for either seasonal or cyclical fluctuations in employment, it is necessary not merely to know the facts as a basis for planning, but also to know them each step of the way in carrying out a policy. For instance, if public works are to be pushed forward in dull periods, it is necessary, not only to know that dull periods recur at more or less regular intervals, but also to know at any one moment whether the curve of employment is going down or up and whether a program for construction or road building should be expanded or contracted. The same information is needed by the business man who plans construction work in connection with his own business and finds it good policy to do it in periods when employment is less extensive. This is but one of the uses of employment statistics to the business man. He must know the trend if he is to stabilize his own output whether he is selling goods or services. No matter what he sells, it is important to him also to know whether the wage-earners of the country, who will be included among his ultimate customers, have the money to buy, and this is largely dependent upon the state of employment. Finally, the facts are needed for employment exchanges in order that they may move employees from one place to another or from one occupation to another when the dull season in one happens to come at the time of a busy season elsewhere.

If the facts are to be useful for any of these purposes they must report fairly all the important industries of the country; they must be widely enough scattered geographically not to be over-influenced by conditions which may be merely local in one section of the country; they must be made available by some central agency which can correlate and interpret them; and, perhaps most important of all, they must be made public with sufficient promptness to be approximately true measures of the state of employment at the time when they are issued. Thus the problem of extending and improving employment statistics is less statistical in its nature than it is administrative. It demands a machinery strong enough and simple enough to work smoothly and rapidly without breakdowns.

The Committee on the Business Cycle undertook to examine the available data and the methods of their collection in order to set up a plan which might be recommended with confidence as a feasible task in the numerous states which at present have no provision for collecting statistics of employment. The Russell Sage Foundation was requested by the Chairman of the President's Conference on Unemployment,

Herbert Hoover, to make the investigation necessary for the development of such a plan, in cooperation with the National Bureau of Economic Research.

At about the same time the American Statistical Association appointed a Committee on Employment Statistics, composed of members of the Association who were either responsible for the collection of employment statistics in state or federal bureaus or engaged in using them so intensively as to give a basis for judgment of their value.[1] This committee has served in an advisory capacity in the preparation of this chapter and in the inquiry which preceded it.

### IV. STATISTICS NOW AVAILABLE

The governmental agencies concerned at present in the collection of statistics, from which the trend of employment can be estimated, include the federal Bureau of Labor Statistics, the New York State Department of Labor, the Industrial Commission of Wisconsin, the Illinois State Department of Labor, the Division of Statistics of the Massachusetts Department of Labor and Industries, and for special industries the Interstate Commerce Commission and the Geological Survey in the Department of the Interior. Certain states in addition to those listed are collecting facts about the state of employment, either through their employment offices or their statistical bureaus, but these statistics are not discussed in this chapter because they are not uniform and therefore not usable in charting the course of employment for the country as a whole. The figures of the United States Employment Service are not now being published but they will be included in this discussion because the experience in collecting them is suggestive.

**The Federal Bureau of Labor Statistics.**—It was at the time of the unemployment crisis of 1914 and 1915 that plans were developed for the

[1] The membership of this committee is as follows: A. J. Altmeyer, Secretary, Industrial Commission of Wisconsin; Charles E. Baldwin, Chief Statistician, U. S. Bureau of Labor Statistics; Joseph A. Becker, Statistician, Bureau of Agricultural Economics, U. S. Department of Agriculture; W. A. Berridge, Assistant Professor of Economics, Brown University; R. D. Cahn, Statistician in Charge, General Advisory Board, Illinois Department of Labor; Frederick E. Croxton, Assistant Professor of Economics, Ohio State University; Ralph G. Hurlin, Director, Division of Statistics, Russell Sage Foundation; Don D. Lescohier, Professor of Economics, University of Wisconsin; Max O. Lorenz, Director, Bureau of Statistics, Interstate Commerce Commission; Eugene B. Patton, Chief Statistician, New York Department of Labor; Roswell F. Phelps, Director, Division of Statistics, Massachusetts Department of Labor and Industries; W. H. Steiner, formerly Acting Chief of the Division of Analysis and Research, Federal Reserve Board; W. W. Stewart, Director, Division of Analysis and Research, Federal Reserve Board; F. G. Tryon, in charge of Coal and Coke Statistics, U. S. Geological Survey; Leo Wolman, New School for Social Research; Mary Van Kleeck, Chairman, Director, Department of Industrial Studies, Russell Sage Foundation.

collection of employment statistics by the federal government. At that time the Mayor's Committee on Unemployment in New York City obtained data from establishments in various industries through a questionnaire, and to supplement this information the Committee asked the federal Bureau of Labor Statistics to take a census, block by block, in certain sections of the city to determine how many were out of work. The facts were interesting, but the whole experience showed that a census of the unemployed was a time-consuming and expensive undertaking and that a count of the number on the pay-rolls was more feasible and likely to be as significant, if carefully interpreted.

It was for these reasons that Royal Meeker, who was then Commissioner of Labor Statistics, decided to ask employers in the more important industries of the country to furnish information monthly as to the number of persons in their employ and the amount of their pay-rolls. The plan was to select a large enough number of establishments in each industry to constitute a fair sample, but it was a sample of the industry which was selected, regardless of possible geographical differences in employment in different sections of the country. The first reports, for October, 1915, included only four industries—cotton, cotton finishing, hosiery, and boots and shoes. In the following month iron and steel were added, and gradually the list was extended until in the early part of 1921 it included thirteen manufacturing industries, with reports from 700 establishments employing about 500,000 wage-earners. Coal mining was added in May, 1920, but discontinued at the time of the strike of 1922. In the latter part of 1922 the list was again expanded to forty-three industries, with reports from 3,233 establishments employing more than 1,500,000 persons, and having an actual weekly pay-roll of approximately $50,000,000,

The questions asked employers are exceedingly simple. The two important items are: (1) "amount of pay-roll" for the pay-roll period nearest the fifteenth of the month and (2) "total number of persons who worked the whole or any part of this period." To throw light on these two facts the schedule provides also for a statement of the length of the pay-roll period, any change in rates of wages and the date on which it was made, and an explanation of any marked increase or decrease in the amount of the pay-roll or the number of persons employed since the preceding month.

The question about total wages paid is asked primarily in order to check the data on number employed. The number on the pay-roll includes usually some who have been employed for only part of the pay-roll period. The count of the number employed is important in showing how many individuals actually worked for any length of time during the pay-roll period, but the total wage bill is a more accurate measure of the volume of employment, provided of course there has not been a change in wage rates. The total pay-roll is not a safe measure of the trend of wages and should not be so used without careful interpretation. It has, however, some use in measuring the trend of the purchasing power of wage-earners.

In the beginning it was difficult to persuade employers to answer even these simple questions. It was necessary to send agents to the establishments to secure the information. It has been the experience of the bureau that with the increasing interest in unemployment and with the development of appreciation of statistics in business, employers have become convinced that employment statistics have practical uses for them.

After the cooperation of employers was secured, it was possible to maintain the work by sending a questionnaire by mail each month. In general the Bureau of Labor Statistics does not collect facts by correspondence, and they believe that the questionnaire method is feasible for the collection of employment statistics only if the questions are simple and few.

The figures which, as we have seen, are taken for the pay-roll period nearest the fifteenth of the month, are made available early in the following month in mimeographed form and given out to the newspapers, but it is usually about two months before the report is printed in the *Monthly Labor Review*. How the federal bureau cooperates with state bureaus will be discussed after the work of the state bureaus has been described.

**Employment Statistics in New York.**—The statistics now gathered by the New York State Department of Labor are similar to those gathered by the federal bureau, and the series was begun at about the same time. The total number of firms reporting since early in 1917 has been 1,648, employing about 500,000 wage-earners and the list has not been changed, except for a few necessary substitutions. In sending out the first questionnaire in June, 1915, firms were asked to report for the corresponding month in the preceding year, so that data are available since 1914. The two facts—number of employees on the pay-roll and the total pay-roll for the pay-roll period nearest the fifteenth of the month— are asked in substantially the same form as on the schedule of the federal bureau, except that New York asks for the numbers and wages for shop and office force separately.

It is the experience of the New York department that it would not be possible to extend the number of questions asked in this monthly report without going through a long process to convince the firms that the additions were worth while. For instance, the department is often asked whether there are fewer women employed than there were during the war. The reports of numbers of employees monthly include both men and women without separating the numbers of each. Many firms do not keep their pay-rolls separately for men and women, and for them it would be very difficult to report total wages for each sex. The significant point is that if any governmental bureau desires a periodic report as frequently as every month, the questions must be simple and must be framed so as to ask for facts which are readily obtainable from the customary records of an industry.

It is the theory of the Department of Labor in New York, as it is in the federal bureau, that the wages paid, taken in relation to the number of employees, show the effect of part-time or overtime employment on earnings. In order to test out the importance of part time, the bureau prepared in December, 1921, and again in June, 1922, a separate schedule which asked specifically the normal number of weekly hours, and the number of employees actually working each specified schedule of hours in a week for which the report was made. Some of the employers had been asked in advance whether they would be willing to have these questions added and the form of questions was discussed with them. The additional data required on these schedules to show part time took a considerably longer time to report, and the bureau had to extend the period for reporting. This again illustrated the necessity for simplicity in the monthly questionnaire. To 1,600 inquiries about 1,350 replies were received. This was the first time that any information had been secured on part time other than that reflected in changes in the pay-rolls. The survey was made because of the emphasis given by the President's Conference on Unemployment to the need for facts about part time. In general the conclusion was that part time was a minor factor in the amount of unemployment as compared with the total loss of employment of workers who are laid off, which is indicated in the reports of numbers on the pay-roll. The department has concluded, however, that it might be desirable to make a special survey of part time and overtime twice or possibly four times a year. This suggests the feasibility of adding to the periodical collection of employment statistics occasional special inquiries of this kind which make interpretation of the periodical figures more adequate.

**Employment Statistics in Wisconsin.**—The collection of employment statistics in Wisconsin was first proposed in the spring of 1920, and to get it under way a conference of manufacturers and labor leaders was called. The manufacturers were reluctant to promise cooperation. The representatives of the unions wished very detailed information. Fortunately, a number of the manufacturing industries of the state were represented in the groups of employers carrying their own insurance under the Workmen's Compensation Act. It was possible to require these employers to make a monthly report of the number of the employees. A few other employers consented to cooperate, and the reporting was started in July, 1920. It was found that the smaller establishments were not proportionately represented, and in December, 1921 the reports were extended to include the smaller industries and small establishments. Trade associations gave assistance in arousing the interest of employers. Representatives of the Industrial Commission spoke at meetings of employers in order to make them see the value of employment statistics. For a month and a half the work of preparing lists, estimating the size of establishments, and writing letters to employers whose reports were desired, took the entire time of the statistician of the commission, two clerks, and a stenographer. After the first month, the routine was more and more definitely established so that by the spring of 1922, two clerks giving half their time could handle the work under the direction of the statistician of the commission, who, also, took care of special correspondence in connection with it and wrote the text for the monthly bulletin.

The questions asked in the schedule used in Wisconsin are practically identical with those in New York State, excepting that employees are classified as "clerical and manual" instead of as "office and shop." This choice of terms in Wisconsin was due to the expectation that other forms of employment besides manufacturing would be included.

Perhaps the most interesting experiment which Wisconsin is making in the collection of employment statistics is its recent effort to include enough different occupations of the state to constitute an inclusive index for the state, Wisconsin. Beginning with January, 1922, monthly statistics of employment have been collected not only for mining, quarrying, and manufacturing, but for agriculture, logging, construction including the building trades, transportation including steam railroads, electric railroads, and express, telephone and telegraph offices, wholesale trade, hotels and restaurants, retail trade (the sales force only), teaching and miscellaneous professional services. The number of employers reporting was 850 by May, 1922. Except in agriculture, building trades, and miscellaneous professional services, the reports for each employment group cover at least one-third of the total number of wage-earners in that employment in the state. The smallest representation is in agriculture, as the 498 farmers who report to the Industrial Commission employ only 0.5 per cent of the farm laborers in Wisconsin.

The base month for the new index is January, 1922, and the expectation is that the same establishments will report every month. At this time, the single index number for all groups has not yet been prepared as it is necessary first to assign the proper weighting to each of the groups, and this weighting has not yet been finally determined.

**Employment Statistics in Illinois.**—Illinois' published employment statistics began in the September, 1921 issue of the employment bulletin published for the employment offices of the state. The work was undertaken at the suggestion of the Advisory Board for the Free Employment Offices, which had as members two representatives of employers, two employees, and a representative of the public as chairman. Facts about the trend of employment were needed in the administration of employment offices, and in May, 1921 the board decided to make an employment survey periodically. Questionnaires were sent in that month to 1,000 firms having one hundred or more employees. The list was made up from directories prepared by manufacturers' associations and lists submitted by the superintendents of employment offices. Of the 1,000 firms circularized, in the first month 425 reported. In the second survey, which was made at the end of August, the first request brought 275 reports and the follow-up 125 more.

In the questionnaire employers were asked to report "the number on pay-roll on last day" of each month, as men, women, and total. No question was asked at first about wages as it was felt in the early months that this would jeopardize the collection of the statistics because of the possible unwillingness of employers to report wages, but in July, 1922, this question was added and other changes made to conform with the schedule used by the federal Bureau of Labor Statistics. Somewhat over 1,400 firms employing 343,000 were reporting by October, 1922.

In addition to manufacturing establishments the Illinois Department of Labor secures reports from the building trades and from public utilities including street railways, mainly in Chicago. Plans are under way for extending the inquiry to other industries, possibly to include mining.

One of the serious difficulties encountered in Illinois has been duplication by different governmental agencies who have asked the same business establishments to report employment statistics. The federal Bureau of Labor Statistics had been collecting data in Illinois long before the state began and could not relinquish its work so long as the state schedule excluded wages, as the material would not have been comparable with that gathered by the federal bureau. At the time when the state began its collection, the United States Employment Service was conducting a monthly survey which included Illinois firms. The Federal Reserve Bank in Chicago was also collecting similar data for the Federal Reserve district which includes Iowa, Michigan, and parts of Illinois, Indiana, and Wisconsin. One of the largest companies in the state refused to give information to the state bureau on the ground that the different official agencies should get together and have only one questionnaire filled by each employer instead of having the same question asked by several different bureaus.

**Employment Statistics in Massachusetts.**—Massachusetts began its monthly collection and publication of statistics of employment in September, 1922, and at this writing therefore the work is in its beginnings. The feature which is new for Massachusetts is the monthly publication of the data, for Massachusetts has had employment statistics covering a very much longer period than any other state. They were, however, collected annually and published only once a year.

Since 1886 Massachusetts has taken an annual census of manufactures. One of the questions asked is the number of employees on the pay-roll each month in the preceding year. From 1889 to 1907 each report contained monthly figures which compared identical establishments for two years, but beginning with 1907 the reports gave the figures for one year for a list of establishments which was intended to be all-inclusive for manufacturing in the state. Since 1907, therefore, the comparison between identical firms has not been possible. As employment statistics are only one item in the census, and the material handled is extensive, the results are not available in print until twelve months or more after the close of the year. Therefore, it is good news that Massachusetts has begun the separate collection of employment statistics so that they may be currently available to the people of the state in letting them know month by month the trend of employment. Nevertheless, the information secured in the annual census will continue to be of great value in the future, as it has been in the past, in charting the course of employment, covering, as it does, a larger proportion of the manufacturing industries than any of the series of employment statistics which are collected monthly. It serves as a check on these other series, and aids in their interpretation. It is a unique, historical record.

Massachusetts has also a series of facts about unemployment which is unique and important to everybody concerned in the prevention of unemployment. These are the reports of the number of unemployed members in the trade unions of Massachusetts, which have been furnished to the Division of Statistics by the trade unions quarterly since 1908. As the facts are collected from officials of labor organizations they refer solely to organized wage-earners, and the question has been raised as to whether they are indicative of employment conditions in the unorganized trades. On this point the director of the Division of Statistics reports that the figures furnished by the trade unions follow closely the data in the annual census for the same industries, indicating that the reports for union membership are fairly typical for each trade as a whole. No other state in the union now collects data periodically from officials of labor unions. New York discontinued the practice when its present employment statistics were begun because the department lacked funds for both series. Students of employment statistics are earnestly hoping that Massachusetts will continue this series, since it now offers an unusual basis for charting unemployment over a period of fourteen years, and its value will be the greater as it is continued longer.

**Cooperation between State and Federal Bureaus.**—These four states, New York, Wisconsin, Illinois, and Massachusetts, have a plan of cooperation with the federal Bureau of Labor Statistics which eliminates duplication of reporting by firms and makes the statistics more useful from the two-fold point of view of state and nation. This plan provides

that the collection in a state will be made by the state bureau and dupli-
cates of the reports will be sent by the state bureau to the federal Bureau
of Labor Statistics. The state is likely to need reports from a larger
number of establishments in its borders than are included in the federal
list. The federal bureau is concerned primarily with securing a fair
sample of establishments in important industries. The state bureau
must have a picture of the industries in its own territory. New York,
for instance, covers a third of its manufacturing industries but sends
a comparatively small number of these reports to Washington. This
plan of cooperation has been in effect between the federal bureau and
New York since February, 1917, Wisconsin since July, 1920, Illinois since
July, 1922, and Massachusetts since September, 1922.[1]

This use of detailed statistics for one state, part of which are used in
combination with other data to indicate the national trend, illustrates
the two-fold need which must be kept in mind in discussing an adequate
system of employment statistics. A state and its citizens need enough
facts to show them the condition of employment within their own borders,
but they also need to know of the condition of business throughout the
country. Thus, not only is a national index important for use as a
barometer, but the detailed facts about a section of the country or an
industry are also necessary as a basis for action.

**The Cost of Collection.**—We have secured figures showing the approximate cost per month of collecting, publishing, and distributing statistics
of employment by the federal bureau and by the cooperating bureaus in
New York, Wisconsin, Illinois, and Massachusetts. The information
was supplied us in December, 1922. It can be regarded only as approximate because members of the staffs of these bureaus who take part in the
work on employment statistics are sometimes employed in other work.
The total expense per month reported by the federal Bureau of Labor
Statistics was $766; by the New York Department of Labor, $743; by
the Illinois Department of Labor, $590; by the Wisconsin Industrial
Commission, $234; and by the Massachusetts Department of Labor and
Industries in its first three months, $110. The number of firms covered
will be increased very soon in Massachusetts so that this figure of cost
will increase.

The federal bureau employs five persons on full time and covered
at the time when these figures were supplied 2,000 firms in addition to
1,200 reached through state bureaus. The New York Department of
Labor with reports from 1,648 firms employed for this work one person
on full time and five on part time. The Illinois Department of Labor
for 2,000 firms has two persons on full time and one on part time. In

[1] Similar arrangements have been made with Maryland but the collection of the
statistics has not yet begun at this writing. Other states have the matter under
consideration.

Wisconsin for 1,300 firms three persons gave part time. In several instances the part time represented approximately half the month. In the Massachusetts bureau the work was not yet finally organized. At that time five members of the staff were giving one to four days each month.

The significant fact brought out in this information is that the collection of adequate statistics of employment is not an expensive undertaking.

**Special Industries.**—In addition to the material gathered by these states and by the federal bureau for manufacturing, certain special industries are covered by other departments of the federal government or offer problems for consideration in the effort to improve employment statistics.

*Steam Railroads.*—In July, 1921, the Interstate Commerce Commission began the collection of statistics of employment on railroads which are more comprehensive than the data for any other industry in the country. The facts are secured from every railroad having an annual operating revenue of $1,000,000 or more, and 90 per cent of the roads are included in this classification. The number of employees in each of 148 classes of railroad labor is reported for the middle of each month. Not merely the persons actually at work on that day are counted, but all employees, including those on vacation or sick leave. Reports are also received of the number of full-time positions in each occupation. This is estimated by dividing the total number of straight-time hours actually worked in each shop or department for the preceding month by the number of hours per man required by the normal schedule for a month. In other words, this gives the total number of men who would be required to do that month's work if no time were lost by absence. Stated more simply, this is intended to be a measure of the normal number of employees for that month. A much more complicated procedure has to be followed in reports for train service employees whose hours are dependent upon more uncertain factors. The compensation earned in each class is also reported.

Up to date no index has been computed on the basis of these figures. They are reported in detail about a month and a half or longer after the close of each month. Their immediate purpose is to provide data for the use of the Railway Labor Board, but they might be made to furnish the information desired as part of a national index of employment.

The chief difficulty in these figures at present is that their comprehensiveness causes a good deal of delay. For instance, on May 19, 1922, statistics for February were the latest available. It is the opinion of the statistician of the Interstate Commerce Commission that data as to the number of men on the railroads could be secured more promptly if a representative list of roads were to report this one item in advance

23

of their complete reports immediately after the count is taken, and this could then be used by a central agency in combination with the indexes for all other forms of employment.

*Mining.*—About 1,000,000 men are employed in mining in this country, of whom approximately 70 per cent mine coal. The Geological Survey collects weekly reports showing the production of coal in tons for the week, the total working hours for the mine, and the causes of lost time. The Survey has not gathered figures showing the number of workers or the wages paid. At the time of the President's Conference on Unemployment figures showing the production of coal in tons were used to estimate the number of men employed. To make the estimate, the total tonnage was divided by the average tonnage per man as shown in data collected by the Geological Survey.

In anthracite mining, reports from forty large producers would probably cover 95 per cent of the number of employees and the total pay-roll of that branch of the coal industry. In the production of oil and gas and the mining of iron, copper, and precious metals, control by a few large organizations would also make the collection of representative statistics comparatively easy.

The serious problem is to get the facts for the 630,000 workers in the bituminous coal industry. In that industry part-time employment is very common. A coal mine that has no orders does not discharge its working force, but tries to retain as many men as possible, and part-time operation may be said to be the normal practice. One reason for this is the fact that the distribution of railroad cars in times of car shortage is determined in accordance with the rating of the mine which varies with the total working force employed. The rating is determined by the railroads. This arrangement puts a premium upon the retention of a large number of names on the pay-roll and the giving of part-time employment. When cars are scarce and prices high, a company is eager for as many cars as possible. Thus the number of names on the pay-rolls would not be so significant for the bituminous coal industry as in manufacturing, but combined with figures showing the number of tons produced and the wages paid they would give a good index of actual employment. The bituminous mines number about 12,000, of which about 3,000 produce 60 per cent of the tonnage.

As already noted, the Bureau of Labor Statistics began in 1920 to collect facts showing numbers employed and total wages in the bituminous coal mines, but this work was interrupted by the coal strike of 1922 and has not yet been resumed. It has been suggested that the most economical arrangement would be for the Geological Survey to add these two facts to the report which they now secure and then to give the data to the Bureau of Labor Statistics to incorporate with the facts about other industries.

*Agriculture.*—Agriculture presents a baffling problem in the effort to complete the statistics of employment for the country. No data whatever exist which can be called an index of the trend of employment of farm labor month by month or year by year.[1] The decennial census shows the numbers employed. The Crop Estimate Service of the federal Department of Agriculture gives an estimate in the spring of the relation between the prospective demand for farm labor and the probable supply, and in December another statement is issued which describes the ease or difficulty of securing labor in the preceding harvest. The employment offices of several states and of the federal government afford another source of information, and some of these furnish valuable forecasts of demand. In Iowa, for instance, the Department of Labor issues a questionnaire to farmers which asks them to forecast their needs. In other states the employment offices have practically no record except that of orders for farm placements, and this is more significant of the activities of the employment office than of the condition of employment on the farms. As already stated, Wisconsin now includes a small proportion of the agricultural industry in the state in its collection of employment statistics. The Wisconsin Crop Reporting Service is cooperating with the Industrial Commission in sending out questionnaires to farmers. But this is the only part of the country where an effort is made to give agriculture a place in the general description of the state of employment.

The peculiar difficulty of collecting the figures is the reason why agriculture has not been included. No record exists in a central place comparable with the pay-roll of a manufacturing establishment and men employed on the farms are so scattered that only a census could give information as accurate as that supplied by the more highly organized industrial establishments. A forecast based on the probable size of crops often proves inaccurate. A farmer, for instance, may state his needs in advance, but when harvest time comes, even though the crops are equal to his expectations, he may find that he has not the money to pay for extra labor, so that his own family does the work. Variations in the general labor supply and in the rate of wages in other industries have their effect, as do also the prices secured for farm products.

The encouraging fact to report at this moment is the keen interest of the federal Department of Agriculture in working out some method of charting the course of agricultural employment. A representative of the Department has indicated to us that as soon as a feasible plan can be developed, data will be collected on this subject. The Department is now making certain special studies of the amount of labor required for a given acreage of particular crops in different sections of the country. Information is also being collected regarding the supply of farm labor. Out of these inquiries will probably come suggestions as to the type of

[1] But see the data for 1920–1922 in Chap. VI above.

information which will most accurately measure fluctuations in employment on the farms.

**Other Federal Agencies Interested.**—Other federal agencies which have a vital interest in the use of employment statistics are the United States Employment Service, the Department of Commerce, and the Federal Reserve Board.

*United States Employment Service.*—The importance of statistics of employment as a guide in the work of a system of employment exchanges has already been indicated. In Canada it is the employment service of the Dominion which collects the facts about employment and its work has set a high standard of speed and effectiveness in making the facts available. The United States Employment Service began in January, 1921, local monthly surveys in the typical industrial centers of the country. Local agents were appointed to collect the facts. The telephone and the telegraph were used to insure speed. The results were published in a monthly bulletin of the Employment Service. The publication of this information was discontinued in June, 1922 because the work duplicated the efforts of the federal Bureau of Labor Statistics and state bureaus, and this duplication seemed likely to prevent the expansion of these other series of employment statistics. It was also felt that unless the United States had a fully developed national system of employment exchanges, it would be wiser to concentrate responsibility for statistical work in bureaus of labor statistics.

Certain defects in the data collected by the Employment Service have been pointed out by those who have studied the data. The most important of them are: (1) collection of the information under circumstances which failed to insure absolute accuracy in reporting; (2) exclusion of establishments employing less than 500 wage-earners; (3) inaccurate industrial weighting for individual cities. The achievements of the United States Employment Service in this work should be emphasized because they are suggestive for its further development by the federal Bureau of Labor Statistics. These are: (1) promptness in reporting and in publishing; (2) making information available regarding the state of employment in particular localities instead of supplying the facts only for industries without geographical classification.

*The Department of Commerce.*—The importance of employment statistics to the business men who seek information from the Department of Commerce is obvious. The *Survey of Current Business*, now published monthly by the Department is a recognition of the need for supplying facts about the condition of business. It is the policy of the Department to secure information from all possible sources and to make its own inquiry only when the data are not available elsewhere. The *Survey of Current Business*, therefore, is a medium through which facts about employment, as collected by the federal Bureau of Labor Statistics, may be combined with the facts about production and the condition of business which are compiled by the Department of Commerce.

*Federal Reserve Board.*—The monthly bulletins published by the Federal Reserve Board and Banks give further evidence of the demand for statistics concerning the condition of business. It is the policy of the Federal Reserve Board to use the available data gathered by other agencies rather than to collect the facts itself. This is true also of the various Federal Reserve Banks. In New York, for instance, the bank uses the employment statistics supplied by the state Department of Labor.

The chief difficulty at present is that for so many districts of the Federal Reserve System employment statistics are not collected by the states nor does the federal Bureau of Labor Statistics classify its data by districts. This is why the Chicago bank for instance, collects facts for its own area, since two of the five states covered wholly or in part by the bank district publish no facts whatever about the state of employment.

Another difficulty is the date of publication of the employment statistics which are now collected. As they are gathered for the week including the fifteenth of the month, it has not been found possible to publish them before the tenth of the following month. They cannot appear, therefore, in the bulletins of the Federal Reserve System until six weeks after the date for which the returns are made. This is one of the problems which are now under consideration by the various state and federal bureaus concerned. It serves to emphasize the great importance of making employment statistics available promptly. One reason for delay is the tardiness of business establishments in making their reports, but it seems likely that this can be overcome as the practical importance of timely statistics is recognized.

## V. NEXT STEPS SUGGESTED

In the past the forward steps in the collection of employment statistics have usually been taken when unemployment was serious enough to arouse interest in the facts about it. Judging by this past experience, we may watch with confidence for the strengthening at this time of our collections of employment statistics as one result of the stress of unemployment which the country has been feeling.

The Committee on Employment Statistics of the American Statistical Association, which, as has been said, includes in its membership statisticians responsible for the collection of employment statistics in state and federal bureaus, has not yet completed its work, but the following suggestions which they have under consideration will serve to indicate next steps in the extension of facts about employment:

1. That a uniform schedule be adopted as the standard, containing the facts now asked for by the federal Bureau of Labor Statistics and by the states cooperating with it, namely:

(*a*) Total number of wage-earners on the pay-roll for the period including the fifteenth of the month.

(*b*) Total wages paid in the same pay-roll period.

The supplementary information which now appears on the schedule of the federal bureau should also be included, showing whether in the period for which the report is made the establishment was operating full time or part time; whether there has been any change in wage rates during the month, and, if so, how much of a change; and whether there have been any special circumstances, such as the opening or closing of departments or branch factories, strikes or lock-outs, or other reasons for unusual increases or decreases in the number of employees or the amount of the pay-roll.

2. That the federal Bureau of Labor Statistics be the coordinating center; that data collected by the Interstate Commerce Commission and the Geological Survey be reported promptly to the federal Bureau of Labor Statistics to be combined with the information now collected by the federal bureau for issuance in one report.

3. That as rapidly as possible states not now collecting these figures be urged to join in the plan, adopting the same methods and the same form of collection as has now been agreed upon by the federal Bureau of Labor Statistics working with the bureaus in New York, Wisconsin, Illinois, and Massachusetts. In order that representative sections of the country may be included soon it is hoped that the next states to join in the plan will be Pennsylvania, California, Ohio, North Carolina, Georgia, Washington, New Jersey, Michigan, Connecticut, Oregon, Kansas, and North Dakota.

4. That promptness of publication by federal and state bureaus be the immediate goal and that to make feasible the issuance of at least preliminary statements as soon as possible after the date of reporting, extraordinary efforts be put forth to eliminate delays in the original reporting by firms and to facilitate prompt tabulation and publication of results.

5. That the consideration of government officials be given to the importance of prompt printing by federal and state printing offices so that periodic statistics of employment and other data regarding conditions of business and of employment may be published in time to have current significance.

6. That consideration be given by the federal Bureau of Labor Statistics to the possibility of classifying by states or by geographical zones other than states, the statistics which are now published for each industry as a whole without regard to geographical location. The Committee believes that local statistics, applying even in some instances to a single city or to an area considerably smaller than a state, are of great importance to those who are responsible for programs of prevention or relief of unemployment. It would seem possible so to plan the classification of indus-

tries as to give the facts for small areas first and then to draw the totals for the country from the sum of the facts for the smaller sections.

7. That attention now be concentrated upon making more adequate the information regarding manufacturing in its main industrial groups, mining, transportation, and agriculture. The probability that wage-earners laid off from one type of employment find work in other industries makes it essential that enough industries be included in the scope of employment statistics to give a fair picture of the conditions of employment in industry as a whole.

8. The Committee believes that ultimately all industries should be included in a national measurement of employment and it suggests the following list which they have arranged in an order determined by (a) the desirability of its inclusion in employment statistics; (b) feasibility of securing the facts: (1) manufacturing (divided into its main industrial groups in accordance with a uniform classification); (2) mining and quarrying; (3) transportation and other forms of communication; (4) building and construction; (5) wholesale trade; (6) retail trade; (7) logging; (8) agriculture. It will be noticed that agriculture is placed last on the list, not because we regard it as comparatively unimportant but because it will probably be impossible to collect the facts on a basis strictly comparable with those relating to other industries. The three criteria of desirability whereby the Committee rated the industries in this list were (a) comparative number employed; (b) strategical position in relation to other industrial groups in a business cycle; (c) extent of fluctuations in numbers employed.

9. The importance of uniform classification of manufacturing industries must be stressed here. This is a problem in which uniformity in the various bureaus has not yet been achieved, but until a classification is adopted which gives the essential facts for the same industries in different states, sound interpretation of the facts will continue to be difficult.

10. In urging inclusion of more industrial groups it should be pointed out that it is not considered necessary to include all the establishments or even a majority of the wage-earners in any industry or in any geographical division. The Committee believes that approximately thirty-three and a third per cent of the employees in any given industrial group may be assumed to constitute a safe sample, provided typical establishments of the varying sizes characteristic of the industry be selected.

11. That the Department of Agriculture be urged to develop as speedily as possible its plans for the collection of facts about employment in agricultural districts. The Committee recognizes that in agriculture and possibly in some other industries it is impossible to conform exactly to the methods of reporting which are recommended for manufacturing, since on the farms pay-roll figures similar to those in factories would not

be available.  It should be possible, however, to secure facts which measure accurately the condition of employment on the farms and then to publish them in connection with pay-roll data from other industries, though the two series of facts would not necessarily be combined in a single index.

In the technical discussion of all the details of collection of employment statistics the important point to keep in mind is the purpose of collecting them.  This study of the business cycle and unemployment is directed toward the possibility of action to prevent the extreme fluctuations which are described as the business cycle.  As we have already indicated, the trend of employment is one of the indexes of business which managers are finding reliable as a guide in determining policies.  Meanwhile, until some measure of control can be established, local communities will be responsible for relief and business itself may devise means of setting aside reserves so that men and women out of work because of conditions of business will not be called upon to bear the whole financial loss.  Whatever plans for prevention or relief are contemplated, it is essential to know how many wage-earners are out of work at any given time.  The difficulty of finding this out by a direct count of the unemployed has been shown.  A feasible substitute for this kind of information is to be found in the statistics showing the trend of employment. The extension of these statistics of employment is urged, because they are needed in approaching constructively the problem of preventing unemployment.

# CHAPTER XX

# STATISTICAL INDEXES OF BUSINESS CONDITIONS AND THEIR USES

## By Oswald W. Knauth

### National Bureau of Economic Research

This chapter treats the question whether, and in how far, the use of general statistics may be expected to lessen the violent fluctuations of the business cycle. Before attempting an answer, it is necessary to recall what statistical data are now available to the business public, as well as the gaps in our information.

## I. WHAT THESE STATISTICAL INDEXES ARE

General business statistics come from three main sources—government, trade associations, and private organizations. In their publications, each agency utilizes extensively data obtained from others, so that the line of demarcation in regard to the source of the data which each presents is not clear. For instance, the *Survey of Current Business* published by the Department of Commerce draws heavily on trade associations, on such private sources as the F. W. Dodge Company for building statistics, on *Bradstreet's* and *Dun's Review* for price indexes and commercial failures, and on the *Journal of Commerce* for dividends paid by corporations. In turn, of course, the trade associations and private organizations utilize each others' and the government's material wherever possible.

**Government Series.**—The main government sources of current statistics are as follows:[1]

1. The Department of Commerce publishes each month (*a*) *The Survey of Current Business*, which is perhaps the most comprehensive single report on business conditions. Started in July, 1921, it is constantly expanding its scope. In addition to current monthly figures, comparative data covering a period of years are given at quarterly intervals. The circulation does not yet exceed five thousand. (*b*) *Commerce Reports*, giving a survey of foreign trade and a variety of notes on business conditions. This series dates back to 1880. (*c*) *Monthly Summary of Foreign Commerce of the United States*. (*d*) The Bureau of the Census not only

[1] A more detailed statement of sources may be had by referring to the *Survey of Current Business*. Only currnet information is here listed.

361

supplies the fundamental data for all statistics of population, agriculture and manufacturers; but it also compiles a variety of monthly reports, such as cotton ginned, cotton consumed, and stocks of coal.

2. The Department of Agriculture publishes each week *Weather, Crops and Markets*, a compilation of the most recent news concerning agricultural conditions and prospects.

3. The Department of Labor publishes the *Monthly Labor Review*, which contains a large amount of information on labor conditions, as well as data on cost of living and an index number of wholesale prices.

4. The Federal Reserve Board publishes monthly the *Federal Reserve Bulletin* which contains a wealth of statistics concerning the banks, prices in the United States and foreign countries, production, stocks, and shipments. Its publication was begun in May, 1915.

5. The Bulletins of the twelve Federal Reserve Banks have attained a high standard of excellence, and are fairly uniform in the material they cover. Besides showing the financial condition of the banks in each section, they also collect many trade statistics, such as samples of the volume of retail and wholesale trade, commercial loans, and commercial paper outstanding.

6. The Interstate Commerce Commission publishes a *Preliminary Statement* of the Operations of Class I Railroads.

**Trade Association Series.**—The information published by trade associations and trade journals is so extended as to defy detailed description in a short space. Trade journals are frequently, though not always, closely connected with associations. The inter-relations of business are such as to make much of this information referring primarily to a particular industry of interest to all business men. This is, of course, particularly true of the basic industries, and the production of pig iron, copper, coal, and petroleum receive wide publicity. But much of the yet unpublished material collected by trade associations would be valuable to a wide circle of allied industries. Of late the Department of Commerce has secured the wider dissemination of some of this material. Nevertheless, much remains to be done in making available to all business enterprises data now confined to a few.

The degree of excellence of the statistical material gathered by trade associations is very uneven. An examination of the work of a considerable number of associations indicates that over one-half do not gather general statistical data of any kind. Only a small proportion—not over one-fourth—collect consecutive material of a comparable nature. Most of the statistics date back only to 1917, though in a few cases compilation was begun before the war. This does not mean that trade associations themselves are of such recent growth but that only during the last few years have they begun to collect data concerning their industries on a large scale.

The data covered by the more ambitious associations—and these are few in number—cover the following items:

| | |
|---|---|
| Consumption of raw material | Capacity of normal production |
| Raw materials on hand | Orders received |
| Output of finished product | Unfilled orders |
| Finished product on hand | Actual rate of consumption |
| Finished product sold | Normal rate of consumption |
| Shipments | |

In most cases, however, statistics are confined to current production and stocks of goods. These data, of course, are valuable as far as they go. This is not the place to discuss government policy toward the publication of prices. But it is proper to note that, as a result of this policy, nearly all executives who have been approached have disavowed any attempt to gather price data. Many would like to do so, for they regard their information as defective without the inclusion of this item. Were prices not practically ascertainable in some other way, the defect would be most serious. But the statistical loss is tempered by the fact that many trade journals as well as other agencies supply market quotations. They do not, it is true, cover this field as completely and efficiently as could the associations. Still, a casual acquaintance with the market will keep a dealer in touch with price developments, whereas he would have little chance of obtaining reliable data in regard to stocks, raw material, and rate of production without the aid of a central agency.

Of secondary importance in hindering the gathering of price statistics is the reported unwillingness of individuals to disclose the facts, except where they are available generally through advertising. And many prices are special prices.

Other obstacles which are reported by trade associations as increasing the difficulty of gathering general information are:

Considerations of individual credit. This obstacle is especially serious in industries in which the unit of production is relatively small.

In many industries, the tradition under which the leaders have grown up has been to favor complete secrecy concerning the operations of individual plants, and this tradition yields ground but slowly.

Fear on the part of many individuals that they might disclose the existence of surplus stock and thus influence prices to their own disadvantage.

The lack of standardization of certain industries.

Inadequate help on the part of individual concerns to get out reports.

Inability of the secretaries of some associations to find simple units of production.

**Series Compiled by Private Organizations.**—Private organizations which publish statistical series are of two kinds—those which gather some type of specific information and those which attempt broad generalization and interpretation.

*Organizations Publishing Specific Information.*—Some of the more important original compilations of statistics are:

The index of construction costs made by the Aberthaw Construction Company of Boston and published in the *Survey of Current Business.*

The freight car loadings published weekly by the American Railway Association, of Washington, D. C.

The monthly index number of prices and business failures published by both *Bradstreet's* and *Dun's Review.*

The record of building activities in twenty-seven states published monthly by the F. W. Dodge Company, of New York.

The record of building expenditures in certain selected cities published by *Bradtsreet's.*

The monthly dividends of corporations published by the *Journal of Commerce* of New York.

The "unfilled orders" published monthly by the United States Steel Corporation.

The course of bank clearings in leading cities given in the *Commerical and Financial Chronicle.*

In addition, many trade journals collect and publish fundamental statistics for their industries; the monthly reviews of certain large banks contribute to the available fund of information; and the current service of such organizations as Babson's Statistical Organization, Moody's Investor's Service, Poor's Publishing Company, and Standard Statistics Company contain a variety of specific data.

*Organizations Making General Analyses of Business Prospects.*—The outstanding attempts to produce broad generalizations of the present and future trend of business are described as typical of the methods employed. They are taken up in alphabetical order as follows:[1]

Babson's Statistical Organization, Wellesley Hills, Mass.

Brookmire Economic Service, 25 West 45 Street, New York, N. Y.

Business Barometer Dial, 347 Fifth Avenue, New York, N. Y.

Harvard Economic Service, Cambridge, Mass.

Moody's Investors Service, 35 Nassau Street, New York, N. Y.

Poor's Publishing Company, 33 Broadway, New York, N. Y.

Standard Statistics Company, 47 West Street, New York, N. Y.

These organizations attempt not merely to present the current statistics of business—they do that; but in addition they attempt to present the information in such form that it may be used for forecasting business conditions. In considering the influence of their work in regard to lessening the cyclical fluctuations of business, it must be noted that the number of concerns which these agencies reach is not large. It is estimated that their total circulation, including duplications, is about 40,000. Their

---

[1] The descriptions have in each case been submitted to and passed upon by the organizations named.

influence, however, extends beyond their immediate mailing lists. Many of their subscribers, especially trade associations and large firms, pass along to their members or agents the conclusions reached.

Babson's Statistical Organization.—The mainstay of the Babson system is the assumption that in business, as in physics, the law holds that "action and reaction are equal." For every period of prosperity, by which is really meant "over-expansion," there must be an equal period of depression or contraction.

This equality has not been proved but is assumed at the outset. The problem is, then, to find statistical measurements whereby it can be determined when we are in a period of over-expansion and how great is its intensity and duration. This period is shown on the chart as an area. The area covered by the period of depression—determined by its intensity and duration—must equal in area the preceding over-expansion before the next upward movement may be expected.

The component parts of this system are two. First is the line of business activity made up from the following twelve items:

> Immigration
> New Building
> Failures
> Bank Clearings[1]
> Yield of Leading Crops
> Railroad Earnings
> Commodity Prices
> Total Foreign Trade
> Foreign Money Rates
> Domestic Money Rates
> Canadian Conditions
> Stock Market Conditions

Each of these items is expressed in terms of the highest and lowest variations during the period 1901–1911, and the last series in each division is given a double weighting. The weighted average is then used to establish the line of business activity. The average condition of the years 1903–1904 is taken as an arbitrary starting point. Variations are expressed in terms of dollars, on the ground that business is conducted in money terms and that any business barometer must be constructed so as to indicate this fact.

The second part of the system is the line of growth from which prosperity or depression is measured. It must comprise such a series as will express not only physical growth but also changes in money values. Bank clearings outside New York City were first chosen to represent this line. Since 1919 check transactions, adjusted so as to cause no break with the earlier years, have been substituted.

[1] Check Transactions substituted Jan. 1, 1919.

In order to fit this line of normal growth, or $x - y$ line, as Mr. Babson calls it, to the line of business activity, the years 1905–1908 were selected, on the ground that they included a complete business cycle. According to the assumption that action and reaction are equal, there must during this period have been as great an area between the two lines above the $x - y$ line as below it. The $x - y$ line was so placed as to produce this result.

It was then found that a change of 1 per cent in check transactions for succeeding years was equal to one-half a point on the barometer scale used, and the line of business activity for the following years was plotted on this basis.

The first test of the system came after the cycle containing the years 1909–1915 was finally completed. Then it was found that the area above the line during this period was almost exactly equal to the area below the line. Accordingly, it is held that the present system functions in a satisfactory manner. However, the system is not taken as final. As Mr. Babson puts it, "We are all in the elementary stage of economic study, and when some better method has been devised by economic research for locating the $x - y$ line, we shall adopt it." It is predicted that the current depression must complete an area, measured in terms of intensity and duration equal to the preceding period of over-expansion before a new period of expansion can set in.

Several points must be borne in mind to understand what this system shows, and what it does not pretend to show.

It does not forecast the length or intensity of a period of expansion. It forecasts only the length and intensity of a depression after the previous period of over-expansion has been completed.

The line of normal growth ($x - y$ line) is considered the level of true prosperity.

Security values usually reach their high and low points during the first quarter of periods of over-expansion and depression.

The course of any period of over-expansion or depression cannot be foretold. It can only be said that the area of the depression as measured by length times intensity will be the same as the preceding area of over-expansion.

Periods of depression can be mitigated only by changing the slope of the line of normal growth, which in turn according to Mr. Babson can be accomplished only by increasing per capita production, by eliminating waste, and by right living.

**Brookmire Economic Service.**—Two years ago, the Brookmire Economic Service discontinued its curve of business activity because it failed to forecast movements during the violent price changes which accompanied the war. Since then, this agency has centered its attention on the construction of a forecasting curve of stock and commodity prices. This forecasting curve is to be sharply distinguished from a curve of business activity. It is not that. But the expectation is that its movement will precede changes in business activity, and its component parts are selected with this end in view.

The curve is made from a simple average of the following six series:

> Speculative activity
>> (Average price of forty stocks and number of shares
>> sold on the New York Stock Exchange)
>
> Domestic production and marketing
>> (A composite of many items)
>
> Ratio of imports to exports
>
> The speed of turnover of bank deposits
>> (Ratio of bank deposits to total clearings)
>
> American commercial paper rates
>> (Four to six months commercial paper)
>
> The open money-market rate in London

Two of these series—the third and fourth—are expressed in terms of ratios. In the first, fifth, and sixth, no secular trend is discernible. Only one series, the second, is expressed in terms of production and this line is corrected for secular trend. The importance to the general average of all six series of any possible error in the secular trend chosen for this single series is held to be very small.

The averages for current months are compared with the average of the base years 1904–1913, and relative fluctuations are expressed in terms of the maximum fluctuations. In this way an equal weighting of the fluctuations is accomplished.[1] Then the points are plotted on a semilogarithmic (natural $x$, log $y$) chart, in order that the importance of extreme fluctuations in any one of the series may be lessened.

A special device is introduced to guard against over-emphasizing the importance of minor fluctuations which might erroneously be thought to indicate a change in trend.

When the average of the six factors used is above the 1904–1913 base, then the slope is upward, and it continues to be upward *as long as* the average is above the 1904–1913 base. In order to plot this upward movement on the chart, the amounts are cumulated so long as the averages are above the base. For instance, if the final figures obtained for the first three months of the upward movement are +125, +100, +150, then the actual points plotted are +125, +225, +375. And this cumulation continues until the average is below the 1904–1913 base. The slope of the curve and its place on the chart thus has no significance.

One further caution. A neutral zone, extending about 3 per cent of the range of fluctuation above and below the base-line has been established. When the average is within this zone, it is held to have no significance, and the next point on the forecasting curve moves directly sideways. When, however, the cumulative total of points within the

---

[1] An exception is the ratio of imports to exports, which is given one-half the weighting of the other items.

neutral zone is such as to bring this total out of the zone, then the effect is recognized as significant.

The vital point in this system is, therefore, a crossing of the neutral zone by the average. And even here one further safeguard is introduced. If within four months the neutral zone is again crossed, then the entire movement is to be disregarded. As a matter of fact, the effect of this change in warning signals is apt not to be serious, for few business men are in such a liquid condition that they can entirely reverse their position in less than four months.

Constructed in this way, the forecasting curve is expected to precede a change in stock prices by one month and in commodity prices by six or seven months. Special emphasis is laid on the statement that this is only approximately true and that action based on the curve must be tempered by judgment. It is held that the extent of a movement can never be foretold, for there are no natural limits to either a rise or a fall in prices. The problem therefore resolves itself into discovering the time when a change in movement will take place; and even the time sequence of business movements, while following recognized grooves, may be hastened or retarded by particular circumstances.

The test of the method is in its capacity to function. And the way in which it has functioned in the past may be seen by reference to Ray Vance's "Business and Investment Forecasting," recently published by the Brookmire Service.

Business Barometer Dial.—The Dial Analysis uses a clock on which are shown the movements of twelve basic factors. These factors are grouped under three main heads:

Indexes of General Confidence: railroad earnings, bank clearings, bank balances, bond sales, stock sales, new securities, new building.
Indexes of Business Conditions: crops, exports, labor conditions, failures.
Index of General Conditions: commodity prices.

The index of each of these factors is shown on the Dial; first, as a percentage change from the previous month, and next, as an average of the previous twelve months compared with an average of the preceding sixty months. This moving "normal" of the preceding sixty months is a distinctive feature of the system. That period is chosen as being not too far in the past to invalidate comparison, and yet long enough to furnish a fair base-line for comparison with the present.

These twelve series are then studied singly and in relation to each other to determine the future trend of business which is discussed in detail in the text of the bulletins.

Harvard Economic Service.—The Harvard Economic Service places its main reliance for the forecasting of business conditions upon the cyclical fluctuations shown by its three major curves, representing (A)

Speculation, (B) Business Activity and (C) Banking and Money Conditions, and upon the time sequence between the changes of trend in these curves.

The statistical series used in making each of these curves are first corrected for their seasonal and secular trends, and are then expressed in terms of their pre-war standard deviations.

After careful study and comparison of the different series,[1] it was decided to use the following data for the construction of each of the post-war indexes:

(A) Speculation
    Bank clearings in New York City
    Prices of twenty industrial stocks
    Number of shares traded on the New York Stock Exchange.
(B) Business Activity
    Bradstreet's price index
    Bank clearings outside New York City.
(C) Banking and Money Conditions
    Four to six months commercial paper rates (New York)
    Sixty to ninety days commercial paper rates (New York).

The five recurrent phases of the business cycle are depression, revival, business prosperity, financial strain and liquidation of securities, industrial crisis and liquidation of commodities.

In the interpretation of these curves, the movements of each must be considered in relation to the movements of the others. Normally, for instance, a trend downward of curve (C) (money) should forecast an upward trend in curve (A) (speculation). Similarly, a pronounced trend in (C) (money), occurring with an upward trend in (A) (speculation) and (B) (business), will forecast a change of trend first in (A) and then in (B). If any of the curves may be considered of primary importance, it is curve (C) ( money). However, an upward movement of curve (C) (money) at a time when curves (A) (speculation) and (B) (business) are both low and tending downward cannot be permanent, and so the movements of (A) and (B) forecast the movement of (C).

In this method of forecasting, then, the direction of movement of each curve is far more important than its absolute position. The order of importance may be stated as follows: First, the direction of movement of each curve considered in connection with the direction of movement of the other curves. Second, the direction of the immediately preceding movements. Third, the magnitude of such movements from the last turning-point. Minor fluctuations do not denote a long-term swing, but a persistent movement covering several months is significant.

While the series used in making the curves are corrected for secular trend, the experience of the service shows that any possible error in this

[1] *The Review of Economic Statistics*, January and April, 1919.

24

correction will not affect the results within a short period of three to five years. That there is danger of error in measuring these secular trends is frankly pointed out. A recent bulletin issued by the Service, entitled *Interpretation of the Index of General Business Conditions* by Warren M. Persons, explains the use of this system in detail.

Moody's Investors Service.—Moody's Investors Service publishes as part of its service a *Monthly Analysis of Business Conditions*, which is primarily intended for investors. The developments in financial conditions, production, foreign trade, the labor market, etc., are briefly discussed. In connection with this work, but considered as of secondary importance, there is presented a trade barometer which is used to indicate "the rise and fall of business prosperity." The items used in this barometer are:

Average daily bank exchanges for the United States
Gross revenue of class I railroads
Merchandise exports
Merchandise imports
Gross value of the monthly iron output of the United States
Dun's index number of commodity prices
A four-month average of liabilities of commercial failures (a negative quantity)

The method of weighting and combining these series is not made public.

Poor's Investment Service.—Poor's Investment Service concentrates on specific information. In addition to *Special Letters* on the outlook for certain securities, Poor's publish a *Weekly Letter* which contains their forecast regarding the business of a large number of corporations. General business conditions are also discussed in the *Weekly Investment Letter* as well as in their *Monthly Mercantile Letters*. The aim is to present the conclusions of the staff in a manner easily understood by business men without entering into the technicalities which have led to these conclusions. The underlying principles on which these letters are based are (a) that business conditions are too complex to be analyzed by any short-cut method, (b) that practical considerations can only be properly weighed and summarized by practical men and (c) that only long-term movements of the market can be foretold with any regular degree of assurance.

Standard Statistics Company, Inc.—The Standard Daily Trade Service's study of the business cycle (in the course of which they have minutely examined, classified, and interpreted voluminous data extending back over a period of more than thirty years) has led to the conclusion that the supply of money and credit available at any given time is the governing force in business activity, prices, and security market movements.

The movements denoting depression and inflation are represented on their chart by three curves which show the money supply, stock prices and business. By hypothesis, the money-supply curve is the controlling factor, and its movements are reflected, after a lag, in the other two curves.

These curves are made ás follows:

Money-supply Curve.—A line representing, from 1901 to 1915, a thirteen-weeks moving average of the ratio of deposits to loans of the New York City Clearing House banks, and from 1918 to date a thirteen-weeks moving average in terms of the standard deviation of first, the ratio of deposits to loans of between six hundred and eight hundred and twenty Federal Reserve Member banks and second, the ratio of total reserves of the twelve Federal Reserve banks to deposit and federal reserve note liabilities combined.

The base-line for the first period was an average for the years 1901–1913. But in computing a base of the post-war period, it was found that the data were insufficient to permit the application of mathematical methods. Accordingly, the base was determined by inspection after a careful study of the years 1919–1921.

The money-supply curve breaks off in the year 1915 and is not resumed until 1918. This interval was the formative period of the Federal Reserve System. Because of this factor as well as the war, the old monetary relationships were in a state of flux, and the new relationships had not yet taken definite shape.

Stock-price Curve.—This is a line representing the actual monthly range from 1901 to 1914 of twenty railroad and twelve industrial stocks and, from 1915 to date, the actual monthly range of twenty-five rail and twenty-five industrial stocks.

Business Curve.—This is a line representing a monthly average of the ratio of the value of bank clearings outside of New York City to normal conditions. The normal conditions line about which the business curve moves was drawn on a logarithmic scale over a period of thirteen years (from 1901 to 1913 inclusive) with secular growth and seasonal variations eliminated. For the years since 1913, normal is estimated by a projection of the previously calculated curve.

All three of these curves swing generally in rythmic movement. As said, however, the money-supply curve is the indicator and points the way. By crossing its own normal line in a downward direction, the money-supply curve gives the signal that stock prices are at or near the top and that the strategic moment for selling has arrived. The same movement indicates that, from three to nine months later (roughly) business expansion will have reached its maximum and that a contraction may be expected to begin.

By crossing its normal line in an upward direction, the money-supply curve gives the signal that stocks are at, or close to, the bottom, that rising prices are in prospect, and that the time to buy has arrived. By the same signal, a broad recovery of business is indicated a few months later.

The position of the money-supply curve at a given time indicates the relative plenitude or shortage of the credit supply. It is to be borne in mind, however, that the position of this curve above or below the normal line is not of great significance. The vital point is the direction in which the curve is moving and the time at which it actually crosses the normal line.

The movements of the different curves take no account of mere fluctuations and short-time breaks and swings. They give no signals for buying or selling securities for day-to-day or week-to-week rises and breaks. What they do give are indications which the investor and business man, having in mind the broader aspects of the situation and the long pull, may well take into consideration.

The faithfulness with which the various curves have usually reflected actual conditions may be gaged by reference to the chart which is published by the Service.

The conception which underlies this system is that the business cycle is a series of responses to money conditions. In a depression, money is plentiful, stock prices are low, and business is at a standstill. Money first flows into stocks, then into business. As the momentum of business increases, it absorbs money from the banks and from stocks. Then banks seek to protect themselves and drain money away from business, producing a recurrence of depression.

## II. DATA WHICH ARE LACKING

Readers who have waded through the preceding pages may get the impression that the business public is already provided with far more statistics and interpretations of statistics than it can assimilate. Certainly the business public does not make the full use of what is now available, and certainly much may be done by compact presentation to make the existing figures more serviceable. Yet it remains true that the man who tries to forecast the probable future developments of practical importance to his own affairs finds that he needs data not to be had.

To list all the important subjects concerning which statistical information is lacking would be impossible. But a few of the gaps in the present array may be noted.

1. While American index numbers of wholesale prices are relatively good, those data do not make possible comparisons between the course of prices in different industries or in different sections of the country. The distinction, important in many trades, between "contract" and "market" prices is not brought out. Comparatively few manufactured articles appear in the price records. The differences between manufacturers' prices and jobbers' prices are not shown. Finally, the accuracy

of the quotations used is not always above suspicion, for the figures are often collected from secondary sources.

2. Available retail prices are confined mainly to foods and fuels, and even this limited range of quotations is obtained only from cities and towns of considerable size.

3. While a marked improvement has been made of late in collecting commodity statistics, the list of articles concerning which production, shipments, and stocks are known is still very short. And the statistics of this sort now compiled usually omit stocks in the hands of merchants —not to speak of consumers.

4. Unfilled orders are among the most important data for avoiding business disasters; yet the statistics now published are limited to a very few industries—or rather a few establishments.

5. As shown more fully in other chapters, the United States lags far behind several other countries in the fullness and accuracy of its statistics of employment, which are a most valuable index of business conditions in general and of consumers' demand in particular.

6. We have no adequate data concerning the credit condition of business enterprises.

7. The condition of banks not connected with the Federal Reserve System is reported by the Comptroller of the Currency only once a year.

8. The statistics of savings and investments are both fragmentary and ambiguous.

This list of gaps in the data needed for the intelligent guiding of economic activities sounds formidable, though it is far from complete. It should be remembered, however, that the ideal of providing exhaustive data is very recent, and that rapid progress has been made towards its realization within the last generation. Nor is there reason to believe that this progress will slacken in the future. Indeed we may count upon the continued improvement of our statistical equipment with as much confidence as we may count upon the advance of any industrial art.

### III. HOW STATISTICAL DATA CAN BE USED

How can the available data be used by the business community? Does their use tend to stabilize production and employment?

If we grant for the moment that the indexes of general business conditions collected by public and private agencies are substantially accurate, then it should be possible to determine from them whether the general trend at a given time is toward greater or less activity. In reaching this judgment, it is of primary importance to locate the approximate position of general business in the current business cycle.

The second step is to learn the relation of the particular industry to the general business cycle. Is depression in this industry likely to come relatively early or relatively late? Is a recovery likely to precede or to follow a general upward movement? Does the industry drop sharply from its peak production, or has it a gradual decline? What are the industries which are so related that a sudden expansion or decline in one will give a warning of change in another? Or is the industry in question a specialty for which no close relation to the business cycle may be discernible?

The third step is to study the technical position within the industry itself. In this respect the data provided by the trade associations which are actively engaged in statistical work often suffice to indicate the probable course of demand and production. But frequently one must go further and analyze the different parts of an industry. For example, the course of prices and production of expensive and of cheap machine tools vary widely and the demand that may be forecast at various stages of the cycle for the two types of product is quite different. Similarly, the demand for expensive and cheap automobiles, for long distance and local telephone calls, for high-grade and low-grade tires, may fluctuate in widely different degrees and even in different directions.

Lastly, it is necessary to know the position of the particular establishment in regard to production, shipments, new orders, unfilled orders, and work in process. To illustrate one method of handling this problem, Chart 56, suggested by Ernest F. DuBrul, is reprinted from *Machinery*, February, 1922. Each of the items plotted is cumulative, net orders being the only one that can show a decrease, owing to cancellations. This chart indicates that in the establishment represented the production and sales have become badly dislocated.

If the establishment is keeping pace with its industry and adjusting its operations to the current phase of the general cycle of business, the sailing is clear. When such is not the case, careful interpretation is called for. For example, if while the industry is expanding, the factory is not getting its proportionate share of new business, then something is wrong either with the service, the sales methods, or the prices, unless the industry as a whole is over-expanding. In considering such problems, not only the status of the particular establishment, but also the position of the industry as a whole and the general business situation should be considered.

Other illustrations of the successful application of statistics to the control of purchases of raw materials, production of finished goods, pricing of products, advertising, extension of plant, and the like are given in numerous industries in the preceding chapters—especially Chapters IX and X. Here it is less necessary to argue the profitableness of good statistical work than to point out some of the difficulties in way of accomplishing it. Many complaints are made regarding the inability of business men to understand statistical reports. This difficulty is serious. The other side of the difficulty is the inability of statisticians to show clearly the lessons to be drawn from their work. Yet even when the

## CHART 56.—CONTROLLING PRODUCTION TO SUIT DEMAND

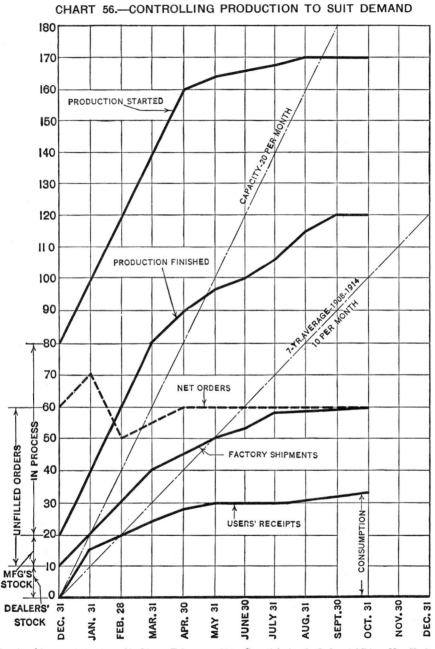

Reprinted by permission from *Machinery*, February, 1922. Copyright by the Industrial Press, New York.

meaning of the figures is clear, it is difficult to give practical effect to their warnings. Contract positions cannot easily be altered and often cover periods six months to a year ahead. Few businesses are so liquid that instantaneous adjustments can be made. Of course occasionally, established concerns may sell out and close up temporarily or permanently. And this has sometimes been done to advantage, though it breaks the continuity of business. A shipping company of seventy years standing is reported to have sold all its ships in 1919 and bought them back at less than half the sales price in 1921. A few manufacturing concerns sold all their stock profitably in 1919 and closed their doors. But such actions require extraordinary courage and involve a risk of losing the intangible elements of organization. They cannot be generally adopted.

Another difficulty in arriving at correct conclusions regarding the future is the dynamic nature of industry. The interplay of forces renders it impossible to isolate any force or situation and determine its future course. Situations are the result of a conjuncture of many forces and depend for their outcomes on the relative strength of the many elements which unite to form them. The mere regrouping of the same forces, or an ability of business men to alter their time sequence, may greatly change the course of events.

The crux of the problem lies in a successful interpretation of what is "normal" in industry. Obviously, in a new industry the "normal" cannot be estimated with assurance. Successful forecasting based on the past is only possible where the past shows a regular movement within well-defined limits and where general conditions warrant the expectation that past movements will be repeated. Such regular growth can only be found in basic commodities and in standardized products whose demand is due to, and limited by, the activity of other factors in the industrial organization. The record of pig iron production for example, goes back to 1854 and shows a remarkably even trend. One can extend the curve and predict the "normal" of 1928 or 1930 with considerable confidence. The "normal" of certain other basic commodities can be foretold with a working degree of precision. To a less degree, the like can be done with standardized products, such as freight cars, radiators, paint, cereals, shoes, ships, and so on. And these standardized goods form the bulk of our production. From this range we pass into the uncertain and the unascertainable, the production of goods such as radio apparatus, 75 mm. cannon, and steel helmets. In regard to the latter we cannot even guess at the "normal" production. In these cases the past gives no guide as to the movement of the future.

If the work of applying statistics to the guiding of business affairs were easy and obvious, it would long ago have been undertaken as universally as bookkeeping. The difficulties just mentioned have so far limited the systematic use of statistics to a comparatively few concerns managed with exceptional skill. But in many if not in most lines of business, these difficulties are of the kind that yield to persistent effort. The gains to be achieved and the losses to be avoided by the successful application of business statistics are so large that efforts to attain success will be persistent.

In many lines, and these the most important, information is already obtainable with which to substitute reasoned forecasting for "hunches." Will the further dissemination of these data enable business men to guide their conduct so intelligently that they will foresee and prepare against the extreme movements which make for prolonged periods of unemployment?

We cannot answer this question positively, because the experiment has not been tried on a large scale. If it is tried, we surmise that the prevision of the future on the part of a large element of the business community will lessen the extremes of prosperity and depression. But such a result is a matter of speculation. We can only say positively, first, that no stabilizing effect of this sort has been noted as yet in industry at large; and second, that numerous concerns in various industries have made use of statistical data and statistical analysis with profit to themselves.[1] The number of such concerns, moreover, is growing and we may look forward to still further growth. Such a cumulative movement, especially if vigorously supported by the government agencies in collecting and disseminating data, has promise of producing important effects upon the future course of business cycles.

[1] On the extent to which statistical information is now used see the data presented in Sec. II, Chap. XXI.

# CHAPTER XXI

## VARIOUS DEVICES USED FOR STABILIZING BUSINESS

By a Committee of the Federated American Engineering Societies

J. H. Van Wagenen, E. F. Wendt, W. H. Herschel and
L. W. Wallace, Executive Secretary of the Federation, Member *ex officio*[1]

This chapter is based on three sources of information: (1) sixteen answers received in reply to a questionnaire sent to a list of selected firms by the Taylor Society; (2) statements received from twenty-five editors of trade journals; and (3) answers to a series of questions sent out by the Committee to which ninety-four replies were received.

The answers received from the several firms will be considered in the order in which the questions were put by the Committee.

### I. THE PREVALENCE OF EFFORTS TO STABILIZE PRODUCTION AND EMPLOYMENT

Question 1. Is special effort made to stabilize production and employment throughout the business cycle? (*a*) If so, what devices have proved successful? (*b*) If not successful, what are the obstacles?

Of the one hundred and seven replies received to this question, fifty-nine answer "Yes" to the first part of the question and thirteen answer "No." Out of the total number of replies received, thirteen are based on seasonal fluctuations rather than the major business cycle. Five firms, representing the following lines of business; electric light and power, telephone, laundry, bakery, and cement mill, consider that they are in the fortunate position of having no need of stabilization.

The belief of thirteen firms is that business depends upon supply and demand and that nothing can be done to modify this condition. In several answers it is shown that the nature of the business to a large extent precludes the use of the more usual methods of stabilization. For example, three firms cannot manufacture for stock because they make goods only to special order, and a firm dealing in crushed stone cannot store such bulky material. In giving a general answer to the question as a whole, a manufacturer of valves and pipe fittings concludes:

It is not possible to stabilize production and employment throughout a major business cycle. We stabilize production through short periods by running a

---

[1] The members of the Committee were named by the Washington Society of Engineers. The Committee was aided in collecting data by similar committees appointed by thirty other engineering societies.

certain percentage of output, based on long-term averages, which percentage is revised every three months according to conditions.

To give a general picture of the information derived from Question 1, the replies are classified (Table LII) according to the character of the various methods of stabilization which the answers show to be in use. A glance indicates that several of these so-called methods are only expedients made necessary during the recent business depression and are not methods deliberately planned in advance.

TABLE LII.—CLASSIFICATION OF REPLIES WITH REFERENCE TO METHODS OF STABILIZATION

|  | NUMBER OF ANSWERS |
|---|---|
| Manufacturing to stock | 18 |
| Increasing variety of product | 12 |
| Selling on a smaller margin of profit | 10 |
| Working the sales department harder | 9 |
| Elimination of waste | 3 |
| Reduction in hours, part-time employment | 3 |
| Planning ahead | 3 |
| Standardization of stock | 2 |
| Transfer and training of understudies | 2 |
| Extending manufacturing facilities during dull times | 1 |
| Regulation of production and development | 1 |
| Employing only skilled labor and paying good wages | 1 |
| "Cut employment to the quick and reduce pay-roll" | 1 |
| "Hard work and effort" | 1 |
| Curtailment of research in dull times | 1 |
| "Change selling policy, retailer to wholesaler, increasing output and getting cash" | 1 |

The answers received by the Taylor Society indicate practices very much the same as those shown in Table LII; also some new ideas are brought out. A rubber company reports:

The sales are handled through a selling company. Production requirements for the year are established by analysis of customers' requirements, checked by factory facilities, and a minimum and maximum manufacturing program approved by the management. If market conditions of the season prevent customers from ordering from the selling company, the selling company acts as a customer in furnishing stock orders to the factory to keep uniform production. Responsibility for stocks and distribution lie entirely with the selling company. Responsibility for keeping the production up rests entirely with the manufacturing company.

Among those who sent the answers in Table LII, a few mentioned advertising. These replies are listed under the general method indicated in one of the answers, "working the sales department harder." The answers received by the Taylor Society bring out various other ideas about advertising and methods of stabilization, as described in the following quotations:

> Localize entire advertising efforts from national to particular districts not producing normal amount of business.
> Use of prize contests.
> Participating in retail marketing of product so as to provide constant outlet.
> By good planning and study and some stocking up, we have found natural turnover of labor in departments without any replacement to cut down production adequate to our requirements. In pre-war days we had an absolutely perfect record for thirteen and one-half years. During that time we did not work a single department even a day of short time, nor lay off an individual because of insufficient work.
> As we are manufacturers and not distributors, our problem is quite complex. The best we have been able to accomplish is to plan our orders ahead, plotting them on advance period charts, and then endeavoring to sell the unfilled departments' output in order to give continuous employment.

The replies of business editors furnish a specially clear view of the difficulties and possibilities as regards different industries. Apparently no effort is made to stabilize the machinery and jewelry industries, and the textile industry finds it impossible to anticipate the fashions. The steam and electric roads can only take business as it comes because "car miles cannot be stored."

The special possibilities of the steel mills are described as follows:

> I believe more attention will be paid in the future to the economics to be had from accumulating pig iron stocks and stocks of semi-finished steel. It is possible to borrow money on pig iron where it would not be easy to borrow on piles of iron ore. Finishing capacity should be larger than steel-making capacity, and if rolling mills could draw on accumulated supplies, it would lessen the outlay for new blast furnaces and new steel plants which are more expensive per ton of output than finishing mills.

The above quotation seems to indicate that the time to prepare for the storm is during fair weather.

## II. THE USE OF STATISTICAL INFORMATION

Question 2.  Is use made of statistical information as a basis for studying and forecasting business conditions?  (*a*) If so, what information is most useful for this purpose?  (*b*) What additional information, not now available, would be useful?  (*c*) How and by whom could it be compiled?

Of ninety-eight replies to this question, fifty-seven indicate the use of some form of statistical information and twenty-six answer "No." One the of parties answering "No" suggests the following cure for present conditions:

Some of the conservatism practiced during dull times injected into business during good times would create more of a balance.

Twenty-one firms use the business reports and forecast of one or more of several well-known professional economic services, and twenty-two make use of various other statistical information, while three use statistics "only to a limited extent." Seven firms appear to rely mostly upon trade journals and fifteen upon other records. Of the remaining three answers, a cigar manufacturer relies wholly on the quarterly report of the Census Bureau, a foundry company declares that its work is 95 per cent special and, therefore, its production and employment cannot be stabilized, and a flour mill is happily free from care because a bakery, belonging to the same owners, takes its entire output.

One of the firms which uses statistics suggests that the ordinary business man needs instruction in regard to the proper interpretation of facts revealed by statistics. The most complete reply is from a manufacturer of hoisting machinery who believes the most useful information is that obtainable from

Curves of general business conditions, of conditions in the iron and steel industry and particularly of employment conditions, due to the fact that our product is primarily labor-saving machinery and its sale depends upon whether employment of labor is above or below normal; comparative curves of labor rates also of great importance for the same reason, for high labor rates will cause stimulated demand for labor-saving equipment.

He also expresses the opinion that the Department of Commerce at Washington, through cooperation with chambers of commerce, trade associations, and engineering societies, might furnish valuable data regarding stocks on hand in various industries, both of raw materials and finished product and stocks in the hands of distributors, which when compared with normal are a guide in determining production programs.

While the answers convey the general impression that information in regard to the amount of stocks on hand in the various industries is of great value, it is pointed out by the editor of one of the trade journals that adequate information may be obtained in regard to the cost of raw material of textiles, but it is "difficult to get data on stocks on hand which manufacturers do not wish to divulge." Also, an editor of a chemical journal asserts that "traditions in industry favor secrecy rather than publicity and exchange of information in regard to consumption, production, and costs." That there is some tendency, however, to modify this practice is shown by an answer from the petroleum industry, in which the statement is made that data are now being gathered by the American Petroleum Institute which were "heretofore looked upon by major companies as confidential to them." Some of the more important kinds of statistical information found useful in forecasting business conditions by firms answering Question 2 are as follows:

Reports of professional forecasting and statistical services
Agricultural statistics
Firm's own records
Production of pig iron
Production of steel
Unfilled steel orders
Trade journals
Territorial and sales analysis
Lumber statistics
Prices of materials
Mining statistics
Labor conditions
Federal Reserve Bank figures
Money market
Car loadings
Trend of business in all lines other than our own
Market reports
Crop reports
New building
Trend of stock market
Prices of farm products
Bank bulletins
Reports of copper and brass research associations
Commerce reports
Statistics gathered from firm's branch managers
Information from all sources as to what has happened under similar conditions in the past
Weather and crop reports
Quarterly reports of Census Bureau
Daily newspapers

The suggestions received as to what additional information not now available would be useful, and how and by what agency it could be collected, are shown in a general way in the following table:

TABLE LIII.—SUGGESTIONS RECEIVED AS TO ADDITIONAL INFORMATION DESIRED

| Trade | Desired statistics | Collecting agency |
|---|---|---|
| Automobile.............. | Production and sale of farm tractors, various automotive parts, units, accessories. | Bureau of Foreign and Domestic Commerce (U. S. Department of Commerce) with co-operation of trade associations. |
| Lumber................ | Consumption, and stock in retail establishments. | Lumbermen's Association. |
| Engineering and mining... | Production, consumption, and stocks. | |
| Foundry trades.......... | Statistics in regard to production of pig iron and stock on hand, now available only to producers of pig iron. | |
| Furniture.............. | Wages and hours of labor in the furniture industry. Production and sales of hardwood lumber. | U. S. Department of Labor and Department of Commerce. |

In contrast to the replies generalized in the above table, one firm states, "We do not require any additional information, and would not have the time or inclination to read any more than we now use." Some of the firms advance the proposition that a general statistical and forecasting service, of the type now furnished by several professional agencies, should be maintained by the government and the reports disseminated widely throughout the country.

From the foregoing discussion of the replies to Question 2, one gathers the general impression that manufacturers recognize the need of extensive use of statistical information in formulating their production programs and business policies, and that it undoubtedly would be a service to the country if this information could be compiled and disseminated by some public agency. It is pointed out in one answer to Question 2 that the services of professional statistical, and forecasting agencies are too expensive for the small firm and for the individual, and that a cheaper source of this information should be devised. It is also pointed out that the average business man should have such statistics interpreted as well as made available for him, as he has not the time or, in most cases, the specialized knowledge necessary to do this correctly for himself. In this connection, it might be said that to make statistics and their meaning most valuable to the public, the agency compiling them should, when feasible, take the responsibility of making forecasts of business conditions from them. The government forecasts weather conditions from meteorological data, why not also business conditions from suitable statistics?

Among the questions sent out by the Taylor Society is the following: Do you employ an officer to study business conditions?

Of fifteen answers received, four are affirmative and four negative without details. One contains the statement that the firm has a sales engineering department, and two say that it is part of the business of all executives in main charge of the production, management, and distribution departments to study business conditions. One answer sets forth that the firm "holds frequent discussions by means of a docket method for determining such policies."

### III. RESERVE FUNDS AND THEIR USES

Question 3. Is a reserve fund accumulated during periods of prosperity to take care of continuation of the business during subsequent depression when interest rates are high and capital scarce? If so, how is this fund used?

Out of eighty-six replies received to the first part of the question, twenty-three were affirmative and the same number were negative; no details given.

To the second part of the question, the answers are varied and interesting, some indicating only a small conception of what the question means. Eight use the surplus to manufacture for stock, "conversion of surplus into inventory;" another uses it for "capital expansion;" one "places it in interest bearing accounts;" and six others say that the fund is invested in various ways.   One uses it to keep up dividends; one to keep the plant going; one "to equalize returns to stockholders so as to give at least a small return on investment during poor business." One firm makes the statement, "any gain is used to keep the banks good natured," and three report that they do not need a reserve as they never have to borrow in dull times.   Two others would gladly have saved a surplus if they could, but this was impossible, one finding business too poor and the other, taxes too high.   One reply states that the surplus was used

to stabilize production and employment and to offset extreme price fluctuations by averaging overhead charges over the business cycle instead of allowing them to fluctuate from unusually low overhead costs in time of abnormal business to extremely high overhead costs in times of subnormal business.

A manufacturer of fire engines says:

Question not clear.   Capital tends to become plenty and interest rates low during periods of depression rather than scarce and high, as stated in your question.   If the earlier part of a period of depression is referred to, we doubt whether as a rule it is possible to accumulate reserves.   On the contrary, during periods of prosperity and the first part of a period of depression, when capital is scarce and rates are high, a manufacturing industry such as ours is usually under a severe strain in the direction of expansion of production, while conditions are usually favorable for financing.   If profits are high, reserves may be accumulated.   Generally, however, we would say that the tendency was toward a severe financial strain to be followed by liquidation as prosperity passes away, and by permanent financing during the period of depression to the extent that liquidation has not solved the problem.

From the answers received, the general impression is gathered that the basis for almost any method of alleviating the effects of the cyclical period of depression requires capital surplus or some other form of financing.   The Committee believes, however, that capital thus used would be most effective if its accumulation and purpose were deliberately planned over a period of years, with the whole problem in mind, rather than if reliance is placed on the hand-to-mouth method of meeting depression emergencies only when they arrive.

## IV. THE PREVALENCE OF LONG-RANGE PLANNING OF CONSTRUCTION WORK

Question 4.   Is construction work planned ahead so as to secure advantage of the lower costs of material and labor during times of depression?

Among the ninety-four replies to this question, fourteen indicate that attempt is made to take advantage of low construction costs as much as possible, or at least to do so to a limited extent according to circumstances.  Seven of the firms report adequate facilities for some time to come, some of them saying such conditions are due to expansion during the war.   One firm is growing so rapidly that it is continuously extending its plant in order to keep up with business.   One buys machinery when prices are low; another buys supplies; but these statements do not really answer the question.   The direct answers are thirty-four "Yes" and twenty-five "No."

Among the general comments received on the subject, six express doubts of the advantage of saving construction work for dull times. Four state that extensions should be made only when production warrants, one of them remarking that he prefers to use funds for manufacture during dull times.   A manufacturer of pumps, tanks, and filtering equipment, and a manufacturer of crackers and cakes, declare the policy impossible; and, in contrast to these, we have the reply of a manufacturer of chemicals who says:

All good and successful employers of labor must plan construction work ahead so as to secure advantage of the lower costs of material and labor during times of depression.

The question brought forth several statements from business editors as to the reasons construction work is not to a greater extent reserved for periods of depression.   The reasons are summarized as follows:

TABLE LIV.—REASONS GIVEN FOR NOT PLANNING CONSTRUCTION WORK FOR PERIODS OF DEPRESSION

| Industry | Comments of editors |
| --- | --- |
| Automobiles | Business grows too rapidly. |
| Coal | It is done by larger units in coal industry.   Only obstacle, lack of vision on part of executives. |
| Chemistry | Expansion cannot be foreseen or planned far in advance. |
| Furniture | Lack of capital and incentive. |
| Iron and steel | Very costly to carry surplus idle capacity due to wide and abrupt fluctuations of demand. |
| Iron and steel | Andrew Carnegie believed emphatically in this policy. Several large steel companies follow this policy, but no important consumer of iron and steel. |
| Power plants | It is customary to put up buildings in dull times and install machinery when needed. |
| Railroads | Restriction of earnings prevents accumulation of funds. |
| Textiles | Majority of manufacturers delay building operations until forced by circumstances to begin them. |

It would appear that the majority of the editors believe that construction work should be undertaken to a greater extent than it is at present in advance of the increased needs for production.

### V. EFFORTS TO RELIEVE WORKMEN LAID OFF

In the two remaining questions asked by the Committee an attempt is made to ascertain to what extent any plans are made use of by manufacturers to relieve the laborer who is thrown out of employment during periods of depression. It goes without saying that no such plan would be quite so satisfactory as one which would be big enough to preclude any possibility of unemployment. Undoubtedly one of the first things to be dealt with in any broad business policy looking to the prevention of acute depressions is the status of the laborer, keeping him employed at all costs. A large percentage of business comes from the laboring man, and one of the essentials is that he should be kept employed so that he can buy.

To the first of these questions, which is, Has any plan been used looking to the relief of employees who have been laid off during slack times? eighty-nine answers were received. Two answered "Yes" without details and forty-two answered "No," but, unfortunately, it is not clear how many of the forty-two firms never lay off employees at all and how many do lay them off without giving them any assistance. Nine firms reported that practically none of their employees are laid off, and an equal number reported laying off only a few, keeping the best men and letting the "floaters" go. Three reported that no relief is necessary because the men get jobs elsewhere. The means of helping the employees most generally used appear to be by part time or rotation of jobs as reported by eleven firms. In two cases there are no definite plans, but individuals are helped as occasion demands. Construction work is mentioned twice and general repair work twice. Each of the following means of helping is mentioned once:

Cutting prices to keep work going
Free life insurance
Free rent
Relief from a benefit association supported by dues from both employer and employees
Use of a charity fund

The report of a manufacturer of garments also gives a number of ideas concerning methods of helping employees:

We have slack periods each spring and fall, and we attempt to fill these in two ways: by manufacturing allied products which will not conflict with our regular business at a cost to cover direct labor and as much of our indirect expenses as possible; and secondly, it has been our policy for a great many years to manufacture for stock in advance of orders. In addition to this, all employees receive a week's vacation with pay after two years' service and two weeks' vacation with pay after three years' service. These vacations of course are usually given in the slack periods. We also pay a service bonus of 50 cents after three years. $1.00 after five years, $2.00 after ten years, and $3.00 after fifteen years, respectively.

We have found during this slack period that, in order to keep our plant going at its normal capacity, it was necessary for us to cut the price of our product radically. In order to effect this we made very drastic cuts in our overhead and operating expenses, however cutting direct wages only 10 per cent. This 10 per cent cut has not been felt by the employees, inasmuch as they have worked so much the harder in order to earn the same amount of money as before.

### VI. USE OF UNEMPLOYMENT OR DEPRESSION INSURANCE

The second question regarding the welfare of the laborer during depressions is:

Is unemployment or depression insurance made use of?

The outstanding feature in the one hundred and two replies to this question is that ninety-three answer "No" and one answer is "do not know what you mean." Only in nine cases are any details given, and in no case is unemployment insurance reported or wage guaranty, or so many weeks employment guaranteed throughout the year. One firm says unemployment insurance is not necessary; another that it is too expensive; and a third thinks the recent depression was too severe to be remedied by insurance.

The forms of insurance reported include insurance for sickness, life, and accident insurance paid by the employees, and group insurance paid by the company. The indications are that unemployment insurance has not been taken up in the United States except in a very few cases. This deduction is confirmed, at least in so far as the textile industry is concerned, by the following comment of one of the trade journal editors:

Unemployment insurance is not very popular with manufacturers in the textile industry, the feeling being, whether warranted or not, that the adherent of such insurance would be playing into the hands of Union Labor. There are a few concerns in the industry that have adopted such a plan.[1]

### VII. CONCLUSION

In considering the foregoing resumé, it should be kept in mind that the data used are very limited, both in number of firms replying and their geographical distribution. The geographical distribution is shown in Table LV (excluding the comments of the editors), and Table LVI shows the extent of diversification of the industries covered by the investigation.

[1] For the details of these plans, see Chap. XVIII, above.

The investigation has revealed few indications of any organized or individual effort being made by American business enterprises to anticipate changes in business conditions. Such activities as are developed, are, for the most part, expedients to ameliorate adverse conditions due to poor business and unemployment attending the periods of depression. The necessity for predicting and preparing for approaching changes in the major cycle and taking business advantage of them before the changes occur appears not yet to be recognized as a business principle.

TABLE LV.—GEOGRAPHICAL DISTRIBUTION OF FIRMS WHICH ANSWERED THE QUESTIONS

| State | Number of replies | State | Number of replies |
|---|---|---|---|
| Alabama | 1 | Michigan | 6 |
| Arizona | 1 | Minnesota | 13 |
| California | 1 | Missouri | 4 |
| Connecticut | 10 | Nebraska | 1 |
| District of Columbia | 1 | New Jersey | 1 |
| Georgia | 1 | New York | 12 |
| Illinois | 2 | Ohio | 6 |
| Indiana | 5 | Pennsylvania | 1 |
| Iowa | 33 | Texas | 4 |
| Massachusetts | 4 | Vermont | 2 |

TABLE LVI.—THE KINDS OF INDUSTRIES AND THE NUMBER OF REPLIES RECEIVED
FROM EACH

| Business | Number of replies | Business | Number of replies |
|---|---|---|---|
| Advertising novelties.......... | | Glass..................... | 1 |
| Automobile assembling........ | 1 | Harness and saddles....... | 1 |
| Awnings, tents, canvas........ | 2 | Heating and ventilating...... | 1 |
| Bakeries.................... | 1 | Hoisting machines........... | 2 |
| Baskets.................... | 2 | Hosiery.................... | 1 |
| Biscuit companies........... | 2 | Ice and fuel............... | 1 |
| Bleachery.................. | 1 | Laundries.................. | 2 |
| Blowers, cleaning systems..... | 1 | Lubricating oils............. | 1 |
| Books..................... | 3 | Lumber.................... | 1 |
| Bookkeeping and filing equipment, office desks.......... | 2 | Machine tools, hardware.... | 5 |
| Brass..................... | 1 | Milling.................... | 1 |
| Brooms................... | 1 | Monuments............... | 1 |
| Buttons................... | 1 | Musical instruments........ | 1 |
| Candy manufacturers, ice cream, bottling works....... | 3 | Oil producing and refining.... | 1 |
| | | Packers................... | 1 |
| Carpets................... | 1 | Paper products............. | 3 |
| Cement................... | 1 | Public service.............. | 2 |
| Chains.................... | 2 | Pulleys.................... | 1 |
| Chemicals................. | 1 | Quarrying and stone crushing. | 1 |
| Cigars.................... | 1 | Retailers' tea, coffee, and spices................... | 2 |
| Cooperage................. | 1 | Rubber................... | 1 |
| Construction............... | 2 | Shoes..................... | 1 |
| Copper.................... | 1 | Silk...................... | 1 |
| Dairy machinery............ | 1 | Silverware................. | 1 |
| Electrical goods............. | 3 | Soap..................... | 1 |
| Fiber cans................. | 1 | Steam turbines............. | 1 |
| Firearms.................. | 2 | Steel construction.......... | 6 |
| Fire engines............... | 1 | Typewriters............... | 1 |
| Food products, canning....... | 4 | Valves and fittings......... | 3 |
| Foundries................. | 1 | Wire and rope............. | 1 |
| Furniture.................. | 2 | Woodwork milling.......... | 2 |
| Garments................. | 5 | Water supply systems....... | 1 |
| Gas appliances............. | 1 | Miscellaneous.............. | 4 |
| Gasoline engines............ | 1 | | |

# INDEX

## A

Abbott, Grace, effect of unemployment on health, 105
Aberthaw Construction Co., building, seasonal work in, 192
labor force for, 194
Acknowledgments, general, by Berridge, 43
Federated Amer. Eng. Soc., 378
Harrison, 272
King, 81
Mallory, 233
Natl. Bur. of Econ. Res., 3
Rice, 101
Stone, 123
Thompson, 169
Adams, T. S., acknowledgment of services of, 3
comments on Chapter III, 32, 38
on Chapter XVIII, 302, 340
reference to Chapter XV by, 114
Advertising, annual fluctuation (Chart 20), 124
costs, 125, 128
during depression, 123, 125, 127
monthly fluctuation (Chart 19), 124
production stabilized by, 123-6
Agriculture, statistics of employment, 355
hours worked by employees in, 86; (Table XVIII), 87
Alameda, Cal., public works, 258
Altmeyer, A. J., employment index, 54
Amalgamated Carpenters, out-of-work benefit plan, 295; (Table XLIII), 297
American Assn. for Labor Legis., acknowledgment to, 3
advocate of Kenyon bill, 248
American Civic Assn., city planning, 257
American Federation of Labor, advocate of Kenyon bill, 248, 284
American Institute of Architects, city planning, 257

American Railway Engineering Assn., seasonal fluctuations in railway employment, 227
American Society for Municipal Improvements, city planning, 257
American Statistical Assn., Committee on Employment Statistics, advisory capacity in preparing Chapter XIX, 345
members, 345
suggestions, 357-8
Andrews, J. B., acknowledgment of services of, 3
reference to Chapter XVII by, 115
Army personnel, period of war, 57; (Chart 7), 58
Assets, conservation of, 146
Associated General Contractors of America, advocates of Kenyon bill, 248
Associates for Government Service, Inc., state and municipal purchasing, 255
Australia, business cycles in, 6
Austria, business cycles in, 5
Automobiles, effect of selling price on sales of (Chart 27), 146
Ayres, Leonard C., labor cost in building, 182

## B

Babson's Statistical Organization, 365-6
Baltimore, Md., public works, 242
Bank credit, control of, 262-7
adjusting discount rates, 263
increasing sensitiveness of deposit-reserve ratios, 265
raising legal reserve against notes, 264
Barometers, business (see Forecaster).
Baxter Bros., building repair in slack times, 195
Belgium, public works, 240
Bell Telephone Companies, planning ahead for depression, 191

Benefits, out-of-work, trade union, 293–301 (*see* also Unemployment insurance).

Bently & Sons Co., A., building during depression, 197

Berridge, W. A., reference to Chapter IV by, 10, 78

Beveridge, W. H., central employment office, 290

Board of Trade employment bureaus, 280

Boot and shoe establishment, earnings and number employed (Chart 28), 147; (Chart 33), 154

Booth, Charles, on selective unemployment, 99

Boulder canyon dam, Arizona, public works, 246, 252

Bowley, A. L., public works, 237

Boyd, D. Knickerbacker, builders' exchange, 199

Bradford, E. S., reference to Chapter XII by, 114

Bridgeport, Conn., public works, 242

Brissenden, P. F., 44

Brookmire Economic Service, 366–8

Budget, value of, 139

Buell, J. B., 272

Buffalo, N. Y., public works, 242

Builders' exchanges, purpose of, 199

Building, additions, alterations and repairs, 176; (Table XXV), 178
  contracts awarded (Chart 44), 177
  construction costs, 183; (Table XXVIII), 184
  costs, 182; (Chart 45), 183
    index of (Table XXIV), 175, 182; (Table XXVIII), 184
  definition, 174
  education of public regarding, 199
  financing, 184
  increase of population and value of (Chart 43), 175
  industry, the, 174–9
  material industries, 179–85
  permits, value of (Chart 42), 174; (Table XXIV), 175
  prices of materials (Chart 45), 183
  program of Dennison Mfg. Co. (Chart 22), 131
  projects contemplated (Chart 44), 177
  Public Commission, municipal public works of federal government, 252, 260

Building, rents, 183; (Table XXVIII), 184
  sources of information on, 177
  stabilizing, 174–200
    methods of, 189–200
    standardizing materials, 198
    statistics, 199
    study of market, 199
    trades, unemployment, 185–89; (Chart 46), 186; (Chart 47), 187
  value, 1910–1921; (Table XXV), 178
  volume of, 174–5
  wage rates (Chart 45), 183

Buildings, as public works, 246
  kinds of, 179; (Table XXVI), 180
  purposes, 178–9

Bureau of Railway Economics, acknowledgment to, 3
  data furnished by, 81

Bureaus, employment, employer's, 280
  fee-charging, 283
  number placed, 286
  philanthropic, 282
  professional, 281
  public, 283–5
  trade union, 281
  types, 273

Business Barometer Dial, 368

Business conditions, indexes of, 361–77
  statistics available, 361–72
    lacking, 372–3

Business cycles, adjusting banking to, 268
  commitments adjusted to, 269
  diversity among industries and enterprises, 19–31; (Tables I and II), 21, 23
  financial devices for mitigating, 262–71
  losses from, 32–40
  nature of, 5–7
  phases of, 6–18
  recent books on, 7
  relation of railway purchases to, 224, 228

Buying, according to cycle, 127
  power and employment cycles, 64–5
  (*see* also Purchasing).

C

Cadbury Bros., Ltd., unemployment insurance scheme, 308

California, Board of Control, public works guidance, 254, 260

Canada, business cycles in, 6
  public works, 240

Cancellation of orders, economic consequences, 173
legal aspect, 170
prevalence in 1920–1921, 171
problem of, 170–3
Carnegie Corporation, acknowledgment to, 3
Charting the course of employment, 342–60
Charts, value of graphic, 36–7
Chicago, Ill., public works, 242
Cigar Makers Union, out-of-work benefits, 294, 295; (Table XLIII), 297, 298
Cincinnati, Ohio, labor turnover study in, 286
City Managers' Assn., city planning, 257
City planning, 256–9
advocates of, 257
Clark, J. Maurice, 13
Cleveland, Ohio, labor turnover study in, 286
trade union bureaus, 281
Clothing industry, stabilizing production in, 116–33
Coal Hoisting Engineers, out-of-work benefits, 294
Coal mines, bituminous, days in operation, 69, 71
Coal used by railroads, 210
Columbus, Ohio, Mayor's Unemployment Committee, 68
public works, 242
Commitments, adjusted to business cycle, 269
Commodities, peak months, 1919–1922; (Table IV), 26–7; (Table V), 29
percentage declines, 1919–1922 (Table VI), 30
percentage rises and declines, 1913–1922 (Table III), 24
statistical position, knowledge of, 163
Commodity prices, fluctuation in individual, 23–7
statistics, collection of, 373
Connecticut, per cent of wage-earners in mfg. in (Table X), 45
Construction, prevalence of long-range planning, 384–6
railway, 225
work as a balance wheel, 114 (*see* also Building).
Contracting close to cost, 194

Contracts, types that tempt cancellation, 172
Contributions to insurance fund, sources, 309–11
Cooley, Edwin J., effect of unemployment on number of court cases, 102
on commitment of children, 106
Credit, bank, control of, 262–7
adjusting discount rates, 263
increasing sensitiveness of deposit-reserve ratios, 265
raising legal reserve against notes, 264
Credit, bank, condition of business enterprises, data on, 373
control of granting, 267–9
adjusting to cycle, 268–9
raising tests, 268
expansion during prosperity, 11
policy during phases of business cycle, 132
supply, 263
tests during expansion, 268
Crisis, bred by prosperity, 10–15
cause of, 114
description, 15
regularity, 6
variation in, 6, 16
years of, in U. S., 5
Crop Reporters, questionnaires filled out by, 81
Curtis Publishing Company, magazine advertisers spending over $10,000 per annum, 125
Customers, service to, during prosperity, 154
Cycles, employment and buying power, 64
employment and public works, 233–6
employment, forecasting, 65–6
index, 49–57
since 1914, 57–9
Cyclical fluctuations, prevention in textile, clothing and novelty industries, 120–32
railway activities, 218–20
under-employment, data on, 76
unemployment, checked by public works, 233–6
Czecho-Slovakia, public works, 240

**D**

Day, Edmund E., index of production, 35; (Chart 8), 60

Days in operation, a measure of under-employment, 69; (Table XIV), 76

Dayton, Ohio, public works, 242

Deering, Milliken Co., unemployment insurance scheme, 337

Delaware and Hudson Co., unemployment insurance scheme, 338

Demand, elasticity of, 121

Demobilization, effect on industrial situation, 58–9

Dennison Manufacturing Co., advertising policy, 126
buying (Chart 21), 128
credit policy, 132
cyclical fluctuation prevented, 120, 122–3
plant construction, 130; (Chart 22), 131
regulating inventories, 128
seasonal production stabilized, 118–9
selling expense, 126
unemployment insurance scheme, 337

Department store, employment in (Charts 40 and 41), 167–8
index numbers of monthly sales (Charts 35–38), 158–60
peak month of sales (Table VII), 30
sales, purchases and inventories in a (Chart 39), 166

Deposit-reserve ratios of Federal Reserve Banks, 265–7

Depression, administrative policies used during, 149
advertising during, 125, 167
description of, 16–8
industries affected most by, 98
labor policy for, 156
manufacturers' policies during, 145–57
for prevention of, 136–45
methods of meeting, in building trades, 189–91
minimizing effects of, in retail stores, 161–3
numbers employed in a large establishment during, 97
per cent of employment decline from boom to (Table XI), 59
relief of workmen during, 386
stabilizing by building during, 191

Detroit, Mich., labor turnover study, 286
public works, 242

Deutsch-Amerikanische Typographia, out-of-work benefits, 294, 295; (Table XLIII), 297

Diamond Workers' Protective Union of America, out-of-work benefit, 294; (Chart 55), 296; (Table XLIII), 297, 299

Director's footnotes, Adams, T. S., 32, 38, 302, 340
Ingalls, W. R., Prefactory note, xxxix
Laidler, H. W., 232, 283
Roberts, G. E., Prefactory note, xxxix
Rorty, M. C., 97, 189, 200, 231
Shaw, A. W., 246

Discount rates, adjusting, 263
raising, 262

Discounts, purchase, 165

Distribution of wage-earners, geographical (Table X), 45

Dodge Company, F. W., building projects contemplated in 50 cities (Chart 44), 177
figures used by Dept. of Commerce, 361
public works figures, 241, 243

Dollar, proposals to stabilize the, 270–1

Domestic difficulties during unemployment, 102–3

Downey, E. H., on prevention in workmen's compensation legislation, 341

DuBrul, Ernest F., condition of a particular establishment, 374; (Chart 56), 375
effect of depression on machine tool manufacture, 121

Duluth Boiler Works, meeting depression, 191

Duncan, James A., effect of unemployment on the individual, 108

E

Economic basis of planning public works, 231–3
consequences of cancellation, 173
losses caused by business cycles, 32–40

Education of public on time to build or repair, 199

Efficiency of labor in prosperity and depression, 10, 61, 105

Elasticity of demand, 121

Emergency Public Works Board, a proposed federal, 240

Employed, number, building industry, 174, 189
building material industries, 180; (Table XXVII), 181
industries subsidiary to railways, 206

Employed, 1920–1922 (Tables XV–XXIII and Charts 14–18), 78–98
  railway industry (Tables XXX and XXXI ), 204
Employees, importance of railways as, 203
Employer's association employment bureaus, 280
Employment, bureaus, employer's, 280
  fee-charging, 283
  fraternal organization, 281
  philanthropic, 282
  professional, 281
  public, 283–5, 289–92
  trade union, 281
Employment, buying power and, 64–5
  changes, 1920–1922, 78–98
  charting the course of, 342–60
  contacts, unorganized, 274–7
  cycles, forecasting, 65–6
    index, 49–57
    since 1914, 57–9
  data (*see* Employment statistics).
  effect of depression on, 86
  exchanges (*see* Exchanges).
  fluctuations in, 43
  forecasting cycles of, 65–6
  indexes of, 43–65; (Charts 2–13 and Table XI)
  measurability, 78, 94, 98
  more steady in small than large establishments, 98
  railway, 211–13, 353–4
  retail store, 168
  securing, 274–7
  service, case for public, 285–9
    methods, 274–85
    nature of, 273–4
    need of organized, 277–9
    "want-ad," 280
    workers placed, 277–9, 286–7
  stabilizing, 378–80
  statistics of, 42–66, 345–57
  volume (*see* Employed, number).
*Engineering News-Record*, public works figures, 241
England, business cycles in, 5
  profit-sharing for executives, 145
  public works, 237–8 (*see* Unemployment insurance).
Enterprise, individual, in the business cycle, 19–31

Equipment, nature of the demand for, 12–3
  railway, 225
Exchanges (England), cost (Table LI), 335
  organization, 305
  work, 317, 333–4

F

Farm employees, hours worked, 86; (Table XVIII), 87
Farmer's families, members of, distributed by industries, 1920–1922; (Table XVII), 85
Federal government, public works, 233–6, 240, 243–53
  road building, 243–4, 246
  statistics, 361–2
Federal Purchasing Board, 255
Federal Reserve Bank of Chicago, employment statistics, 350
Federal Reserve Bank of New York, labor cost in building, 182
Federal Reserve Banks, deposit-reserve ratio, 265
  discount ratio, 262
Federal Reserve Board, employment statistics, 357
  indexes of business conditions, 362
Federal reserve notes and deposits, raising legal reserve against, 264
Federated American Engineering Societies, acknowledgment to, 3
  advocate of Kenyon bill, 248
  city planning, 257
  reference to chapter by, 115, 377
Feiker, F. M., acknowledgment of services of, 3
Financial activities adjusted to business cycle, 269
  devices for mitigating severity of cycle, 262–71
  obstacles to stabilizing railway activities, 229
  policies for stabilizing business, 146
Financing building, 184
  assistance to customers in, 196
Financing business to meet depression, 130
  municipal public works, 257–8
Fisher, Irving, stabilizing the dollar, 270
Fitchburg, Mass., public works, 242

Flood control, public works, 246
Flour State Baking Company, meeting depression, 191
Forecaster, business, Harvard, 65
use to retail trade, 161
Forecasting, business, 137, 364–72
employment cycles, 65–6
information needed for, 156
Forests, public work in, 246
Foster & Creighton Co., building contracts taken at cost, 194
France, business cycles in, 5
public works, 238
Fraternal organization employment bureaus, 281
Frey, John P., Iron Molders' out-of-work stamp system, 300
Fullerton, High, efficiency during unemployment, 105
Full time, compared with actual time, 69–73; (Table XII), 72
per cent worked each quarter, 1920–1922 in each industry (Table XXI), 95
Funds, revolving, 250
use of reserve, 383–6
Future discounted by unemployed worker, 105–7

**G**

Gay, Edwin F., some salutary effects of business cycles, 32
Geographical distribution of wage earners, 45
Germany, business cycles in, 5
public works, 238
Gloucester, Mass., public works, 242
Goldsborough, T. Alan, bill to stabilize the dollar, 270
Gompers, Samuel, benefit plan for Cigar Makers' Union, 294
Goods on order, at different periods of cycle, 129
Government, supplies, control of purchasing, 254–6
versus private efforts to cope with cycle, 132 (*see* also Federal government).
Graphic charts, value of, 136
Great Britain, cancellation of orders in, 171 (*see* also England).

Guibbin, J. A. T., unpublished data for New Jersey supplied by, 54
Guis, J. M., standardization of building materials, 198

**H**

Harding, President, first object of Conference on Unemployment, 342
letter regarding public works, 244
Harriman, E. H., policy of buying in depressions, 228
Harrison, M., effects of unemployment on the individual, 102, 104
Harrison, Shelby M., reference to Chapter XVI by, 115
Harvard Economic Service, 368–70
Haverty, Co., Thomas, new kinds of contracting work done during depression, 195
Health and vitality of unemployed worker, 105
Hickey-Freeman Company, acknowledgment to, 3
methods used to stabilize seasonal production, 119
Hoggson Bros., meeting depression, 192
Hoover,, Herbert, 243
Hours worked, as a measurement of work done, 94, 98
at trough and peak of cycle (Charts 15–17 and Table XXIII), 97
by farm employees, 86; (Table XVIII), 87
each quarter by industry (Table XX), 92
per cent of, at trough and peak (Chart 18), 94
relative changes (Chart 17), 93
Housing, relation to construction costs, 183
Huber, Senator, unemployment insurance bill, 339
Hunt, Edward Eyre, acknowledgment by Natl. Bur. of Econ. Res. to, 4
contribution to Chapter XIV, 233

**I**

Illinois, employment statistics, 349
monthly cost, 352

Illinois, private employment agencies placements, 1917–1918, 287

handling unskilled labor, 278

Illinois wage earners in manufacturing (Table X), 45

Impartiality required in employment service, 289

Improved machinery introduced to stimulate sales, 149; (Chart 30), 150

Income, national, basis for estimating losses, 37–38; (Table IX), 39

Indexes, building costs since 1913, 182

employment (Charts 2–13 and Table XI), 45–65

production (Chart 1), 35; (Table VIII), 36; (Chart 8), 60

statistical, government, 361

private organizations, 363–72

trade assn., 362

uses of business, 361–77

India, business cycles in, 6

Individual industries and enterprises in cycle, 19–31

Industrial equipment, nature of demand for, 12–3

Information, kind needed to forecast trend, 156 (*see* also Statistics).

Ingalls, W. R., Prefactory note, xxxix

Inglenock Construction Co., fire-damages handled as fill-in, 196

Insurance, social, 303–4, 320

unemployment (*see* Unemployment insurance).

International Ladies Garment Workers' Union (Cleveland), unemployment insurance scheme, 338–9

Interstate Commerce Commission, control of railroad rates, 229

employment statistics, 342, 353

railway employees and compensation, 203

tentative value of railway property, 201

Inventory control, 127–30

shrinkage of values, 158

I. O. O. F., employment bureaus, 282

Iowa, farm labor questionnaire, 355

Iron and steel industry employment in, 75

Iron and steel used by railroads, 211

Iron Molders' Union, out-of-work stamp system, 299–300

Irrigation, as public works, 246

Italy, business cycles in, 5

public works, 239

**J**

Jackson, James F., effect of unemployment on domestic relations, 102

Japan, business cycles in, 6

Jewelry Workers, out-of-work benefits, 294

Johnson, Alba B., long-range planning in railway industry, 227

Joseph and Feiss Co., methods used to stabilize seasonal production, 119

Jute prices, 128

**K**

Kelly-Atkinson Construction Co., The, building repairs done during depression, 195

Kemmerer, E. W., adjusting banking to the business cycle, 269

Kenyon, Senator, introduced bill creating Emergency Public Works Board, 240, 247–9

Kenyon-Nolan bill, national employment service, 273, 284

King, W. I., contribution to Chapter XIV, 233

estimated number of workers in building trades, 189

reference to Chapter VI by, 68, 235

Knauth, O. W., reference to Chapter XX by, 66, 115, 127

Koss Construction Co., building repairs done during depression, 195

Kuehnle (Philadelphia), planning for depression, 193

**L**

Labor, cost in building, 179, 181–3

efficiency, 10, 61, 105

policy for depression, 156, 386

Lackland, Rev. G. S., unemployment and radicalism, 103

Laidler, H. W., comment on Chapter XIV, 232

comment on Chapter XVI, 283

Lambie & Co., C. S., customers assisted in financing building during depression, 196

Legislation, national employment bureaus, 273

public works, 1921, 247

Leigh, E. B., railway purchases and business, 221

Libbey Glass Co., meeting depression, 191

Liquidation, effect of prompt (Chart 29), 148

Lithographers, out-of-work benefits, 294, 296; (Table XLIII), 297

Long-range planning, prevalence in construction work, 384–6
public works, 231–61
railways, 228–30

Losses, economic, 32–40
estimated on index numbers of production, 34–7
estimated on total income of nation, 37–9

Luethi, M. E., effects of unemployment, 100

Lumber, mill work, and furniture industries, overtime in, 75
used by railroads, 212

Lynchburg, Va., public works, 242

M

Macaulay, Frederick R., reference to Chapter II by, 7

MacDonald, Thomas H., federal public works aid to states supervised by, 243

Magazine advertising, increased cost, 125
U. S. annual (Chart 20), 124
U. S. monthly (Chart 19), 124

Maintenance, railway, 226

Malingering under insurance (English), 313

Mallery, Otto T., acknowledgment of services of, 3
references to Chapter XIV by, 80, 114

Mann, Lawrence B., analysis of dep't store sales (Table VII), 30

Manufacturing, effect of depression, 1921, 98
policies contributing to success (Chart 31), 151
policies during depression, 145–57
administrative, 149–51
financial, 146–9
labor, 156, 386
manufacturing, 151–2
selling, 152–6

Manufacturing, policies for prevention of depression, 136–45
policies for production and orders, 140–1
purchasing, 141–3
selling, 143–5
use of statistics, 136–9
value of budget, 139–40
stabilizing production through, 135–57

Mark-downs, effect of, 159–60, 166

Masons, employment bureaus, 282

Massachusetts, days in operation in mfg. industries, 69
employment index, 45; (Chart 2), 46, 185, 350
industrial specialization, 47
overtime among metal trade workers (Table XIII), 75
per cent of wage-earners in mfg. (Table X), 45
state employment bureaus, attitude of employers, 284
unemployment, in building trades, 185; (Chart 47), 187–8
insurance bill, 339
in trade unions (Chart 3), 46, 48; (Chart 6), 55
in transportation, 213
statistics, 342
cost, 352

Match industry (England), unemployment insurance scheme, 309

Material and labor costs in building, 179, 181–3
building industries, 179–85

Materials used, purchased and inventoried (Chart 24), 142

Meeker, Royal, collection of monthly employment statistics, 346

Mental results of unemployment, 107–8

Merchandizing, retail methods of, 163
stabilizing production through, 120–7, 157–68

Metal products used by railways, 212
trades workers, overtime, 75

Meyer, Andries, trade union out-of-work benefits, 297

Middletown, Ohio, public works, 242

Migration of workers between industries, 82; (Table XVI), 84; (Table XVII), 85, 98

Miller, A. C., deposit-reserve ratios, 265–7

Miller, Christian, employment insurance bill (Pa.), 339

Milwaukee, Wis., emergency fund for public works, 258

Mines, bituminous coal, days in operation, 69, 71

Mining, effect of depression of 1921 on, 98

employment statistics, 354

Mitchell, Jr., David, effect of unemployment on the individual, 107

Mitchell, T. W., contribution to Chapter XIV, 233

Mitchell, W. C., contribution to Chapter XIV, 233

Montague, Gilbert H., acknowledgment of services of, 3

reference to Chapter XI by, 114

Moody's Investors Service, 370

Morley, Felix, number engaged in public works, Germany, 239

Municipal bonds for public works, 241

Murdock bill, 1914, 273

Murray, Nat C., acknowledgment of services of, 4

Muscle Shoals proposal, public works, 246, 252

**N**

National Assn. of Credit Men, acknowledgment to, 4

National Board of Fire Underwriters, losses from fire, 176

National Bureau of Economic Research, acknowledgments by, 3

method of preparation of this investigation, 1

organization of, 1

plan of investigation, 3

scope of investigation, 2

National Conference of Business Paper Editors, acknowledgment to, 3

National Conference on City Planning, 257

National Federation of Construction Industries, building cost index, 181

National income, basis for estimated losses, 37–8

National Municipal League, city planning, 257

Netherlands, business cycles in, 5

New Jersey, employment index, 45; (Chart 2), 46; (Chart 5), 52, 54

overtime and time lost in mfg. establishments (Table XIV), 76

per cent of wage-earners in mfg., (Table X), 45

State Board of Control of Institutions and Agencies, public works program, 254, 260

Newspaper advertising in 23 cities, annual (Chart 20), 124

in 1920 and 1921, 125

monthly (Chart 19), 124

New York City, Mayor's Committee on Unemployment, 346

public works, 242

rents, index of (Table XXVIII), 184

New York (state), central purchasing of state supplies, 254–5, 260

employment index, 45; (Chart 5), 52, 56

monthly cost, 352

statistics, 347–8

overtime in telephone industry, 75

part-time study, 348

pay roll and total earnings in mfg., 342

per cent of wage-earners in mfg., (Table X), 45

state employment bureaus, attitude of employers, 284

proportion of common labor among men placed, 278

study of under-employment, 1921, 69, 71

unemployment, in building trades 185; (Chart 46), 186

in trade unions (Chart 3), 46

Northwestern University, Bureau of Business Research, acknowledgment to, 4

Novelties, stabilizing production of, 116–33

**O**

Odencrantz, Louise C., mental effects of unemployment, 107

Ohio, state employment bureaus, attitude of employers, 284

proportion of common labor among men placed, 278

Oil used by railways, 211

Orders, cancellation of, 129, 170–3
  controlling production through, 140
  effect of selling price on new (Chart 32), 153
  legal contracts, 114
  unfilled, statistics collected, 373
O'Shaughnessy, James, increased cost of magazine advertising, 125
Outlays upon public works (Table XLI), 233
Out-of-work benefits, trade union, adequacy, 295
  administration, 298
  as a preventative to unemployment, 300
  income and expenditure (Chart 55), 296
  number protected, 294
Out-of-work donations scheme (English), amount paid out, 326
  cost borne by state, 310
  rates of benefit, 309
  working of, 317
Out-of-work stamp system, 299–300
Overtime, 68, 71; (Tables XIII and XIV), 74–6

P

Parmelee, Julius H., acknowledgment of services of, 3
  reference to Chapter XIII by, 114
Parsons Housing Co., The W. J., during winter a lower profit taken on building, 197
Part time, 67; (Table XII), 72
  during depression, 90, 98
  industries which use, 93
  study of New York Dept. of Labor, 348
Pay-roll statistics, 79
Peak months for different commodities, 1919–1922 (Table IV), 26-7; (Table V), 29
Pennsylvania, Emergency Public Works Cons., 253–4, 260
  employment statistics, 45
  Industrial Board, advocate of Kenyon bill, 248
  unemployment insurance bill, 339
Peoria, Ill., public works, 242
Perkins, George, burden of out-of-work benefits, 298

Persons, H. S., acknowledgment of services of, 4
Persons, Warren M., business forecaster (Chart 13), 65
Philadelphia, investigation of unemployment, 70
  public works, 242
Philanthropic organizations employment bureaus, 282
Pig iron production and employment (Chart 11), 63
Planning (*see* Public works and long-range planning).
Plant construction, Dennison Mfg. Co., 130; (Chart 22), 131
Poor's Investment Service, 370
Population, increased, compared with value of building permits (Chart 43), 176
Potters, National Brotherhood of Operative, out-of-work benefit scheme, 294; (Table XLIII), 297
President's Conference on Unemployment, favored a system of public employment offices, 273
  first object, 342
  number employed in building trades, 189
  recommendations of Committee on Unemployment Statistics, 343
  upheld Kenyon bill, 248
Price levels, before a crisis, 14
  during depression, 17
  during revivals, 8
Price reductions, 167
Prices, cause of break in retail, 162
  commodity, fluctuation in, 23–7
  index numbers of retail, character of, 373
  of wholesale, character of, 372
  months of highest and lowest, for 62 commodities (Table IV), 26–7
  of building materials (Chart 45), 183
  percentage rise from 1913 to peak and drop to 1922 (Table III), 24–5
  selling, effect on employment of (Chart 26), 144
    effect on new orders of (Chart 32), 153
    effect on sales of reductions in (Chart 27), 146
  stabilizing demand through, 143
Printz-Biederman Co., methods used to stabilize seasonal production, 119

Production, and distribution, stabilizing, 134–70
  and employment, cycles of, 59–63
  control of, 129; (Chart 56), 375
  fluctuation in, 28–30
  held close to orders (Chart 23), 140
  high and low points, 1919–1922 (Tables V and VI), 29, 30
  index of, 34–7; (Table VIII), 36) (Chart 8), 60; (Charts 9 and 10) 62, 63
  merchandizing that stabilizes, 120–7; 156–68
  possible compared with actual (Chart 1), 35, 36
  stabilizing, devices, 113
    prevalence of efforts, 378–80 (*see* also Manufacturing policies).
  statistics for retail trade, 163
Products, proper time to introduce new, 121–3
Profit-sharing for executives, 145
Profit, small margin and early recovery (Chart 29), 148
Profits, factor in business cycle, 6
Prosperity, breeding a crisis, 10–15
  cumulation, 8–10
Public employment bureaus (*see* Employment bureaus).
Public works, administrative measures, county, 259
  federal appropriation policy, 248
  bond issues, 245, 253
  centralization, 246
  legislation, 246
  "reserve" clause, 245, 253
  road building aid, 244
  municipal, city planning, 256
  financing, 257
  political consideration, 258
  state, production of supplies, 254–6
  programs for institutions, 254
  responsibility, 253
Public works, bibliography, 260
  bill introduced by Kenyon, 240, 247–9
  buildings, federal, 244
  cyclical unemployment checked by, 233–6
  Department Assn., 247
  distribution of, 237–44
  Canada, 240
  England, 237–8
  France, 238

Public works, distribution of, Germany, 238–9
  Distribution of Italy, 239
  U. S., 240–4
  Emergency Board proposed, 240
  federal aid for, 243–4
  long-range planning, economic basis, 231–3
  summary of practical measures, 259
  municipal bonds for, 241
  Reclamation Service, revolving funds, 250; (Chart 54), 251
  relief, 236–7
  "reserve" fund, 234–6
  river and harbor, federal aid, 244
  road building, federal, 243
Puget Sound Bridge and Dredging Co., during depression securities taken in payment for building, 197
Purchasers, railways as, 206–12, 220–1
Purchases, relation of materials used to (Chart 24), 142
  unfilled orders as a basis for (Chart 25), 143
Purchasing, Associates for Government Service, Inc., 255
  centralized in the states, 255
  Federal Board, for coordinating, 255
  methods and policies, 164
  Navy Department's advance, 256
  of manufacturers, 141–5
  Post Office Department's advance, 256
  power, stabilizing, 220
  of wages, 64, 232

**Q**

Questionnaires, sent out for Chapter VI, 80–1
  results of Horace Secrist's (Table I), 21–2
  results of John Whyte's (Table II), 23
  sent out for Chapter XXI, 378
Quick, W. J., building repairs during depression, 195

**R**

Railway, activities, cyclical fluctuations (Charts 51 and 52), 218–20
  obstacles to stabilization of, 229
  seasonal fluctuations (Charts 48, 49 and Table XXXVIII), 213–7
  secular fluctuations, 217–8
  stabilization of, 201–30

Railway Business Assn., estimated number employed in subsidiary industries, 206

Railway construction, 255
employees, overtime, 76
employment, seasonal fluctuation (Table XXXVIII), 215, 223
stability of, 211–13
statistics, 353–4
equipment (Tables XXXIII and XXXIV), 207–8, 225
Labor Board, I. C. C. statistics prepared for, 353
wages and working conditions, 229
maintenance, 226
materials used by, 210–12
purchases and business, 220–1
trackage (Table XXXVI), 209
traffic growth (Chart 50), 217
value of prosperity of, 201

Railways, as employers, 203–6
as manufacturers, 202–3
as purchasers, 206–12

Reconstruction Commission (New York), recommend development of state employment offices, 273

Recruiting for war, effect on industrial situation, 57–8

Rectanus, S. R., benefits of unemployment, 100

Relief work, public, 236–7

Remedies for cyclical employment, Part III, 111ff.

Rents, index in New York City (Table XXVIII), 184

Repairs, proper time for, 157
value of, in building industry, 176, 178

Reserve funds, and their uses by manufacturers, 383–4
for public works, 234–6

Retail stores and manufacturing employment compared (Chart 41), 168
average monthly sales (Charts 35–7), 158–9
earnings and employees (Chart 40), 167
methods of minimizing depressions in, 161–3
sales and prices (Chart 38), 160
sales, purchases and inventories (Chart 39), 166

Retail trade, essentials of stabilizing, 157
fluctuations in (Charts 35–8), 158–61
(*see* also Merchandizing).

Revivals, trade, 8–10, 18

Revolving funds, 250

Richmond, Va., public works, 242

Road building, federal aid appropriation for, 243–4

Roberts, G. E., *see* Prefactory notes, xxxix

Rochester, N. Y., public works, 242

Root, W. A. and H. A:, during winter a lower profit in building taken, 197

Rorty, M. C., commentson Chapter VI, 97
comments on Chapter XII, 189, 200
comments on Chapter XIV, 231

Rowntree & Co., Ltd., unemployment insurance scheme, 308–9, 319

Rowntree, B. Seebohm, contributions and benefits, unemployment insurance, 311

Russell Sage Foundation, acknowledgment to, 3

Russia, business cycles in, 6

S

Salaries, wages and hours worked (Chart 17), 93

Sales, analysis, use of, 164
average monthly, chain stores (Chart 37), 154
department stores (Chart 35), 158
growing stores (Chart 36), 159
methods used to stabilize, 166
purchases made just preceding (Chart 39), 166
reduction of price used to stimulate (Chart 27), 146

Sandus, Virgil A., acknowledgment of services of, 4

San Francisco, Cal., public employment bureaus, 278

Scandinavian countries, business cycles in, 6

Schedules (*see* Questionnaires).

Seasonal fluctuations, exclusion of, from considerations, 6
in retail trade, 161
causes of, 116
results of, 117
prevention of, 116–20
railway activity, 213–7
employment (Table XXXVIII), 215

Secrist, Horace, acknowledgment of services of, 4, 20
classification of answers to questionnaire sent out by (Table I), 21

Secular fluctuations, railway activity, 217

Self-respect, effect of unemployment on, 108–9

Selling policies, 126, 152–6

prices (*see* Prices).

Service to customers during prosperity, 154; (Chart 34), 155

Shattuck, Representative, unemployment insurance bill (Mass.), 339

Shaw, A. W., comment on Chapter XIV, 246

Short selling (Chart 30), 150

Short time, 67, 68, 71, 74

Smallman-Bruce Construction Co., Inc., building repair during depression, 195

Smelser, David P., trade union out-of-work benefits, 293, 295, 298, 299

Soule, George, efficiency of labor, 10

relation of wages and prices, 17

South America, business cycles in, 6

Spain, business cycles in, 5

Spencer, Judge A. C., railway purchases and business, 220

Sprague, O. M. W. discount rate proposal, 263–4

raising credit tests during expansion, 268

reserve ratios, 264

supply of credit, 263

Stability of railway employment, 211–3

Stabilization, building, 174–200

business, devices used, 378–89

dollar, the, 270

employment, prevalence of efforts, 378–80

methods of (Table LII), 379

production, 116–169, 378–80

railway operations, 201–30

retail trade, 157

sales, 166

Stack Construction Co., new kinds of construction work done during depression, 196

Standardization of building materials, 198

Standard of living, lowered by unemployment, 104

Standard Statistics Co., 370–2

Statistics, building, use of, 199

business conditions, available, 361–72

lacking, 372–3

cost of collection, 352–3

Statistics, employment, available, 43–66, 345–57

employment, lacking, 342–3

exchange of between stores, 165

government series of, 361

private organizations, 363–72

trade association, 362–3

use of, 136, 373–7, 380

Steam railroad (*see* Railway).

Steele & Sons Co., meeting depression, 1920, 192

Steuart, W. M., acknowledgment of services of, 4

Stewart, Ethelbert, figures supplied by, 53

Stewart, Walter W., index of production, 35

Stock turnover, 164–5

Stocks, accumulation of, 162

Stone & Webster, meeting depression, 190

Stone, N. I., acknowledgment of services of, 3

reference to Chapter XI, 374

Store management, 163

Strover, Carl, stabilizing the dollar, 270

Surplus (*see* Reserve funds).

Switzerland, public works, 240

**T**

Taylor, Lea D., effects of unemployment on individual, 103

Taylor Society, acknowledgment to, 3

questionnaire sent out by, 378, 379

Taylor, W. R., relation of railway purchases to business, 220

Telephone operators, overtime, 75

Territorial differences in business, 30–1

Textile industry, stabilizing production of, 116–33

types of contracts, 172

Thompson, S. E., reference to Chapter X, 114, 374

Toledo, Ohio, public works, 242

Trade association aid in collection of employment statistics, 349

resolutions against cancellation, 171

statistics, 362–3

Trade union, bureaus of employment, 281

out-of-work benefit, 293–301, 304–5, 329–33; (Table L), 332

unemployment in, 46–7; (Chart 46), 186; (Chart 47), 187–8; (Table XLVI), 324

Transportation (*see* Railway).

Turnover, investigation, 73
stock, 164

Typographical Assn. of N. Y., benefits, 294, 295

## U

Umpire (English) on insurance claims, 314–5

Under-employment, 67–77
conclusions to, 77
data on, 68–76
days in operation, 67, 69, 76
full time, 69–73; (Table XII), 72
overtime, 68, 71; (Tables XIII and XIV), 74–6
part time, 67; (Table XII), 72
phases of, 67
relation to unemployment, 67
short time, 67, 68, 71, 74
turnover, 73

Unemployed, estimated number, 43 (*see* also Employed, number).

Unemployment, and the worker, 99–**109**
as an insurable risk, 303
beneficial effects, 100
building trades, 185–9
curtailed through insurance, 320–2
cyclical, checked by public works, 233–6
defining, general, 78–9
definition for insurance, 311–20
effect on children, 99
factors in investigation, 80
insurance, American experiments, 304, 336–40
English, administration, 333–6
benefits (Table XLIII), 307, 323; (Table XLVII), 325; (Table XLVIII), 327; (Table XLIX), 331
cost, 310, 326; (Table LI), 335
courts of referees, 313
fund, 322–9
persons covered, 323
prevention of unemployment, 320–2, 340–1
umpire's . decisions regarding claims, 313–6
measurability, 78
mental results, 107–8
relation to under-employment, 67
seasonal need for further study, 2

Unemployment, selective, 99–101
Statistics, Committee, recommendations, 343
trade union (Chart 3), 46; (Table XLVI), 324

Union, trade (*see* Trade union).

United States Chamber of Commerce, acknowledgment to, 4
advocate of Kenyon bill, 248
questionnaires distributed through, 81

United States Children's Bureau, study of effect of unemployment on children, 99, 103, 104
Bureau of Labor Statistics, building material prices and wages, 182–3
employment index (Chart 5), 52, 56
estimate of under-employment, 68, 70
overtime in lumber, mill work, etc., 75
rate of labor turnover, 73, 286
statistics of employment, 343, 345–7, 352
union wages in building trades, 189
Bureau of Market and Crop Estimates, acknowledgment to, 4
farm labor, 355
questionnaires distributed through, 81
Bureau of the Census, acknowledgment to, 4
questionnaires distributed through, 81
tabulation of material for Chapter VI, 81
Census of Manufacturers, employment, 50, 53; (Chart 6), 55, 56
Department of Agriculture, employment, 355
indexes of business conditions, 362
Department of Commerce, employment statistics, 356
indexes of business conditions, 361
Department of Labor, indexes of business conditions, 362
Emergency Public Works Board proposed, 240
Employment Service, attitude toward, 284
employment statistics (Chart 5), 52, 54, 56, 212, 291, 342, 356
use after Armistice, 272

United States Geological Survey, employment statistics, 345, 354

Railroad Administration, r a i l w a y maintenance under, 225

Reclamation Service, revolving funds, 250; (Chart 54), 251

War Labor Policies Board, public works, 240 (*see* also Interstate Commerce Commission and Railway Labor Board).

V

Vance, Ray, forecasting, 368

Van Kleek, Mary, acknowledgment of services of, 3

Villain, George, budgets and five-year program suggested for French railways, 228

Voluntary insurance (England), encouragement, 329–33

W

Wage-earners, geographical distribution (Table X), 45 (*see* also Employed, number).

Wage rates, building (Chart 45), 183
per hour (Chart 12), 64

Wages, purchasing power of, 64, 232
salaries and hours worked (Chart 17), 93

Wainright Commission, public employment offices recommended, 272

Walbridge-Aldinger Co., buildings closed before cold weather for interior work, 197

Wall, Alexander, acknowledgment of services of, 4

Wallace, L. W., acknowledgment of services of, 3

"Want-add" employment service, 280

War, effect on industrial situation, 57–9

Warner Co., Charles, meeting depression, 189

Washington, D. C., city plan, 252, 260

Wason, L. C., planning work in building, 192, 194

Waste in industry, Committee on the Elimination of, loss of time on the job, 74

Whyte, John, acknowledgment of services of, 4, 20
classification of answers to questionnaire sent out by (Table II), 23

Williams Whiting, importance of the job, 108

Willits, Joseph H., investigation in Philadelphia, 70

Wilmington, Del., public works, 242

Winston-Dear Co., deferred payment plan in building, 196

Wisconsin, employment statistics (Chart 5), 52, 348–9, 352
pay-roll and total earnings in mfg., 342
per cent of wage-earners in mfg., (Table X), 45
private employment agencies, placements, 287
questionnaire to farmers, 355
state employment bureaus, attitude of employers, 284
unemployment insurance bill, 339

Wolman, Leo, reference to Chapter XVIII by, 79, 80, 115, 387

Woods, Arthur, public works, 240

Worker, and his family during unemployment, 99–109
domestic troubles, 101–3
future discounted, 105
losses, physical, 103–4
mental results, 107
relief for, 386–7
self-respect lost, 108

Wright, Carroll D., under-employment, 1885, 68

# NATIONAL BUREAU OF ECONOMIC RESEARCH PUBLICATIONS IN REPRINT

*An Arno Press Series*

Barger, Harold. **The Transportation Industries, 1889-1946:** A Study of Output, Employment, and Productivity. 1951

Barger, Harold and Hans H. Landsberg. **American Agriculture, 1899-1939:** A Study of Output, Employment, and Productivity. 1942

Barger, Harold and Sam H. Schurr. **The Mining Industries, 1899-1939:** A Study of Output, Employment, and Productivity. 1944

Burns, Arthur F. **The Frontiers of Economic Knowledge.** 1954

Committee of the President's Conference on Unemployment. **Business Cycles and Unemployment.** 1923

Conference of the Universities-National Bureau Committee for Economic Research. **Aspects of Labor Economics.** 1962

Conference of the Universities-National Bureau Committee for Economic Research. **Business Concentration and Price Policy.** 1955

Conference of the Universities-National Bureau Committee for Economic Research. **Capital Formation and Economic Growth.** 1955

Conference of the Universities-National Bureau Committee for Economic Research. **Policies to Combat Depression.** 1956

Conference of the Universities-National Bureau Committee for Economic Research. **The State of Monetary Economics.** [1963]

Conference of the Universities-National Bureau Committee for Economic Research and the Committee on Economic Growth of the Social Science Research Council. **The Rate and Direction of Inventive Activity:** Economic and Social Factors. 1962

Conference on Research in Income and Wealth. **Input-Output Analysis:** An Appraisal. 1955

Conference on Research in Income and Wealth. **Problems of Capital Formation:** Concepts, Measurement, and Controlling Factors. 1957

Conference on Research in Income and Wealth. **Trends in the American Economy in the Nineteenth Century.** 1960

Conference on Research in National Income and Wealth. **Studies in Income and Wealth.** 1937

Copeland, Morris A. **Trends in Government Financing.** 1961

Fabricant, Solomon. **Employment in Manufacturing, 1899-1939:** An Analysis of Its Relation to the Volume of Production. 1942

Fabricant, Solomon. **The Output of Manufacturing Industries, 1899-1937.** 1940

Goldsmith, Raymond W.   **Financial Intermediaries in the American Economy Since 1900.** 1958

Goldsmith, Raymond W.   **The National Wealth of the United States in the Postwar Period.** 1962

Kendrick, John W.   **Productivity Trends in the United States.** 1961

Kuznets, Simon.   **Capital in the American Economy:** Its Formation and Financing. 1961

Kuznets, Simon.   **Commodity Flow and Capital Formation.** Vol. One. 1938

Kuznets, Simon.   **National Income:** A Summary of Findings. 1946

Kuznets, Simon.   **National Income and Capital Formation, 1919-1935:** A Preliminary Report. 1937

Kuznets, Simon.   **National Product in Wartime.** 1945

Kuznets, Simon.   **National Product Since 1869.** 1946

Kuznets, Simon.   **Seasonal Variations in Industry and Trade.** 1933

Long, Clarence D.   **Wages and Earnings in the United States, 1860-1890.** 1960

Mendershausen, Horst.   **Changes in Income Distribution During the Great Depression.** 1946

Mills, Frederick C.   **Economic Tendencies in the United States:** Aspects of Pre-War and Post-War Changes. 1932

Mills, Frederick C.   **Price-Quantity Interactions in Business Cycles.** 1946

Mills, Frederick C.   **The Behavior of Prices.** 1927

Mitchell, Wesley C.   **Business Cycles:** The Problem and Its Setting. [1927]

Mitchell, Wesley C., et al.   **Income in the United States:** Its Amount and Distribution 1909-1919. Volume One, Summary. [1921]

Mitchell, Wesley C., editor.   **Income in the United States:** Its Amount and Distribution 1909-1919. Volume Two, Detailed Report. 1922

National Accounts Review Committee of the National Bureau of Economic Research.   **The National Economic Accounts of the United States.** 1958

Rees, Albert.   **Real Wages in Manufacturing, 1890-1914.** 1961

Stigler, George J.   **Capital and Rates of Return in Manufacturing Industries.** 1963

Wealth Inventory Planning Study, The George Washington University.   **Measuring the Nation's Wealth.** 1964

Williams, Pierce.   **The Purchase of Medical Care Through Fixed Periodic Payment.** 1932

Wolman, Leo.   **The Growth of American Trade Unions, 1880-1923.** 1924

Woolley, Herbert B.   **Measuring Transactions Between World Areas.** 1966